Valuentum's

MOST EXCITING STOCKS

2021 EDITION

VALUENTUM SECURITIES, INC.

ILLINOIS

For information about permission to reproduce selections from this book, write to
info@valuentum.com.

For more information about special discounts for bulk purchases, please contact
info@valuentum.com.

ISBN 978-0-9980384-7-6

Published by Valuentum Securities, Inc.
Woodstock, Illinois 60098
www.valuentum.com

Contributors

Brian Nelson, CFA
President, Investment Research and Stock Analysis at Valuentum Securities

Callum Turcan
Associate Director of Research, Co-Editor of Newsletters, Portfolio Manager at Valuentum Securities

Chris Araos
Associate Stock and Dividend Analyst at Valuentum Securities

Anne Redd
Newsletter Assistant at Valuentum Securities

Table of Contents

Brian Nelson, CFA
*President, Investment
Research and Stock
Analysis*

Valuentum Securities, Inc.
brian@valuentum.com

How to Use the *Most Exciting Stocks*

Welcome to the 2021 edition of Valuentum's *Most Exciting Stocks*!

Investing is difficult but it doesn't have to be. It seems like most of what the financial media does these days is just make a lot of noise, seemingly to only confuse investors. Savers simply have a firehose of information at their fingertips from last quarter's GDP to the forward earnings multiple on S&P 500 stocks and beyond, but it's hard to know what's material and what's not.

Financial advisors don't have it any easier. They have lots of resources and thousands of stocks--large and small, domestic and foreign--to choose from to build custom client portfolios to meet best interest standards, but oftentimes, there's little systematic way to compare stocks across one robust methodological framework. Where to begin?

In the *Most Exciting Stocks*, we include analysis on some of the strongest and most exciting stocks on the market through the lens of our systematic stock-selection framework. We hope doing so will help investors cut through a lot of the noise out there to make more informed research decisions that will lead to better investment outcomes.

Which Stocks Are Highlighted?

Stocks that make the cut for this publication are generally best-in-class within their respective sectors when it comes to their economic return and financial risk characteristics, or they may fit the profile of an up-and-comer that's locked into long-term secular growth trends tied to disruptive innovation. In this book, we include many companies that are simply taking their industries by storm.

Here are just a few examples. Carvana (CVNA) is changing how consumers buy used cars, Roku (ROKU) is leading the streaming charge against linear TV, Teradyne's (TER) industrial robotics technology may change how workplaces operate, Beyond Meat (BYND) is striving to alter the substance of the meat products industry, Virgin Galactic (SPCE) wants to make spaceflight accessible for private individuals, while Uber (UBER) is changing how we think about getting from point A to point B through ridesharing.

Penn National (PENN) is aggressively expanding into sports betting with its investment in Barstool Sports, CRISPR Therapeutics' (CRSP) revolutionary gene-editing technology may offer a path to curative solutions for the worst diseases, Wayfair (W) is disrupting how we buy home goods, ETSY (ETSY) is carving out a niche online marketplace in craft items, while Zoom Video (ZM) has come of age during the outbreak of COVID-19. Others have been around for a while. Monster Beverage (MNST) continues to innovate within the energy drink market, while Boston Beer (SAM) has found new life with its Truly brand.

All of the aforementioned companies are analyzed in this publication and many more. There are more than 100 exciting companies in this book. Whether you're looking to build a diversified portfolio of the highest-quality stocks on the market, or simply seeking to augment your existing portfolio with a few solid (or exciting) ideas, the *Most Exciting Stocks* publication is an essential resource for any investor. Before we jump into the analysis of some of our favorite stocks, let's outline a few key components of this publication and explain how you can get the most from each of one.

Introductory Articles to Offer Context

We don't spend much time analyzing the broader macro environment. Famous investor Peter Lynch has been credited in saying, "If you spend more than 13 minutes analyzing economic and market forecasts, you've wasted 10 minutes." Our process at Valuentum is very much of the bottom-up variety, meaning that we focus on individual stock analysis and roll up those opinions into a broader market assessment. In this book, we include our "Stock Market Outlook for 2021," which we think is a must-read to help with context behind the company analysis. We also include several selected articles to help guide you on your way, with a focus on the concept of luck and the often-overlooked importance of the "too hard bucket."

A Company Index and Key Fundamental Data

We believe stocks are businesses, not pieces of paper or squiggly lines, and we despise backtests and data mining. The Valuentum methodology is purely forward-looking in substance. It combines a discounted cash-flow (DCF) and relative-valuation process with technical and momentum analysis to offer a view of a company's investment merits. In layman's terms, we calculate what we think a company is worth, use multiple analysis to double-check that estimate, and then evaluate technical and momentum indicators to add greater conviction to the process.

In the *Most Exciting Stocks,* we showcase a selection of some of the highest quality and most exciting ideas as well as their ratings on the Valuentum Buying Index (VBI) rating system, a methodology that puts our analysis together into one number (1=worst; 10=best) to assess the timeliness of a stock investment. Stocks with the highest Valuentum Buying Index ratings may be among the timeliest investment opportunities to consider, in our opinion. Facebook (FB), Alphabet (GOOG) (GOOGL) and Korn/Ferry (KFY) are three that currently score well.

We hope you're anxious to dig in, but before you jump into the stock pages of this expansive document, it may be useful to first start with the company index at the front of the publication. The company index showcases some of the most important information and data about each stock. The Economic Castle column unveils companies that have the greatest value-creation potential, helping readers quickly identify some of the highest-quality stocks, while the high and low fair value estimates help to sort the most undervalued companies from those that may be quite expensive, in our view.

Forward-Looking Stock Report Pages

In the heart of the *Most Exciting Stocks*, we include the forward-looking stock report page on companies that have made the cut for inclusion. (The full 16-page report of each company can be found at www.valuentum.com with a paid membership.) On each page, we include a fair value estimate of what we think the stock is worth, assess the attractiveness of the stock based on a fair value estimate range, and provide a relative valuation comparison in the context of the company's broader sector.

With each idea highlighted in this publication, we evaluate the company's competitive advantages (ROIC less WACC spread) and risk profiles (our ValueRisk rating). We also assess the expected volatility of key valuation drivers such as revenue and earnings to arrive at an appropriate risk assessment for each stock, too. When combined, the cross section of the ValueCreation and ValueRisk ratings provide a financial assessment of a company's business quality and competitive position. A ValueTrend rating offers insight into the trajectory of a company's economic profit creation.

Included on each page is one of our favorite metrics, a stock's rating on the Valuentum Buying Index (VBI). We believe the VBI helps identify the most attractive stocks from a valuation perspective at the best time to consider buying them, in our view, helping to avoid "value traps" (falling knives) and lagging performance due to the opportunity cost of holding a stock with great potential but at an inopportune time.

Always Work with Your Financial Professional

As a financial publisher, Valuentum can never know what stock or stocks may be right for you, and it's almost a certainty that not all stocks in this publication will be right for your personal goals and risk tolerances. Many of them have tremendous risks that could never be fully captured within a single stock report page.

Always do your own due diligence, and please be sure to work with your personal financial advisor in deciding whether any idea or investment strategy may be right for you. If at any time you need further clarification about the analysis or data in this publication, please be sure to contact us at info@valuentum.com or refer to the Glossary at the end of the publication for more information.

Thank you!

Brian Nelson, CFA
President, Investment Research and Stock Analysis

Valuentum Securities, Inc.
brian@valuentum.com

The Role of Luck in Investing and How To Think About It

For every Amazon (AMZN) that made it, there are hundreds, maybe thousands, from the dot-com era that didn't. Very few remember Pets.com or etoys.com, both of which went belly up during the dot-com meltdown. For every Tesla (TSLA), there is a DeLorean Motor Co. We might have completely forgotten about DeLorean were it not for the blockbuster movie, *Back To The Future*, that immortalized its futuristic sports car.

For every streaming enterprise like Netflix (NFLX), there is a Napster that failed. Most of us probably don't even remember the original Napster, which encountered legal troubles before closing shop shortly after the dot-com bust. For every Alphabet (GOOG, GOOGL), there's an AltaVista or Netscape. For every Apple (AAPL), there is a Palm or Blackberry (BB). Who remembers how popular the Palm Pilot and Blackberry were? How about the Motorola (MSI) Razr? For every Facebook (FB), there is a Myspace or Friendster.

As investors, we underestimate the role of luck in a company's long-term success. In February 2000, a month before the dot-com market crash, a fledgling Amazon raised $672 million in convertible notes to European investors. If the company hadn't done so, there'd likely be no Amazon today, and one of the wealthiest men in the world, Jeff Bezos, might have just been a mere footnote in stock market history. Amazon would have been insolvent in 2001-2002 just like many of its other dot-com peers.

Tesla might not have cut it decades ago. Many baby boomers preferred their gas-guzzling muscle cars and big SUVs. If crude oil prices hadn't soared during the energy resource bubble during the 2000s (sparking memories of the Oil Embargo of 1973), there might not be as much appetite for electric vehicles as there is today (putting aside, of course, the environment-conscious reasons). After all, the first electric vehicle was invented in the early 19th century, and an electric carriage was a big hit at the 1893 Chicago World's Fair.

What if Netflix had stuck to snail mail with its DVD delivery service, instead of innovating into streaming? Another company would have certainly eaten its lunch, and Neflix may have lived up to what many pessimistic analysts were expecting in its early years. In 2004, for example, some analysts pegged the company's fair value at just $8 per share. Netflix is now a far different company than it was years ago, even creating its own movies. The company is trading at nearly $480 per share, after a 7:1 stock split in 2015.

Google's search algorithm has changed the world, but at one point we had AltaVista and Netscape and even Yahoo. We didn't know that we needed Google when we had Yahoo, just like people didn't know they preferred an automobile even though they had a great stable of horses. Myspace and Friendster controlled the social media game years ago, but they just couldn't keep up with Facebook's technological innovation. We sometimes forget that Yahoo had a chance to buy both Google and Facebook, the former on two occasions (the first time for just $1 million) and the latter for $1 billion or so in 2006. Alphabet's market cap is now north of $1 trillion, while Facebook's is now nearly $800 billion.

Everybody loved their Blackberry in 2010-2011, but when Apple's click-wheel technology became mainstream, there was no going back. Any one of the smartphone makers could have been the "Apple" of today, however. Apple didn't have to be the winner. After all, the company lost the PC game in the 1990s, as Compaq, Dell (DELL) and IBM (IBM) reigned supreme. Things could have gone a far different way for Apple.

How many of us have heard the story of someone who bought and held Amazon from the dot-com bubble, or that got in on Tesla "early," or that continued to add to Netflix during the large drawdowns of the past decade. How many have owned shares of Apple from the mid-1990s? You probably don't hear stories of people who lost it all in Pets.com or etoys.com, or find many books written about investors that went all-in on electric vehicle technology in the late 19th century, even though it was the way of the future.

Luck plays a big role in which companies excel and which companies fail. If things had gone only slightly differently, the companies that we think of as huge successes today might not even be in existence. Even studying economic moats (competitive advantages) isn't a foolproof strategy of protecting one's portfolio from uncertainty. Warren Buffett's recent forays into IBM, the airlines (JETS), and Kraft Heinz (KHC) are subtle reminders that even the best of the best can't always anticipate what the future holds. That's why we pay close attention to the Economic Castle rating, which considers the ROIC-WACC spread over the foreseeable next five years, not into perpetuity.

But as investors, we cannot fall into the trap of ignoring the future either, and we certainly cannot fool ourselves into believing we know what will happen 10 to 20 years from now. We simply don't. What if Myspace gained a technological edge against Facebook? What if Amazon didn't get its funding in February 2000? What if Netflix stood still and failed to innovate? What if Yahoo had actually bought Google or Facebook for a fraction of what they are worth today (and not Mark Cuban's now-defunct Broadcast.com)? What would the FAANGs look like today if things had gone just a bit differently? Who would own the Mavericks?

So, if luck is so predominant in outcomes, how should we approach the role of luck in investing? For starters, we can't be too confident in what we think the future might hold (that's obvious), even for moaty companies (i.e. what a company's fundamentals in the next 10 to 20 years will look like). Think again about all the moaty restaurants, REITs (VNQ) and airlines that have suffered immensely during the COVID-19 pandemic. Likewise, we also know that we need to consider future forecasts, as past data only provides some vague context and isn't the slightest bit useful when it comes to asset pricing.

But this is okay. For long-term investors, what actually happens to future fundamentals may not be the most important consideration. You read that correctly. What drives stock values and prices today (and at every point in time in the future) is what people think will happen to fundamentals in the future (and in each iteration of a "new" future as time passes and expectations change). Investing is not about predicting future reality, but rather about reading expectations, and anticipating expectations revisions.

Therefore, it becomes crucial to know how future expectations impact the valuation construct. Let's walk through an example. During March and April of 2020, when the Fed and Treasury provided a backstop to the markets, many continued to focus on the uncertainty of the present economic conditions. Nobody truly knew what the economic data in the next two quarters would look like. But the more important consideration was that the long-term component within equity valuation was being enhanced as interest rates fell and inflationary expectations increased.

Investors didn't need to know what the economic data would look like in the second quarter or even for 2020--or even 2021--to know that stock values were advancing within the enterprise valuation construct as a result of Fed/Treasury actions and changes in long-run expectations. Here's the takeaway: You don't need to know future fundamentals with precision to be successful in the markets. Don't fear forecasts and the role of luck. You do, however, need to know how future expectations (and changes in future expectations) impact stock values and prices.

That's why the construct of enterprise valuation, or the discounted cash-flow model, is so important. Enterprise valuation is so much more than the tool to arrive at a fair value estimate of a company. As I write in the book *Value Trap: Theory of Universal Valuation* (ISBN-13: 978-0998038483), the process of enterprise valuation helps to inform the investor of the key drivers behind stock market movements and how one can assess pricing movements via changes in future expectations. Luck plays too big of a role in the long run than to rely on anything else but a strong understanding of the discounted cash-flow model (enterprise valuation), and how to interpret price movements through such an analytical lens.

Brian Nelson, CFA
President, Investment Research and Stock Analysis

Valuentum Securities, Inc.
brian@valuentum.com

Thinking Slow: 3 Research Blind Spots That Changed the Investment World

Daniel Kahneman in his text *Thinking, Fast and Slow* divided the human psyche into two systems. The first system is instinctive and emotional, often set on autopilot, while the second system is slower and more logical, requiring a calculating conscious. Many of the maxims the investment world takes for granted today suffer from conclusions that are made rapidly, almost without thinking, driven by our first system, creating what I call research blind spots.

In World War II, Allied bombing raids were suffering from very high casualty rates. It was estimated that for those pilots that were flying at the beginning of the war, only about 10% survived, a terrible loss rate. Bombing was crucial to the Allied effort, however, so high command sought to cut the number of casualties with a focus on where to put the armor on the bomber. But where should they put it? One couldn't arm the entire bomber as it would be too heavy to take off.

They studied the planes that came back from their missions and found that there were concentrations in bullet holes on the fuselage, wings and the tail. Instinctively, it seemed obvious that to reduce casualties, one should arm these heavily damaged areas. However, what was missing was the data on the planes that hadn't returned. It turned out that the areas that actually needed to be heavily armed were the cockpit and engines. The planes that sustained damage in these areas never made it back.

These types of biases, or research blind spots, as I call them, are everywhere in finance, and there in the most common places--sometimes with respect to your most treasured beliefs. For the researcher, it's very hard to see them, much like a driver can't see a blind spot on the road, but it's so very important to be aware of them. As I was writing my book *Value Trap: Theory of Universal Valuation* in 2018, I often wondered how so many investors could miss so many obvious things, but it turns out, biases and blind spots are more common than I believed. Let's talk about three big ones.

Research Blind Spot #1: Active Management and Missing Data

In the widely-publicized active versus passive debate, many from Jack Bogle and Burton Malkiel to prominent index fund licensers have studied the performance of professional active fund managers. The takeaway goes that after fees, many active fund managers don't perform all that well. But just like in the Allied bomber example, their work only covers a part of the market where the data is abundant, similar to concluding that armor should be placed on the fuselage, wings and tail given the evidence on planes that returned.

The stock market, however, is much bigger than professional active management. In fact, active domestic equity mutual funds and ETFs represent just 15% of the stock market--hardly enough data to make any conclusions about the merits of individual stock selection--and when professional active management underperforms, another part of the 70% of the stock market actually outperforms (e.g. the individual investor, hedge funds, pension funds, life insurance companies, etc.).

With our mental research systems on autopilot, however, popular studies defer to incomplete data sets to defend the efficient markets hypothesis, creating research blind spots completely overlooking a part of the market that's nearly 5 times bigger than professional active management--or what one might say, the critical data on the planes that didn't return. Our biases lead us to believe one thing almost unconsciously, but we must be aware that our brains are wired for autopilot, unless we truly challenge assumptions and parameters and "think slow."

For example, instead of asking what percentage of the market these studies cover, finance has hastily jumped to conclusions on incomplete data to support a bias. Studies on just 15% of the stock market tell us next to nothing about the merits of stock selection, but this research blind spot has changed the investment world. Indexing and passive management continue to proliferate.

Research Blind Spot #2: ETFs and the Wrong Construct

In the physical world, we take for granted empirical and evidence-based analysis. Studies in chemistry, medicine and beyond provide answers to questions that we knew next to nothing just a few decades ago. Our brains therefore have become hardwired to trust data, any data, as a result.

However, this isn't always a good thing in the world of investments. Perhaps one of the best-selling books to read is Darrell Huff's 1954 classic, *How to Lie with Statistics*, which explains the hazards of confusing correlation with causation. Yet, like the Sirens in Greek mythology, investors are lured to more and more data.

The field of finance took a turn toward empirical work sometime in the 1960s as computers (and data) became more widely available for number crunching. With more and more data, the field arrived at more and more "conclusions," paying little mind to the actual construct of the market, which is based on future expectations. Here is a quote from Peter L. Bernstein's *Capital Ideas Evolving*:

> Sharpe is concerned that too many practitioners--and a large number of the business school professors from whom they learned their trade--tend to forget that all asset pricing models are about expectations. And how in the world can you measure expectations, which are a look forward, not backward? You cannot just look at history and deduce much about what expectations have been--or will be. The whole matter revolves around the future. Therefore, the historical data on which we all depend so heavily may be useless for asset pricing. As we never know with certainty what the future holds, all we have to rely on is a sense of the probabilities of future events.
>
> "You are just reduced to a religious statement," Sharpe concludes. "I have been around long enough to see empirical results that seem to be really solid until you try a different country or different statistical method or different time period. Maybe that's why Fischer Black said you should put your trust only in logic and theory and forget about statistical empirical results."

What Bernstein and Sharpe indicate in this excerpt is that empirical, evidence-based analysis using realized data may tell us little about the stock market, asset pricing, or much of anything. The market, itself, is a function of future expectations, and some of the "conclusions" we hold dear based on realized data may very well be wrong. There may be nothing wrong with the data and analysis, but everything wrong with the construct.

Empirical researchers, when using realized data, suffer from a research blind spot, or a bias for realized data. They hastily use it in developing new products without "thinking slow" about whether such data makes sense or not. Backtesting and data mining of realized data have nonetheless changed the investment world, fueling the big business of ETF fees, despite The Smart Beta Mirage (July 2020):

> We document sharp performance deterioration of smart beta indexes after the corresponding smart beta ETFs are listed for investments. Adjusted by aggregate market return, the average return of smart beta indexes drops from 2.77% per year "on paper" before ETF listing to −0.44% per year after ETF listing. This performance deterioration cannot be explained by strategic timing in ETF listing nor explained by time trend in factor premia. We find evidence of data mining in constructing smart beta indexes as the post-ETF-listing performance decline is much sharper for indexes that are more susceptible to data mining in backtests. Our results caution the risk of data mining in the proliferation of ETF offerings as investors respond strongly to the stellar performance in backtests (Huang, Song, Xiang).

Research Blind Spot #3: Multiples and Short Cuts

Our brains are hard-wired for short cuts.

There are helpful short cuts like the Rule of 72 as it relates to how long it takes to double one's money given an annual rate of return, and good rules of thumb for how much one should save for an emergency fund or what percentage of your gross income should be devoted to housing expenses, but there are also harmful short cuts. With our brains on autopilot, we might think a stock that is trading at 10x earnings is more attractive than another stock trading at 20x earnings.

We hastily jumped to this conclusion without "thinking slow" about what is implied by those multiples. For example, the stock trading at 10x earnings might truly be overvalued, sporting the characteristics of a value trap with a huge net debt position, while the stock trading at 20x earnings might have a tremendous net cash position and huge free cash flow prospects that are undervalued by the market. Only through the process of enterprise valuation (i.e. the discounted cash flow method) can one understand those multiples and what they imply with respect to a company's valuation.

Humans' bias for short cuts has resulted in the behavior of preferring low-multiple entities regardless of their underlying characteristics. Furthermore, we support this bias with decades of backward-looking data, but it's likely what we're looking at with many studies is nothing more than randomness. Even with statistical evidence now suggesting that the "value" factor has not held up in walk forward studies, by Eugene Fama and Kenneth French, themselves, investors cannot overcome their bias toward short cut evidence-based analysis supported by backward-looking data mining efforts. Factor investing, nonetheless, continues to change the investment world.

Concluding Thoughts

We have to be on high alert about how our minds work. When it comes to the active versus passive debate, does the analysis suffer from parameter risk? With respect to empirical, evidence-based analysis, does the analysis have the entire construct wrong? When it comes to short-cut multiples, are we falling into the behavioral trap of thinking on autopilot? Don't let your mind get hacked!

Brian Nelson, CFA
President, Investment Research and Stock Analysis

Valuentum Securities, Inc.
brian@valuentum.com

How Big Is Your "Too Hard" Bucket?

In a prior note, we learned about the role of luck in investing. Even minor changes in the history of the path of successful companies would have relegated them to mere footnotes in the annals of time. Amazon (AMZN), as probably the best example, may not have made it past the dot-com bust without some timely financing just before the dot-com crash in 2000, while other companies may have looked a whole lot different today had just a few things not gone their way, from Apple (AAPL) and Facebook (FB) to Alphabet (GOOG, GOOGL) and beyond.

In investing, it's okay to admit that there are some things that investors can't know. It's not a poor reflection of one's analytical ability or a possible shortcoming of one's experience, but rather quite the contrary: Understanding and accepting that some things are "unknowable" is a sign of the quality of one's judgment. Quite simply, certain critical components of the equity evaluation process are more "unknowable" than others. The intelligent investor recognizes the variance (fair value estimate ranges) and the magnitude of the "unknowable" between companies and generally tries to identify entities that have the least "unknowable" characteristics as possible or situations where the "unknowable" might actually be weighted in their favor (an asymmetric fair value distribution).

For example, trying to predict the timing of a turnaround at General Electric (GE) based on historical data is a fool's errand, in our view (it's an entirely different company than what it was even 10 years ago), while assessing what may happen with healthcare laws in 2021, let alone 2025, may make many entities in the healthcare space largely "uninvestable." What may happen to the yield curve and loan loss reserves through the course of the next recession is hard to know for sure, perhaps precluding banking (KBE, KRE) ideas from long-term consideration. The huge leverage on the books at MLPs (AMLP) coupled with their meager free cash flow generation almost certainly makes them an "avoid," in our assessment, but they can turn things around over time.

How well General Motors (GM) will compete against Tesla (TSLA) in the next 20 years is at best a coin toss, while the path of the price of crude oil (USO) or gold (GLD) prices--not to mention cryptocurrency--is nearly impossible to predict with any sort of precision. There are some things that can influence commodity prices one way or another, and for every investor that thinks crude oil will be over $40 in 2025, another investor might believe it will be under. No matter what a mining entity's cost structure, their economic profit is going to be impacted by the price of the rocks and minerals they pull out of the ground.

How should you think about these types of companies? Warren Buffett and Charlie Munger put stocks that fall into this "unknowable" category in the "Too Hard" pile or "Too Hard" bucket. It is extremely important for you to have your own "Too Hard" bucket, too, and it should be large. Jason Zweig writes in *Your Money and Your Brain*:

> ...your investing workspace should have a small "In" box with a handful of ideas to consider, a little "Out" box holding another few ideas you've already approved or rejected--and an enormous "Too Hard" pile for everything else.

I'm not talking about a "Too Hard" pile of 50% of companies you've looked at; I'm talking 90%, or perhaps maybe 99%!

It's likely that there are probably 150 stocks in our coverage of hundreds and hundreds of stocks that meet the qualifications to be in your "In" box. The rest may fall into a "Too Hard" pile. In our "Too Hard" pile, for example, we put most of the energy sector--including metals, mining and chemical companies--as well as banks and financials (including insurance), and a large number of "old economy" names, including the legacy automakers and General Electric, as examples.

We're not going to pretend that we know what will happen to healthcare laws in 2025, and for certain situations like this, we like broad-based exposure to healthcare as in the Health Select Sector SPDR (XLV). We may stretch into the "Too Hard" pile for yield and income at times, but we're aware of the many incremental risks of doing so. You should be aware of them, too.

Throughout 2020, the market largely agreed with our assessment regarding many of the "Too Hard" sectors. Energy (XLE) and financials (XLF) were among the worst performing sectors, many capital-intensive "old economy" names have been out of favor, and the market continues to prefer ideas in the Best Ideas Newsletter portfolio--and for good reason. The names in our newsletter portfolios are rather easy to understand, have strong balance sheets, considerable future free cash flow potential, excellent visibility into their growth prospects (recurring revenue models) and competitively advantaged operations.

Valuentum's BEST IDEAS -- as of January 15, 2021

Portfolio Holdings	Symbol	Div Yield %	Fair Value	Economic Castle	VBI Rating	P/FV	Last Close ($)	% of Portfolio
Alphabet - Class C	GOOG	-	$2493.00	Very Attractive	7	0.70	1,736.19	8%-13%
Facebook	FB	-	$413.00	Very Attractive	10	0.61	251.36	8%-13%
Visa	V	0.63%	$219.00	Very Attractive	6	0.92	201.59	8%-13%
Apple	AAPL	0.64%	$140.00	Highest Rated	6	0.91	127.14	6.5%-8%
Health Care ETF	XLV	1.49%	-	-	-	-	116.97	6.5%-8%
Microsoft	MSFT	1.05%	$236.00	Very Attractive	6	0.90	212.65	6.5%-8%
PayPal	PYPL	-	$215.00	Very Attractive	6	1.12	239.79	6.5%-8%
Cisco	CSCO	3.19%	$51.00	Very Attractive	7	0.89	45.43	5%-6.75%
Johnson & Johnson	JNJ	2.51%	$143.00	Attractive	3	1.12	160.30	5%-6.75%
Berkshire Hathaway	BRK-B	-	$229.00	Very Attractive	5	1.02	233.74	3.5%-5%
Disney	DIS	-	$150.00	Attractive	6	1.14	171.44	3.5%-5%
Dollar General	DG	0.68%	$186.00	Attractive	5	1.14	211.44	3.5%-5%
Korn/Ferry *NEW*	KFY	0.82%	$66.00	Very Attractive	9	0.72	47.19	1.5%-2.5%
Chipotle *NEW*	CMG	-	$1178.00	Very Attractive	6	1.19	1,405.74	1.5%-2.5%
Domino's *NEW*	DPZ	0.83%	$369.00	Highest Rated	7	1.02	375.23	1.5%-2.5%
Vertex Pharma *NEW*	VRTX	-	$229.00	Very Attractive	3	0.98	225.55	1.5%-2.5%
Energy Select SPDR *NEW*	XLE	5.62%	-	-	-	-	42.75	1.5%-2.5%
Financial Select SPDR *NEW*	XLF	2.03%	-	-	-	-	30.94	1.5%-2.5%
Cash consideration	-	-	-	-	-	-	-	~0%

UR = Under Review
This portfolio is not a real money portfolio. Data as of January 15, 2021, retrieved from YF, Valuentum.

Image: Valuentum's simulated Best Ideas Newsletter portfolio. This is not a real money portfolio.

The riskiest types of companies, however, should be in your "Too Hard" pile, and you might find these are companies that have those "tricky" low earnings multiples--and all the makings of value traps. These companies aren't cheap; they're just riskier with more "unknowable" aspects to their business models. For every Facebook or Alphabet in your "In" box that you might like, there should be 20-30, or more, in your "Too Hard" pile.

Our brains on autopilot might try to lure us into the low P/Es across some of these "Too Hard" sectors, but our experience, judgment, and "slow thinking" might instead point to big cap tech and large cap growth as where the true long-term bargains might be had. These areas, to little surprise, have heavily outperformed quite a bit since the beginning of 2020 through the time of this publishing.

There are "unknowable" aspects to many names in our "In" box, too, but we try to keep the degree of the "unknowable" as small as possible, and we weigh the upside of the "unknowable" with the potential downside. For example, we might fully accept the "unknowable" aspect of whether Facebook might be broken up due to antitrust measures because this could potentially be another catalyst for upside (as the market is forced to value the company on a sum of the parts basis). On the other hand, the upside for many "zombie" companies in the energy space may not be much, and the "unknowable" in this case might be more heavily weighted to the downside (if energy resource prices continue to tumble). Where possible, we prefer the "unknowable" to be weighted to the upside.

The role of luck will always play an important role in any investment outcome, but in my view, when it comes to stocks in your "In" box, they should be ones with strong net cash positions, solid expected future free cash flows, impressive competitively-advantaged business models with strong visibility into future growth (and dividend/income potential, where applicable). As in the nature of fat pitch investing, you don't have to swing at every pitch, or concern yourself with companies in the "Too Hard" pile. If something has a huge net debt position or doesn't generate sufficient free cash flow to comfortably cover its dividend, put it in the "Too Hard" bucket and move on. Treat your "In" box to companies in our newsletter portfolios for consideration.

Your "Too Hard" bucket should nonetheless be enormous!

Stock Market Outlook for 2021

Brian Nelson, CFA
President, Investment Research and Stock Analysis at Valuentum Securities

Callum Turcan
Associate Director of Research, Co-Editor of Newsletters, Portfolio Manager at Valuentum Securities

Chris Araos
Associate Stock and Dividend Analyst at Valuentum Securities

Anne Redd
Newsletter Assistant at Valuentum Securities

2020 was one for the history books.

We covered our thoughts and reflections on the past year in our "2020 Won't Soon Be Forgotten" article, and now we are looking towards the future. Global health authorities should be able to bring an end to the ongoing coronavirus ('COVID-19') pandemic sooner than many had expected as several vaccines have already been approved for emergency use and several others appear increasingly likely to get approved. Global vaccine distribution activities are currently underway, and this should allow the world to slowly return to pre-pandemic activities. Before then, immense stimulus measures launched primarily in developed nations should support global economic activities until the public health crisis is put to an end, establishing a positive outlook for the upcoming year.

With that said, 2021 may be no less stressful of an environment than 2020, with systemic risk rearing its ugly head. In the early days of 2021 "bull raids," or aggressive and orchestrated "short squeezes" on stocks, have translated into excessive volatility and irrational market behavior--driven in part by Reddit WallStreetBets (WSB) users and Robinhood traders and exacerbated by price-agnostic trading from traditional quant algorithms. The poster child of the times has been GameStop (GME). The used game retailer's shares went from a 52-week low of $2.57 in March 2020 to a 52-week high of $159.18 in January. At that time of this writing, they are trading at ~$50-$80 per share-- still far above what may be considered a fair value estimate of the equity.

There have been more instances of crazy market behavior so far in 2021, too. Other heavily shorted stocks--including Express (EXPR), Macerich (MAC), Bed Bath & Beyond (BBBY), and AMC Entertainment (AMC)--have become tools of trading madness. As with the "fad" of investing in bankrupt or near-bankrupt companies in 2020--when the Robinhood crowd whipsawed prices of Hertz (HYZ), Whiting Petroleum (WLL), GNC (GNC), and Chesapeake Energy (CHKAQ) among others--in early 2021, the trading sharks circled heavily shorted names to drive aggressive short squeezes, often in conjunction with the application of deep out of the money call options. Several overextended hedge funds felt the pain.

Though we reiterate our fair value estimate of the S&P 500 is 3,530-3,920 based on common-sense normalized expectations, we also believe that systematic risk is increasing as price-agnostic trading continues to proliferate across the market. Fewer and fewer investors are paying attention to intrinsic value estimates, and this could have severe implications on the health of the global financial system. With that said, let's walk through key fundamental themes touching on the spaces of technology, e-commerce and retail, fintech and payment processing, energy and oil/gas, green energy, utilities, biotech and healthcare, 5G wireless, old industrial, video streaming, traditional banking, and cryptocurrencies.

We hope you enjoy. Here's to a great 2021!

Technology

All things considered, stocks in the information technology sector performed incredibly well in 2020, and we expect that will continue in 2021. Though one could argue that the COVID-19 pandemic pulled forward demand for certain tech offerings, meaning growth will be harder for certain firms to come by going forward, we see recent trends as a sign that the digital transition is accelerating.

For instance, digital advertising was already steadily becoming a larger part of total advertising spending given the highly targeted and flexible nature of these campaigns. GroupM, a division of WPP (WPP), believes that 2020 could be the first year where digital advertising represents over half of all advertising spending in the US (excluding political ad spending). Looking ahead, we expect digital advertising will continue to grow in both relative (as a percent of total ad spending) and nominal terms. GroupM forecasts US digital advertising to continue to take market share in 2021.

The outlook for the global digital advertising market is quite promising due to the rise of the "global middle class" (higher incomes supports greater revenue per user) and rising Internet penetration rates in emerging economies (creating new growth opportunities). We continue to be huge fans of Alphabet (GOOG) (GOOGL) and Facebook (FB) given their dominant positions in the digital ad industry.

Both Alphabet and Facebook have pristine balance sheets, stellar cash flow profiles, high-margin businesses, promising growth outlooks, and are trading well below their intrinsic value estimates (as of this writing). This is why we include both Alphabet Class C shares and shares of Facebook in the portfolio of the *Best Ideas Newsletter*, which we publish for members on the 15th of each month. As it relates to anti-trust concerns facing Facebook, we are not too concerned. A breakup of the social media giant could counterintuitively see its share price converge toward our estimate of its intrinsic value at a faster pace than as a standalone company due to sum-of-the-parts evaluations.

Another realm that has experienced strong growth of late, and will likely continue to do so, is cloud computing. Microsoft (MSFT), supported by its big data analytics offerings, has witnessed sales at its cloud-focused Azure business segment surge higher in the recent past. Though Amazon (AMZN) has long been a leader in the cloud-computing space in terms of market share, Microsoft is starting to catch up. Even Alphabet is starting to see its Google Cloud unit start to gain some traction while Oracle's (ORCL) cloud-oriented businesses have performed well of late, which helped lead to management issuing favorable near-term guidance during Oracle's latest earnings call. We include shares of ORCL in the portfolio of the *Dividend Growth Newsletter*, which we publish for members on the first of every month.

Research and Markets, a third-party market research service, forecasts the global cloud-computing market in terms of revenues will post compound annual growth rates in the high teens through 2025 (versus 2020 levels). With a greater number of employees now working from home, enterprise IT needs have fundamentally changed as there is a greater need for securely accessible flexible productivity offerings.

Microsoft's telecommunications-focused Teams service is integrated with its other products and services, such as Dynamics 365 (focuses on enterprise resource planning and customer relationship management applications), highlighting the company's ability to cross-sell and upsell its various offerings to enterprises large and small (made possible by Microsoft's focus on cloud-oriented services). We include Microsoft in both the *Best Ideas Newsletter* and *Dividend Growth Newsletter* portfolios.

Cybersecurity needs are on the rise. The recent SolarWinds (SWI) hack, which US intelligence agencies view as being conducted by Russian entities with ties to the Russian government, further highlights the need for top-tier cybersecurity offerings. Crowdstrike (CRWD), Okta (OKTA), and Zscaler (ZS) are three top-tier cybersecurity-oriented companies that provide their offerings via Software-as-a-Service ('SaaS') delivery methods. The Russian hacking group attempted to break into Crowdstrike's operations via the SolarWinds hack but was ultimately unsuccessful. All three of these companies were investor favorites in 2020, and we expect that interest in companies operating in the cybersecurity space will remain elevated throughout 2021, especially for SaaS firms.

In our view, demand for dynamic cybersecurity services will continue to grow at a brisk clip going forward. The need to secure sensitive information, and the potential cost of that sensitive information getting stolen underpins our optimistic outlook towards the space. Sony (SNE) was hacked by a North Korea entity in 2014 that saw sensitive information about Sony's employees released to the public along with several movies that had yet to be released.

The potential damage hacks can have on a company is immense, especially if that company's core business model is built around storing sensitive information regarding its customer or user base. Equifax's (EFX) public image took a big hit when it was hacked (the hack was announced back in 2017), and the company was forced into a multimillion-dollar settlement.

Third-party research service Grand View Research expects the global cybersecurity market will increase by a 10% compound annual growth rate from 2020 to 2027. In our view, companies are likely willing to pay up for top-tier cybersecurity offerings, which further supports the outlook for the industry given the favorable impact pricing power can have on operating margins.

E-Commerce & Retail

Pivoting to e-commerce, the recent surge in households turning to Internet giants such as Amazon to meet their routine needs such as groceries, toilet paper, and other consumer staples products via home delivery options has legs. Third-party market researcher eMarketer predicts that US e-commerce sales grew over 32% annually in 2020, climbing to north of $790 billion from about $600 billion in 2019.

By 2024, eMarketer views US e-commerce sales hitting $1.2 *trillion*. An increasing number of purchases across all types of product categories (from groceries, to clothes, to appliances and more) will be made online all over the world going forward, in our view.

Traditional retailers that invested heavily in their home-delivery, curbside pickup, in-store pickup fulfillment options, and their digital operations more broadly (having an e-commerce platform that is easy to use) were well prepared when the COVID-19 pandemic hit. Dick's Sporting Goods (DKS) and Home Depot (HD) are two prime examples of companies that were able to lean on their past investments in omni-channel sales capabilities and meaningful digital investments to ride out the storm while generating impressive same-store sales growth.

Dick's Sporting Goods has placed a big emphasis on improving its mobile app over the years (the source of over half of its e-commerce sales in the third quarter of fiscal 2020), such as integrating the app with its popular customer loyalty program. This strategy has proven to be a boon for the company. Home Depot continues to benefit from strong do-it-yourself ('DIY') demands as households pursue home improvement projects while stuck indoors due to COVID-19. These customers are increasingly turning to Home Depot's e-commerce platform to place orders online and pick up in-store. Additionally, Home Depot is well-positioned to meet the strong demand from the domestic housing market as it has a top-notch professional facing business. We include both firms in our *Dividend Growth Newsletter* portfolio.

Dollar General (DG) has made significant improvements to its digital operations in recent years, though the company still relies on its physical presence to meet demand. Given that Dollar General focuses on small cities and towns in the US with populations of 20,000 or less, we view its business model as being well-insulated from e-commerce competition due to the logistical hurdles that companies face when attempting to meet demand in these remote regions via home delivery fulfillment options. We include Dollar General in the *Best Ideas Newsletter* portfolio and continue to be impressed with the stellar same-store sales growth the retailer has put up of late.

Fintech and Payment Processing

One of the dynamic effects the rise of e-commerce has had on the global economy involves creating greater demand for online-oriented payment processing services. PayPal (PYPL) is one of our favorite companies in this space as its growth outlook is stellar, supported by its high-quality cash flow profile and pristine balance sheet. The firm also owns Venmo, the popular peer-to-peer money transfer mobile-oriented app, and we are excited about the numerous ways PayPal could monetize this business. After separating from eBay (EBAY) in 2015, PayPal has steadily grown its total payment volume ('TPV'). Its TPV was up 36% year-over-year on a constant currency basis in the third quarter of 2020.

The ultimate end game of the fintech and payment processing space is to create a "walled garden" where companies can provide multiple services at once with limited competition in certain instances. For instance, if a customer buys something online and that product is located overseas in a country with a different currency, PayPal can make money both by processing the payment and by providing foreign currency transaction solutions, along with any other required service (without necessarily being compelled to provide other options to the customer for each individual service).

We are also big fans of Visa (V). As households get ready to resume pre-pandemic activities such as business trips and vacations in the wake of global health authorities eventually putting an end to the public health crisis, Visa's lucrative travel-oriented businesses should stage a strong recovery. In the meantime, its online-facing businesses continue to do well, and the firm does not have any credit risk exposure as it does not lend money. PayPal has a relatively small lending operation. We include both PayPal and Visa in the *Best Ideas Newsletter* portfolio and are big fans of both companies.

Apple (AAPL), a holding in both the *Best Ideas Newsletter* and *Dividend Growth Newsletter* portfolios, sought to grow its fintech business when it partnered with Goldman Sachs (GS) to launch the Apple Card. The company also has its Apple Pay service, and the Apple Card is a logical extension of its efforts in this space. By leveraging its large hardware user base, Apple aims to grow its service-oriented revenues over time, and its foray into fintech is part of that strategy. We are keeping a close eye on Apple's growing services business given the high-margin nature of these revenue streams and the long growth runway the iPhone giant has on this front if successful.

Facebook aims to grow its payment processing business with an eye towards its WhatsApp messenger service. In 2020, Facebook partnered up with Jio Platforms (acquiring a ~10% equity stake in the firm for about $5.7 billion), an Indian telecommunications and digital platform company. The goal appears to be built around creating a sizable e-commerce and payment processing business in India by connecting WhatsApp users with small and large stores across the country. While these are still early days, we are incredibly excited at the potential WhatsApp offers Facebook in terms of building up e-commerce and payment processing business, leveraging WhatsApp large active user base to do so.

Reportedly Jamie Dimon, CEO of JPMorgan Chase (JPM), noted that key fintech players such as PayPal, Square (SQ), Stripe, and Ant Financial along with the fintech divisions of major tech giants needed to be monitored given their potential ability to completely disrupt the financial services sector. For instance, Square, which is run by Jack Dorsey who also runs Twitter (TWTR) (Mr. Dorsey is CEO of both firms and co-founded/founded both firms), plans to launch its own bank this year. Known as Square Financial Services, the bank will operate as an independently run subsidiary of Square and "its primary purpose will be to offer small business loans for Square Capital's commercial lending business, and to offer deposit products."

The Federal Deposit Insurance Corporation ('FDIC') conditionally approved Square Financial Services' deposit insurance application (as it concerns the firm's industrial loan bank charter) in March 2020, and Square has already received charter approval from the Utah Department of Financial Institutions. We are intrigued by this news given the implications it has for the broader fintech space.

We're closely monitoring how the fintech and payment processing landscape will continue to evolve in 2021. The resumption of travel activities will be a major boon for credit card networks Visa and MasterCard (MA), and more broadly, the secular transition away from cash (which picked up steam in 2020) continues to support the long-term outlook of both companies. The growing prevalence of e-commerce will continue to provide PayPal with a massive tailwind (same goes for Visa and MasterCard), as will slowly unlocking the full revenue generation potential of PayPal's Venmo service. We're keeping a very close eye on this situation as Venmo recently launched its own branded credit card on October 5, 2020, which is issued by Synchrony Financial (SYF) and backed by Visa's payment network.

We added Financial Select Sector SPDR (XLF) to the *Best Ideas Newsletter* portfolio on January 12. The improving outlook for the banking space is a product of expectations that the global economy will recover, which in turn should limit credit write-offs while putting upward pressure on interest rates (off a low base) which supports the outlook for net interest margins ('NIMs').

Energy, Oil & Gas

The ongoing recovery in raw energy resources pricing (crude oil, liquified natural gas, natural gas, natural gas liquids) has gone a long way to improve the outlook for upstream firms--companies involved in the extraction of oil & gas from the ground--albeit off an incredibly low base. Expectations that energy demand will recover meaningfully in the coming quarters due to a combination of the COVID-19 vaccine distribution efforts currently underway and actions taken by the OPEC+ oil cartel to limit global oil supplies (for an extended period) have been key to supporting the market.

In our view, the outlook for the upstream oil & gas industry has shifted from dire to manageable with WTI and Brent pushing back into the $50 per-barrel range. Higher raw energy resources pricing needs to be combined with disciplined capital investment strategies for the heavily indebted upstream oil & gas industry to truly take advantage of the upturn. Significant headwinds remain, however. For the recovery to have legs, the recent increase in raw energy resources pricing needs to be sustained.

The outlook for integrated energy companies has also improved significantly of late. Integrated energy firms generally have large upstream divisions alongside substantial midstream (pipelines, storage facilities, and processing plants), downstream (refineries and petrochemical plants), and retail (gas stations and related convenience stores) operations. Integrated energy companies often generate an outsized portion of their operating cash flows from their upstream operations, so any improvement on this front can go a long way to improve their company-wide financial performance.

As it concerns the midstream and downstream industries, the resumption of pre-pandemic activities should lead to a recovery in gasoline and diesel demand in the near term, with demand for jet fuel (made from kerosene) potentially recovering in the medium term given the headwinds facing commercial airliners will likely linger. This in turn should benefit both refineries and the pipelines that transport refined petroleum products to end buyers, along with the related energy infrastructure such as storage facilities and marine terminals. Rising oil & gas production levels support midstream assets that cater to the upstream industry such as gathering & processing ('G&P') operations along with long haul pipelines.

Petrochemical plant operators should benefit from a recovering global economy given that the industry produces the building blocks of modern society (such as plastics, adhesives, detergents, and more), as should the midstream assets that support petrochemical operations. That includes cryogenic processing plants that separate "dry" natural gas (methane) from "wet" natural gas (mixed Y-grade natural gas liquids), and fractionators that separate the various natural gas liquids (e.g., propane, butane, or ethane) from the Y-grade natural gas liquids into standalone products.

Rising input prices for the downstream space (i.e., higher raw energy resources pricing) will likely be offset by higher utilization rates, which generally provides an uplift to operating margins given the high fixed costs the industry faces. This will be made possible by expected demand growth creating a need for greater production volumes.

The potential for the COVID-19 pandemic to end sooner than expected supports the entire oil & gas industry. On January 12, we added Energy Select Sector SPDR (XLE) to the *Best Ideas Newsletter* portfolio to gain broad exposure to the space and the potential for a sustained recovery. Our favorite midstream firms are Enterprise Products Partners LP (EPD) and Magellan Midstream Partners LP (MMP), two top-tier companies that are included in the *High Yield Dividend Newsletter* portfolio.

Green Energy

The dichotomy between stocks in the green energy space and stocks in the oil & gas energy space couldn't be more apparent. A prolonged period of low raw energy resources pricing (the downturn began back in late-2014) and sharp improvements in the economics of green energy operations led investors to shift capital away from equities in the fossil fuel space towards equities with exposure to renewable energy. Several provisions geared toward supporting the green energy space were included in the recently passed omnibus spending and emergency fiscal relief package in the US.

Electric vehicles ('EVs') are clearly an investor favorite with shares of Tesla (TSLA), Li Auto (LI), Lordstown Motors (RIDE), Nio (NIO), BYD Group (BYDDF), Xpeng (XPEV), and Workhorse Group (WKHS) all moving sharply higher over the past year. Looking ahead, the long-term outlook for EVs remains bright as does the outlook for companies with exposure to the space (though many companies in this space are currently trading at arguably generous valuations). In terms of units, the EV market remains relatively small as things stand today, though we expect that to change over time. By some estimates the EV market in terms of unit sales should rise by more than ten-fold from 2020 to 2030, at least according to privately held Deloitte.

There are several things we're keeping a close eye on in 2021, including 1) how effective the EV industry is at scaling up manufacturing activities, 2) how the EV sales growth trajectory is evolving in key growth markets (China, Western Europe, and the US), 3) what kind of EV investments traditional automakers are making, and 4) what level of interest there is in EV pickup offerings. Tesla has the Cybertruck, General Motors (GM) has its all-electric Hummer pickup truck, and privately held Rivian has its all-electric R1T pickup truck offering, though note that it will be at least a few years until these offerings are readily available (meaning short delivery times instead of long waits). General Motors has recently rotated towards EVs, as have other traditional automakers with Ford (F) partnering up with Volkswagen (VWAPY) to assist in their collective EV and autonomous vehicle efforts.

Utilities

Pivoting now to electric utilities, firms that prioritized green energy investments were clearly investor favorites in 2020, and we expect that to continue into 2021. NextEra Energy (NEE) owns two Florida-focused electric utilities and a large economic stake in NextEra Energy Partners (NEP), which is focused on renewable energy generation assets. During the past five years the share price of NEE (adjusted for stock splits) and the unit price of NEP have both more than tripled as of this writing. The NextEra Energy family continues to invest large sums toward growing its green energy operations by building new solar plants, wind farms, and battery storage facilities (which underpins the electric utility family's promising growth outlook). We include Utilities Select Sector SPDR Fund (XLU) in the *High Yield Dividend Newsletter* portfolio, published for members on the first of every month, to gain broad exposure to the space.

NextEra Energy is not alone in its green energy push. American Electric Power (AEP) aggressively highlights its plan to fundamentally change its power generation mix. From 2020 to 2030, the utility aims to reduce coal power to 24% from 43% of its company-wide power generation capacity while electric generated by 'Hydro, Wind, Solar and Pumped' are forecasted to rise from 18% to 39% of its company-wide power generation capacity during this period. Nuclear power is expected to remain at a high-single digit percentage of its power generation mix during this period as nuclear power can continue meeting demand when the wind isn't blowing, and the sun isn't shining.

Even Berkshire Hathaway (BRK.A) (BRK.B), an idea in the *Best Ideas Newsletter* portfolio, is directing its majority-owned Berkshire Hathaway Energy unit to invest heavily in green energy with an eye towards wind farms in Iowa and Alberta, Canada. In the recent past, Berkshire Hathaway has hyped the sharp improvements in the economics of its wind farms as a way to save its customers money while creating growth opportunities for its energy operations. An enormous part of that improvement in power generation economics is due to innovation at firms like General Electric (GE) and Siemens (SIEGY), which manufacture the turbines used in wind farms.

First Solar (FSLR), a US-based manufacturer of solar modules, is excited about the kinds of economic improvements its copper replacement project could yield. Copper prices have been strong of late, and reducing solar module costs while improving cell efficiency could go a long way to improve the industry's outlook. The National Renewable Energy Laboratory ('NREL') and First Solar aim to reduce the amount of copper used in cadmium telluride solar cells by "placing... elements from the fifth column of the periodic table... such as antimony or arsenic, onto tellurium crystal sites at extremely high speeds by low-cost methods required for mass production." Though copper is still an essential part of the industry as an electrical conductor, it appears the industry is beginning to challenge old habits.

Biotech and Healthcare

One of our favorite biotech ideas is Vertex Pharmaceuticals (VRTX). Vertex's commercialized therapeutics portfolio is heavily weighted towards treating cystic fibrosis ('CF') across various age groups including: TRIKAFTA/KAFTRIO (age 12 and older), SYMDEKO/SYMKEVI (age six and older), ORKAMBI (age two and older), and KALYDECO (age four months and older). In October 2019, Vertex's TRIKAFTA offering was approved by the US Food and Drug Administration ('FDA').

CF is a profoundly serious disease. Recent pharmaceutical breakthroughs have significantly advanced the ability for healthcare providers to treat and manage patients with CF, with Vertex leading the way on this front. The approval in the US and Europe covered slightly different applications of Vertex's TRIKAFTA/KAFTRIO treatments. In August 2020, the European Commission ('EC') approved KAFTRIO (the European-branded name of the TRIKAFTA therapeutic) to treat certain forms of CF in patients aged 12 and older in combination with KALYDECO.

In October 2015, Vertex and CRISPR Therapeutics AG (CRSP) announced a strategic partnership that aimed to use "CRISPR's gene editing technology, known as CRISPR-Cas9, to discover and develop potential new treatments aimed at the underlying genetic causes of human disease." CRISPR focuses on gene therapies. The partnership is currently working on treating transfusion-dependent beta thalassemia ('TDT'), CF and SCD. We are intrigued by the potential therapeutic breakthroughs that the Vertex-CRISPR partnership could uncover.

Among the pharma giants, Johnson & Johnson's (JNJ) recent performance has been better than expected. Within the company's earnings presentation covering the final quarter of fiscal 2020, Johnson & Johnson noted it generated ~$20.0 billion in free cash flow last fiscal year and exited fiscal 2020 with a ~$10.0 billion net debt position. Given its ability to generate meaningful free cash flow in almost any environment, a product of its impressive business model, we view Johnson & Johnson as well-positioned to manage its net debt load and dividend obligations going forward.

Johnson & Johnson is working on its own COVID-19 vaccine, and interim clinical trial data has been promising. The company's management team noted that it was getting ready to share data from its Phase 3 clinical trial soon, which could add yet another arrow to the quiver of global health authorities assuming the clinical trial provides promising efficacy and safety results. Though we do not expect Johnson & Johnson to generate needle-moving revenue from the potential COVID-19 vaccine should the vaccine candidate receive emergency authorization, if the company proves to be successful on this front, that will go a long way to improving its corporate image worldwide.

Vertex and Johnson & Johnson weren't the only ones showcasing exciting fundamentals during 2020, as several biotech and pharmaceutical companies also revealed the resilience of their business models in a year posing severe exogenous headwinds created by the coronavirus ('COVID-19') pandemic. For broad-based diversified exposure tied to secular growth tailwinds across the largest drug development companies in the world (and their robust pipelines of drugs and therapies), we include the Health Care Select Sector SPDR ETF (XLV) in both the *Best Ideas Newsletter* and *Dividend Growth Newsletter* portfolios.

5G Wireless

Next-generation 5G wireless technology has been highlighted as a game-changer for much more than just smartphones, a sentiment we generally agree with. Apple, another one of our favorite companies, launched its first-ever 5G iPhone when releasing its iPhone 12 line-up in October 2020. Channel checks indicate that demand for the iPhone 12 has held up well in China and elsewhere, and the company reportedly plans to boost production. We expect the iPhone 12 will post strong sales performance in the US as well, aided by both the technological improvements of 5G technology and consumers saving money on discretionary activities (travel or eating out) during the pandemic (meaning they have more money to spend on new items like a premium smartphone).

The adoption rate of 5G wireless technology companies is uncertain, though the COVID-19 pandemic created turbulence that is unprecedented. We expect that 5G adoption will pick up steam in 2021. AT&T (T), Verizon (VZ), and T-Mobile (TMUS) are all aggressively advertising their 5G wireless services, and many of those ads focus on the new 5G-capable iPhone 12 lineup. We include AT&T in the *High Yield Dividend Newsletter* portfolio due to its impressive free cash flow generating abilities, potential upside from its nascent HBO Max video streaming service, and the expected uplift from 5G wireless adoption.

Going forward, the number of 5G-capable smartphones on the market will likely continue to grow. Samsung (SSNFL) offers various 5G-capable smartphone offerings and competes with Apple by selling both low- and high-end offerings. There is room for multiple winners in this space, and we continue to be impressed with Apple's ability to monetize the success of its hardware sales to create new growth opportunities.

Cisco Systems (CSCO) provides some of the software that supports 5G operations including its Cisco ONE architecture offering, which is "a cloud-first, software-defined architecture that spans enterprise and service provider deployments seamlessly--this includes open roaming between cellular and Wi-Fi, including the new Wi-Fi 6." We include shares of CSCO in the *Best Ideas Newsletter* and *Dividend Growth Newsletter* portfolios.

We're big fans of Cisco's pristine balance sheet and stellar cash flow profile. Its near-term outlook indicates the company is putting the worst of the COVID-19 pandemic behind it (the pandemic weighted negatively on Cisco's total product sales performance due to soft demand in certain enterprise and commercial markets). The company's software business has continued to move in the right direction of late, supported by its cybersecurity and telecommunications offerings, along with its exposure to the rollout of 5G wireless infrastructure and related activities.

Qualcomm (QCOM) is a leader in 5G modem and radio frequency ('RF") technology and is a leading supplier of the related semiconductor components to smartphone manufacturers. It also has a very lucrative licensing business. The company's recent truce with Apple and Huawei supports its outlook, and Qualcomm stands to be a big winner from the adoption of 5G technology. We are big fans of Qualcomm and include the firm in the *Dividend Growth Newsletter* portfolio.

Old Industrial

The ongoing coronavirus ('COVID-19') has weighed negatively on the industrial sector for most of 2020, before the space started to recover during the latter part of the year. Industrial conglomerate General Electric's (GE) fourth-quarter earnings for 2020 showed the beaten-down firm may be on the rebound. What really impressed us was that GE Industrial's free cash flow came in at $4.4 billion in the final quarter of last year which pushed the segment's full year free cash flow up to a positive $0.6 billion in 2020. GE may be starting its long-awaited comeback.

Caterpillar (CAT) and Honeywell (HON) have been communicating to investors that 2021 will likely be a year of recovery. Caterpillar expects its financial performance to improve as it is seeing signs of better end-user demand and the need for dealers to restock their inventories (after dealer inventories declined in the final quarter of 2020). Honeywell expects its financial performance will rebound in 2021 with management guiding for both organic sales growth and margin expansion. Cost structure improvements, particularly those embarked on during the COVID-19 pandemic, will also be key for both entities. Honeywell is included in the *Dividend Growth Newsletter* portfolio.

One storied industrial firm that may continue to struggle to right the ship in 2021 is Boeing (BA). Problems at its 737 MAX offering, delays in aircraft deliveries due to the COVID-19 pandemic (resulting in a large inventory buildup), and sharp reductions in its monthly aircraft production rates (reduced economies of scale) have weighed very heavily on its operational and financial performance. At the end of 2020, Boeing's net debt load stood at $38.0 billion (inclusive of short-term debt) and that is on top of hefty long-term pension and retiree health care obligations. The company is far from out of the woods.

Other industrial names have held up much better during the COVID-19 crisis. 3M (MMM), for example, has a meaningful personal protective equipment ('PPE') business and has raced to keep up with elevated demand due to the pandemic. Looking ahead, 3M aims to grow its total sales by 5%-8% annually in 2021, with annual organic currency-neutral growth forecasted at 3%-6%. The company expects earnings per share will come in between $9.20-$9.75 this year, a meaningful increase from its adjusted non-GAAP EPS of $8.74 in 2020 (3M posted $9.25 in diluted EPS on a GAAP basis in 2020).

Video Streaming

We are optimistic that video streaming services will maintain their recent gains in terms of paying subscriber growth throughout 2021. Disney (DIS), an idea in the *Best Ideas Newsletter* portfolio, is one of our favorite ways to consider playing the space as its Hulu, Disney+, and ESPN+ video streaming services have posted tremendous paid subscriber growth of late. For refence, Disney owns 67% of Hulu and 80% of ESPN, and uses its controlling stake in those businesses to generate synergies by bundling those services with its Disney+ service.

Even more importantly, Disney's forecasted paid subscriber growth through fiscal 2024 is stunning. By fiscal 2024, Disney aims to have 300-350 million in total paid subscribers across its core video streaming services. Launching new video streaming services (such as its pending Star and Star+ services that are geared towards international markets) while expanding its existing services into new markets will support Disney's paid subscriber growth trajectory going forward.

Disney intends to prioritize investments in original content in the coming years to keep the momentum going in the right direction. For that reason, Disney expects its video streaming services will incur meaningful operating losses (on a standalone basis) in the next couple of fiscal years before becoming sizable profit generators. We see these investments as a good use of capital. A resumption of pre-pandemic activities does not mean that households will shed their preference for video streaming services, and we expect many subscribers will stay around for the original content.

As an aside, note that Disney's financial performance should improve considerably in the coming quarters as global health authorities work to bring an end to the COVID-19 pandemic. When Disney can resume operations at its theme parks and resorts at or near pre-pandemic capacity levels, its financials should experience a material tailwind given that these assets have historically been its major profit generators. Furthermore, sporting events will be able to resume in earnest (though many already have) and the threat of sporting events getting cancelled will diminish significantly.

Netflix (NFLX) should also continue to do well as it is now finally able to go from burning through vast amounts of cash on an annual basis to generating positive free cash flows. Sharp growth in its net paid subscriber base (up about 17% from the end of 2019 to the end of the third quarter of 2020) combined with the delay of some production activities which reduced content development costs enabled Netflix to generate about $2.6 billion in positive net operating cash flow and $2.2 billion in free cash flow during the first three quarters of 2020. Back during the first three quarters of 2019, Netflix posted -$1.4 billion (negative $1.4 billion) in net operating cash flow, resulting in a large negative free cash flow figure.

Though competition in the industry continues to grow, as witnessed through the recent launch of AT&T's HBO Max service and the recent launch of Comcast's (CMCSA) NBCUniversal segment's Peacock service, we see room for multiple winners in this space. Bundling live TV packages with existing video streaming content further eliminates the need for households to retain a cable package, and Hulu offers these types of services. Apple has its Apple TV+ service, Amazon has Amazon Prime, and even Roku (ROKU) is getting ready to push into the space after reportedly acquiring the failed startup Quibi's streaming content. The industry's growth outlook is bright and once scale is achieved the video streaming business can be quite lucrative.

Traditional Banking

Though we're generally cautious on traditional banking business models due to the arbitrary nature of cash-flow generation within the banking system and the difficulty in valuing such entities on the basis of a free cash flow to the firm (enterprise valuation) framework, the traditional banking system held up quite well during 2020 thanks in large part to a backstop by the Federal Reserve and Treasury.

We think Morgan Stanley (MS) is executing well, and its return on tangible equity of 17.7% during the fourth quarter of 2020 speaks to solid economic-value creation. Goldman Sachs (GS) annualized return on total equity (ROTE) was an impressive 22.5% during its fourth quarter, helping drive the full-year measure to 11.1% for 2020. Bank of America (BAC) was an idea in the *Best Ideas Newsletter* portfolio in the past, but we removed the company on June 11, 2020, as it has continued to disappoint.

Citigroup (C), however, remains among our least favorite banking entities as it struggles with legacy issues, and while Wells Fargo (WFC) used to be a well-run bank, consumer perception has certainly changed with its "fake account scandal" that cost it $3 billion to settle criminal and civil charges. JP Morgan's return metrics have been solid like Morgan Stanley's and Goldman's, with return on equity (ROE) coming in at 19% and return on total common equity (ROTCE) coming in at 24% in the quarter.

We continue to view the banking system more as utility-like serving as an extension of the federal government (e.g., Paycheck Protection Program loans), and as such, we generally don't think the group will be able to muster above-average returns in the long run. That said, we still include diversified exposure to the financial sector in the *Best Ideas Newsletter* portfolio via the Financial Select Sector SPDR (XLF), but only for diversification purposes.

Cryptocurrencies

With the Federal Reserve and Treasury continuing to flood the market system with excess liquidity and stimulus, money is flowing into assets that perhaps it shouldn't. The prices of cryptocurrencies of all kinds from Bitcoin (GBTC), to Ethereum, and to Dogecoin have been skyrocketing. These instruments are more like trading vehicles than assets with intrinsic worth.

They depend entirely on the confidence that at some point in the future, they will become viable currencies with widespread consumer and merchant adoption. Until then, their prices are merely being propelled by the "greater fool theory," meaning that someone else must be willing to buy at a higher price to take existing holders out. Situations such as these generally don't end well, but we cannot rule out their long-term survival.

In light of the proliferation of price-agnostic trading for the past many decades that has catapulted the conversation of "value versus growth" to headlines, offering a foundation for many quant funds that specialize in these areas to thrive, it would not be surprising for similar dynamics to take hold in the cryptocurrency markets, whereupon "castles in the air" provide enough support for such instruments to become more commonplace within the global financial system than they otherwise should.

Celebrities are backing crypto, and even Tesla has added Bitcoin to its balance sheet. With so much money sloshing around, even the value of baseball cards has started to surge. When combined with the irrational trading of bankrupt stocks and what looks to be coordinated short squeezes by market participants, the markets have become a playground, or better yet a casino, for many. We continue to believe that those that focus on intrinsic values will come out ahead in the long run, and a market system that prioritizes intrinsic value analysis will ultimately be the healthiest.

Concluding Thoughts

2020 was one from the history books and a year that will live on in infamy. That said, we are excited for the future as global health authorities are steadily putting an end to the public health crisis created by COVID-19, aided by the quick discovery of safe and viable vaccines.

Tech, fintech, and payment processing firms were all big winners in 2020, and we expect that to continue being the case in 2021. Digital advertising, cloud-computing, and e-commerce activities are set to continue dominating their respective fields. Cybersecurity demand is moving higher and the constant threats posed by both governments (usually nations that are hostile to Western interests) and non-state actors highlights how crucial these services are.

Retailers with omni-channel selling capabilities are well-positioned to ride the global economic recovery upwards. Green energy firms will continue to grow at a brisk pace in 2021, though the oil & gas industry appears ready for a comeback. The adoption of 5G wireless technologies and smartphones will create immense growth opportunities for smartphone makers, semiconductor players and telecommunications giants. Video streaming services have become ubiquitous over the past decade with room to continue growing as households "cut the cord" and instead opt for several video streaming packages.

We're not too big of fans of old industrial names given their capital-intensive nature relative to capital-light technology or fintech, but there are select names that have appeal. Cryptocurrencies have taken the market by storm as we turn the calendar into 2021, but the traditional banking system remains healthy enough to withstand another shock should it be on the horizon. Our fair value estimate of the S&P 500 remains 3,530-3,920, as it has been since June 2020, but we may still be on a roller coaster ride.

Here's to a great 2021!

To learn more about Valuentum and its services, please visit us at www.valuentum.com or contact a sales representative at info@valuentum.com.

Company Index – Sorted by Symbol

Company Name	Symbol	Industry	VBI	Est. Div Yield	Economic Castle	Low Fair Value	High Fair Value
Apple	AAPL	Technology Giants	6	0.7%	Highest Rated	112.00	168.00
Adobe Systems	ADBE	Technology Giants	6	0.0%	Highest Rated	374.00	560.00
Analog Devices	ADI	Technology Giants	5	1.6%	Very Attractive	108.00	162.00
Automatic Data Processing	ADP	Technology Giants	6	2.1%	Highest Rated	134.00	200.00
Albemarle	ALB	Mining & Chemicals	6	1.0%	Attractive	85.00	177.00
Applied Materials	AMAT	Technology Giants	7	1.0%	Very Attractive	64.00	106.00
Advanced Micro Devices	AMD	Technology Giants	6	0.0%	Attractive	51.00	105.00
American Tower	AMT	Telecom Services	3	2.2%	Attractive	186.00	280.00
Amazon.com	AMZN	Technology Giants	6	0.0%	Attractive	2,510.00	4,183.00
AptarGroup	ATR	Mining & Chemicals	5	1.1%	Attractive	95.00	149.00
Activision	ATVI	Discretionary Spending	3	0.5%	Very Attractive	53.00	89.00
Broadcom	AVGO	Technology Giants	7	3.3%	Very Attractive	281.00	469.00
AutoZone	AZO	Discretionary Spending	6	0.0%	Very Attractive	1,144.00	1,716.00
Alibaba	BABA	Technology Giants	3	0.0%	Highest Rated	202.00	336.00
Baxter Intl	BAX	Health Care Bellwethers	3	1.2%	Attractive	60.00	96.00
Becton, Dickinson	BDX	Health Care Bellwethers	3	1.3%	Attractive	173.00	289.00
Baidu	BIDU	Technology Giants	6	0.0%	Very Attractive	123.00	229.00
Booking Holdings	BKNG	Technology Giants	6	0.0%	Very Attractive	1,661.00	2,491.00
Boston Scientific	BSX	Health Care Bellwethers	3	0.0%	Attractive	23.00	39.00
Beyond Meat	BYND	Disruptive Innovation	1	0.0%	Unattractive	65.00	135.00
Casey's General	CASY	Recession Resistant	4	0.8%	Attractive	151.00	227.00
Caterpillar	CAT	Industrial Leaders	5	2.4%	Attractive	137.00	205.00
Crown Castle	CCI	Telecom Services	3	3.5%	Attractive	126.00	210.00
Church & Dwight	CHD	Recession Resistant	3	1.1%	Attractive	60.00	90.00
Colgate-Palmolive	CL	Recession Resistant	4	2.2%	Attractive	48.00	72.00
Clorox	CLX	Recession Resistant	6	2.0%	Very Attractive	158.00	238.00
Chipotle	CMG	Discretionary Spending	6	0.0%	Very Attractive	825.00	1,531.00
Costco	COST	Recession Resistant	4	0.7%	Attractive	250.00	374.00
Campbell Soup	CPB	Recession Resistant	7	2.8%	Attractive	34.00	54.00
Salesforce.com	CRM	Technology Giants	3	0.0%	Attractive	177.00	265.00
CRISPR Therapeutics	CRSP	Disruptive Innovation	6	0.0%	Unattractive	130.00	270.00
Cisco	CSCO	Technology Giants	7	3.3%	Very Attractive	41.00	61.00
Cintas Corp	CTAS	Discretionary Spending	4	1.0%	Very Attractive	202.00	302.00
Carvana Co.	CVNA	Disruptive Innovation	6	0.0%	Unattractive	170.00	352.00
Deere	DE	Industrial Leaders	5	1.2%	Attractive	187.00	281.00
Dollar General	DG	Discretionary Spending	5	0.7%	Attractive	149.00	223.00
Danaher	DHR	Industrial Leaders	6	0.3%	Attractive	137.00	228.00
Disney	DIS	Discretionary Spending	6	0.0%	Attractive	116.00	184.00
Dick's Sporting	DKS	Discretionary Spending	6	2.1%	Attractive	54.00	80.00
Dunkin' Brands	DNKN	Discretionary Spending	5	2.0%	Attractive	51.00	85.00
DocuSign	DOCU	Disruptive Innovation	6	0.0%	Very Attractive	177.00	295.00
eBay	EBAY	Technology Giants	4	1.3%	Attractive	41.00	69.00
ETSY	ETSY	Disruptive Innovation	6	0.0%	Very Attractive	107.00	223.00
Expeditors Intl	EXPD	Industrial Leaders	6	1.1%	Very Attractive	71.00	107.00
Facebook	FB	Technology Giants	10	0.0%	Very Attractive	310.00	516.00
F5 Networks	FFIV	Technology Giants	7	0.0%	Highest Rated	157.00	235.00
First Solar	FSLR	Disruptive Innovation	6	0.0%	Attractive	74.00	138.00
Graco	GGG	Mining & Chemicals	6	1.0%	Very Attractive	46.00	76.00
General Mills	GIS	Recession Resistant	6	3.3%	Attractive	46.00	68.00
Alphabet	GOOG	Technology Giants	7	0.0%	Very Attractive	1,870.00	3,116.00
Global Payments	GPN	Disruptive Innovation	7	0.4%	Attractive	167.00	251.00
W.W. Grainger	GWW	Industrial Leaders	6	1.5%	Attractive	278.00	416.00
Hasbro	HAS	Discretionary Spending	6	3.2%	Attractive	71.00	107.00
Home Depot	HD	Discretionary Spending	7	2.1%	Very Attractive	212.00	318.00
Honeywell	HON	Industrial Leaders	5	1.8%	Very Attractive	162.00	242.00
Hormel Foods	HRL	Recession Resistant	6	1.8%	Attractive	35.00	53.00
IntercontinentalExchange	ICE	Disruptive Innovation	7	1.2%	Attractive	80.00	120.00
Intuitive Surgical	ISRG	Health Care Bellwethers	6	0.0%	Very Attractive	442.00	822.00
JD.com	JD	Disruptive Innovation	6	0.0%	Attractive	70.00	116.00
Johnson & Johnson	JNJ	Health Care Bellwethers	3	2.8%	Attractive	114.00	172.00

The pages that follow are organized alphabetically according to each company's ticker symbol.

Company Name	Symbol	Industry	VBI	Est. Div Yield	Economic Castle	Low Fair Value	High Fair Value
Kellogg	K	Recession Resistant	7	3.4%	Attractive	45.00	67.00
Keurig Dr Pepper	KDP	Recession Resistant	7	2.0%	Attractive	22.00	32.00
Korn/Ferry	KFY	Technology Giants	9	1.0%	Very Attractive	53.00	79.00
KLA-Tencor	KLAC	Technology Giants	5	1.4%	Very Attractive	181.00	271.00
Kimberly-Clark	KMB	Recession Resistant	4	2.8%	Attractive	96.00	144.00
Kinder Morgan	KMI	Oil & Gas Complex	6	7.7%	Neutral	12.00	26.00
CarMax	KMX	Discretionary Spending	7	0.0%	Attractive	88.00	146.00
Coca-Cola	KO	Recession Resistant	4	3.3%	Attractive	30.00	48.00
Kroger	KR	Recession Resistant	4	2.1%	Attractive	23.00	39.00
Lowe's	LOW	Discretionary Spending	7	1.4%	Attractive	126.00	198.00
Lam Research	LRCX	Technology Giants	6	1.1%	Very Attractive	342.00	512.00
Lululemon	LULU	Disruptive Innovation	6	0.0%	Very Attractive	242.00	450.00
Mastercard	MA	Technology Giants	6	0.5%	Very Attractive	275.00	413.00
McDonald's	MCD	Discretionary Spending	6	2.2%	Attractive	158.00	250.00
Mondelez Intl	MDLZ	Recession Resistant	6	2.2%	Attractive	40.00	60.00
Medtronic	MDT	Health Care Bellwethers	3	2.2%	Attractive	76.00	114.00
Mercadolibre	MELI	Disruptive Innovation	6	0.0%	Attractive	1,193.00	1,988.00
McCormick	MKC	Recession Resistant	3	1.5%	Attractive	63.00	97.00
3M	MMM	Industrial Leaders	7	3.4%	Attractive	131.00	219.00
Monster Beverage	MNST	Disruptive Innovation	7	0.0%	Very Attractive	60.00	100.00
Altria Group	MO	Recession Resistant	3	8.7%	Very Attractive	34.00	50.00
Microsoft	MSFT	Technology Giants	6	1.0%	Very Attractive	189.00	283.00
Mettler-Toledo	MTD	Health Care Bellwethers	4	0.0%	Very Attractive	696.00	1,044.00
Micron Technology	MU	Technology Giants	7	0.0%	Neutral	45.00	83.00
Netflix	NFLX	Discretionary Spending	6	0.0%	Attractive	317.00	659.00
Nike	NKE	Discretionary Spending	5	0.8%	Very Attractive	99.00	149.00
Nvidia	NVDA	Technology Giants	6	0.1%	Very Attractive	394.00	672.00
Oracle	ORCL	Technology Giants	6	1.6%	Very Attractive	54.00	80.00
Palo Alto	PANW	Disruptive Innovation	5	0.0%	Very Attractive	276.00	438.00
Paychex	PAYX	Technology Giants	6	2.7%	Attractive	59.00	93.00
Penn National	PENN	Disruptive Innovation	6	0.0%	Attractive	56.00	94.00
PepsiCo	PEP	Recession Resistant	6	2.9%	Attractive	101.00	151.00
Procter & Gamble	PG	Recession Resistant	2	2.2%	Attractive	80.00	120.00
Pinterest	PINS	Disruptive Innovation	5	0.0%	Attractive	50.00	92.00
Philip Morris	PM	Recession Resistant	6	6.1%	Very Attractive	61.00	91.00
Proto Labs	PRLB	Disruptive Innovation	6	0.0%	Attractive	110.00	183.00
Phillips 66	PSX	Oil & Gas Complex	6	5.1%	Attractive	58.00	96.00
PayPal	PYPL	Technology Giants	6	0.0%	Very Attractive	172.00	258.00
QUALCOMM	QCOM	Technology Giants	7	1.7%	Very Attractive	131.00	197.00
Roku	ROKU	Disruptive Innovation	6	0.0%	Very Attractive	206.00	343.00
Boston Beer	SAM	Disruptive Innovation	6	0.0%	Attractive	688.00	1,210.00
SBA Comm	SBAC	Telecom Services	3	0.7%	Attractive	172.00	286.00
Starbucks	SBUX	Discretionary Spending	6	1.9%	Very Attractive	60.00	100.00
Stitch Fix	SFIX	Disruptive Innovation	6	0.0%	Very Attractive	39.00	65.00
Sherwin-Williams	SHW	Mining & Chemicals	4	0.7%	Attractive	414.00	690.00
Smucker	SJM	Recession Resistant	6	3.0%	Attractive	84.00	126.00
Virgin Galactic	SPCE	Disruptive Innovation	6	0.0%	Unattractive	13.00	38.00
Splunk	SPLK	Disruptive Innovation	6	0.0%	Attractive	171.00	285.00
Stryker	SYK	Health Care Bellwethers	6	1.1%	Attractive	157.00	261.00
Sysco	SYY	Recession Resistant	6	2.4%	Attractive	57.00	91.00
Teradyne	TER	Disruptive Innovation	5	0.3%	Very Attractive	73.00	121.00
Target	TGT	Recession Resistant	5	1.6%	Attractive	122.00	182.00
Tesla	TSLA	Discretionary Spending	2	0.0%	Neutral	335.00	695.00
Taiwan Semiconductor	TSM	Technology Giants	5	1.7%	Attractive	71.00	118.00
Twitter	TWTR	Technology Giants	6	0.0%	Attractive	35.00	59.00
Texas Instruments	TXN	Technology Giants	6	2.5%	Very Attractive	107.00	187.00
Uber	UBER	Disruptive Innovation	5	0.0%	Unattractive	29.00	87.00
UnitedHealth Group	UNH	Health Care Bellwethers	7	1.4%	Very Attractive	241.00	401.00
Visa	V	Technology Giants	6	0.6%	Very Attractive	175.00	263.00
VF Corp	VFC	Discretionary Spending	6	2.3%	Attractive	70.00	104.00
Verisk	VRSK	Disruptive Innovation	7	0.5%	Very Attractive	149.00	248.00
VeriSign	VRSN	Disruptive Innovation	7	0.0%	Highest Rated	129.00	215.00
Vertex Pharma	VRTX	Health Care Bellwethers	3	0.0%	Very Attractive	137.00	321.00
Wayfair	W	Disruptive Innovation	3	0.0%	Very Attractive	225.00	375.00
Wal-Mart	WMT	Recession Resistant	4	1.5%	Attractive	89.00	133.00
Slack Tech	WORK	Disruptive Innovation	6	0.0%	Attractive	34.00	56.00
Williams-Sonoma	WSM	Discretionary Spending	7	1.9%	Attractive	94.00	140.00
Zimmer Biomet	ZBH	Health Care Bellwethers	3	0.7%	Attractive	108.00	162.00
Zoom Video	ZM	Disruptive Innovation	3	0.0%	Highest Rated	273.00	455.00
Zoetis	ZTS	Health Care Bellwethers	6	0.5%	Attractive	109.00	203.00

Apple AAPL   FAIRLY VALUED

Buying Index™ 6   Value Rating 🟡

Economic Castle	Estimated Fair Value	Fair Value Range	Investment Style	Sector	Industry
Highest Rated	$140.00	$112.00 - $168.00	MEGA-CAP BLEND	Information Technology	Technology Giants

The iPhone maker is one of the strongest companies in the world and has what it takes to navigate through the COVID-19 crisis.

Stock Chart (weekly)

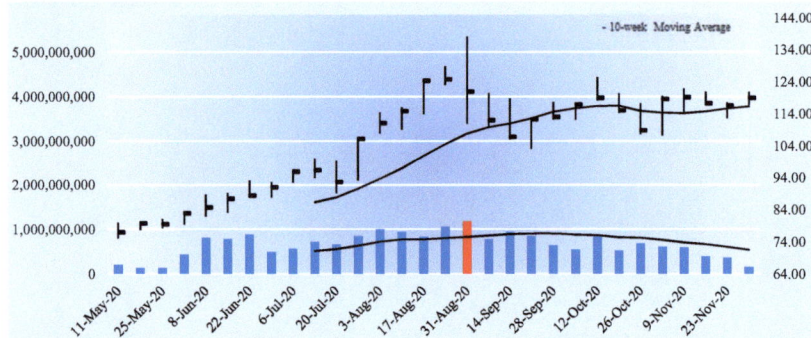

The week with the highest trading volume out of the last 30 weeks was a week of heavy selling, or distribution (red bar).

Investment Considerations

DCF Valuation	**FAIRLY VALUED**
Relative Valuation	**NEUTRAL**
ValueCreation™	**EXCELLENT**
ValueRisk™	**LOW**
ValueTrend™	**POSITIVE**
Cash Flow Generation	**STRONG**
Financial Leverage	**LOW**
Growth	**HIGH**
Technical Evaluation	**BULLISH**
Relative Strength	**NEUTRAL**
Money Flow Index (MFI)	**NEUTRAL**
Upside/Downside Volume (U/D)	**DETERIORATING**
Near-term Technical Support, 10-week MA	**116.00**

DCF = Discounted Cash Flow; MFI, U/D = Please see glossary. MA = Moving Average

Business Quality

ValueRisk™	ValueCreation™			
	Very Poor	Poor	Good	Excellent
Low				■
Medium				
High				
Very High				

Firms that generate economic profits with little operating variability score near the top right of the matrix.

Company Vitals

Market Cap (USD)	$2,086,734
Avg Weekly Vol (30 wks)	654,595
30-week Range (USD)	75.05 - 137.98
Valuentum Sector	Information Technology
5-week Return	9.1%
13-week Return	4.5%
30-week Return	54.6%
Dividend Yield %	0.7%
Dividends per Share	0.82
Forward Dividend Payout Ratio	20.6%
Est. Normal Diluted EPS	5.22
P/E on Est. Normal Diluted EPS	22.8
Est. Normal EBITDA	115,304
Forward EV/EBITDA	21.7
EV/Est. Normal EBITDA	17.4
Forward Revenue Growth (5-yr)	9.9%
Forward EPS Growth (5-yr)	15.2%

NMF = Not Meaningful; Est. = Estimated; FY = Fiscal Year

Returns Summary
3-year Historical Average

Return on Equity	59.7%
Return on Assets	16.4%
ROIC, with goodwill	46.0%
ROIC, without goodwill	46.1%

ROIC = Return on Invested Capital; NMF = Not Meaningful

Leverage, Coverage, and Liquidity
In Millions of USD

Total Debt	112,436
Net Debt	-79,394
Total Debt/EBITDA	1.5
Net Debt/EBITDA	NMF
EBITDA/Interest	26.9
Current Ratio	1.4
Quick Ratio	2.2

NMF = Not Meaningful

Investment Highlights

• Apple is as much a brand as it is one of the world's most innovative companies. The firm is no longer known for its iPods and personal computers thanks to the proliferation of the iPhone over the past decade. The company's execution remains top notch, and we expect it to continue to roll out innovative products in smartphones and wearable technology.

• Apple's rollout of future iterations of the iPhone (including 5G-enabled) should propel fundamentals. Though we're not embedding another blockbuster hit in our model, we wouldn't be surprised if Apple delivers another. The sky is the limit when it comes to innovation at Apple.

• Apple's growing Services segment bodes well for its long-term profitability, and the segment is growing like a weed. Apple Pay is now accepted by a large percentage of US retailers, and paid subscriptions are surging. Wearables has been an area of strength, and Apple holds a large share of global smartwatch market. Its customer loyalty and installed base of devices are key competitive advantages.

• Though we're not too worried given Apple's bargaining power over suppliers, investors should pay close attention to the firm's gross margin. Pricing and cost pressures may be unavoidable at times, and currency exchange rates should not be ignored as Apple generates ~60% of its revenue outside the US.

• Apple's cash hoard is more than the market caps of some of the largest firms in the S&P 500. It retains tremendous flexibility, and its dividend growth potential may be unmatched. Buybacks have averaged an amazing ~$70 billion during fiscal 2018-2020.

Relative Valuation

	Forward P/E	PEG	Price / FV
Facebook	31.0	1.8	69.6%
Alphabet	34.9	1.8	73.3%
Amazon.com	NMF	3.3	95.7%
Microsoft	31.6	2.5	91.6%
Peer Median	31.6	2.2	82.5%
Apple	**29.8**	**2.4**	**85.0%**

Price / FV = Current Stock Price divided by Estimated Fair Value

Financial Summary

	----- Actual -----			Projected
Fiscal Year End:		Sep-19	Sep-20	Sep-21
Revenue		260,174	274,515	314,869
Revenue, YoY%		-2.0%	5.5%	14.7%
Operating Income		63,930	66,288	79,734
Operating Margin %		24.6%	24.1%	25.3%
Net Income		55,256	57,411	68,530
Net Income Margin %		21.2%	20.9%	21.8%
Diluted EPS		2.97	3.28	3.99
Diluted EPS, YoY %		-0.2%	10.2%	21.8%
Free Cash Flow (CFO-capex)		58,896	73,365	86,191
Free Cash Flow Margin %		22.6%	26.7%	27.4%

In Millions of USD (except for per share items)

Structure of the Computer Hardware Industry   NEUTRAL

The computer hardware space, which spans the personal computer to the iPhone and iPad, is highly competitive. The industry is characterized by frequent product introductions and rapid technological advances that can cause dramatic market share shifts. Though some firms benefit from a strong brand, participants often price aggressively, pressuring margins. Firms are also subject to potential component shortages/disruptions, which can punish performance. Obsolescence may be an eventuality for some, and services revenue has become critical for others. We're neutral on the space.

Adobe Systems ADBE FAIRLY VALUED

Buying Index™ 6 **Value Rating** 🟡

Economic Castle	Estimated Fair Value	Fair Value Range	Investment Style	Sector	Industry
Highest Rated	$467.00	$374.00 - $560.00	MEGA-CAP GROWTH	Information Technology	Technology Giants

Adobe Systems' asset-light operations facilitate significant free cash flow generation, and its total addressable market continues to present notable growth opportunities.

Stock Chart (weekly)

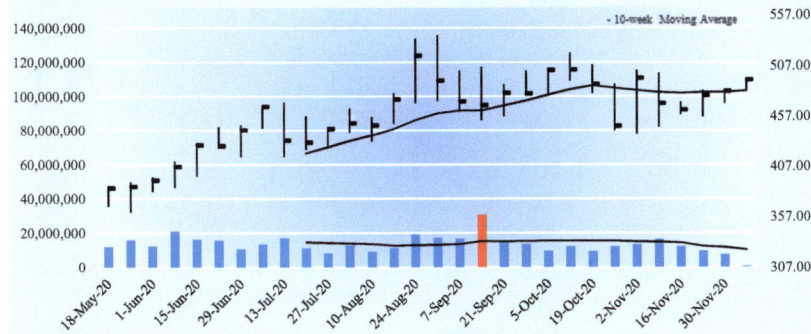

The week with the highest trading volume out of the last 30 weeks was a week of heavy selling, or distribution (red bar).

Investment Considerations

DCF Valuation	FAIRLY VALUED
Relative Valuation	UNATTRACTIVE
ValueCreation™	EXCELLENT
ValueRisk™	LOW
ValueTrend™	NEGATIVE
Cash Flow Generation	STRONG
Financial Leverage	LOW
Growth	HIGH
Technical Evaluation	VERY BULLISH
Relative Strength	WEAK
Money Flow Index (MFI)	NEUTRAL
Upside/Downside Volume (U/D)	BEARISH
Near-term Technical Support, 10-week MA	482.00

DCF = Discounted Cash Flow; MFI, U/D = Please see glossary. MA = Moving Average

Business Quality

ValueRisk™	Very Poor	Poor	Good	Excellent
Low				■
Medium				
High				
Very High				

ValueCreation™

Firms that generate economic profits with little operating variability score near the top right of the matrix.

Relative Valuation

	Forward P/E	PEG	Price / FV
Apple	29.8	2.4	85.0%
Alphabet	34.9	1.8	73.3%
Amazon.com	NMF	3.3	95.7%
Microsoft	31.6	2.5	91.6%
Peer Median	31.6	2.5	88.3%
Adobe Systems	**49.1**	**3.0**	**105.5%**

Price / FV = Current Stock Price divided by Estimated Fair Value

Company Vitals

Market Cap (USD)	$242,139
Avg Weekly Vol (30 wks)	13,303
30-week Range (USD)	361.44 - 536.88
Valuentum Sector	Information Technology
5-week Return	-0.4%
13-week Return	1.6%
30-week Return	32.6%
Dividend Yield %	0.0%
Dividends per Share	0.00
Forward Dividend Payout Ratio	0.0%
Est. Normal Diluted EPS	14.31
P/E on Est. Normal Diluted EPS	34.4
Est. Normal EBITDA	8,538
Forward EV/EBITDA	38.9
EV/Est. Normal EBITDA	28.4
Forward Revenue Growth (5-yr)	14.1%
Forward EPS Growth (5-yr)	27.6%

NMF = Not Meaningful; Est. = Estimated; FY = Fiscal Year

Returns Summary
3-year Historical Average

Return on Equity	26.7%
Return on Assets	14.3%
ROIC, with goodwill	28.4%
ROIC, without goodwill	93.1%

ROIC = Return on Invested Capital; NMF = Not Meaningful

Leverage, Coverage, and Liquidity
In Millions of USD

Total Debt	4,138
Net Debt	-39
Total Debt/EBITDA	1.0
Net Debt/EBITDA	NMF
EBITDA/Interest	25.5
Current Ratio	0.8
Quick Ratio	0.7

NMF = Not Meaningful

Investment Highlights

• Adobe is one of the largest software companies in the world. The firm's flagship offering in its digital media business is Adobe Creative Cloud, which allows customers to download the latest version of Adobe Creative Suite products. The firm also continues to focus on digital marketing solutions. It was founded in 1982 and is based in San Jose, California.

• There are not many business models as lucrative as Adobe's. Roughly 90% of its revenue comes from recurring sources. Asset-light operations enable significant cash-flow generation. We like its potential margin expansion as recurring revenue continues to ramp.

• Adobe continues to gain traction with respect to Creative Cloud subscriptions, and we love this recurring, subscription-based model. Adobe Marketing Cloud is becoming a favorite of Chief Marketing Officers, as digital marketing bookings continue to expand at a nice clip. The firm expects years of growth ahead of it.

• Adobe believes its Creative Cloud has a total addressable market (TAM) of ~$29 billion, including ~$14.5 billion in its core opportunity, by 2021. It expects its Document Cloud TAM will expand to ~$7.5 billion by 2021, while its largest opportunity, Experience Cloud, is expected to grow to a TAM of ~$71 billion.

• Adobe's cash-rich business model throws off gobs of excess capital. Traditional free cash flow has averaged ~$3.5 billion during the past three fiscal years (2017-2019), helping it repurchase ~$5.9 billion in treasury stock over that time.

Financial Summary

	----- Actual -----		Projected
Fiscal Year End:	Nov-18	Nov-19	Nov-20
Revenue	9,030	11,171	12,802
Revenue, YoY%	23.7%	23.7%	14.6%
Non-GAAP Operating Income	2,840	3,268	5,405
Non-GAAP EBIT %	31.5%	29.3%	42.2%
Non-GAAP Net Income	2,591	2,951	4,893
Non-GAAP NI Margin %	28.7%	26.4%	38.2%
Non-GAAP Diluted EPS	5.20	6.00	10.04
Non-GAAP Dil EPS, YoY %	54.0%	15.4%	67.2%
Non-GAAP FCF (CFO-capex)	3,762	4,027	5,486
Non-GAAP FCF Margin %	41.7%	36.1%	42.9%

In Millions of USD (except for per share items)

Structure of the Software Industry VERY GOOD

Firms that serve the mature software markets—or those consisting of basic business applications—have powerful distribution channels, large installed bases, and fortress balance sheets. These entrenched competitors benefit from significant customer switching costs, which make it nearly impossible for new entrants to gain a foothold. Participants generally benefit from high-margin license revenue and generate significant returns on investment. Still, the shift to cloud computing has created both opportunities and challenges, and the enterprise software landscape continues to evolve. We like the group.

VALUENTUM

Analog Devices ADI   FAIRLY VALUED

Buying Index™   **5**   *Value Rating*   ⬤

Economic Castle	Estimated Fair Value	Fair Value Range	Investment Style	Sector	Industry
Very Attractive	$135.00	$108.00 - $162.00	LARGE-CAP CORE	Information Technology	Technology Giants

Analog Devices is a free-cash-flow generating machine. Its free cash flow as a percentage of revenue has been north of 30% during the past couple years. Analog is quite acquisitive, however, with Maxim its latest deal.

Stock Chart (weekly)

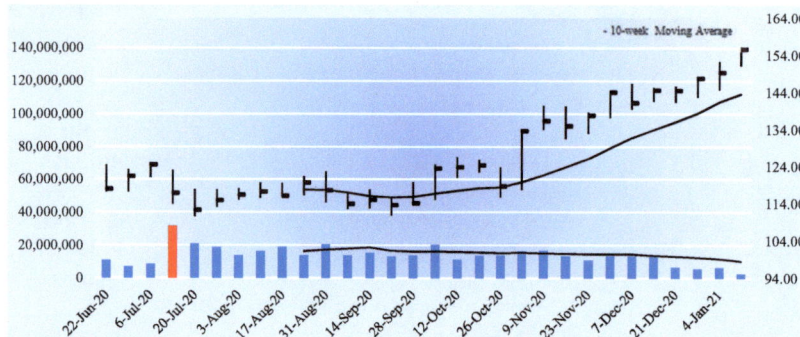

The week with the highest trading volume out of the last 30 weeks was a week of heavy selling, or distribution (red bar).

Investment Considerations

DCF Valuation	**FAIRLY VALUED**
Relative Valuation	**ATTRACTIVE**
ValueCreation™	**EXCELLENT**
ValueRisk™	**LOW**
ValueTrend™	**NEGATIVE**
Cash Flow Generation	**STRONG**
Financial Leverage	**MEDIUM**
Growth	**MODEST**
Technical Evaluation	**NEUTRAL**
Relative Strength	**STRONG**
Money Flow Index (MFI)	**OVERBOUGHT**
Upside/Downside Volume (U/D)	**BULLISH**
Near-term Technical Support, 10-week MA	**144.00**

DCF = Discounted Cash Flow; MFI, U/D = Please see glossary. MA = Moving Average

Company Vitals

Market Cap (USD)	$57,883
Avg Weekly Vol (30 wks)	13,848
30-week Range (USD)	110.47 - 156.21
Valuentum Sector	Information Technology
5-week Return	9.5%
13-week Return	24.9%
30-week Return	29.7%
Dividend Yield %	1.6%
Dividends per Share	2.48
Forward Dividend Payout Ratio	43.1%
Est. Normal Diluted EPS	7.01
P/E on Est. Normal Diluted EPS	22.2
Est. Normal EBITDA	3,806
Forward EV/EBITDA	19.0
EV/Est. Normal EBITDA	16.3
Forward Revenue Growth (5-yr)	7.0%
Forward EPS Growth (5-yr)	20.2%

NMF = Not Meaningful; Est. = Estimated; FY = Fiscal Year

Returns Summary
3-year Historical Average

Return on Equity	12.1%
Return on Assets	6.5%
ROIC, with goodwill	12.2%
ROIC, without goodwill	35.3%

ROIC = Return on Invested Capital; NMF = Not Meaningful

Leverage, Coverage, and Liquidity
In Millions of USD

Total Debt	5,145
Net Debt	4,089
Total Debt/EBITDA	2.3
Net Debt/EBITDA	1.8
EBITDA/Interest	11.5
Current Ratio	1.8
Quick Ratio	1.3

NMF = Not Meaningful

Investment Highlights

• Analog Devices makes high-performance analog, mixed-signal and digital signal processing integrated circuits used by over 125,000 end customers. It has 45,000+ SKUs and derives roughly two thirds of sales from data converters and high-performance amplifiers. Most of its revenue comes from the business-to-business space. It was founded in 1965 and is headquartered in Massachusetts.

• Analog expects its business-to-business markets, including industrial, automotive, and communications, to grow at a double-digit rate in the near term and account for a larger mix of its business. Its strong position in wireless (5G communications) should continue driving outperformance there.

• The 2014 deal with Hittite Microwave and the 2017 purchase of Linear Tech have created an analog industry giant, almost doubling its addressable market to $60 billion. Analog's 2021 purchase of Maxim will further strengthen its position. On a proforma basis, Analog expects $8.2 billion in sales and $2.7 billion in free cash flow after the Maxim combination, reflecting a robust 30%+ free cash flow margin.

• Analog's net debt load of ~$4.1 billion at the end of fiscal 2020 reflects balance sheet deterioration from its net cash position of $2.3+ billion at the end of fiscal 2016. The company has made notable progress in deleveraging since the Linear Tech deal, however, and its all-stock transaction to acquire Maxim seems prudent given existing leverage.

• Analog's Dividend Cushion ratio is strong thanks to its robust free cash flow generation. Investors should be cognizant of pricing pressure across its product line-up, however. We'll be paying close attention to whether it can deliver on the $275 million in estimated synergies related to the Maxim tie-up.

Business Quality

ValueRisk™	Very Poor	Poor	Good	Excellent
Low				▓
Medium				
High				
Very High				

ValueCreation™

Firms that generate economic profits with little operating variability score near the top right of the matrix.

Relative Valuation

	Forward P/E	PEG	Price / FV
Apple	29.8	2.4	85.0%
Alphabet	34.9	1.8	73.3%
Amazon.com	NMF	3.3	95.7%
Microsoft	31.6	2.5	91.6%
Peer Median	31.6	2.5	88.3%
Analog Devices	**27.0**	**2.3**	**115.3%**

Price / FV = Current Stock Price divided by Estimated Fair Value

Financial Summary

	----- Actual -----		Projected
Fiscal Year End:	Oct-19	Oct-20	Oct-21
Revenue	5,991	5,603	6,253
Revenue, YoY%	-3.4%	-6.5%	11.6%
Non-GAAP Operating Income	1,806	1,551	2,574
Non-GAAP EBIT %	30.1%	27.7%	41.2%
Non-GAAP Net Income	1,363	1,221	2,141
Non-GAAP NI Margin %	22.8%	21.8%	34.2%
Non-GAAP Diluted EPS	3.66	3.28	5.76
Non-GAAP Dil EPS, YoY %	-8.3%	-10.2%	75.4%
Non-GAAP FCF (CFO-capex)	1,977	1,843	2,703
Non-GAAP FCF Margin %	33.0%	32.9%	43.2%

In Millions of USD (except for per share items)

Structure of the Integrated Circuits Industry   **VERY POOR**

Firms in the integrated circuits industry make components that form the electronic building blocks used in electronic systems and equipment. The industry is notoriously cyclical and subject to significant economic upturns and downturns, as well as rapid technological changes. Firms must innovate to survive, and products stocked in inventory can sometimes become obsolete before they are even shipped. Severe pricing competition and lengthy manufacturing cycles only add uncertainty to the mix. We're not fans of the structure of the integrated circuits space.

VALUENTUM

Automatic Data Processing ADP   FAIRLY VALUED

	Buying Index™	6	Value Rating	●

Economic Castle	Estimated Fair Value	Fair Value Range	Investment Style	Sector	Industry
Highest Rated	$167.00	$134.00 - $200.00	LARGE-CAP CORE	Information Technology	Technology Giants

Automatic Data Processing boasts a large, recurring revenue base resulting in strong, consistent cash flow generation.

Stock Chart (weekly)

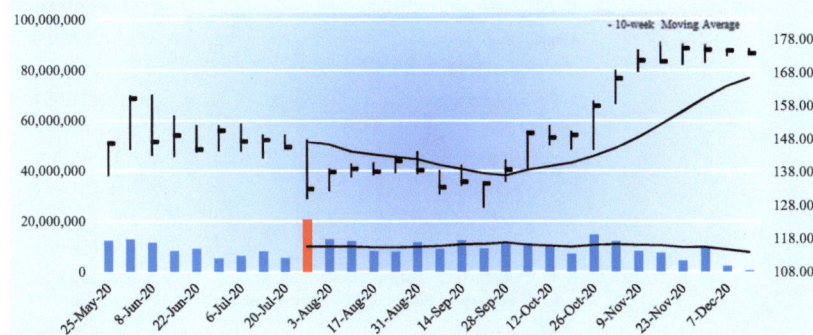

The week with the highest trading volume out of the last 30 weeks was a week of heavy selling, or distribution (red bar).

Investment Considerations

DCF Valuation	FAIRLY VALUED
Relative Valuation	NEUTRAL
ValueCreation™	EXCELLENT
ValueRisk™	LOW
ValueTrend™	NEGATIVE
Cash Flow Generation	STRONG
Financial Leverage	LOW
Growth	MODEST
Technical Evaluation	BULLISH
Relative Strength	STRONG
Money Flow Index (MFI)	NEUTRAL
Upside/Downside Volume (U/D)	BULLISH
Near-term Technical Support, 10-week MA	166.00

DCF = Discounted Cash Flow; MFI, U/D = Please see glossary. MA = Moving Average

Company Vitals

Market Cap (USD)	$75,137
Avg Weekly Vol (30 wks)	9,415
30-week Range (USD)	127.31 - 177.19
Valuentum Sector	Information Technology
5-week Return	-0.2%
13-week Return	31.3%
30-week Return	25.8%
Dividend Yield %	2.1%
Dividends per Share	3.72
Forward Dividend Payout Ratio	65.4%
Est. Normal Diluted EPS	7.31
P/E on Est. Normal Diluted EPS	23.8
Est. Normal EBITDA	4,588
Forward EV/EBITDA	20.8
EV/Est. Normal EBITDA	16.4
Forward Revenue Growth (5-yr)	4.6%
Forward EPS Growth (5-yr)	9.7%

NMF = Not Meaningful; Est. = Estimated; FY = Fiscal Year

Returns Summary

3-year Historical Average

Return on Equity	46.5%
Return on Assets	5.4%
ROIC, with goodwill	69.6%
ROIC, without goodwill	177.4%

ROIC = Return on Invested Capital; NMF = Not Meaningful

Leverage, Coverage, and Liquidity

In Millions of USD

Total Debt	2,005
Net Debt	96
Total Debt/EBITDA	0.6
Net Debt/EBITDA	0.0
EBITDA/Interest	32.8
Current Ratio	1.0
Quick Ratio	0.1

NMF = Not Meaningful

Investment Highlights

• Automatic Data Processing (ADP) is one of the world's largest providers of business outsourcing solutions. It offers a wide range of easy-to-use human resource, payroll, tax and benefits administration solutions from a single source. It has ~700,000 clients in 110+ countries, and ~80% of the Fortune 100 use at least one ADP service. The company was founded in 1949 and is based in New Jersey.

• The US human cloud capital management (HCM) market is expected to grow to ~$80 billion by early this decade, while the multi-national and international HCM market is expected to grow to well over $45 billion in coming years. ADP has a huge opportunity for future growth.

• ADP's operating environment is evolving. The increasing complexity of regulatory compliance, trends toward the use of big data, and the globalization of businesses and the additional complexities that come along with cross-border operations are all expected to help drive demand. Reported revenue is expected to be roughly flat in fiscal 2021 due to the impact of COVID-19.

• ADP boasts a large, recurring revenue base resulting in strong, consistent cash flow generation. The firm's business model has low capital requirements. It has minimal long-term obligations and has been paying dividends continuously since 1974. It's hard not to like ADP's investment profile.

• ADP will face headwinds in fiscal 2021 as a result of the COVID-19 pandemic, but the company's unmatched scale and diversification will help it weather the storm. Adjusted diluted earnings per share is expected to decline modestly in fiscal 2021.

Business Quality

ValueRisk™	Very Poor	Poor	Good	Excellent
Low				■
Medium				
High				
Very High				

Firms that generate economic profits with little operating variability score near the top right of the matrix.

Relative Valuation

	Forward P/E	PEG	Price / FV
Apple	29.8	2.4	85.0%
Alphabet	34.9	1.8	73.3%
Amazon.com	NMF	3.3	95.7%
Microsoft	31.6	2.5	91.6%
Peer Median	31.6	2.5	88.3%
Automatic Data Processing	**30.5**	**2.5**	**104.0%**

Price / FV = Current Stock Price divided by Estimated Fair Value

Financial Summary

	----- Actual -----		Projected
Fiscal Year End:	Jun-19	Jun-20	Jun-21
Revenue	14,110	14,590	14,590
Revenue, YoY%	5.9%	3.4%	0.0%
Operating Income	3,024	3,142	3,250
Operating Margin %	21.4%	21.5%	22.3%
Net Income	2,293	2,467	2,436
Net Income Margin %	16.2%	16.9%	16.7%
Diluted EPS	5.24	5.70	5.69
Diluted EPS, YoY %	43.3%	8.8%	-0.2%
Free Cash Flow (CFO-capex)	2,122	2,410	2,709
Free Cash Flow Margin %	15.0%	16.5%	18.6%

In Millions of USD (except for per share items)

Structure of the Staffing Services Industry   NEUTRAL

The staffing services industry spans firms that provide business outsourcing services to those that offer talent management solutions. Providers of business outsourcing solutions compete with a variety of independent firms as well as captive in-house functions. Their businesses are characterized by long-term client relationships and recurring revenue. Talent management firms offer executive recruitment and consulting services and face emerging competition from professional networking website providers. Attracting consultants is particularly important for executive recruitment entities. We're neutral on the group.

Albemarle ALB   FAIRLY VALUED

Buying Index™ 6   **Value Rating** ○

Economic Castle	Estimated Fair Value	Fair Value Range	Investment Style	Sector	Industry
Attractive	$131.00	$85.00 - $177.00	LARGE-CAP CORE	Materials	Mining & Chemicals

Albermarle's long-term growth trajectory is supported by rising lithium demand to produce batteries for electric vehicles. Our forecasts are aggressive so investors should take note of its large fair value estimate range.

Investment Considerations

DCF Valuation	FAIRLY VALUED
Relative Valuation	UNATTRACTIVE
ValueCreation™	GOOD
ValueRisk™	HIGH
ValueTrend™	NEGATIVE
Cash Flow Generation	STRONG
Financial Leverage	MEDIUM
Growth	MODEST
Technical Evaluation	BULLISH
Relative Strength	STRONG
Money Flow Index (MFI)	NEUTRAL
Upside/Downside Volume (U/D)	BULLISH
Near-term Technical Support, 10-week MA	131.00

DCF = Discounted Cash Flow; MFI, U/D = Please see glossary. MA = Moving Average

Stock Chart (weekly)

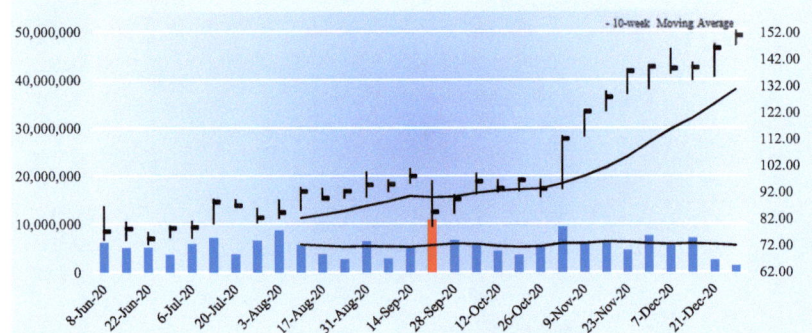

The week with the highest trading volume out of the last 30 weeks was a week of heavy selling, or distribution (red bar).

Business Quality

ValueRisk™	Very Poor	Poor	Good	Excellent
Low				
Medium				
High			▓	
Very High				

ValueCreation™

Firms that generate economic profits with little operating variability score near the top right of the matrix.

Company Vitals

Market Cap (USD)	$16,517
Avg Weekly Vol (30 wks)	5,487
30-week Range (USD)	72.39 - 152.82
Valuentum Sector	Materials
5-week Return	9.9%
13-week Return	65.4%
30-week Return	78.3%
Dividend Yield %	1.0%
Dividends per Share	1.54
Forward Dividend Payout Ratio	30.7%
Est. Normal Diluted EPS	5.10
P/E on Est. Normal Diluted EPS	29.6
Est. Normal EBITDA	867
Forward EV/EBITDA	20.1
EV/Est. Normal EBITDA	20.4
Forward Revenue Growth (5-yr)	1.6%
Forward EPS Growth (5-yr)	1.4%

NMF = Not Meaningful; Est. = Estimated; FY = Fiscal Year

Returns Summary
3-year Historical Average

Return on Equity	10.1%
Return on Assets	4.5%
ROIC, with goodwill	7.5%
ROIC, without goodwill	11.1%

ROIC = Return on Invested Capital; NMF = Not Meaningful

Leverage, Coverage, and Liquidity
In Millions of USD

Total Debt	1,705
Net Debt	1,150
Total Debt/EBITDA	1.9
Net Debt/EBITDA	1.3
EBITDA/Interest	17.2
Current Ratio	1.7
Quick Ratio	1.0

NMF = Not Meaningful

Investment Highlights

• Albemarle is a leading supplier of lithium and lithium products, including battery components to electric vehicle manufacturers. Performance catalysts for use by the oil refining industry and bromine derivatives for fire safety solutions represent its other key businesses. The firm was founded in 1994 and is headquartered in Baton Rouge, Louisiana.

• The company has a competitively-advantaged (low cost) and diverse lithium derivatives portfolio with a strong leadership team and attractive growth opportunities. Albemarle's largest segment, 'Lithium', carries the highest adjusted EBITDA margin out of its three core segments.

• Albermarle has ambitious corporate goals through 2021: annual sales growth of 7%-10% and adjusted EBITDA margins in the 32%-35% range. Management has also set its long-term leverage target as a net debt-to-adjusted EBITDA ratio of 2.0x-2.5x. Recent transactions saw the firm's pro forma leverage ratio increase materially. The firm has raised its dividend for 25+ consecutive years.

• Albermarle expects growth in its 'Lithium' and 'Advanced Materials' business to be driven by opportunities in battery applications (electric vehicles, storage, etc.) for lithium over both the near term and long term. The firm claims it has the world's best raw material reserves for bromine and lithium and is in the midst of a sizable capex build.

• Concerns have cropped up over a potential oversupply issue in the global lithium markets as capacity growth projects could outpace demand. According to some estimates, electric vehicles will have to make up ~31% of global auto sales by 2025 (~2% currently) to account for increased supply.

Relative Valuation

	Forward P/E	PEG	Price / FV
Air Products & Chemicals	27.5	2.3	130.9%
DuPont	29.2	3.7	108.9%
BHP Billiton	20.3	1.9	107.6%
Sherwin-Williams	43.9	2.4	131.2%
Peer Median	28.3	2.4	119.9%
Albemarle	**30.1**	**3.0**	**115.2%**

Price / FV = Current Stock Price divided by Estimated Fair Value

Financial Summary

	----- Actual -----		Projected
Fiscal Year End:	Dec-17	Dec-18	Dec-19
Revenue	3,072	3,375	3,598
Revenue, YoY%	14.7%	9.9%	6.6%
Non-GAAP Operating Income	588	701	665
Non-GAAP EBIT %	19.1%	20.8%	18.5%
Non-GAAP Net Income	55	694	546
Non-GAAP NI Margin %	1.8%	20.6%	15.2%
Non-GAAP Diluted EPS	0.49	6.34	5.02
Non-GAAP Dil EPS, YoY %	-87.5%	1198.2%	-20.8%
Non-GAAP FCF (CFO-capex)	-14	-154	-132
Non-GAAP FCF Margin %	-0.5%	-4.6%	-3.7%

In Millions of USD (except for per share items)

Structure of the Chemicals Industry   POOR

The chemicals (mid/small) industry includes firms that make thousands of different chemical substances, ranging from basic raw materials to advanced specialty chemicals. Making chemicals is a cyclical and energy-intensive business, with volatile oil/gas prices influencing feedstock, operation, and transportation costs. Specialty providers can carve out niches, but commodity chemicals producers are largely undifferentiated, making it impossible to gain a sustainable competitive edge. The industry is very capital intensive, and large swings in prices and volume should be expected. We don't like the industry structure.

Applied Materials AMAT   FAIRLY VALUED

Buying Index™ 7 **Value Rating** ●

Economic Castle	Estimated Fair Value	Fair Value Range	Investment Style	Sector	Industry
Very Attractive	$85.00	$64.00 - $106.00	LARGE-CAP CORE	Information Technology	Technology Giants

Applied Materials continues to invest to deliver solutions for its customers in the "AI-Big Data" era. Management noted in November 2020 that 'its future opportunities have never looked better.'

Stock Chart (weekly)

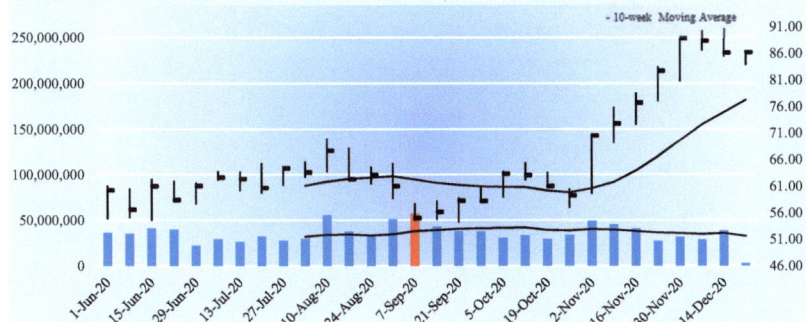

The week with the highest trading volume out of the last 30 weeks was a week of heavy selling, or distribution (red bar).

Investment Considerations

DCF Valuation	**FAIRLY VALUED**
Relative Valuation	**ATTRACTIVE**
ValueCreation™	**EXCELLENT**
ValueRisk™	**MEDIUM**
ValueTrend™	**POSITIVE**
Cash Flow Generation	**STRONG**
Financial Leverage	**LOW**
Growth	**MODEST**
Technical Evaluation	**BULLISH**
Relative Strength	**STRONG**
Money Flow Index (MFI)	**NEUTRAL**
Upside/Downside Volume (U/D)	**BULLISH**
Near-term Technical Support, 10-week MA	**77.00**

DCF = Discounted Cash Flow; MFI, U/D = Please see glossary. MA = Moving Average

Company Vitals

Market Cap (USD)	$88,390
Avg Weekly Vol (30 wks)	35,420
30-week Range (USD)	54.15 - 90.61
Valuentum Sector	Information Technology
5-week Return	11.9%
13-week Return	47.8%
30-week Return	54.9%
Dividend Yield %	1.0%
Dividends per Share	0.88
Forward Dividend Payout Ratio	30.8%
Est. Normal Diluted EPS	4.72
P/E on Est. Normal Diluted EPS	18.3
Est. Normal EBITDA	5,911
Forward EV/EBITDA	23.0
EV/Est. Normal EBITDA	15.2
Forward Revenue Growth (5-yr)	6.1%
Forward EPS Growth (5-yr)	14.2%

NMF = Not Meaningful; Est. = Estimated; FY = Fiscal Year

Returns Summary
3-year Historical Average

Return on Equity	35.2%
Return on Assets	16.5%
ROIC, with goodwill	49.5%
ROIC, without goodwill	95.3%

ROIC = Return on Invested Capital; NMF = Not Meaningful

Leverage, Coverage, and Liquidity
In Millions of USD

Total Debt	5,309
Net Debt	1,279
Total Debt/EBITDA	1.0
Net Debt/EBITDA	0.2
EBITDA/Interest	22.4
Current Ratio	2.6
Quick Ratio	1.6

NMF = Not Meaningful

Investment Highlights

• Applied Materials is the largest supplier of semi equipment, LCD fabrication equipment to the flat panel display industry and photovoltaic manufacturing systems to the solar industry. Substantial competition exists in all areas of its business, but it is working hard to accelerate its customers' ambitions. The firm was founded in 1967 and is headquartered in Santa Clara, California.

• In both semiconductor and display, major changes in device technology provide a catalyst for the firm's growth. With the coming of artificial intelligence, an explosion of data generation from machines is expected to drive demand for data storage and compute models and architectures.

• Fiscal 2020 was a banner year for Applied Materials but risks such as economic growth during COVID-19, global trade tensions, and a potential pullback in memory investments are not to be ignored. The company continues to execute well, however, and it is working to deliver solutions for its customers in the 'AI-Big Data era.' Management recently noted 'its future opportunities have never looked better.'

• Applied's growth will largely be driven by the proliferation of connected (mobile) devices in the 'Internet of Things.' It is optimistic about the long-term opportunity of the display market as the industry moves through technology transitions. Operating cash flow generation remains strong, with the company setting a record high in fiscal 2020.

• The semiconductor industry has been increasingly driven by consumer demand for lower-cost electronic products with increased capability. The rapid pace of technological change can quickly diminish the value of Applied Materials' current technologies.

Business Quality

ValueCreation™

ValueRisk™	Very Poor	Poor	Good	Excellent
Low				
Medium				■
High				
Very High				

Firms that generate economic profits with little operating variability score near the top right of the matrix.

Relative Valuation

	Forward P/E	PEG	Price / FV
Apple	29.8	2.4	85.0%
Alphabet	34.9	1.8	73.3%
Amazon.com	NMF	3.3	95.7%
Microsoft	31.6	2.5	91.6%
Peer Median	31.6	2.5	88.3%
Applied Materials	**30.1**	**1.2**	**101.4%**

Price / FV = Current Stock Price divided by Estimated Fair Value

Financial Summary

	----- Actual -----		Projected
Fiscal Year End:	Oct-17	Oct-18	Oct-19
Revenue	14,537	17,253	14,608
Revenue, YoY%	34.3%	18.7%	-15.3%
Non-GAAP Operating Income	3,868	4,796	3,483
Non-GAAP EBIT %	26.6%	27.8%	23.8%
Non-GAAP Net Income	3,434	3,313	2,874
Non-GAAP NI Margin %	23.6%	19.2%	19.7%
Non-GAAP Diluted EPS	3.17	3.23	2.86
Non-GAAP Dil EPS, YoY %	105.4%	1.9%	-11.5%
Non-GAAP FCF (CFO-capex)	3,264	3,165	2,806
Non-GAAP FCF Margin %	22.5%	18.3%	19.2%

In Millions of USD (except for per share items)

Structure of the Semiconductor Equipment Industry   **VERY POOR**

The semiconductor equipment industry is highly competitive and characterized by rapid technological change. Success hinges on the ability to commercialize new technology in a timely manner, continuously enhance products to improve efficiency of customer fab operations, and manage costs and inventory effectively. Performance of constituents is heavily influenced by manufacturing capacity and fab utilization rates, which together create volatile demand cycles. The potential for unexpected shifts in demand for the group's products leaves us unexcited about the industry's structural characteristics.

Advanced Micro Devices AMD   FAIRLY VALUED

Buying Index™ 6   **Value Rating** 🟡

Economic Castle	Estimated Fair Value	Fair Value Range	Investment Style	Sector	Industry
Attractive	$78.00	$51.00 - $105.00	LARGE-CAP GROWTH	Information Technology	Technology Giants

We are raising our fair value estimate (again) for AMD as its outlook continues to improve. AMD is acquiring Xilinx for ~$35 billion in stock.

Stock Chart (weekly)

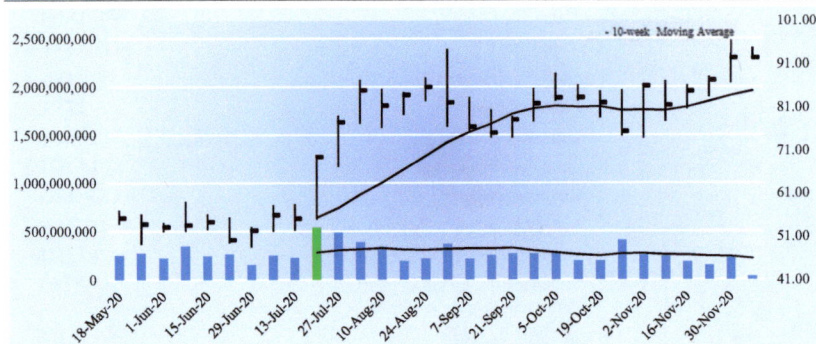

The week with the highest trading volume out of the last 30 weeks was a week of heavy selling, or distribution (red bar).

Company Vitals

Market Cap (USD)	$103,387
Avg Weekly Vol (30 wks)	264,274
30-week Range (USD)	48.42 - 96.37
Valuentum Sector	Information Technology
5-week Return	9.6%
13-week Return	20.2%
30-week Return	67.9%
Dividend Yield %	0.0%
Dividends per Share	0.00
Forward Dividend Payout Ratio	0.0%
Est. Normal Diluted EPS	2.65
P/E on Est. Normal Diluted EPS	34.8
Est. Normal EBITDA	4,185
Forward EV/EBITDA	49.9
EV/Est. Normal EBITDA	24.5
Forward Revenue Growth (5-yr)	24.5%
Forward EPS Growth (5-yr)	69.4%

NMF = Not Meaningful; Est. = Estimated; FY = Fiscal Year

Returns Summary
3-year Historical Average

Return on Equity	20.8%
Return on Assets	5.4%
ROIC, with goodwill	12.6%
ROIC, without goodwill	15.5%

ROIC = Return on Invested Capital; NMF = Not Meaningful

Leverage, Coverage, and Liquidity
In Millions of USD

Total Debt	486
Net Debt	-1,017
Total Debt/EBITDA	0.6
Net Debt/EBITDA	NMF
EBITDA/Interest	8.8
Current Ratio	1.9
Quick Ratio	1.4

NMF = Not Meaningful

Investment Highlights

• AMD is a global semiconductor company. The firm makes x86 microprocessors as well as graphics, video, and multimedia products for desktop and mobile devices. Its solutions, for example, power the newest gaming and entertainment consoles from Microsoft and Sony. The company was founded in 1969 and is headquartered in Sunnyvale, California.

• AMD is in the process of acquiring Xilinx through an all-stock transaction worth ~$35 billion. Xilinx's offerings include field-programmable gate arrays, or FPGAs, that can be configured by the customer after the manufacturing process is complete.

• Intel has dominated the microprocessor market for years, holding a commanding market share position. Intel's market share and significant financial resources will continue to pose serious headwinds for pricing and profits at AMD. However, AMD has made some share gains against Intel in PCs and CPUs of late, and it has an opportunity to take additional share.

• Please be aware that our enterprise cash flow models assume AMD posts double-digit annual revenue growth and significant operating margin expansion over the coming fiscal years. Should AMD stumble for any reason, its intrinsic value would face material headwinds.

• A few missteps at Intel have opened the door at AMD, and there could be further upside at the company. Though technology changes fast, AMD is well-positioned in the near term, and our recent fair value estimate increases reflect that dynamic.

Investment Considerations

DCF Valuation	FAIRLY VALUED
Relative Valuation	UNATTRACTIVE
ValueCreation™	EXCELLENT
ValueRisk™	HIGH
ValueTrend™	POSITIVE
Cash Flow Generation	WEAK
Financial Leverage	LOW
Growth	AGGRESSIVE
Technical Evaluation	BULLISH
Relative Strength	STRONG
Money Flow Index (MFI)	NEUTRAL
Upside/Downside Volume (U/D)	DETERIORATING
Near-term Technical Support, 10-week MA	85.00

DCF = Discounted Cash Flow; MFI, U/D = Please see glossary. MA = Moving Average

Business Quality
ValueCreation™

ValueRisk™	Very Poor	Poor	Good	Excellent
Low				
Medium				
High				▓▓
Very High				

Firms that generate economic profits with little operating variability score near the top right of the matrix.

Relative Valuation

	Forward P/E	PEG	Price / FV
Apple	29.8	2.4	85.0%
Alphabet	34.9	1.8	73.3%
Amazon.com	NMF	3.3	95.7%
Microsoft	31.6	2.5	91.6%
Peer Median	31.6	2.5	88.3%
Advanced Micro Devices	**74.3**	**4.4**	**118.3%**

Price / FV = Current Stock Price divided by Estimated Fair Value

Financial Summary

	----- Actual -----		Projected
Fiscal Year End:	Dec-18	Dec-19	Dec-20
Revenue	6,475	6,731	9,531
Revenue, YoY%	21.5%	4.0%	41.6%
Non-GAAP Operating Income	451	541	1,671
Non-GAAP EBIT %	7.0%	8.0%	17.5%
Non-GAAP Net Income	337	341	1,419
Non-GAAP NI Margin %	5.2%	5.1%	14.9%
Non-GAAP Diluted EPS	0.32	0.30	1.24
Non-GAAP Dil EPS, YoY %	665.3%	-3.9%	NMF
Non-GAAP FCF (CFO-capex)	-129	276	1,101
Non-GAAP FCF Margin %	-2.0%	4.1%	11.6%

In Millions of USD (except for per share items)

Structure of the Broad Line Semiconductor Industry
POOR

The broad line semiconductor industry is characterized by intense competition, rapid technological change, and frequent product introductions. The number and variety of computing devices have expanded rapidly, creating a connected landscape between suppliers and competitors. New market segments have emerged rapidly (smartphones, tablets), and constituents must continuously innovate to maintain share as traditional PC demand faces pressure. Though some firms may gain advantages via the combination of their manufacturing/test facilities with their design teams, we think the structure of the group is poor.

VALUENTUM

American Tower AMT   FAIRLY VALUED

Buying Index™   3   Value Rating

Economic Castle	Estimated Fair Value	Fair Value Range	Investment Style	Sector	Industry
Attractive	$233.00	$186.00 - $280.00	LARGE-CAP BLEND	Telecom Services	Telecom Services - diversified

We significantly increased our fair value estimate for American Tower. Its outlook is supported by the rollout of 5G operations in the US and elsewhere.

Stock Chart (weekly)

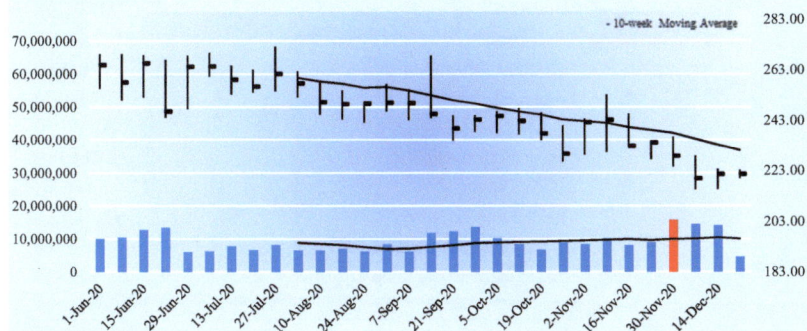

The week with the highest trading volume out of the last 30 weeks was a week of heavy selling, or distribution (red bar).

Investment Considerations

DCF Valuation	FAIRLY VALUED
Relative Valuation	NEUTRAL
ValueCreation™	GOOD
ValueRisk™	LOW
ValueTrend™	POSITIVE
Cash Flow Generation	STRONG
Financial Leverage	HIGH
Growth	HIGH
Technical Evaluation	BEARISH
Relative Strength	WEAK
Money Flow Index (MFI)	NEUTRAL
Upside/Downside Volume (U/D)	BEARISH
Near-term Technical Resistance, 10-wk MA	231.00

DCF = Discounted Cash Flow; MFI, U/D = Please see glossary. MA = Moving Average

Business Quality

ValueRisk™	ValueCreation™			
	Very Poor	Poor	Good	Excellent
Low			▓	
Medium				
High				
Very High				

Firms that generate economic profits with little operating variability score near the top right of the matrix.

Company Vitals

Market Cap (USD)	$98,692
Avg Weekly Vol (30 wks)	9,259
30-week Range (USD)	215.41 - 272.20
Valuentum Sector	Telecom Services
5-week Return	-5.2%
13-week Return	-8.9%
30-week Return	-14.1%
Dividend Yield %	2.2%
Dividends per Share	4.84
Forward Dividend Payout Ratio	58.8%
Est. Normal Diluted EPS	6.43
P/E on Est. Normal Diluted EPS	34.5
Est. Normal EBITDA	6,132
Forward EV/EBITDA	25.3
EV/Est. Normal EBITDA	19.8
Forward Revenue Growth (5-yr)	9.0%
Forward EPS Growth (5-yr)	15.2%

NMF = Not Meaningful; Est. = Estimated; FY = Fiscal Year

Returns Summary
3-year Historical Average

Return on Equity	23.2%
Return on Assets	4.2%
ROIC, with goodwill	8.9%
ROIC, without goodwill	11.2%

ROIC = Return on Invested Capital; NMF = Not Meaningful

Leverage, Coverage, and Liquidity
In Millions of USD

Total Debt	24,055
Net Debt	22,477
Total Debt/EBITDA	5.4
Net Debt/EBITDA	5.0
EBITDA/Interest	5.5
Current Ratio	0.5
Quick Ratio	0.4

NMF = Not Meaningful

Investment Highlights

• American Tower is a REIT that owns wireless and broadcast communications real estate. The firm has a global portfolio of ~181k properties (including ~41k in the US) that includes wireless and broadcast towers, and distributed antenna systems (DAS). The firm leases antenna space on multitenant communication sites and has a high quality US asset base.

• The attractive characteristics of scalable tower operations (operating leverage), long-term contracts, built-in escalators, high operating margins, and low customer churn highlight American Tower's high quality business model.

• American Tower has made significant progress in expanding its global growth platform over the past several years through various acquisitions. For instance, in early-January 2020, American Tower closed on its acquisition of Eaton Tower Holdings which significantly grew its presence in Africa. American Tower's global growth runway is impressive.

• Competition is present, and customer concentration is real. The company competes with other public tower companies, wireless carrier tower consortiums such as Indus Towers, and private tower companies. Significant customer concentration risk exists in every major geographical market American Tower operates in.

• Domestic carriers such as Verizon and AT&T continue to spend to improve their networks, which is a positive for American Tower. The continued evolution of fixed to mobile and increasing number of advanced devices will continue to drive industry spending.

Relative Valuation

	Forward P/E	PEG	Price / FV
AT&T	12.1	4.3	89.1%
Comcast	20.0	1.2	110.7%
Verizon	12.3	3.1	100.8%
Crown Castle	25.8	1.4	91.6%
Peer Median	16.2	2.2	96.2%
American Tower	**26.9**	**1.8**	**95.1%**

Price / FV = Current Stock Price divided by Estimated Fair Value

Financial Summary

	----- Actual -----		Projected
Fiscal Year End:	Dec-18	Dec-19	Dec-20
Revenue	7,440	7,580	8,042
Revenue, YoY%	11.6%	1.9%	6.1%
Adjusted Operating Income	1,905	2,688	2,935
Adj. Operating Margin %	25.6%	35.5%	36.5%
Funds from Operations	3,539	3,521	3,742
FFO Margin %	47.6%	46.5%	46.5%
Diluted FFO per share	7.99	7.90	8.23
Diluted FFO, YoY %	18.9%	-1.1%	4.2%
Free Cash Flow (CFO-capex)	2,835	2,762	2,926
Free Cash Flow Margin %	38.1%	36.4%	36.4%

In Millions of USD (except for per share items)

Structure of the Wireless Telecom Services Industry   GOOD

Most firms in the wireless telecom services industry lease antenna space on communication sites/towers to wireless service providers, radio and television broadcast companies, and tenants in other industries. Tenant leases are typically long-term, non-cancellable, have high renewal rates (98%+) and include attractive built-in annual rent escalations. Tower operators enjoy consistent demand for their sites, have high operating leverage (incremental costs to add new tenants are minimal), and require little capital expenditures to maintain their communication sites. We like the structure of the group.

Amazon.com AMZN   FAIRLY VALUED

Buying Index™   6   Value Rating

Economic Castle	Estimated Fair Value	Fair Value Range	Investment Style	Sector	Industry
Attractive	$3346.00	$2510.00 - $4183.00	MEGA-CAP BLEND	Information Technology	Technology Giants

Amazon's outlook is supported by its growing e-commerce, logistics, cloud-computing, digital subscription services and digital advertising business.

Stock Chart (weekly)

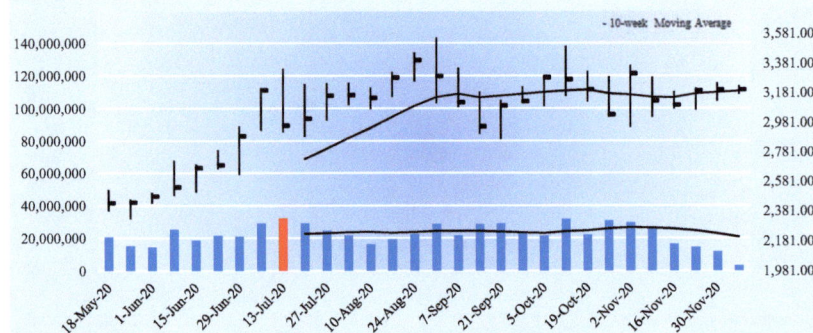

The week with the highest trading volume out of the last 30 weeks was a week of heavy selling, or distribution (red bar).

Company Vitals

Market Cap (USD)	$1,614,579
Avg Weekly Vol (30 wks)	22,288
30-week Range (USD)	2,330.00 - 3,552.25
Valuentum Sector	Information Technology
5-week Return	-0.9%
13-week Return	1.0%
30-week Return	33.2%
Dividend Yield %	0.0%
Dividends per Share	0.00
Forward Dividend Payout Ratio	0.0%
Est. Normal Diluted EPS	76.42
P/E on Est. Normal Diluted EPS	41.9
Est. Normal EBITDA	90,156
Forward EV/EBITDA	31.1
EV/Est. Normal EBITDA	18.0
Forward Revenue Growth (5-yr)	20.1%
Forward EPS Growth (5-yr)	41.9%

NMF = Not Meaningful; Est. = Estimated; FY = Fiscal Year

Returns Summary
3-year Historical Average

Return on Equity	21.0%
Return on Assets	5.2%
ROIC, with goodwill	18.5%
ROIC, without goodwill	22.3%

ROIC = Return on Invested Capital; NMF = Not Meaningful

Leverage, Coverage, and Liquidity
In Millions of USD

Total Debt	63,205
Net Debt	8,184
Total Debt/EBITDA	1.7
Net Debt/EBITDA	0.2
EBITDA/Interest	22.8
Current Ratio	1.1
Quick Ratio	0.9

NMF = Not Meaningful

Investment Highlights

• Amazon seeks to be the center for four primary customer sets: consumers, sellers, enterprises, and content creators. The company also provides advertising services and co-branded credit card agreements in addition to its Amazon Web Services, a suite of on demand cloud-based services. It stands as the best example as to why the dot-com boom of the late 1990s wasn't a complete bust.

• Amazon Web Services is becoming an increasingly important part of Amazon's business. Revenue growth in the segment is outpacing overall company growth, and AWS accounts for a substantial percentage of the tech giant's operating income.

• In the past, Amazon has notoriously been less concerned with maximizing profits, but free cash flow has now become a welcome abundance. Our fair value estimate is highly sensitive to our long-term/mid-cycle operating margin assumptions. For example, a one percentage point change in our mid-cycle operating margin assumption results in a ~$230 change in Amazon's fair value estimate.

• The online retailer continues to focus on taking market share and damaging its brick-and-mortar competitors. Its $13.7 billion purchase of Whole Foods speaks directly to this as the firm continues to compete aggressively for market share. The company continues to work to disrupt a number of other verticals, including pharmacy and shipping.

• Amazon is truly a special entity. From millions of new Prime members, to creating its own content, to delivering packages via drones, to its rapidly expanding AWS business and beyond, Amazon is a wonder of an enterprise. The Internet giant is working to enter the digital ad market in a big way.

Investment Considerations

DCF Valuation	FAIRLY VALUED
Relative Valuation	UNATTRACTIVE
ValueCreation™	EXCELLENT
ValueRisk™	MEDIUM
ValueTrend™	NEGATIVE
Cash Flow Generation	STRONG
Financial Leverage	MEDIUM
Growth	AGGRESSIVE
Technical Evaluation	BULLISH
Relative Strength	WEAK
Money Flow Index (MFI)	NEUTRAL
Upside/Downside Volume (U/D)	BEARISH
Near-term Technical Support, 10-week MA	3194.00

DCF = Discounted Cash Flow; MFI, U/D = Please see glossary. MA = Moving Average

Business Quality

ValueRisk™	Very Poor	Poor	Good	Excellent
Low				
Medium				▓
High				
Very High				

ValueCreation™ column header above Very Poor/Poor/Good/Excellent.

Firms that generate economic profits with little operating variability score near the top right of the matrix.

Relative Valuation

	Forward P/E	PEG	Price / FV
Facebook	31.0	1.8	69.6%
Apple	29.8	2.4	85.0%
Alphabet	34.9	1.8	73.3%
Microsoft	31.6	2.5	91.6%
Peer Median	31.3	2.1	79.2%
Amazon.com	NMF	3.3	95.7%

Price / FV = Current Stock Price divided by Estimated Fair Value

Financial Summary

	----- Actual -----		Projected
Fiscal Year End:	Dec-18	Dec-19	Dec-20
Revenue	232,887	280,552	379,867
Revenue, YoY%	30.9%	20.5%	35.4%
Operating Income	12,717	14,742	22,637
Operating Margin %	5.5%	5.3%	6.0%
Net Income	10,073	11,588	17,881
Net Income Margin %	4.3%	4.1%	4.7%
Diluted EPS	20.15	22.99	35.13
Diluted EPS, YoY %	NMF	NMF	52.8%
Free Cash Flow (CFO-capex)	17,296	21,653	39,822
Free Cash Flow Margin %	7.4%	7.7%	10.5%

In Millions of USD (except for per share items)

Structure of the Internet & Catalog Retail Industry   GOOD

The Internet and catalog retail industry benefits as a whole from the secular trend toward consumer digital (online) consumption. The industry consists of a number of exclusive online retailers led by Amazon, which continues to disrupt the broader retail space, and businesses that offer Internet travel services such as Booking Holdings, while online auctions are dominated by eBay. The industry generates high returns on investment due to minimal capital costs, but the landscape will be vastly different in the decades ahead. Still, we like the group.

AptarGroup ATR FAIRLY VALUED

Buying Index™ 5 **Value Rating** ○

Economic Castle	Estimated Fair Value	Fair Value Range	Investment Style	Sector	Industry
Attractive	$122.00	$95.00 - $149.00	MID-CAP CORE	Materials	Mining & Chemicals

Aptar expects the global packaging market to grow at a 3%-5% CAGR through 2022. The company had put up a very nice track record of consecutive annual dividend increases until the COVID-19 outbreak.

Stock Chart (weekly)

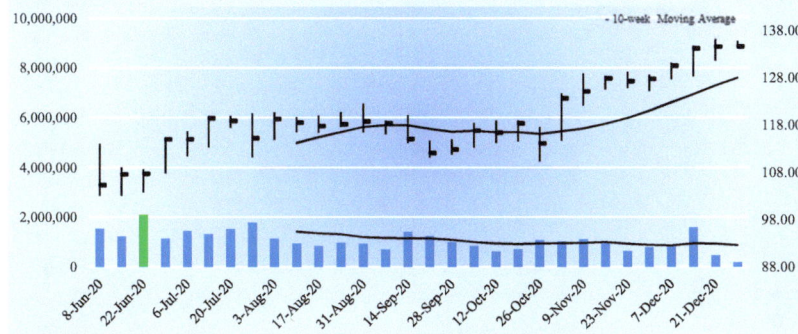

The week with the highest trading volume out of the last 30 weeks was a week of heavy selling, or distribution (red bar).

Investment Considerations

DCF Valuation	FAIRLY VALUED
Relative Valuation	UNATTRACTIVE
ValueCreation™	EXCELLENT
ValueRisk™	MEDIUM
ValueTrend™	NEGATIVE
Cash Flow Generation	STRONG
Financial Leverage	MEDIUM
Growth	MODEST
Technical Evaluation	NEUTRAL
Relative Strength	STRONG
Money Flow Index (MFI)	OVERBOUGHT
Upside/Downside Volume (U/D)	BULLISH
Near-term Technical Support, 10-week MA	128.00

DCF = Discounted Cash Flow; MFI, U/D = Please see glossary. MA = Moving Average

Company Vitals

Market Cap (USD)	$8,739
Avg Weekly Vol (30 wks)	1,066
30-week Range (USD)	103.07 - 136.22
Valuentum Sector	Materials
5-week Return	6.1%
13-week Return	18.7%
30-week Return	19.2%
Dividend Yield %	1.1%
Dividends per Share	1.44
Forward Dividend Payout Ratio	39.4%
Est. Normal Diluted EPS	4.95
P/E on Est. Normal Diluted EPS	27.2
Est. Normal EBITDA	622
Forward EV/EBITDA	19.5
EV/Est. Normal EBITDA	15.7
Forward Revenue Growth (5-yr)	4.8%
Forward EPS Growth (5-yr)	18.5%

NMF = Not Meaningful; Est. = Estimated; FY = Fiscal Year

Returns Summary

3-year Historical Average

Return on Equity	16.5%
Return on Assets	7.3%
ROIC, with goodwill	16.0%
ROIC, without goodwill	21.1%

ROIC = Return on Invested Capital; NMF = Not Meaningful

Leverage, Coverage, and Liquidity

In Millions of USD

Total Debt	1,290
Net Debt	1,028
Total Debt/EBITDA	2.5
Net Debt/EBITDA	2.0
EBITDA/Interest	16.0
Current Ratio	1.9
Quick Ratio	1.2

NMF = Not Meaningful

Investment Highlights

• Aptar is a leading global supplier of a broad range of innovative dispensing systems for the fragrance/cosmetic, personal care, pharmaceutical, household and food/beverage markets. Its delivery solutions include aerosol valves, nasal pumps, and lotion dispensers, among others. The company was founded in 1992 and is based in northern Illinois.

• Aptar is #1 or #2 in the markets in which it serves. No competitor fully matches the firm's broad product offering, geographic presence, and the number of markets served. We think its position as a leader in the dispensing solutions niche of the packaging industry is quite advantageous.

• Aptar's strategy is to invest meaningfully in R&D at a pace of about 3% of sales, make key acquisitions of well-managed companies with unique technology, and expand close to its customers. The company has expertise in design and prototyping, precision injection molding and high-speed assembly of creative solutions. It expects the global packaging market to grow at a 3%-5% CAGR through 2022.

• Aptar has a number of drivers for achieving its growth targets. It is aiming to maintain market share leadership in its key applications, grow its market applications where it is not already a leader, and expand its presence in Asia. Long-term financial targets include 4%-7% core sales growth and an adjusted EBITDA margin of 20%-22%.

• Aptar's Dividend Cushion ratio remains strong, despite it pausing its payout growth in 2020 after 25+ consecutive years of increases. Management has set its target dividend payout ratio at 30%-40% and leverage target ratio at 1x-3x. ROIC is targeted at 13%-15%.

Business Quality

ValueCreation™

ValueRisk™	Very Poor	Poor	Good	Excellent
Low				
Medium				▓
High				
Very High				

Firms that generate economic profits with little operating variability score near the top right of the matrix.

Relative Valuation

	Forward P/E	PEG	Price / FV
Air Products & Chemicals	27.5	2.3	130.9%
DuPont	29.2	3.7	108.9%
BHP Billiton	20.3	1.9	107.6%
Sherwin-Williams	43.9	2.4	131.2%
Peer Median	28.3	2.4	119.9%
AptarGroup	36.8	2.4	110.3%

Price / FV = Current Stock Price divided by Estimated Fair Value

Financial Summary

	----- Actual -----		Projected
Fiscal Year End:	Dec-17	Dec-18	Dec-19
Revenue	2,469	2,765	2,859
Revenue, YoY%	5.9%	12.0%	3.4%
Operating Income	324	350	323
Operating Margin %	13.1%	12.7%	11.3%
Net Income	220	195	237
Net Income Margin %	8.9%	7.0%	8.3%
Diluted EPS	3.41	3.00	3.66
Diluted EPS, YoY %	7.6%	-12.1%	22.0%
Free Cash Flow (CFO-capex)	168	103	273
Free Cash Flow Margin %	6.8%	3.7%	9.5%

In Millions of USD (except for per share items)

Structure of the Containers & Packaging Industry — NEUTRAL

Firms in the containers and packaging industry are highly competitive and operate capital intensive businesses characterized by facilities that run continuously to remain profitable. Firms are exposed to the costs of aluminum, steel and other materials, though many can pass through price changes thanks to contractual provisions. Still, cost containment is critical, as increases in productivity, combined with capacity changes, can create significant pricing pressures. Metal, plastic, glass and flexible materials are essentially substitutes, and differentiation can be difficult to achieve. We're generally neutral on the group.

Activision ATVI FAIRLY VALUED

Buying Index™ 3 Value Rating ○

Economic Castle	Estimated Fair Value	Fair Value Range	Investment Style	Sector	Industry
Very Attractive	$71.00	$53.00 - $89.00	LARGE-CAP CORE	Consumer Discretionary	Discretionary Spending

We recently increased our fair value estimate for Activision Blizzard as the company is well-positioned to navigate headwinds created by COVID-19.

Stock Chart (weekly)

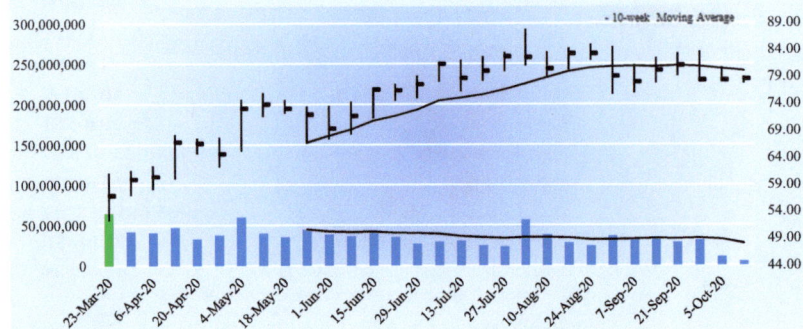

The week with the highest trading volume out of the last 30 weeks was a week of heavy selling, or distribution (red bar).

Investment Considerations

DCF Valuation	**FAIRLY VALUED**
Relative Valuation	**NEUTRAL**
ValueCreation™	**EXCELLENT**
ValueRisk™	**MEDIUM**
ValueTrend™	**NEGATIVE**
Cash Flow Generation	**STRONG**
Financial Leverage	**LOW**
Growth	**MODEST**
Technical Evaluation	**BEARISH**
Relative Strength	**WEAK**
Money Flow Index (MFI)	**NEUTRAL**
Upside/Downside Volume (U/D)	**BEARISH**
Near-term Technical Resistance, 10-wk MA	**80.00**

DCF = Discounted Cash Flow; MFI, U/D = Please see glossary. MA = Moving Average

Business Quality

ValueRisk™	Very Poor	Poor	Good	Excellent
Low				
Medium				▉
High				
Very High				

Firms that generate economic profits with little operating variability score near the top right of the matrix.

Company Vitals

Market Cap (USD)	$60,500
Avg Weekly Vol (30 wks)	35,123
30-week Range (USD)	52.33 - 87.73
Valuentum Sector	Consumer Discretionary
5-week Return	-0.7%
13-week Return	-0.8%
30-week Return	48.6%
Dividend Yield %	0.5%
Dividends per Share	0.41
Forward Dividend Payout Ratio	14.7%
Est. Normal Diluted EPS	3.37
P/E on Est. Normal Diluted EPS	23.3
Est. Normal EBITDA	4,029
Forward EV/EBITDA	17.0
EV/Est. Normal EBITDA	14.2
Forward Revenue Growth (5-yr)	8.1%
Forward EPS Growth (5-yr)	15.8%

NMF = Not Meaningful; Est. = Estimated; FY = Fiscal Year

Returns Summary
3-year Historical Average

Return on Equity	10.9%
Return on Assets	6.5%
ROIC, with goodwill	14.0%
ROIC, without goodwill	54.8%

ROIC = Return on Invested Capital; NMF = Not Meaningful

Leverage, Coverage, and Liquidity
In Millions of USD

Total Debt	2,675
Net Debt	-3,119
Total Debt/EBITDA	1.2
Net Debt/EBITDA	NMF
EBITDA/Interest	25.5
Current Ratio	2.5
Quick Ratio	2.3

NMF = Not Meaningful

Investment Highlights

• Activision is a worldwide publisher of online, personal computer, console, handheld, and mobile interactive entertainment products. The firm currently offers games that operate on PlayStation, Nintendo Wii, Microsoft Xbox, and smartphones, among others. Revenue from digital channels continue to represent a larger portion of sales at the company.

• The interactive entertainment industry is competitive, and new entertainment software products are introduced frequently. Adding to risk is that Activision's business is primarily 'hit' driven, which can create extremely volatile results at times. The firm has traditionally generated a significant portion of revenue from just four franchises: Call of Duty, World of Warcraft, Destiny, and Skylanders, though this is changing as the company pushes deeper into the smartphone/mobile gaming industry. This dependence increases the company's uncertainty relative to firms in other industries, and developing new gaming franchises is no easy feat...even for experienced publishers.

• In February 2016, Activision completed its acquisition of King Digital Entertainment through a deal worth $5.9 billion by equity value. Activision is now a big player in the mobile phone gaming space. The firm released the free-to-play Call of Duty: Mobile videogame in October 2019.

• Activision competes with various forms of entertainment. Not only does it bump heads with the likes of Electronic Arts (Madden NFL) and Take-Two (Grand Theft Auto), but pretty much anything from movies to board games can steal customers' attention.

Relative Valuation

	Forward P/E	PEG	Price / FV
Disney	75.6	0.3	98.3%
Home Depot	22.9	1.9	106.7%
McDonald's	38.5	1.1	111.0%
Nike	52.8	2.5	104.9%
Peer Median	45.6	1.5	105.8%
Activision	**28.1**	**2.5**	**110.5%**

Price / FV = Current Stock Price divided by Estimated Fair Value

Financial Summary

	----- Actual -----		Projected
Fiscal Year End:	Dec-18	Dec-19	Dec-20
Revenue	7,500	6,489	8,007
Revenue, YoY%	6.9%	-13.5%	23.4%
Non-GAAP Operating Income	1,988	1,739	2,746
Non-GAAP EBIT %	26.5%	26.8%	34.3%
Non-GAAP Net Income	1,813	1,503	2,178
Non-GAAP NI Margin %	24.2%	23.2%	27.2%
Non-GAAP Diluted EPS	2.35	1.95	2.80
Non-GAAP Dil EPS, YoY %	559.8%	-17.1%	43.5%
Non-GAAP FCF (CFO-capex)	1,659	1,715	2,932
Non-GAAP FCF Margin %	22.1%	26.4%	36.6%

In Millions of USD (except for per share items)

Structure of the Software (graphics) Industry   POOR

The software (graphics) industry is composed of a variety of firms from online gaming entities to technology-based-language learning companies. Industry constituents compete for the leisure time, attention and discretionary spending of consumers. The social gaming space, in particular, is evolving rapidly, and new entrants will inevitably drive down outsize returns over time. Performance of many participants is "hit" driven. If companies don't deliver "hit" products to the market, operating results will suffer. Rapid technological change makes obsolescence a possibility. We don't like the group's structure.

Broadcom AVGO   FAIRLY VALUED

Buying Index™ 7   **Value Rating** 🟡

Economic Castle	Estimated Fair Value	Fair Value Range	Investment Style	Sector	Industry
Very Attractive	$375.00	$281.00 - $469.00	LARGE-CAP CORE	Information Technology	Technology Giants

We increased our fair value estimate for Broadcom (again) as the firm continues to grow its infrastructure software business.

Stock Chart (weekly)

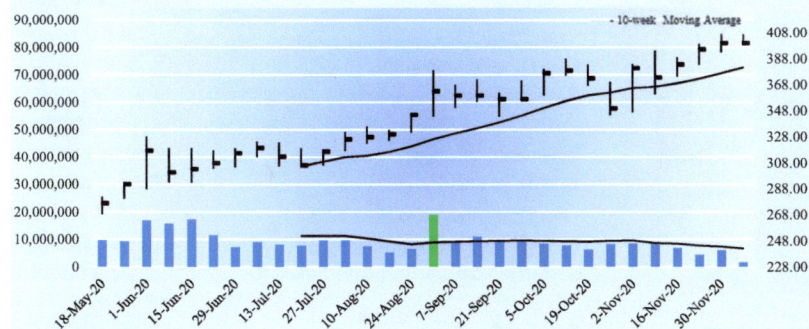

The week with the highest trading volume out of the last 30 weeks was a week of heavy selling, or distribution (red bar).

Company Vitals

Market Cap (USD)	$167,516
Avg Weekly Vol (30 wks)	9,158
30-week Range (USD)	268.00 - 406.68
Valuentum Sector	Information Technology
5-week Return	2.7%
13-week Return	9.7%
30-week Return	48.8%
Dividend Yield %	3.3%
Dividends per Share	13.00
Forward Dividend Payout Ratio	58.5%
Est. Normal Diluted EPS	26.45
P/E on Est. Normal Diluted EPS	15.1
Est. Normal EBITDA	14,594
Forward EV/EBITDA	16.0
EV/Est. Normal EBITDA	13.7
Forward Revenue Growth (5-yr)	6.6%
Forward EPS Growth (5-yr)	34.9%

NMF = Not Meaningful; Est. = Estimated; FY = Fiscal Year

Returns Summary
3-year Historical Average

Return on Equity	24.5%
Return on Assets	10.7%
ROIC, with goodwill	20.5%
ROIC, without goodwill	53.4%

ROIC = Return on Invested Capital; NMF = Not Meaningful

Leverage, Coverage, and Liquidity
In Millions of USD

Total Debt	37,641
Net Debt	32,548
Total Debt/EBITDA	3.7
Net Debt/EBITDA	3.2
EBITDA/Interest	7.0
Current Ratio	1.4
Quick Ratio	1.2

NMF = Not Meaningful

Investment Highlights

- Broadcom is a leading diversified communications semiconductor company with a broad portfolio of category-leading franchises. It serves markets in China, the US, Singapore, among others across the globe. The company is headquartered in Singapore and has a long history, with some of its divisions tracing their roots to the 1960s.

- Its 'Wired Infrastructure' segment is well-positioned for the long run. Key drivers for the segment include increasing use of cloud, social media, and video streaming, big data and corresponding analytics, and the adoption of connected home technology.

- Broadcom acquired Brocade in an all-cash deal worth ~$5.5 billion in November 2017. In November 2018, Broadcom continued its acquisitive streak with the purchase of CA Tech for ~$18.9 billion in cash. Broadcom acquired the 'Enterprise Security' business from then-Symantec in November 2019 for ~$10.7 billion in cash.

- Broadcom is using acquisitions to grow its infrastructure software business, which should help the firm grow its operating margins over time. Please note that our free flow model assumes Broadcom grows its revenues and operating margins significantly over the coming fiscal years.

- Broadcom's capital allocation plan includes paying 50% of prior fiscal year's free cash flow as dividends, the flexibility to use the balance of free cash flow to fund repurchases and acquisitions, and to maintain an investment-grade credit rating.

Investment Considerations

DCF Valuation	FAIRLY VALUED
Relative Valuation	ATTRACTIVE
ValueCreation™	EXCELLENT
ValueRisk™	MEDIUM
ValueTrend™	POSITIVE
Cash Flow Generation	STRONG
Financial Leverage	HIGH
Growth	MODEST
Technical Evaluation	BULLISH
Relative Strength	STRONG
Money Flow Index (MFI)	NEUTRAL
Upside/Downside Volume (U/D)	DETERIORATING
Near-term Technical Support, 10-week MA	381.00

DCF = Discounted Cash Flow; MFI, U/D = Please see glossary. MA = Moving Average

Business Quality
ValueCreation™

ValueRisk™	Very Poor	Poor	Good	Excellent
Low				
Medium				■
High				
Very High				

Firms that generate economic profits with little operating variability score near the top right of the matrix.

Relative Valuation

	Forward P/E	PEG	Price / FV
Apple	29.8	2.4	85.0%
Alphabet	34.9	1.8	73.3%
Amazon.com	NMF	3.3	95.7%
Microsoft	31.6	2.5	91.6%
Peer Median	31.6	2.5	88.3%
Broadcom	**18.0**	**1.8**	**106.6%**

Price / FV = Current Stock Price divided by Estimated Fair Value

Financial Summary

	----- Actual -----		Projected
Fiscal Year End:	Oct-18	Oct-19	Oct-20
Revenue	20,848	22,597	23,840
Revenue, YoY%	18.2%	8.4%	5.5%
Non-GAAP Operating Income	5,368	4,257	11,910
Non-GAAP EBIT %	25.7%	18.8%	50.0%
Non-GAAP Net Income	12,278	2,707	9,314
Non-GAAP NI Margin %	58.9%	12.0%	39.1%
Non-GAAP Diluted EPS	28.49	6.46	22.23
Non-GAAP Dil EPS, YoY %	NMF	NMF	NMF
Non-GAAP FCF (CFO-capex)	8,245	9,265	10,239
Non-GAAP FCF Margin %	39.5%	41.0%	42.9%

In Millions of USD (except for per share items)

Structure of the Broad Line Semiconductor Industry   POOR

The broad line semiconductor industry is characterized by intense competition, rapid technological change, and frequent product introductions. The number and variety of computing devices have expanded rapidly, creating a connected landscape between suppliers and competitors. New market segments have emerged rapidly (smartphones, tablets), and constituents must continuously innovate to maintain share as traditional PC demand faces pressure. Though some firms may gain advantages via the combination of their manufacturing/test facilities with their design teams, we think the structure of the group is poor.

AutoZone AZO   FAIRLY VALUED

Buying Index™ 6   **Value Rating** ◯

Economic Castle	Estimated Fair Value	Fair Value Range	Investment Style	Sector	Industry
Very Attractive	$1430.00	$1144.00 - $1716.00	LARGE-CAP VALUE	Consumer Discretionary	Discretionary Spending

AutoZone expects continued earnings growth despite challenges caused by COVID-19. Its expansion into commercial sales further brightens its long-term outlook.

Stock Chart (weekly)

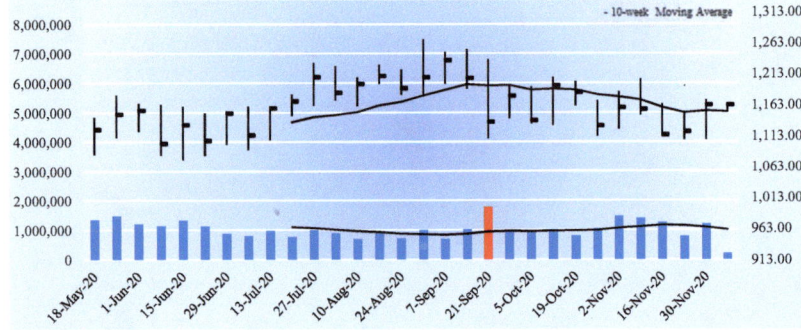

The week with the highest trading volume out of the last 30 weeks was a week of heavy selling, or distribution (red bar).

Company Vitals

Market Cap (USD)	$28,011
Avg Weekly Vol (30 wks)	1,025
30-week Range (USD)	1,074.45 - 1,267.93
Valuentum Sector	Consumer Discretionary
5-week Return	-1.7%
13-week Return	-6.9%
30-week Return	5.9%
Dividend Yield %	0.0%
Dividends per Share	0.00
Forward Dividend Payout Ratio	0.0%
Est. Normal Diluted EPS	90.77
P/E on Est. Normal Diluted EPS	12.8
Est. Normal EBITDA	3,278
Forward EV/EBITDA	10.8
EV/Est. Normal EBITDA	9.7
Forward Revenue Growth (5-yr)	3.6%
Forward EPS Growth (5-yr)	7.6%

NMF = Not Meaningful; Est. = Estimated; FY = Fiscal Year

Returns Summary   3-year Historical Average

Return on Equity	-108.2%
Return on Assets	15.1%
ROIC, with goodwill	51.6%
ROIC, without goodwill	56.1%

ROIC = Return on Invested Capital; NMF = Not Meaningful

Leverage, Coverage, and Liquidity

In Millions of USD

Total Debt	5,513
Net Debt	3,763
Total Debt/EBITDA	2.0
Net Debt/EBITDA	1.3
EBITDA/Interest	14.0
Current Ratio	1.1
Quick Ratio	0.3

NMF = Not Meaningful

Investment Highlights

• AutoZone is a leading retailer and distributor of auto replacement parts in the US. Though the firm tries to differentiate itself with customer service, we don't think this is necessarily a competitive advantage versus peers such as Advance Auto and Pep Boys. Its US retail business is its #1 priority. The company was founded in 1979 and is based in Tennessee.

• AutoZone has been aggressively investing in the highly-fragmented commercial segment of its industry in order to drive share gains. The efforts have resulted in a doubling of sales to this industry segment since 2010, which has grown at a ~4.5% annual rate over the past 20 years.

• AutoZone is a fantastic growth story. It has grown revenue ~10-fold since 1990 as it continues to grab a larger share of the huge 'Do-It-Yourself' auto aftermarket industry. Its expansion is not over yet either. AutoZone's US retail business can be expected to grow ~3% annually, while its commercial business offers solid growth potential. The commercial industry is estimated at a size of ~$76 billion.

• AutoZone's margins have been impacted by increased wage pressure and rising transportation costs, but it continues to work to improve merchandising and supply chain costs and holds an optimistic near-term outlook. Concerns over the US used auto market in coming years are rising and could impact demand for AutoZone.

• AutoZone is working to build a best-in-class B2B sales organization as a driver of commercial sales, which accounts for a small portion of domestic sales. Its market share in the commercial industry stands at only ~4%. Cost management will be key.

Investment Considerations

DCF Valuation	**FAIRLY VALUED**
Relative Valuation	**NEUTRAL**
ValueCreation™	**EXCELLENT**
ValueRisk™	**LOW**
ValueTrend™	**POSITIVE**
Cash Flow Generation	**STRONG**
Financial Leverage	**MEDIUM**
Growth	**MODEST**
Technical Evaluation	**VERY BULLISH**
Relative Strength	**WEAK**
Money Flow Index (MFI)	**NEUTRAL**
Upside/Downside Volume (U/D)	**BEARISH**
Near-term Technical Support, 10-week MA	**1152.00**

DCF = Discounted Cash Flow; MFI, U/D = Please see glossary. MA = Moving Average

Business Quality   ValueCreation™

ValueRisk™	Very Poor	Poor	Good	Excellent
Low				■
Medium				
High				
Very High				

Firms that generate economic profits with little operating variability score near the top right of the matrix.

Relative Valuation

	Forward P/E	PEG	Price / FV
Disney	75.6	0.3	98.3%
Home Depot	22.9	1.9	106.7%
McDonald's	38.5	1.1	111.0%
Nike	52.8	2.5	104.9%
Peer Median	45.6	1.5	105.8%
AutoZone	**15.2**	**2.1**	**81.3%**

Price / FV = Current Stock Price divided by Estimated Fair Value

Financial Summary

Fiscal Year End:	Actual Aug-19	Actual Aug-20	Projected Aug-21
Revenue	11,864	12,632	13,099
Revenue, YoY%	5.7%	6.5%	3.7%
Operating Income	2,216	2,418	2,522
Operating Margin %	18.7%	19.1%	19.3%
Net Income	1,617	1,733	1,810
Net Income Margin %	13.6%	13.7%	13.8%
Diluted EPS	63.43	71.93	76.68
Diluted EPS, YoY %	30.1%	13.4%	6.6%
Free Cash Flow (CFO-capex)	1,633	2,263	2,140
Free Cash Flow Margin %	13.8%	17.9%	16.3%

In Millions of USD (except for per share items)

Structure of the Retail Auto Parts Industry   GOOD

The retail auto parts industry is characterized by stiff competition in many areas, including brand recognition, customer service, and price. The industry is impacted by both the age and number of vehicles in service, especially those that are no longer under manufacturer's warranties (typically seven years old and older). Demand for retail auto parts can best be described as counter-cyclical: as consumers' cash flows decrease, drivers tend to keep their vehicles longer, leading to more retail auto parts sales. Though competition among constituents is intense, we like the industry's defensive characteristics.

Alibaba BABA   FAIRLY VALUED

Buying Index™   3   **Value Rating**   🟡

Economic Castle	Estimated Fair Value	Fair Value Range	Investment Style	Sector	Industry
Highest Rated	$269.00	$202.00 - $336.00	MEGA-CAP BLEND	Information Technology	Technology Giants

Alibaba Cloud has posted impressive sales growth of late, which supports the firm's outlook and our fair value estimate range.

Stock Chart (weekly)

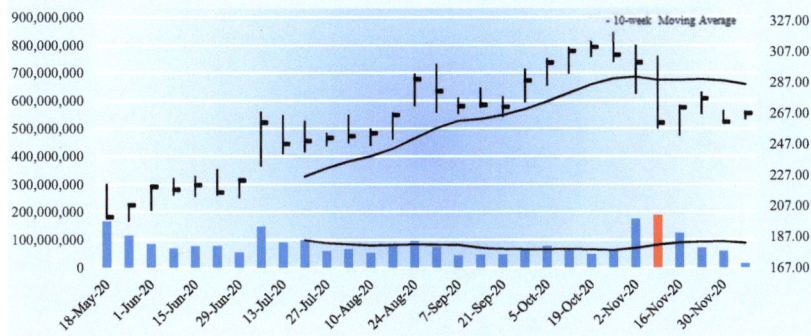

The week with the highest trading volume out of the last 30 weeks was a week of heavy selling, or distribution (red bar).

Company Vitals

Market Cap (USD)	$712,183
Avg Weekly Vol (30 wks)	83,061
30-week Range (USD)	196.70 - 319.32
Valuentum Sector	Information Technology
5-week Return	-12.1%
13-week Return	-3.1%
30-week Return	25.6%
Dividend Yield %	0.0%
Dividends per Share (in CNY)	0.00
Forward Dividend Payout Ratio	0.0%
Est. Normal Diluted EPS (in CNY)	91.73
P/E on Est. Normal Diluted EPS	20.5
Est. Normal EBITDA (in CNY)	371,671
Forward EV/EBITDA	17.0
EV/Est. Normal EBITDA	12.8
Forward Revenue Growth (5-yr)	22.4%
Forward EPS Growth (5-yr)	13.2%

NMF = Not Meaningful; Est. = Estimated; FY = Fiscal Year

Returns Summary

3-year Historical Average

Return on Equity	19.8%
Return on Assets	10.6%
ROIC, with goodwill	21.5%
ROIC, without goodwill	40.9%

ROIC = Return on Invested Capital; NMF = Not Meaningful

Leverage, Coverage, and Liquidity

In Millions of CNY

Total Debt	125,430
Net Debt	-253,264
Total Debt/EBITDA	0.9
Net Debt/EBITDA	NMF
EBITDA/Interest	26.0
Current Ratio	1.9
Quick Ratio	1.6

NMF = Not Meaningful

Investment Highlights

• Alibaba has been generating significant economic value during the past few years. The company benefits from a network effect and will continue to benefit from favorable demographic trends in China. Altaba (formerly Yahoo!) and Softbank own a nice slice of the firm. The firm also explores next-generation technology applications in its 'Innovation Initiatives' segment.

• Alibaba is widely known as being synonymous with e-commerce in China. The firm owns Taobao.com, the country's largest online shopping destination, Tmall, China's largest third-party plaform for brands and retailers, and Juhuasuan, China's most popular group buying marketplace.

• One upside catalyst to Alibaba's shares rests on its monetization rate. Though the firm manages its business for growth in GMV and active buyers, the Street is laser-focused on this metric. Segments outside its core commerce business such as 'Cloud Computing' and 'Digital Media and Entertainment' could be sources of upside as well.

• Alibaba has a robust marketplaces operation and is a mobile commerce leader. Total gross merchandising volume (GMV) on its China retail marketplaces is staggeringly large. The company hit $1+ trillion in GMV (May 2020), up from $768 billion in fiscal 2018.

• Risks are abundant with firms in China (regulatory/legal/governance), and the company's standing within the political structure of the country could be worth watching. It would take a massive event to derail the firm at this point though.

Investment Considerations

DCF Valuation	**FAIRLY VALUED**
Relative Valuation	**NEUTRAL**
ValueCreation™	**EXCELLENT**
ValueRisk™	**MEDIUM**
ValueTrend™	**NEGATIVE**
Cash Flow Generation	**STRONG**
Financial Leverage	**LOW**
Growth	**AGGRESSIVE**
Technical Evaluation	**BEARISH**
Relative Strength	**WEAK**
Money Flow Index (MFI)	**NEUTRAL**
Upside/Downside Volume (U/D)	**BEARISH**
Near-term Technical Resistance, 10-wk MA	**#REF!**

DCF = Discounted Cash Flow; MFI, U/D = Please see glossary. MA = Moving Average

Business Quality

ValueCreation™

ValueRisk™	Very Poor	Poor	Good	Excellent
Low				
Medium				■
High				
Very High				

Firms that generate economic profits with little operating variability score near the top right of the matrix.

Relative Valuation

	Forward P/E	PEG	Price / FV
Apple	29.8	2.4	85.0%
Alphabet	34.9	1.8	73.3%
Amazon.com	NMF	3.3	95.7%
Microsoft	31.6	2.5	91.6%
Peer Median	31.6	2.5	88.3%
Alibaba	**25.9**	**2.5**	**99.2%**

Price / FV = Current Stock Price divided by Estimated Fair Value

Financial Summary

	----- Actual -----		Projected
Fiscal Year End:	Mar-19	Mar-20	Mar-21
Revenue (CNY)	376,844	509,711	746,727
Revenue, YoY%	50.6%	35.3%	46.5%
Non-GAAP Operating Income	57,084	92,006	217,879
Non-GAAP EBIT Margin %	15.1%	18.1%	29.2%
Non-GAAP Net Income	87,590	149,263	194,573
Non-GAAP NI Margin %	23.2%	29.3%	26.1%
Non-GAAP Diluted EPS (CNY)	33.39	55.94	72.56
Non-GAAP Dil EPS, YoY %	36.2%	67.6%	29.7%
Non-GAAP Free Cash Flow	101,332	135,221	200,782
Non-GAAP FCF Margin %	26.9%	26.5%	26.9%

In Millions of CNY (except for per share items)

Structure of the Internet & Catalog Retail Industry   GOOD

The Internet and catalog retail industry benefits as a whole from the secular trend toward consumer digital (online) consumption. The industry consists of a number of exclusive online retailers led by Amazon, which continues to disrupt the broader retail space, and businesses that offer Internet travel services such as Booking Holdings, while online auctions are dominated by eBay. The industry generates high returns on investment due to minimal capital costs, but the landscape will be vastly different in the decades ahead. Still, we like the group.

VALUENTUM

Baxter Intl BAX   FAIRLY VALUED

Buying Index™ 3   Value Rating ⬤

Economic Castle	Estimated Fair Value	Fair Value Range	Investment Style	Sector	Industry
Attractive	$78.00	$60.00 - $96.00	LARGE-CAP CORE	Health Care	Health Care Bellwethers

Baxter suspended its share buyback program to conserve cash during the COVID-19 pandemic.

Stock Chart (weekly)

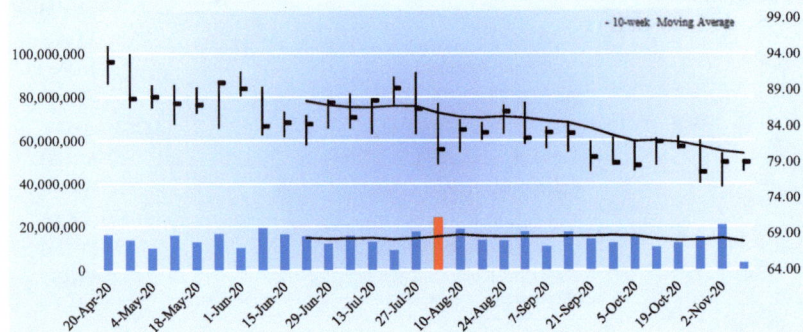

The week with the highest trading volume out of the last 30 weeks was a week of heavy selling, or distribution (red bar).

Investment Considerations

DCF Valuation	**FAIRLY VALUED**
Relative Valuation	**NEUTRAL**
ValueCreation™	**EXCELLENT**
ValueRisk™	**MEDIUM**
ValueTrend™	**POSITIVE**
Cash Flow Generation	**STRONG**
Financial Leverage	**MEDIUM**
Growth	**MODEST**
Technical Evaluation	**BEARISH**
Relative Strength	**WEAK**
Money Flow Index (MFI)	**NEUTRAL**
Upside/Downside Volume (U/D)	**BEARISH**
Near-term Technical Resistance, 10-wk MA	**80.00**

DCF = Discounted Cash Flow; MFI, U/D = Please see glossary. MA = Moving Average

Company Vitals

Market Cap (USD)	$40,965
Avg Weekly Vol (30 wks)	14,325
30-week Range (USD)	75.51 - 95.19
Valuentum Sector	Health Care
5-week Return	0.1%
13-week Return	-5.3%
30-week Return	-15.0%
Dividend Yield %	1.2%
Dividends per Share	0.98
Forward Dividend Payout Ratio	31.7%
Est. Normal Diluted EPS	4.29
P/E on Est. Normal Diluted EPS	18.4
Est. Normal EBITDA	3,413
Forward EV/EBITDA	15.9
EV/Est. Normal EBITDA	12.6
Forward Revenue Growth (5-yr)	5.5%
Forward EPS Growth (5-yr)	23.3%

NMF = Not Meaningful; Est. = Estimated; FY = Fiscal Year

Returns Summary
3-year Historical Average

Return on Equity	12.7%
Return on Assets	6.4%
ROIC, with goodwill	12.4%
ROIC, without goodwill	17.6%

ROIC = Return on Invested Capital; NMF = Not Meaningful

Leverage, Coverage, and Liquidity
In Millions of USD

Total Debt	5,350
Net Debt	2,015
Total Debt/EBITDA	2.2
Net Debt/EBITDA	0.8
EBITDA/Interest	34.1
Current Ratio	2.3
Quick Ratio	1.6

NMF = Not Meaningful

Investment Highlights

• Baxter has a broad portfolio of essential renal and hospital products. Its global footprint helps it play a key role in expanding access to healthcare in emerging and developed countries alike. The majority of the firm's revenue is generated from products in market-leading positions. The company split via a tax-free distribution to shareholders in 2015.

• Baxter's strong image and brand is augmented by an extensive global footprint and channel strength. The company continues to focus on growing international sales, which should be helped by its strong pipeline of new product launches.

• Baxter is dedicated to maintaining disciplined capital allocation after its split with Baxalta, which was acquired by Shire. It will continue reinvesting in its business to expand margins, though when faced with headwinds from the COVID-19 pandemic, management kept a lid on operating expenses to better position the firm to ride out the storm.

• Over the long haul, Baxter aims to maintain a dividend payout ratio of approximately 35%. Baxter temporarily suspended its share repurchasing program in 2020 due to headwinds caused by the COVID-19 pandemic as management wanted to conserve cash on the balance sheet.

• Please be aware that our free cash flow model assumes Baxter realizes significant revenue growth and margin expansion over the coming years. Should the firm stumble for any reason, its intrinsic value would face significant pressure.

Business Quality   ValueCreation™

ValueRisk™	Very Poor	Poor	Good	Excellent
Low				
Medium				▓
High				
Very High				

Firms that generate economic profits with little operating variability score near the top right of the matrix.

Relative Valuation

	Forward P/E	PEG	Price / FV
Johnson & Johnson	17.6	1.8	99.5%
Medtronic	25.6	2.2	109.0%
Merck	21.5	2.2	100.5%
Pfizer	20.1	0.8	93.3%
Peer Median	22.5	3.1	97.2%
Baxter Intl	**25.5**	**1.8**	**101.2%**

Price / FV = Current Stock Price divided by Estimated Fair Value

Financial Summary

	----- Actual -----		Projected
Fiscal Year End:	Dec-18	Dec-19	Dec-20
Revenue	11,099	11,362	11,419
Revenue, YoY%	4.9%	2.4%	0.5%
Operating Income	1,485	1,631	1,904
Operating Margin %	13.4%	14.4%	16.7%
Net Income	1,552	1,001	1,603
Net Income Margin %	14.0%	8.8%	14.0%
Diluted EPS	2.84	1.93	3.09
Diluted EPS, YoY %	NMF	NMF	NMF
Free Cash Flow (CFO-capex)	1,358	1,408	1,726
Free Cash Flow Margin %	12.2%	12.4%	15.1%

In Millions of USD (except for per share items)

Structure of the Medical Instruments Industry   GOOD

The medical instrument industry is heavily regulated and characterized by rapid technological change. Firms have been forced to compete on price due to economically-motivated buyers, consolidation among healthcare providers, and declining reimbursement rates. Healthcare reform measures have put additional pressure on procedure rates and market sizes. Still, firms can gain advantages by developing products with differentiated clinical outcomes or by creating patent-protected technology. Since most constituents hold important patents or trade secrets, we tend to like the group.

Becton, Dickinson BDX   FAIRLY VALUED

Buying Index™   3   Value Rating 🟡

Economic Castle	Estimated Fair Value	Fair Value Range	Investment Style	Sector	Industry
Attractive	$231.00	$173.00 - $289.00	LARGE-CAP CORE	Health Care	Health Care Bellwethers

We moderately increased our fair value estimate for Becton, Dickinson as its outlook is improving.

Stock Chart (weekly)

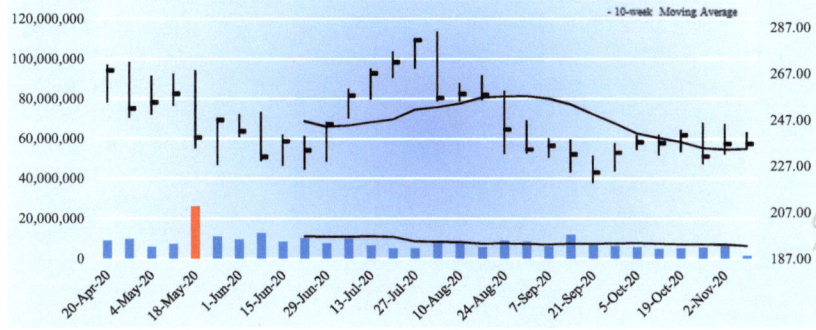

The week with the highest trading volume out of the last 30 weeks was a week of heavy selling, or distribution (red bar).

Investment Considerations

DCF Valuation	**FAIRLY VALUED**
Relative Valuation	**NEUTRAL**
ValueCreation™	**EXCELLENT**
ValueRisk™	**MEDIUM**
ValueTrend™	**NEGATIVE**
Cash Flow Generation	**STRONG**
Financial Leverage	**HIGH**
Growth	**MODEST**
Technical Evaluation	**BEARISH**
Relative Strength	**WEAK**
Money Flow Index (MFI)	**NEUTRAL**
Upside/Downside Volume (U/D)	**BEARISH**
Near-term Technical Support, 10-week MA	**234.00**

DCF = Discounted Cash Flow; MFI, U/D = Please see glossary. MA = Moving Average

Business Quality

ValueRisk™	Very Poor	Poor	Good	Excellent
Low				
Medium				▓
High				
Very High				

Firms that generate economic profits with little operating variability score near the top right of the matrix.

Company Vitals

Market Cap (USD)	$65,017
Avg Weekly Vol (30 wks)	8,135
30-week Range (USD)	219.50 - 284.97
Valuentum Sector	Health Care
5-week Return	-0.6%
13-week Return	-8.6%
30-week Return	-9.7%
Dividend Yield %	1.3%
Dividends per Share	3.16
Forward Dividend Payout Ratio	31.4%
Est. Normal Diluted EPS	13.56
P/E on Est. Normal Diluted EPS	17.4
Est. Normal EBITDA	7,743
Forward EV/EBITDA	13.8
EV/Est. Normal EBITDA	10.8
Forward Revenue Growth (5-yr)	7.1%
Forward EPS Growth (5-yr)	32.0%

NMF = Not Meaningful; Est. = Estimated; FY = Fiscal Year

Returns Summary
3-year Historical Average

Return on Equity	6.1%
Return on Assets	2.2%
ROIC, with goodwill	8.7%
ROIC, without goodwill	15.4%

ROIC = Return on Invested Capital; NMF = Not Meaningful

Leverage, Coverage, and Liquidity
In Millions of USD

Total Debt	19,390
Net Debt	18,770
Total Debt/EBITDA	3.8
Net Debt/EBITDA	3.6
EBITDA/Interest	8.1
Current Ratio	1.2
Quick Ratio	0.5

NMF = Not Meaningful

Investment Highlights

• Becton, Dickinson and Co is a medical technology company that sells medical devices, instrument systems and reagents. 'Medical' is the firm's largest division at more than half of revenue. The segment focuses on advancing medication delivery, reducing the risk of medication errors and enhancing diabetes treatment, and sells items such as needles, syringes, catheters, and sharps disposal containers. 'Life Sciences' is its second-largest segment and provides integrated systems for specimen collection, safety-engineered blood collection, automated blood culturing and tuberculosis culturing, and a vast range of other applications.

• Becton, Dickinson's outlook is supported by its merger with C.R. Bard, a ~$24 billion cash and stock deal completed in December 2017. Please note that our cash flow models assume that Becton, Dickson generates significant margin expansion and revenue growth over the coming fiscal years. We caution that should the firm stumble, its intrinsic value would face significant pressure.

• The C.R. Bard deal strengthened Becton, Dickinson's position outside the US with strong regional teams in Europe and China. However, the COVID-19 pandemic has created significant headwinds for Becton, Dickinson's business. Its international growth ambitions stalled in fiscal 2020.

• Looking ahead, Becton, Dickinson aims to simply its business processes and utilize digital offerings to improve its growth outlook while keeping a lid on costs. The resumption of elective procedures worldwide supports its near-term outlook.

Relative Valuation

	Forward P/E	PEG	Price / FV
Johnson & Johnson	17.6	1.8	99.5%
Medtronic	25.6	2.2	109.0%
Merck	21.5	2.2	100.5%
Pfizer	20.1	0.8	93.3%
Peer Median	22.5	3.1	97.2%
Becton, Dickinson	**23.5**	**1.9**	**102.4%**

Price / FV = Current Stock Price divided by Estimated Fair Value

Financial Summary

	----- Actual -----		Projected
Fiscal Year End:	Sep-18	Sep-19	Sep-20
Revenue	15,983	17,290	16,823
Revenue, YoY%	32.2%	8.2%	-2.7%
Operating Income	2,249	2,894	3,888
Operating Margin %	14.1%	16.7%	23.1%
Net Income	311	1,233	2,761
Net Income Margin %	1.9%	7.1%	16.4%
Diluted EPS	0.60	3.93	10.05
Diluted EPS, YoY %	-87.0%	NMF	NMF
Free Cash Flow (CFO-capex)	1,970	2,373	3,540
Free Cash Flow Margin %	12.3%	13.7%	21.0%

In Millions of USD (except for per share items)

Structure of the Medical Instruments Industry   GOOD

The medical instrument industry is heavily regulated and characterized by rapid technological change. Firms have been forced to compete on price due to economically-motivated buyers, consolidation among healthcare providers, and declining reimbursement rates. Healthcare reform measures have put additional pressure on procedure rates and market sizes. Still, firms can gain advantages by developing products with differentiated clinical outcomes or by creating patent-protected technology. Since most constituents hold important patents or trade secrets, we tend to like the group.

Baidu BIDU   FAIRLY VALUED

Buying Index™   6   Value Rating 🟡

Economic Castle	Estimated Fair Value	Fair Value Range	Investment Style	Sector	Industry
Very Attractive	$176.00	$123.00 - $229.00	LARGE-CAP VALUE	Information Technology	Technology Giants

Baidu is making significant investments in artifical intelligence to support its online search operations.

Stock Chart (weekly)

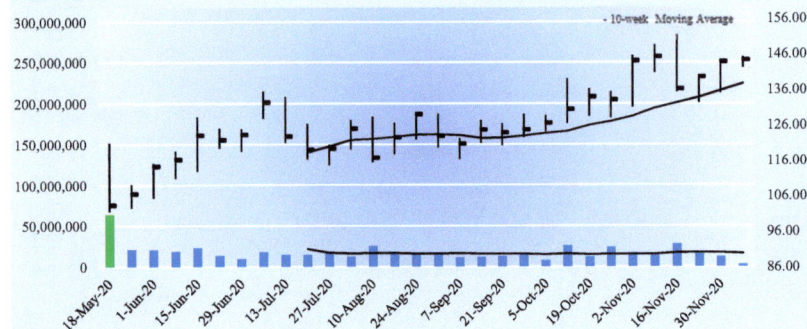

The week with the highest trading volume out of the last 30 weeks was a week of heavy selling, or distribution (red bar).

Company Vitals

Market Cap (USD)	$50,318
Avg Weekly Vol (30 wks)	17,795
30-week Range (USD)	101.51 - 151.18
Valuentum Sector	Information Technology
5-week Return	-2.8%
13-week Return	18.9%
30-week Return	41.6%
Dividend Yield %	0.0%
Dividends per Share	0.00
Forward Dividend Payout Ratio	0.0%
Est. Normal Diluted EPS	7.23
P/E on Est. Normal Diluted EPS	20.0
Est. Normal EBITDA	6,057
Forward EV/EBITDA	5.8
EV/Est. Normal EBITDA	6.4
Forward Revenue Growth (5-yr)	6.8%
Forward EPS Growth (5-yr)	27.2%

NMF = Not Meaningful; Est. = Estimated; FY = Fiscal Year

Returns Summary   3-year Historical Average

Return on Equity	10.9%
Return on Assets	5.3%
ROIC, with goodwill	32.5%
ROIC, without goodwill	42.0%

ROIC = Return on Invested Capital; NMF = Not Meaningful

Leverage, Coverage, and Liquidity
In Millions of USD

Total Debt	9,590
Net Debt	-11,578
Total Debt/EBITDA	2.3
Net Debt/EBITDA	NMF
EBITDA/Interest	9.6
Current Ratio	2.9
Quick Ratio	2.7

NMF = Not Meaningful

Investment Highlights

• Baidu provides its users with many channels to find and share information. In addition to its core Chinese web search product, where it controls 60%-80% share, the firm powers many popular community-based products, such as Baidu PostBar, Baidu Knows, and Baidu Encyclopedia. The company was founded in 2000 and is headquartered in Beijing.

• Baidu continues to execute on its vast growth opportunities and is investing to carry the momentum forward. The Internet is going mobile, and a significant portion of the company's revenue comes from its vibrant mobile ecosystem.

• With the world's largest Internet user population, and a long way to go to reach the penetration levels of developed countries, China's Internet is growing in both influence and sophistication. Baidu is at the forefront of this trend. We doubt any firm not natively based in China will ever develop a search platform that better serves the country. Sogou and Tencent are tough rivals though.

• The pace of economic growth in China has the potential to impact consumer confidence and discretionary spending in the country. The middle class that has been growing and spending at a rapid rate could slow its Internet shopping budget should the economy hit difficult times.

• Very few management teams are more excited than Baidu's. The executive suite is working on building an ecosystem to drive more 'closed loop transactions.' Exploiting the huge growth potential ahead is a key priority, and adjusted EBITDA margins remain impressive.

Investment Considerations

DCF Valuation	FAIRLY VALUED
Relative Valuation	NEUTRAL
ValueCreation™	EXCELLENT
ValueRisk™	MEDIUM
ValueTrend™	NEGATIVE
Cash Flow Generation	STRONG
Financial Leverage	MEDIUM
Growth	MODEST
Technical Evaluation	BULLISH
Relative Strength	STRONG
Money Flow Index (MFI)	NEUTRAL
Upside/Downside Volume (U/D)	DETERIORATING
Near-term Technical Support, 10-week MA	138.00

DCF = Discounted Cash Flow; MFI, U/D = Please see glossary. MA = Moving Average

Business Quality   ValueCreation™

ValueRisk™	Very Poor	Poor	Good	Excellent
Low				
Medium				▉
High				
Very High				

Firms that generate economic profits with little operating variability score near the top right of the matrix.

Relative Valuation

	Forward P/E	PEG	Price / FV
Apple	29.8	2.4	85.0%
Alphabet	34.9	1.8	73.3%
Amazon.com	NMF	3.3	95.7%
Microsoft	31.6	2.5	91.6%
Peer Median	31.6	2.5	88.3%
Baidu	**15.5**	**6.3**	**82.0%**

Price / FV = Current Stock Price divided by Estimated Fair Value

Financial Summary

	----- Actual -----			Projected
Fiscal Year End:	Dec-18	Dec-19	Dec-20	
Revenue	14,876	15,429	16,308	
Revenue, YoY%	14.1%	3.7%	5.7%	
Operating Income	2,259	906	3,509	
Operating Margin %	15.2%	5.9%	21.5%	
Net Income	4,010	296	3,246	
Net Income Margin %	27.0%	1.9%	19.9%	
Diluted EPS	11.40	0.85	9.29	
Diluted EPS, YoY %	41.7%	-92.6%	995.1%	
Free Cash Flow (CFO-capex)	3,955	3,165	5,336	
Free Cash Flow Margin %	26.6%	20.5%	32.7%	

In Millions of USD (except for per share items)

Structure of the Internet Software & Services Industry   NEUTRAL

The Internet software/services industry is composed of a variety of companies with rapidly-changing business models. Most focus on improving the ways people connect with information, either via Internet search or by social media platforms, and generate revenue primarily by delivering cost-effective online advertising. Constituents earn significant returns on invested capital due to their capital-light operations, though competition remains fierce. We expect most companies in this group to look substantially different 10 years from now than they do today. Overall, we're neutral on the structure.

Booking Holdings BKNG FAIRLY VALUED

Buying Index™ 6   **Value Rating** ○

Economic Castle	Estimated Fair Value	Fair Value Range	Investment Style	Sector	Industry
Very Attractive	$2076.00	$1661.00 - $2491.00	LARGE-CAP CORE	Information Technology	Technology Giants

We moderately increased our fair value estimate for Booking Holdings as its outlook has improved due to recent COVID-19 vaccine candidate news.

Stock Chart (weekly)

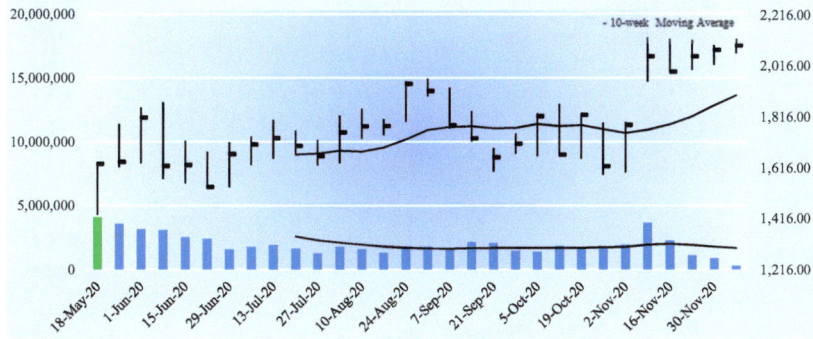

The week with the highest trading volume out of the last 30 weeks was a week of heavy selling, or distribution (red bar).

Investment Considerations

DCF Valuation	**FAIRLY VALUED**
Relative Valuation	**UNATTRACTIVE**
ValueCreation™	**EXCELLENT**
ValueRisk™	**LOW**
ValueTrend™	**NEGATIVE**
Cash Flow Generation	**STRONG**
Financial Leverage	**MEDIUM**
Growth	**MODEST**
Technical Evaluation	**BULLISH**
Relative Strength	**STRONG**
Money Flow Index (MFI)	**NEUTRAL**
Upside/Downside Volume (U/D)	**BEARISH**
Near-term Technical Support, 10-week MA	**1899.00**

DCF = Discounted Cash Flow; MFI, U/D = Please see glossary. MA = Moving Average

Company Vitals

Market Cap (USD)	$91,222
Avg Weekly Vol (30 wks)	1,972
30-week Range (USD)	1,430.00 - 2,128.02
Valuentum Sector	Information Technology
5-week Return	2.3%
13-week Return	16.3%
30-week Return	46.6%
Dividend Yield %	0.0%
Dividends per Share	0.00
Forward Dividend Payout Ratio	0.0%
Est. Normal Diluted EPS	66.65
P/E on Est. Normal Diluted EPS	31.5
Est. Normal EBITDA	4,286
Forward EV/EBITDA	112.3
EV/Est. Normal EBITDA	21.6
Forward Revenue Growth (5-yr)	1.2%
Forward EPS Growth (5-yr)	-1.1%

NMF = Not Meaningful; Est. = Estimated; FY = Fiscal Year

Returns Summary
3-year Historical Average

Return on Equity	42.7%
Return on Assets	16.3%
ROIC, with goodwill	74.1%
ROIC, without goodwill	130.7%

ROIC = Return on Invested Capital; NMF = Not Meaningful

Leverage, Coverage, and Liquidity
In Millions of USD

Total Debt	8,628
Net Debt	1,318
Total Debt/EBITDA	1.4
Net Debt/EBITDA	0.2
EBITDA/Interest	22.7
Current Ratio	1.8
Quick Ratio	1.7

NMF = Not Meaningful

Investment Highlights

• Booking Holdings is a leader in global online hotel reservations. The firm is composed of four primary brands--Booking.com, Booking Holdings.com, Agoda.com, Kayak and Rentalcars.com--and several ancillary brands. Booking growth continues to be excellent across its platforms. The company was founded in 1997 and is headquartered in Connecticut.

• Demand in Booking Holdings' business model is boosted by a virtuous cycle. Its partnerships allow it to offer an enhanced customer experience, driving increased conversion and traffic. Growing traffic levels give it the opportunity to test and improve customer and partner satisfaction.

• Booking Holdings has made a habit of issuing conservative quarterly guidance, which the market tends not to like. Investors should be prepared for material swings on quarterly reports due to such guidance, and the firm's equity may be better served by management not issuing such punitive quarterly guidance. Nevertheless, we continue to have confidence in the firm's fundamentals.

• Booking.com, the company's largest subsidiary and reason behind its name change, accounts for the majority of its gross bookings and operating income with more than 1.5 million listed properties and an average of 1 million bookings per day. Management has suggested that it is open to acquisitions to further expand its portfolio.

• As it rides the wave of secular growth in Internet penetration in travel, Booking Holdings will also benefit from expansion into new markets in North America, the Asia Pacific, and South America. Increasing competition and potentially slowing global economic activity should not be ignored, however.

Business Quality
ValueCreation™

ValueRisk™	Very Poor	Poor	Good	Excellent
Low				■
Medium				
High				
Very High				

Firms that generate economic profits with little operating variability score near the top right of the matrix.

Relative Valuation

	Forward P/E	PEG	Price / FV
Apple	29.8	2.4	85.0%
Alphabet	34.9	1.8	73.3%
Amazon.com	NMF	3.3	95.7%
Microsoft	31.6	2.5	91.6%
Peer Median	31.6	2.5	88.3%
Booking Holdings	**906.5**	**NMF**	**101.0%**

Price / FV = Current Stock Price divided by Estimated Fair Value

Financial Summary

	Actual		Projected
Fiscal Year End:	Dec-18	Dec-19	Dec-20
Revenue	14,527	15,066	6,735
Revenue, YoY%	16.9%	3.7%	-55.3%
Operating Income	5,341	5,345	384
Operating Margin %	36.8%	35.5%	5.7%
Net Income	3,998	4,865	101
Net Income Margin %	27.5%	32.3%	1.5%
Diluted EPS	83.26	111.82	2.31
Diluted EPS, YoY %	77.7%	34.3%	-97.9%
Free Cash Flow (CFO-capex)	4,896	4,497	1,167
Free Cash Flow Margin %	33.7%	29.8%	17.3%

In Millions of USD (except for per share items)

Structure of the Internet & Catalog Retail Industry   GOOD

The Internet and catalog retail industry benefits as a whole from the secular trend toward consumer digital (online) consumption. The industry consists of a number of exclusive online retailers led by Amazon, which continues to disrupt the broader retail space, and businesses that offer Internet travel services such as Booking Holdings, while online auctions are dominated by eBay. The industry generates high returns on investment due to minimal capital costs, but the landscape will be vastly different in the decades ahead. Still, we like the group.

Boston Scientific BSX   FAIRLY VALUED

Buying Index™	**3**	**Value Rating** ●

Economic Castle	Estimated Fair Value	Fair Value Range	Investment Style	Sector	Industry
Attractive	$31.00	$23.00 - $39.00	LARGE-CAP CORE	Health Care	Health Care Bellwethers

We reduced our fair value estimate for Boston Scientific. The COVID-19 pandemic created material headwinds for its business.

Stock Chart (weekly)

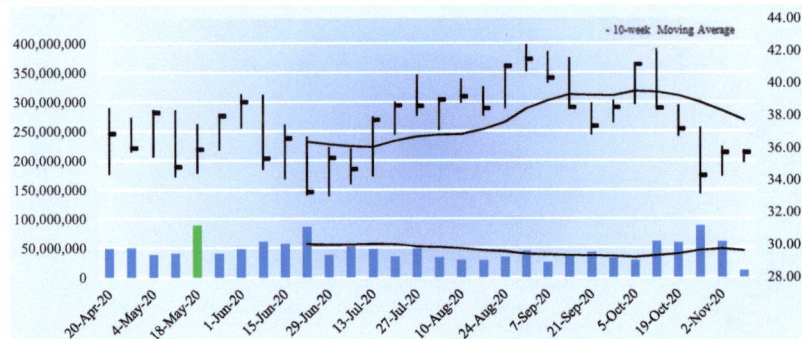

The week with the highest trading volume out of the last 30 weeks was a week of heavy selling, or distribution (red bar).

Company Vitals

Market Cap (USD)	$50,358
Avg Weekly Vol (30 wks)	46,595
30-week Range (USD)	33.00 - 42.37
Valuentum Sector	Health Care
5-week Return	-13.9%
13-week Return	-8.7%
30-week Return	-5.6%
Dividend Yield %	0.0%
Dividends per Share	0.00
Forward Dividend Payout Ratio	0.0%
Est. Normal Diluted EPS	1.69
P/E on Est. Normal Diluted EPS	21.1
Est. Normal EBITDA	4,322
Forward EV/EBITDA	19.3
EV/Est. Normal EBITDA	13.9
Forward Revenue Growth (5-yr)	4.6%
Forward EPS Growth (5-yr)	-9.4%

NMF = Not Meaningful; Est. = Estimated; FY = Fiscal Year

Returns Summary
3-year Historical Average

Return on Equity	21.4%
Return on Assets	9.0%
ROIC, with goodwill	7.6%
ROIC, without goodwill	14.3%

ROIC = Return on Invested Capital; NMF = Not Meaningful

Leverage, Coverage, and Liquidity
In Millions of USD

Total Debt	10,008
Net Debt	9,791
Total Debt/EBITDA	3.6
Net Debt/EBITDA	3.6
EBITDA/Interest	5.8
Current Ratio	1.0
Quick Ratio	0.4

NMF = Not Meaningful

Investment Highlights

• Boston Scientific is a major provider in the coronary stent and cardiac rhythm management (CRM) market. Interventional cardiology, CRM, endoscopy, and peripheral interventions are its largest divisions. Over half of Boston Scientific's annual revenues come from the US and its emerging markets revenues are modest. The company was founded in 1979.

• In August 2019, Boston Scientific closed its all-cash ~$4.2 billion acquisition of BTG plc. The deal added a large 'Interventional Medicine' to Boston Scientific's portfolio that is geared towards oncology and vascular-related medical needs.

• Boston Scientific expects the acquisition of BTG plc will generate ~$175 million in cost synergies by August 2022, with 80% of those synergies expected to be realized by August 2021. New product launches are expected over the coming years as Boston Scientific plans to leverage its global reach to grow sales of BTG products now owned by Boston Scientific.

• Boston Scientific has a strong product pipeline. Management is targeting sustained adjusted operating margin expansion, organic revenue growth, double-digit EPS growth, and strong free cash flows over the long haul. The company faced significant headwinds due to the COVID-19 pandemic, however.

• Boston Scientific does not have a significant amount of debt coming due until 2022 due to recent refinancing maneuvers. The company is managing its debt maturity profile and liquidity levels to ride out the storm caused by the COVID-19 pandemic.

Investment Considerations

DCF Valuation	**FAIRLY VALUED**
Relative Valuation	**UNATTRACTIVE**
ValueCreation™	**GOOD**
ValueRisk™	**MEDIUM**
ValueTrend™	**POSITIVE**
Cash Flow Generation	**STRONG**
Financial Leverage	**HIGH**
Growth	**MODEST**
Technical Evaluation	**BEARISH**
Relative Strength	**WEAK**
Money Flow Index (MFI)	**NEUTRAL**
Upside/Downside Volume (U/D)	**BEARISH**
Near-term Technical Resistance, 10-wk MA	**38.00**

DCF = Discounted Cash Flow; MFI, U/D = Please see glossary. MA = Moving Average

Business Quality

ValueRisk™	ValueCreation™			
	Very Poor	Poor	Good	Excellent
Low				
Medium			▓	
High				
Very High				

Firms that generate economic profits with little operating variability score near the top right of the matrix.

Relative Valuation

	Forward P/E	PEG	Price / FV
Johnson & Johnson	17.6	1.8	99.5%
Medtronic	25.6	2.2	109.0%
Merck	21.5	2.2	100.5%
Pfizer	20.1	0.8	93.3%
Peer Median	20.8	2.0	100.0%
Boston Scientific	**35.0**	**NMF**	**115.2%**

Price / FV = Current Stock Price divided by Estimated Fair Value

Financial Summary

	----- Actual -----			Projected
Fiscal Year End:		Dec-18	Dec-19	Dec-20
Revenue		9,823	10,735	10,069
Revenue, YoY%		8.6%	9.3%	-6.2%
Non-GAAP Operating Income		1,506	1,741	2,125
Non-GAAP EBIT %		15.3%	16.2%	21.1%
Non-GAAP Net Income		1,670	4,700	1,453
Non-GAAP NI Margin %		17.0%	43.8%	14.4%
Non-GAAP Diluted EPS		1.19	3.33	1.02
Non-GAAP Dil EPS, YoY %		NMF	NMF	NMF
Non-GAAP Free Cash Flow		-6	1,420	2,371
Non-GAAP FCF Margin %		-0.1%	13.2%	23.6%

In Millions of USD (except for per share items)

Structure of the Medical Instruments Industry   GOOD

The medical instrument industry is heavily regulated and characterized by rapid technological change. Firms have been forced to compete on price due to economically-motivated buyers, consolidation among healthcare providers, and declining reimbursement rates. Healthcare reform measures have put additional pressure on procedure rates and market sizes. Still, firms can gain advantages by developing products with differentiated clinical outcomes or by creating patent-protected technology. Since most constituents hold important patents or trade secrets, we tend to like the group.

Beyond Meat BYND   OVERVALUED 3.3%

Buying Index™ 1   **Value Rating** ✖

Economic Castle	Estimated Fair Value	Fair Value Range	Investment Style	Sector	Industry
Unattractive	$100.00	$65.00 - $135.00	MID-CAP GROWTH	Next Generation	Disruptive Innovation

Beyond Meat's shares will be volatile, and its fundamentals may not live up to the market's expectations. Long term, conventional animal-protein companies may eventually become fierce rivals with their own plant-based offerings.

Stock Chart (weekly)

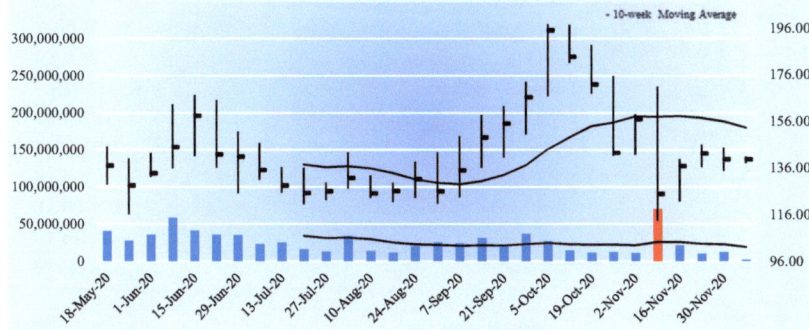

The week with the highest trading volume out of the last 30 weeks was a week of heavy selling, or distribution (red bar).

Company Vitals

Market Cap (USD)	$5,902
Avg Weekly Vol (30 wks)	25,302
30-week Range (USD)	113.26 - 197.50
Valuentum Sector	Next Generation
5-week Return	-15.1%
13-week Return	2.5%
30-week Return	1.5%
Dividend Yield %	0.0%
Dividends per Share	0.00
Forward Dividend Payout Ratio	0.0%
Est. Normal Diluted EPS	1.06
P/E on Est. Normal Diluted EPS	131.4
Est. Normal EBITDA	86
Forward EV/EBITDA	1889.9
EV/Est. Normal EBITDA	66.0
Forward Revenue Growth (5-yr)	38.6%
Forward EPS Growth (5-yr)	-257.4%

NMF = Not Meaningful; Est. = Estimated; FY = Fiscal Year

Returns Summary
3-year Historical Average

Return on Equity	13.3%
Return on Assets	-16.4%
ROIC, with goodwill	-78.7%
ROIC, without goodwill	-78.7%

ROIC = Return on Invested Capital; NMF = Not Meaningful

Leverage, Coverage, and Liquidity
In Millions of USD

Total Debt	31
Net Debt	-245
Total Debt/EBITDA	3.9
Net Debt/EBITDA	NMF
EBITDA/Interest	2.5
Current Ratio	8.5
Quick Ratio	NA

NMF = Not Meaningful

Investment Highlights

• Beyond Meat is revolutionizing the food industry with plant-based meats. The company makes meat from plants that tastes similar to animal-based meat products that have nutritional and environmental benefits (animal welfare). Its flagship product is the Beyond Burger found in grocery stores (about two thirds of total revenue), and it also makes other plant-based meat products (sausage, beef, and the like).

• The company's 'Restaurant and Foodservice' business (about half of 2019 sales) has been struggling of late. Quick service restaurants ('QSRs') account for about one third of Beyond Meat's sales in this category, and the remaining two thirds are made to a wide variety of customers including bars, lodging establishments, and restaurants--the kind of entities that have been hit hard by the COVID-19 pandemic. Pressures on this front will likely continue until global health authorities bring the pandemic under control. Renewed lockdowns in Europe and the potential for renewed lockdowns in the US are likely going to continue to be hurdles for Beyond Meat in the near term.

• The company is one of the greatest innovators of the 21st century, but its market opportunity may be much smaller than the $1.4 trillion global meat industry that bullish investors are betting on. We believe Beyond Meat will remain a niche operator in the beef, pork and poultry categories, not a mainstream enterprise.

• Beyond Meat must continue to innovate with hefty R&D expenses as competition is fierce. Such considerable investment will pressure profitability. Direct rivals include Impossible Foods, but also most other conventional animal-protein companies out there (e.g. Cargill, Hormel, Tyson, etc.)

Investment Considerations

DCF Valuation	OVERVALUED
Relative Valuation	NEUTRAL
ValueCreation™	VERY POOR
ValueRisk™	HIGH
ValueTrend™	NEGATIVE
Cash Flow Generation	WEAK
Financial Leverage	LOW
Growth	AGGRESSIVE
Technical Evaluation	BEARISH
Relative Strength	NEUTRAL
Money Flow Index (MFI)	NEUTRAL
Upside/Downside Volume (U/D)	DETERIORATING
Near-term Technical Resistance, 10-wk MA	153.00

DCF = Discounted Cash Flow; MFI, U/D = Please see glossary. MA = Moving Average

Business Quality

ValueRisk™	ValueCreation™ Very Poor	Poor	Good	Excellent
Low				
Medium				
High	▓			
Very High				

Firms that generate economic profits with little operating variability score near the top right of the matrix.

Relative Valuation

	Forward P/E	PEG	Price / FV
Wayfair	56.3	NMF	84.2%
Zoom Video	170.7	28.8	120.8%
Roku	-338.4	NMF	96.0%
Monster Beverage	36.0	2.9	104.4%
Peer Median	46.1	15.9	100.2%
Beyond Meat	**-553.0**	**NMF**	**139.6%**

Price / FV = Current Stock Price divided by Estimated Fair Value

Financial Summary

	----- Actual -----		Projected
Fiscal Year End:	Dec-18	Dec-19	Dec-20
Revenue	88	298	411
Revenue, YoY%	169.9%	238.8%	37.9%
Operating Income	-28	0	-8
Operating Margin %	-31.8%	-0.2%	-2.0%
Net Income	-30	-12	-11
Net Income Margin %	-34.0%	-4.2%	-2.7%
Diluted EPS	-4.75	-0.29	-0.25
Diluted EPS, YoY %	-14.6%	-93.8%	-14.2%
Free Cash Flow (CFO-capex)	-60	-71	-118
Free Cash Flow Margin %	-68.2%	-23.8%	-28.8%

In Millions of USD (except for per share items)

Structure of the Internet & Catalog Retail Industry   GOOD

The Internet and catalog retail industry benefits as a whole from the secular trend toward consumer digital (online) consumption. The industry consists of a number of exclusive online retailers led by Amazon, which continues to disrupt the broader retail space, and businesses that offer Internet travel services such as Booking Holdings, while online auctions are dominated by eBay. The industry generates high returns on investment due to minimal capital costs, but the landscape will be vastly different in the decades ahead. Still, we like the group.

Casey's General CASY   FAIRLY VALUED

Buying Index™   **4**   **Value Rating**

Economic Castle	Estimated Fair Value	Fair Value Range	Investment Style	Sector	Industry
Attractive	$189.00	$151.00 - $227.00	MID-CAP VALUE	Consumer Staples	Recession Resistant

Casey's consistent unit store growth, inside same-store sales growth, and consecutive years of dividend increases are admirable. It's targeting a 10% EBITDA CAGR and 4% store count CAGR in the long run.

Stock Chart (weekly)

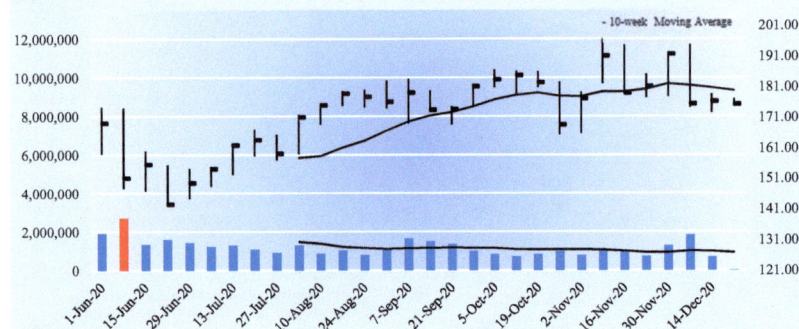

The week with the highest trading volume out of the last 30 weeks was a week of heavy selling, or distribution (red bar).

Company Vitals

Market Cap (USD)	$6,518
Avg Weekly Vol (30 wks)	1,163
30-week Range (USD)	142.34 - 196.58
Valuentum Sector	Consumer Staples
5-week Return	-2.6%
13-week Return	0.2%
30-week Return	8.9%
Dividend Yield %	0.8%
Dividends per Share	1.36
Forward Dividend Payout Ratio	16.5%
Est. Normal Diluted EPS	12.39
P/E on Est. Normal Diluted EPS	14.2
Est. Normal EBITDA	940
Forward EV/EBITDA	11.6
EV/Est. Normal EBITDA	8.3
Forward Revenue Growth (5-yr)	6.6%
Forward EPS Growth (5-yr)	21.4%

NMF = Not Meaningful; Est. = Estimated; FY = Fiscal Year

Returns Summary
3-year Historical Average

Return on Equity	19.4%
Return on Assets	7.4%
ROIC, with goodwill	9.5%
ROIC, without goodwill	10.0%

ROIC = Return on Invested Capital; NMF = Not Meaningful

Leverage, Coverage, and Liquidity
In Millions of USD

Total Debt	1,405
Net Debt	1,327
Total Debt/EBITDA	2.2
Net Debt/EBITDA	2.1
EBITDA/Interest	12.1
Current Ratio	0.4
Quick Ratio	0.1

NMF = Not Meaningful

Investment Highlights

• Casey's General operates ~2,200 convenience stores mostly in the Midwestern states. The stores offer self-service gasoline, a wide variety of grocery items, and prepared foods such as made-from-scratch pizza and donuts, chicken tenders, and sandwiches. The company was founded in 1959, is headquartered in Iowa, and employs over 38,000.

• Casey's goal is to serve 1.5 billion customers per year by fiscal 2030. Such a target will involve significant expansion efforts, both in total number of stores and number of stores operating 24 hours per day. The firm is the 4th largest convenience store in North America and serves 665+ million customers per year.

• Casey's success largely depends on improving margins on grocery and prepared food/fountain goods. This may be difficult due to competition from other convenience stores and gas stations as well as other external forces such as a rising wage floor. Increasing sales of gasoline and the margin attained on pump sales--both key levers to profits--are mostly out of its control.

• We like several of Casey's initiatives, but we are also building in optimistic rates of sales and margin expansion. The firm is looking to increase prepared food sales, and expanding stores to 24-hour operations and adding pizza delivery and an online ordering app should boost help. Price increases are sticking, giving EPS and gross margin a boost.

• Digital connectivity with customers will be key to its success going forward (restaurant digital orders are soaring). The company has identified opportunities for an additional 1,150 store locations that have populations greater than 10k within 400 miles of a distribution center.

Investment Considerations

DCF Valuation	**FAIRLY VALUED**
Relative Valuation	**ATTRACTIVE**
ValueCreation™	**GOOD**
ValueRisk™	**MEDIUM**
ValueTrend™	**NEGATIVE**
Cash Flow Generation	**WEAK**
Financial Leverage	**MEDIUM**
Growth	**MODEST**
Technical Evaluation	**BEARISH**
Relative Strength	**WEAK**
Money Flow Index (MFI)	**NEUTRAL**
Upside/Downside Volume (U/D)	**DETERIORATING**
Near-term Technical Resistance, 10-wk MA	**180.00**

DCF = Discounted Cash Flow; MFI, U/D = Please see glossary. MA = Moving Average

Business Quality

ValueRisk™	ValueCreation™			
	Very Poor	Poor	Good	Excellent
Low				
Medium			▮	
High				
Very High				

Firms that generate economic profits with little operating variability score near the top right of the matrix.

Relative Valuation

	Forward P/E	PEG	Price / FV
Coca-Cola	34.3	1.5	128.0%
Procter & Gamble	26.5	3.3	144.1%
Philip Morris	15.4	2.4	104.3%
Wal-Mart	26.8	2.3	130.2%
Peer Median	26.7	2.4	129.1%
Casey's General	**21.2**	**1.2**	**92.7%**

Price / FV = Current Stock Price divided by Estimated Fair Value

Financial Summary

	----- Actual -----		Projected
Fiscal Year End:	Apr-19	Apr-20	Apr-21
Revenue	9,353	9,175	8,469
Revenue, YoY%	11.5%	-1.9%	-7.7%
Operating Income	319	395	447
Operating Margin %	3.4%	4.3%	5.3%
Net Income	204	264	307
Net Income Margin %	2.2%	2.9%	3.6%
Diluted EPS	5.51	7.10	8.26
Diluted EPS, YoY %	-33.9%	28.7%	16.4%
Free Cash Flow (CFO-capex)	136	65	44
Free Cash Flow Margin %	1.5%	0.7%	0.5%

In Millions of USD (except for per share items)

Structure of the Food Retailers Industry   NEUTRAL

Firms in the mature food retailers industry generally have slim profit margins and face significant competition from brick-and-mortar locations (discount, department, drug, dollar, warehouse clubs and supermarkets) as well as Internet-based retailers (including Amazon). Though the industry is not terribly cyclical, economic conditions, disposable income, credit availability, fuel prices, and unemployment levels drive ticket size and traffic trends. Offering consumers a compelling value proposition is a must, even as higher-priced organic food offerings proliferate. We're generally neutral on the group.

Caterpillar CAT FAIRLY VALUED

Buying Index™ 5 **Value Rating** ○

Economic Castle	Estimated Fair Value	Fair Value Range	Investment Style	Sector	Industry
Attractive	$171.00	$137.00 - $205.00	LARGE-CAP CORE	Industrials	Industrial Leaders

Caterpillar's shares have bounced back from the COVID-19 crisis, but its ultra-cyclical operations are concerning. We've fine-tuned our future assumptions from the last report update, driving the latest fair value estimate increase.

Stock Chart (weekly)

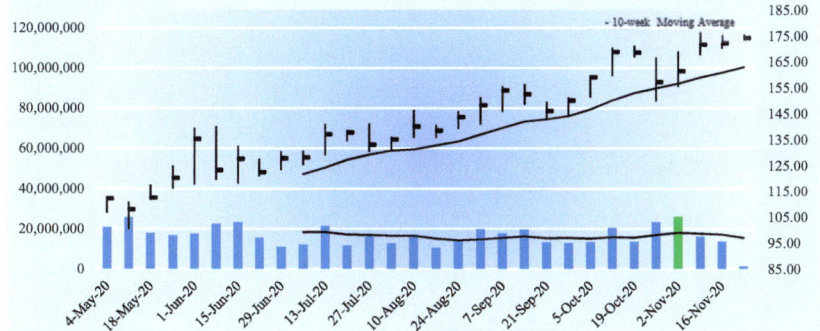

The week with the highest trading volume out of the last 30 weeks was a week of heavy selling, or distribution (red bar).

Company Vitals

Market Cap (USD)	$98,856
Avg Weekly Vol (30 wks)	16,554
30-week Range (USD)	100.22 - 176.37
Valuentum Sector	Industrials
5-week Return	4.5%
13-week Return	21.4%
30-week Return	58.3%
Dividend Yield %	2.4%
Dividends per Share	4.12
Forward Dividend Payout Ratio	75.0%
Est. Normal Diluted EPS	8.90
P/E on Est. Normal Diluted EPS	19.6
Est. Normal EBITDA	9,031
Forward EV/EBITDA	16.1
EV/Est. Normal EBITDA	11.2
Forward Revenue Growth (5-yr)	0.6%
Forward EPS Growth (5-yr)	2.1%

NMF = Not Meaningful; Est. = Estimated; FY = Fiscal Year

Returns Summary
3-year Historical Average

Return on Equity	30.7%
Return on Assets	5.5%
ROIC, with goodwill	20.3%
ROIC, without goodwill	27.3%

ROIC = Return on Invested Capital; NMF = Not Meaningful

Leverage, Coverage, and Liquidity
In Millions of USD

Total Debt	10,715
Net Debt	2,431
Total Debt/EBITDA	1.0
Net Debt/EBITDA	0.2
EBITDA/Interest	25.8
Current Ratio	1.5
Quick Ratio	1.0

NMF = Not Meaningful; Debt excludes debt associated with the finance sub.

Investment Highlights

• Caterpillar makes construction and mining equipment, diesel and natural gas engines, industrial gas turbines and diesel-electric locomotives. The company also owns Caterpillar Financial Services (Cat Financial). The machinery giant's operations are tied to cyclical end markets, and results are not immune to geopolitical risks either. It is based in Deerfield, Illinois.

• Cat's dealer network is a significant competitive advantage. Its reach is phenomenal, with ~50 dealers in the US and 120+ outside the US (serving ~190 countries). Mining equipment sales remain tied to expectations of commodity prices, and the period 2013-2016 is exemplary of the pain this can cause.

• Drivers of demand at Cat of late include continued strength in the North American construction market, new equipment sales momentum in resource industries, and demand for rebuilds of well-serving equipment in the energy space. Higher material and freight costs have the potential to weigh on bottom-line results in the near term.

• Caterpillar is quite effective at managing costs through the course of the economic cycle. Part of Caterpillar's strategy when faced with revenue declines is to manage the fall such that the decrease in operating profit is less than 30% of the decline in revenue. We also like the focus on driving strong inventory turns.

• Cat Financial's exposure to weak credits in the mining and energy arenas will always have us concerned. The hidden captive finance arms across the broader machinery group may put surprising pressure on performance in the event of a downturn.

Investment Considerations

DCF Valuation	FAIRLY VALUED
Relative Valuation	NEUTRAL
ValueCreation™	EXCELLENT
ValueRisk™	LOW
ValueTrend™	POSITIVE
Cash Flow Generation	STRONG
Financial Leverage	LOW
Growth	MODEST
Technical Evaluation	NEUTRAL
Relative Strength	STRONG
Money Flow Index (MFI)	OVERBOUGHT
Upside/Downside Volume (U/D)	DETERIORATING
Near-term Technical Support, 10-week MA	163.00

DCF = Discounted Cash Flow; MFI, U/D = Please see glossary. MA = Moving Average

Business Quality
ValueCreation™

ValueRisk™	Very Poor	Poor	Good	Excellent
Low				■
Medium				
High				
Very High				

Firms that generate economic profits with little operating variability score near the top right of the matrix.

Relative Valuation

	Forward P/E	PEG	Price / FV
Danaher	36.3	3.0	121.5%
Honeywell	28.8	1.7	101.3%
Lockheed Martin	15.0	2.3	96.3%
Union Pacific	25.9	1.4	119.1%
Peer Median	27.3	1.7	110.2%
Caterpillar	31.7	0.8	101.9%

Price / FV = Current Stock Price divided by Estimated Fair Value

Financial Summary

	----- Actual -----		Projected
Fiscal Year End:	Dec-18	Dec-19	Dec-20
Revenue	54,722	53,800	41,534
Revenue, YoY%	20.4%	-1.7%	-22.8%
Non-GAAP Operating Income	8,293	8,290	4,313
Non-GAAP EBIT %	15.2%	15.4%	10.4%
Non-GAAP Net Income	6,148	6,094	3,102
Non-GAAP NI Margin %	11.2%	11.3%	7.5%
Non-GAAP Diluted EPS	10.26	10.74	5.49
Non-GAAP Dil EPS, YoY %	NMF	NMF	NMF
Non-GAAP FCF (CFO-capex)	5,282	5,856	6,155
Non-GAAP FCF Margin %	9.7%	10.9%	14.8%

In Millions of USD (except for per share items)

Structure of the Agricultural Machinery Industry
NEUTRAL

The agricultural machinery industry is composed of firms that make farm and construction equipment. Demand for agricultural equipment is levered to farm incomes and commodity prices, while purchases of construction equipment are dependent on global economic health. Population growth and the increasing need for food/energy are the major long-term drivers for new orders across the industry. Still, firms are competitive, capital intensive, and possess significant operating leverage. A strong/dependable brand and an expansive distribution network are keys to success. We're neutral on the group.

Crown Castle CCI   FAIRLY VALUED

Buying Index™   **3**   **Value Rating** ⬤

Economic Castle	Estimated Fair Value	Fair Value Range	Investment Style	Sector	Industry
Attractive	$168.00	$126.00 - $210.00	LARGE-CAP VALUE	Telecom Services	Telecom Services - diversified

We significantly increased our fair value estimate for Crown Castle as its long-term growth outlook has improved considerably.

Stock Chart (weekly)

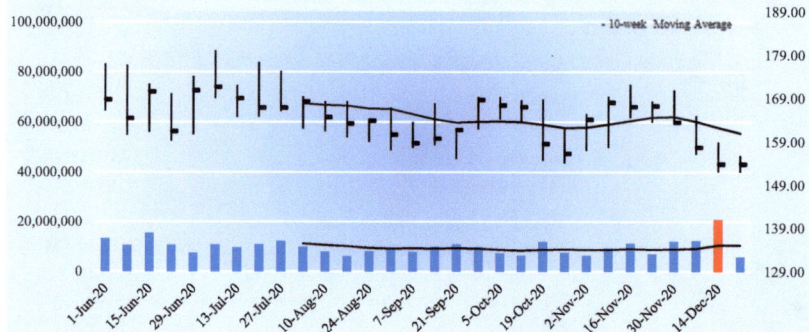

The week with the highest trading volume out of the last 30 weeks was a week of heavy selling, or distribution (red bar).

Company Vitals

Market Cap (USD)	$64,293
Avg Weekly Vol (30 wks)	9,926
30-week Range (USD)	152.09 - 180.00
Valuentum Sector	Telecom Services
5-week Return	-8.2%
13-week Return	-6.2%
30-week Return	-10.4%
Dividend Yield %	3.5%
Dividends per Share	5.32
Forward Dividend Payout Ratio	89.1%
Est. Normal Diluted EPS	2.95
P/E on Est. Normal Diluted EPS	52.1
Est. Normal EBITDA	4,184
Forward EV/EBITDA	24.9
EV/Est. Normal EBITDA	19.6
Forward Revenue Growth (5-yr)	7.5%
Forward EPS Growth (5-yr)	19.0%

NMF = Not Meaningful; Est. = Estimated; FY = Fiscal Year

Returns Summary
3-year Historical Average

Return on Equity	5.8%
Return on Assets	2.0%
ROIC, with goodwill	6.2%
ROIC, without goodwill	9.3%

ROIC = Return on Invested Capital; NMF = Not Meaningful

Leverage, Coverage, and Liquidity
In Millions of USD

Total Debt	18,121
Net Debt	17,788
Total Debt/EBITDA	5.7
Net Debt/EBITDA	5.6
EBITDA/Interest	4.6
Current Ratio	0.6
Quick Ratio	0.5

NMF = Not Meaningful

Investment Highlights

• Crown Castle operates shared wireless infrastructure, including towers and a variety of other structures. The company's core business is providing access to its towers via long-term contracts in various forms (licenses, sub-leases, etc). The company commenced operating as a REIT in January 2014 and is headquartered in Houston.

• Crown Castle's long-term goal is to grow its per share dividend by 7%-8% per year. Management expects to significantly grow the REIT's asset base over the coming years through a combination of acquisitions and meaningful capital expenditures.

• Crown Castle boasts an attractive business model and is well-positioned to capitalize on the launch of 5G wireless services in the US. Approximately 40% of the REIT's 'Towers site rental gross margin' is generated from towers on land and properties owned by Crown Castle. However, we caution that Crown Castle has meaningful customer concentration risk.

• Crown Castle has a lot of debt on the books. We're generally debt-averse (think of what happened during the Great Financial Crisis), though Crown Castle's long-term recurring revenue streams, hefty incremental margins on new business, and high-quality customer base help mitigate some of the financial risk.

• Crown Castle remains acquisitive as it continues to work to meet rapidly growing mobile data demand. Crown Castle initiated a dividend in the first quarter of 2014 when it was organized as a REIT. We like its renewed focus on delivering cash back to shareholders.

Investment Considerations

DCF Valuation	FAIRLY VALUED
Relative Valuation	NEUTRAL
ValueCreation™	GOOD
ValueRisk™	MEDIUM
ValueTrend™	POSITIVE
Cash Flow Generation	STRONG
Financial Leverage	HIGH
Growth	MODEST
Technical Evaluation	BEARISH
Relative Strength	WEAK
Money Flow Index (MFI)	NEUTRAL
Upside/Downside Volume (U/D)	BEARISH
Near-term Technical Resistance, 10-wk MA	161.00

DCF = Discounted Cash Flow; MFI, U/D = Please see glossary. MA = Moving Average

Business Quality

ValueRisk™	Very Poor	Poor	Good	Excellent
Low				
Medium			▓	
High				
Very High				

ValueCreation™

Firms that generate economic profits with little operating variability score near the top right of the matrix.

Relative Valuation

	Forward P/E	PEG	Price / FV
AT&T	12.1	4.3	89.1%
Comcast	20.0	1.2	110.7%
Verizon	12.3	3.1	100.8%
American Tower	26.9	1.8	95.1%
Peer Median	16.2	2.5	97.9%
Crown Castle	**25.8**	**1.4**	**91.6%**

Price / FV = Current Stock Price divided by Estimated Fair Value

Financial Summary

	Actual		Projected
Fiscal Year End:	Dec-18	Dec-19	Dec-20
Revenue	5,370	5,763	5,907
Revenue, YoY%	23.3%	7.3%	2.5%
Adjusted Operating Income	1,436	1,591	1,530
Adj. Operating Margin %	26.7%	27.6%	25.9%
Funds from Operations	2,228	2,376	2,594
FFO Margin %	41.5%	41.2%	43.9%
Diluted FFO per share	5.37	5.68	5.97
Diluted FFO, YoY %	10.6%	5.9%	5.0%
Free Cash Flow (CFO-capex)	761	641	979
Free Cash Flow Margin %	14.2%	11.1%	16.6%

In Millions of USD (except for per share items)

Structure of the Wireless Telecom Services Industry   GOOD

Most firms in the wireless telecom services industry lease antenna space on communication sites/towers to wireless service providers, radio and television broadcast companies, and tenants in other industries. Tenant leases are typically long-term, non-cancellable, have high renewal rates (98%+) and include attractive built-in annual rent escalations. Tower operators enjoy consistent demand for their sites, have high operating leverage (incremental costs to add new tenants are minimal), and require little capital expenditures to maintain their communication sites. We like the structure of the group.

Church & Dwight CHD   FAIRLY VALUED

Buying Index™ 3   **Value Rating** ◯

Economic Castle	Estimated Fair Value	Fair Value Range	Investment Style	Sector	Industry
Attractive	$75.00	$60.00 - $90.00	LARGE-CAP CORE	Consumer Staples	Recession Resistant

Organic performance at Church & Dwight is expected to be solid in the near term thanks in part to pricing expansion. Consumer product demand from COVID-19 panic buying has helped sales.

Stock Chart (weekly)

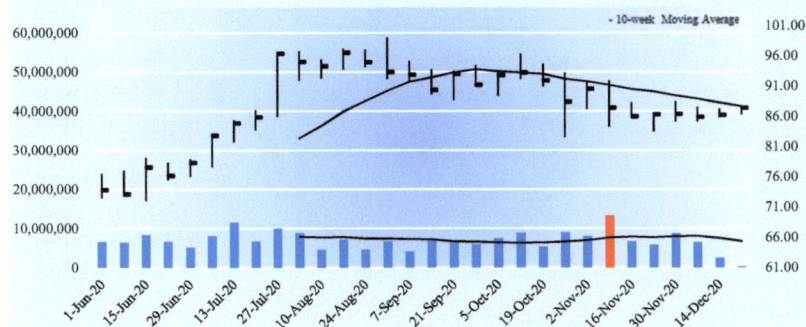

The week with the highest trading volume out of the last 30 weeks was a week of heavy selling, or distribution (red bar).

Investment Considerations

DCF Valuation	**FAIRLY VALUED**
Relative Valuation	**UNATTRACTIVE**
ValueCreation™	**EXCELLENT**
ValueRisk™	**LOW**
ValueTrend™	**POSITIVE**
Cash Flow Generation	**STRONG**
Financial Leverage	**MEDIUM**
Growth	**MODEST**
Technical Evaluation	**BEARISH**
Relative Strength	**WEAK**
Money Flow Index (MFI)	**NEUTRAL**
Upside/Downside Volume (U/D)	**BEARISH**
Near-term Technical Resistance, 10-wk MA	**88.00**

DCF = Discounted Cash Flow; MFI, U/D = Please see glossary. MA = Moving Average

Business Quality

ValueRisk™	ValueCreation™			
	Very Poor	Poor	Good	Excellent
Low				■
Medium				
High				
Very High				

Firms that generate economic profits with little operating variability score near the top right of the matrix.

Company Vitals

Market Cap (USD)	$22,016
Avg Weekly Vol (30 wks)	6,912
30-week Range (USD)	72.03 - 98.96
Valuentum Sector	Consumer Staples
5-week Return	2.0%
13-week Return	-6.7%
30-week Return	16.5%
Dividend Yield %	1.1%
Dividends per Share	0.96
Forward Dividend Payout Ratio	33.7%
Est. Normal Diluted EPS	3.45
P/E on Est. Normal Diluted EPS	25.3
Est. Normal EBITDA	1,358
Forward EV/EBITDA	20.7
EV/Est. Normal EBITDA	17.6
Forward Revenue Growth (5-yr)	6.7%
Forward EPS Growth (5-yr)	11.1%

NMF = Not Meaningful; Est. = Estimated; FY = Fiscal Year

Returns Summary
3-year Historical Average

Return on Equity	27.9%
Return on Assets	11.1%
ROIC, with goodwill	16.0%
ROIC, without goodwill	26.7%

ROIC = Return on Invested Capital; NMF = Not Meaningful

Leverage, Coverage, and Liquidity
In Millions of USD

Total Debt	2,063
Net Debt	1,907
Total Debt/EBITDA	2.0
Net Debt/EBITDA	1.9
EBITDA/Interest	13.8
Current Ratio	0.9
Quick Ratio	0.5

NMF = Not Meaningful

Investment Highlights

• Church & Dwight is a leader in the household products industry and boasts such strong brands as Arm & Hammer, First Response, Nair, OxiClean, and Orajel. It is the top US producer of baking soda. The company operates under two segments: 'Consumer Domestic' and 'Consumer International.' The firm has significant financial capacity and is an investment grade credit (A3/BBB+).

• Church & Dwight is not opposed to acquisitions, and it has bought 11 of its 12 'Power Brands' since 2001 with Water Pik among the most recent (2017). In March 2019, it also agreed to acquire the Flawless (and Finishing Touch) hair removal brand for ~$475 million and another earn-out of up to $425 million.

• Church & Dwight is looking to international markets and e-commerce for growth. Management has set an 'evergreen' target of 6% annual organic growth for its international business. More than 35% of its advertising spend is online, and its online sales account for ~12% of total sales in 2020, up from just 1% in 2015. The company has maintained a balanced and diversified portfolio throughout the years.

• Church & Dwight's 12 'Power Brands' account for ~80% of sales. Almost all of its revenue comes from household/personal care products with the balance from specialty products. Its product portfolio is split 60/40 between premium and value. It continues to focus on acquiring power brands and expanding categories (e.g. gummy vitamins through vitafusion).

• Its asset-light business model (capex runs at ~2% of sales) throws off considerable free cash flow that will help drive its goal of having 20 'Power Brands' in the future! Church & Dwight has paid a dividend for 115+ consecutive years, and it registers a solid Dividend Cushion ratio, too.

Relative Valuation

	Forward P/E	PEG	Price / FV
Coca-Cola	34.3	1.5	128.0%
Procter & Gamble	26.5	3.3	144.1%
Philip Morris	15.4	2.4	104.3%
Wal-Mart	26.8	2.3	130.2%
Peer Median	26.7	2.4	129.1%
Church & Dwight	**30.7**	**3.2**	**116.4%**

Price / FV = Current Stock Price divided by Estimated Fair Value

Financial Summary

	----- Actual -----		Projected
Fiscal Year End:	Dec-18	Dec-19	Dec-20
Revenue	4,146	4,358	4,854
Revenue, YoY%	9.8%	5.1%	11.4%
Operating Income	792	840	974
Operating Margin %	19.1%	19.3%	20.1%
Net Income	569	616	718
Net Income Margin %	13.7%	14.1%	14.8%
Diluted EPS	2.27	2.44	2.85
Diluted EPS, YoY %	-21.9%	7.7%	16.6%
Free Cash Flow (CFO-capex)	704	791	904
Free Cash Flow Margin %	17.0%	18.2%	18.6%

In Millions of USD (except for per share items)

Structure of the Household Products Industry   GOOD

Firms in the household products industry sell some of the most recognized branded consumer packaged goods in the world and often hold a significant market share position in a variety of product categories. Though the industry is characterized by stiff competition from retailers' private-label brands, constituents tend to boast meaningful competitive advantages due to their brand strength/reputation and generate high returns on invested capital. Household products companies remain tied to the vicissitudes of consumer spending, but we tend to like the structure of the group.

Colgate-Palmolive CL   OVERVALUED 10.1%

Buying Index™   **4**   **Value Rating**   ✕

Economic Castle	Estimated Fair Value	Fair Value Range	Investment Style	Sector	Industry
Attractive	$60.00	$48.00 - $72.00	LARGE-CAP CORE	Consumer Staples	Recession Resistant

Colgate-Palmolive's pet nutrition business, led by its Hill's brand, has posted strong sales growth of late. Shares still look pricey, in our view.

Stock Chart (weekly)

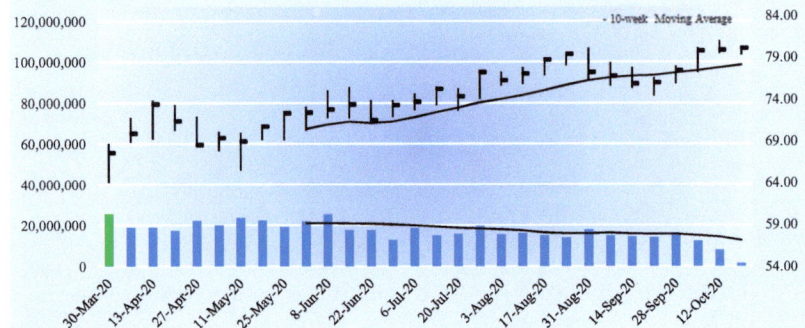

The week with the highest trading volume out of the last 30 weeks was a week of heavy selling, or distribution (red bar).

Company Vitals

Market Cap (USD)	$68,940
Avg Weekly Vol (30 wks)	17,051
30-week Range (USD)	64.08 - 80.98
Valuentum Sector	Consumer Staples
5-week Return	6.3%
13-week Return	8.0%
30-week Return	21.3%
Dividend Yield %	2.2%
Dividends per Share	1.76
Forward Dividend Payout Ratio	58.9%
Est. Normal Diluted EPS	3.71
P/E on Est. Normal Diluted EPS	21.6
Est. Normal EBITDA	5,105
Forward EV/EBITDA	17.5
EV/Est. Normal EBITDA	14.9
Forward Revenue Growth (5-yr)	3.3%
Forward EPS Growth (5-yr)	11.2%

NMF = Not Meaningful; Est. = Estimated; FY = Fiscal Year

Returns Summary   3-year Historical Average

Return on Equity	9700.1%
Return on Assets	18.9%
ROIC, with goodwill	35.7%
ROIC, without goodwill	51.7%

ROIC = Return on Invested Capital; NMF = Not Meaningful

Leverage, Coverage, and Liquidity
In Millions of USD

Total Debt	7,847
Net Debt	6,964
Total Debt/EBITDA	1.8
Net Debt/EBITDA	1.6
EBITDA/Interest	29.4
Current Ratio	1.0
Quick Ratio	0.6

NMF = Not Meaningful

Investment Highlights

• Colgate is a leader in oral/personal care with the top toothpaste, manual toothbrush, and liquid hand soap brands across the world. Its portfolio includes Colgate Total, Colgate Plax, and Palmolive. Worldwide, the firm has ~40% of toothpaste share and ~31% manual toothbrush share. The company was founded in 1806 and is headquartered in New York, New York.

• Colgate estimates the size world's middle class stood at ~1.8 billion in 2009 and will grow to ~4.9 billion by 2030. Rising incomes and the emergence of a global middle class underpins Colgate's long-term trajectory. Foreign currency movements need to be monitored.

• Core drivers of Colgate's profitable growth moving forward include customer engagement, pricing, and revenue growth management. Colgate's GAAP gross margins improved during the first half of 2020 on a year-over-year basis as households stockpiled consumer staples products in the wake of COVID-19. Colgate's advertising expenses continue to grow.

• In 2019, Colgate acquired Laboratoires Filorga Cosmétiques, a skin care company, for ~USD$1.7 billion in cash. In 2020, Colgate acquired Hello Products, an oral care company, for ~USD$0.35 billion in cash. Colgate is a serial acquirer and acquisitions represent a core part of its business strategy.

• Colgate has raised its dividend every year for the past 55+ years, a remarkable track record. The firm is revamping its IT operations to place a greater focus on analytics in order to stay competitive and to speed up product development timetables.

Investment Considerations

DCF Valuation	OVERVALUED
Relative Valuation	UNATTRACTIVE
ValueCreation™	EXCELLENT
ValueRisk™	LOW
ValueTrend™	NEGATIVE
Cash Flow Generation	STRONG
Financial Leverage	MEDIUM
Growth	MODEST
Technical Evaluation	BULLISH
Relative Strength	WEAK
Money Flow Index (MFI)	NEUTRAL
Upside/Downside Volume (U/D)	DETERIORATING
Near-term Technical Support, 10-week MA	78.00

DCF = Discounted Cash Flow; MFI, U/D = Please see glossary. MA = Moving Average

Business Quality   ValueCreation™

ValueRisk™	Very Poor	Poor	Good	Excellent
Low				■
Medium				
High				
Very High				

Firms that generate economic profits with little operating variability score near the top right of the matrix.

Relative Valuation

Relative Valuation	Forward P/E	PEG	Price / FV
Coca-Cola	34.3	1.5	128.0%
Procter & Gamble	26.5	3.3	144.1%
Philip Morris	15.4	2.4	104.3%
Wal-Mart	26.8	2.3	130.2%
Peer Median	26.7	2.4	129.1%
Colgate-Palmolive	**26.8**	**2.6**	**133.4%**

Price / FV = Current Stock Price divided by Estimated Fair Value

Financial Summary

	----- Actual -----			Projected
Fiscal Year End:	Dec-18	Dec-19	Dec-20	
Revenue	15,544	15,693	15,991	
Revenue, YoY%	0.6%	1.0%	1.9%	
Operating Income	3,842	3,750	3,805	
Operating Margin %	24.7%	23.9%	23.8%	
Net Income	2,400	2,367	2,549	
Net Income Margin %	15.4%	15.1%	15.9%	
Diluted EPS	2.75	2.75	2.99	
Diluted EPS, YoY %	20.6%	0.0%	8.8%	
Free Cash Flow (CFO-capex)	2,620	2,798	2,946	
Free Cash Flow Margin %	16.9%	17.8%	18.4%	

In Millions of USD (except for per share items)

Structure of the Household Products Industry   GOOD

Firms in the household products industry sell some of the most recognized branded consumer packaged goods in the world and often hold a significant market share position in a variety of product categories. Though the industry is characterized by stiff competition from retailers' private-label brands, constituents tend to boast meaningful competitive advantages due to their brand strength/reputation and generate high returns on invested capital. Household products companies remain tied to the vicissitudes of consumer spending, but we tend to like the structure of the group.

Clorox CLX   FAIRLY VALUED

Buying Index™   6   Value Rating

Economic Castle	Estimated Fair Value	Fair Value Range	Investment Style	Sector	Industry
Very Attractive	$198.00	$158.00 - $238.00	LARGE-CAP CORE	Consumer Staples	Recession Resistant

Clorox's margins are steadily improving, aided by its ongoing cost savings program. We've recently raised our fair value estimate.

Stock Chart (weekly)

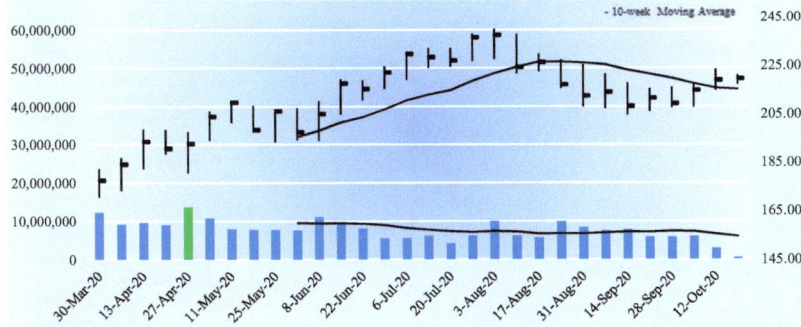

The week with the highest trading volume out of the last 30 weeks was a week of heavy selling, or distribution (red bar).

Investment Considerations

DCF Valuation	FAIRLY VALUED
Relative Valuation	UNATTRACTIVE
ValueCreation™	EXCELLENT
ValueRisk™	LOW
ValueTrend™	POSITIVE
Cash Flow Generation	STRONG
Financial Leverage	MEDIUM
Growth	MODEST
Technical Evaluation	VERY BULLISH
Relative Strength	WEAK
Money Flow Index (MFI)	NEUTRAL
Upside/Downside Volume (U/D)	BEARISH
Near-term Technical Support, 10-week MA	215.00

DCF = Discounted Cash Flow; MFI, U/D = Please see glossary. MA = Moving Average

Company Vitals

Market Cap (USD)	$28,029
Avg Weekly Vol (30 wks)	7,577
30-week Range (USD)	70.69 - 239.86
Valuentum Sector	Consumer Staples
5-week Return	5.1%
13-week Return	-3.2%
30-week Return	23.6%
Dividend Yield %	2.0%
Dividends per Share	4.44
Forward Dividend Payout Ratio	57.2%
Est. Normal Diluted EPS	9.05
P/E on Est. Normal Diluted EPS	24.2
Est. Normal EBITDA	1,743
Forward EV/EBITDA	19.7
EV/Est. Normal EBITDA	17.2
Forward Revenue Growth (5-yr)	3.6%
Forward EPS Growth (5-yr)	8.0%

NMF = Not Meaningful; Est. = Estimated; FY = Fiscal Year

Returns Summary

3-year Historical Average

Return on Equity	128.5%
Return on Assets	16.6%
ROIC, with goodwill	27.9%
ROIC, without goodwill	49.4%

ROIC = Return on Invested Capital; NMF = Not Meaningful

Leverage, Coverage, and Liquidity

In Millions of USD

Total Debt	2,780
Net Debt	1,909
Total Debt/EBITDA	1.9
Net Debt/EBITDA	1.3
EBITDA/Interest	14.7
Current Ratio	1.4
Quick Ratio	1.1

NMF = Not Meaningful

Investment Highlights

• Clorox's brands includes its namesake bleach and cleaning products, Pine-Sol cleaners, Fresh Step cat litter, Glad bags, Kingsford charcoal, and KC Masterpiece sauces. ~80% of the company's revenue is generated by brands that hold the #1 or #2 market share positions in their categories. Clorox was founded in 1913 and is headquartered in Oakland, California.

• Clorox, like many other big brand companies, realized the importance of the shift to e-commerce and digital marketing several years ago. It continues to invest heavily in its digital operations, and its e-commerce sales have grown at a brisk CAGR since fiscal 2015.

• Clorox has noteworthy long-term annual financial goals: organic sales growth of 2%-4%, EBIT margin improvement of 25-50 basis points, and free cash flow of 11%-13% of sales. US retail sales represent ~85% of its revenues. Clorox expects sales growth at its domestic operations will outpace growth at its international operations over the coming fiscal years.

• Clorox's financials have held up well in the face of COVID-19 due to surging demand for consumer staples products in the US, especially hygiene offerings. The firm is committed to maintaining the fundamental strength of its business via pricing, cost savings, margin accretive innovation and 'going lean' initiatives.

• Clorox has raised its annual dividend each year since 1977. It also has a target for a 175 basis point annual EBIT margin benefit from cost savings. SG&A spend is targeted at less than 14% of sales, and gross debt-to-EBITDA is targeted at 2.0x-2.5x.

Business Quality

ValueCreation™

ValueRisk™	Very Poor	Poor	Good	Excellent
Low				■
Medium				
High				
Very High				

Firms that generate economic profits with little operating variability score near the top right of the matrix.

Relative Valuation

	Forward P/E	PEG	Price / FV
Coca-Cola	34.3	1.5	128.0%
Procter & Gamble	26.5	3.3	144.1%
Philip Morris	15.4	2.4	104.3%
Wal-Mart	26.8	2.3	130.2%
Peer Median	26.7	2.4	129.1%
Clorox	**28.3**	**3.7**	**110.9%**

Price / FV = Current Stock Price divided by Estimated Fair Value

Financial Summary

	----- Actual -----		Projected
Fiscal Year End:	Jun-19	Jun-20	Jun-21
Revenue	6,214	6,721	6,943
Revenue, YoY%	1.5%	8.2%	3.3%
Operating Income	1,124	1,274	1,337
Operating Margin %	18.1%	19.0%	19.3%
Net Income	820	939	990
Net Income Margin %	13.2%	14.0%	14.3%
Diluted EPS	6.32	7.36	7.76
Diluted EPS, YoY %	1.0%	16.4%	5.5%
Free Cash Flow (CFO-capex)	786	1,292	1,009
Free Cash Flow Margin %	12.6%	19.2%	14.5%

In Millions of USD (except for per share items)

Structure of the Household Products Industry   GOOD

Firms in the household products industry sell some of the most recognized branded consumer packaged goods in the world and often hold a significant market share position in a variety of product categories. Though the industry is characterized by stiff competition from retailers' private-label brands, constituents tend to boast meaningful competitive advantages due to their brand strength/reputation and generate high returns on invested capital. Household products companies remain tied to the vicissitudes of consumer spending, but we tend to like the structure of the group.

Chipotle CMG   FAIRLY VALUED

Buying Index™ 6   **Value Rating** ⬤

Economic Castle	Estimated Fair Value	Fair Value Range	Investment Style	Sector	Industry
Very Attractive	$1178.00	$825.00 - $1531.00	LARGE-CAP GROWTH	Consumer Discretionary	Discretionary Spending

We recently raised our fair value estimate significantly due to Chipotle's encouraging performance on the digital front.

Stock Chart (weekly)

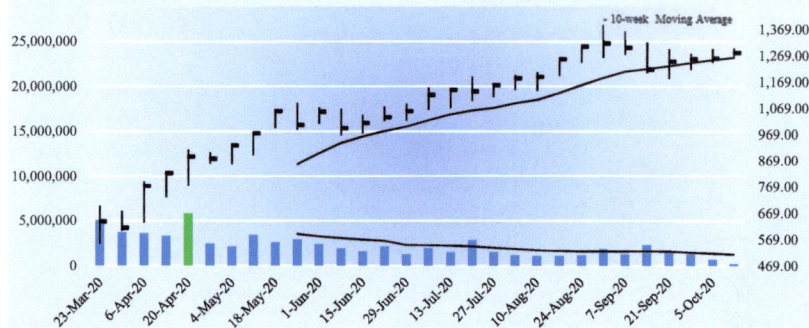

The week with the highest trading volume out of the last 30 weeks was a week of heavy selling, or distribution (red bar).

Company Vitals

Market Cap (USD)	$36,180
Avg Weekly Vol (30 wks)	2,185
30-week Range (USD)	51.21 - 1,384.45
Valuentum Sector	Consumer Discretionary
5-week Return	-2.5%
13-week Return	11.2%
30-week Return	127.8%
Dividend Yield %	0.0%
Dividends per Share	0.00
Forward Dividend Payout Ratio	0.0%
Est. Normal Diluted EPS	32.20
P/E on Est. Normal Diluted EPS	39.7
Est. Normal EBITDA	1,378
Forward EV/EBITDA	58.2
EV/Est. Normal EBITDA	25.6
Forward Revenue Growth (5-yr)	12.8%
Forward EPS Growth (5-yr)	35.0%

NMF = Not Meaningful; Est. = Estimated; FY = Fiscal Year

Returns Summary   3-year Historical Average

Return on Equity	15.9%
Return on Assets	8.8%
ROIC, with goodwill	32.8%
ROIC, without goodwill	33.4%

ROIC = Return on Invested Capital; NMF = Not Meaningful

Leverage, Coverage, and Liquidity

In Millions of USD

Total Debt	0
Net Debt	-881
Total Debt/EBITDA	0.0
Net Debt/EBITDA	NMF
EBITDA/Interest	Excellent
Current Ratio	1.6
Quick Ratio	1.5

NMF = Not Meaningful

Investment Highlights

• Chipotle serves a focused menu of burritos, tacos, burrito bowls (a burrito without the tortilla) and salads, made using fresh ingredients. It prides itself on trying to find the highest-quality ingredients ('Food With Integrity') and providing an exceptional restaurant experience. The company was founded in 1993 and is based in Denver, Colorado.

• Chipotle reported that its digital sales grew by over 216% year-over-year in the second quarter of 2020, highlighting the firm's ability to navigate headwinds created by COVID-19. The firm continues to grow its physical store count.

• Chipotle has been on a rollercoaster ride in the past few years--beginning with the food safety scandal that caused substantial drops in same-store sales starting late 2015--and the restaurant is facing strengthened competition from Yum! Brands' Taco Bell, and Qdoba. However, top-line growth is back on track in a big way, and the company is re-focused on innovation.

• Chipotle's growth story rests on its ability to continue growing its physical store count while also expanding its digital operations. The company recently signed new delivery partnerships with Uber Eats and Grubhub, while also expanding its digital operations into Canada. Innovations on the digital front will be key.

• Investors should be aware of the generosity in our assumptions. We are expecting low double-digit annual revenue growth through 2024 and assume Chipotle significantly expands its operating margin over this period, aided by economies of scale.

Investment Considerations

DCF Valuation	FAIRLY VALUED
Relative Valuation	NEUTRAL
ValueCreation™	EXCELLENT
ValueRisk™	MEDIUM
ValueTrend™	POSITIVE
Cash Flow Generation	STRONG
Financial Leverage	LOW
Growth	HIGH
Technical Evaluation	BULLISH
Relative Strength	NEUTRAL
Money Flow Index (MFI)	NEUTRAL
Upside/Downside Volume (U/D)	DETERIORATING
Near-term Technical Support, 10-week MA	1260.00

DCF = Discounted Cash Flow; MFI, U/D = Please see glossary. MA = Moving Average

Business Quality   ValueCreation™

ValueRisk™	Very Poor	Poor	Good	Excellent
Low				
Medium				▓
High				
Very High				

Firms that generate economic profits with little operating variability score near the top right of the matrix.

Relative Valuation

	Forward P/E	PEG	Price / FV
Disney	75.6	0.3	98.3%
Home Depot	22.9	1.9	106.7%
McDonald's	38.5	1.1	111.0%
Nike	52.8	2.5	104.9%
Peer Median	45.6	NMF	105.8%
Chipotle	**117.3**	**2.1**	**108.5%**

Price / FV = Current Stock Price divided by Estimated Fair Value

Financial Summary

	----- Actual -----		Projected
Fiscal Year End:	Dec-18	Dec-19	Dec-20
Revenue	4,865	5,586	5,977
Revenue, YoY%	8.7%	14.8%	7.0%
Operating Income	334	478	379
Operating Margin %	6.9%	8.6%	6.3%
Net Income	177	350	303
Net Income Margin %	3.6%	6.3%	5.1%
Diluted EPS	6.31	12.38	10.90
Diluted EPS, YoY %	NMF	NMF	-11.9%
Free Cash Flow (CFO-capex)	335	388	576
Free Cash Flow Margin %	6.9%	6.9%	9.6%

In Millions of USD (except for per share items)

Structure of the Restaurants Industry - Fast Casual & Full Service   NEUTRAL

The restaurant industry has benefited from a long-term trend toward eating out, but the space has become increasingly more competitive as new concepts are introduced and successful chains expand. Not only are there pricing pressures and trade-down threats, but rising costs for commodities and labor have pressured profits. Barriers to entry are low, and many constituents have a difficult time differentiating themselves. We tend to like larger chains that benefit from scale advantages and international expansion opportunities, though niche franchises can be appealing. We're neutral on the structure of the group.

Costco COST   OVERVALUED 0.7%

Buying Index™   **4**   **Value Rating** ✕

Economic Castle	Estimated Fair Value	Fair Value Range	Investment Style	Sector	Industry
Attractive	$312.00	$250.00 - $374.00	LARGE-CAP CORE	Consumer Staples	Recession Resistant

Costco posted strong e-commerce sales growth in fiscal 2020. We've recently increased our fair value estimate.

Stock Chart (weekly)

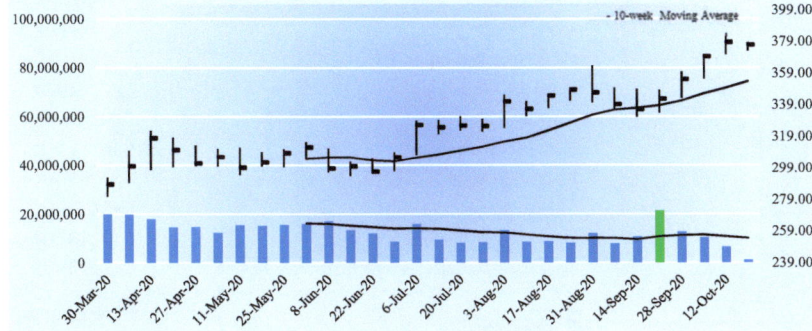

The week with the highest trading volume out of the last 30 weeks was a week of heavy selling, or distribution (red bar).

Company Vitals

Market Cap (USD)	$166,893
Avg Weekly Vol (30 wks)	12,499
30-week Range (USD)	80.89 - 383.86
Valuentum Sector	Consumer Staples
5-week Return	12.8%
13-week Return	15.7%
30-week Return	31.1%
Dividend Yield %	0.7%
Dividends per Share	2.80
Forward Dividend Payout Ratio	30.7%
Est. Normal Diluted EPS	13.78
P/E on Est. Normal Diluted EPS	27.3
Est. Normal EBITDA	9,895
Forward EV/EBITDA	23.5
EV/Est. Normal EBITDA	16.6
Forward Revenue Growth (5-yr)	7.4%
Forward EPS Growth (5-yr)	20.0%

NMF = Not Meaningful; Est. = Estimated; FY = Fiscal Year

Returns Summary
3-year Historical Average

Return on Equity	25.7%
Return on Assets	8.2%
ROIC, with goodwill	29.5%
ROIC, without goodwill	29.5%

ROIC = Return on Invested Capital; NMF = Not Meaningful

Leverage, Coverage, and Liquidity
In Millions of USD

Total Debt	6,823
Net Debt	-2,621
Total Debt/EBITDA	1.1
Net Debt/EBITDA	NMF
EBITDA/Interest	41.5
Current Ratio	1.0
Quick Ratio	0.5

NMF = Not Meaningful

Investment Highlights

• Costco operates an international chain of warehouses, mainly under the 'Costco Wholesale' name. Costco is open only to members and offers three types of membership: Business, Gold Star (individual) and the Executive membership. It has more than 105 million loyal cardholders. The company was founded in 1976 and is headquartered in Washington.

• Costco's business proved very resilient during the initial stages of the COVID-19 pandemic. Its adjusted company-wide comparable sales grew by 9.2% year-over-year in fiscal 2020, led by its e-commerce comparable sales rising by 50.1% year-over-year.

• Costco targets merchandise that produces high sales volumes and rapid inventory turnover. This turnover, when combined with efficiencies achieved by volume purchasing, efficient distribution and reduced handling of merchandise in no-frills, self-service warehouses, enables Costco to operate profitably at significantly lower gross margins than peers.

• Costco has a number of strengths: strong member renewals, fantastic employees that enjoy the higher-than-average pay, great merchandise, and a treasure-hunt atmosphere that consumers love. Its image speaks of quality, and the public often uses Costco as an example for excellent employee relations.

• Large scale food retailers were put on notice with Amazon's 2017 acquisition of Whole Foods. Costco has staying power, in our view, and the firm continues to resonate with all of its stakeholders. The company continues to grow its e-commerce operations.

Investment Considerations

DCF Valuation	OVERVALUED
Relative Valuation	NEUTRAL
ValueCreation™	EXCELLENT
ValueRisk™	LOW
ValueTrend™	NEGATIVE
Cash Flow Generation	MEDIUM
Financial Leverage	LOW
Growth	MODEST
Technical Evaluation	BULLISH
Relative Strength	STRONG
Money Flow Index (MFI)	NEUTRAL
Upside/Downside Volume (U/D)	DETERIORATING
Near-term Technical Support, 10-week MA	354.00

DCF = Discounted Cash Flow; MFI, U/D = Please see glossary. MA = Moving Average

Business Quality

ValueRisk™	Very Poor	Poor	Good	Excellent
Low				■
Medium				
High				
Very High				

ValueCreation™

Firms that generate economic profits with little operating variability score near the top right of the matrix.

Relative Valuation

	Forward P/E	PEG	Price / FV
Coca-Cola	34.3	1.5	128.0%
Procter & Gamble	26.5	3.3	144.1%
Philip Morris	15.4	2.4	104.3%
Wal-Mart	26.8	2.3	130.2%
Peer Median	26.7	2.4	129.1%
Costco	41.4	2.3	120.8%

Price / FV = Current Stock Price divided by Estimated Fair Value

Financial Summary

	----- Actual -----		Projected
Fiscal Year End:	Aug-18	Aug-19	Aug-20
Revenue	141,576	152,703	165,225
Revenue, YoY%	9.7%	7.9%	8.2%
Operating Income	4,480	4,737	5,381
Operating Margin %	3.2%	3.1%	3.3%
Net Income	3,134	3,659	4,035
Net Income Margin %	2.2%	2.4%	2.4%
Diluted EPS	7.09	8.26	9.11
Diluted EPS, YoY %	16.7%	16.5%	10.3%
Free Cash Flow (CFO-capex)	2,805	3,368	3,829
Free Cash Flow Margin %	2.0%	2.2%	2.3%

In Millions of USD (except for per share items)

Structure of the Food Retailers Industry   NEUTRAL

Firms in the mature food retailers industry generally have slim profit margins and face significant competition from brick-and-mortar locations (discount, department, drug, dollar, warehouse clubs and supermarkets) as well as Internet-based retailers (including Amazon). Though the industry is not terribly cyclical, economic conditions, disposable income, credit availability, fuel prices, and unemployment levels drive ticket size and traffic trends. Offering consumers a compelling value proposition is a must, even as higher-priced organic food offerings proliferate. We're generally neutral on the group.

Campbell Soup CPB   FAIRLY VALUED

Buying Index™ 7   **Value Rating** ○

Economic Castle	Estimated Fair Value	Fair Value Range	Investment Style	Sector	Industry
Attractive	$44.00	$34.00 - $54.00	LARGE-CAP CORE	Consumer Staples	Recession Resistant

Campbell Soup sees its ongoing cost saving and efficiency programs more than offsetting potential cost inflation pressures in the near term.

Stock Chart (weekly)

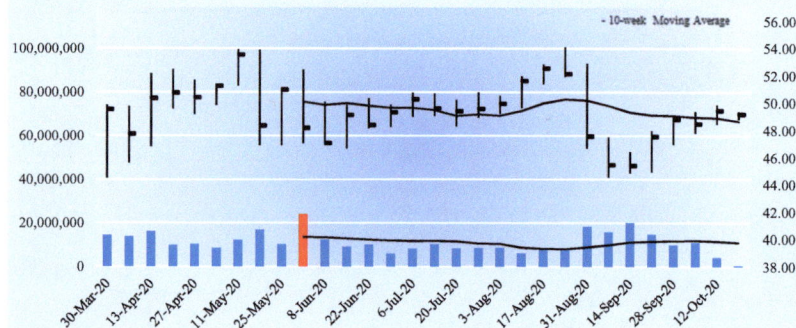

The week with the highest trading volume out of the last 30 weeks was a week of heavy selling, or distribution (red bar).

Investment Considerations

DCF Valuation	**FAIRLY VALUED**
Relative Valuation	**ATTRACTIVE**
ValueCreation™	**EXCELLENT**
ValueRisk™	**MEDIUM**
ValueTrend™	**NEGATIVE**
Cash Flow Generation	**STRONG**
Financial Leverage	**HIGH**
Growth	**MODEST**
Technical Evaluation	**VERY BULLISH**
Relative Strength	**WEAK**
Money Flow Index (MFI)	**NEUTRAL**
Upside/Downside Volume (U/D)	**BEARISH**
Near-term Technical Support, 10-week MA	**49.00**

DCF = Discounted Cash Flow; MFI, U/D = Please see glossary. MA = Moving Average

Company Vitals

Market Cap (USD)	$14,858
Avg Weekly Vol (30 wks)	11,065
30-week Range (USD)	44.52 - 54.08
Valuentum Sector	Consumer Staples
5-week Return	8.6%
13-week Return	0.0%
30-week Return	9.5%
Dividend Yield %	2.8%
Dividends per Share	1.40
Forward Dividend Payout Ratio	47.5%
Est. Normal Diluted EPS	3.31
P/E on Est. Normal Diluted EPS	14.9
Est. Normal EBITDA	1,877
Forward EV/EBITDA	11.6
EV/Est. Normal EBITDA	10.8
Forward Revenue Growth (5-yr)	1.6%
Forward EPS Growth (5-yr)	13.9%

NMF = Not Meaningful; Est. = Estimated; FY = Fiscal Year

Returns Summary

3-year Historical Average

Return on Equity	29.4%
Return on Assets	3.5%
ROIC, with goodwill	12.6%
ROIC, without goodwill	20.6%

ROIC = Return on Invested Capital; NMF = Not Meaningful

Leverage, Coverage, and Liquidity

In Millions of USD

Total Debt	6,196
Net Debt	5,337
Total Debt/EBITDA	3.7
Net Debt/EBITDA	3.2
EBITDA/Interest	4.8
Current Ratio	0.8
Quick Ratio	0.5

NMF = Not Meaningful

Investment Highlights

• Campbell Soup reports in the following segments: 'Meals & Beverages' and 'Snacks.' Its products include Campbell's Chunky soup, Goldfish crackers, Swanson broth and stocks, Prego pasta sauces, Snyder's of Hanover pretzels, Lance sandwich crackers, Milano cookies, and V8 juice, among others. The company was founded in 1869.

• In March 2018, Campbell acquired Snyder's-Lance through a ~$6.1 billion deal by enterprise value as part of its strategy to expand its faster-growing better-for-you snack portfolio. $295 million in total cost synergies are expected by the end of fiscal 2022.

• Campbell seeks to realize an incremental $75 - $85 million in cost savings in fiscal 2021 as management aims to generate $850 million in total cumulative cost savings by the end of fiscal 2022. Some of the targeted savings from Campbell's purchase of Snyder-Lance are from initiatives that were underway before Campbell acquired the firm.

• Campbell is responding to dramatic shifts impacting the food industry from changing consumer behavior and demographics to the shift to digital. The company is working to reduce costs in its efforts to permanently return to profitable growth, though it must continue to innovate as well to stay ahead of its peers.

• From the end of fiscal 2019 to the end of fiscal 2020, Campbell reduced its net debt to adjusted EBITDA ratio from 5.2x to 3.0x, aided by the use of divestment proceeds to pare down its debt load. The company is considering additional bolt-on acquisitions.

Business Quality

ValueCreation™

ValueRisk™	Very Poor	Poor	Good	Excellent
Low				
Medium				▓
High				
Very High				

Firms that generate economic profits with little operating variability score near the top right of the matrix.

Relative Valuation

	Forward P/E	PEG	Price / FV
Coca-Cola	34.3	1.5	128.0%
Procter & Gamble	26.5	3.3	144.1%
Philip Morris	15.4	2.4	104.3%
Wal-Mart	26.8	2.3	130.2%
Peer Median	26.7	2.4	129.1%
Campbell Soup	**16.7**	**1.8**	**111.8%**

Price / FV = Current Stock Price divided by Estimated Fair Value

Financial Summary

	----- Actual -----		Projected
Fiscal Year End:	Jul-19	Jul-20	Jul-21
Revenue	8,107	8,691	8,352
Revenue, YoY%	-6.7%	7.2%	-3.9%
Operating Income	1,150	1,337	1,425
Operating Margin %	14.2%	15.4%	17.1%
Net Income	474	592	886
Net Income Margin %	5.8%	6.8%	10.6%
Diluted EPS	1.57	1.96	2.95
Diluted EPS, YoY %	82.2%	24.5%	50.4%
Free Cash Flow (CFO-capex)	985	1,086	790
Free Cash Flow Margin %	12.1%	12.5%	9.5%

In Millions of USD (except for per share items)

Structure of the Food Products Industry

NEUTRAL

The food products industry is composed of a number of firms with strong brand names. However, market supply/demand dynamics and intense competition still impact product prices, while fluctuations in commodity costs can make earnings quite volatile. Private-label competition, competitors' promotional spending, and changing consumer preferences often drive demand trends. The group's customers—such as supermarkets, warehouses, and food distributors—continue to consolidate, increasing buying power over constituents and hurting margins. Still, we're generally neutral on the group.

VALUENTUM

Salesforce.com CRM   FAIRLY VALUED

Buying Index™ 3   **Value Rating** ⬤

Economic Castle	Estimated Fair Value	Fair Value Range	Investment Style	Sector	Industry
Attractive	$221.00	$177.00 - $265.00	LARGE-CAP BLEND	Information Technology	Technology Giants

We've raised our fair value estimate for Salesforce (again) due to its improving growth outlook. Salesforce is acquiring Slack for ~$27.7 billion.

Stock Chart (weekly)

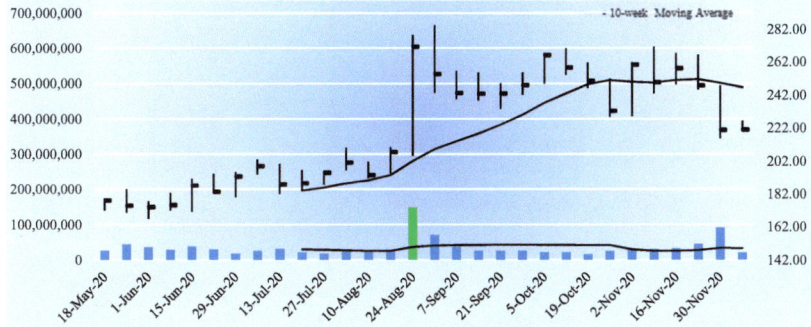

The week with the highest trading volume out of the last 30 weeks was a week of heavy selling, or distribution (red bar).

Company Vitals

Market Cap (USD)	$187,825
Avg Weekly Vol (30 wks)	35,024
30-week Range (USD)	167.00 - 284.50
Valuentum Sector	Information Technology
5-week Return	-15.3%
13-week Return	-10.3%
30-week Return	27.0%
Dividend Yield %	0.0%
Dividends per Share	0.00
Forward Dividend Payout Ratio	0.0%
Est. Normal Diluted EPS	5.35
P/E on Est. Normal Diluted EPS	41.3
Est. Normal EBITDA	10,910
Forward EV/EBITDA	21.3
EV/Est. Normal EBITDA	16.7
Forward Revenue Growth (5-yr)	17.6%
Forward EPS Growth (5-yr)	119.8%

NMF = Not Meaningful; Est. = Estimated; FY = Fiscal Year

Returns Summary   *3-year Historical Average*

Return on Equity	3.6%
Return on Assets	1.7%
ROIC, with goodwill	11.3%
ROIC, without goodwill	27.7%

ROIC = Return on Invested Capital; NMF = Not Meaningful

Leverage, Coverage, and Liquidity
In Millions of USD

Total Debt	2,673
Net Debt	-5,274
Total Debt/EBITDA	0.8
Net Debt/EBITDA	NMF
EBITDA/Interest	26.5
Current Ratio	1.1
Quick Ratio	1.0

NMF = Not Meaningful

Investment Highlights

- Salesforce.com is a provider of enterprise cloud computing (software) solutions. The company delivers customer relationship management, or CRM, applications via the Internet, or 'cloud.' The company sells to businesses of all sizes across industries on a subscription basis. The Americas remains its dominant geography.

- Salesforce has done well in expanding its CRM market leadership. Recently, the company's market share sat at ~20%, up from 6.3% in 2009, which is higher than its closest rivals Oracle, SAP, and Microsoft. Further share gains won't come easy, but Salesforce is up to the task.

- Salesforce put up another year of robust revenue growth in fiscal 2020 (up materially over fiscal 2019). Salesforce is one of the fastest enterprise software companies in the word and one of the fastest to reach $16 billion in revenue. Minor acquisitions have helped it get there, and its recent acquisition of Slack will only bolster its product suite.

- The company's deferred revenue and backlog continue to grow, revealing material future expansion potential. Salesforce.com expects fiscal 2022 sales to be in a range of $21-$23 billion as its addressable market grows to ~$120 billion. Cloud software companies may be largely recession-resistant.

- Revenue growth is the company's current top priority. Long-term, however, Salesforce.com is targeting a mid-30% operating margin. If it hits this, significant upside to our fair value estimate may exist.

Investment Considerations

DCF Valuation	**FAIRLY VALUED**
Relative Valuation	**UNATTRACTIVE**
ValueCreation™	**EXCELLENT**
ValueRisk™	**LOW**
ValueTrend™	**NEGATIVE**
Cash Flow Generation	**STRONG**
Financial Leverage	**LOW**
Growth	**AGGRESSIVE**
Technical Evaluation	**BEARISH**
Relative Strength	**WEAK**
Money Flow Index (MFI)	**NEUTRAL**
Upside/Downside Volume (U/D)	**BEARISH**
Near-term Technical Resistance, 10-wk MA	**246.00**

DCF = Discounted Cash Flow; MFI, U/D = Please see glossary. MA = Moving Average

Business Quality

ValueRisk™ / ValueCreation™	Very Poor	Poor	Good	Excellent
Low				■
Medium				
High				
Very High				

Firms that generate economic profits with little operating variability score near the top right of the matrix.

Relative Valuation

	Forward P/E	PEG	Price / FV
Apple	29.8	2.4	85.0%
Alphabet	34.9	1.8	73.3%
Amazon.com	NMF	3.3	95.7%
Microsoft	31.6	2.5	91.6%
Peer Median	31.6	2.5	88.3%
Salesforce.com	49.3	12.4	100.0%

Price / FV = Current Stock Price divided by Estimated Fair Value

Financial Summary

	Actual		Projected
Fiscal Year End:	Jan-19	Jan-20	Jan-21
Revenue	13,282	17,098	21,065
Revenue, YoY%	26.7%	28.7%	23.2%
Non-GAAP Operating Income	535	463	5,084
Non-GAAP EBIT %	4.0%	2.7%	24.1%
Non-GAAP Net Income	1,110	126	3,888
Non-GAAP NI Margin %	8.4%	0.7%	18.5%
Non-GAAP Diluted EPS	1.43	0.15	4.48
Non-GAAP Dil EPS, YoY %	NMF	NMF	NMF
Non-GAAP FCF (CFO-capex)	2,803	3,688	7,263
Non-GAAP FCF Margin %	21.1%	21.6%	34.5%

In Millions of USD (except for per share items)

Structure of the Software Industry   **VERY GOOD**

Firms that serve the mature software markets—or those consisting of basic business applications—have powerful distribution channels, large installed bases, and fortress balance sheets. These entrenched competitors benefit from significant customer switching costs, which make it nearly impossible for new entrants to gain a foothold. Participants generally benefit from high-margin license revenue and generate significant returns on investment. Still, the shift to cloud computing has created both opportunities and challenges, and the enterprise software landscape continues to evolve. We like the group.

CRISPR Therapeutics CRSP   FAIRLY VALUED

Buying Index™ 6   Value Rating ◯

Economic Castle	Estimated Fair Value	Fair Value Range	Investment Style	Sector	Industry
Unattractive	$200.00	$130.00 - $270.00	LARGE-CAP BLEND	Next Generation	Disruptive Innovation

CRISPR Therapeutics is working to translate its gene-editing platform into treatments for diabetes, cancer and other diseases. An investment comes with substantial risk as its financials reflect an early stage company.

Stock Chart (weekly)

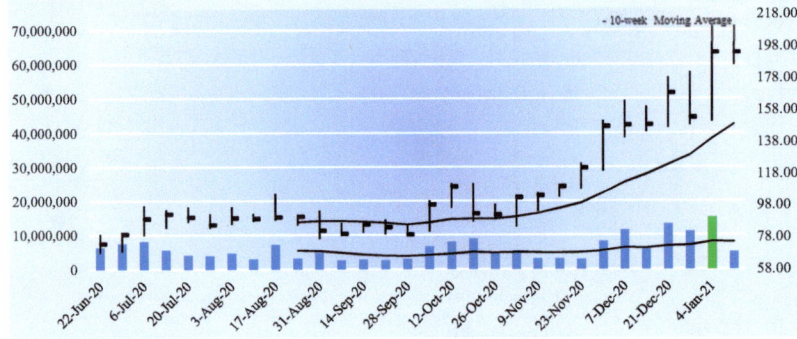

The week with the highest trading volume out of the last 30 weeks was a week of heavy selling, or distribution (red bar).

Investment Considerations

DCF Valuation	**FAIRLY VALUED**
Relative Valuation	**NEUTRAL**
ValueCreation™	**VERY POOR**
ValueRisk™	**HIGH**
ValueTrend™	**POSITIVE**
Cash Flow Generation	**WEAK**
Financial Leverage	**LOW**
Growth	**AGGRESSIVE**
Technical Evaluation	**BULLISH**
Relative Strength	**STRONG**
Money Flow Index (MFI)	**NEUTRAL**
Upside/Downside Volume (U/D)	**BULLISH**
Near-term Technical Support, 10-week MA	**149.00**

DCF = Discounted Cash Flow; MFI, U/D = Please see glossary. MA = Moving Average

Business Quality   ValueCreation™

ValueRisk™	Very Poor	Poor	Good	Excellent
Low				
Medium				
High	▓			
Very High				

Firms that generate economic profits with little operating variability score near the top right of the matrix.

Company Vitals

Market Cap (USD)	$11,035
Avg Weekly Vol (30 wks)	6,098
30-week Range (USD)	68.01 - 210.39
Valuentum Sector	Next Generation
5-week Return	26.3%
13-week Return	74.1%
30-week Return	178.9%
Dividend Yield %	0.0%
Dividends per Share	0.00
Forward Dividend Payout Ratio	0.0%
Est. Normal Diluted EPS	-1.10
P/E on Est. Normal Diluted EPS	NMF
Est. Normal EBITDA	-94
Forward EV/EBITDA	-24.5
EV/Est. Normal EBITDA	-106.8
Forward Revenue Growth (5-yr)	25.9%
Forward EPS Growth (5-yr)	26.6%

NMF = Not Meaningful; Est. = Estimated; FY = Fiscal Year

Returns Summary   3-year Historical Average

Return on Equity	-16.5%
Return on Assets	-13.0%
ROIC, with goodwill	-128.7%
ROIC, without goodwill	-128.7%

ROIC = Return on Invested Capital; NMF = Not Meaningful

Leverage, Coverage, and Liquidity
In Millions of USD

Total Debt	0
Net Debt	-949
Total Debt/EBITDA	0.0
Net Debt/EBITDA	NMF
EBITDA/Interest	Excellent
Current Ratio	17.3
Quick Ratio	NA

NMF = Not Meaningful

Investment Highlights

• CRISPR stands for 'Clustered Regularly Interspaced Short Palindromatic Repeats' and CRISPR Therapeutics is working to use CRISPR-based gene-editing technology to alter sequences of genomic DNA to create more advanced and potentially curative therapies for both rare and common diseases. The company is headquartered in Switzerland with offices in the US and UK.

• CRISPR Therapeutics is furtherst along in developing treatments for TDT (transfusion-dependent beta thalassemia) and SCD (severe sickle cell disease). It is also progressing its gene-editing technology with three CAR-T candidates for hematological and solid cancer tumors.

• We're not talking science fiction. Gene-editing technology may be the way of the future, and CRISPR Therapeutics is at the forefront of the CRISPR/Cas9 (CRISPR-associated protein 9) revolution. In layman's terms, the company's technology cuts double-stranded DNA at a specific location, which allows natural cellular processes to repair the DNA and correct undesirable sequences.

• CRISPR Therapeutics has partnerships with Vertex for TDT, SCD, and cystic fibrosis, ViaCyte for diabetes, and option agreements with Bayer for certain disorders. Its pipeline spans hemoglobinopathies (CTX001), immuno-oncology (CTX110, 120, 130), regenerative (Type I diabetes), and in vivo approaches (cystic fibrosis).

• Shares of CRISPR Therapeutics are nearly impossible to value with any sort of precision, and our valuation assumptions are highly subjective and certain to change in coming updates. Though its technology is revolutionary, CRSP's shares are ultra-speculative.

Relative Valuation

	Forward P/E	PEG	Price / FV
Wayfair	56.3	NMF	84.2%
Zoom Video	170.7	28.8	120.8%
Roku	-338.4	NMF	96.0%
Monster Beverage	36.0	2.9	104.4%
Peer Median	46.1	15.9	100.2%
CRISPR Therapeutics	**-38.2**	**NMF**	**96.9%**

Price / FV = Current Stock Price divided by Estimated Fair Value

Financial Summary

	----- Actual -----		Projected
Fiscal Year End:	Dec-18	Dec-19	Dec-20
Revenue	3	290	3
Revenue, YoY%	-92.4%	9169.8%	-99.1%
Operating Income	-159	47	-411
Operating Margin %	-5087.8%	16.1%	-15772.3%
Net Income	-165	67	-332
Net Income Margin %	-5281.1%	23.1%	-12736.8%
Diluted EPS	-3.44	1.17	-5.07
Diluted EPS, YoY %	101.6%	-134.1%	-532.0%
Free Cash Flow (CFO-capex)	-99	50	-214
Free Cash Flow Margin %	-3169.4%	17.3%	-8226.9%

In Millions of USD (except for per share items)

Structure of the Biotechnology Industry   **GOOD**

Firms in the biotechnology industry face no certain future. Drug development is complex, difficult, and risky, and failure rates are high. Product development cycles are extended—approximately 10 to 15 years from discovery to market. A potential new medicine must undergo years of testing to establish safety/efficacy. Sales depend on reimbursement from third-party payers. Competition can be fierce when biosimilar products exist, though patents are material competitive advantages. We like the group on the basis of patent protection, but the timing of expiration of such patents should be watched closely.

Cisco CSCO   FAIRLY VALUED

Buying Index™ 7   Value Rating 🟡

Economic Castle	Estimated Fair Value	Fair Value Range	Investment Style	Sector	Industry
Very Attractive	$51.00	$41.00 - $61.00	LARGE-CAP VALUE	Information Technology	Technology Giants

Cisco seeks to grow its subscription software revenue as recurring sales provide for stronger cash flow profiles.

Stock Chart (weekly)

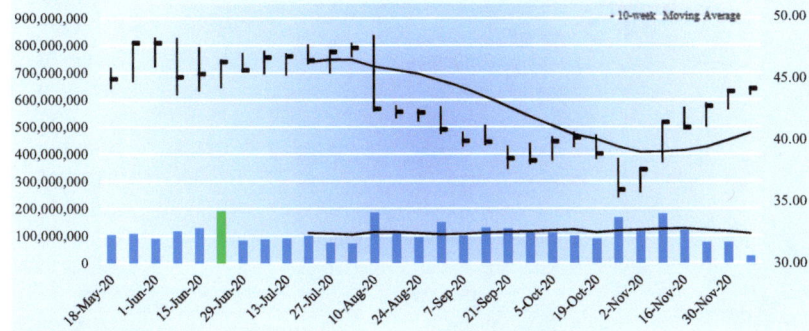

The week with the highest trading volume out of the last 30 weeks was a week of heavy selling, or distribution (red bar).

Company Vitals

Market Cap (USD)	$187,644
Avg Weekly Vol (30 wks)	110,527
30-week Range (USD)	35.28 - 48.45
Valuentum Sector	Information Technology
5-week Return	10.5%
13-week Return	9.7%
30-week Return	-2.4%
Dividend Yield %	3.3%
Dividends per Share	1.44
Forward Dividend Payout Ratio	45.1%
Est. Normal Diluted EPS	3.71
P/E on Est. Normal Diluted EPS	11.9
Est. Normal EBITDA	18,783
Forward EV/EBITDA	9.5
EV/Est. Normal EBITDA	9.2
Forward Revenue Growth (5-yr)	1.4%
Forward EPS Growth (5-yr)	10.5%

NMF = Not Meaningful; Est. = Estimated; FY = Fiscal Year

Returns Summary
3-year Historical Average

Return on Equity	20.6%
Return on Assets	7.7%
ROIC, with goodwill	23.7%
ROIC, without goodwill	66.6%

ROIC = Return on Invested Capital; NMF = Not Meaningful

Leverage, Coverage, and Liquidity
In Millions of USD

Total Debt	14,583
Net Debt	-14,836
Total Debt/EBITDA	0.9
Net Debt/EBITDA	NMF
EBITDA/Interest	27.2
Current Ratio	1.7
Quick Ratio	1.6

NMF = Not Meaningful

Investment Highlights

• Cisco sells Internet Protocol based networking and other products related to the communications and IT industry. The firm provides a broad line of products for transporting data, voice, and video. It is #1 or #2 across a wide variety of architectures, and we like the progress it is making in its transition to a software and subscription based business model. It was founded in 1984 and is headquartered in California.

• Cisco has been acquisitive as of late. Instead of targeting suppliers to improve its gross margin, the firm's M&A strategy will be focused on disruptive technology and software and cloud acquisitions that will positively impact gross margins.

• Cisco has been aggressively buying back stock. For example, in fiscal 2019 and fiscal 2018, it repurchased ~$20.7 billion and ~$17.5 billion of its shares, respectively (repurchases slowed in fiscal 2020). Cisco's business transition is also gaining positive momentum. Recurring revenue accounts for 30%+ of total sales, and subscriptions as a percentage of software revenue continues to climb.

• Cisco had $29.4 billion in cash and investments at the end of fiscal 2020 (and a very nice net cash position). Such a cash hoard gives it financial flexibility to pursue value-creating acquisitions and/or significantly grow the dividend. While we like shares, we're watching closely the impact buybacks have on its balance sheet.

• Cisco is not immune to the COVID-19 pandemic. The outbreak will pressure revenue in fiscal 2021, but non-GAAP gross margins and non-GAAP earnings per share will remain resilient. The company continues to return cash to shareholders.

Investment Considerations

DCF Valuation	FAIRLY VALUED
Relative Valuation	ATTRACTIVE
ValueCreation™	EXCELLENT
ValueRisk™	LOW
ValueTrend™	POSITIVE
Cash Flow Generation	STRONG
Financial Leverage	LOW
Growth	MODEST
Technical Evaluation	BULLISH
Relative Strength	STRONG
Money Flow Index (MFI)	NEUTRAL
Upside/Downside Volume (U/D)	IMPROVING
Near-term Technical Support, 10-week MA	41.00

DCF = Discounted Cash Flow; MFI, U/D = Please see glossary. MA = Moving Average

Business Quality

ValueRisk™	ValueCreation™			
	Very Poor	Poor	Good	Excellent
Low				▓▓
Medium				
High				
Very High				

Firms that generate economic profits with little operating variability score near the top right of the matrix.

Relative Valuation

	Forward P/E	PEG	Price / FV
Apple	29.8	2.4	85.0%
Alphabet	34.9	1.8	73.3%
Amazon.com	NMF	3.3	95.7%
Microsoft	31.6	2.5	91.6%
Peer Median	31.6	2.5	88.3%
Cisco	**13.8**	**1.6**	**86.5%**

Price / FV = Current Stock Price divided by Estimated Fair Value

Financial Summary

	----- Actual -----		Projected
Fiscal Year End:	Jul-19	Jul-20	Jul-21
Revenue	51,904	49,301	48,759
Revenue, YoY%	5.2%	-5.0%	-1.1%
Non-GAAP Operating Income	14,541	14,101	16,421
Non-GAAP EBIT %	28.0%	28.6%	33.7%
Non-GAAP Net Income	11,621	11,196	12,827
Non-GAAP NI Margin %	22.4%	22.7%	26.3%
Non-GAAP Diluted EPS	2.61	2.63	3.19
Non-GAAP Dil EPS, YoY %	11480.0%	NMF	NMF
Non-GAAP FCF (CFO-capex)	14,922	14,656	13,893
Non-GAAP FCF Margin %	28.7%	29.7%	28.5%

In Millions of USD (except for per share items)

Structure of the Networking Equipment Industry   POOR

Firms in the networking equipment industry provide products for transporting data, voice, and video within businesses and around the world. Participants must adapt to address virtualization/cloud-driven needs in the enterprise data center market; the convergence of video, collaboration, and networked mobility technologies; and the move toward programmable, virtual networks. The industry is characterized by low barriers to entry, rapid technological change and significant pricing competition. Gross margins can be volatile and should be watched closely. We don't like the structure of the group.

VALUENTUM

Cintas Corp CTAS   OVERVALUED 14.8%

Buying Index™ 4   Value Rating ✗

Economic Castle	Estimated Fair Value	Fair Value Range	Investment Style	Sector	Industry
Very Attractive	$252.00	$202.00 - $302.00	LARGE-CAP CORE	Consumer Discretionary	Discretionary Spending

Cintas continues to generate enormous amounts of free cash flow, despite the outbreak of COVID-19, but shares aren't cheap. We think investors are paying up for Cintas' excellent dividend growth track record.

Stock Chart (weekly)

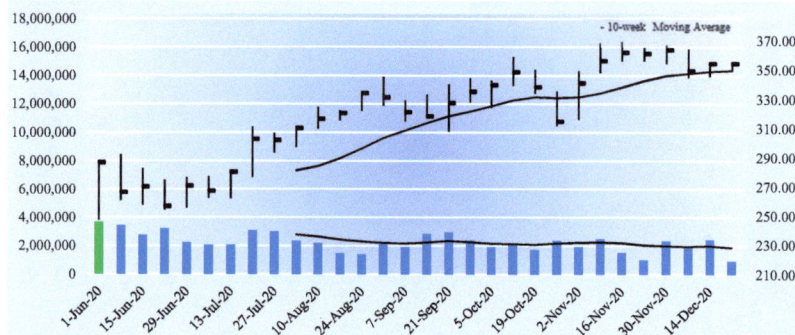

The week with the highest trading volume out of the last 30 weeks was a week of heavy selling, or distribution (red bar).

Investment Considerations

DCF Valuation	OVERVALUED
Relative Valuation	NEUTRAL
ValueCreation™	EXCELLENT
ValueRisk™	LOW
ValueTrend™	NEGATIVE
Cash Flow Generation	STRONG
Financial Leverage	MEDIUM
Growth	MODEST
Technical Evaluation	BULLISH
Relative Strength	STRONG
Money Flow Index (MFI)	NEUTRAL
Upside/Downside Volume (U/D)	BULLISH
Near-term Technical Support, 10-week MA	349.00

DCF = Discounted Cash Flow; MFI, U/D = Please see glossary. MA = Moving Average

Company Vitals

Market Cap (USD)	$38,800
Avg Weekly Vol (30 wks)	2,264
30-week Range (USD)	247.11 - 369.20
Valuentum Sector	Consumer Discretionary
5-week Return	-2.6%
13-week Return	7.4%
30-week Return	42.6%
Dividend Yield %	1.0%
Dividends per Share	3.51
Forward Dividend Payout Ratio	43.3%
Est. Normal Diluted EPS	10.39
P/E on Est. Normal Diluted EPS	34.1
Est. Normal EBITDA	1,873
Forward EV/EBITDA	26.8
EV/Est. Normal EBITDA	22.2
Forward Revenue Growth (5-yr)	4.7%
Forward EPS Growth (5-yr)	10.2%

NMF = Not Meaningful; Est. = Estimated; FY = Fiscal Year

Returns Summary

3-year Historical Average

Return on Equity	27.0%
Return on Assets	10.7%
ROIC, with goodwill	16.8%
ROIC, without goodwill	32.3%

ROIC = Return on Invested Capital; NMF = Not Meaningful

Leverage, Coverage, and Liquidity

In Millions of USD

Total Debt	2,850
Net Debt	2,753
Total Debt/EBITDA	1.9
Net Debt/EBITDA	1.8
EBITDA/Interest	14.7
Current Ratio	2.0
Quick Ratio	0.9

NMF = Not Meaningful

Investment Highlights

• Cintas primarily provides uniform rental services, but it also has first aid, safety, fire protection, and document management service operations. The company serves more than one million businesses of all types, boasting significant customer diversity. It was founded in 1968 and is headquartered in Cincinnati, Ohio.

• Cintas is the largest company in the uniform industry, and its top line and diluted earnings per share have expanded at a nice mid-single-digit annual clip during the past 10 years. With the exception of its 'Uniform Direct Sales' business, gross margins run in the ~45% range.

• Total debt has expanded significantly since the Great Recession, checking in at more than $2.5 billion at the end of August 2020. The firm's credit ratings remain firmly in investment grade territory, however, and its debt-to-EBITDA ratio remains reasonable. Management continues to buy back stock, a move we do not like given our opinion of its valuation.

• In 2017, Cintas purchased rival G&K Services for approximately $2.2 billion, including acquired net debt. The acquisition strengthened Cintas' position in US and Canada, and the company expects to realize annual synergies in a range of $130-$140 million in their entirety in the fourth full year after closing.

• The G&K deal should help with fuel savings due to better route density and reduced redundant capacity. Free cash flow at Cintas remains top notch, despite the COVID-19 outbreak, and its dividend growth track record makes it a Dividend Aristocrat.

Business Quality

ValueCreation™

ValueRisk™	Very Poor	Poor	Good	Excellent
Low				■
Medium				
High				
Very High				

Firms that generate economic profits with little operating variability score near the top right of the matrix.

Relative Valuation

	Forward P/E	PEG	Price / FV
Disney	104.2	NMF	117.1%
Home Depot	22.9	1.9	106.7%
McDonald's	38.5	1.1	111.0%
Nike	52.8	2.5	104.9%
Peer Median	45.6	1.9	108.9%
Cintas Corp	**43.7**	**4.3**	**140.6%**

Price / FV = Current Stock Price divided by Estimated Fair Value

Financial Summary

	----- Actual -----		Projected
Fiscal Year End:	May-18	May-19	May-20
Revenue	6,477	6,892	7,085
Revenue, YoY%	21.7%	6.4%	2.8%
Operating Income	992	1,134	1,183
Operating Margin %	15.3%	16.4%	16.7%
Net Income	784	883	888
Net Income Margin %	12.1%	12.8%	12.5%
Diluted EPS	7.14	8.06	8.11
Diluted EPS, YoY %	68.3%	12.9%	0.6%
Free Cash Flow (CFO-capex)	692	791	1,161
Free Cash Flow Margin %	10.7%	11.5%	16.4%

In Millions of USD (except for per share items)

Structure of the Commercial Services Industry

NEUTRAL

The commercial services industry runs the gamut of firms from those that provide document management services and/or mail-related operations to entities that offer records management solutions and corporate uniforms. Though there are pockets of strength, a number of participants must reinvent themselves to survive over the long haul. Industry constituents are levered to business spending and are not immune to competitive forces. Carving out a sustainable competitive advantage is difficult to do in this group, though returns on invested capital have been satisfactory. We're neutral on the industry's structure.

Carvana Co. CVNA FAIRLY VALUED

Buying Index™ 6 **Value Rating** 🟡

Economic Castle	Estimated Fair Value	Fair Value Range	Investment Style	Sector	Industry
Unattractive	$261.00	$170.00 - $352.00	LARGE-CAP GROWTH	Next Generation	Disruptive Innovation

Carvana is disrupting the process by which consumers buy used cars with its e-commerce platform that emphasizes transparent pricing and a no-pressure experience.

Stock Chart (weekly)

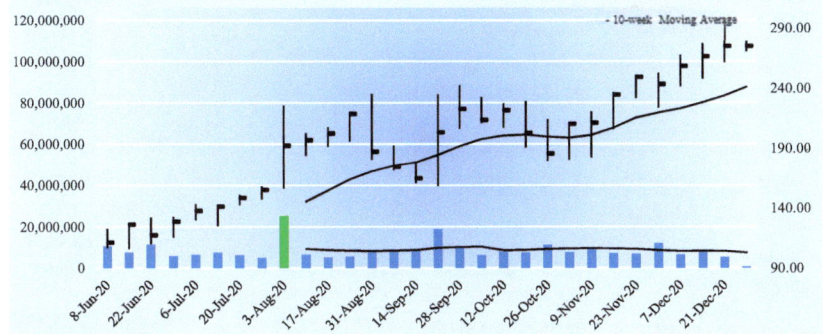

The week with the highest trading volume out of the last 30 weeks was a week of heavy selling, or distribution (red bar).

Investment Considerations

DCF Valuation	FAIRLY VALUED
Relative Valuation	NEUTRAL
ValueCreation™	VERY POOR
ValueRisk™	HIGH
ValueTrend™	NEGATIVE
Cash Flow Generation	WEAK
Financial Leverage	HIGH
Growth	AGGRESSIVE
Technical Evaluation	BULLISH
Relative Strength	STRONG
Money Flow Index (MFI)	NEUTRAL
Upside/Downside Volume (U/D)	BULLISH
Near-term Technical Support, 10-week MA	241.00

DCF = Discounted Cash Flow; MFI, U/D = Please see glossary. MA = Moving Average

Business Quality

ValueCreation™

ValueRisk™	Very Poor	Poor	Good	Excellent
Low				
Medium				
High	■			
Very High				

Firms that generate economic profits with little operating variability score near the top right of the matrix.

Company Vitals

Market Cap (USD)	$12,869
Avg Weekly Vol (30 wks)	8,390
30-week Range (USD)	106.14 - 292.76
Valuentum Sector	Next Generation
5-week Return	9.4%
13-week Return	21.6%
30-week Return	132.9%
Dividend Yield %	0.0%
Dividends per Share	0.00
Forward Dividend Payout Ratio	0.0%
Est. Normal Diluted EPS	0.51
P/E on Est. Normal Diluted EPS	537.0
Est. Normal EBITDA	1
Forward EV/EBITDA	-49.3
EV/Est. Normal EBITDA	27,302.1
Forward Revenue Growth (5-yr)	37.4%
Forward EPS Growth (5-yr)	-216.0%

NMF = Not Meaningful; Est. = Estimated; FY = Fiscal Year

Returns Summary

3-year Historical Average

Return on Equity	-119.4%
Return on Assets	-22.1%
ROIC, with goodwill	-61.4%
ROIC, without goodwill	-62.0%

ROIC = Return on Invested Capital; NMF = Not Meaningful

Leverage, Coverage, and Liquidity

In Millions of USD

Total Debt	1,501
Net Debt	1,382
Total Debt/EBITDA	NMF
Net Debt/EBITDA	-5.7
EBITDA/Interest	-3.0
Current Ratio	2.4
Quick Ratio	NA

NMF = Not Meaningful

Investment Highlights

- Carvana was formed in 2016 and is listed on the NYSE. The company offers an online platform for buying/selling used cars. Its e-commerce initiatives focus on giving consumers a wide selection of vehicles, transparent pricing, and a no-haggle experience. Its technology can facilitate a transaction, including scheduled delivery, in as little as 10 minutes. Its principal offices are in Tempe, Arizona.
- Carvana's proprietary alogorithms optimize its inventory of 25,000+ vehicles, and its logistics network can offer next-day delivery saving consumers lots ot time. It has a patented 360-degree vehicle imaging feature whereby consumers can research and evaluate a vehicle.
- The company is disrupting a huge market. The US automotive industry generates ~$1 trillion in sales each year, and the used car retail industry is highly fragmented, with over 40,000+ used car dealerships in the US. Consumers generally don't like the existing used-car buying process, and Carvana is working hard to solve this problem with an easy end-to-end online solution.
- An investment in Carvana is about as risky as it gets, however. The company is burning through cash, generating losses, and diluting shareholders with new equity to offset losses and capital investment. We're building in very optimistic long-term assumptions to derive our fair value estimate, and we assign the stock a large fair value estimate range.
- Its vertically-integrated e-commerce platform, in-house logistics network, and financing solutions with fast decisions on credit are key advantages, but the company has a lot to prove. It also has a dual-class share structure, with the Garcia family controlling 90%+ of voting power.

Relative Valuation

	Forward P/E	PEG	Price / FV
Wayfair	56.3	NMF	84.2%
Zoom Video	170.7	28.8	120.8%
Roku	-338.4	NMF	96.0%
Monster Beverage	36.0	2.9	104.4%
Peer Median	46.1	15.9	100.2%
Carvana Co.	**-115.3**	**NMF**	**105.3%**

Price / FV = Current Stock Price divided by Estimated Fair Value

Financial Summary

	----- Actual -----		Projected
Fiscal Year End:	Dec-18	Dec-19	Dec-20
Revenue	1,955	3,940	5,354
Revenue, YoY%	127.7%	101.5%	35.9%
Operating Income	-230	-284	-347
Operating Margin %	-11.7%	-7.2%	-6.5%
Net Income	-55	-115	-156
Net Income Margin %	-2.8%	-2.9%	-2.9%
Diluted EPS	-1.85	-2.45	-2.38
Diluted EPS, YoY %	-55.2%	32.5%	-2.6%
Free Cash Flow (CFO-capex)	-558	-988	-1,560
Free Cash Flow Margin %	-28.5%	-25.1%	-29.1%

In Millions of USD (except for per share items)

Structure of the Internet & Catalog Retail Industry GOOD

The Internet and catalog retail industry benefits as a whole from the secular trend toward consumer digital (online) consumption. The industry consists of a number of exclusive online retailers led by Amazon, which continues to disrupt the broader retail space, and businesses that offer Internet travel services such as Booking Holdings, while online auctions are dominated by eBay. The industry generates high returns on investment due to minimal capital costs, but the landscape will be vastly different in the decades ahead. Still, we like the group.

Deere DE FAIRLY VALUED

| | Buying Index™ | 5 | Value Rating | ⬤ |

Economic Castle	Estimated Fair Value	Fair Value Range	Investment Style	Sector	Industry
Attractive	$234.00	$187.00 - $281.00	LARGE-CAP CORE	Industrials	Industrial Leaders

Worldwide sales of agriculture/turf equipment and construction/forestry equipment have slowed during the COVID-19 pandemic, but we expect Deere's performance to bounce back considerably.

Stock Chart (weekly)

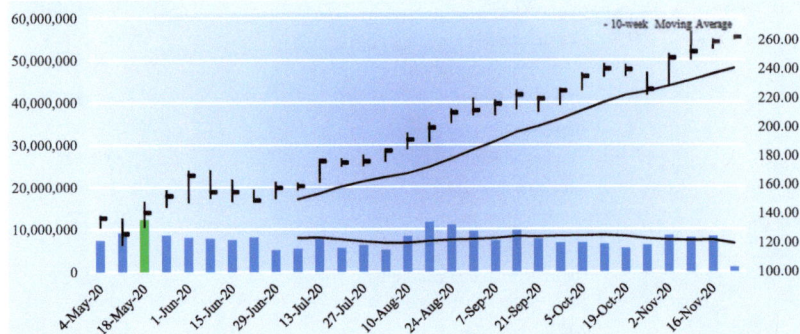

The week with the highest trading volume out of the last 30 weeks was a week of heavy selling, or distribution (red bar).

Investment Considerations

DCF Valuation	**FAIRLY VALUED**
Relative Valuation	**NEUTRAL**
ValueCreation™	**EXCELLENT**
ValueRisk™	**LOW**
ValueTrend™	**NEGATIVE**
Cash Flow Generation	**WEAK**
Financial Leverage	**LOW**
Growth	**MODEST**
Technical Evaluation	**NEUTRAL**
Relative Strength	**STRONG**
Money Flow Index (MFI)	**OVERBOUGHT**
Upside/Downside Volume (U/D)	**BULLISH**
Near-term Technical Support, 10-week MA	**240.00**

DCF = Discounted Cash Flow; MFI, U/D = Please see glossary. MA = Moving Average

Company Vitals

Market Cap (USD)	$83,944
Avg Weekly Vol (30 wks)	7,551
30-week Range (USD)	117.85 - 265.87
Valuentum Sector	Industrials
5-week Return	10.4%
13-week Return	24.7%
30-week Return	92.0%
Dividend Yield %	1.2%
Dividends per Share	3.04
Forward Dividend Payout Ratio	39.1%
Est. Normal Diluted EPS	13.34
P/E on Est. Normal Diluted EPS	19.6
Est. Normal EBITDA	9,001
Forward EV/EBITDA	14.0
EV/Est. Normal EBITDA	9.9
Forward Revenue Growth (5-yr)	2.2%
Forward EPS Growth (5-yr)	11.7%

NMF = Not Meaningful; Est. = Estimated; FY = Fiscal Year

Returns Summary
3-year Historical Average

Return on Equity	26.0%
Return on Assets	3.8%
ROIC, with goodwill	25.9%
ROIC, without goodwill	30.5%

ROIC = Return on Invested Capital; NMF = Not Meaningful

Leverage, Coverage, and Liquidity
In Millions of USD

Total Debt	9,301
Net Debt	4,863
Total Debt/EBITDA	1.2
Net Debt/EBITDA	0.6
EBITDA/Interest	5.2
Current Ratio	2.0
Quick Ratio	1.8

NMF = Not Meaningful; Debt excludes debt associated with the finance sub.

Investment Highlights

• Deere operates in three business segments. Its agricultural/turf segment makes tractors, loaders, combines, and harvesters. Its construction/forestry segment produces earthmoving machines, loaders and excavators, while its financial operation supports its dealer network via wholesale financing. The company was founded in 1837 and is based in Illinois.

• Though Deere investors will feel the up's and down's of the economic cycle, the firm's strong brand name and extensive dealer network are key competitive strengths. We like the company's fundamentals, but its financial services operation adds a degree of credit risk to its operations.

• Deere is tied to the changing worldwide demand for farm outputs that are required to meet the population's growing food and bio-energy needs. Fluctuating agricultural commodity prices directly impact sales of Deere's equipment and are largely responsible for the cyclical tendencies of its operations. Management targets a 25%-35% payout ratio of mid-cycle earnings.

• Trade tensions and related tariffs have the potential to impact both demand for Deere's products and input costs. Rising raw material and logistics costs are also weighing on its near-term margin outlook. Management expects cost pressures to ease in the near term, but geopolitical uncertainty is causing customers to delay big spending plans.

• The market for agricultural/turf equipment is competitive and includes rivals such as AGCO, CNH Global, Kubota, and Toro. The construction/forestry segment is also highly competitive, and Deere bumps heads in this market with Caterpillar, Komatsu, and Volvo, among others.

Business Quality

ValueRisk™	Very Poor	Poor	Good	Excellent
Low				▨
Medium				
High				
Very High				

ValueCreation™

Firms that generate economic profits with little operating variability score near the top right of the matrix.

Relative Valuation

	Forward P/E	PEG	Price / FV
Danaher	36.3	3.0	121.5%
Honeywell	28.8	1.7	101.3%
Lockheed Martin	15.0	2.3	96.3%
Union Pacific	25.9	1.4	119.1%
Peer Median	27.3	NMF	110.2%
Deere	**33.7**	**1.1**	**111.9%**

Price / FV = Current Stock Price divided by Estimated Fair Value

Financial Summary

	----- Actual -----		Projected
Fiscal Year End:	Oct-18	Oct-19	Oct-20
Revenue	37,358	39,258	34,037
Revenue, YoY%	25.6%	5.1%	-13.3%
Operating Income	5,274	5,554	4,593
Operating Margin %	14.1%	14.1%	13.5%
Net Income	2,371	3,253	2,518
Net Income Margin %	6.3%	8.3%	7.4%
Diluted EPS	7.24	10.15	7.78
Diluted EPS, YoY %	8.5%	40.1%	-23.4%
Free Cash Flow (CFO-capex)	-1,128	-37	3,816
Free Cash Flow Margin %	-3.0%	-0.1%	11.2%

In Millions of USD (except for per share items)

Structure of the Agricultural Machinery Industry   NEUTRAL

The agricultural machinery industry is composed of firms that make farm and construction equipment. Demand for agricultural equipment is levered to farm incomes and commodity prices, while purchases of construction equipment are dependent on global economic health. Population growth and the increasing need for food/energy are the major long-term drivers for new orders across the industry. Still, firms are competitive, capital intensive, and possess significant operating leverage. A strong/dependable brand and an expansive distribution network are keys to success. We're neutral on the group.

Dollar General DG   FAIRLY VALUED

Buying Index™   5   Value Rating ◐

Economic Castle	Estimated Fair Value	Fair Value Range	Investment Style	Sector	Industry
Attractive	$186.00	$149.00 - $223.00	LARGE-CAP CORE	Consumer Discretionary	Discretionary Spending

We once again raised our fair value estimate as Dollar General as its growth outlook continues to get brighter.

Stock Chart (weekly)

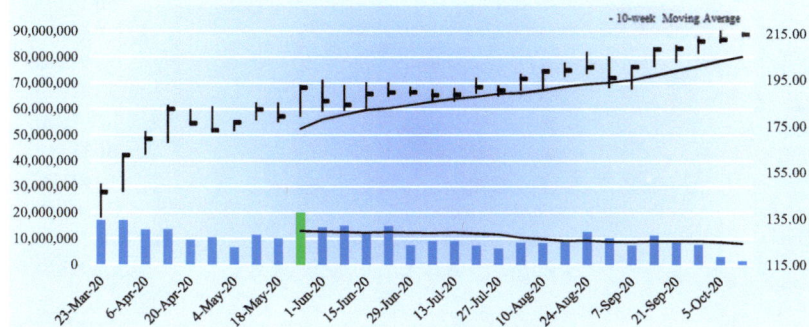

The week with the highest trading volume out of the last 30 weeks was a week of heavy selling, or distribution (red bar).

Company Vitals

Market Cap (USD)	$55,360
Avg Weekly Vol (30 wks)	10,406
30-week Range (USD)	35.25 - 216.47
Valuentum Sector	Consumer Discretionary
5-week Return	6.7%
13-week Return	13.1%
30-week Return	53.4%
Dividend Yield %	0.7%
Dividends per Share	1.44
Forward Dividend Payout Ratio	14.0%
Est. Normal Diluted EPS	12.26
P/E on Est. Normal Diluted EPS	17.5
Est. Normal EBITDA	4,447
Forward EV/EBITDA	14.6
EV/Est. Normal EBITDA	13.0
Forward Revenue Growth (5-yr)	6.6%
Forward EPS Growth (5-yr)	19.3%

NMF = Not Meaningful; Est. = Estimated; FY = Fiscal Year

Returns Summary
3-year Historical Average

Return on Equity	26.0%
Return on Assets	11.5%
ROIC, with goodwill	18.3%
ROIC, without goodwill	33.3%

ROIC = Return on Invested Capital; NMF = Not Meaningful

Leverage, Coverage, and Liquidity
In Millions of USD

Total Debt	2,912
Net Debt	2,672
Total Debt/EBITDA	1.0
Net Debt/EBITDA	1.0
EBITDA/Interest	27.8
Current Ratio	1.1
Quick Ratio	0.1

NMF = Not Meaningful

Investment Highlights

• Dollar General is the largest discount retailer in the US by number of stores with over 16,700 neighborhood stores in 46 states. It provides products that are frequently used and replenished such as food, snacks, and health and beauty aids. The company helps shoppers: 'Save time, Save money, Every day.' It was founded in 1939 and is headquartered in Tennessee.

• Dollar General's strategy is built on catering to regions that e-commerce offerings are less viable in, particularly towns with populations of 20,000 or less. The company recently opened its first stores in Washington State and Wyoming.

• Dollar General has put up roughly 30 consecutive years of same-store sales growth. The firm continues to add new stores to its portfolio and plans to add many more, in addition to remodeling and relocations. The company's free cash flow generating capacity in the midst of such a robust expansion program is impressive and a testament to its consistency.

• Dollar General sees the opportunity for an additional 10,000+ store locations across the US which supports its long-term growth trajectory. The firm has performed well in the face of COVID-19 and posted 18.8% year-over-year same-store sales growth in the second quarter of fiscal 2020, an impressive figure.

• Dollar General is steadily adding new consumable products to its stores (frozen food products and fresh foods like vegetables) while investing significantly in its digital operations. Its various strategic initiatives have proven highly effective of late.

Investment Considerations

DCF Valuation	**FAIRLY VALUED**
Relative Valuation	**ATTRACTIVE**
ValueCreation™	**EXCELLENT**
ValueRisk™	**LOW**
ValueTrend™	**POSITIVE**
Cash Flow Generation	**STRONG**
Financial Leverage	**LOW**
Growth	**MODEST**
Technical Evaluation	**NEUTRAL**
Relative Strength	**NEUTRAL**
Money Flow Index (MFI)	**OVERBOUGHT**
Upside/Downside Volume (U/D)	**BULLISH**
Near-term Technical Support, 10-week MA	**205.00**

DCF = Discounted Cash Flow; MFI, U/D = Please see glossary. MA = Moving Average

Business Quality
ValueCreation™

ValueRisk™	Very Poor	Poor	Good	Excellent
Low				■
Medium				
High				
Very High				

Firms that generate economic profits with little operating variability score near the top right of the matrix.

Relative Valuation

	Forward P/E	PEG	Price / FV
Disney	75.6	0.3	98.3%
Home Depot	22.9	1.9	106.7%
McDonald's	38.5	1.1	111.0%
Nike	52.8	2.5	104.9%
Peer Median	45.6	NMF	105.8%
Dollar General	**20.8**	**1.7**	**115.3%**

Price / FV = Current Stock Price divided by Estimated Fair Value

Financial Summary

	----- Actual -----		Projected
Fiscal Year End:	Jan-19	Jan-20	Jan-21
Revenue	25,625	27,754	33,194
Revenue, YoY%	9.2%	8.3%	19.6%
Operating Income	2,116	2,302	3,358
Operating Margin %	8.3%	8.3%	10.1%
Net Income	1,589	1,713	2,605
Net Income Margin %	6.2%	6.2%	7.8%
Diluted EPS	5.97	6.64	10.30
Diluted EPS, YoY %	6.1%	11.1%	55.2%
Free Cash Flow (CFO-capex)	1,410	1,453	1,971
Free Cash Flow Margin %	5.5%	5.2%	5.9%

In Millions of USD (except for per share items)

Structure of the Multiline Retail (discount) Industry   GOOD

The retail discount store industry provides consumable basic needs to customers primarily in the low- and middle-income brackets. More than one third of the industry's customers live in households that earn less than $20,000 per year, making the group's results counter-cyclical--as more households generate lower income due to poor economic conditions, store growth and same-store-sales opportunities increase. Still, competition is fierce among constituents and with many other retailers, including grocery stores. But given the niche low-price strategy of participants and their counter-cyclical nature, we like the group.

Danaher DHR   FAIRLY VALUED

Buying Index™ 6   **Value Rating** ⬤

Economic Castle	Estimated Fair Value	Fair Value Range	Investment Style	Sector	Industry
Attractive	$182.00	$137.00 - $228.00	LARGE-CAP GROWTH	Industrials	Industrial Leaders

Danaher makes savvy acquisitions and applies its 'Danaher Business System' tools to carve out competitive advantages. Its business continues to shift as it buys new assets and divests others.

Stock Chart (weekly)

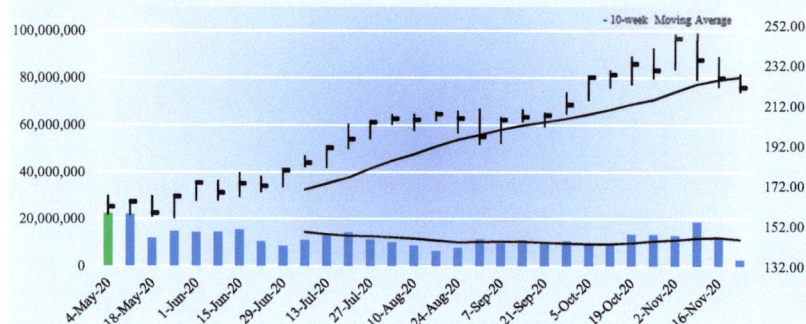

The week with the highest trading volume out of the last 30 weeks was a week of heavy selling, or distribution (red bar).

Investment Considerations

DCF Valuation	**FAIRLY VALUED**
Relative Valuation	**UNATTRACTIVE**
ValueCreation™	**EXCELLENT**
ValueRisk™	**MEDIUM**
ValueTrend™	**POSITIVE**
Cash Flow Generation	**STRONG**
Financial Leverage	**HIGH**
Growth	**HIGH**
Technical Evaluation	**BULLISH**
Relative Strength	**STRONG**
Money Flow Index (MFI)	**NEUTRAL**
Upside/Downside Volume (U/D)	**DETERIORATING**
Near-term Technical Resistance, 10-wk MA	**226.00**

DCF = Discounted Cash Flow; MFI, U/D = Please see glossary. MA = Moving Average

Company Vitals

Market Cap (USD)	$160,394
Avg Weekly Vol (30 wks)	11,974
30-week Range (USD)	155.61 - 248.32
Valuentum Sector	Industrials
5-week Return	-4.5%
13-week Return	7.3%
30-week Return	37.2%
Dividend Yield %	0.3%
Dividends per Share	0.72
Forward Dividend Payout Ratio	11.8%
Est. Normal Diluted EPS	7.86
P/E on Est. Normal Diluted EPS	28.1
Est. Normal EBITDA	9,577
Forward EV/EBITDA	22.5
EV/Est. Normal EBITDA	17.1
Forward Revenue Growth (5-yr)	13.1%
Forward EPS Growth (5-yr)	22.3%

NMF = Not Meaningful; Est. = Estimated; FY = Fiscal Year

Returns Summary
3-year Historical Average

Return on Equity	8.7%
Return on Assets	4.7%
ROIC, with goodwill	7.3%
ROIC, without goodwill	19.0%

ROIC = Return on Invested Capital; NMF = Not Meaningful

Leverage, Coverage, and Liquidity
In Millions of USD

Total Debt	21,729
Net Debt	1,817
Total Debt/EBITDA	4.9
Net Debt/EBITDA	0.4
EBITDA/Interest	41.1
Current Ratio	5.2
Quick Ratio	4.7

NMF = Not Meaningful

Investment Highlights

• Danaher makes innovative products and provides services to professional, medical, industrial, and commercial customers. Its portfolio of premier brands, including Pall, Cepheid, and Beckman Coulter, is among the most highly recognized in each of the markets it serves. The company was founded in 1969 and is headquartered in Washington, D.C.

• Danaher spun off its 'Dental' segment into an independent, publicly-traded company in the second half of 2019. The segment had accounted for ~14.5% of Danaher's total revenue, and it expects a more refined focus to benefit its business moving forward.

• Danaher boasts a strong portfolio of brands and an extensive installed base that helps it drive recurring revenue. Roughly 70% of its revenue is generated direct from customers (as opposed to distributors) and recurring. Its portfolio is geographically diverse as North America accounts for ~40% of revenue, high growth markets for ~30%, and Western Europe for ~25%.

• Danaher's portfolio is exposed to secular growth drivers such as increasing environmental, healthcare, and food safety regulatory requirements, and China offers long-term expansion opportunities for the firm. We also applaud the firm's free cash flow conversion efforts as free cash flow consistently exceeds net income.

• In 2020, Danaher bought GE's BioPharma unit, which is a leading provider of instruments, consumables, and software that support biologic production workflows, for ~$21 billion. $100+ million in annual cost savings are expected by year three after closing.

Business Quality

ValueRisk™	Very Poor	Poor	Good	Excellent
Low				
Medium				▓▓
High				
Very High				

ValueCreation™

Firms that generate economic profits with little operating variability score near the top right of the matrix.

Relative Valuation

	Forward P/E	PEG	Price / FV
Honeywell	28.8	1.7	101.3%
Lockheed Martin	15.0	2.3	96.3%
Union Pacific	25.9	1.4	119.1%
United Parcel Service	22.0	1.4	124.5%
Peer Median	23.9	1.6	110.2%
Danaher	**36.3**	**3.0**	**121.5%**

Price / FV = Current Stock Price divided by Estimated Fair Value

Financial Summary

	----- Actual -----		Projected
Fiscal Year End:	Dec-18	Dec-19	Dec-20
Revenue	17,049	17,911	21,959
Revenue, YoY%	9.9%	5.1%	22.6%
Non-GAAP Operating Income	3,055	3,269	5,979
Non-GAAP EBIT %	17.9%	18.3%	27.2%
Non-GAAP Net Income	2,406	2,432	4,507
Non-GAAP NI Margin %	14.1%	13.6%	20.5%
Non-GAAP Diluted EPS	3.39	3.35	6.09
Non-GAAP Dil EPS, YoY %	10.1%	-1.1%	81.7%
Non-GAAP FCF (CFO-capex)	3,438	3,325	4,970
Non-GAAP FCF Margin %	20.2%	18.6%	22.6%

In Millions of USD (except for per share items)

Structure of the Conglomerates Industry   GOOD

The industrial conglomerate industry is characterized by firms that operate various business lines on a global scale. Demand for industrial products tends to be cyclical in nature, and most firms couple their manufacturing operations with generally more stable services businesses to mitigate fundamental volatility. Firms tend to have bargaining power over suppliers due to industry dominance and boast substantial resources to adapt to changing conditions or competitive threats. Most sell products under powerful and recognizable brand names and look to emerging markets for future growth. We like the group.

Disney DIS   FAIRLY VALUED

Buying Index™   6   Value Rating   🌕

Economic Castle	Estimated Fair Value	Fair Value Range	Investment Style	Sector	Industry
Attractive	$150.00	$116.00 - $184.00	MEGA-CAP GROWTH	Consumer Discretionary	Discretionary Spending

Disney's video streaming services (Disney+, ESPN+, Hulu) are performing well in the face of COVID-19. We've raised our fair value estimate on significantly higher projections related to its successful streaming services.

Stock Chart (weekly)

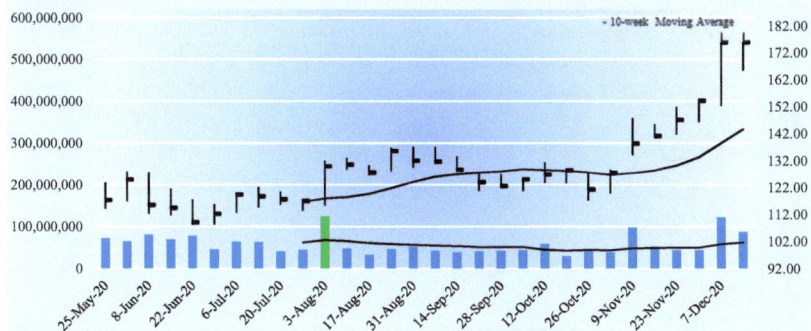

The week with the highest trading volume out of the last 30 weeks was a week of heavy selling, or distribution (red bar).

Investment Considerations

DCF Valuation	**FAIRLY VALUED**
Relative Valuation	**UNATTRACTIVE**
ValueCreation™	**EXCELLENT**
ValueRisk™	**MEDIUM**
ValueTrend™	**NEGATIVE**
Cash Flow Generation	**STRONG**
Financial Leverage	**HIGH**
Growth	**HIGH**
Technical Evaluation	**BULLISH**
Relative Strength	**STRONG**
Money Flow Index (MFI)	**NEUTRAL**
Upside/Downside Volume (U/D)	**BULLISH**
Near-term Technical Support, 10-week MA	**144.00**

DCF = Discounted Cash Flow; MFI, U/D = Please see glossary. MA = Moving Average

Business Quality

ValueRisk™	Very Poor	Poor	Good	Excellent
Low				
Medium				▓
High				
Very High				

ValueCreation™

Firms that generate economic profits with little operating variability score near the top right of the matrix.

Company Vitals

Market Cap (USD)	$317,702
Avg Weekly Vol (30 wks)	58,509
30-week Range (USD)	108.02 - 179.45
Valuentum Sector	Consumer Discretionary
5-week Return	24.1%
13-week Return	39.5%
30-week Return	45.2%
Dividend Yield %	0.0%
Dividends per Share	0.00
Forward Dividend Payout Ratio	0.0%
Est. Normal Diluted EPS	6.75
P/E on Est. Normal Diluted EPS	26.0
Est. Normal EBITDA	26,143
Forward EV/EBITDA	31.4
EV/Est. Normal EBITDA	13.7
Forward Revenue Growth (5-yr)	12.3%
Forward EPS Growth (5-yr)	-244.8%

NMF = Not Meaningful; Est. = Estimated; FY = Fiscal Year

Returns Summary   3-year Historical Average

Return on Equity	14.0%
Return on Assets	6.6%
ROIC, with goodwill	7.3%
ROIC, without goodwill	15.0%

ROIC = Return on Invested Capital; NMF = Not Meaningful

Leverage, Coverage, and Liquidity

In Millions of USD

Total Debt	58,628
Net Debt	40,714
Total Debt/EBITDA	6.4
Net Debt/EBITDA	4.5
EBITDA/Interest	6.1
Current Ratio	1.3
Quick Ratio	1.1

NMF = Not Meaningful

Investment Highlights

• Disney is a diversified entertainment company with operations in five segments: Media Networks, Parks and Resorts, Studio Entertainment, Consumer Products, and Interactive. Video streaming services are now a core part of Disney's business model, supported by its well-known brand. It was founded in 1923 and is headquartered in California.

• Disney has an innate ability to leverage creative success across its entire company. For example, its 'Consumer Products' division has created 11 major franchises that each generate more than $1 billion in annual global retail sales. The timing of movie releases can make such sales somewhat lumpy, however.

• Strong performance at Disney's video streaming services offset some of the headwinds created by COVID-19, which hit its 'Parks and Resorts' segment particularly hard. The resumption of live sporting events and ongoing net paid subscriber gains at its video streaming services supports its near-term outlook, though significant hurdles remain.

• Disney acquired 21st Century Fox for $71.3 billion in cash and stock at an overall 50/50 mix of cash and stock after 21st Century was spun off from Fox. Disney now owns Fox's film and TV studio, along with FX and National Geographic networks. $2 billion in cost synergies are expected by 2021, and $13.8 billion in 21st Century Fox's debt was assumed.

• Disney launched an ESPN-branded sports streaming service in 2018 and a Disney-branded service in 2019. It also owns ~67% of Hulu. Disney offers a streaming bundle with all three services combined, and these offerings support its long-term growth trajectory.

Relative Valuation

	Forward P/E	PEG	Price / FV
Home Depot	22.9	1.9	106.7%
McDonald's	38.5	1.1	111.0%
Nike	52.8	2.5	104.9%
Starbucks	92.2	0.6	110.6%
Peer Median	45.6	1.5	108.6%
Disney	**104.2**	**NMF**	**117.1%**

Price / FV = Current Stock Price divided by Estimated Fair Value

Financial Summary

	----- Actual -----		Projected
Fiscal Year End:	Sep-19	Sep-20	Sep-21
Revenue	69,570	65,388	68,069
Revenue, YoY%	17.1%	-6.0%	4.1%
Operating Income	11,830	3,794	5,867
Operating Margin %	17.0%	5.8%	8.6%
Net Income	10,425	-2,832	3,111
Net Income Margin %	15.0%	-4.3%	4.6%
Diluted EPS	6.26	-1.57	1.69
Diluted EPS, YoY %	-25.1%	-125.0%	-207.7%
Free Cash Flow (CFO-capex)	1,108	3,594	8,371
Free Cash Flow Margin %	1.6%	5.5%	12.3%

In Millions of USD (except for per share items)

Structure of the Media (entertainment) Industry   NEUTRAL

The media (entertainment) industry spans firms with diversified worldwide entertainment operations to those that specialize primarily in motion picture production and technologies. Firms with media network businesses compete for viewers with other networks, while companies with studio entertainment businesses compete with all forms of entertainment. A significant number of companies produce theatrical/television films, and success depends on unpredictable public preferences. The strongest participants will consistently create filmed entertainment and/or cable programming that consumers want. We're neutral on the group.

Dick's Sporting DKS FAIRLY VALUED

Buying Index™ 6   **Value Rating** ◯

Economic Castle	Estimated Fair Value	Fair Value Range	Investment Style	Sector	Industry
Attractive	$67.00	$54.00 - $80.00	MID-CAP VALUE	Consumer Discretionary	Discretionary Spending

Dick's Sporting Goods' e-commerce sales growth remains incredible, and its brick-and-mortar stores are doing great, too.

Stock Chart (weekly)

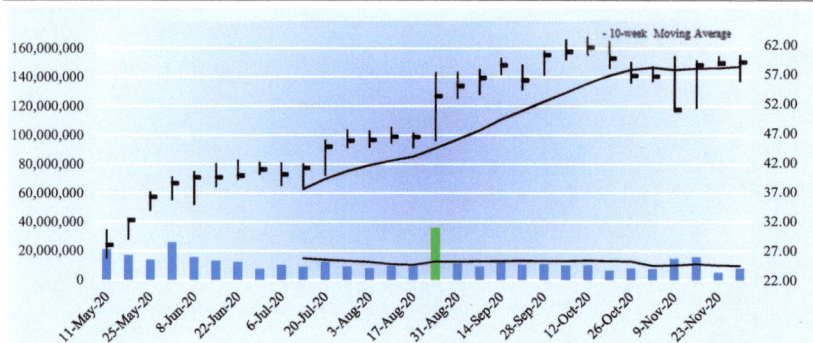

The week with the highest trading volume out of the last 30 weeks was a week of heavy selling, or distribution (red bar).

Investment Considerations

DCF Valuation	**FAIRLY VALUED**
Relative Valuation	**NEUTRAL**
ValueCreation™	**GOOD**
ValueRisk™	**LOW**
ValueTrend™	**NEGATIVE**
Cash Flow Generation	**MEDIUM**
Financial Leverage	**LOW**
Growth	**MODEST**
Technical Evaluation	**VERY BULLISH**
Relative Strength	**STRONG**
Money Flow Index (MFI)	**NEUTRAL**
Upside/Downside Volume (U/D)	**DETERIORATING**
Near-term Technical Support, 10-week MA	**58.00**

DCF = Discounted Cash Flow; MFI, U/D = Please see glossary. MA = Moving Average

Business Quality

ValueCreation™

ValueRisk™	Very Poor	Poor	Good	Excellent
Low			▓	
Medium				
High				
Very High				

Firms that generate economic profits with little operating variability score near the top right of the matrix.

Company Vitals

Market Cap (USD)	$5,254
Avg Weekly Vol (30 wks)	12,347
30-week Range (USD)	25.59 - 63.29
Valuentum Sector	Consumer Discretionary
5-week Return	3.4%
13-week Return	9.7%
30-week Return	103.1%
Dividend Yield %	2.1%
Dividends per Share	1.25
Forward Dividend Payout Ratio	30.5%
Est. Normal Diluted EPS	4.69
P/E on Est. Normal Diluted EPS	12.6
Est. Normal EBITDA	839
Forward EV/EBITDA	7.0
EV/Est. Normal EBITDA	6.4
Forward Revenue Growth (5-yr)	3.2%
Forward EPS Growth (5-yr)	9.3%

NMF = Not Meaningful; Est. = Estimated; FY = Fiscal Year

Returns Summary

3-year Historical Average

Return on Equity	16.6%
Return on Assets	7.0%
ROIC, with goodwill	12.1%
ROIC, without goodwill	13.5%

ROIC = Return on Invested Capital; NMF = Not Meaningful

Leverage, Coverage, and Liquidity

In Millions of USD

Total Debt	224
Net Debt	155
Total Debt/EBITDA	0.3
Net Debt/EBITDA	0.2
EBITDA/Interest	38.0
Current Ratio	1.2
Quick Ratio	0.1

NMF = Not Meaningful

Investment Highlights

• Dick's Sporting Goods is a full-line sporting goods retailer offering a broad assortment of brand name sporting goods equipment, apparel and footwear. The company also owns and operates Golf Galaxy, a golf specialty retailer, and Field & Stream, a hunting and fishing specialty retailer. The firm was founded in 1948 and is headquartered in Pennsylvania.

• Dick's Sporting Goods has an industry-leading omni-channel platform, and its focus is on serving athletes regardless of how they choose to shop with them (in-store, curbside, online). The firm continues to work on building brand loyalty and a seamless shopping experience.

• Dick's e-commerce performance is worth emphasizing. During the third quarter of 2020, for example, e-commerce sales increased 95% as compared to the third quarter of 2019. E-commerce penetration of its total sales is ~20%-25%, and we expect this to continue to become a larger part of its operations.

• Athletes go to Dick's to buy some of the top brands, including adidas, Callaway, olumbia, Nike, The North Face, Titleist, Under Armour and Yeti, among others. It also has a number of private label offerings not available elsewhere such as Second Skin, DSG, and Top-Flite.

• Though Dick's Sporting Goods is succeeding in both e-commerce and brick-and-mortar, the retail sporting goods market is a tough one. For example, The Sports Authority and Gander Mountain filed for Chapter 11 bankruptcy protection in recent years.

Relative Valuation

	Forward P/E	PEG	Price / FV
Disney	75.6	0.3	98.3%
Home Depot	22.9	1.9	106.7%
McDonald's	38.5	1.1	111.0%
Nike	52.8	2.5	104.9%
Peer Median	45.6	1.5	105.8%
Dick's Sporting	**14.4**	**1.9**	**88.0%**

Price / FV = Current Stock Price divided by Estimated Fair Value

Financial Summary

	----- Actual -----		Projected
Fiscal Year End:	Jan-19	Jan-20	Jan-21
Revenue	8,437	8,751	9,101
Revenue, YoY%	-1.8%	3.7%	4.0%
Operating Income	445	376	494
Operating Margin %	5.3%	4.3%	5.4%
Net Income	320	297	358
Net Income Margin %	3.8%	3.4%	3.9%
Diluted EPS	3.24	3.34	4.10
Diluted EPS, YoY %	7.7%	3.1%	22.8%
Free Cash Flow (CFO-capex)	515	187	433
Free Cash Flow Margin %	6.1%	2.1%	4.8%

In Millions of USD (except for per share items)

Structure of the Retail - Sporting Goods Industry   NEUTRAL

The seasonal retail sporting goods industry is heavily tied to sporting trends and relies on large athletic partners to create desirable athletic goods and apparel. Exclusive licenses can help certain firms achieve competitive advantages, and while scale helps, small companies have been able to carve out favorable niches. Online competition continues to grow from non-traditional retailers, causing potential pressures on margin and pricing performance. Potential firearm regulation could negatively impact sales, but most companies are well diversified. We're neutral on the space, but continued consolidation could ultimately benefit industrywide pricing and margins.

VALUENTUM

Dunkin' Brands DNKN   FAIRLY VALUED

Buying Index™ 5   **Value Rating** ⬤

Economic Castle	Estimated Fair Value	Fair Value Range	Investment Style	Sector	Industry
Attractive	$68.00	$51.00 - $85.00	MID-CAP CORE	Consumer Discretionary	Discretionary Spending

Dunkin' Brands is utilizing digital sales channels to offset headwinds created by the COVID-19 pandemic.

Stock Chart (weekly)

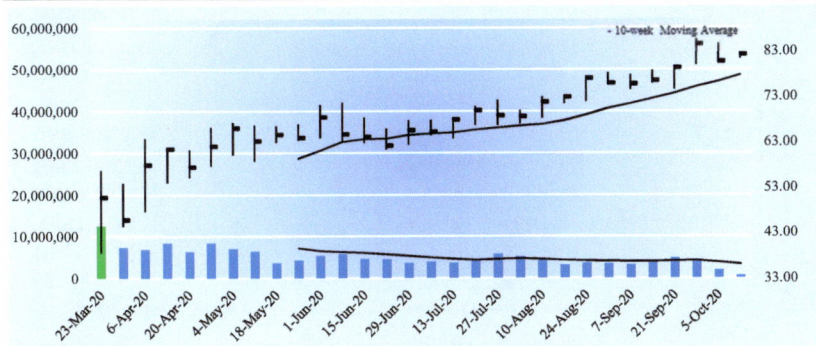

The week with the highest trading volume out of the last 30 weeks was a week of heavy selling, or distribution (red bar).

Investment Considerations

DCF Valuation	FAIRLY VALUED
Relative Valuation	NEUTRAL
ValueCreation™	EXCELLENT
ValueRisk™	MEDIUM
ValueTrend™	POSITIVE
Cash Flow Generation	STRONG
Financial Leverage	HIGH
Growth	MODEST
Technical Evaluation	NEUTRAL
Relative Strength	STRONG
Money Flow Index (MFI)	OVERBOUGHT
Upside/Downside Volume (U/D)	BULLISH
Near-term Technical Support, 10-week MA	78.00

DCF = Discounted Cash Flow; MFI, U/D = Please see glossary. MA = Moving Average

Company Vitals

Market Cap (USD)	$6,880
Avg Weekly Vol (30 wks)	5,003
30-week Range (USD)	38.52 - 85.55
Valuentum Sector	Consumer Discretionary
5-week Return	7.8%
13-week Return	21.3%
30-week Return	105.0%
Dividend Yield %	2.0%
Dividends per Share	1.61
Forward Dividend Payout Ratio	59.5%
Est. Normal Diluted EPS	3.98
P/E on Est. Normal Diluted EPS	20.7
Est. Normal EBITDA	615
Forward EV/EBITDA	19.4
EV/Est. Normal EBITDA	15.0
Forward Revenue Growth (5-yr)	4.0%
Forward EPS Growth (5-yr)	13.3%

NMF = Not Meaningful; Est. = Estimated; FY = Fiscal Year

Returns Summary   3-year Historical Average

Return on Equity	-252.2%
Return on Assets	7.2%
ROIC, with goodwill	14.9%
ROIC, without goodwill	25.3%

ROIC = Return on Invested Capital; NMF = Not Meaningful

Leverage, Coverage, and Liquidity

In Millions of USD

Total Debt	3,035
Net Debt	2,328
Total Debt/EBITDA	6.5
Net Debt/EBITDA	5.0
EBITDA/Interest	3.7
Current Ratio	1.6
Quick Ratio	1.4

NMF = Not Meaningful

Investment Highlights

• Dunkin' Brands is one of the world's leading franchisors of quick service restaurants serving hot and cold coffee and baked goods, as well as hard-serve ice cream. It truly has a world-class operation and supply chain, and the firm's growth opportunity in China is quite attractive. It was founded in 1950 and is headquartered in Massachusetts.

• The coffee space is not without significant and intense competition. Starbucks continues to dominate the premium space, and McDonald's all day breakfast has increased competition. Even the likes of Taco Bell has stepped up efforts with its new breakfast menu.

• Dunkin' Brands is 100% franchised, including more than 13,000 Dunkin' restaurants and ~8,000 Baskin-Robbins restaurants. We like its asset-light operations, which translates into strong free cash flow. The company's long-term international growth opportunity is also remarkable, though the COVID-19 pandemic has created short-term headwinds on this front.

• The Dunkin' Brands of the future could reach 30,000+ restaurants globally. Its long-term goal includes 17,000+ Dunkin' stores in the US, which may be focused on the currently under-penetrated western US. The company has made significant upgrades to its digital operations recently.

• Dunkin' is leveraging consumer packaged goods to target new markets. Before the pandemic, management noted that roughly 6 out of 10 cups of its coffee consumed in the US was via a consumer packaged-good product.

Business Quality   ValueCreation™

ValueRisk™	Very Poor	Poor	Good	Excellent
Low				
Medium				▓
High				
Very High				

Firms that generate economic profits with little operating variability score near the top right of the matrix.

Relative Valuation

	Forward P/E	PEG	Price / FV
Disney	75.6	0.3	98.3%
Home Depot	22.9	1.9	106.7%
McDonald's	38.5	1.1	111.0%
Nike	52.8	2.5	104.9%
Peer Median	45.6	1.5	105.8%
Dunkin' Brands	**30.4**	**1.5**	**120.9%**

Price / FV = Current Stock Price divided by Estimated Fair Value

Financial Summary

	----- Actual -----		Projected
Fiscal Year End:	Dec-18	Dec-19	Dec-20
Revenue	1,322	1,370	1,286
Revenue, YoY%	53.6%	3.7%	-6.1%
Non-GAAP Operating Income	400	433	440
Non-GAAP EBIT %	30.3%	31.6%	34.2%
Non-GAAP Net Income	230	242	224
Non-GAAP NI Margin %	17.4%	17.7%	17.4%
Non-GAAP Diluted EPS	2.71	2.89	2.71
Non-GAAP Dil EPS, YoY %	-28.7%	6.8%	-6.4%
Non-GAAP Free Cash Flow	217	261	228
Non-GAAP FCF Margin %	16.4%	19.1%	17.7%

In Millions of USD (except for per share items)

Structure of the Restaurants Industry - Fast Food & Coffee   NEUTRAL

The restaurant industry has benefited from a long-term trend toward eating out, but the space has become increasingly more competitive as new concepts are introduced and successful chains expand. Not only are there pricing pressures and trade-down threats, but rising costs for commodities and labor have pressured profits. Barriers to entry are low, and many constituents have a difficult time differentiating themselves. We tend to like larger chains that benefit from scale advantages and international expansion opportunities, though niche franchises can be appealing. We're neutral on the structure of the group.

DocuSign DOCU   FAIRLY VALUED

Buying Index™ 6   **Value Rating** 🟡

Economic Castle	Estimated Fair Value	Fair Value Range	Investment Style	Sector	Industry
Very Attractive	$236.00	$177.00 - $295.00	LARGE-CAP BLEND	Next Generation	Disruptive Innovation

DocuSign's cloud software suite is disrupting the traditional way people conduct business through contracts, offer letters, and other agreements.

Stock Chart (weekly)

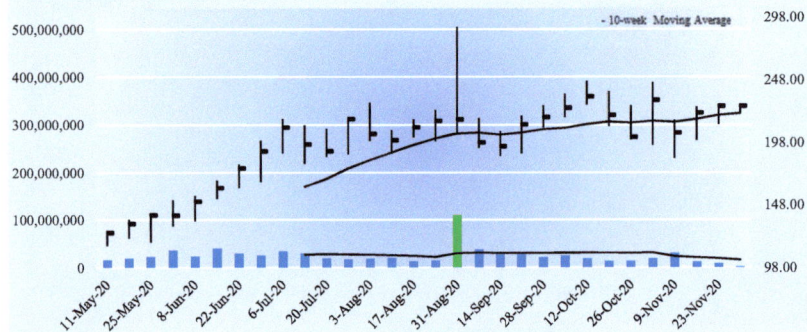

The week with the highest trading volume out of the last 30 weeks was a week of heavy selling, or distribution (red bar).

Company Vitals

Market Cap (USD)	$40,089
Avg Weekly Vol (30 wks)	24,543
30-week Range (USD)	115.57 - 290.23
Valuentum Sector	Next Generation
5-week Return	11.1%
13-week Return	10.1%
30-week Return	92.8%
Dividend Yield %	0.0%
Dividends per Share	0.00
Forward Dividend Payout Ratio	0.0%
Est. Normal Diluted EPS	2.30
P/E on Est. Normal Diluted EPS	98.6
Est. Normal EBITDA	684
Forward EV/EBITDA	195.4
EV/Est. Normal EBITDA	58.3
Forward Revenue Growth (5-yr)	29.5%
Forward EPS Growth (5-yr)	-232.2%

NMF = Not Meaningful; Est. = Estimated; FY = Fiscal Year

Returns Summary
3-year Historical Average

Return on Equity	-37.9%
Return on Assets	-13.8%
ROIC, with goodwill	26.8%
ROIC, without goodwill	55.8%

ROIC = Return on Invested Capital; NMF = Not Meaningful

Leverage, Coverage, and Liquidity
In Millions of USD

Total Debt	465
Net Debt	-191
Total Debt/EBITDA	NMF
Net Debt/EBITDA	NMF
EBITDA/Interest	-4.8
Current Ratio	1.4
Quick Ratio	NA

NMF = Not Meaningful

Investment Highlights

• DocuSign offers a cloud software suite (DocuSign Agreement Cloud) for automating the process by which people do business. Its DocuSign eSignature, which allows a contract or agreement to be signed electronically on virtually any device around the world, is the top electronic signature solution, and its cloud offerings include multiple other features, too.

• DocuSign has a strong first-mover advantage in the electronic signature category that has only been augmented as a result of the outbreak of COVID-19. Its DocuSign Agreement Cloud has ~600,000 customers and hundreds of millions of users.

• DocuSign's long-term growth opportunity is huge and supports our fair value estimate. The firm estimates that its existing customers account for just 1% of total available enterprises and businesses around the world. Not only does it have opportunities with new customers but expanding within its existing customer base is a large opportunity as well. Billings growth has been phenomenal.

• Security is the most important consideration when it comes to doing important business in the cloud. This offers a key risk to the DocuSign story, but the company notes that it uses 'the strongest data encryption technologies commercially available (10-K).' Customers have grown to trust DocuSign.

• The company's primary rival is Adobe via its 2011 acquisition of EchoSign, and while the market opportunity is huge, Adobe is no slouch. DocuSign has a long history of operating losses, and the trajectory of future growth is difficult to predict.

Investment Considerations

DCF Valuation	FAIRLY VALUED
Relative Valuation	UNATTRACTIVE
ValueCreation™	EXCELLENT
ValueRisk™	MEDIUM
ValueTrend™	POSITIVE
Cash Flow Generation	STRONG
Financial Leverage	LOW
Growth	AGGRESSIVE
Technical Evaluation	BULLISH
Relative Strength	STRONG
Money Flow Index (MFI)	NEUTRAL
Upside/Downside Volume (U/D)	BULLISH
Near-term Technical Support, 10-week MA	221.00

DCF = Discounted Cash Flow; MFI, U/D = Please see glossary. MA = Moving Average

Business Quality

ValueRisk™	ValueCreation™			
	Very Poor	Poor	Good	Excellent
Low				
Medium				▓
High				
Very High				

Firms that generate economic profits with little operating variability score near the top right of the matrix.

Relative Valuation

	Forward P/E	PEG	Price / FV
Wayfair	56.3	NMF	84.2%
Zoom Video	170.7	28.8	120.8%
Roku	-338.4	NMF	96.0%
Monster Beverage	36.0	2.9	104.4%
Peer Median	46.1	15.9	100.2%
DocuSign	**387.3**	**NMF**	**96.1%**

Price / FV = Current Stock Price divided by Estimated Fair Value

Financial Summary

	----- Actual -----		Projected
Fiscal Year End:	Jan-19	Jan-20	Jan-21
Revenue	701	974	1,385
Revenue, YoY%	35.2%	38.9%	42.2%
Operating Income	-426	-194	131
Operating Margin %	-60.8%	-19.9%	9.4%
Net Income	-426	-208	109
Net Income Margin %	-60.8%	-21.4%	7.8%
Diluted EPS	-3.16	-1.18	0.59
Diluted EPS, YoY %	94.9%	-62.6%	-149.7%
Free Cash Flow (CFO-capex)	46	44	405
Free Cash Flow Margin %	6.5%	4.5%	29.3%

In Millions of USD (except for per share items)

Structure of the Internet & Catalog Retail Industry   GOOD

The Internet and catalog retail industry benefits as a whole from the secular trend toward consumer digital (online) consumption. The industry consists of a number of exclusive online retailers led by Amazon, which continues to disrupt the broader retail space, and businesses that offer Internet travel services such as Booking Holdings, while online auctions are dominated by eBay. The industry generates high returns on investment due to minimal capital costs, but the landscape will be vastly different in the decades ahead. Still, we like the group.

eBay EBAY   FAIRLY VALUED

Buying Index™   4   Value Rating

Economic Castle	Estimated Fair Value	Fair Value Range	Investment Style	Sector	Industry
Attractive	$55.00	$41.00 - $69.00	LARGE-CAP VALUE	Information Technology	Technology Giants

The COVID-19 pandemic has served as a positive catalyst for eBay's organic top line as consumers transition to e-commerce purchases. eBay's business has undergone a considerable transformation during the past several years.

Stock Chart (weekly)

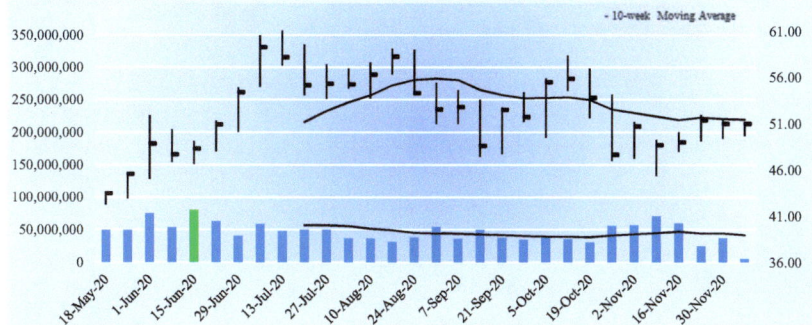

- 10-week Moving Average

The week with the highest trading volume out of the last 30 weeks was a week of heavy selling, or distribution (red bar).

Company Vitals

Market Cap (USD)	$43,630
Avg Weekly Vol (30 wks)	46,292
30-week Range (USD)	42.21 - 61.06
Valuentum Sector	Information Technology
5-week Return	6.2%
13-week Return	-4.4%
30-week Return	19.6%
Dividend Yield %	1.3%
Dividends per Share	0.64
Forward Dividend Payout Ratio	18.7%
Est. Normal Diluted EPS	3.78
P/E on Est. Normal Diluted EPS	13.5
Est. Normal EBITDA	4,569
Forward EV/EBITDA	11.2
EV/Est. Normal EBITDA	10.6
Forward Revenue Growth (5-yr)	2.8%
Forward EPS Growth (5-yr)	13.6%

NMF = Not Meaningful; Est. = Estimated; FY = Fiscal Year

Returns Summary
3-year Historical Average

Return on Equity	21.2%
Return on Assets	5.0%
ROIC, with goodwill	19.6%
ROIC, without goodwill	31.9%

ROIC = Return on Invested Capital; NMF = Not Meaningful

Leverage, Coverage, and Liquidity
In Millions of USD

Total Debt	7,760
Net Debt	4,935
Total Debt/EBITDA	2.6
Net Debt/EBITDA	1.6
EBITDA/Interest	9.7
Current Ratio	1.2
Quick Ratio	0.9

NMF = Not Meaningful

Investment Highlights

- eBay is a online marketplace that connects buyers and sellers worldwide. Activist investor Carl Icahn no longer holds shares in this security, and it has been separated from PayPal since July 2015. It sold its online ticket platform StubHub to Viagogo in February 2020. The company was founded in 1995 and is headquartered in San Jose, California.

- eBay is still a powerhouse even after letting go of its prized PayPal. In 2019, the firm processed $90 billion+ in gross merchandise value, and it exited the year with over 180 million active buyers. Increased competition in e-commerce is impacting expectations, though COVID-19 has been a powerful positive

- After selling Stubhub to Swiss rival Viagogo, eBay announced the sale of its Classified business unit to Norway-based Adevinta for $9.2 billion in July 2020 (eBay will now have a stake in Adevinta). eBay continues to shed assets as a part of its strategic review. The company has also initiated a quarterly dividend and is targeting a 1.5x net debt-to-EBITDA ratio.

- There have been a lot of moving parts in eBay's business during the past several years that have made year-over-year comparisons messy. However, organic (FX-neutral) revenue advanced at a nice clip during 2020, and while consumers staying at home as a result of the outbreak of COVID-19 provided a boost, its core business remains healthy.

- eBay is generating gobs of free cash flow that supports both its new dividend payout and its valuation. The company's free cash flow has averaged $2.35 billion during the past three fiscal years (2017-2019). Niche rivals such as Etsy continue to nip at its heels, however.

Investment Considerations

DCF Valuation	FAIRLY VALUED
Relative Valuation	ATTRACTIVE
ValueCreation™	EXCELLENT
ValueRisk™	MEDIUM
ValueTrend™	POSITIVE
Cash Flow Generation	STRONG
Financial Leverage	MEDIUM
Growth	MODEST
Technical Evaluation	BEARISH
Relative Strength	WEAK
Money Flow Index (MFI)	NEUTRAL
Upside/Downside Volume (U/D)	BEARISH
Near-term Technical Resistance, 10-wk MA	51.00

DCF = Discounted Cash Flow; MFI, U/D = Please see glossary. MA = Moving Average

Business Quality

ValueRisk™	Very Poor	Poor	Good	Excellent
Low				
Medium				▩
High				
Very High				

ValueCreation™

Firms that generate economic profits with little operating variability score near the top right of the matrix.

Relative Valuation

	Forward P/E	PEG	Price / FV
Apple	29.8	2.4	85.0%
Alphabet	34.9	1.8	73.3%
Amazon.com	NMF	3.3	95.7%
Microsoft	31.6	2.5	91.6%
Peer Median	31.6	2.5	88.3%
eBay	14.9	1.8	92.7%

Price / FV = Current Stock Price divided by Estimated Fair Value

Financial Summary

	- Actual -	Split Adjusted	Post - Proj
Fiscal Year End:	Dec-18	Dec-19	Dec-20
Revenue	10,746	10,800	10,184
Revenue, YoY%	12.3%	0.5%	-5.7%
Non-GAAP Operating Income	2,508	2,321	3,676
Non-GAAP EBIT Margin %	23.3%	21.5%	36.1%
Non-GAAP Net Income	2,528	1,792	2,858
Non-GAAP NI Margin %	23.5%	16.6%	28.1%
Non-GAAP Diluted EPS	2.55	2.09	3.42
Non-GAAP Dil EPS, YoY %	NMF	NMF	NMF
Free Cash Flow (CFO-capex)	2,007	2,560	3,264
Free Cash Flow Margin %	18.7%	23.7%	32.1%

In Millions of USD (except for per share items)

Structure of the Internet & Catalog Retail Industry   GOOD

The Internet and catalog retail industry benefits as a whole from the secular trend toward consumer digital (online) consumption. The industry consists of a number of exclusive online retailers led by Amazon, which continues to disrupt the broader retail space, and businesses that offer Internet travel services such as Booking Holdings, while online auctions are dominated by eBay. The industry generates high returns on investment due to minimal capital costs, but the landscape will be vastly different in the decades ahead. Still, we like the group.

ETSY ETSY   FAIRLY VALUED

| | Buying Index™ | 6 | Value Rating | 🟡 |

Economic Castle	Estimated Fair Value	Fair Value Range	Investment Style	Sector	Industry
Very Attractive	$165.00	$107.00 - $223.00	LARGE-CAP BLEND	Next Generation	Disruptive Innovation

Etsy is an online marketplace that is slowly building a strong network effect with a niche in unique and creative goods. Explosive growth suggests a disruptive nature to Etsy's business model.

Stock Chart (weekly)

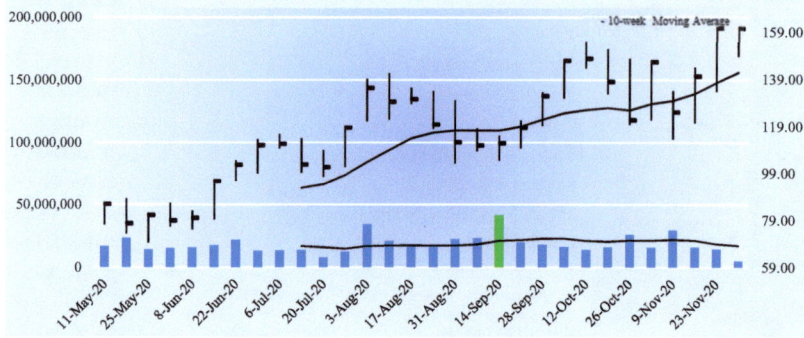

The week with the highest trading volume out of the last 30 weeks was a week of heavy selling, or distribution (red bar).

Investment Considerations

DCF Valuation	FAIRLY VALUED
Relative Valuation	NEUTRAL
ValueCreation™	EXCELLENT
ValueRisk™	HIGH
ValueTrend™	POSITIVE
Cash Flow Generation	STRONG
Financial Leverage	HIGH
Growth	AGGRESSIVE
Technical Evaluation	BULLISH
Relative Strength	STRONG
Money Flow Index (MFI)	NEUTRAL
Upside/Downside Volume (U/D)	DETERIORATING
Near-term Technical Support, 10-week MA	142.00

DCF = Discounted Cash Flow; MFI, U/D = Please see glossary. MA = Moving Average

Company Vitals

Market Cap (USD)	$20,184
Avg Weekly Vol (30 wks)	18,388
30-week Range (USD)	69.35 - 160.63
Valuentum Sector	Next Generation
5-week Return	30.3%
13-week Return	41.6%
30-week Return	99.8%
Dividend Yield %	0.0%
Dividends per Share	0.00
Forward Dividend Payout Ratio	0.0%
Est. Normal Diluted EPS	4.03
P/E on Est. Normal Diluted EPS	39.9
Est. Normal EBITDA	684
Forward EV/EBITDA	55.9
EV/Est. Normal EBITDA	29.5
Forward Revenue Growth (5-yr)	41.8%
Forward EPS Growth (5-yr)	55.6%

NMF = Not Meaningful; Est. = Estimated; FY = Fiscal Year

Returns Summary

	3-year Historical Average
Return on Equity	21.2%
Return on Assets	8.5%
ROIC, with goodwill	47.1%
ROIC, without goodwill	61.7%

ROIC = Return on Invested Capital; NMF = Not Meaningful

Leverage, Coverage, and Liquidity

In Millions of USD

Total Debt	785
Net Debt	-32
Total Debt/EBITDA	5.7
Net Debt/EBITDA	NMF
EBITDA/Interest	5.7
Current Ratio	4.9
Quick Ratio	NA

NMF = Not Meaningful

Investment Highlights

• Etsy operates the online marketplace Etsy.com, which connects creative entrepreneurs with consumers looking to find unique crafts and goods. In August 2019, the company acquired Reverb, an online marketplace dedicated to selling new and used musical instruments. In 2019, both marketplaces connected nearly 3 million sellers with over 45 million buyers.

• Etsy makes money by collecting fees from sellers that use its marketplace services (e.g. listing goods to sell, completing the transaction). The company also generates services revenue such as advertising sales from sellers looking for prominent placement of their products on the Etsy marketplace.

• Buyers are attracted to Etsy because sellers offer items that generally can't be found anywhere else, while Etsy offers sellers a marketplace with millions of buyers. It is building a nice network effect in the niche arena of creative crafts and items. Top categories include home furnishings, jewelry, craft supplies, and apparel, and 80%+ of sellers identify as women.

• A critical component of Etsy's continued growth will be its ongoing relationship with sellers, which remain a strong component of the foundation of its competitive advantage. The unique items on its marketplace are what attracts buyers, and therefore more sellers, and so on and so forth.

• Etsy is making inroads in a niche area within a business model that eBay largely defined a couple decades ago. Global e-commerce penetration is small enough to allow for plenty of winners, but long-term success is not guaranteed.

Business Quality

ValueRisk™	ValueCreation™			
	Very Poor	Poor	Good	Excellent
Low				
Medium				
High				▨
Very High				

Firms that generate economic profits with little operating variability score near the top right of the matrix.

Relative Valuation

	Forward P/E	PEG	Price / FV
Wayfair	56.3	NMF	84.2%
Zoom Video	170.7	28.8	120.8%
Roku	-338.4	NMF	96.0%
Monster Beverage	36.0	2.9	104.4%
Peer Median	46.1	15.9	100.2%
ETSY	**76.1**	**3.8**	**97.3%**

Price / FV = Current Stock Price divided by Estimated Fair Value

Financial Summary

	----- Actual -----		Projected
Fiscal Year End:	Dec-18	Dec-19	Dec-20
Revenue	604	818	1,613
Revenue, YoY%	36.8%	35.6%	97.1%
Operating Income	75	89	264
Operating Margin %	12.4%	10.8%	16.4%
Net Income	77	96	265
Net Income Margin %	12.8%	11.7%	16.5%
Diluted EPS	0.61	0.76	2.11
Diluted EPS, YoY %	-8.9%	25.1%	176.7%
Free Cash Flow (CFO-capex)	198	199	263
Free Cash Flow Margin %	32.8%	24.4%	16.3%

In Millions of USD (except for per share items)

Structure of the Internet & Catalog Retail Industry   GOOD

The Internet and catalog retail industry benefits as a whole from the secular trend toward consumer digital (online) consumption. The industry consists of a number of exclusive online retailers led by Amazon, which continues to disrupt the broader retail space, and businesses that offer Internet travel services such as Booking Holdings, while online auctions are dominated by eBay. The industry generates high returns on investment due to minimal capital costs, but the landscape will be vastly different in the decades ahead. Still, we like the group.

VALUENTUM

Expeditors Intl EXPD   FAIRLY VALUED

Buying Index™   **6**   **Value Rating**   ⬤

Economic Castle	Estimated Fair Value	Fair Value Range	Investment Style	Sector	Industry
Very Attractive	$89.00	$71.00 - $107.00	LARGE-CAP CORE	Industrials	Industrial Leaders

Expeditors has done a nice job executing in the face of highly unpredictable air and ocean markets in recent quarters. The company continues to layer on dividend increase after dividend increase each year, too.

Stock Chart (weekly)

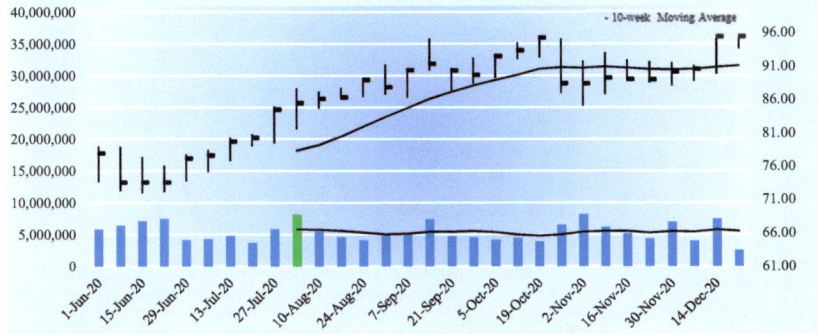

The week with the highest trading volume out of the last 30 weeks was a week of heavy selling, or distribution (red bar).

Investment Considerations

DCF Valuation	**FAIRLY VALUED**
Relative Valuation	**NEUTRAL**
ValueCreation™	**EXCELLENT**
ValueRisk™	**LOW**
ValueTrend™	**NEGATIVE**
Cash Flow Generation	**STRONG**
Financial Leverage	**LOW**
Growth	**MODEST**
Technical Evaluation	**BULLISH**
Relative Strength	**NEUTRAL**
Money Flow Index (MFI)	**NEUTRAL**
Upside/Downside Volume (U/D)	**DETERIORATING**
Near-term Technical Support, 10-week MA	**91.00**

DCF = Discounted Cash Flow; MFI, U/D = Please see glossary. MA = Moving Average

Company Vitals

Market Cap (USD)	$16,965
Avg Weekly Vol (30 wks)	5,404
30-week Range (USD)	71.94 - 95.47
Valuentum Sector	Industrials
5-week Return	6.8%
13-week Return	4.3%
30-week Return	25.5%
Dividend Yield %	1.1%
Dividends per Share	1.04
Forward Dividend Payout Ratio	30.6%
Est. Normal Diluted EPS	5.13
P/E on Est. Normal Diluted EPS	18.6
Est. Normal EBITDA	1,173
Forward EV/EBITDA	19.7
EV/Est. Normal EBITDA	13.7
Forward Revenue Growth (5-yr)	8.1%
Forward EPS Growth (5-yr)	15.3%

NMF = Not Meaningful; Est. = Estimated; FY = Fiscal Year

Returns Summary
3-year Historical Average

Return on Equity	27.1%
Return on Assets	17.3%
ROIC, with goodwill	72.5%
ROIC, without goodwill	72.5%

ROIC = Return on Invested Capital; NMF = Not Meaningful

Leverage, Coverage, and Liquidity
In Millions of USD

Total Debt	0
Net Debt	-924
Total Debt/EBITDA	0.0
Net Debt/EBITDA	NMF
EBITDA/Interest	Excellent
Current Ratio	2.1
Quick Ratio	1.9

NMF = Not Meaningful

Investment Highlights

• Expeditors is a global logistics company. Its services include air and ocean freight consolidation and forwarding, vendor consolidation, customs clearance, cargo insurance, distribution and other value added logistics services. The company was founded in 1979 and is headquartered in Seattle, Washington.

• The company is a non-asset based organization, which affords it considerable flexibility when managing customers' supply chains. Its relationships with suppliers and partners allow it to find some of the best routing and pricing options for customers.

• The global economy, political arena and capital and credit markets continue to experience uncertainty and volatility. Unfavorable changes in economic conditions may result in lower freight volumes and adversely affect Expeditors revenues and operating results, as was the case in 2009 and 2012. The impact of these factors on the company's customers and services providers could compound the effect.

• Management's primary goal is to return the company to sustainable double-digit expansion. Recent demand trends have helped improve volumes, but the potential for excess capacity to impact pricing persists and fuel costs may remain volatile. The executive suite understands the challenges of the global economy well.'

• A focus on controlling costs and overhead expenses will be critical to earnings expansion, especially amid the current unpredictable COVID-19 pandemic. Investors should note the impact air carriers adjusting to buy rates to align with demand increases has had on pricing dynamics.

Business Quality

ValueRisk™	ValueCreation™			
	Very Poor	Poor	Good	Excellent
Low				■
Medium				
High				
Very High				

Firms that generate economic profits with little operating variability score near the top right of the matrix.

Relative Valuation

	Forward P/E	PEG	Price / FV
Danaher	36.3	3.0	121.5%
Honeywell	28.8	1.7	101.3%
Lockheed Martin	15.0	2.3	96.3%
Union Pacific	25.9	1.4	119.1%
Peer Median	27.3	2.0	110.2%
Expeditors Intl	**28.1**	**1.4**	**107.2%**

Price / FV = Current Stock Price divided by Estimated Fair Value

Financial Summary

	----- Actual -----		Projected
Fiscal Year End:	Dec-17	Dec-18	Dec-19
Revenue	6,921	8,138	8,175
Revenue, YoY%	13.5%	17.6%	0.5%
Operating Income	839	975	761
Operating Margin %	12.1%	12.0%	9.3%
Net Income	489	618	591
Net Income Margin %	7.1%	7.6%	7.2%
Diluted EPS	2.69	3.48	3.39
Diluted EPS, YoY %	14.2%	29.1%	-2.4%
Free Cash Flow (CFO-capex)	394	525	633
Free Cash Flow Margin %	5.7%	6.5%	7.7%

In Millions of USD (except for per share items)

Structure of the Air Freight & Logistics Industry   **GOOD**

The highly competitive air freight and logistics industry is heavily tied to cyclical domestic economic expansion (primarily from retail good shipments). The international freight market remains a critical growth engine for air cargo providers, while all constituents deal with the cost of rising fuel (diesel) prices and potentially price-sensitive demand during periods of economic weakness. Firms with freight-forwarding, asset-light operations and/or large difficult-to-replicate shipping networks can carve out sustainable competitive advantages while generating high returns on investment. We generally like the group.

Facebook FB   UNDERVALUED 7.8%

Buying Index™   10   Value Rating ✔

Economic Castle	Estimated Fair Value	Fair Value Range	Investment Style	Sector	Industry
Very Attractive	$413.00	$310.00 - $516.00	MEGA-CAP BLEND	Information Technology	Technology Giants

Facebook may be the most undervalued company in our coverage universe, and it is a top weighting in the Best Ideas Newsletter portfolio. It also benefits from one of the strongest competitive advantages out there: the network effect.

Stock Chart (weekly)

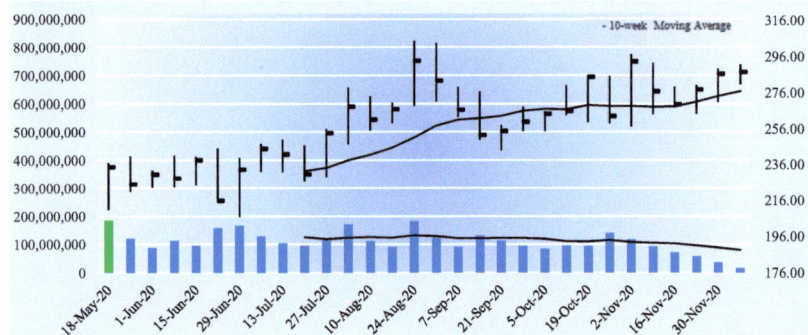

The week with the highest trading volume out of the last 30 weeks was a week of heavy selling, or distribution (red bar).

Investment Considerations

DCF Valuation	UNDERVALUED
Relative Valuation	ATTRACTIVE
ValueCreation™	EXCELLENT
ValueRisk™	MEDIUM
ValueTrend™	NEGATIVE
Cash Flow Generation	STRONG
Financial Leverage	LOW
Growth	AGGRESSIVE
Technical Evaluation	BULLISH
Relative Strength	NEUTRAL
Money Flow Index (MFI)	NEUTRAL
Upside/Downside Volume (U/D)	DETERIORATING
Near-term Technical Support, 10-week MA	277.00

DCF = Discounted Cash Flow; MFI, U/D = Please see glossary. MA = Moving Average

Company Vitals

Market Cap (USD)	$826,907
Avg Weekly Vol (30 wks)	109,720
30-week Range (USD)	207.11 - 304.67
Valuentum Sector	Information Technology
5-week Return	-0.8%
13-week Return	6.1%
30-week Return	35.5%
Dividend Yield %	0.0%
Dividends per Share	0.00
Forward Dividend Payout Ratio	0.0%
Est. Normal Diluted EPS	14.38
P/E on Est. Normal Diluted EPS	20.0
Est. Normal EBITDA	61,895
Forward EV/EBITDA	18.7
EV/Est. Normal EBITDA	12.5
Forward Revenue Growth (5-yr)	17.8%
Forward EPS Growth (5-yr)	24.6%

NMF = Not Meaningful; Est. = Estimated; FY = Fiscal Year

Returns Summary   3-year Historical Average

Return on Equity	23.9%
Return on Assets	20.6%
ROIC, with goodwill	57.6%
ROIC, without goodwill	105.7%

ROIC = Return on Invested Capital; NMF = Not Meaningful

Leverage, Coverage, and Liquidity

In Millions of USD

Total Debt	0
Net Debt	-54,855
Total Debt/EBITDA	0.0
Net Debt/EBITDA	NMF
EBITDA/Interest	Excellent
Current Ratio	4.4
Quick Ratio	4.3

NMF = Not Meaningful

Investment Highlights

• Facebook's mission is to make the world more open and connected. People use Facebook to stay in touch with friends/family, to learn about news, and to share what matters to them. The company continues to expand its reach with businesses such as the popular social media platform Instagram. The company was founded in 2004 and is headquartered in California.

• It may be unfair to lump Facebook in with other weaker social media companies. Facebook is generating tens of billions in revenue and is throwing off gobs of excess free cash flow. The company's balance sheet is pristine, too, with tens of billions in cash and no debt.

• Facebook's number of mobile users continues to grow, with mobile ad revenue surging. Data privacy and security remain paramount, however. Its operating margin guidance for the years ahead may not be as strong as it could be due to increased levels of spending in areas such as product development and infrastructure, safety and security, and AR/VR.

• Facebook's free cash flow generation and balance sheet are amazing, but investors must be cognizant of the low barriers to entry in the social media space and the fickle nature of its users. Recent social and political pressures have impacted public perception, and testifying in Congress has become the norm.

• Facebook's monthly active users (MAUs) count is growing at a solid rate. Concerns over user growth in Europe and US & Canada regions have cropped up, but its advertising business is as strong as ever. E-commerce (Shops) could offer huge upside.

Business Quality   ValueCreation™

ValueRisk™	Very Poor	Poor	Good	Excellent
Low				
Medium				▇
High				
Very High				

Firms that generate economic profits with little operating variability score near the top right of the matrix.

Relative Valuation

	Forward P/E	PEG	Price / FV
Apple	29.8	2.4	85.0%
Alphabet	34.9	1.8	73.3%
Amazon.com	NMF	3.3	95.7%
Microsoft	31.6	2.5	91.6%
Peer Median	31.6	2.5	88.3%
Facebook	**31.0**	**1.8**	**69.6%**

Price / FV = Current Stock Price divided by Estimated Fair Value

Financial Summary

	----- Actual -----			Projected
Fiscal Year End:		Dec-18	Dec-19	Dec-20
Revenue		55,838	70,697	83,917
Revenue, YoY%		37.4%	26.6%	18.7%
Operating Income		24,913	23,986	34,406
Operating Margin %		44.6%	33.9%	41.0%
Net Income		22,111	18,485	26,248
Net Income Margin %		39.6%	26.1%	31.3%
Diluted EPS		7.57	6.43	9.27
Diluted EPS, YoY %		40.6%	-15.1%	44.2%
Free Cash Flow (CFO-capex)		15,359	21,212	23,841
Free Cash Flow Margin %		27.5%	30.0%	28.4%

In Millions of USD (except for per share items)

Structure of the Internet Software & Services Industry   NEUTRAL

The Internet software/services industry is composed of a variety of companies with rapidly-changing business models. Most focus on improving the ways people connect with information, either via Internet search or by social media platforms, and generate revenue primarily by delivering cost-effective online advertising. Constituents earn significant returns on invested capital due to their capital-light operations, though competition remains fierce. We expect most companies in this group to look substantially different 10 years from now than they do today. Overall, we're neutral on the structure.

F5 Networks FFIV   FAIRLY VALUED

Buying Index™ 7   **Value Rating** ◯

Economic Castle	Estimated Fair Value	Fair Value Range	Investment Style	Sector	Industry
Highest Rated	$196.00	$157.00 - $235.00	MID-CAP VALUE	Information Technology	Technology Giants

F5 Networks' transition to more of a SaaS-driven model should bolster recurring revenue and help it deliver on its commitment to double-digit non-GAAP eanings per share growth in coming years.

Stock Chart (weekly)

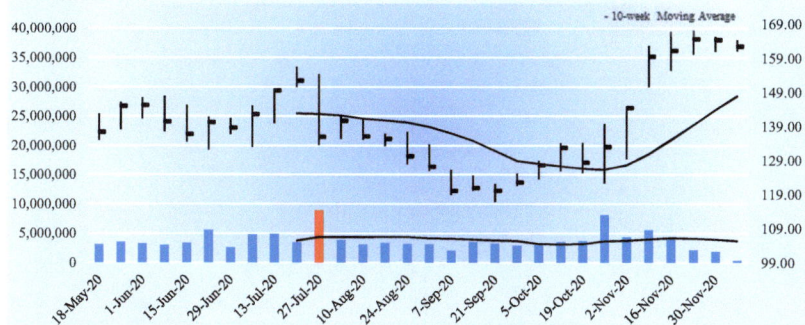

The week with the highest trading volume out of the last 30 weeks was a week of heavy selling, or distribution (red bar).

Company Vitals

Market Cap (USD)	$9,970
Avg Weekly Vol (30 wks)	3,712
30-week Range (USD)	116.79 - 167.00
Valuentum Sector	Information Technology
5-week Return	0.9%
13-week Return	34.2%
30-week Return	14.8%
Dividend Yield %	0.0%
Dividends per Share	0.00
Forward Dividend Payout Ratio	0.0%
Est. Normal Diluted EPS	11.08
P/E on Est. Normal Diluted EPS	14.7
Est. Normal EBITDA	927
Forward EV/EBITDA	10.4
EV/Est. Normal EBITDA	9.9
Forward Revenue Growth (5-yr)	4.8%
Forward EPS Growth (5-yr)	16.9%

NMF = Not Meaningful; Est. = Estimated; FY = Fiscal Year

Returns Summary
3-year Historical Average

Return on Equity	26.5%
Return on Assets	13.2%
ROIC, with goodwill	51.9%
ROIC, without goodwill	158.8%

ROIC = Return on Invested Capital; NMF = Not Meaningful

Leverage, Coverage, and Liquidity
In Millions of USD

Total Debt	388
Net Debt	-822
Total Debt/EBITDA	0.8
Net Debt/EBITDA	NMF
EBITDA/Interest	Excellent
Current Ratio	1.4
Quick Ratio	1.2

NMF = Not Meaningful

Investment Highlights

• F5 Networks is a leader in application delivery services. Its hardware, software, and virtual solutions help organizations address the growth of voice, data, and video traffic to better support mobile workers and applications—in the data center, the network, and the cloud. The firm acquired anti-fraud technology firm Shape Security in January 2020.

• Momentum in F5 Networks' web firewall application offerings has been solid as cybersecurity is as important as ever, but ever-intensifying competition from larger tech giants should be noted. Still, the company has set 8%-9% as a long-term annual revenue growth target.

• F5 is increasingly driving higher-margin software revenue, which is growing at a rapid clip. Greater demand for hybrid solutions that offer flexibility to deploy services in the cloud has been a source of strength. By the middle of this decade, management expects software to account for ~75% of product revenue (up from ~35% today).

• F5 Networks estimates its total addressable market will grow to $28 billion in 2023, a huge opportunity. We also like the company's balance sheet health as it held cash, cash equivalents and short-term investments of more than $1.2 billion and a net cash position of ~$820 million at the end of fiscal 2020.

• The company's transition to more of a SaaS-driven model should bolster recurring revenue and help it deliver on its commitment to double-digit non-GAAP EPS growth in coming years. Management is also committed to returning cash to shareholders.

Investment Considerations

DCF Valuation	FAIRLY VALUED
Relative Valuation	ATTRACTIVE
ValueCreation™	EXCELLENT
ValueRisk™	LOW
ValueTrend™	NEGATIVE
Cash Flow Generation	STRONG
Financial Leverage	LOW
Growth	MODEST
Technical Evaluation	BULLISH
Relative Strength	STRONG
Money Flow Index (MFI)	NEUTRAL
Upside/Downside Volume (U/D)	BULLISH
Near-term Technical Support, 10-week MA	148.00

DCF = Discounted Cash Flow; MFI, U/D = Please see glossary. MA = Moving Average

Business Quality

ValueCreation™			
ValueRisk™	Very Poor	Poor	Good	Excellent
Low				▉
Medium				
High				
Very High				

Firms that generate economic profits with little operating variability score near the top right of the matrix.

Relative Valuation

	Forward P/E	PEG	Price / FV
Apple	29.8	2.4	85.0%
Alphabet	34.9	1.8	73.3%
Amazon.com	NMF	3.3	95.7%
Microsoft	31.6	2.5	91.6%
Peer Median	31.6	2.5	88.3%
F5 Networks	15.9	1.9	82.9%

Price / FV = Current Stock Price divided by Estimated Fair Value

Financial Summary

	----- Actual -----		Projected
Fiscal Year End:	Sep-19	Sep-20	Sep-21
Revenue	2,242	2,351	2,494
Revenue, YoY%	3.7%	4.8%	6.1%
Non-GAAP Operating Income	518	392	781
Non-GAAP EBIT %	23.1%	16.7%	31.3%
Non-GAAP Net Income	428	307	613
Non-GAAP NI Margin %	19.1%	13.1%	24.6%
Non-GAAP Diluted EPS	7.08	5.01	10.19
Non-GAAP Dil EPS, YoY %	-3.3%	-29.2%	103.5%
Non-GAAP FCF (CFO-capex)	644	601	908
Non-GAAP FCF Margin %	28.7%	25.6%	36.4%

In Millions of USD (except for per share items)

Structure of the Software Industry
VERY GOOD

Firms that serve the mature software markets—or those consisting of basic business applications—have powerful distribution channels, large installed bases, and fortress balance sheets. These entrenched competitors benefit from significant customer switching costs, which make it nearly impossible for new entrants to gain a foothold. Participants generally benefit from high-margin license revenue and generate significant returns on investment. Still, the shift to cloud computing has created both opportunities and challenges, and the enterprise software landscape continues to evolve. We like the group.

VALUENTUM

First Solar FSLR   FAIRLY VALUED

	Buying Index™	6	Value Rating	◐

Economic Castle	Estimated Fair Value	Fair Value Range	Investment Style	Sector	Industry
Attractive	$106.00	$74.00 - $138.00	LARGE-CAP VALUE	Next Generation	Broadline Semiconductors

We sharply increased our fair value estimate for First Solar as the US will likely become more accommodative towards the industry going forward.

Stock Chart (weekly)

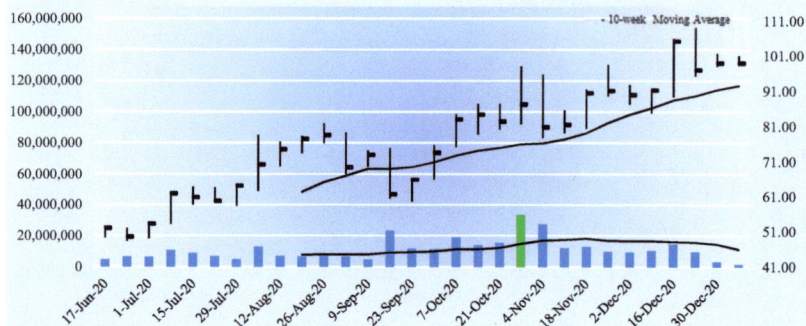

The week with the highest trading volume out of the last 30 weeks was a week of heavy selling, or distribution (red bar).

Company Vitals

Market Cap (USD)	$10,417
Avg Weekly Vol (30 wks)	11,152
30-week Range (USD)	48.30 - 109.09
Valuentum Sector	Next Generation
5-week Return	8.5%
13-week Return	17.5%
30-week Return	90.9%
Dividend Yield %	0.0%
Dividends per Share	0.00
Forward Dividend Payout Ratio	0.0%
Est. Normal Diluted EPS	4.69
P/E on Est. Normal Diluted EPS	21.1
Est. Normal EBITDA	889
Forward EV/EBITDA	12.1
EV/Est. Normal EBITDA	9.8
Forward Revenue Growth (5-yr)	5.5%
Forward EPS Growth (5-yr)	-241.7%

NMF = Not Meaningful; Est. = Estimated; FY = Fiscal Year

Returns Summary

3-year Historical Average

Return on Equity	-1.1%
Return on Assets	-0.8%
ROIC, with goodwill	22.3%
ROIC, without goodwill	22.5%

ROIC = Return on Invested Capital; NMF = Not Meaningful

Leverage, Coverage, and Liquidity

In Millions of USD

Total Debt	472
Net Debt	-1,692
Total Debt/EBITDA	1.2
Net Debt/EBITDA	NMF
EBITDA/Interest	15.0
Current Ratio	2.7
Quick Ratio	2.1

NMF = Not Meaningful

Investment Highlights

• First Solar provides solar energy solutions worldwide. The company's goal is to reduce the cost of solar electricity to levels that compete on a non-subsidized basis with the price of retail electricity. The company operates in two segments, Components and Systems. It was founded in 1999 and is headquartered in Tempe, Arizona.

• Please be aware that our model assumes First Solar realizes material operating margin expansion and revenue growth going forward, underpinned by our expectations that the US federal government will provide additional support to the industry.

• First Solar had a sizable net cash position at the end of September 2020, which provides the firm with significant financial firepower. The company's net bookings have been moving in the right direction of late and its long-term growth outlook is bright, in our view. Its total addressable market in Europe and North America is quite large.

• First Solar's domestic design and manufacturing footprint could prove useful in the coming years as it relates to navigating US-China trade tensions. The company also has a manufacturing footprint in Germany, Malaysia, and Vietnam. Global trade tensions are an ongoing concern.

• First Solar faces intense competition that prices aggressively and seeks to capture market share. The development of other renewable energy technologies adds significant uncertainty to its long-term viability, as does uncertainty related to government incentives.

Investment Considerations

DCF Valuation	FAIRLY VALUED
Relative Valuation	NEUTRAL
ValueCreation™	EXCELLENT
ValueRisk™	MEDIUM
ValueTrend™	NEGATIVE
Cash Flow Generation	WEAK
Financial Leverage	MEDIUM
Growth	MODEST
Technical Evaluation	BULLISH
Relative Strength	STRONG
Money Flow Index (MFI)	NEUTRAL
Upside/Downside Volume (U/D)	BULLISH
Near-term Technical Support, 10-week MA	92.00

DCF = Discounted Cash Flow; MFI, U/D = Please see glossary. MA = Moving Average

Business Quality

ValueCreation™

ValueRisk™	Very Poor	Poor	Good	Excellent
Low				
Medium				▨
High				
Very High				

Firms that generate economic profits with little operating variability score near the top right of the matrix.

Relative Valuation

	Forward P/E	PEG	Price / FV
Wayfair	56.3	NMF	84.2%
Zoom Video	170.7	28.8	120.8%
Roku	-338.4	NMF	96.0%
Monster Beverage	36.0	2.9	104.4%
Peer Median	46.1	15.9	100.2%
First Solar	**26.3**	**NMF**	**93.3%**

Price / FV = Current Stock Price divided by Estimated Fair Value

Financial Summary

	----- Actual -----		Projected
Fiscal Year End:	Dec-18	Dec-19	Dec-20
Revenue	2,244	3,063	2,827
Revenue, YoY%	-23.7%	36.5%	-7.7%
Operating Income	40	201	530
Operating Margin %	1.8%	6.6%	18.8%
Net Income	145	-115	398
Net Income Margin %	6.5%	-3.8%	14.1%
Diluted EPS	1.37	-1.09	3.76
Diluted EPS, YoY %	-186.2%	-179.7%	-444.1%
Free Cash Flow (CFO-capex)	-1,067	-495	206
Free Cash Flow Margin %	-47.5%	-16.2%	7.3%

In Millions of USD (except for per share items)

Structure of the Broad Line Semiconductor Industry   POOR

The broad line semiconductor industry is characterized by intense competition, rapid technological change, and frequent product introductions. The number and variety of computing devices have expanded rapidly, creating a connected landscape between suppliers and competitors. New market segments have emerged rapidly (smartphones, tablets), and constituents must continuously innovate to maintain share as traditional PC demand faces pressure. Though some firms may gain advantages via the combination of their manufacturing/test facilities with their design teams, we think the structure of the group is poor.

VALUENTUM

Graco GGG   FAIRLY VALUED

Buying Index™   6   Value Rating   🟡

Economic Castle	Estimated Fair Value	Fair Value Range	Investment Style	Sector	Industry
Very Attractive	$61.00	$46.00 - $76.00	LARGE-CAP CORE	Materials	Mining & Chemicals

Graco's 'Industrial' segment benefits from a number of drivers: factory movements and upgrades and the integration of equipment with factory data and control systems.

Stock Chart (weekly)

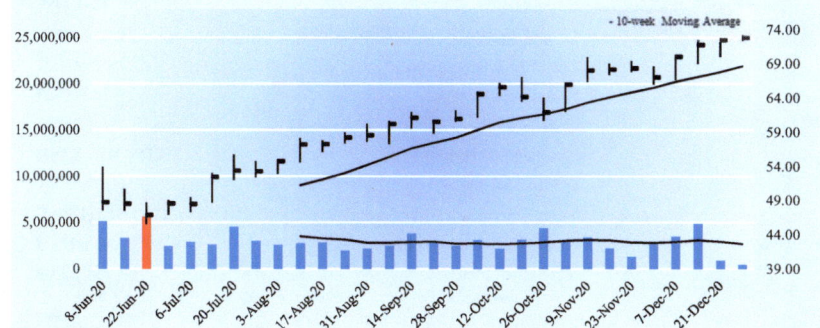

The week with the highest trading volume out of the last 30 weeks was a week of heavy selling, or distribution (red bar).

Company Vitals

Market Cap (USD)	$12,600
Avg Weekly Vol (30 wks)	2,962
30-week Range (USD)	45.48 - 73.17
Valuentum Sector	Materials
5-week Return	6.9%
13-week Return	17.9%
30-week Return	38.2%
Dividend Yield %	1.0%
Dividends per Share	0.75
Forward Dividend Payout Ratio	37.5%
Est. Normal Diluted EPS	2.19
P/E on Est. Normal Diluted EPS	33.3
Est. Normal EBITDA	537
Forward EV/EBITDA	25.7
EV/Est. Normal EBITDA	23.7
Forward Revenue Growth (5-yr)	3.3%
Forward EPS Growth (5-yr)	6.0%

NMF = Not Meaningful; Est. = Estimated; FY = Fiscal Year

Returns Summary   3-year Historical Average

Return on Equity	30.6%
Return on Assets	15.4%
ROIC, with goodwill	38.6%
ROIC, without goodwill	54.3%

ROIC = Return on Invested Capital; NMF = Not Meaningful

Leverage, Coverage, and Liquidity
In Millions of USD

Total Debt	277
Net Debt	145
Total Debt/EBITDA	0.6
Net Debt/EBITDA	0.3
EBITDA/Interest	33.7
Current Ratio	2.4
Quick Ratio	1.4

NMF = Not Meaningful

Investment Highlights

• Graco makes systems and equipment to move, measure, control, dispense and spray fluid and coating materials. The company supplies technology and expertise for the management of fluids and coatings in industrial and commercial applications. The firm was founded in 1926 and is headquartered in Minneapolis, Minnesota. It recently underwent a 3-for-1 stock split.

• Graco is dedicated to growth through new products and markets, and its new product development expenses reflect that. For example, Graco's R&D spending as a percentage of revenue is frequently above the average of that of its peer group. Product development was 4.1% of sales in 2019.

• Graco is targeting a 12%+ earnings CAGR in the coming years. The anticipated drivers of this growth are the 3%-5% industrial production average growth rate, acquisitions, new product development, new markets, global expansion, and end user conversion. The progress of these drivers can provide insight into the potential for an upside surprise.

• The company's 'Industrial' segment benefits from a number of drivers: factory movements and upgrades and the integration of equipment with factory data and control systems. Industrial segment operating margins have been fairly lofty at ~30% of segment sales.

• Graco boasts a high-quality, efficient, and engaged labor force with 80%+ of production based in the US. Such centralization allows for the leverage of overhead costs, though its international sales create a currency mismatch in sales-to-cost of goods sold.

Investment Considerations

DCF Valuation	FAIRLY VALUED
Relative Valuation	UNATTRACTIVE
ValueCreation™	EXCELLENT
ValueRisk™	MEDIUM
ValueTrend™	NEGATIVE
Cash Flow Generation	STRONG
Financial Leverage	LOW
Growth	MODEST
Technical Evaluation	BULLISH
Relative Strength	STRONG
Money Flow Index (MFI)	NEUTRAL
Upside/Downside Volume (U/D)	DETERIORATING
Near-term Technical Support, 10-week MA	69.00

DCF = Discounted Cash Flow; MFI, U/D = Please see glossary. MA = Moving Average

Business Quality   ValueCreation™

ValueRisk™	Very Poor	Poor	Good	Excellent
Low				
Medium				▮
High				
Very High				

Firms that generate economic profits with little operating variability score near the top right of the matrix.

Relative Valuation

	Forward P/E	PEG	Price / FV
Air Products & Chemicals	27.5	2.3	130.9%
DuPont	29.2	3.7	108.9%
BHP Billiton	20.3	1.9	107.6%
Sherwin-Williams	43.9	2.4	131.2%
Peer Median	28.3	2.4	119.9%
Graco	**36.4**	**6.2**	**119.2%**

Price / FV = Current Stock Price divided by Estimated Fair Value

Financial Summary

	----- Actual -----		Projected
Fiscal Year End:	Dec-17	Dec-18	Dec-19
Revenue	1,475	1,653	1,646
Revenue, YoY%	10.9%	12.1%	-0.4%
Operating Income	360	436	447
Operating Margin %	24.4%	26.4%	27.2%
Net Income	252	341	346
Net Income Margin %	17.1%	20.6%	21.0%
Diluted EPS	1.45	1.97	2.00
Diluted EPS, YoY %	102.8%	36.0%	1.6%
Free Cash Flow (CFO-capex)	298	315	291
Free Cash Flow Margin %	20.2%	19.0%	17.7%

In Millions of USD (except for per share items)

Structure of the Machinery & Tools Industry   GOOD

The machinery and tools industry is fragmented and highly competitive. Most constituents offer a wide range of products in a myriad of markets. Firms are heavily exposed to fluctuating raw material prices (steel, resins, chemicals) and the vicissitudes of the global economic cycle, including customer capital/maintenance budgets. Several companies are recognized worldwide for their strong brand names and reputation for quality, innovation and value, and we view such attributes as material competitive advantages. Though pricing competition is not absent, we like the structural characteristics of the group.

General Mills GIS FAIRLY VALUED

Buying Index™ 6   Value Rating 🟡

Economic Castle	Estimated Fair Value	Fair Value Range	Investment Style	Sector	Industry
Attractive	$57.00	$46.00 - $68.00	LARGE-CAP CORE	Consumer Staples	Recession Resistant

We moderately increased our fair value estimate for General Mills. The company has aggressively pared down its leverage ratio recently.

Stock Chart (weekly)

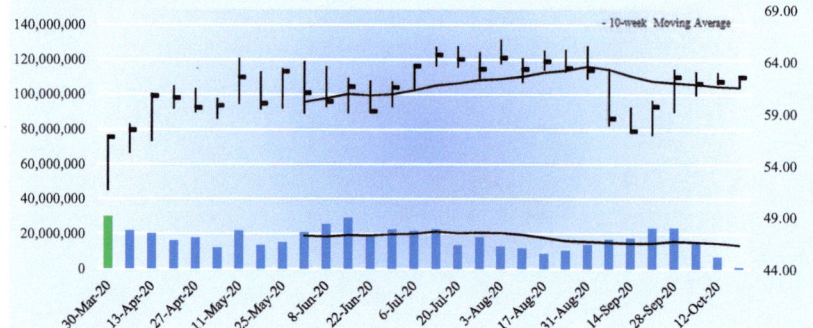

The week with the highest trading volume out of the last 30 weeks was a week of heavy selling, or distribution (red bar).

Investment Considerations

DCF Valuation	**FAIRLY VALUED**
Relative Valuation	**NEUTRAL**
ValueCreation™	**EXCELLENT**
ValueRisk™	**LOW**
ValueTrend™	**POSITIVE**
Cash Flow Generation	**STRONG**
Financial Leverage	**HIGH**
Growth	**MODEST**
Technical Evaluation	**VERY BULLISH**
Relative Strength	**WEAK**
Money Flow Index (MFI)	**NEUTRAL**
Upside/Downside Volume (U/D)	**BEARISH**
Near-term Technical Support, 10-week MA	**62.00**

DCF = Discounted Cash Flow; MFI, U/D = Please see glossary. MA = Moving Average

Business Quality

ValueRisk™	ValueCreation™			
	Very Poor	Poor	Good	Excellent
Low				■
Medium				
High				
Very High				

Firms that generate economic profits with little operating variability score near the top right of the matrix.

Company Vitals

Market Cap (USD)	$38,344
Avg Weekly Vol (30 wks)	17,373
30-week Range (USD)	51.50 - 66.13
Valuentum Sector	Consumer Staples
5-week Return	9.7%
13-week Return	-2.6%
30-week Return	19.0%
Dividend Yield %	3.3%
Dividends per Share	2.04
Forward Dividend Payout Ratio	55.6%
Est. Normal Diluted EPS	4.19
P/E on Est. Normal Diluted EPS	14.9
Est. Normal EBITDA	4,048
Forward EV/EBITDA	13.6
EV/Est. Normal EBITDA	12.4
Forward Revenue Growth (5-yr)	2.1%
Forward EPS Growth (5-yr)	6.8%

NMF = Not Meaningful; Est. = Estimated; FY = Fiscal Year

Returns Summary
3-year Historical Average

Return on Equity	31.2%
Return on Assets	6.8%
ROIC, with goodwill	10.1%
ROIC, without goodwill	23.4%

ROIC = Return on Invested Capital; NMF = Not Meaningful

Leverage, Coverage, and Liquidity
In Millions of USD

Total Debt	13,540
Net Debt	11,862
Total Debt/EBITDA	3.8
Net Debt/EBITDA	3.3
EBITDA/Interest	7.7
Current Ratio	0.7
Quick Ratio	0.4

NMF = Not Meaningful

Investment Highlights

• General Mills has a distinguished portfolio of leading brands, including Cheerios, Betty Crocker, Pillsbury, Yoplait, Nature Valley, Old El Paso and Häagen-Dazs. The firm also owns Blue Buffalo, a leading pet food and nutrition company. Roughly 75% of sales come from the US. The company was founded in 1928 and is headquartered in Minneapolis, Minnesota.

• General Mills has experienced strong demand for its products as US households stocked up on consumer staples product during the COVID-19 pandemic. The company is investing in its digital and e-commerce operations to keep pace with elevated demand.

• General Mills acquired Blue Buffalo Pet Products through an ~$8 billion deal in April 2018. This acquisition was pursued so General Mills could capitalize on the "humanization of pets" trend in the US and improve its long-term growth outlook. Blue Buffalo boasts one of the strongest brands in the space, and sales growth at the unit has been brisk of late.

• General Mills has aggressively reduced its net debt to adjusted EBITDA ratio since closing the Blue Buffalo deal (when that metric sat at ~4.2x on a pro forma basis). By the first quarter of fiscal 2021, General Mills' leverage ratio had declined to ~3.0x. The firm resumed dividend increases in September 2020.

• General Mills dominates the US cereal market with brands such as Cheerios, Lucky Charms, and Cinnamon Toast Crunch. During the initial phases of the COVID-19 pandemic, cereal sales increased significantly in the US, though sales have been slowing recently.

Relative Valuation

	Forward P/E	PEG	Price / FV
Coca-Cola	34.3	1.5	128.0%
Procter & Gamble	26.5	3.3	144.1%
Philip Morris	15.4	2.4	104.3%
Wal-Mart	26.8	2.3	130.2%
Peer Median	26.7	2.4	129.1%
General Mills	**17.1**	**2.6**	**109.7%**

Price / FV = Current Stock Price divided by Estimated Fair Value

Financial Summary

	----- Actual -----		Projected
Fiscal Year End:	May-19	May-20	May-21
Revenue	16,865	17,627	17,504
Revenue, YoY%	7.1%	4.5%	-0.7%
Operating Income	2,821	2,978	3,107
Operating Margin %	16.7%	16.9%	17.8%
Net Income	1,753	2,181	2,226
Net Income Margin %	10.4%	12.4%	12.7%
Diluted EPS	2.90	3.56	3.67
Diluted EPS, YoY %	-17.1%	22.8%	3.1%
Free Cash Flow (CFO-capex)	2,269	3,215	2,427
Free Cash Flow Margin %	13.5%	18.2%	13.9%

In Millions of USD (except for per share items)

Structure of the Food Products Industry   NEUTRAL

The food products industry is composed of a number of firms with strong brand names. However, market supply/demand dynamics and intense competition still impact product prices, while fluctuations in commodity costs can make earnings quite volatile. Private-label competition, competitors' promotional spending, and changing consumer preferences often drive demand trends. The group's customers—such as supermarkets, warehouses, and food distributors—continue to consolidate, increasing buying power over constituents and hurting margins. Still, we're generally neutral on the group.

Alphabet GOOG   UNDERVALUED 2.3%

Buying Index™   7   Value Rating ✔

Economic Castle	Estimated Fair Value	Fair Value Range	Investment Style	Sector	Industry
Very Attractive	$2493.00	$1870.00 - $3116.00	MEGA-CAP BLEND	Information Technology	Technology Giants

Alphabet's shares look very attractive on a discounted cash flow basis. The company's free cash flow generation is top notch, and it remains one of our very best ideas for long-term capital appreciation potential.

Stock Chart (weekly)

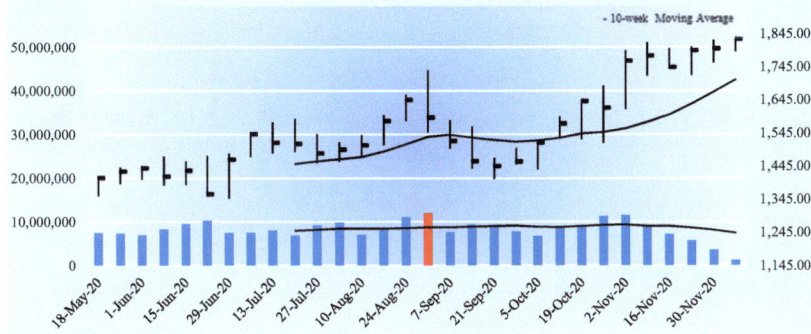

The week with the highest trading volume out of the last 30 weeks was a week of heavy selling, or distribution (red bar).

Investment Considerations

DCF Valuation	UNDERVALUED
Relative Valuation	NEUTRAL
ValueCreation™	EXCELLENT
ValueRisk™	MEDIUM
ValueTrend™	NEGATIVE
Cash Flow Generation	STRONG
Financial Leverage	LOW
Growth	AGGRESSIVE
Technical Evaluation	BULLISH
Relative Strength	STRONG
Money Flow Index (MFI)	NEUTRAL
Upside/Downside Volume (U/D)	DETERIORATING
Near-term Technical Support, 10-week MA	1705.00

DCF = Discounted Cash Flow; MFI, U/D = Please see glossary. MA = Moving Average

Company Vitals

Market Cap (USD)	$1,256,325
Avg Weekly Vol (30 wks)	8,147
30-week Range (USD)	1,347.01 - 1,835.65
Valuentum Sector	Information Technology
5-week Return	2.1%
13-week Return	18.8%
30-week Return	34.2%
Dividend Yield %	0.0%
Dividends per Share	0.00
Forward Dividend Payout Ratio	0.0%
Est. Normal Diluted EPS	84.15
P/E on Est. Normal Diluted EPS	21.7
Est. Normal EBITDA	82,843
Forward EV/EBITDA	21.3
EV/Est. Normal EBITDA	13.8
Forward Revenue Growth (5-yr)	15.7%
Forward EPS Growth (5-yr)	19.8%

NMF = Not Meaningful; Est. = Estimated; FY = Fiscal Year

Returns Summary   3-year Historical Average

Return on Equity	15.1%
Return on Assets	11.6%
ROIC, with goodwill	51.7%
ROIC, without goodwill	70.2%

ROIC = Return on Invested Capital; NMF = Not Meaningful

Leverage, Coverage, and Liquidity
In Millions of USD

Total Debt	4,554
Net Debt	-115,121
Total Debt/EBITDA	0.1
Net Debt/EBITDA	NMF
EBITDA/Interest	Excellent
Current Ratio	3.4
Quick Ratio	3.2

NMF = Not Meaningful

Investment Highlights

• Known for its search dominance, Alphabet is a tech company focused on a number of things: Android, ads, YouTube, Chrome, and research. We think the company will have some megahits in the years ahead. It reports operating losses in its 'Other Bets' category frequently, suggesting core levels of profitability are higher than reported.

• Alphabet offers investors a compelling combination of attractive valuation, growth potential, cash-flow generation and competitive profile. Very few firms are more attractive on a fundamental basis, in our view, and its impressive free cash flow conversion rates (consistently above 100%) speak to this.

• Alphabet is pleased with momentum in its mobile division, particularly within strong mobile advertising revenue. The mobile Internet space will be key for the firm. YouTube and programmatic advertising offer upside potential, too, but we're watching spending levels, which have spiked due in part to higher traffic acquisition costs.

• Alphabet has a strong future in search, and we continue to be in awe of the strength in this division. Its massive net cash position gives the company a substantial cushion to fall back on as it invests in high-return opportunities and new concepts such as smart home features, Glass, Fiber, or other innovative ideas.

• Alphabet has three different stock classes with two different tickers. GOOGL is Class A stock, and GOOG represents the non-voting Class C stock that was created by a stock split in 2014 in order for Google founders to maintain majority control.

Business Quality   ValueCreation™

ValueRisk™	Very Poor	Poor	Good	Excellent
Low				
Medium				▨
High				
Very High				

Firms that generate economic profits with little operating variability score near the top right of the matrix.

Relative Valuation

	Forward P/E	PEG	Price / FV
Facebook	31.0	1.8	69.6%
Apple	29.8	2.4	85.0%
Amazon.com	NMF	3.3	95.7%
Microsoft	31.6	2.5	91.6%
Peer Median	31.0	2.5	88.3%
Alphabet	**34.9**	**1.8**	**73.3%**

Price / FV = Current Stock Price divided by Estimated Fair Value

Financial Summary

	----- Actual -----			Projected
Fiscal Year End:		Dec-18	Dec-19	Dec-20
Revenue		136,819	161,857	178,852
Revenue, YoY%		23.4%	18.3%	10.5%
Operating Income		31,392	34,231	40,751
Operating Margin %		22.9%	21.1%	22.8%
Net Income		30,736	34,343	35,861
Net Income Margin %		22.5%	21.2%	20.1%
Diluted EPS		43.70	49.97	52.44
Diluted EPS, YoY %		142.8%	14.3%	4.9%
Free Cash Flow (CFO-capex)		22,832	30,972	28,394
Free Cash Flow Margin %		16.7%	19.1%	15.9%

In Millions of USD (except for per share items)

Structure of the Internet Software & Services Industry   NEUTRAL

The Internet software/services industry is composed of a variety of companies with rapidly-changing business models. Most focus on improving the ways people connect with information, either via Internet search or by social media platforms, and generate revenue primarily by delivering cost-effective online advertising. Constituents earn significant returns on invested capital due to their capital-light operations, though competition remains fierce. We expect most companies in this group to look substantially different 10 years from now than they do today. Overall, we're neutral on the structure.

Global Payments GPN   FAIRLY VALUED

Buying Index™ 7   **Value Rating** ○

Economic Castle	Estimated Fair Value	Fair Value Range	Investment Style	Sector	Industry
Attractive	$209.00	$167.00 - $251.00	LARGE-CAP BLEND	Next Generation	Disruptive Innovation

Global Payments' global footprint and distribution network are its greatest competitive advantages. The company is a pure play on payments technology, and its merger with Total System Services has been a game changer.

Stock Chart (weekly)

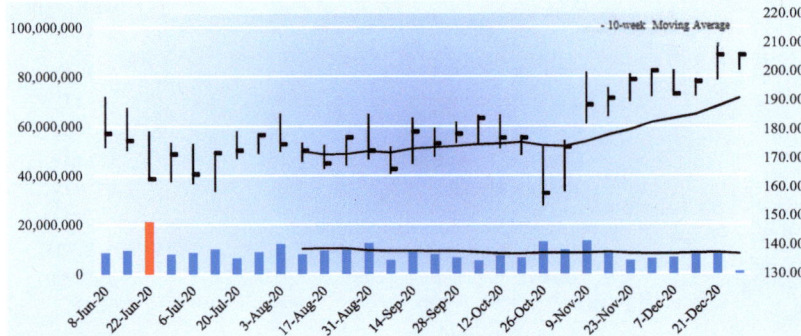

The week with the highest trading volume out of the last 30 weeks was a week of heavy selling, or distribution (red bar).

Company Vitals

Market Cap (USD)	$40,932
Avg Weekly Vol (30 wks)	8,634
30-week Range (USD)	153.33 - 209.66
Valuentum Sector	Next Generation
5-week Return	4.9%
13-week Return	13.4%
30-week Return	9.3%
Dividend Yield %	0.4%
Dividends per Share	0.78
Forward Dividend Payout Ratio	12.1%
Est. Normal Diluted EPS	9.18
P/E on Est. Normal Diluted EPS	22.4
Est. Normal EBITDA	3,584
Forward EV/EBITDA	17.0
EV/Est. Normal EBITDA	13.5
Forward Revenue Growth (5-yr)	15.0%
Forward EPS Growth (5-yr)	40.6%

NMF = Not Meaningful; Est. = Estimated; FY = Fiscal Year

Returns Summary   3-year Historical Average

Return on Equity	10.1%
Return on Assets	3.2%
ROIC, with goodwill	7.3%
ROIC, without goodwill	18.2%

ROIC = Return on Invested Capital; NMF = Not Meaningful

Leverage, Coverage, and Liquidity

In Millions of USD

Total Debt	9,126
Net Debt	7,447
Total Debt/EBITDA	5.3
Net Debt/EBITDA	4.3
EBITDA/Interest	5.7
Current Ratio	1.2
Quick Ratio	0.7

NMF = Not Meaningful

Investment Highlights

• Global Payments has one of our favorite business models, facilitating transaction processing between merchant and card issuer. The majority of its merchant services revenue is generated by services priced as a percentage of transaction value or a fee per transaction. It is designated as a Merchant Service Provider by MasterCard and as an Independent Sales Organization (ISO) by Visa.

• Global Payments' global footprint and distribution network are key competitive advantages, while its scalable infrastructure means operating margins will remain healthy, even if they aren't as large as that of Visa or MasterCard. Its 2019 merger with Total System Services has driven explosive growth.

• We're huge fans of Global Payments' business model and we have no qualms with its acquisition program, but its balance sheet is worth watching closely. The ~$24.5 billion merger with Total System Services in 2019, its ~$4.3 billion purchase of Heartland in 2016 and its ~$1.2 billion acquisition of Active Network have added leverage. Net debt stood at ~$7.4 billion at the end of 2019.

• Global Payments has strong goals for its business in coming years. It is targeting organic adjusted net revenue plus network fees to grow at a high-single to low-double-digit rate, adjusted operating margin expansion of up to 75 basis points per year, and an adjusted earnings per share growth rate in the mid-to-high teens. These goals are achievable.

• The company competes with Fiserv, Fidelity National, Chase Paymentech, and Elevon (US Bancorp). Opportunities in Europe/Asia are growing as institutions outsource merchant payment services to third parties. New entrants such as Square may pose disruptive long-term threats.

Investment Considerations

DCF Valuation	**FAIRLY VALUED**
Relative Valuation	**ATTRACTIVE**
ValueCreation™	**EXCELLENT**
ValueRisk™	**LOW**
ValueTrend™	**NEGATIVE**
Cash Flow Generation	**STRONG**
Financial Leverage	**HIGH**
Growth	**AGGRESSIVE**
Technical Evaluation	**BULLISH**
Relative Strength	**STRONG**
Money Flow Index (MFI)	**NEUTRAL**
Upside/Downside Volume (U/D)	**BULLISH**
Near-term Technical Support, 10-week MA	**191.00**

DCF = Discounted Cash Flow; MFI, U/D = Please see glossary. MA = Moving Average

Business Quality   ValueCreation™

ValueRisk™	Very Poor	Poor	Good	Excellent
Low				■
Medium				
High				
Very High				

Firms that generate economic profits with little operating variability score near the top right of the matrix.

Relative Valuation

	Forward P/E	PEG	Price / FV
Wayfair	56.3	NMF	84.2%
Zoom Video	170.7	28.8	120.8%
Roku	-338.4	NMF	96.0%
Monster Beverage	36.0	2.9	104.4%
Peer Median	46.1	15.9	100.2%
Global Payments	**31.8**	**2.4**	**98.3%**

Price / FV = Current Stock Price divided by Estimated Fair Value

Financial Summary

	----- Actual -----		Projected
Fiscal Year End:	Dec-18	Dec-19	Dec-20
Revenue	3,366	4,912	7,275
Revenue, YoY%	-15.3%	45.9%	48.1%
Non-GAAP Operating Income	737	791	1,803
Non-GAAP EBIT %	21.9%	16.1%	24.8%
Non-GAAP Net Income	452	417	1,300
Non-GAAP NI Margin %	13.4%	8.5%	17.9%
Diluted EPS	2.84	2.09	6.46
Non-GAAP Dil EPS, YoY %	-5.8%	-26.2%	208.6%
Non-GAAP Free Cash Flow	893	1,083	1,923
Non-GAAP FCF Margin %	26.5%	22.1%	26.4%

In Millions of USD (except for per share items)

Structure of the Financial Tech Services Industry   EXCELLENT

The financial tech services industry is primarily composed of firms that generate revenue by charging fees to customers for providing transaction processing and other payment-related services. Constituents operate in a rapidly-evolving legal/regulatory environment, particularly with respect to interchange fees, data protection, and information security. Several participants benefit from a significant competitive advantage – the network effect. As more consumers use credit/debit cards, more merchants accept them, thereby creating a virtuous cycle. The industry is one of the most attractive in our coverage.

W.W. Grainger GWW   FAIRLY VALUED

Buying Index™ 6   **Value Rating** ○

Economic Castle	Estimated Fair Value	Fair Value Range	Investment Style	Sector	Industry
Attractive	$347.00	$278.00 - $416.00	LARGE-CAP CORE	Industrials	Industrial Leaders

W.W. Grainger expects strong top-line growth in its US business in the near term, and it is confident in its ability to pass through cost increases related to tariffs and general inflation. Dividend growth should ensue.

Stock Chart (weekly)

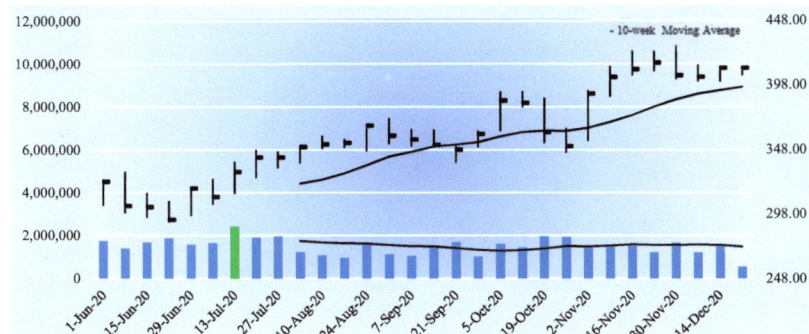

The week with the highest trading volume out of the last 30 weeks was a week of heavy selling, or distribution (red bar).

Investment Considerations

DCF Valuation	FAIRLY VALUED
Relative Valuation	NEUTRAL
ValueCreation™	EXCELLENT
ValueRisk™	LOW
ValueTrend™	POSITIVE
Cash Flow Generation	STRONG
Financial Leverage	MEDIUM
Growth	MODEST
Technical Evaluation	BULLISH
Relative Strength	STRONG
Money Flow Index (MFI)	NEUTRAL
Upside/Downside Volume (U/D)	BEARISH
Near-term Technical Support, 10-week MA	396.00

DCF = Discounted Cash Flow; MFI, U/D = Please see glossary. MA = Moving Average

Business Quality

ValueRisk™	Very Poor	Poor	Good	Excellent
Low				■
Medium				
High				
Very High				

ValueCreation™

Firms that generate economic profits with little operating variability score near the top right of the matrix.

Company Vitals

Market Cap (USD)	$23,191
Avg Weekly Vol (30 wks)	1,500
30-week Range (USD)	291.22 - 427.90
Valuentum Sector	Industrials
5-week Return	-0.2%
13-week Return	16.8%
30-week Return	32.8%
Dividend Yield %	1.5%
Dividends per Share	6.12
Forward Dividend Payout Ratio	35.4%
Est. Normal Diluted EPS	19.84
P/E on Est. Normal Diluted EPS	20.7
Est. Normal EBITDA	1,742
Forward EV/EBITDA	15.5
EV/Est. Normal EBITDA	14.3
Forward Revenue Growth (5-yr)	2.7%
Forward EPS Growth (5-yr)	12.3%

NMF = Not Meaningful; Est. = Estimated; FY = Fiscal Year

Returns Summary   3-year Historical Average

Return on Equity	37.5%
Return on Assets	12.0%
ROIC, with goodwill	24.8%
ROIC, without goodwill	28.5%

ROIC = Return on Invested Capital; NMF = Not Meaningful

Leverage, Coverage, and Liquidity
In Millions of USD

Total Debt	2,220
Net Debt	1,682
Total Debt/EBITDA	1.6
Net Debt/EBITDA	1.2
EBITDA/Interest	16.1
Current Ratio	2.4
Quick Ratio	1.3

NMF = Not Meaningful

Investment Highlights

• W.W. Grainger is a leading distributor of maintenance, repair and operating (MRO) products in North America, with expanding global operations. The worldwide MRO market is estimated to be roughly $560 billion, with North America accounting for ~25% of that figure. Grainger is a Dividend Aristocrat and was founded in Chicago in 1927.

• Grainger uses a multichannel business model (catalogs, e-commerce, etc.) to distribute supplies to customers in the US and internationally. The company is not immune to global economic threats and the risks of unexpected product shortages, however.

• The North American MRO market remains highly fragmented, offering acquisition opportunities for participants. Grainger controls ~8% share of the North American market among large customers, while the other top 10 distributors account for roughly one-quarter of the market. It is executing a complete business model reset in Canada as it works to improve profitability in the country.

• Grainger directly sources roughly 20% of its US segment's COGS from China, and it expects tariffs to increase segment costs by roughly 2%. However, management anticipates price increases and/or alternative supply initiatives will be able to offset the expected cost increase. It expects digital initiatives to improve its return on marketing investment.

• The proliferation of online shopping has made customers more aware of pricing competition, and larger customers are increasingly expecting distributors to cater to their needs. Management is working to cut costs to navigate the competitive environment.

Relative Valuation

	Forward P/E	PEG	Price / FV
Danaher	36.3	3.0	121.5%
Honeywell	28.8	1.7	101.3%
Lockheed Martin	15.0	2.3	96.3%
Union Pacific	25.9	1.4	119.1%
Peer Median	27.3	2.0	110.2%
W.W. Grainger	**23.7**	**2.4**	**118.3%**

Price / FV = Current Stock Price divided by Estimated Fair Value

Financial Summary

	----- Actual -----		Projected
Fiscal Year End:	Dec-17	Dec-18	Dec-19
Revenue	10,425	11,221	11,374
Revenue, YoY%	2.8%	7.6%	1.4%
Operating Income	1,049	1,158	1,349
Operating Margin %	10.1%	10.3%	11.9%
Net Income	586	782	957
Net Income Margin %	5.6%	7.0%	8.4%
Diluted EPS	10.10	13.84	17.29
Diluted EPS, YoY %	1.4%	37.0%	24.9%
Free Cash Flow (CFO-capex)	819	818	1,183
Free Cash Flow Margin %	7.9%	7.3%	10.4%

In Millions of USD (except for per share items)

Structure of the Industrial Distributors Industry   GOOD

Though consolidating, the industrial distributors industry remains fragmented and highly competitive. Delivering cost savings, convenience, and product availability are the major competitive factors. Some rivals use vans to sell products in markets away from their warehouses, while others rely on mail order, websites or telemarketing sales. Still, others operate stores and use centralized distribution centers to supply their networks. The industry is economically-sensitive and exposed to the threat of aggressive pricing strategies, but we generally like the group's massive distribution platforms that are difficult to replicate.

Hasbro HAS   FAIRLY VALUED

Buying Index™   6   Value Rating   🟡

Economic Castle	Estimated Fair Value	Fair Value Range	Investment Style	Sector	Industry
Attractive	$89.00	$71.00 - $107.00	LARGE-CAP VALUE	Consumer Discretionary	Discretionary Spending

Hasbro faces significant headwinds due to COVID-19.

Stock Chart (weekly)

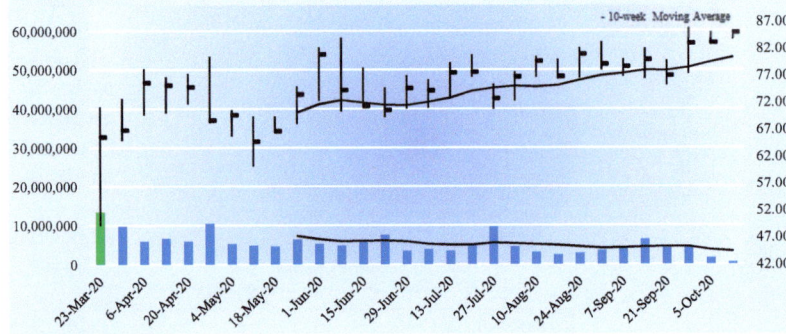

The week with the highest trading volume out of the last 30 weeks was a week of heavy selling, or distribution (red bar).

Company Vitals

Market Cap (USD)	$10,913
Avg Weekly Vol (30 wks)	5,300
30-week Range (USD)	49.23 - 85.82
Valuentum Sector	Consumer Discretionary
5-week Return	7.9%
13-week Return	10.3%
30-week Return	63.1%
Dividend Yield %	3.2%
Dividends per Share	2.72
Forward Dividend Payout Ratio	82.6%
Est. Normal Diluted EPS	4.31
P/E on Est. Normal Diluted EPS	19.7
Est. Normal EBITDA	1,093
Forward EV/EBITDA	11.5
EV/Est. Normal EBITDA	9.5
Forward Revenue Growth (5-yr)	8.7%
Forward EPS Growth (5-yr)	2.7%

NMF = Not Meaningful; Est. = Estimated; FY = Fiscal Year

Returns Summary
3-year Historical Average

Return on Equity	18.6%
Return on Assets	6.4%
ROIC, with goodwill	30.1%
ROIC, without goodwill	40.7%

ROIC = Return on Invested Capital; NMF = Not Meaningful

Leverage, Coverage, and Liquidity
In Millions of USD

Total Debt	4,047
Net Debt	-533
Total Debt/EBITDA	4.4
Net Debt/EBITDA	NMF
EBITDA/Interest	9.0
Current Ratio	5.4
Quick Ratio	4.8

NMF = Not Meaningful

Investment Highlights

• Hasbro's products include toys/games, television programming, motion pictures and digital gaming. The firm owns well-known brands such as Transformers, Nerf, Playskool, My Little Pony, G.I. Joe, Magic: The Gathering, Monopoly, Peppa Pig, and PJ Masks. The company was founded in 1923 and is headquartered in Rhode Island.

• Though concerns over the demise of physical toys may not be completely unfounded in this digital age, Hasbro is less a toy company than it is a licensing firm. Its high-margin 'Entertainment and Licensing' segment performed relatively well in the face of COVID-19.

• Hasbro had a net debt load north of $4.1 billion (inclusive of short-term debt) at the end of the second quarter of fiscal 2020, a product of its recent acquisition activity. Though Hasbro has continued to generate meaningful free cash flows during the initial phases of the COVID-19 pandemic, we caution that this burden needs to be closely monitored.

• Hasbro is not immune from COVID-19. The pandemic prompted households to shift spending away from consumer discretionary products and towards consumer staples goods. Hasbro's supply chain was also negatively impacted by the pandemic, though production activities have ramped back up of late.

• At the start of fiscal 2020, Hasbro completed its acquisition of eOne for a total cash consideration of ~$3.8 billion. The goal is to generate annualized synergies of $130 million by 2022. This deal added properties such as Peppa Pig to Hasbro's portfolio.

Investment Considerations

DCF Valuation	**FAIRLY VALUED**
Relative Valuation	**NEUTRAL**
ValueCreation™	**EXCELLENT**
ValueRisk™	**LOW**
ValueTrend™	**NEGATIVE**
Cash Flow Generation	**STRONG**
Financial Leverage	**HIGH**
Growth	**MODEST**
Technical Evaluation	**BULLISH**
Relative Strength	**NEUTRAL**
Money Flow Index (MFI)	**NEUTRAL**
Upside/Downside Volume (U/D)	**BULLISH**
Near-term Technical Support, 10-week MA	**80.00**

DCF = Discounted Cash Flow; MFI, U/D = Please see glossary. MA = Moving Average

Business Quality

ValueRisk™	Very Poor	Poor	Good	Excellent
Low				
Medium				
High				
Very High				

ValueCreation™

Firms that generate economic profits with little operating variability score near the top right of the matrix.

Relative Valuation

	Forward P/E	PEG	Price / FV
Disney	75.6	0.3	98.3%
Home Depot	22.9	1.9	106.7%
McDonald's	38.5	1.1	111.0%
Nike	52.8	2.5	104.9%
Peer Median	45.6	1.5	105.8%
Hasbro	**25.8**	**2.4**	**95.4%**

Price / FV = Current Stock Price divided by Estimated Fair Value

Financial Summary

	----- Actual -----		Projected
Fiscal Year End:	Dec-18	Dec-19	Dec-20
Revenue	4,580	4,720	5,367
Revenue, YoY%	-12.1%	3.1%	13.7%
Operating Income	331	652	618
Operating Margin %	7.2%	13.8%	11.5%
Net Income	220	520	423
Net Income Margin %	4.8%	11.0%	7.9%
Diluted EPS	1.74	4.05	3.29
Diluted EPS, YoY %	-44.4%	132.9%	-18.6%
Free Cash Flow (CFO-capex)	506	519	482
Free Cash Flow Margin %	11.0%	11.0%	9.0%

In Millions of USD (except for per share items)

Structure of the Leisure Industry   NEUTRAL

The leisure industry is composed of firms that span the cruise line business to those that make toys and children's products. The cruise business has grown significantly in recent years, but still remains relatively small compared to the overall vacation industry (including land-based destinations). Competition among toy companies is intensifying due to recent trends toward shorter toy life cycles, the increasing use of technology in toys, and the proliferation of electronic consumer products and video games. All industry participants compete for consumer discretionary income. We're neutral on the structure of the group.

Home Depot HD   FAIRLY VALUED

| | | Buying Index™ | 6 | Value Rating | ◯ |

Economic Castle	Estimated Fair Value	Fair Value Range	Investment Style	Sector	Industry
Very Attractive	$265.00	$212.00 - $318.00	MEGA-CAP CORE	Consumer Discretionary	Discretionary Spending

Home Depot has performed well in the face of the COVID-19 pandemic, assisted by its digital sales channels.

Stock Chart (weekly)

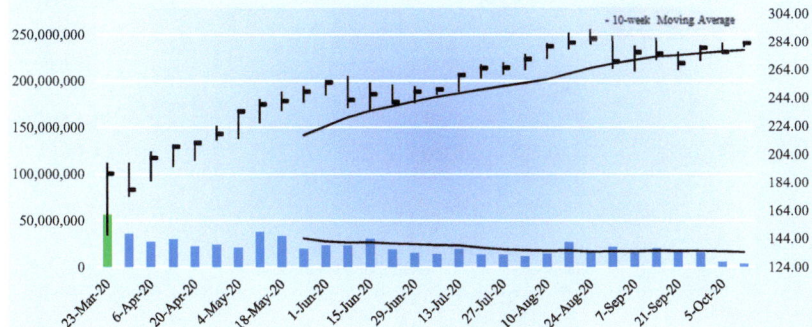

The week with the highest trading volume out of the last 30 weeks was a week of heavy selling, or distribution (red bar).

Company Vitals

Market Cap (USD)	$310,221
Avg Weekly Vol (30 wks)	21,497
30-week Range (USD)	46.33 - 292.95
Valuentum Sector	Consumer Discretionary
5-week Return	1.5%
13-week Return	9.2%
30-week Return	88.5%
Dividend Yield %	2.1%
Dividends per Share	6.00
Forward Dividend Payout Ratio	48.6%
Est. Normal Diluted EPS	15.54
P/E on Est. Normal Diluted EPS	18.2
Est. Normal EBITDA	24,002
Forward EV/EBITDA	16.6
EV/Est. Normal EBITDA	14.1
Forward Revenue Growth (5-yr)	4.6%
Forward EPS Growth (5-yr)	14.5%

NMF = Not Meaningful; Est. = Estimated; FY = Fiscal Year

Returns Summary

3-year Historical Average

Return on Equity	-1799.2%
Return on Assets	22.8%
ROIC, with goodwill	46.5%
ROIC, without goodwill	50.7%

ROIC = Return on Invested Capital; NMF = Not Meaningful

Leverage, Coverage, and Liquidity

In Millions of USD

Total Debt	31,483
Net Debt	29,350
Total Debt/EBITDA	1.8
Net Debt/EBITDA	1.6
EBITDA/Interest	14.8
Current Ratio	1.1
Quick Ratio	0.2

NMF = Not Meaningful

Investment Highlights

• Home Depot is the world's largest home improvement specialty retailer. Its stores sell an assortment of building materials, home improvement and lawn/garden products. Its stores average ~104,000 square feet of enclosed space, with ~24,000 additional square feet of outside garden area. The company was founded in 1978 and is based in Atlanta, Georgia.

• Home Depot's financial performance depends in part on the stability of the housing, residential construction and home improvement markets, which have been resilient of late. However, these markets can and do experience wild swings over the course of a full economic cycle.

• Home Depot intends to spend ~$5.0 billion upgrading and renovating its stores, ~$2.5 billion on technology-related investments, and ~$1.2 billion on enhancing its supply chain over the coming fiscal years after announcing various initiatives in May 2020. The retailer has successfully grow its digital business of late and wants to expand on that success.

• Home Depot serves three primary customer groups: Do-It-Yourself customers, Do-It-For-Me customers, and professional customers (tradesmen). Home Depot plans to focus more on its professional customers, where average tickets are substantially larger. Providing recurring MRO needs is among its core initiatives in this area.

• Home Depot's impressive financial performance of late, specifically its strong free cash flow generation, has allowed it to raise its dividend in a big way. The company is navigating the COVID-19 crisis quite well.

Investment Considerations

DCF Valuation	FAIRLY VALUED
Relative Valuation	NEUTRAL
ValueCreation™	EXCELLENT
ValueRisk™	LOW
ValueTrend™	NEGATIVE
Cash Flow Generation	STRONG
Financial Leverage	MEDIUM
Growth	MODEST
Technical Evaluation	BULLISH
Relative Strength	WEAK
Money Flow Index (MFI)	NEUTRAL
Upside/Downside Volume (U/D)	DETERIORATING
Near-term Technical Support, 10-week MA	278.00

DCF = Discounted Cash Flow; MFI, U/D = Please see glossary. MA = Moving Average

Business Quality

ValueRisk™	ValueCreation™ Very Poor	Poor	Good	Excellent
Low				▓
Medium				
High				
Very High				

Firms that generate economic profits with little operating variability score near the top right of the matrix.

Relative Valuation

	Forward P/E	PEG	Price / FV
Disney	75.6	0.3	98.3%
McDonald's	38.5	1.1	111.0%
Nike	52.8	2.5	104.9%
Starbucks	92.2	0.6	110.6%
Peer Median	64.2	0.8	107.7%
Home Depot	**22.9**	**1.9**	**106.7%**

Price / FV = Current Stock Price divided by Estimated Fair Value

Financial Summary

	----- Actual -----		Projected
Fiscal Year End:	Jan-19	Jan-20	Jan-21
Revenue	108,203	110,225	124,775
Revenue, YoY%	7.2%	1.9%	13.2%
Operating Income	15,777	15,843	18,221
Operating Margin %	14.6%	14.4%	14.6%
Net Income	11,121	11,242	13,275
Net Income Margin %	10.3%	10.2%	10.6%
Diluted EPS	9.73	10.25	12.35
Diluted EPS, YoY %	33.5%	5.3%	20.5%
Free Cash Flow (CFO-capex)	10,596	11,045	13,189
Free Cash Flow Margin %	9.8%	10.0%	10.6%

In Millions of USD (except for per share items)

Structure of the Specialty Retailers Industry   NEUTRAL

The specialty retail segment is fragmented, highly competitive, and economically-sensitive. The group covers a broad array of businesses and is dominated by retailers with large brick-and-mortar store footprints. Though some constituents may be insulated from e-commerce competition, others risk obsolescence as product distribution moves to digital means, and online retailers offer lower prices for identical goods and services. We're fairly neutral on the structure of the industry, though some constituents will inevitably face secular and permanent declines.

VALUENTUM

Honeywell HON   FAIRLY VALUED

			Buying Index™	5	Value Rating	●

Economic Castle	Estimated Fair Value	Fair Value Range	Investment Style	Sector	Industry
Very Attractive	$202.00	$162.00 - $242.00	LARGE-CAP CORE	Industrials	Industrial Leaders

Honeywell's massive installed base and large services business offer considerable competitive advantages.

Stock Chart (weekly)

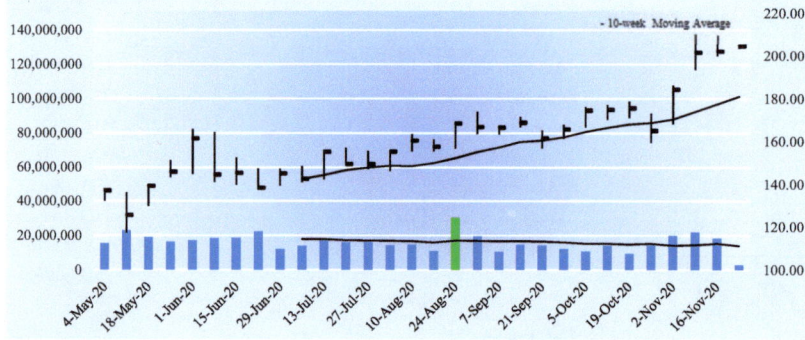

The week with the highest trading volume out of the last 30 weeks was a week of heavy selling, or distribution (red bar).

Investment Considerations

DCF Valuation	FAIRLY VALUED
Relative Valuation	NEUTRAL
ValueCreation™	EXCELLENT
ValueRisk™	LOW
ValueTrend™	POSITIVE
Cash Flow Generation	STRONG
Financial Leverage	MEDIUM
Growth	MODEST
Technical Evaluation	NEUTRAL
Relative Strength	STRONG
Money Flow Index (MFI)	OVERBOUGHT
Upside/Downside Volume (U/D)	BULLISH
Near-term Technical Support, 10-week MA	181.00

DCF = Discounted Cash Flow; MFI, U/D = Please see glossary. MA = Moving Average

Company Vitals

Market Cap (USD)	$149,384
Avg Weekly Vol (30 wks)	16,010
30-week Range (USD)	117.11 - 210.00
Valuentum Sector	Industrials
5-week Return	18.1%
13-week Return	21.4%
30-week Return	52.8%
Dividend Yield %	1.8%
Dividends per Share	3.72
Forward Dividend Payout Ratio	52.4%
Est. Normal Diluted EPS	9.58
P/E on Est. Normal Diluted EPS	21.4
Est. Normal EBITDA	9,934
Forward EV/EBITDA	20.0
EV/Est. Normal EBITDA	15.6
Forward Revenue Growth (5-yr)	1.9%
Forward EPS Growth (5-yr)	7.3%

NMF = Not Meaningful; Est. = Estimated; FY = Fiscal Year

Returns Summary
3-year Historical Average

Return on Equity	27.1%
Return on Assets	8.4%
ROIC, with goodwill	22.4%
ROIC, without goodwill	55.8%

ROIC = Return on Invested Capital; NMF = Not Meaningful

Leverage, Coverage, and Liquidity
In Millions of USD

Total Debt	16,002
Net Debt	5,586
Total Debt/EBITDA	1.8
Net Debt/EBITDA	0.6
EBITDA/Interest	25.2
Current Ratio	1.3
Quick Ratio	1.0

NMF = Not Meaningful

Investment Highlights

• Honeywell operates in four segments: Aerospace, Building Technologies, Performance Materials and Technologies, and Safety and Productivity Solutions. Its aerospace products are used on virtually every aircraft, and its personal protection equipment has been in huge demand due to COVID-19. The firm was founded in 1920 and is based in New Jersey.

• Honeywell generates nice normalized margins. Its 'Performance Materials and Technology' segment boasts its highest profit margins in the low- to mid-20% range, followed by its 'Aerospace' segment in the low 20% range. It is working to optimize fixed costs in its manufacturing and logistics facilities.

• Long term, Honeywell expects strength across is major end markets including commercial aviation, defense, and process automation, which will be driven by flight hours growth, robust defense budgets, and warehouse building. The COVID-19 pandemic will pose challenges, but we like this industrial powerhouse.

• Honeywell's long-term financial targets include 3%-5% annual organic sales growth, 30-50 basis points of margin expansion per year, EPS growth greater than peers, a cash conversion rate greater than 100%, and the maintenance of investment grade credit ratings. Management is also targeting dividend growth in-line with earnings growth.

• In addition to its highly-respected brand name, the company's massive installed base and large services business offer considerable competitive advantages. Its recurring software sales have also been growing at a nice double-digit clip.

Business Quality
ValueCreation™

ValueRisk™	Very Poor	Poor	Good	Excellent
Low				■
Medium				
High				
Very High				

Firms that generate economic profits with little operating variability score near the top right of the matrix.

Relative Valuation

	Forward P/E	PEG	Price / FV
Danaher	36.3	3.0	121.5%
Lockheed Martin	15.0	2.3	96.3%
Union Pacific	25.9	1.4	119.1%
United Parcel Service	22.0	1.4	124.5%
Peer Median	23.9	1.9	120.3%
Honeywell	28.8	1.7	101.3%

Price / FV = Current Stock Price divided by Estimated Fair Value

Financial Summary

	----- Actual -----		Projected
Fiscal Year End:	Dec-18	Dec-19	Dec-20
Revenue	41,802	36,709	32,157
Revenue, YoY%	3.1%	-12.2%	-12.4%
Operating Income	6,705	7,916	6,754
Operating Margin %	16.0%	21.6%	21.0%
Net Income	6,765	6,143	5,159
Net Income Margin %	16.2%	16.7%	16.0%
Diluted EPS	8.98	8.41	7.10
Diluted EPS, YoY %	349.0%	-6.4%	-15.6%
Free Cash Flow (CFO-capex)	5,606	6,058	4,522
Free Cash Flow Margin %	13.4%	16.5%	14.1%

In Millions of USD (except for per share items)

Structure of the Conglomerates Industry   GOOD

The industrial conglomerate industry is characterized by firms that operate various business lines on a global scale. Demand for industrial products tends to be cyclical in nature, and most firms couple their manufacturing operations with generally more stable services businesses to mitigate fundamental volatility. Firms tend to have bargaining power over suppliers due to industry dominance and boast substantial resources to adapt to changing conditions or competitive threats. Most sell products under powerful and recognizable brand names and look to emerging markets for future growth. We like the group.

VALUENTUM

Hormel Foods HRL   FAIRLY VALUED

Buying Index™   6   Value Rating   🟡

Economic Castle	Estimated Fair Value	Fair Value Range	Investment Style	Sector	Industry
Attractive	$44.00	$35.00 - $53.00	LARGE-CAP CORE	Consumer Staples	Recession Resistant

So far, Hormel has done a solid job navigating the storm caused by the COVID-19 pandemic.

Stock Chart (weekly)

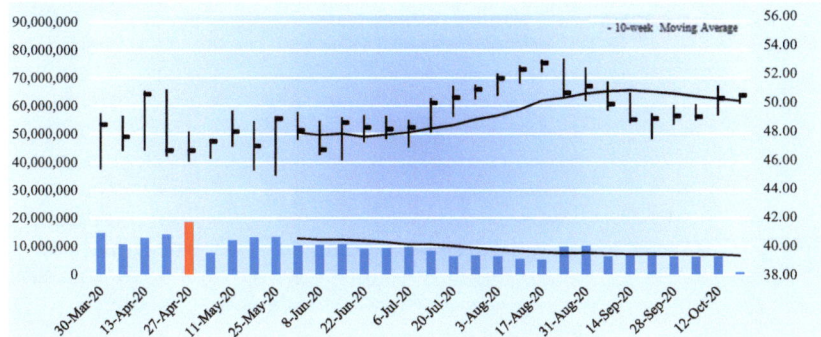

The week with the highest trading volume out of the last 30 weeks was a week of heavy selling, or distribution (red bar).

Company Vitals

Market Cap (USD)	$27,538
Avg Weekly Vol (30 wks)	9,200
30-week Range (USD)	44.90 - 52.97
Valuentum Sector	Consumer Staples
5-week Return	4.0%
13-week Return	0.1%
30-week Return	10.3%
Dividend Yield %	1.8%
Dividends per Share	0.93
Forward Dividend Payout Ratio	55.1%
Est. Normal Diluted EPS	2.37
P/E on Est. Normal Diluted EPS	21.2
Est. Normal EBITDA	1,731
Forward EV/EBITDA	21.3
EV/Est. Normal EBITDA	15.7
Forward Revenue Growth (5-yr)	3.6%
Forward EPS Growth (5-yr)	13.0%

NMF = Not Meaningful; Est. = Estimated; FY = Fiscal Year

Returns Summary
3-year Historical Average

Return on Equity	18.1%
Return on Assets	12.7%
ROIC, with goodwill	19.4%
ROIC, without goodwill	34.6%

ROIC = Return on Invested Capital; NMF = Not Meaningful

Leverage, Coverage, and Liquidity
In Millions of USD

Total Debt	250
Net Debt	-438
Total Debt/EBITDA	0.2
Net Debt/EBITDA	NMF
EBITDA/Interest	73.4
Current Ratio	2.1
Quick Ratio	1.2

NMF = Not Meaningful

Investment Highlights

• Hormel is primarily engaged in the production of a variety of meat and food products and the marketing of those products. Pork and turkey remain the major raw materials for its products. It owns the Skippy peanut butter brand, and the Jenny-O turkey store; the SPAM family of products and Hormel pepperoni and party trays are common offerings as well.

• Hormel has posted 50+ years of consecutive dividend increases. Management has made maintaining Hormel's listing as a Dividend Aristocrat a priority. The company boasts 'A-rated' credit ratings and had a net cash position at the end of FY2019.

• More than 30 brands have #1 or #2 market share positions in their respective categories from grocery products and refrigerated foods to the Jennie-O turkey store. During the initial stages of the COVID-19 pandemic, Hormel's financial performance proved resilient, though the firm has had to contend with significant incremental supply chain expenses.

• Hormel withdrew its FY2020 sales and earnings guidance due to COVID-19 and spent heavily in FY2020 to deal with the pandemic. Elevated levels of worker callouts slowed down operations at some of its plants and reduced capacity, though management expects these hurdles will be short-term in nature.

• Please be aware that our cash flow models assume significant operating margin expansion, supported by cost control measures, and decent revenue growth, supported by organic sales growth and acquisitions, at Hormel over the coming fiscal years.

Investment Considerations

DCF Valuation	FAIRLY VALUED
Relative Valuation	NEUTRAL
ValueCreation™	EXCELLENT
ValueRisk™	LOW
ValueTrend™	NEGATIVE
Cash Flow Generation	STRONG
Financial Leverage	LOW
Growth	MODEST
Technical Evaluation	VERY BULLISH
Relative Strength	WEAK
Money Flow Index (MFI)	NEUTRAL
Upside/Downside Volume (U/D)	BULLISH
Near-term Technical Support, 10-week MA	50.00

DCF = Discounted Cash Flow; MFI, U/D = Please see glossary. MA = Moving Average

Business Quality

ValueRisk™	ValueCreation™			
	Very Poor	Poor	Good	Excellent
Low				■
Medium				
High				
Very High				

Firms that generate economic profits with little operating variability score near the top right of the matrix.

Relative Valuation

	Forward P/E	PEG	Price / FV
Coca-Cola	34.3	1.5	128.0%
Procter & Gamble	26.5	3.3	144.1%
Philip Morris	15.4	2.4	104.3%
Wal-Mart	26.8	2.3	130.2%
Peer Median	26.7	2.4	129.1%
Hormel Foods	**29.9**	**1.5**	**114.6%**

Price / FV = Current Stock Price divided by Estimated Fair Value

Financial Summary

	----- Actual -----		Projected
Fiscal Year End:	Oct-18	Oct-19	Oct-20
Revenue	9,546	9,497	9,772
Revenue, YoY%	4.1%	-0.5%	2.9%
Operating Income	1,157	1,157	1,102
Operating Margin %	12.1%	12.2%	11.3%
Net Income	1,012	979	921
Net Income Margin %	10.6%	10.3%	9.4%
Diluted EPS	1.86	1.80	1.69
Diluted EPS, YoY %	18.5%	-3.5%	-6.1%
Free Cash Flow (CFO-capex)	852	629	770
Free Cash Flow Margin %	8.9%	6.6%	7.9%

In Millions of USD (except for per share items)

Structure of the Food Products Industry   NEUTRAL

The food products industry is composed of a number of firms with strong brand names. However, market supply/demand dynamics and intense competition still impact product prices, while fluctuations in commodity costs can make earnings quite volatile. Private-label competition, competitors' promotional spending, and changing consumer preferences often drive demand trends. The group's customers—such as supermarkets, warehouses, and food distributors—continue to consolidate, increasing buying power over constituents and hurting margins. Still, we're generally neutral on the group.

IntercontinentalExchange ICE   FAIRLY VALUED

Buying Index™   **7**   **Value Rating** ⬤

Economic Castle	Estimated Fair Value	Fair Value Range	Investment Style	Sector	Industry
Attractive	$100.00	$80.00 - $120.00	LARGE-CAP GROWTH	Next Generation	Disruptive Innovation

Intercontinental Exchange's acquisitive behavior and weakening balance sheet have given us pause.

Stock Chart (weekly)

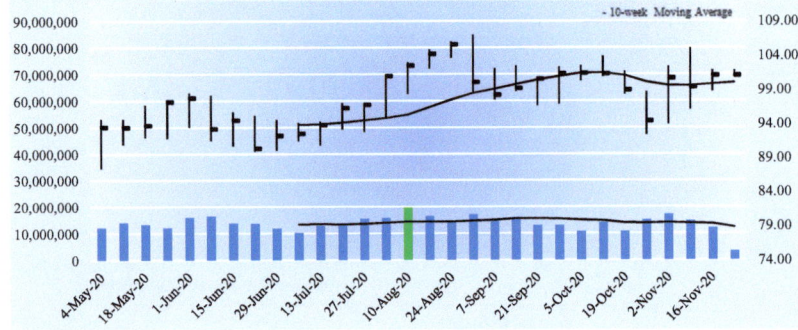

The week with the highest trading volume out of the last 30 weeks was a week of heavy selling, or distribution (red bar).

Investment Considerations

DCF Valuation	**FAIRLY VALUED**
Relative Valuation	**ATTRACTIVE**
ValueCreation™	**EXCELLENT**
ValueRisk™	**LOW**
ValueTrend™	**POSITIVE**
Cash Flow Generation	**STRONG**
Financial Leverage	**MEDIUM**
Growth	**HIGH**
Technical Evaluation	**VERY BULLISH**
Relative Strength	**WEAK**
Money Flow Index (MFI)	**NEUTRAL**
Upside/Downside Volume (U/D)	**DETERIORATING**
Near-term Technical Support, 10-week MA	**100.00**

DCF = Discounted Cash Flow; MFI, U/D = Please see glossary. MA = Moving Average

Company Vitals

Market Cap (USD)	$57,099
Avg Weekly Vol (30 wks)	13,759
30-week Range (USD)	87.51 - 106.99
Valuentum Sector	Next Generation
5-week Return	3.1%
13-week Return	-4.4%
30-week Return	14.6%
Dividend Yield %	1.2%
Dividends per Share	1.20
Forward Dividend Payout Ratio	26.6%
Est. Normal Diluted EPS	5.76
P/E on Est. Normal Diluted EPS	17.6
Est. Normal EBITDA	5,083
Forward EV/EBITDA	15.2
EV/Est. Normal EBITDA	12.4
Forward Revenue Growth (5-yr)	10.6%
Forward EPS Growth (5-yr)	16.3%

NMF = Not Meaningful; Est. = Estimated; FY = Fiscal Year

Returns Summary   3-year Historical Average

Return on Equity	12.9%
Return on Assets	2.5%
ROIC, with goodwill	9.2%
ROIC, without goodwill	19.3%

ROIC = Return on Invested Capital; NMF = Not Meaningful

Leverage, Coverage, and Liquidity

In Millions of USD

Total Debt	7,819
Net Debt	6,035
Total Debt/EBITDA	2.3
Net Debt/EBITDA	1.8
EBITDA/Interest	11.7
Current Ratio	1.0
Quick Ratio	0.0

NMF = Not Meaningful

Investment Highlights

• IntercontinentalExchange is a leading operator of regulated global markets and clearing houses, including futures exchanges, over-the-counter markets, derivatives clearing houses and post-trade services. The company's revenue has expanded at a double-digit CAGR since 2006. It was founded in 2000 and is headquartered in Atlanta, Georgia.

• Revenue in its 'Trading and Clearing' segment comes from fees on futures/options in energy, agricultural, metals, financials, fixed income/credit, and cash equities/options. Its 'Data and Listing' segment provides data/listing services.

• Intercontinental Exchange expanded into the mortgage services market with its full acquisitions of MERS (2018) and Simplifile (2019), and then further increased its exposure to this area with its September 2020 buyout of Ellie Mae, a cloud-based platform serving the mortgage finance industry. We're not entirely excited about ICE's new strategic direction.

• In light of its acquisition frenzy and move to acquire Ellie Mae, Intercontinental Exchange now has a meaningful leverage position, with billions in net debt (inclusive of short-term debt) and an adjusted debt-to-EBITDA measure of 4.2x at the end of the third quarter of 2020.

• The increased leverage is concerning, but ICE has a good track record, and it has put up impressive GAAP operating margins consistently north of 50% in recent years. We also like the company's free cash flow generating capacity.

Business Quality   ValueCreation™

ValueRisk™	Very Poor	Poor	Good	Excellent
Low				▨
Medium				
High				
Very High				

Firms that generate economic profits with little operating variability score near the top right of the matrix.

Relative Valuation

	Forward P/E	PEG	Price / FV
Wayfair	56.3	NMF	84.2%
Zoom Video	170.7	28.8	120.8%
Roku	-338.4	NMF	96.0%
Monster Beverage	36.0	2.9	104.4%
Peer Median	46.1	15.9	100.2%
IntercontinentalExchange	**22.4**	**1.8**	**101.1%**

Price / FV = Current Stock Price divided by Estimated Fair Value

Financial Summary

		----- Actual -----		Projected
Fiscal Year End:		Dec-18	Dec-19	Dec-20
Revenue		6,276	6,547	7,457
Revenue, YoY%		7.6%	4.3%	13.9%
Operating Income		2,617	2,673	3,433
Operating Margin %		41.7%	40.8%	46.0%
Net Income		1,988	1,933	2,520
Net Income Margin %		31.7%	29.5%	33.8%
Diluted EPS		3.43	3.42	4.50
Diluted EPS, YoY %		-18.9%	-0.4%	31.7%
Free Cash Flow (CFO-capex)		2,253	2,354	2,907
Free Cash Flow Margin %		35.9%	36.0%	39.0%

In Millions of USD (except for per share items)

Structure of the Exchanges Industry   GOOD

The exchanges industry consists of firms that deliver trading, clearing, exchange technology, and regulatory securities listing. Industry constituents operate some of the most well-known exchanges including the NASDAQ, Chicago Board Options Exchange, and the Chicago Mercantile Exchange. Firms carve out competitive advantages via scale (operating the largest market for a given financial instrument) and via technological superiority (transaction speeds and reliability). The securities markets are intensely competitive, but new entrants tend to have limited liquidity/capability. We like the industry structure.

Intuitive Surgical ISRG   FAIRLY VALUED

				Buying Index™ 6		***Value Rating***	⊙

Economic Castle	Estimated Fair Value	Fair Value Range	Investment Style	Sector	Industry
Very Attractive	$632.00	$442.00 - $822.00	LARGE-CAP GROWTH	Health Care	Health Care Bellwethers

We've increased our fair value estimate for Intuitive Surgical. We caution that the COVID-19 pandemic is a significant headwind for the firm.

Stock Chart (weekly)

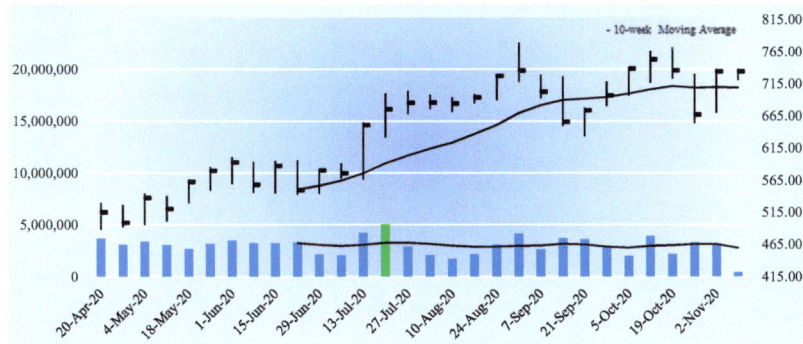

The week with the highest trading volume out of the last 30 weeks was a week of heavy selling, or distribution (red bar).

Investment Considerations

DCF Valuation	**FAIRLY VALUED**
Relative Valuation	**UNATTRACTIVE**
ValueCreation™	**EXCELLENT**
ValueRisk™	**MEDIUM**
ValueTrend™	**NEGATIVE**
Cash Flow Generation	**STRONG**
Financial Leverage	**LOW**
Growth	**HIGH**
Technical Evaluation	**BULLISH**
Relative Strength	**WEAK**
Money Flow Index (MFI)	**NEUTRAL**
Upside/Downside Volume (U/D)	**DETERIORATING**
Near-term Technical Support, 10-week MA	**709.00**

DCF = Discounted Cash Flow; MFI, U/D = Please see glossary. MA = Moving Average

Company Vitals

Market Cap (USD)	$87,697
Avg Weekly Vol (30 wks)	2,969
30-week Range (USD)	488.00 - 778.83
Valuentum Sector	Health Care
5-week Return	-2.0%
13-week Return	7.1%
30-week Return	40.2%
Dividend Yield %	0.0%
Dividends per Share	0.00
Forward Dividend Payout Ratio	0.0%
Est. Normal Diluted EPS	17.91
P/E on Est. Normal Diluted EPS	41.0
Est. Normal EBITDA	2,687
Forward EV/EBITDA	55.3
EV/Est. Normal EBITDA	31.4
Forward Revenue Growth (5-yr)	10.7%
Forward EPS Growth (5-yr)	18.4%

NMF = Not Meaningful; Est. = Estimated; FY = Fiscal Year

Returns Summary
3-year Historical Average

Return on Equity	17.5%
Return on Assets	14.8%
ROIC, with goodwill	72.2%
ROIC, without goodwill	85.5%

ROIC = Return on Invested Capital; NMF = Not Meaningful

Leverage, Coverage, and Liquidity
In Millions of USD

Total Debt	0
Net Debt	-3,222
Total Debt/EBITDA	0.0
Net Debt/EBITDA	NMF
EBITDA/Interest	Excellent
Current Ratio	4.5
Quick Ratio	3.8

NMF = Not Meaningful

Investment Highlights

- Intuitive Surgical is a leader in the field of robotic-assisted minimally invasive surgery. Since it shipped its first da Vinci System, Intuitive Surgical has expanded its installed base to more than 5,850 sites. The company underwent a 3-for-1 stock split in 2017. It was founded in 1995 and is headquartered in Sunnyvale, California.

- Our forecasts assume Intuitive Surgical continues to grow its installed base at a decent clip over the coming years, which in turn underpins our expectations that the company keeps growing its revenues by double-digits annually going forward.

- The clinical benefits of da Vinci prostatectomy and hysterectomy versus open surgery are many, including shorter hospital stays and less blood loss. Growth in the number of da Vinci surgeries for both procedures has been exponential. New da Vinci Xi Surgical System products continue to be developed, offering a growing market and up-selling opportunities for the firm.

- Intuitive Surgical continues to grow the installed base of its new Ion system, a robotic-assisted minimally invasive biopsy platform. As of the third quarter of 2020, Intuitive Surgical's installed Ion system base stood at over 30. The COVID-19 pandemic has created headwinds on this front.

- Utilization rates of Intuitive Surgical's da Vinci systems have been negatively impacted by the COVID-19 pandemic and should future waves of infections shut down global economies, that would pose serious short-term headwinds for the firm.

Business Quality

ValueRisk™	Very Poor	Poor	Good	Excellent
Low				
Medium				▓
High				
Very High				

ValueCreation™

Firms that generate economic profits with little operating variability score near the top right of the matrix.

Relative Valuation

	Forward P/E	PEG	Price / FV
Johnson & Johnson	17.6	1.8	99.5%
Medtronic	25.6	2.2	109.0%
Merck	21.5	2.2	100.5%
Pfizer	20.1	0.8	93.3%
Peer Median	20.8	2.0	100.0%
Intuitive Surgical	**75.0**	**2.2**	**116.1%**

Price / FV = Current Stock Price divided by Estimated Fair Value

Financial Summary

	----- Actual -----		Projected
Fiscal Year End:	Dec-18	Dec-19	Dec-20
Revenue	3,724	4,479	4,291
Revenue, YoY%	19.0%	20.3%	-4.2%
Operating Income	1,199	1,375	1,332
Operating Margin %	32.2%	30.7%	31.1%
Net Income	1,128	1,379	1,170
Net Income Margin %	30.3%	30.8%	27.3%
Diluted EPS	9.49	11.54	9.79
Diluted EPS, YoY %	48.2%	21.5%	-15.2%
Free Cash Flow (CFO-capex)	982	1,172	1,220
Free Cash Flow Margin %	26.4%	26.2%	28.4%

In Millions of USD (except for per share items)

Structure of the Medical Devices Industry   GOOD

The medical devices industry is heavily regulated and characterized by rapid technological change. Firms have been forced to compete on price due to economically-motivated buyers, consolidation among healthcare providers, and declining reimbursement rates. Healthcare reform measures have put additional pressure on procedure rates and market sizes. Still, firms can gain advantages by developing products with differentiated clinical outcomes or by creating patent-protected technology. Since most constituents hold important patents or trade secrets, we tend to like the group.

JD.com JD   FAIRLY VALUED

Buying Index™ 6   **Value Rating** 🟡

Economic Castle	Estimated Fair Value	Fair Value Range	Investment Style	Sector	Industry
Attractive	$93.00	$70.00 - $116.00	LARGE-CAP BLEND	Next Generation	Disruptive Innovation

JD.com is the leading e-commerce company in China. It continues to invest in supply chain-based technology and infrastructure to further support its strong top-line growth trajectory. Free cash flow generation is impressive.

Stock Chart (weekly)

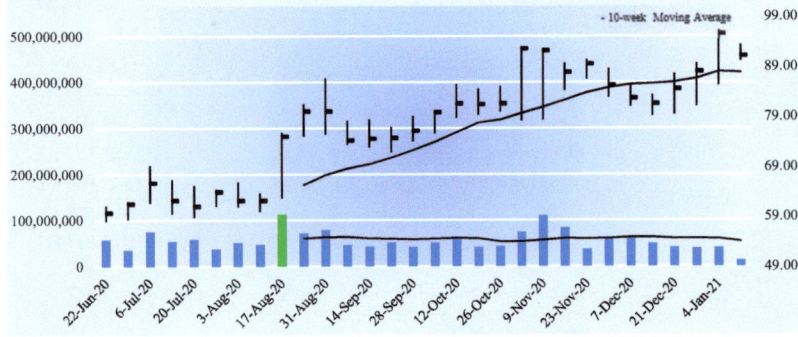

The week with the highest trading volume out of the last 30 weeks was a week of heavy selling, or distribution (red bar).

Investment Considerations

DCF Valuation	**FAIRLY VALUED**
Relative Valuation	**NEUTRAL**
ValueCreation™	**GOOD**
ValueRisk™	**MEDIUM**
ValueTrend™	**NEGATIVE**
Cash Flow Generation	**MEDIUM**
Financial Leverage	**MEDIUM**
Growth	**AGGRESSIVE**
Technical Evaluation	**BULLISH**
Relative Strength	**STRONG**
Money Flow Index (MFI)	**NEUTRAL**
Upside/Downside Volume (U/D)	**BEARISH**
Near-term Technical Support, 10-week MA	**88.00**

DCF = Discounted Cash Flow; MFI; U/D = Please see glossary. MA = Moving Average

Company Vitals

Market Cap (USD)	$133,086
Avg Weekly Vol (30 wks)	55,611
30-week Range (USD)	57.94 - 96.20
Valuentum Sector	Next Generation
5-week Return	11.7%
13-week Return	11.0%
30-week Return	53.9%
Dividend Yield %	0.0%
Dividends per Share	0.00
Forward Dividend Payout Ratio	0.0%
Est. Normal Diluted EPS	3.41
P/E on Est. Normal Diluted EPS	26.7
Est. Normal EBITDA	7,871
Forward EV/EBITDA	30.0
EV/Est. Normal EBITDA	15.9
Forward Revenue Growth (5-yr)	21.4%
Forward EPS Growth (5-yr)	35.8%

NMF = Not Meaningful; Est. = Estimated; FY = Fiscal Year

Returns Summary

	3-year Historical Average
Return on Equity	3.9%
Return on Assets	1.2%
ROIC, with goodwill	12.1%
ROIC, without goodwill	13.1%

ROIC = Return on Invested Capital; NMF = Not Meaningful

Leverage, Coverage, and Liquidity

In Millions of USD

Total Debt	1,444
Net Debt	-7,823
Total Debt/EBITDA	0.9
Net Debt/EBITDA	NMF
EBITDA/Interest	15.1
Current Ratio	1.0
Quick Ratio	0.5

NMF = Not Meaningful

Investment Highlights

• JD.com is China's largest e-commerce company and its biggest retailer by revenue. Its goal is to offer an enjoyable online experience through its content-rich and user-friendly website and mobile apps. The company has its own fulfillment infrastructure in China, supporting both online direct sales and online marketplace businesses. Electronics and home appliance sales account for about half of revenue.

• In 2015, JD.com opened its first US facility, an R&D center in Silicon Valley. It allows for easier interactions between the company and US retailers, partners, as well as brands seeking to expand their presence in China. Subscribers of JD Plus surpassed 20 million in October 2020.

• Though explosive growth at JD.com is anticipated to continue, there are risks associated with the pace of economic growth in China. The fragmented Chinese retail market provides ongoing opportunity, however. China's online retail penetration has grown to 15%-20% in recent years compared to ~6% in 2012. Annual active customer accounts totaled 441.6 million in September 2020, up 30%+ year over year.

• In ten years, JD.com plans to have revenue split 50/50 between domestic and foreign markets. It plans to take on Amazon in the US, a bold yet risky strategy. Significant investments are being made in its logistics segment, but this may not prove to be a sustainable competitive advantage over Amazon. Impressive growth continues in any case.

• JD.com expects international momentum to blossom, and this should enable the firm to attract world-class products. Multiple luxury and fashion brands recently launched stores on JD.com, for example. Headline risk related to US-China relations could create a volatile environment for shares.

Business Quality

ValueRisk™	Very Poor	Poor	Good	Excellent
Low				
Medium			■	
High				
Very High				

Firms that generate economic profits with little operating variability score near the top right of the matrix.

Relative Valuation

	Forward P/E	PEG	Price / FV
Wayfair	56.3	NMF	84.2%
Zoom Video	170.7	28.8	120.8%
Roku	-338.4	NMF	96.0%
Monster Beverage	36.0	2.9	104.4%
Peer Median	46.1	15.9	100.2%
JD.com	**54.3**	**2.2**	**97.9%**

Price / FV = Current Stock Price divided by Estimated Fair Value

Financial Summary

	----- Actual -----		Projected
Fiscal Year End:	Dec-18	Dec-19	Dec-20
Revenue	67,198	82,865	115,099
Revenue, YoY%	20.7%	23.3%	38.9%
Operating Income	-381	734	3,010
Operating Margin %	-0.6%	0.9%	2.6%
Net Income	-362	1,708	2,476
Net Income Margin %	-0.5%	2.1%	2.2%
Diluted EPS	-0.25	1.17	1.68
Diluted EPS, YoY %	NMF	NMF	NMF
Free Cash Flow (CFO-capex)	549	2,267	4,445
Free Cash Flow Margin %	0.8%	2.7%	3.9%

In Millions of USD (except for per share items)

Structure of the Internet Software & Services Industry   **NEUTRAL**

The Internet software/services industry is composed of a variety of companies with rapidly-changing business models. Most focus on improving the ways people connect with information, either via Internet search or by social media platforms, and generate revenue primarily by delivering cost-effective online advertising. Constituents earn significant returns on invested capital due to their capital-light operations, though competition remains fierce. We expect most companies in this group to look substantially different 10 years from now than they do today. Overall, we're neutral on the structure.

Johnson & Johnson JNJ   FAIRLY VALUED

Buying Index™ 4   **Value Rating** ⬤

Economic Castle	Estimated Fair Value	Fair Value Range	Investment Style	Sector	Industry
Attractive	$143.00	$114.00 - $172.00	MEGA-CAP VALUE	Health Care	Health Care Bellwethers

J&J's financials have held up well in the face of the COVID-19 pandemic, and the firm is actively working on developing a COVID-19 vaccine.

Stock Chart (weekly)

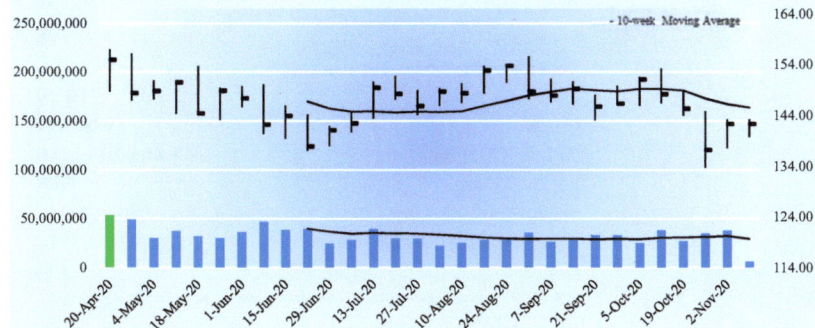

The week with the highest trading volume out of the last 30 weeks was a week of heavy selling, or distribution (red bar).

Investment Considerations

DCF Valuation	FAIRLY VALUED
Relative Valuation	ATTRACTIVE
ValueCreation™	EXCELLENT
ValueRisk™	LOW
ValueTrend™	NEGATIVE
Cash Flow Generation	STRONG
Financial Leverage	LOW
Growth	MODEST
Technical Evaluation	BEARISH
Relative Strength	WEAK
Money Flow Index (MFI)	NEUTRAL
Upside/Downside Volume (U/D)	BEARISH
Near-term Technical Resistance, 10-wk MA	145.00

DCF = Discounted Cash Flow; MFI, U/D = Please see glossary. MA = Moving Average

Company Vitals

Market Cap (USD)	$381,842
Avg Weekly Vol (30 wks)	32,415
30-week Range (USD)	133.64 - 157.00
Valuentum Sector	Health Care
5-week Return	-6.2%
13-week Return	-4.1%
30-week Return	-5.8%
Dividend Yield %	2.8%
Dividends per Share	4.04
Forward Dividend Payout Ratio	49.9%
Est. Normal Diluted EPS	9.60
P/E on Est. Normal Diluted EPS	14.8
Est. Normal EBITDA	37,494
Forward EV/EBITDA	12.0
EV/Est. Normal EBITDA	10.4
Forward Revenue Growth (5-yr)	3.6%
Forward EPS Growth (5-yr)	14.0%

NMF = Not Meaningful; Est. = Estimated; FY = Fiscal Year

Returns Summary

3-year Historical Average

Return on Equity	17.6%
Return on Assets	6.8%
ROIC, with goodwill	20.5%
ROIC, without goodwill	29.6%

ROIC = Return on Invested Capital; NMF = Not Meaningful

Leverage, Coverage, and Liquidity

In Millions of USD

Total Debt	27,696
Net Debt	8,409
Total Debt/EBITDA	1.0
Net Debt/EBITDA	0.3
EBITDA/Interest	85.2
Current Ratio	1.3
Quick Ratio	0.9

NMF = Not Meaningful

Investment Highlights

• J&J has built one of the most comprehensive health care businesses. The firm's three core business operating segments are as follows: Consumer Health, Pharmaceuticals, and Medical Devices. Its Pharmaceuticals segment generates about half of its annual revenues. The company was founded in 1885 and is headquartered in New Brunswick, New Jersey.

• J&J is actively working on developing a COVID-19 vaccine. In the event it gets approved by regulators, we do not expect the vaccine to generate needle-moving revenue as it will be sold on a not-for-profit basis. However, it would earn J&J goodwill worldwide.

• J&J's pharma portfolio is impressive. STELARA (exclusivity through 2023 in US) and SIMPONI (exclusivity through 2024 in US) are key profit drivers. Biosimilars competition is accelerating, but J&J's Oncology division is growing at a tremendous pace. DARZALEX (treats certain types of blood cancer) has recently been gaining market share.

• J&J's Consumer Health segment is home to numerous top-tier brands including: TYLENOL, LISTERINE, BAND-AID, PEPCID, NEUTROGENA, NEOSPORIN, and ZYRTEC. Sales at its OTC, Oral Care, and Wound Care/Other divisions within its Consumer Health segment have performed well of late.

• J&J is a Dividend Aristocrat and has raised its dividend for 55+ years consecutive years. Its annual payout has advanced from just $0.43/share in 1997 to its current robust payout. J&J's dividend is supported by its robust free cash flow generating abilities.

Business Quality

ValueRisk™	Very Poor	Poor	Good	Excellent
Low				■
Medium				
High				
Very High				

ValueCreation™

Firms that generate economic profits with little operating variability score near the top right of the matrix.

Relative Valuation

	Forward P/E	PEG	Price / FV
Medtronic	25.6	2.2	109.0%
Abbott	34.1	2.2	110.0%
Merck	21.5	2.2	100.5%
Pfizer	20.1	0.8	93.3%
Peer Median	23.5	2.2	104.7%
Johnson & Johnson	**17.6**	**1.8**	**99.5%**

Price / FV = Current Stock Price divided by Estimated Fair Value

Financial Summary

	----- Actual -----		Projected
Fiscal Year End:	Dec-18	Dec-19	Dec-20
Revenue	81,581	82,059	81,813
Revenue, YoY%	6.7%	0.6%	-0.3%
Non-GAAP Operating Income	21,175	20,080	25,611
Non-GAAP EBIT %	26.0%	24.5%	31.3%
Non-GAAP Net Income	15,297	15,119	21,499
Non-GAAP NI Margin %	18.8%	18.4%	26.3%
Non-GAAP Diluted EPS	5.61	5.63	8.09
Non-GAAP Dil EPS, YoY %	1083.9%	0.5%	NMF
Non-GAAP FCF (CFO-capex)	18,531	19,918	17,735
Non-GAAP FCF Margin %	22.7%	24.3%	21.7%

In Millions of USD (except for per share items)

Structure of the Household Products Industry   GOOD

Firms in the household products industry sell some of the most recognized branded consumer packaged goods in the world and often hold a significant market share position in a variety of product categories. Though the industry is characterized by stiff competition from retailers' private-label brands, constituents tend to boast meaningful competitive advantages due to their brand strength/reputation and generate high returns on invested capital. Household products companies remain tied to the vicissitudes of consumer spending, but we tend to like the structure of the group.

Kellogg K OVERVALUED 0.3%

Buying Index™ 7 **Value Rating** ✕

Economic Castle	Estimated Fair Value	Fair Value Range	Investment Style	Sector	Industry
Attractive	$56.00	$45.00 - $67.00	LARGE-CAP CORE	Consumer Staples	Recession Resistant

Kellogg has aggressively improved its cost structure over the past several fiscal years, though we want to see if those improvements stick.

Stock Chart (weekly)

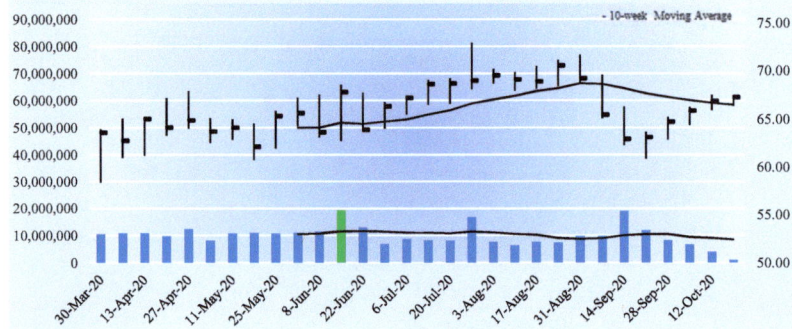

The week with the highest trading volume out of the last 30 weeks was a week of heavy selling, or distribution (red bar).

Company Vitals

Market Cap (USD)	$23,060
Avg Weekly Vol (30 wks)	9,898
30-week Range (USD)	58.36 - 72.87
Valuentum Sector	Consumer Staples
5-week Return	7.7%
13-week Return	-1.9%
30-week Return	11.3%
Dividend Yield %	3.4%
Dividends per Share	2.28
Forward Dividend Payout Ratio	57.3%
Est. Normal Diluted EPS	4.55
P/E on Est. Normal Diluted EPS	14.8
Est. Normal EBITDA	2,639
Forward EV/EBITDA	12.5
EV/Est. Normal EBITDA	11.6
Forward Revenue Growth (5-yr)	1.3%
Forward EPS Growth (5-yr)	14.2%

NMF = Not Meaningful; Est. = Estimated; FY = Fiscal Year

Returns Summary
3-year Historical Average

Return on Equity	48.5%
Return on Assets	6.8%
ROIC, with goodwill	10.7%
ROIC, without goodwill	21.6%

ROIC = Return on Invested Capital; NMF = Not Meaningful

Leverage, Coverage, and Liquidity
In Millions of USD

Total Debt	7,922
Net Debt	7,525
Total Debt/EBITDA	4.2
Net Debt/EBITDA	4.0
EBITDA/Interest	6.6
Current Ratio	0.7
Quick Ratio	0.4

NMF = Not Meaningful

Investment Highlights

• Kellogg has a number of iconic brands. Pop-Tarts is a great example and has an impressive 80%+ share in the toaster pastries market thanks to strong advertising and innovation efforts. Other brands include Kelloggs, Keebler, Cheez-It, Murray, Austin, and Famous Amos. More than 100 years ago, W.K. Kellogg founded the company, and it is based in Michigan.

• Kellogg's strategy is simple: win in breakfast and in emerging markets. Becoming a global snacks leader and growing frozen foods are other priorities. India, Brazil, and the Middle East offer large opportunities, as does the emerging global middle class at-large.

• Kellogg generated over 40% of its net sales outside the US in fiscal 2019. The company's business in West Africa has been performing well of late, supported by its stake in Multipro, a leading food product sales and distribution company, and its stake in Tolaram Africa Foods, a holding company that owns a large economic interest in an affiliated food manufacturer.

• Kellogg is investing in its brands and capabilities to return to consistent top-line growth. The firm is placing a greater focus on improving its analytics, digital, and e-commerce operations to better retain new and existing customers. Kellogg has been steadily overhauling and improving its packaging operations.

• At the end of fiscal 2019, Kellogg had completed 'Project K' which is expected to result in annualized cost savings of ~$700 million going forward. Kellogg's financial performance during the COVID-19 pandemic has held up relatively well so far.

Investment Considerations

DCF Valuation	OVERVALUED
Relative Valuation	ATTRACTIVE
ValueCreation™	EXCELLENT
ValueRisk™	LOW
ValueTrend™	NEGATIVE
Cash Flow Generation	STRONG
Financial Leverage	HIGH
Growth	MODEST
Technical Evaluation	VERY BULLISH
Relative Strength	WEAK
Money Flow Index (MFI)	NEUTRAL
Upside/Downside Volume (U/D)	DETERIORATING
Near-term Technical Support, 10-week MA	66.00

DCF = Discounted Cash Flow; MFI, U/D = Please see glossary. MA = Moving Average

Business Quality

ValueRisk™	Very Poor	Poor	Good	Excellent
Low				■
Medium				
High				
Very High				

ValueCreation™

Firms that generate economic profits with little operating variability score near the top right of the matrix.

Relative Valuation

	Forward P/E	PEG	Price / FV
Coca-Cola	34.3	1.5	128.0%
Procter & Gamble	26.5	3.3	144.1%
Philip Morris	15.4	2.4	104.3%
Wal-Mart	26.8	2.3	130.2%
Peer Median	26.7	2.4	129.1%
Kellogg	**16.9**	**1.7**	**120.1%**

Price / FV = Current Stock Price divided by Estimated Fair Value

Financial Summary

	----- Actual -----		Projected
Fiscal Year End:	Dec-18	Dec-19	Dec-20
Revenue	13,547	13,578	13,659
Revenue, YoY%	4.8%	0.2%	0.6%
Operating Income	1,706	1,401	1,952
Operating Margin %	12.6%	10.3%	14.3%
Net Income	1,140	960	1,351
Net Income Margin %	8.4%	7.1%	9.9%
Diluted EPS	3.28	2.80	3.98
Diluted EPS, YoY %	-9.6%	-14.6%	42.2%
Free Cash Flow (CFO-capex)	762	590	1,013
Free Cash Flow Margin %	5.6%	4.3%	7.4%

In Millions of USD (except for per share items)

Structure of the Food Products Industry
NEUTRAL

The food products industry is composed of a number of firms with strong brand names. However, market supply/demand dynamics and intense competition still impact product prices, while fluctuations in commodity costs can make earnings quite volatile. Private-label competition, competitors' promotional spending, and changing consumer preferences often drive demand trends. The group's customers—such as supermarkets, warehouses, and food distributors—continue to consolidate, increasing buying power over constituents and hurting margins. Still, we're generally neutral on the group.

Keurig Dr Pepper KDP   FAIRLY VALUED

Buying Index™ 7   **Value Rating** ○

Economic Castle	Estimated Fair Value	Fair Value Range	Investment Style	Sector	Industry
Attractive	$27.00	$22.00 - $32.00	LARGE-CAP CORE	Consumer Staples	Recession Resistant

Keurig Dr Pepper aims to reduce its net debt to EBITDA ratio below 3.0x by the end of 2021.

Stock Chart (weekly)

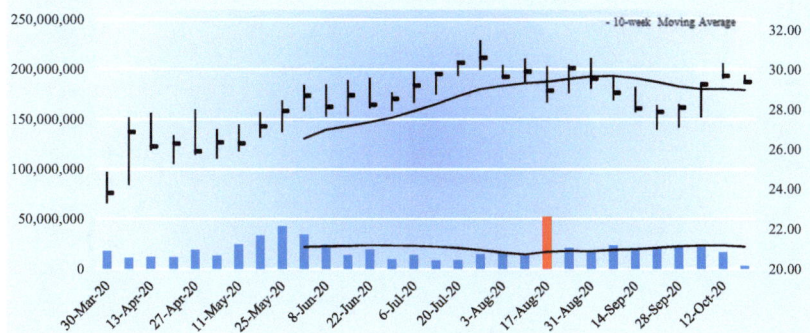

The week with the highest trading volume out of the last 30 weeks was a week of heavy selling, or distribution (red bar).

Investment Considerations

DCF Valuation	**FAIRLY VALUED**
Relative Valuation	**ATTRACTIVE**
ValueCreation™	**EXCELLENT**
ValueRisk™	**LOW**
ValueTrend™	**NEGATIVE**
Cash Flow Generation	**STRONG**
Financial Leverage	**HIGH**
Growth	**MODEST**
Technical Evaluation	**VERY BULLISH**
Relative Strength	**WEAK**
Money Flow Index (MFI)	**NEUTRAL**
Upside/Downside Volume (U/D)	**BEARISH**
Near-term Technical Support, 10-week MA	**29.00**

DCF = Discounted Cash Flow; MFI, U/D = Please see glossary. MA = Moving Average

Business Quality

ValueRisk™	Very Poor	Poor	Good	Excellent
Low				■
Medium				
High				
Very High				

ValueCreation™

Firms that generate economic profits with little operating variability score near the top right of the matrix.

Company Vitals

Market Cap (USD)	$41,686
Avg Weekly Vol (30 wks)	19,540
30-week Range (USD)	23.29 - 31.46
Valuentum Sector	Consumer Staples
5-week Return	5.8%
13-week Return	-3.8%
30-week Return	19.5%
Dividend Yield %	2.0%
Dividends per Share	0.60
Forward Dividend Payout Ratio	51.2%
Est. Normal Diluted EPS	1.54
P/E on Est. Normal Diluted EPS	19.1
Est. Normal EBITDA	4,309
Forward EV/EBITDA	15.7
EV/Est. Normal EBITDA	13.1
Forward Revenue Growth (5-yr)	4.7%
Forward EPS Growth (5-yr)	16.6%

NMF = Not Meaningful; Est. = Estimated; FY = Fiscal Year

Returns Summary
3-year Historical Average

Return on Equity	19.1%
Return on Assets	5.1%
ROIC, with goodwill	7.9%
ROIC, without goodwill	14.0%

ROIC = Return on Invested Capital; NMF = Not Meaningful

Leverage, Coverage, and Liquidity
In Millions of USD

Total Debt	14,741
Net Debt	14,640
Total Debt/EBITDA	4.8
Net Debt/EBITDA	4.8
EBITDA/Interest	4.7
Current Ratio	0.4
Quick Ratio	0.2

NMF = Not Meaningful

Investment Highlights

• Keurig Dr Pepper is a leading coffee and beverage company in the US. The firm's expansive brand portfolio includes Dr Pepper, Keurig, Green Mountain Coffee Roasters, Canada Dry, Snapple, Hawaiian Punch, Mott's, Clamato, 7UP, Squirt, Crush, A&W, and Schweppes. The company was incorporated in 2007 and is based in Plano, Texas.

• The company's largest brand, Dr Pepper, is the #2 flavored CSD in the US, and the firm's Snapple brand is a leading ready-to-drink tea. More than 80% of volume is generated by brands that hold either the #1 or #2 position in their category.

• JAB and its partners, the former owners of Keurig Green Mountain, own ~66% of Keurig Dr Pepper. The new company is committed to maintaining investment grade credit ratings as it targets a net debt/EBTIDA ratio below 3.0x by the end of 2021. By 2021, the firm also aims to realize $600 million in annualized synergies.

• Keurig Dr Pepper has exposure to high growth markets such as ready-to-drink coffee and tea, which will be enhanced by innovation and brand consolidation. Point-of-sale reach will be materially enhanced as a result of increased scale, which will bring an unrivaled nationwide distribution network.

• Keurig Dr Pepper's financials held up relatively well during the initial phases of the COVID-19 pandemic, though we caution its investment grade credit ratings (Baa2/BBB) have a negative outlook. Deleveraging activities remain a priority.

Relative Valuation

	Forward P/E	PEG	Price / FV
Coca-Cola	34.3	1.5	128.0%
Procter & Gamble	26.5	3.3	144.1%
Philip Morris	15.4	2.4	104.3%
Wal-Mart	26.8	2.3	130.2%
Peer Median	26.7	2.4	129.1%
Keurig Dr Pepper	**25.1**	**2.0**	**108.8%**

Price / FV = Current Stock Price divided by Estimated Fair Value

Financial Summary

	----- Actual -----		Projected
Fiscal Year End:	Dec-18	Dec-19	Dec-20
Revenue	7,442	11,120	11,476
Revenue, YoY%	11.2%	49.4%	3.2%
Operating Income	1,247	2,380	2,870
Operating Margin %	16.8%	21.4%	25.0%
Net Income	586	1,254	1,662
Net Income Margin %	7.9%	11.3%	14.5%
Diluted EPS	0.53	0.88	1.17
Diluted EPS, YoY %	-90.9%	65.5%	32.6%
Free Cash Flow (CFO-capex)	1,204	2,144	2,034
Free Cash Flow Margin %	16.2%	19.3%	17.7%

In Millions of USD (except for per share items)

Structure of the Nonalcoholic Beverages Industry   GOOD

The nonalcoholic beverage segment of the commercial beverage industry is highly competitive, consisting of numerous companies that make various sparkling beverages, water products, juices, fruit drinks, energy and other performance-enhancing drinks. Pricing, advertising, product innovation, the availability of in-store private-label beverages, and health concerns about sugar-sweetened beverages are key drivers that impact demand. Leading brands with high levels of consumer acceptance and an expansive distribution network are sources of competitive strengths. We like the structure of the group.

Korn/Ferry KFY   UNDERVALUED 29.6%

Buying Index™   **9**   **Value Rating** ✔

Economic Castle	Estimated Fair Value	Fair Value Range	Investment Style	Sector	Industry
Very Attractive	$66.00	$53.00 - $79.00	MID-CAP VALUE	Information Technology	Technology Giants

Korn/Ferry's shares are super cheap in part because the market is overlooking its very healthy net cash position. COVID-19 will pose both opportunities and challenges as its customers rethink their organizational structures.

Stock Chart (weekly)

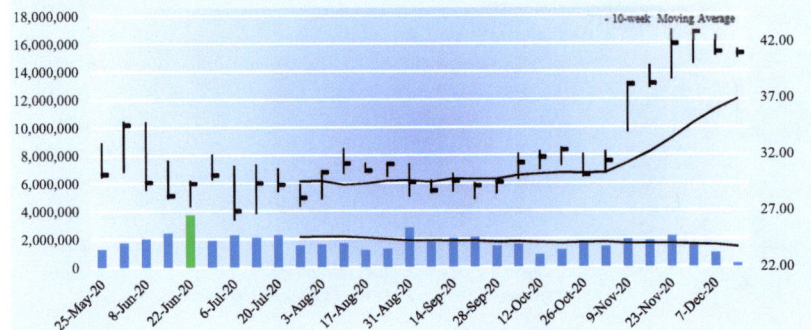

The week with the highest trading volume out of the last 30 weeks was a week of heavy selling, or distribution (red bar).

Investment Considerations

DCF Valuation	UNDERVALUED
Relative Valuation	ATTRACTIVE
ValueCreation™	EXCELLENT
ValueRisk™	LOW
ValueTrend™	POSITIVE
Cash Flow Generation	STRONG
Financial Leverage	MEDIUM
Growth	MODEST
Technical Evaluation	BULLISH
Relative Strength	STRONG
Money Flow Index (MFI)	NEUTRAL
Upside/Downside Volume (U/D)	BULLISH
Near-term Technical Support, 10-week MA	37.00

DCF = Discounted Cash Flow; MFI, U/D = Please see glossary. MA = Moving Average

Business Quality

ValueRisk™	ValueCreation™ Very Poor	Poor	Good	Excellent
Low				▓
Medium				
High				
Very High				

Firms that generate economic profits with little operating variability score near the top right of the matrix.

Company Vitals

Market Cap (USD)	$2,241
Avg Weekly Vol (30 wks)	1,760
30-week Range (USD)	26.14 - 43.01
Valuentum Sector	Information Technology
5-week Return	4.0%
13-week Return	41.3%
30-week Return	33.4%
Dividend Yield %	1.0%
Dividends per Share	0.40
Forward Dividend Payout Ratio	28.3%
Est. Normal Diluted EPS	2.69
P/E on Est. Normal Diluted EPS	15.2
Est. Normal EBITDA	249
Forward EV/EBITDA	11.1
EV/Est. Normal EBITDA	7.1
Forward Revenue Growth (5-yr)	0.3%
Forward EPS Growth (5-yr)	13.7%

NMF = Not Meaningful; Est. = Estimated; FY = Fiscal Year

Returns Summary

3-year Historical Average

Return on Equity	9.7%
Return on Assets	5.0%
ROIC, with goodwill	25.4%
ROIC, without goodwill	84.4%

ROIC = Return on Invested Capital; NMF = Not Meaningful

Leverage, Coverage, and Liquidity

In Millions of USD

Total Debt	394
Net Debt	-469
Total Debt/EBITDA	1.7
Net Debt/EBITDA	NMF
EBITDA/Interest	10.4
Current Ratio	0.8
Quick Ratio	0.6

NMF = Not Meaningful

Investment Highlights

- Korn/Ferry helps its clients recruit world-class leadership talent. The firm is a single source for a wide range of leadership and talent consulting services. Its fee revenue is well-diversified by specialty practice. 'Industrial' is its largest end market at ~30% of fee revenue. The company was founded in 1969 and is based in Los Angeles, California.

- Korn/Ferry believes it has some significant growth opportunities ahead of it, one of which is its products business. As the company works to optimize the bundling and integration of its offerings, management believes the business can triple from recent levels, though it may take some time.

- Korn/Ferry has evolved into an organizational consulting firm. More than half of its revenue now comes from sources other than its core offering of executive search, and this will continue to grow as recent acquisitions are integrated. It is less mono-line and more a multi-solutions organization. Korn/Ferry continues to pursue assets and intellectual property to help deliver a comprehensive approach to talent.

- The acquisition of Hay Group more evenly splits Korn/Ferry's focus between recruiting and human capital management. The acquisition will play a key role in the firm's business transformation. Hay Group's portfolio of intellectual property includes several of the world's most comprehensive databases.

- The firm's cash and marketable securities balance continues to be a source of equity value. In March 2015, Korn/Ferry declared its first quarterly dividend in company history. We think the company has room for material future dividend growth, but its yield is unappealing for the time being.

Relative Valuation

	Forward P/E	PEG	Price / FV
Apple	29.8	2.4	85.0%
Alphabet	34.9	1.8	73.3%
Amazon.com	NMF	3.3	95.7%
Microsoft	31.6	2.5	91.6%
Peer Median	31.6	2.5	88.3%
Korn/Ferry	**28.9**	**0.8**	**62.0%**

Price / FV = Current Stock Price divided by Estimated Fair Value

Financial Summary

	----- Actual -----		Projected
Fiscal Year End:	Apr-19	Apr-20	Apr-21
Revenue	1,974	1,977	1,675
Revenue, YoY%	8.5%	0.2%	-15.3%
Operating Income	141	176	127
Operating Margin %	7.1%	8.9%	7.6%
Net Income	103	105	76
Net Income Margin %	5.2%	5.3%	4.6%
Diluted EPS	1.83	1.92	1.41
Diluted EPS, YoY %	-23.1%	4.7%	-26.2%
Free Cash Flow (CFO-capex)	212	195	112
Free Cash Flow Margin %	10.8%	9.9%	6.7%

In Millions of USD (except for per share items)

Structure of the Staffing Services Industry   NEUTRAL

The staffing services industry spans firms that provide business outsourcing services to those that offer talent management solutions. Providers of business outsourcing solutions compete with a variety of independent firms as well as captive in-house functions. Their businesses are characterized by long-term client relationships and recurring revenue. Talent management firms offer executive recruitment and consulting services and face emerging competition from professional networking website providers. Attracting consultants is particularly important for executive recruitment entities. We're neutral on the group.

KLA-Tencor KLAC   FAIRLY VALUED

Buying Index™ 5   **Value Rating** ○

Economic Castle	Estimated Fair Value	Fair Value Range	Investment Style	Sector	Industry
Very Attractive	$226.00	$181.00 - $271.00	LARGE-CAP GROWTH	Information Technology	Technology Giants

In 2019, KLA-Tencor acquired Orbotech, which has augmented its prospects in the high-growth printed circuit board, flat panel display, and semi manufacturing segments.

Stock Chart (weekly)

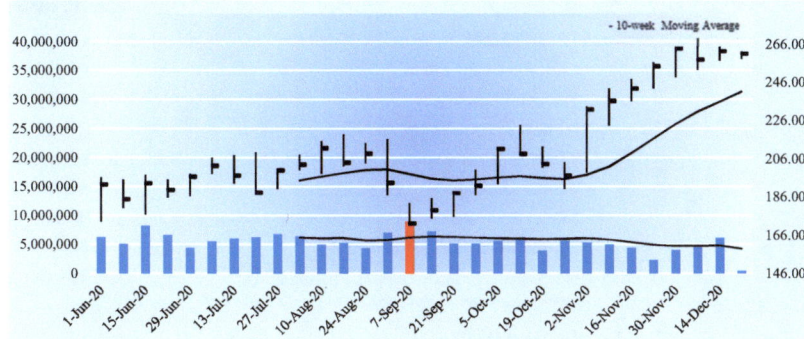

The week with the highest trading volume out of the last 30 weeks was a week of heavy selling, or distribution (red bar).

Investment Considerations

DCF Valuation	**FAIRLY VALUED**
Relative Valuation	**NEUTRAL**
ValueCreation™	**EXCELLENT**
ValueRisk™	**LOW**
ValueTrend™	**POSITIVE**
Cash Flow Generation	**STRONG**
Financial Leverage	**MEDIUM**
Growth	**HIGH**
Technical Evaluation	**NEUTRAL**
Relative Strength	**STRONG**
Money Flow Index (MFI)	**OVERBOUGHT**
Upside/Downside Volume (U/D)	**BULLISH**
Near-term Technical Support, 10-week MA	**241.00**

DCF = Discounted Cash Flow; MFI, U/D = Please see glossary. MA = Moving Average

Business Quality   ValueCreation™

ValueRisk™	Very Poor	Poor	Good	Excellent
Low				■
Medium				
High				
Very High				

Firms that generate economic profits with little operating variability score near the top right of the matrix.

Company Vitals

Market Cap (USD)	$41,767
Avg Weekly Vol (30 wks)	5,440
30-week Range (USD)	171.31 - 268.89
Valuentum Sector	Information Technology
5-week Return	7.2%
13-week Return	38.6%
30-week Return	49.0%
Dividend Yield %	1.4%
Dividends per Share	3.60
Forward Dividend Payout Ratio	48.0%
Est. Normal Diluted EPS	11.07
P/E on Est. Normal Diluted EPS	23.6
Est. Normal EBITDA	2,235
Forward EV/EBITDA	28.4
EV/Est. Normal EBITDA	19.4
Forward Revenue Growth (5-yr)	11.9%
Forward EPS Growth (5-yr)	23.3%

NMF = Not Meaningful; Est. = Estimated; FY = Fiscal Year

Returns Summary   3-year Historical Average

Return on Equity	91.1%
Return on Assets	15.5%
ROIC, with goodwill	87.6%
ROIC, without goodwill	119.7%

ROIC = Return on Invested Capital; NMF = Not Meaningful

Leverage, Coverage, and Liquidity
In Millions of USD

Total Debt	3,470
Net Debt	1,489
Total Debt/EBITDA	2.2
Net Debt/EBITDA	0.9
EBITDA/Interest	14.0
Current Ratio	3.7
Quick Ratio	2.9

NMF = Not Meaningful

Investment Highlights

• KLA-Tencor is among the largest semiconductor equipment companies in the world. The firm supplies process control and yield management solutions for a variety of segments, including integrated circuits, LED, data storage, printed circuit boards and photovoltaic. The company dates back to 1975 and was formed through a merger of KLA and Tencor in 1997. It is headquartered in California.

• Purchasing decisions of KLA-Tencor's customers make the timing, length, and severity of up-and-down cycles difficult to predict. The market for process control and yield management systems is highly competitive, but the company expects increasing cost/complexity to offer new opportunities.

• KLA-Tencor's 2019 acquisition of Orbotech added ~$2.5 billion to its addressable market in the high-growth printed circuit board, flat panel display, and semi manufacturing segments. Annual cost synergies have been solid, and the company's recent free cash flow generation has been impressive, north of $1.6 billion in fiscal 2020. Capex as a percentage of sales has averaged ~2.5%-3% post merger.

• KLA-Tencor is one of the more attractively-positioned semiconductor capital equipment firms. It has invested $2+ billion in R&D during the past three fiscal years (2018-2020), which speaks to its customer focus. End market demand can be choppy, but we expect its revenue growth to do better than industry trends. It refers to China as 'fertile ground.'

• Long-term demand in wafer fab equipment remains strong thanks to more diversified end markets driving demand, but WFE spending will ebb and flow with the cycle at times. US-China trade tensions could continue to complicate industry-wide demand trends.

Relative Valuation

	Forward P/E	PEG	Price / FV
Apple	29.8	2.4	85.0%
Alphabet	34.9	1.8	73.3%
Amazon.com	NMF	3.3	95.7%
Microsoft	31.6	2.5	91.6%
Peer Median	31.6	2.5	88.3%
KLA-Tencor	**34.8**	**2.2**	**115.4%**

Price / FV = Current Stock Price divided by Estimated Fair Value

Financial Summary

	----- Actual -----		Projected
Fiscal Year End:	Jun-17	Jun-18	Jun-19
Revenue	3,480	4,037	4,568
Revenue, YoY%	16.6%	16.0%	13.2%
Operating Income	1,276	1,537	1,461
Operating Margin %	36.7%	38.1%	32.0%
Net Income	926	802	1,176
Net Income Margin %	26.6%	19.9%	25.7%
Diluted EPS	5.88	5.10	7.49
Diluted EPS, YoY %	30.9%	-13.3%	47.0%
Free Cash Flow (CFO-capex)	1,042	1,162	1,022
Free Cash Flow Margin %	29.9%	28.8%	22.4%

In Millions of USD (except for per share items)

Structure of the Semiconductor Equipment Industry   **VERY POOR**

The semiconductor equipment industry is highly competitive and characterized by rapid technological change. Success hinges on the ability to commercialize new technology in a timely manner, continuously enhance products to improve efficiency of customer fab operations, and manage costs and inventory effectively. Performance of constituents is heavily influenced by manufacturing capacity and fab utilization rates, which together create volatile demand cycles. The potential for unexpected shifts in demand for the group's products leaves us unexcited about the industry's structural characteristics.

Kimberly-Clark KMB OVERVALUED 7%

Buying Index™ 4 **Value Rating** ✖

Economic Castle	Estimated Fair Value	Fair Value Range	Investment Style	Sector	Industry
Attractive	$120.00	$96.00 - $144.00	LARGE-CAP CORE	Consumer Staples	Recession Resistant

Kimberly-Clark launched a major restructuring program back in 2018 to steadily improve its margins over time, though shares are not cheap.

Stock Chart (weekly)

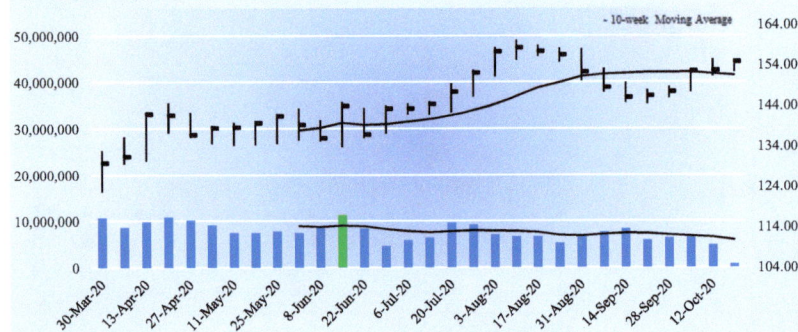

The week with the highest trading volume out of the last 30 weeks was a week of heavy selling, or distribution (red bar).

Company Vitals

Market Cap (USD)	$53,485
Avg Weekly Vol (30 wks)	7,530
30-week Range (USD)	22.76 - 160.16
Valuentum Sector	Consumer Staples
5-week Return	6.1%
13-week Return	5.2%
30-week Return	20.0%
Dividend Yield %	2.8%
Dividends per Share	4.28
Forward Dividend Payout Ratio	62.1%
Est. Normal Diluted EPS	8.50
P/E on Est. Normal Diluted EPS	18.2
Est. Normal EBITDA	4,844
Forward EV/EBITDA	14.5
EV/Est. Normal EBITDA	12.6
Forward Revenue Growth (5-yr)	2.6%
Forward EPS Growth (5-yr)	9.8%

NMF = Not Meaningful; Est. = Estimated; FY = Fiscal Year

Returns Summary
3-year Historical Average

Return on Equity	117.3%
Return on Assets	13.4%
ROIC, with goodwill	27.8%
ROIC, without goodwill	34.0%

ROIC = Return on Invested Capital; NMF = Not Meaningful

Leverage, Coverage, and Liquidity
In Millions of USD

Total Debt	7,747
Net Debt	7,305
Total Debt/EBITDA	2.1
Net Debt/EBITDA	2.0
EBITDA/Interest	14.2
Current Ratio	0.7
Quick Ratio	0.4

NMF = Not Meaningful

Investment Highlights

• Kimberly-Clark is best known for its personal care and consumer tissue brands. The firm's products are used by one-quarter of the world's population. Its 'Personal Care' division accounts for ~50% of revenue. The company spun-off its KC-Health Care operations into Halyard Health (HYH) in 2014. It was founded in 1872 and is based in Dallas, Texas.

• In 2018, Kimberly-Clark launched its '2018 Global Restructuring Program' which involves the firm exiting some low-margin businesses. This program is forecasted to yield $500-$550 million in annualized cost savings by late-2021 or 2022.

• Kimberly-Clark has a #1 or #2 position in 80+ countries, and it has five distinct billion-dollar brands: Huggies, Kleenex, Kimberly-Clark, Scott, and Kotex. The company seeks to generate long-term growth in developing and emerging markets. Kimberly-Clark estimates its products are used by one-quarter of the world's population.

• About half of Kimberly-Clark's sales come from its domestic operations. Its domestic operations carries significantly higher margins than its international operations. Through 2022, Kimberly-Clark seeks to grow its organic sales by 1%-3% per year and its operating profit by 3%-5% per year.

• Kimberly-Clark is targeting a long-term payout ratio of ~60% (dividends per share divided by EPS). Through 2022, the firm aims to generate mid-single digit annual EPS growth which supports Kimberly-Clark's dividend growth trajectory.

Investment Considerations

DCF Valuation	OVERVALUED
Relative Valuation	NEUTRAL
ValueCreation™	EXCELLENT
ValueRisk™	LOW
ValueTrend™	NEGATIVE
Cash Flow Generation	STRONG
Financial Leverage	MEDIUM
Growth	MODEST
Technical Evaluation	VERY BULLISH
Relative Strength	WEAK
Money Flow Index (MFI)	NEUTRAL
Upside/Downside Volume (U/D)	DETERIORATING
Near-term Technical Support, 10-week MA	151.00

DCF = Discounted Cash Flow; MFI, U/D = Please see glossary. MA = Moving Average

Business Quality

ValueRisk™	ValueCreation™			
	Very Poor	Poor	Good	Excellent
Low				■
Medium				
High				
Very High				

Firms that generate economic profits with little operating variability score near the top right of the matrix.

Relative Valuation

	Forward P/E	PEG	Price / FV
Coca-Cola	34.3	1.5	128.0%
Procter & Gamble	26.5	3.3	144.1%
Philip Morris	15.4	2.4	104.3%
Wal-Mart	26.8	2.3	130.2%
Peer Median	26.7	2.4	129.1%
Kimberly-Clark	**22.5**	**2.5**	**129.0%**

Price / FV = Current Stock Price divided by Estimated Fair Value

Financial Summary

	----- Actual -----		Projected
Fiscal Year End:	Dec-18	Dec-19	Dec-20
Revenue	18,486	18,450	18,764
Revenue, YoY%	1.2%	-0.2%	1.7%
Operating Income	2,230	2,781	3,257
Operating Margin %	12.1%	15.1%	17.4%
Net Income	1,410	2,157	2,357
Net Income Margin %	7.6%	11.7%	12.6%
Diluted EPS	4.03	6.24	6.89
Diluted EPS, YoY %	-37.0%	54.7%	10.4%
Free Cash Flow (CFO-capex)	2,093	1,527	2,027
Free Cash Flow Margin %	11.3%	8.3%	10.8%

In Millions of USD (except for per share items)

Structure of the Household Products Industry   GOOD

Firms in the household products industry sell some of the most recognized branded consumer packaged goods in the world and often hold a significant market share position in a variety of product categories. Though the industry is characterized by stiff competition from retailers' private-label brands, constituents tend to boast meaningful competitive advantages due to their brand strength/reputation and generate high returns on invested capital. Household products companies remain tied to the vicissitudes of consumer spending, but we tend to like the structure of the group.

Kinder Morgan KMI   FAIRLY VALUED

Buying Index™   6   Value Rating ⦿

Economic Castle	Estimated Fair Value	Fair Value Range	Investment Style	Sector	Industry
Neutral	$19.00	$12.00 - $26.00	LARGE-CAP VALUE	Energy	Oil & Gas Complex

Kinder Morgan scaled back its capital expenditure expectations which should improve its cash flow profile going forward.

Stock Chart (weekly)

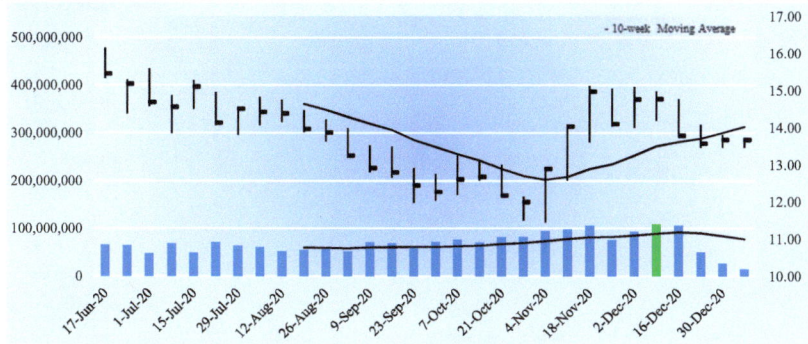

The week with the highest trading volume out of the last 30 weeks was a week of heavy selling, or distribution (red bar).

Company Vitals

Market Cap (USD)	$30,949
Avg Weekly Vol (30 wks)	68,943
30-week Range (USD)	11.45 - 16.14
Valuentum Sector	Energy
5-week Return	-7.8%
13-week Return	7.6%
30-week Return	-14.1%
Dividend Yield %	7.7%
Dividends per Share	1.05
Forward Dividend Payout Ratio	123.9%
Est. Normal Diluted EPS	0.84
P/E on Est. Normal Diluted EPS	16.4
Est. Normal EBITDA	6,634
Forward EV/EBITDA	8.8
EV/Est. Normal EBITDA	8.6
Forward Revenue Growth (5-yr)	-0.9%
Forward EPS Growth (5-yr)	-4.2%

NMF = Not Meaningful; Est. = Estimated; FY = Fiscal Year

Returns Summary   3-year Historical Average

Return on Equity	4.3%
Return on Assets	1.9%
ROIC, with goodwill	5.0%
ROIC, without goodwill	7.2%

ROIC = Return on Invested Capital; NMF = Not Meaningful

Leverage, Coverage, and Liquidity

In Millions of USD

Total Debt	30,670
Net Debt	25,814
Total Debt/EBITDA	4.8
Net Debt/EBITDA	4.1
EBITDA/Interest	3.5
Current Ratio	0.6
Quick Ratio	0.5

NMF = Not Meaningful; Debt excludes debt associated with the finance sub.

Investment Highlights

• Kinder Morgan is one of the largest midstream energy companies in North America, with ~80,000 miles of pipelines (including ~70,000 miles of natural gas pipelines) and ~150 terminals. It re-consolidated its holdings in Kinder Morgan Energy Partners (KMP), El Paso Pipeline Partners (EPB) and Kinder Morgan Management (KMR). Kinder Morgan exited Canada in 2019 and is now focused on growing its natural gas business, particularly in Texas. Kinder Morgan is directly exposed to fluctuations in raw energy resources pricing via its upstream segment that utilizes CO2 injection extraction methods.

• Kinder Morgan's business strategy is to 1) focus on stable, fee-based energy transportation/storage assets, 2) increase utilization of its assets while controlling costs, 3) leverage scale from incremental acquisitions and expansions of assets that fit within its strategy, and 4) maximize the benefits of its financial structure. The company is doing a good job executing upon its strategy, but its capital structure has worked against dividend growth plans, creating a not-so-virtuous cycle for stakeholders. The company significantly reduced its capital expenditure expectations going forward, which benefits its free cash flow outlook.

• Looking ahead, Kinder Morgan's growth portfolio is heavily concentrated on infrastructure projects catering to natural gas. Transporting natural gas production out of the Permian Basin, situated in West Texas and Southeast New Mexico, via long haul pipelines to LNG export facilities along the US Gulf Coast is a big part of this strategy. Permian natural gas production growth through 2030 is expected to be quite significant.

Investment Considerations

DCF Valuation	FAIRLY VALUED
Relative Valuation	NEUTRAL
ValueCreation™	POOR
ValueRisk™	HIGH
ValueTrend™	POSITIVE
Cash Flow Generation	STRONG
Financial Leverage	HIGH
Growth	DECLINING
Technical Evaluation	BULLISH
Relative Strength	NEUTRAL
Money Flow Index (MFI)	NEUTRAL
Upside/Downside Volume (U/D)	BULLISH
Near-term Technical Resistance, 10-wk MA	14.00

DCF = Discounted Cash Flow; MFI, U/D = Please see glossary. MA = Moving Average

Business Quality

ValueRisk™	ValueCreation™			
	Very Poor	Poor	Good	Excellent
Low				
Medium				
High		▇		
Very High				

Firms that generate economic profits with little operating variability score near the top right of the matrix.

Relative Valuation

	Forward P/E	PEG	Price / FV
Schlumberger	27.1	NMF	80.6%
Chevron	-198.5	NMF	111.0%
Exxon Mobil	-102.5	NMF	100.4%
Enterprise Product Partners	9.7	NMF	98.1%
Peer Median	-46.4	NMF	99.2%
Kinder Morgan	**16.1**	**NMF**	**71.9%**

Price / FV = Current Stock Price divided by Estimated Fair Value

Financial Summary

	----- Actual -----		Projected
Fiscal Year End:	Dec-18	Dec-19	Dec-20
Revenue	14,144	13,209	11,505
Revenue, YoY%	3.2%	-6.6%	-12.9%
Operating Income	3,958	3,928	4,352
Operating Margin %	28.0%	29.7%	37.8%
Net Income	1,609	2,190	1,967
Net Income Margin %	11.4%	16.6%	17.1%
Diluted EPS	0.67	0.97	0.85
Diluted EPS, YoY %	NMF	44.7%	-12.4%
Free Cash Flow (CFO-capex)	2,139	2,478	3,184
Free Cash Flow Margin %	15.1%	18.8%	27.7%

In Millions of USD (except for per share items)

Structure of the Oil & Gas Pipeline Industry   NEUTRAL

Firms in the oil and gas pipeline industry own or operate thousands of miles of pipelines and terminals—assets that are nearly impossible/uneconomical to replicate. Most companies act as a toll road and receive a fee for transporting natural gas, crude oil and other refined products (and generally avoid commodity price risk). Though there is much to like, most constituents operate as master limited partnerships and pay out hefty distributions that can stretch their balance sheets. Additional unit issuance (dilution) has become common, and capital-market dependence is a key risk. We're neutral on the group.

CarMax KMX   FAIRLY VALUED

Buying Index™ 7   Value Rating

Economic Castle	Estimated Fair Value	Fair Value Range	Investment Style	Sector	Industry
Attractive	$117.00	$88.00 - $146.00	LARGE-CAP VALUE	Consumer Discretionary	Discretionary Spending

CarMax has put new store openings on hold until fiscal 2022 as it navigates the COVID-19 pandemic. The company's new omni-channel strategy gives it a huge opportunity in the used car industry.

Stock Chart (weekly)

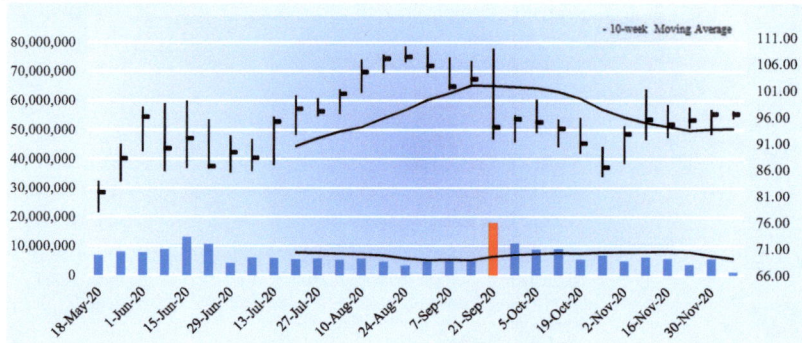

The week with the highest trading volume out of the last 30 weeks was a week of heavy selling, or distribution (red bar).

Investment Considerations

DCF Valuation	**FAIRLY VALUED**
Relative Valuation	**ATTRACTIVE**
ValueCreation™	**VERY POOR**
ValueRisk™	**MEDIUM**
ValueTrend™	**NEGATIVE**
Cash Flow Generation	**WEAK**
Financial Leverage	**MEDIUM**
Growth	**MODEST**
Technical Evaluation	**BULLISH**
Relative Strength	**WEAK**
Money Flow Index (MFI)	**NEUTRAL**
Upside/Downside Volume (U/D)	**BEARISH**
Near-term Technical Support, 10-week MA	**94.00**

DCF = Discounted Cash Flow; MFI, U/D = Please see glossary. MA = Moving Average

Company Vitals

Market Cap (USD)	$16,098
Avg Weekly Vol (30 wks)	6,696
30-week Range (USD)	77.79 - 109.31
Valuentum Sector	Consumer Discretionary
5-week Return	-0.2%
13-week Return	-5.3%
30-week Return	20.6%
Dividend Yield %	0.0%
Dividends per Share	0.00
Forward Dividend Payout Ratio	0.0%
Est. Normal Diluted EPS	6.64
P/E on Est. Normal Diluted EPS	14.5
Est. Normal EBITDA	1,661
Forward EV/EBITDA	15.0
EV/Est. Normal EBITDA	10.7
Forward Revenue Growth (5-yr)	6.0%
Forward EPS Growth (5-yr)	10.3%

NMF = Not Meaningful; Est. = Estimated; FY = Fiscal Year

Returns Summary

3-year Historical Average

Return on Equity	23.6%
Return on Assets	4.4%
ROIC, with goodwill	-0.7%
ROIC, without goodwill	-0.7%

ROIC = Return on Invested Capital; NMF = Not Meaningful

Leverage, Coverage, and Liquidity

In Millions of USD

Total Debt	2,212
Net Debt	1,673
Total Debt/EBITDA	2.2
Net Debt/EBITDA	1.7
EBITDA/Interest	12.0
Current Ratio	2.4
Quick Ratio	0.5

NMF = Not Meaningful

Investment Highlights

• CarMax is the largest retailer of used cars in the US and one of the largest vehicle auction operators. The firm differentiates itself through no-haggle pricing and a customer-friendly sales process in ~220 stores. The used car market (~85% of its sales), however, is highly competitive. The company was founded in 1993 and is headquartered in Richmond, Virginia.

• CarMax is focusing on tech and using big data capabilities to leverage its core strengths. An enhanced mobile platform is expected to help drive omni-channel selling opportunities as a growing number of consumers use mobile as a first line of investigation into the buying process.

• In addition to being highly competitive, CarMax's business is sensitive to interest rates, unemployment, gas prices, discretionary spending, and consumer credit health. Store growth and share gains will drive most of its future growth. Investors can expect 8-15 store openings in a 'normal' fiscal year, though it has currently paused store openings due to COVID-19 (new store growth will resume in fiscal 2022).

• The US used car market could come under pressure in coming years as a result of rapidly advancing next-gen tech in new cars and a supply glut of vehicles coming off leases from the recent strength in the US new vehicle market. However, momentum in used vehicle unit sales has held up better than we had anticipated in recent quarters.

• Investors should be aware that CarMax's business is dependent upon capital to fund growth and to support the activities of its CAF segment. Changes in capital and credit markets could adversely impact its business, sales, results of operations and financial condition.

Business Quality

ValueRisk™	Very Poor	Poor	Good	Excellent
Low				
Medium	▉			
High				
Very High				

ValueCreation™

Firms that generate economic profits with little operating variability score near the top right of the matrix.

Relative Valuation

	Forward P/E	PEG	Price / FV
Disney	75.6	0.3	98.3%
Home Depot	22.9	1.9	106.7%
McDonald's	38.5	1.1	111.0%
Nike	52.8	2.5	104.9%
Peer Median	45.6	1.5	105.8%
CarMax	**22.4**	**0.9**	**82.5%**

Price / FV = Current Stock Price divided by Estimated Fair Value

Financial Summary

	----- Actual -----		Projected
Fiscal Year End:	Feb-19	Feb-20	Feb-21
Revenue	18,173	20,320	18,837
Revenue, YoY%	6.1%	11.8%	-7.3%
Operating Income	750	782	987
Operating Margin %	4.1%	3.8%	5.2%
Net Income	842	888	705
Net Income Margin %	4.6%	4.4%	3.7%
Diluted EPS	4.79	5.33	4.31
Diluted EPS, YoY %	33.0%	11.2%	-19.0%
Free Cash Flow (CFO-capex)	-142	-568	1,162
Free Cash Flow Margin %	-0.8%	-2.8%	6.2%

In Millions of USD (except for per share items)

Structure of the Retail Auto Parts Industry   GOOD

The retail auto parts industry is characterized by stiff competition in many areas, including brand recognition, customer service, and price. The industry is impacted by both the age and number of vehicles in service, especially those that are no longer under manufacturer's warranties (typically seven years old and older). Demand for retail auto parts can best be described as counter-cyclical: as consumers' cash flows decrease, drivers tend to keep their vehicles longer, leading to more retail auto parts sales. Though competition among constituents is intense, we like the industry's defensive characteristics.

Coca-Cola KO   OVERVALUED 3.8%

Buying Index™ 4   **Value Rating ✕**

Economic Castle	Estimated Fair Value	Fair Value Range	Investment Style	Sector	Industry
Attractive	$39.00	$30.00 - $48.00	MEGA-CAP CORE	Consumer Staples	Recession Resistant

Shares of Coca-Cola remain pricey, in our view, and the COVID-19 pandemic has weighed negatively on its financial performance.

Stock Chart (weekly)

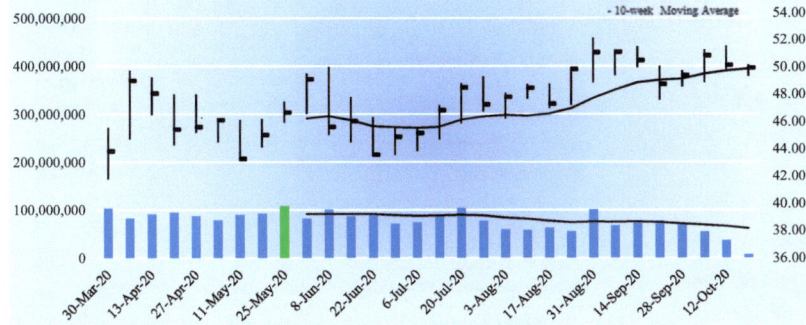

The week with the highest trading volume out of the last 30 weeks was a week of heavy selling, or distribution (red bar).

Investment Considerations

DCF Valuation	**OVERVALUED**
Relative Valuation	**NEUTRAL**
ValueCreation™	**EXCELLENT**
ValueRisk™	**MEDIUM**
ValueTrend™	**NEGATIVE**
Cash Flow Generation	**STRONG**
Financial Leverage	**HIGH**
Growth	**MODEST**
Technical Evaluation	**BULLISH**
Relative Strength	**WEAK**
Money Flow Index (MFI)	**NEUTRAL**
Upside/Downside Volume (U/D)	**DETERIORATING**
Near-term Technical Support, 10-week MA	**50.00**

DCF = Discounted Cash Flow; MFI, U/D = Please see glossary. MA = Moving Average

Business Quality

ValueCreation™

ValueRisk™	Very Poor	Poor	Good	Excellent
Low				
Medium				▓
High				
Very High				

Firms that generate economic profits with little operating variability score near the top right of the matrix.

Company Vitals

Market Cap (USD)	$215,333
Avg Weekly Vol (30 wks)	77,270
30-week Range (USD)	41.79 - 52.13
Valuentum Sector	Consumer Staples
5-week Return	0.3%
13-week Return	3.6%
30-week Return	16.0%
Dividend Yield %	3.3%
Dividends per Share	1.64
Forward Dividend Payout Ratio	112.5%
Est. Normal Diluted EPS	2.12
P/E on Est. Normal Diluted EPS	23.5
Est. Normal EBITDA	13,435
Forward EV/EBITDA	24.8
EV/Est. Normal EBITDA	18.4
Forward Revenue Growth (5-yr)	2.8%
Forward EPS Growth (5-yr)	4.7%

NMF = Not Meaningful; Est. = Estimated; FY = Fiscal Year

Returns Summary
3-year Historical Average

Return on Equity	31.8%
Return on Assets	6.6%
ROIC, with goodwill	26.9%
ROIC, without goodwill	40.9%

ROIC = Return on Invested Capital; NMF = Not Meaningful

Leverage, Coverage, and Liquidity
In Millions of USD

Total Debt	42,763
Net Debt	31,588
Total Debt/EBITDA	3.6
Net Debt/EBITDA	2.7
EBITDA/Interest	12.6
Current Ratio	0.8
Quick Ratio	0.6

NMF = Not Meaningful

Investment Higlights

• Coca-Cola is the world's largest beverage company. The firm owns and markets four of the world's top five nonalcoholic sparkling beverage brands: Coca-Cola, Diet Coke, Fanta, and Sprite. Coca-Cola is getting ready to launch hard seltzer products under the Topo Chico brand in the US. Coca-Cola was founded in 1886 and is based in Atlanta, Georgia.

• The company boasts a number of competitive advantages: its brands, financial strength, distribution system, and global reach. Coca-Cola decided to directly enter the domestic energy drink market by launching its Coca-Cola Energy offering nationwide in 2020.

• Coca-Cola's financials have taken a big hit from the COVID-19 pandemic, though the firm has been able to offset some of those headwinds by significantly reducing its SG&A expenses. The company retains ample liquidity to ride out the storm, though its dividend growth rate will likely slowdown in the medium-term in order to adjust to the new normal.

• We are big fans of Coca-Cola's business model and ability to generate significant free cash flows. The firm "refranchised" its bottling operations in the US and we like the strategic pivot. Additionally, Coca-Cola has steadily been divesting its international bottling operations over the years.

• Coca-Cola has raised its dividend in each of the past 55 years. Investors, however, should be cognizant of the generosity embedded in its fair value estimate, originating from a low discount rate and elevated expected top-line growth and margin enhancement.

Relative Valuation

	Forward P/E	PEG	Price / FV
Anheuser-Busch InBev	27.2	0.5	101.7%
Procter & Gamble	26.5	3.3	144.1%
Philip Morris	15.4	2.4	104.3%
Wal-Mart	26.8	2.3	130.2%
Peer Median	26.7	2.4	117.2%
Coca-Cola	**34.3**	**1.5**	**128.0%**

Price / FV = Current Stock Price divided by Estimated Fair Value

Financial Summary

	----- Actual -----		Projected
Fiscal Year End:	Dec-18	Dec-19	Dec-20
Revenue	31,856	37,266	32,794
Revenue, YoY%	-10.0%	17.0%	-12.0%
Non-GAAP Operating Income	9,779	10,544	8,758
Non-GAAP EBIT %	30.7%	28.3%	26.7%
Non-GAAP Net Income	6,685	8,920	6,224
Non-GAAP NI Margin %	21.0%	23.9%	19.0%
Non-GAAP Diluted EPS	1.56	2.07	1.46
Non-GAAP Dil EPS, YoY %	486.2%	33.0%	-29.5%
Non-GAAP FCF (CFO-capex)	5,973	8,417	6,588
Non-GAAP FCF Margin %	18.8%	22.6%	20.1%

In Millions of USD (except for per share items)

Structure of the Nonalcoholic Beverages Industry   GOOD

The nonalcoholic beverage segment of the commercial beverage industry is highly competitive, consisting of numerous companies that make various sparkling beverages, water products, juices, fruit drinks, energy and other performance-enhancing drinks. Pricing, advertising, product innovation, the availability of in-store private-label beverages, and health concerns about sugar-sweetened beverages are key drivers that impact demand. Leading brands with high levels of consumer acceptance and an expansive distribution network are sources of competitive strengths. We like the structure of the group.

Kroger KR   FAIRLY VALUED

Buying Index™   4   Value Rating ☀

Economic Castle	Estimated Fair Value	Fair Value Range	Investment Style	Sector	Industry
Attractive	$31.00	$23.00 - $39.00	LARGE-CAP CORE	Consumer Staples	Recession Resistant

Kroger's business model proved resilient during the initial stages of the COVID-19 pandemic.

Stock Chart (weekly)

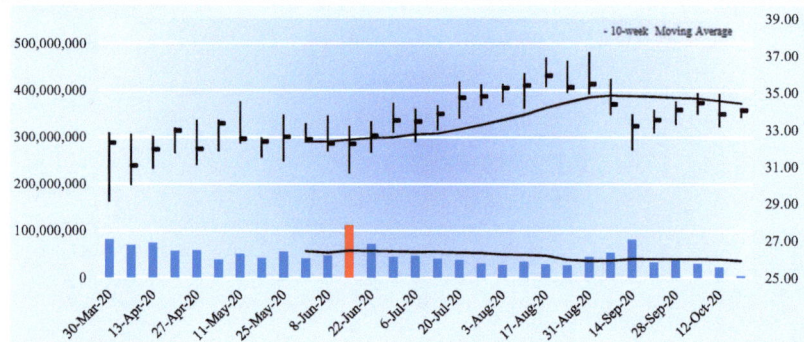

The week with the highest trading volume out of the last 30 weeks was a week of heavy selling, or distribution (red bar).

Company Vitals

Market Cap (USD)	$27,410
Avg Weekly Vol (30 wks)	46,987
30-week Range (USD)	29.10 - 37.22
Valuentum Sector	Consumer Staples
5-week Return	3.4%
13-week Return	-1.9%
30-week Return	13.5%
Dividend Yield %	2.1%
Dividends per Share	0.72
Forward Dividend Payout Ratio	21.9%
Est. Normal Diluted EPS	3.08
P/E on Est. Normal Diluted EPS	11.1
Est. Normal EBITDA	6,237
Forward EV/EBITDA	6.2
EV/Est. Normal EBITDA	6.6
Forward Revenue Growth (5-yr)	1.3%
Forward EPS Growth (5-yr)	10.5%

NMF = Not Meaningful; Est. = Estimated; FY = Fiscal Year

Returns Summary
3-year Historical Average

Return on Equity	29.2%
Return on Assets	5.6%
ROIC, with goodwill	9.4%
ROIC, without goodwill	10.6%

ROIC = Return on Invested Capital; NMF = Not Meaningful

Leverage, Coverage, and Liquidity
In Millions of USD

Total Debt	14,076
Net Debt	13,677
Total Debt/EBITDA	2.9
Net Debt/EBITDA	2.8
EBITDA/Interest	8.1
Current Ratio	0.8
Quick Ratio	0.1

NMF = Not Meaningful

Investment Highlights

• Kroger is one of the largest retailers in the US. The firm spans many states with store formats that include grocery and multi-department stores, and jewelry stores. We think it is doing a good job capturing value, health, and convenience trends. The company was founded in 1883 and is based in Cincinatti, Ohio.

• We like Kroger, but the company operates in an intensely competitive environment. Profit margins are extremely narrow. Amazon's purchase of Whole Foods in 2017 accelerated technology investments from incumbents like Kroger.

• Kroger has been put up years of market share gains. This strength in operating performance includes periods where the industry declined materially. The firm is working on a virtuous cycle in its business as it invests in technology by developing partnerships and services that allow it to monetize data and leverage its current grocery assets.

• Kroger's business proved resilient during the initial stages of the COVID-19 pandemic. Its past digital investments improved its omni-channel sales capabilities and helped the firm grow its identical store sales by double-digits year-over-year during the second quarter of fiscal 2020.

• Kroger has increased its dividend over the past 10+ consecutive years and we expect management will continue pushing through payout increases over the coming fiscal years. Kroger's net debt load needs to be monitored, however.

Investment Considerations

DCF Valuation	FAIRLY VALUED
Relative Valuation	ATTRACTIVE
ValueCreation™	GOOD
ValueRisk™	MEDIUM
ValueTrend™	NEGATIVE
Cash Flow Generation	WEAK
Financial Leverage	MEDIUM
Growth	MODEST
Technical Evaluation	BEARISH
Relative Strength	WEAK
Money Flow Index (MFI)	NEUTRAL
Upside/Downside Volume (U/D)	BULLISH
Near-term Technical Resistance, 10-wk MA	34.00

DCF = Discounted Cash Flow; MFI, U/D = Please see glossary. MA = Moving Average

Business Quality

ValueRisk™	Very Poor	Poor	Good	Excellent
Low				
Medium			▮	
High				
Very High				

ValueCreation™

Firms that generate economic profits with little operating variability score near the top right of the matrix.

Relative Valuation

	Forward P/E	PEG	Price / FV
Coca-Cola	34.3	1.5	128.0%
Procter & Gamble	26.5	3.3	144.1%
Philip Morris	15.4	2.4	104.3%
Wal-Mart	26.8	2.3	130.2%
Peer Median	26.7	2.4	129.1%
Kroger	10.3	1.6	109.8%

Price / FV = Current Stock Price divided by Estimated Fair Value

Financial Summary

	----- Actual -----		Projected
Fiscal Year End:	Jan-19	Jan-20	Jan-21
Revenue	121,162	122,286	132,191
Revenue, YoY%	-1.2%	0.9%	8.1%
Operating Income	2,614	2,251	3,738
Operating Margin %	2.2%	1.8%	2.8%
Net Income	3,110	1,659	2,624
Net Income Margin %	2.6%	1.4%	2.0%
Diluted EPS	3.80	2.06	3.29
Diluted EPS, YoY %	80.2%	-45.8%	59.8%
Free Cash Flow (CFO-capex)	1,197	1,536	2,085
Free Cash Flow Margin %	1.0%	1.3%	1.6%

In Millions of USD (except for per share items)

Structure of the Food Retailers Industry   NEUTRAL

Firms in the mature food retailers industry generally have slim profit margins and face significant competition from brick-and-mortar locations (discount, department, drug, dollar, warehouse clubs and supermarkets) as well as Internet-based retailers (including Amazon). Though the industry is not terribly cyclical, economic conditions, disposable income, credit availability, fuel prices, and unemployment levels drive ticket size and traffic trends. Offering consumers a compelling value proposition is a must, even as higher-priced organic food offerings proliferate. We're generally neutral on the group.

VALUENTUM

Lowe's LOW   FAIRLY VALUED

Buying Index™ 6   **Value Rating** ◯

Economic Castle	Estimated Fair Value	Fair Value Range	Investment Style	Sector	Industry
Attractive	$162.00	$126.00 - $198.00	LARGE-CAP CORE	Consumer Discretionary	Discretionary Spending

Lowe's has performed well in the face of COVID-19, assisted by its growing e-commerce operations. We recently raised Lowe's fair value estimate.

Stock Chart (weekly)

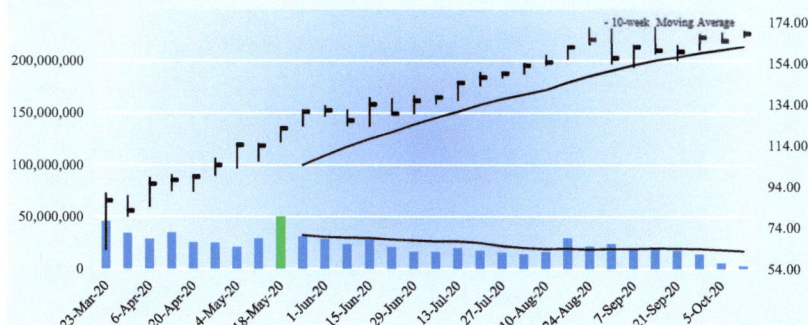

The week with the highest trading volume out of the last 30 weeks was a week of heavy selling, or distribution (red bar).

Investment Considerations

DCF Valuation	FAIRLY VALUED
Relative Valuation	NEUTRAL
ValueCreation™	EXCELLENT
ValueRisk™	MEDIUM
ValueTrend™	NEGATIVE
Cash Flow Generation	STRONG
Financial Leverage	MEDIUM
Growth	MODEST
Technical Evaluation	BULLISH
Relative Strength	STRONG
Money Flow Index (MFI)	NEUTRAL
Upside/Downside Volume (U/D)	DETERIORATING
Near-term Technical Support, 10-week MA	162.00

DCF = Discounted Cash Flow; MFI, U/D = Please see glossary. MA = Moving Average

Company Vitals

Market Cap (USD)	$131,070
Avg Weekly Vol (30 wks)	23,088
30-week Range (USD)	63.04 - 171.72
Valuentum Sector	Consumer Discretionary
5-week Return	3.2%
13-week Return	17.5%
30-week Return	158.3%
Dividend Yield %	1.4%
Dividends per Share	2.40
Forward Dividend Payout Ratio	27.9%
Est. Normal Diluted EPS	10.24
P/E on Est. Normal Diluted EPS	16.4
Est. Normal EBITDA	11,830
Forward EV/EBITDA	14.1
EV/Est. Normal EBITDA	12.6
Forward Revenue Growth (5-yr)	6.2%
Forward EPS Growth (5-yr)	18.4%

NMF = Not Meaningful; Est. = Estimated; FY = Fiscal Year

Returns Summary
3-year Historical Average

Return on Equity	85.7%
Return on Assets	9.4%
ROIC, with goodwill	24.2%
ROIC, without goodwill	25.1%

ROIC = Return on Invested Capital; NMF = Not Meaningful

Leverage, Coverage, and Liquidity
In Millions of USD

Total Debt	19,306
Net Debt	18,430
Total Debt/EBITDA	2.5
Net Debt/EBITDA	2.4
EBITDA/Interest	11.0
Current Ratio	1.0
Quick Ratio	0.1

NMF = Not Meaningful

Investment Highlights

• Lowe's is the world's second largest home improvement retailer. It operates over 1,700 stores in the US and ~250 in Canada (including under the RONA brand). The company strives to be its customer's first choice for home improvement. Lowe's recently exited Mexico. It was founded in 1946 and is headquartered in North Carolina.

• Lowe's is a fantastic company, and one that continues to benefit from the housing recovery. We're expecting the home improvement retail group to continue outperforming the broader retail space, which continues to struggle, thanks in part to the lack of a meaningful online threat at this point in time.

• Lowe's embarked on a major restructuring program in fiscal 2018 and 2019 that saw the firm close down underperforming stores and exit Mexico. This program has already started to yield significant cost savings. Lowe's has made significant digital investments over the past few years, which better positioned the firm to navigate the COVID-19 pandemic.

• Lowe's plans to continue to grow sales through improving its customer experience as it continues to develop omni-channel capabilities. It has additional opportunity in improving its product and service offering for the Pro customer. Pros are relatively underrepresented in Lowe's customer base, but Pro comps have outperformed company averages of late.

• Aside from return on invested capital, one of the key metrics we look at in the retail space is 'sales per selling square foot.' For Lowe's, this metric has steadily advanced since 2009. Lowe's is customer-focused with an emphasis on simplicity as it helps consumers tackle large projects.

Business Quality

ValueRisk™	Very Poor	Poor	Good	Excellent
Low				
Medium				■
High				
Very High				

ValueCreation™ (column header)

Firms that generate economic profits with little operating variability score near the top right of the matrix.

Relative Valuation

	Forward P/E	PEG	Price / FV
Disney	75.6	0.3	98.3%
Home Depot	22.9	1.9	106.7%
McDonald's	38.5	1.1	111.0%
Nike	52.8	2.5	104.9%
Peer Median	45.6	1.5	105.8%
Lowe's	**19.6**	**1.7**	**104.0%**

Price / FV = Current Stock Price divided by Estimated Fair Value

Financial Summary

	----- Actual -----		Projected
Fiscal Year End:	Jan-19	Jan-20	Jan-21
Revenue	71,309	72,148	84,918
Revenue, YoY%	3.9%	1.2%	17.7%
Operating Income	4,018	6,314	9,112
Operating Margin %	5.6%	8.8%	10.7%
Net Income	2,314	4,281	6,569
Net Income Margin %	3.2%	5.9%	7.7%
Diluted EPS	2.85	5.50	8.62
Diluted EPS, YoY %	-30.6%	93.1%	56.6%
Free Cash Flow (CFO-capex)	5,019	2,812	6,689
Free Cash Flow Margin %	7.0%	3.9%	7.9%

In Millions of USD (except for per share items)

Structure of the Specialty Retailers Industry

NEUTRAL

The specialty retail segment is fragmented, highly competitive, and economically-sensitive. The group covers a broad array of businesses and is dominated by retailers with large brick-and-mortar store footprints. Though some constituents may be insulated from e-commerce competition, others risk obsolescence as product distribution moves to digital means, and online retailers offer lower prices for identical goods and services. We're fairly neutral on the structure of the industry, though some constituents will inevitably face secular and permanent declines.

Lam Research LRCX   FAIRLY VALUED

Buying Index™ 6   Value Rating ⬤

Economic Castle	Estimated Fair Value	Fair Value Range	Investment Style	Sector	Industry
Very Attractive	$427.00	$342.00 - $512.00	LARGE-CAP CORE	Information Technology	Technology Giants

We're huge fans of Lam Research's technical advantages and tremendous free cash flow generation. Its free cash flow margin is consistently north of 20%, averaging 23.5% during the past three fiscal years (2018-2020).

Stock Chart (weekly)

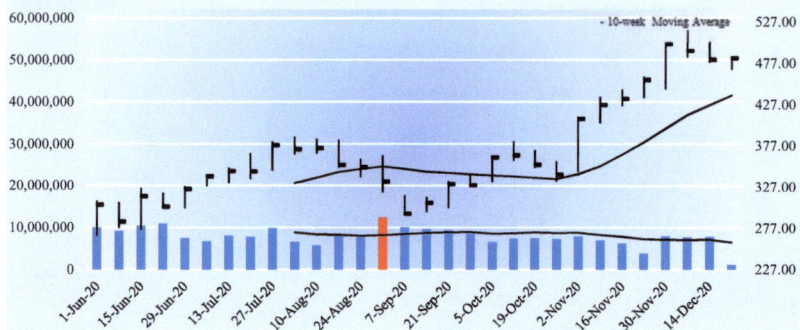

The week with the highest trading volume out of the last 30 weeks was a week of heavy selling, or distribution (red bar).

Investment Considerations

DCF Valuation	FAIRLY VALUED
Relative Valuation	NEUTRAL
ValueCreation™	EXCELLENT
ValueRisk™	LOW
ValueTrend™	POSITIVE
Cash Flow Generation	STRONG
Financial Leverage	LOW
Growth	MODEST
Technical Evaluation	BULLISH
Relative Strength	STRONG
Money Flow Index (MFI)	NEUTRAL
Upside/Downside Volume (U/D)	BULLISH
Near-term Technical Support, 10-week MA	438.00

DCF = Discounted Cash Flow; MFI, U/D = Please see glossary. MA = Moving Average

Company Vitals

Market Cap (USD)	$87,278
Avg Weekly Vol (30 wks)	7,895
30-week Range (USD)	267.10 - 516.65
Valuentum Sector	Information Technology
5-week Return	10.6%
13-week Return	45.7%
30-week Return	78.4%
Dividend Yield %	1.1%
Dividends per Share	5.20
Forward Dividend Payout Ratio	38.0%
Est. Normal Diluted EPS	20.79
P/E on Est. Normal Diluted EPS	23.2
Est. Normal EBITDA	4,617
Forward EV/EBITDA	27.6
EV/Est. Normal EBITDA	18.4
Forward Revenue Growth (5-yr)	6.1%
Forward EPS Growth (5-yr)	15.8%

NMF = Not Meaningful; Est. = Estimated; FY = Fiscal Year

Returns Summary

	3-year Historical Average
Return on Equity	26.4%
Return on Assets	13.9%
ROIC, with goodwill	57.8%
ROIC, without goodwill	92.9%

ROIC = Return on Invested Capital; NMF = Not Meaningful

Leverage, Coverage, and Liquidity

In Millions of USD

Total Debt	2,417
Net Debt	-2,533
Total Debt/EBITDA	0.7
Net Debt/EBITDA	NMF
EBITDA/Interest	36.5
Current Ratio	2.9
Quick Ratio	2.3

NMF = Not Meaningful

Investment Highlights

- Lam Research makes wafer fabrication equipment and serves the global semiconductor industry. The firm has been the leading supplier of high-throughput plasma etch equipment for more than a decade. Its customers make non-volatile memory (NVM), dynamic random-access memory (DRAM) and logic devices. It was founded in 1980 and is headquartered in Fremont, California.

- The memory markets continue to benefit from growth in density as part of the ongoing shift to what management calls the new data-enabled economy. The growing interconnectedness of our world is producing never before seen levels of data, which will required data storage.

- The company's exposure to the 'Memory' end market has fallen from 70%+ of revenue in recent years to under 60%, with increasing revenue from 'Foundry' operations. Logic/integrated circuit making accounts for ~10% of its business. We like its emphasis on R&D (~10-13% of sales), which has enhanced its core competencies in nanoscale applications, plasma and fluidics, among other areas.

- Lam Research has deals with all of the largest semiconductor makers, but it does have a degree of customer concentration. As of fiscal 2020, Micron Tech, Samsung Electronics, SK hynix, and TSM each accounted for more than 10% of total revenue. China and Korea account for ~30% and ~25% of revenue, respectively.

- Lam Research is well-positioned in the right segments of the market with significant know-how and a broad installed base. Demand from applications in the cloud and the 'Internet of Things' (IOT) is driving the need for more powerful semiconductors that are more cost efficient.

Business Quality

ValueRisk™	Very Poor	Poor	Good	Excellent
Low				⬛
Medium				
High				
Very High				

ValueCreation™

Firms that generate economic profits with little operating variability score near the top right of the matrix.

Relative Valuation

	Forward P/E	PEG	Price / FV
Apple	29.8	2.4	85.0%
Alphabet	34.9	1.8	73.3%
Amazon.com	NMF	3.3	95.7%
Microsoft	31.6	2.5	91.6%
Peer Median	31.6	2.5	88.3%
Lam Research	**35.3**	**2.3**	**113.1%**

Price / FV = Current Stock Price divided by Estimated Fair Value

Financial Summary

	----- Actual -----		Projected
Fiscal Year End:	Jun-17	Jun-18	Jun-19
Revenue	8,014	11,077	9,654
Revenue, YoY%	36.1%	38.2%	-12.9%
Operating Income	1,902	3,213	2,924
Operating Margin %	23.7%	29.0%	30.3%
Net Income	1,698	2,381	2,476
Net Income Margin %	21.2%	21.5%	25.6%
Diluted EPS	9.24	13.17	13.70
Diluted EPS, YoY %	77.0%	42.5%	4.0%
Free Cash Flow (CFO-capex)	1,872	2,383	2,872
Free Cash Flow Margin %	23.4%	21.5%	29.8%

In Millions of USD (except for per share items)

Structure of the Semiconductor Equipment Industry   VERY POOR

The semiconductor equipment industry is highly competitive and characterized by rapid technological change. Success hinges on the ability to commercialize new technology in a timely manner, continuously enhance products to improve efficiency of customer fab operations, and manage costs and inventory effectively. Performance of constituents is heavily influenced by manufacturing capacity and fab utilization rates, which together create volatile demand cycles. The potential for unexpected shifts in demand for the group's products leaves us unexcited about the industry's structural characteristics.

Lululemon LULU FAIRLY VALUED

Buying Index™ 6 **Value Rating** 🟡

Economic Castle	Estimated Fair Value	Fair Value Range	Investment Style	Sector	Industry
Very Attractive	$346.00	$242.00 - $450.00	LARGE-CAP BLEND	Next Generation	Disruptive Innovation

Lululemon has recently moved into the in-home fitness space with its acquisition of Mirror.

Stock Chart (weekly)

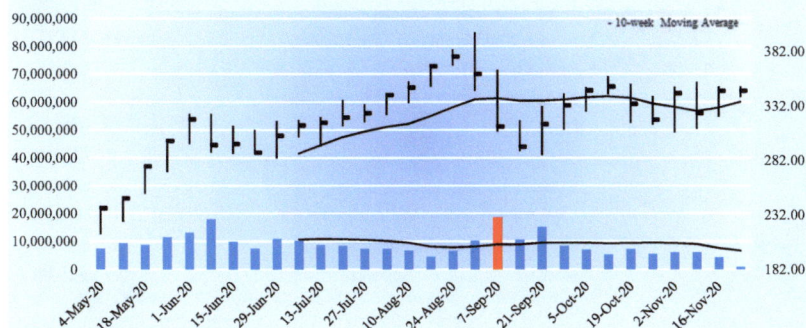

The week with the highest trading volume out of the last 30 weeks was a week of heavy selling, or distribution (red bar).

Investment Considerations

DCF Valuation	**FAIRLY VALUED**
Relative Valuation	**NEUTRAL**
ValueCreation™	**EXCELLENT**
ValueRisk™	**MEDIUM**
ValueTrend™	**NEGATIVE**
Cash Flow Generation	**STRONG**
Financial Leverage	**LOW**
Growth	**AGGRESSIVE**
Technical Evaluation	**BULLISH**
Relative Strength	**WEAK**
Money Flow Index (MFI)	**NEUTRAL**
Upside/Downside Volume (U/D)	**BEARISH**
Near-term Technical Support, 10-week MA	**336.00**

DCF = Discounted Cash Flow; MFI, U/D = Please see glossary. MA = Moving Average

Business Quality

ValueRisk™	Very Poor	Poor	Good	Excellent
Low				
Medium				▓
High				
Very High				

ValueCreation™

Firms that generate economic profits with little operating variability score near the top right of the matrix.

Company Vitals

Market Cap (USD)	$45,276
Avg Weekly Vol (30 wks)	8,737
30-week Range (USD)	213.97 - 399.90
Valuentum Sector	Next Generation
5-week Return	2.9%
13-week Return	-8.4%
30-week Return	60.7%
Dividend Yield %	0.0%
Dividends per Share	0.00
Forward Dividend Payout Ratio	0.0%
Est. Normal Diluted EPS	9.20
P/E on Est. Normal Diluted EPS	37.6
Est. Normal EBITDA	1,808
Forward EV/EBITDA	50.3
EV/Est. Normal EBITDA	24.8
Forward Revenue Growth (5-yr)	16.5%
Forward EPS Growth (5-yr)	24.6%

NMF = Not Meaningful; Est. = Estimated; FY = Fiscal Year

Returns Summary
3-year Historical Average

Return on Equity	29.1%
Return on Assets	20.6%
ROIC, with goodwill	79.9%
ROIC, without goodwill	82.8%

ROIC = Return on Invested Capital; NMF = Not Meaningful

Leverage, Coverage, and Liquidity
In Millions of USD

Total Debt	611
Net Debt	-482
Total Debt/EBITDA	0.6
Net Debt/EBITDA	NMF
EBITDA/Interest	Excellent
Current Ratio	2.9
Quick Ratio	1.8

NMF = Not Meaningful

Investment Highlights

• Lululemon athletica is a designer and retailer of technical athletic apparel operating primarily in North America and Australia. Its yoga-inspired apparel is marketed under the 'lululemon athletica' and 'ivivva' athletica brand names. The firm continues to drive global brand awareness. It was founded in the late 1990s and is based in Vancouver, Canada.

• The yoga-pants maker posts strong margins, continues to invest in innovation across its business, while pursuing an omni-channel guest-centric approach. Leadership is decentralized and purpose driven, emphasizing every guest point. We like the customer focus.

• Lululemon underscores the shift in consumption habits occurring in the US. Consumers are opting for more fashionable brand-oriented items, which is allowing affordable luxury to prosper. Near-term drivers include international expansion, product innovation, and digital initiatives on the top line, and sourcing and supply chain benefits, among others, on the bottom line.

• Lululemon is ramping up its marketing efforts towards men. The firm continues to tout its product innovation as a key driver of the strong momentum it is seeing in this category, and it believes it has a $1+ billion opportunity. Its men's division accounts for ~20% of its total business, but men account for nearly 30% of all new guests.

• Lululemon expects to raise its men's category, e-commerce, and international businesses to ~25% of total revenue each, up from 19%, 20%, and 20%, respectively. It recently moved into the in-home fitness space by buying Mirror.

Relative Valuation

	Forward P/E	PEG	Price / FV
Wayfair	56.3	NMF	84.2%
Zoom Video	170.7	28.8	120.8%
Roku	-338.4	NMF	96.0%
Monster Beverage	36.0	2.9	104.4%
Peer Median	46.1	15.9	100.2%
Lululemon	**81.5**	**1.9**	**99.9%**

Price / FV = Current Stock Price divided by Estimated Fair Value

Financial Summary

	----- Actual -----		Projected
Fiscal Year End:	Jan-19	Jan-20	Jan-21
Revenue	3,288	3,979	4,138
Revenue, YoY%	24.1%	21.0%	4.0%
Operating Income	706	889	764
Operating Margin %	21.5%	22.3%	18.5%
Net Income	484	646	550
Net Income Margin %	14.7%	16.2%	13.3%
Diluted EPS	3.61	4.93	4.24
Diluted EPS, YoY %	90.2%	36.5%	-14.0%
Free Cash Flow (CFO-capex)	517	386	604
Free Cash Flow Margin %	15.7%	9.7%	14.6%

In Millions of USD (except for per share items)

Structure of the Luxury Goods Industry   **GOOD**

Luxury goods firms differentiate themselves based on brand name, perception, and quality in order to generate excess returns on invested capital through the economic cycle. Building a large, successful luxury brand is difficult, leaving those that possess them with intangible competitive advantages that are not easily overcome by new entrants. Growth in emerging middle classes and China will be the key demand drivers going forward, though the strongest brands will also successfully via market share gains. Though changes in consumer preferences should be watched closely, we like the structure of the group.

Mastercard MA   FAIRLY VALUED

Buying Index™ 6   Value Rating 🟡

Economic Castle	Estimated Fair Value	Fair Value Range	Investment Style	Sector	Industry
Very Attractive	$344.00	$275.00 - $413.00	MEGA-CAP BLEND	Information Technology	Technology Giants

Mastercard's outlook remains bright as rising e-commerce demand underpins its growth trajectory.

Stock Chart (weekly)

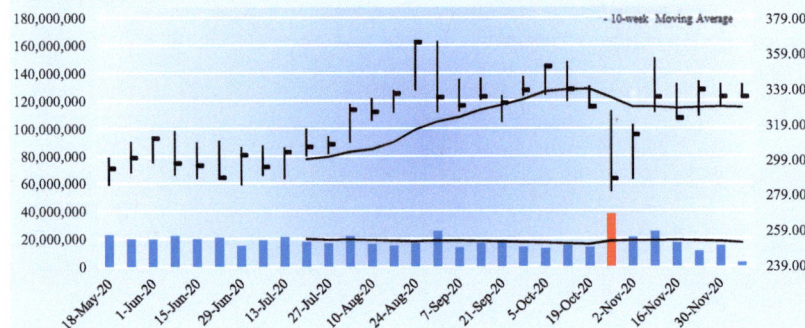

The week with the highest trading volume out of the last 30 weeks was a week of heavy selling, or distribution (red bar).

Company Vitals

Market Cap (USD)	$342,513
Avg Weekly Vol (30 wks)	17,976
30-week Range (USD)	281.2 - 367.25
Valuentum Sector	Information Technology
5-week Return	-3.4%
13-week Return	0.1%
30-week Return	17.4%
Dividend Yield %	0.5%
Dividends per Share	1.60
Forward Dividend Payout Ratio	24.9%
Est. Normal Diluted EPS	10.89
P/E on Est. Normal Diluted EPS	30.8
Est. Normal EBITDA	15,035
Forward EV/EBITDA	34.7
EV/Est. Normal EBITDA	22.8
Forward Revenue Growth (5-yr)	11.5%
Forward EPS Growth (5-yr)	14.4%

NMF = Not Meaningful; Est. = Estimated; FY = Fiscal Year

Returns Summary
3-year Historical Average

Return on Equity	107.4%
Return on Assets	25.0%
ROIC, with goodwill	86.5%
ROIC, without goodwill	128.6%

ROIC = Return on Invested Capital; NMF = Not Meaningful

Leverage, Coverage, and Liquidity
In Millions of USD

Total Debt	8,527
Net Debt	267
Total Debt/EBITDA	0.8
Net Debt/EBITDA	0.0
EBITDA/Interest	50.6
Current Ratio	1.4
Quick Ratio	1.2

NMF = Not Meaningful

Investment Highlights

• Mastercard is a payments industry leader. Every day, the firm's network makes payments happen. It doesn't issue cards, set interest rates or establish annual fees. Mastercard generates revenue by charging fees to issuers and acquirers for providing transaction processing and other payment-related services based on the gross dollar volume of activity.

• Please note our cash flow model assumes Mastercard grows its revenues by double-digits annually and significant expands its operating margins over the coming years. Should the firm stumble for any reason, its intrinsic value would face significant headwinds.

• The larger secular trend moving society towards electronic payments accelerated during the COVID-19 pandemic due to surging e-commerce demand. Technological advances and demand for adjacent services will continue to drive growth opportunities for MasterCard, and these secular growth tailwinds underpin the firm's very promising outlook.

• Mastercard benefits from one of the strongest competitive advantages out there – the network effect. As more consumers use credit/debit cards, more merchants accept them, thereby creating a virtuous cycle. Mastercard's financials have held up well so far in the face of the COVID-19 pandemic.

• When it comes to the credit-card processing space, we generally prefer Visa and Mastercard, which do not take on credit risk like Discover or American Express. This shields those firms from credit quality concerns. Subdued travel demand is a near-term headwind.

Investment Considerations

DCF Valuation	FAIRLY VALUED
Relative Valuation	NEUTRAL
ValueCreation™	EXCELLENT
ValueRisk™	LOW
ValueTrend™	NEGATIVE
Cash Flow Generation	STRONG
Financial Leverage	LOW
Growth	HIGH
Technical Evaluation	BULLISH
Relative Strength	WEAK
Money Flow Index (MFI)	NEUTRAL
Upside/Downside Volume (U/D)	BEARISH
Near-term Technical Support, 10-week MA	329.00

DCF = Discounted Cash Flow; MFI, U/D = Please see glossary. MA = Moving Average

Business Quality

ValueRisk™	Very Poor	Poor	Good	Excellent
Low				■
Medium				
High				
Very High				

Firms that generate economic profits with little operating variability score near the top right of the matrix.

Relative Valuation

	Forward P/E	PEG	Price / FV
Apple	29.8	2.4	85.0%
Alphabet	34.9	1.8	73.3%
Amazon.com	NMF	3.3	95.7%
Microsoft	31.6	2.5	91.6%
Peer Median	31.6	2.5	88.3%
Mastercard	52.2	1.7	97.4%

Price / FV = Current Stock Price divided by Estimated Fair Value

Financial Summary

	Actual		Projected
Fiscal Year End:	Dec-18	Dec-19	Dec-20
Revenue	14,950	16,883	15,228
Revenue, YoY%	19.6%	12.9%	-9.8%
Operating Income	8,410	9,664	8,266
Operating Margin %	56.3%	57.2%	54.3%
Net Income	5,859	8,118	6,434
Net Income Margin %	39.2%	48.1%	42.2%
Diluted EPS	5.60	7.94	6.42
Diluted EPS, YoY %	53.2%	41.9%	-19.1%
Free Cash Flow (CFO-capex)	5,719	7,455	8,144
Free Cash Flow Margin %	38.3%	44.2%	53.5%

In Millions of USD (except for per share items)

Structure of the Financial Tech Services Industry   EXCELLENT

The financial tech services industry is primarily composed of firms that generate revenue by charging fees to customers for providing transaction processing and other payment-related services. Constituents operate in a rapidly-evolving legal/regulatory environment, particularly with respect to interchange fees, data protection, and information security. Several participants benefit from a significant competitive advantage – the network effect. As more consumers use credit/debit cards, more merchants accept them, thereby creating a virtuous cycle. The industry is one of the most attractive in our coverage.

McDonald's MCD   FAIRLY VALUED

Buying Index™ 7   **Value Rating**

Economic Castle	Estimated Fair Value	Fair Value Range	Investment Style	Sector	Industry
Attractive	$204.00	$158.00 - $250.00	LARGE-CAP CORE	Consumer Discretionary	Discretionary Spending

We've raised McDonald's fair value estimate as its outlook is improving, though headwinds from COVID-19 remain.

Stock Chart (weekly)

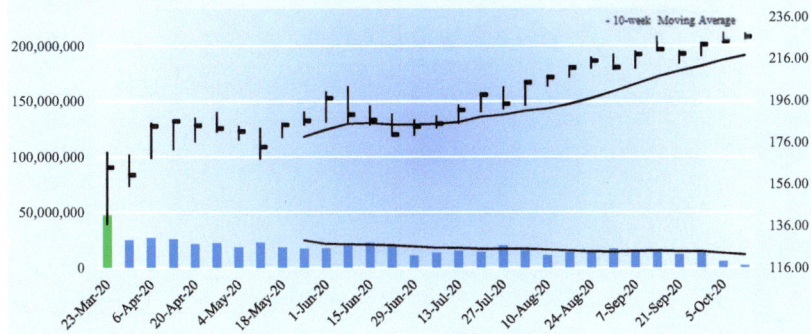

The week with the highest trading volume out of the last 30 weeks was a week of heavy selling, or distribution (red bar).

Company Vitals

Market Cap (USD)	$173,235
Avg Weekly Vol (30 wks)	17,670
30-week Range (USD)	136.50 - 228.66
Valuentum Sector	Consumer Discretionary
5-week Return	3.1%
13-week Return	18.6%
30-week Return	58.4%
Dividend Yield %	2.2%
Dividends per Share	5.00
Forward Dividend Payout Ratio	84.9%
Est. Normal Diluted EPS	10.62
P/E on Est. Normal Diluted EPS	21.3
Est. Normal EBITDA	12,558
Forward EV/EBITDA	25.3
EV/Est. Normal EBITDA	16.4
Forward Revenue Growth (5-yr)	6.0%
Forward EPS Growth (5-yr)	14.5%

NMF = Not Meaningful; Est. = Estimated; FY = Fiscal Year

Returns Summary
3-year Historical Average

Return on Equity	-132.5%
Return on Assets	16.3%
ROIC, with goodwill	27.1%
ROIC, without goodwill	30.0%

ROIC = Return on Invested Capital; NMF = Not Meaningful

Leverage, Coverage, and Liquidity
In Millions of USD

Total Debt	34,177
Net Debt	33,278
Total Debt/EBITDA	3.3
Net Debt/EBITDA	3.2
EBITDA/Interest	9.4
Current Ratio	1.0
Quick Ratio	0.9

NMF = Not Meaningful

Investment Highlights

• Home of the Big Mac, McDonald's is the world's largest quick-service restaurant brand. The firm's management is extremely shareholder-friendly, returning billions to shareholders annually. At the end of 2019, McDonald's had ~38,700 restaurants in 119 countries. The company was founded in 1940 and is based in Oak Brook, Illinois.

• At the end of 2019, ~93% of McDonald's restaurant locations were franchised, including ~95% of its US locations. In 2019, McDonald's net restaurant count grew by over 800 after adding over 600 net new restaurant locations to its business in 2018.

• Though it will be hard to produce another gem to the same success as McCafe, 'all-day breakfast' has been a needle-mover, and its refranchising efforts are moving the operating line. Industry-wide traffic weakness and competitive pricing in the US are worth noting as they relate to comp performance. McDonald's seeks to franchise ~95% of its total restaurant count.

• McDonald's continues to modernize its stores and upgrade its digital operations. The company's drive-thru operations were essential in meeting customer demand during the initial phases of the COVID-19 pandemic, though headwinds from COVID-19 have been a major drag on its financials of late.

• Labor/wage market developments are worth keeping an eye on, and increasing competition from fast-casual and healthier menus is a permanent, structural change. McDonald's is slowly reopening its in-store dining areas that were shut down due to COVID-19.

Investment Considerations

DCF Valuation	FAIRLY VALUED
Relative Valuation	ATTRACTIVE
ValueCreation™	EXCELLENT
ValueRisk™	MEDIUM
ValueTrend™	POSITIVE
Cash Flow Generation	STRONG
Financial Leverage	HIGH
Growth	MODEST
Technical Evaluation	BULLISH
Relative Strength	STRONG
Money Flow Index (MFI)	NEUTRAL
Upside/Downside Volume (U/D)	BULLISH
Near-term Technical Support, 10-week MA	217.00

DCF = Discounted Cash Flow; MFI, U/D = Please see glossary. MA = Moving Average

Business Quality

ValueRisk™	Very Poor	Poor	Good	Excellent
Low				
Medium				▨
High				
Very High				

Firms that generate economic profits with little operating variability score near the top right of the matrix.

Relative Valuation

	Forward P/E	PEG	Price / FV
Disney	75.6	0.3	98.3%
Home Depot	22.9	1.9	106.7%
Nike	52.8	2.5	104.9%
Starbucks	92.2	0.6	110.6%
Peer Median	64.2	1.2	105.8%
McDonald's	**38.5**	**1.1**	**111.0%**

Price / FV = Current Stock Price divided by Estimated Fair Value

Financial Summary

	----- Actual -----		Projected
Fiscal Year End:	Dec-18	Dec-19	Dec-20
Revenue	21,025	21,077	19,075
Revenue, YoY%	-7.9%	0.2%	-9.5%
Operating Income	8,586	8,886	6,709
Operating Margin %	40.8%	42.2%	35.2%
Net Income	5,924	6,025	4,414
Net Income Margin %	28.2%	28.6%	23.1%
Diluted EPS	7.54	7.88	5.89
Diluted EPS, YoY %	18.4%	4.5%	-25.2%
Free Cash Flow (CFO-capex)	4,226	5,728	4,676
Free Cash Flow Margin %	20.1%	27.2%	24.5%

In Millions of USD (except for per share items)

Structure of the Restaurants Industry - Fast Food & Coffee   NEUTRAL

The restaurant industry has benefited from a long-term trend toward eating out, but the space has become increasingly more competitive as new concepts are introduced and successful chains expand. Not only are there pricing pressures and trade-down threats, but rising costs for commodities and labor have pressured profits. Barriers to entry are low, and many constituents have a difficult time differentiating themselves. We tend to like larger chains that benefit from scale advantages and international expansion opportunities, though niche franchises can be appealing. We're neutral on the structure of the group.

Mondelez Intl MDLZ   FAIRLY VALUED

Buying Index™ 7   **Value Rating** 🟡

Economic Castle	Estimated Fair Value	Fair Value Range	Investment Style	Sector	Industry
Attractive	$50.00	$40.00 - $60.00	LARGE-CAP CORE	Consumer Staples	Recession Resistant

Mondelez is focused on growing its organic sales while better controlling costs going forward. We moderately increased our fair value estimate.

Stock Chart (weekly)

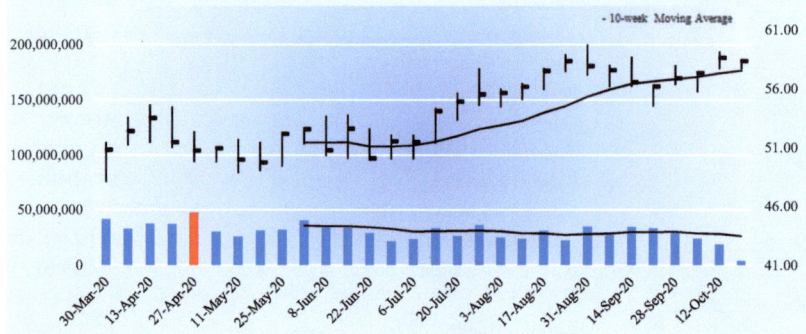

The week with the highest trading volume out of the last 30 weeks was a week of heavy selling, or distribution (red bar).

Company Vitals

Market Cap (USD)	$85,023
Avg Weekly Vol (30 wks)	30,085
30-week Range (USD)	48.00 - 59.72
Valuentum Sector	Consumer Staples
5-week Return	4.1%
13-week Return	6.3%
30-week Return	19.5%
Dividend Yield %	2.2%
Dividends per Share	1.26
Forward Dividend Payout Ratio	48.2%
Est. Normal Diluted EPS	3.15
P/E on Est. Normal Diluted EPS	18.5
Est. Normal EBITDA	6,862
Forward EV/EBITDA	17.2
EV/Est. Normal EBITDA	14.9
Forward Revenue Growth (5-yr)	3.2%
Forward EPS Growth (5-yr)	7.1%

NMF = Not Meaningful; Est. = Estimated; FY = Fiscal Year

Returns Summary

	3-year Historical Average
Return on Equity	11.7%
Return on Assets	4.8%
ROIC, with goodwill	8.5%
ROIC, without goodwill	16.2%

ROIC = Return on Invested Capital; NMF = Not Meaningful

Leverage, Coverage, and Liquidity

In Millions of USD

Total Debt	18,426
Net Debt	17,135
Total Debt/EBITDA	3.5
Net Debt/EBITDA	3.3
EBITDA/Interest	11.5
Current Ratio	0.5
Quick Ratio	0.3

NMF = Not Meaningful

Investment Highlights

• Mondelez is a global snacks powerhouse. Its 'Biscuits' and 'Chocolate' product categories generate roughly two-thirds of its revenues combined. The company generates about three-quarters of its segment operating income from its 'Europe' and 'North America' divisions. Going forward, Mondelez is targeting international growth opportunities.

• It's hard not to like the firm's product line-up. Mondelez boasts many of the world's favorite snack brands: Oreo, Triscuit, Honey Maid, Toblerone, Chips Ahoy, Wheat Thins, Newtons, Ritz, and Nabisco. Consumers continue to love its products.

• Over the long haul, Mondelez is targeting 3%+ annual organic net revenue growth, annual adjusted earnings per share growth at a high-single-digit rate, and free cash flow of $3+ billion per year. Mondelez owns a large equity stake in both Keurig Dr Pepper and JDE Peet's, indicating its balance sheet is stronger than it first appears.

• Mondelez is investing in its digital capabilities to improve its advertising campaigns, adjust its brand messaging, and better position the firm to capitalize on the shift towards e-commerce. Cost control measures, supply chain efficiencies, and better inventory management systems are being pursued.

• Mondelez has been putting up decent organic rates of late. During the first half of fiscal 2020, organic net revenue growth came in at 3.7%. As with most companies, however, its outlook remains murky due to COVID-19.

Investment Considerations

DCF Valuation	**FAIRLY VALUED**
Relative Valuation	**ATTRACTIVE**
ValueCreation™	**EXCELLENT**
ValueRisk™	**LOW**
ValueTrend™	**POSITIVE**
Cash Flow Generation	**STRONG**
Financial Leverage	**HIGH**
Growth	**MODEST**
Technical Evaluation	**BULLISH**
Relative Strength	**WEAK**
Money Flow Index (MFI)	**NEUTRAL**
Upside/Downside Volume (U/D)	**BULLISH**
Near-term Technical Support, 10-week MA	**57.00**

DCF = Discounted Cash Flow; MFI, U/D = Please see glossary. MA = Moving Average

Business Quality

ValueCreation™

ValueRisk™	Very Poor	Poor	Good	Excellent
Low				■
Medium				
High				
Very High				

Firms that generate economic profits with little operating variability score near the top right of the matrix.

Relative Valuation

	Forward P/E	PEG	Price / FV
Coca-Cola	34.3	1.5	128.0%
Procter & Gamble	26.5	3.3	144.1%
Philip Morris	15.4	2.4	104.3%
Wal-Mart	26.8	2.3	130.2%
Peer Median	26.7	2.4	129.1%
Mondelez Intl	**22.3**	**2.4**	**116.6%**

Price / FV = Current Stock Price divided by Estimated Fair Value

Financial Summary

	----- Actual -----		Projected
Fiscal Year End:	Dec-18	Dec-19	Dec-20
Revenue	25,938	25,868	26,230
Revenue, YoY%	0.2%	-0.3%	1.4%
Operating Income	3,701	4,027	4,695
Operating Margin %	14.3%	15.6%	17.9%
Net Income	3,391	3,870	3,776
Net Income Margin %	13.1%	15.0%	14.4%
Diluted EPS	2.28	2.65	2.62
Diluted EPS, YoY %	NMF	16.3%	-1.4%
Free Cash Flow (CFO-capex)	2,853	3,040	4,611
Free Cash Flow Margin %	11.0%	11.8%	17.6%

In Millions of USD (except for per share items)

Structure of the Food Products Industry   NEUTRAL

The food products industry is composed of a number of firms with strong brand names. However, market supply/demand dynamics and intense competition still impact product prices, while fluctuations in commodity costs can make earnings quite volatile. Private-label competition, competitors' promotional spending, and changing consumer preferences often drive demand trends. The group's customers—such as supermarkets, warehouses, and food distributors—continue to consolidate, increasing buying power over constituents and hurting margins. Still, we're generally neutral on the group.

VALUENTUM

Medtronic MDT FAIRLY VALUED

Buying Index™ 3 **Value Rating** 🟡

Economic Castle	Estimated Fair Value	Fair Value Range	Investment Style	Sector	Industry
Attractive	$95.00	$76.00 - $114.00	LARGE-CAP CORE	Health Care	Health Care Bellwethers

We moderately raised our fair value estimate for Medtronic as the company's near-term outlook continues to improve.

Stock Chart (weekly)

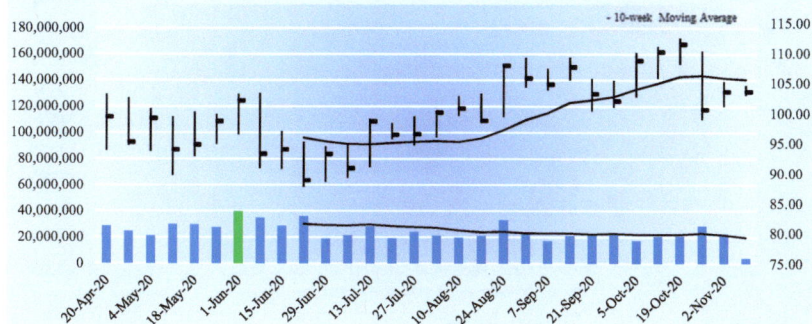

The week with the highest trading volume out of the last 30 weeks was a week of heavy selling, or distribution (red bar).

Company Vitals

Market Cap (USD)	$139,920
Avg Weekly Vol (30 wks)	24,324
30-week Range (USD)	87.68 - 112.48
Valuentum Sector	Health Care
5-week Return	-5.5%
13-week Return	1.4%
30-week Return	1.5%
Dividend Yield %	2.2%
Dividends per Share	2.32
Forward Dividend Payout Ratio	57.3%
Est. Normal Diluted EPS	5.87
P/E on Est. Normal Diluted EPS	17.7
Est. Normal EBITDA	12,971
Forward EV/EBITDA	15.1
EV/Est. Normal EBITDA	11.9
Forward Revenue Growth (5-yr)	5.5%
Forward EPS Growth (5-yr)	13.4%

NMF = Not Meaningful; Est. = Estimated; FY = Fiscal Year

Returns Summary
3-year Historical Average

Return on Equity	8.3%
Return on Assets	4.6%
ROIC, with goodwill	9.8%
ROIC, without goodwill	22.4%

ROIC = Return on Invested Capital; NMF = Not Meaningful

Leverage, Coverage, and Liquidity
In Millions of USD

Total Debt	24,797
Net Debt	13,849
Total Debt/EBITDA	3.1
Net Debt/EBITDA	1.7
EBITDA/Interest	7.3
Current Ratio	2.1
Quick Ratio	1.5

NMF = Not Meaningful

Investment Highlights

• Medtronic is a global leader in medical technology. The company functions in four operating segments: Cardiac & Vascular, Minimally Invasive Therapies, Restorative Therapies, and Diabetes. Medtronic bought Covidien in a tax-inversion deal in 2015 through a cash-and-stock deal worth ~$42.9 billion. Medtronic traces its roots back to the late 1940s.

• Medtronic is a Dividend Aristocrat. It has grown its per-share dividend at an ~17% CAGR by increasing its dividend over the past 43 consecutive years (as of calendar year 2020). Management remains committed to returning free cash flow to shareholders.

• Medtronic's long-term free cash flow conversion target is 80%, and in fiscal 2020, the company easily exceeded that goal by generating a free cash flow conversion rate of ~97%. The firm's product pipeline remains robust, with an eye towards its 'Deep Brian Stimulation System,' pacemaker, atrial fibrillation, and pelvic health offerings.

• Medtronic sees emerging markets underpinning its long-term growth trajectory, which represented a relatively small portion of its fiscal 2020 revenues. The firm identified three things to work on to improve its performance in these markets: channel optimization, functional capabilities, and localization.

• The COVID-19 pandemic has been disruptive to Medtronic, consistent with the pain felt across the rest of the MedTech industry. Medtronic has a strong financial profile to deal with weakness as a result of deferred procedures from the pandemic.

Investment Considerations

DCF Valuation	FAIRLY VALUED
Relative Valuation	UNATTRACTIVE
ValueCreation™	EXCELLENT
ValueRisk™	LOW
ValueTrend™	NEGATIVE
Cash Flow Generation	STRONG
Financial Leverage	MEDIUM
Growth	MODEST
Technical Evaluation	VERY BEARISH
Relative Strength	WEAK
Money Flow Index (MFI)	NEUTRAL
Upside/Downside Volume (U/D)	DETERIORATING
Near-term Technical Resistance, 10-wk MA	106.00

DCF = Discounted Cash Flow; MFI, U/D = Please see glossary. MA = Moving Average

Business Quality

ValueRisk™	ValueCreation™			
	Very Poor	Poor	Good	Excellent
Low				■
Medium				
High				
Very High				

Firms that generate economic profits with little operating variability score near the top right of the matrix.

Relative Valuation

	Forward P/E	PEG	Price / FV
Johnson & Johnson	17.6	1.8	99.5%
Abbott	34.1	2.2	110.0%
Merck	21.5	2.2	100.5%
Pfizer	20.1	0.8	93.3%
Peer Median	20.8	2.0	100.0%
Medtronic	**25.6**	**2.2**	**109.0%**

Price / FV = Current Stock Price divided by Estimated Fair Value

Financial Summary

	----- Actual -----		Projected
Fiscal Year End:	Apr-19	Apr-20	Apr-21
Revenue	30,557	28,913	29,202
Revenue, YoY%	2.0%	-5.4%	1.0%
Operating Income	6,268	5,293	7,485
Operating Margin %	20.5%	18.3%	25.6%
Net Income	4,631	4,789	5,417
Net Income Margin %	15.2%	16.6%	18.6%
Diluted EPS	3.41	3.54	4.05
Diluted EPS, YoY %	50.4%	3.9%	14.3%
Free Cash Flow (CFO-capex)	5,873	6,021	4,300
Free Cash Flow Margin %	19.2%	20.8%	14.7%

In Millions of USD (except for per share items)

Structure of the Medical Devices Industry
GOOD

The medical devices industry is heavily regulated and characterized by rapid technological change. Firms have been forced to compete on price due to economically-motivated buyers, consolidation among healthcare providers, and declining reimbursement rates. Healthcare reform measures have put additional pressure on procedure rates and market sizes. Still, firms can gain advantages by developing products with differentiated clinical outcomes or by creating patent-protected technology. Since most constituents hold important patents or trade secrets, we tend to like the group.

VALUENTUM

Mercadolibre MELI FAIRLY VALUED

Buying Index™ 6   **Value Rating** ○

Economic Castle	Estimated Fair Value	Fair Value Range	Investment Style	Sector	Industry
Attractive	$1590.00	$1193.00 - $1988.00	LARGE-CAP GROWTH	Next Generation	Disruptive Innovation

The growing prevalence of e-commerce benefits Mercadolibre's outlook, and we once again raised our fair value estimate of the stock.

Stock Chart (weekly)

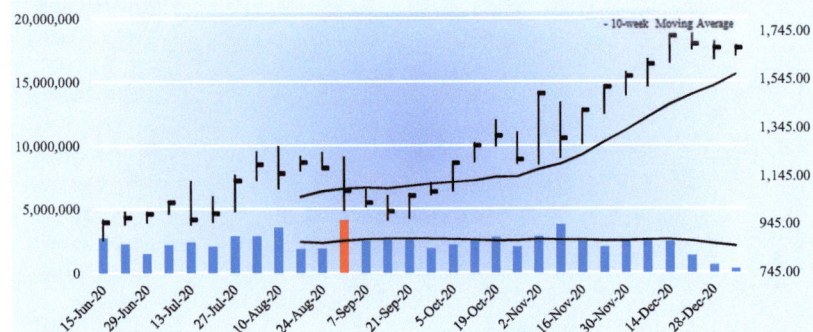

The week with the highest trading volume out of the last 30 weeks was a week of heavy selling, or distribution (red bar).

Investment Considerations

DCF Valuation	**FAIRLY VALUED**
Relative Valuation	**UNATTRACTIVE**
ValueCreation™	**EXCELLENT**
ValueRisk™	**MEDIUM**
ValueTrend™	**POSITIVE**
Cash Flow Generation	**STRONG**
Financial Leverage	**HIGH**
Growth	**AGGRESSIVE**
Technical Evaluation	**BULLISH**
Relative Strength	**STRONG**
Money Flow Index (MFI)	**NEUTRAL**
Upside/Downside Volume (U/D)	**BULLISH**
Near-term Technical Support, 10-week MA	**1564.00**

DCF = Discounted Cash Flow; MFI, U/D = Please see glossary. MA = Moving Average

Company Vitals

Market Cap (USD)	$81,487
Avg Weekly Vol (30 wks)	2,325
30-week Range (USD)	877.02 - 1,735.75
Valuentum Sector	Next Generation
5-week Return	7.5%
13-week Return	35.4%
30-week Return	88.9%
Dividend Yield %	0.0%
Dividends per Share	0.00
Forward Dividend Payout Ratio	0.0%
Est. Normal Diluted EPS	12.45
P/E on Est. Normal Diluted EPS	134.4
Est. Normal EBITDA	1,459
Forward EV/EBITDA	270.9
EV/Est. Normal EBITDA	54.3
Forward Revenue Growth (5-yr)	34.8%
Forward EPS Growth (5-yr)	-251.9%

NMF = Not Meaningful; Est. = Estimated; FY = Fiscal Year

Returns Summary   3-year Historical Average

Return on Equity	-7.2%
Return on Assets	-2.0%
ROIC, with goodwill	30.3%
ROIC, without goodwill	33.5%

ROIC = Return on Invested Capital; NMF = Not Meaningful

Leverage, Coverage, and Liquidity
In Millions of USD

Total Debt	817
Net Debt	-2,231
Total Debt/EBITDA	NMF
Net Debt/EBITDA	NMF
EBITDA/Interest	-1.2
Current Ratio	2.2
Quick Ratio	2.1

NMF = Not Meaningful

Investment Highlights

• Mercadolibre is the largest e-commerce ecosystem in Latin America. The company benefits from positive demographic/income trends and rising internet penetration in the region. The firm was founded in 1999 and is headquartered in Argentina. It suspended its dividend in 2018 to focus on other, more opportunistic investments.

• The company operates a high-margin and strong cash-generating business. Its brand is well-known, and the firm boasts a strong marketplace business in Latin America. It has a huge opportunity for growth, though it operates in economically volatile markets.

• The firm aims to keep growing the penetration of its payments, shipping and financing solutions as strategic facilitators of e-commerce both on and off its platforms, persistent development of its mobile product offering, category-specific verticalization capabilities to gain wallet share, and continuing to expand and develop its relationship with large retail brands.

• Growth in key areas of Mercadolibre's business has been explosive in recent years. GMV has grown at a robust pace of late. Economic uncertainty in key markets can impact results. Additionally, Amazon seeks to grow its Brazilian operations and could prove to be a significant competitor in an important market.

• The Latin American e-commerce industry is growing at a brisk clip and the industry's promising outlook underpins our optimistic assumptions regarding Mercadolibre's future revenue growth and potential room for margin expansion.

Business Quality

	ValueCreation™			
ValueRisk™	Very Poor	Poor	Good	Excellent
Low				
Medium				■
High				
Very High				

Firms that generate economic profits with little operating variability score near the top right of the matrix.

Relative Valuation

	Forward P/E	PEG	Price / FV
Wayfair	56.3	NMF	84.2%
Zoom Video	170.7	28.8	120.8%
Roku	-338.4	NMF	96.0%
Monster Beverage	36.0	2.9	104.4%
Peer Median	46.1	15.9	100.2%
Mercadolibre	**NMF**	**NMF**	**105.3%**

Price / FV = Current Stock Price divided by Estimated Fair Value

Financial Summary

	----- Actual -----		Projected
Fiscal Year End:	Dec-18	Dec-19	Dec-20
Revenue	1,440	2,296	3,834
Revenue, YoY%	3.0%	59.4%	67.0%
Operating Income	-69	-153	171
Operating Margin %	-4.8%	-6.7%	4.5%
Net Income	-37	-172	79
Net Income Margin %	-2.6%	-7.5%	2.0%
Diluted EPS	-0.83	-3.53	1.47
Diluted EPS, YoY %	-366.3%	325.1%	NMF
Free Cash Flow (CFO-capex)	138	314	919
Free Cash Flow Margin %	9.6%	13.7%	24.0%

In Millions of USD (except for per share items)

Structure of the Financial Tech Services Industry   **EXCELLENT**

The financial tech services industry is primarily composed of firms that generate revenue by charging fees to customers for providing transaction processing and other payment-related services. Constituents operate in a rapidly-evolving legal/regulatory environment, particularly with respect to interchange fees, data protection, and information security. Several participants benefit from a significant competitive advantage – the network effect. As more consumers use credit/debit cards, more merchants accept them, thereby creating a virtuous cycle. The industry is one of the most attractive in our coverage.

McCormick MKC FAIRLY VALUED

Buying Index™ 3　　**Value Rating**　○

Economic Castle	Estimated Fair Value	Fair Value Range	Investment Style	Sector	Industry
Attractive	$80.00	$63.00 - $97.00	LARGE-CAP CORE	Consumer Staples	Recession Resistant

McCormick announced a 2:1 stock split for shareholder on record as of November 20, 2020. Our fair value estimate has been adjusted for the split.

Stock Chart (weekly)

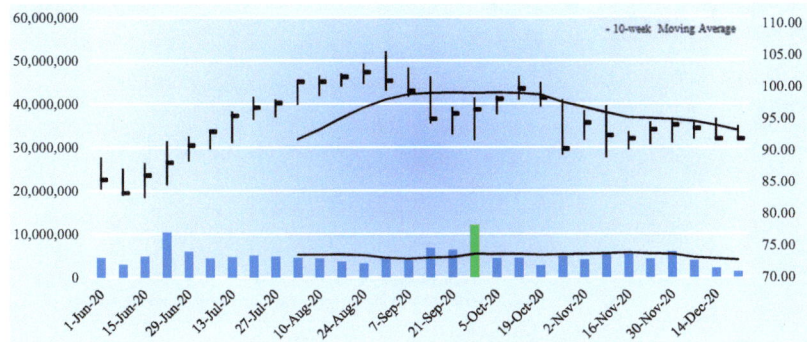

The week with the highest trading volume out of the last 30 weeks was a week of heavy selling, or distribution (red bar).

Company Vitals

Market Cap (USD)	$24,613
Avg Weekly Vol (30 wks)	4,826
30-week Range (USD)	82.52 - 105.53
Valuentum Sector	Consumer Staples
5-week Return	-0.4%
13-week Return	-5.8%
30-week Return	4.3%
Dividend Yield %	1.5%
Dividends per Share	1.36
Forward Dividend Payout Ratio	47.1%
Est. Normal Diluted EPS	3.26
P/E on Est. Normal Diluted EPS	28.2
Est. Normal EBITDA	1,502
Forward EV/EBITDA	21.6
EV/Est. Normal EBITDA	19.2
Forward Revenue Growth (5-yr)	4.6%
Forward EPS Growth (5-yr)	7.7%

NMF = Not Meaningful; Est. = Estimated; FY = Fiscal Year

Returns Summary
3-year Historical Average

Return on Equity	25.1%
Return on Assets	7.3%
ROIC, with goodwill	9.2%
ROIC, without goodwill	19.9%

ROIC = Return on Invested Capital; NMF = Not Meaningful

Leverage, Coverage, and Liquidity
In Millions of USD

Total Debt	4,327
Net Debt	4,172
Total Debt/EBITDA	3.8
Net Debt/EBITDA	3.7
EBITDA/Interest	6.9
Current Ratio	0.7
Quick Ratio	0.3

NMF = Not Meaningful

Investment Highlights

• McCormick makes spices, seasoning mixes, condiments and other flavorful products and distributes them to the entire food industry. Shareholders are rewarded by the firm's strong free cash flow distributed as dividends and repurchases. McCormick is targeting meaningful margin expansion in the coming years. It was founded in 1889 and is based in Maryland.

• McCormick has increased its annual dividend in each of the past 30+ consecutive years, earning the firm coveted Dividend Aristocrat status. The company's dividend health is weakened by its significant net debt load (~$3.9 billion at the end of August 2020), but free cash flow generation is robust.

• McCormick posted strong revenue growth during the first three quarters of fiscal 2020 as demand for consumer staples products surged during the initial phases of the COVID-19 pandemic. Going forward, the company is investing heavily in targeted media campaigns that showcase how McCormick's products can be used while cooking at home.

• McCormick is a global leader in flavor, and we're huge fans of its broad portfolio to meet demand across the globe. Please note our free cash flow model assumes McCormick realizes meaningful margin expansion and revenue growth going forward, and its valuation could face significant headwinds should the firm stumble.

• McCormick completed its purchase of Reckitt Benckiser's food division for ~$4.2 billion in August 2017. The deal brought Frank's RedHot, French's Mustard, and other well-known condiment brands into the McCormick portfolio.

Investment Considerations

DCF Valuation	FAIRLY VALUED
Relative Valuation	UNATTRACTIVE
ValueCreation™	EXCELLENT
ValueRisk™	MEDIUM
ValueTrend™	POSITIVE
Cash Flow Generation	STRONG
Financial Leverage	HIGH
Growth	MODEST
Technical Evaluation	BEARISH
Relative Strength	WEAK
Money Flow Index (MFI)	NEUTRAL
Upside/Downside Volume (U/D)	DETERIORATING
Near-term Technical Resistance, 10-wk MA	93.00

DCF = Discounted Cash Flow; MFI, U/D = Please see glossary. MA = Moving Average

Business Quality

ValueRisk™	Very Poor	Poor	Good	Excellent
Low				
Medium				▮
High				
Very High				

Firms that generate economic profits with little operating variability score near the top right of the matrix.

Relative Valuation

	Forward P/E	PEG	Price / FV
Coca-Cola	34.3	1.5	128.0%
Procter & Gamble	26.5	3.3	144.1%
Philip Morris	15.4	2.4	104.3%
Wal-Mart	26.8	2.3	130.2%
Peer Median	26.7	2.4	129.1%
McCormick	31.8	4.5	114.7%

Price / FV = Current Stock Price divided by Estimated Fair Value

Financial Summary

	----- Actual -----		Projected
Fiscal Year End:	Nov-18	Nov-19	Nov-20
Revenue	5,409	5,347	5,609
Revenue, YoY%	11.9%	-1.1%	4.9%
Operating Income	942	979	1,168
Operating Margin %	17.4%	18.3%	20.8%
Net Income	933	703	782
Net Income Margin %	17.3%	13.1%	14.0%
Diluted EPS	3.50	2.62	2.89
Diluted EPS, YoY %	88.5%	-25.2%	10.2%
Free Cash Flow (CFO-capex)	652	773	1,016
Free Cash Flow Margin %	12.1%	14.5%	18.1%

In Millions of USD (except for per share items)

Structure of the Food Products Industry　　　　NEUTRAL

The food products industry is composed of a number of firms with strong brand names. However, market supply/demand dynamics and intense competition still impact product prices, while fluctuations in commodity costs can make earnings quite volatile. Private-label competition, competitors' promotional spending, and changing consumer preferences often drive demand trends. The group's customers—such as supermarkets, warehouses, and food distributors—continue to consolidate, increasing buying power over constituents and hurting margins. Still, we're generally neutral on the group.

3M MMM   FAIRLY VALUED

Buying Index™   7   Value Rating ⬤

Economic Castle	Estimated Fair Value	Fair Value Range	Investment Style	Sector	Industry
Attractive	$175.00	$131.00 - $219.00	LARGE-CAP VALUE	Industrials	Industrial Leaders

3M has raised its dividend for 60+ consecutive years. Its respirator masks have seen increased demand as a result of the COVID-19 pandemic.

Stock Chart (weekly)

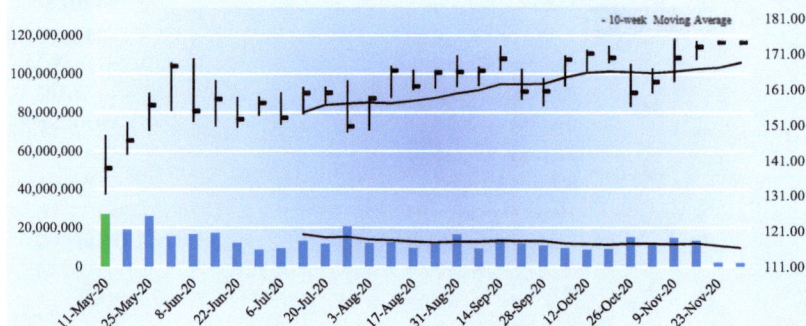

The week with the highest trading volume out of the last 30 weeks was a week of heavy selling, or distribution (red bar).

Investment Considerations

DCF Valuation	**FAIRLY VALUED**
Relative Valuation	**ATTRACTIVE**
ValueCreation™	**EXCELLENT**
ValueRisk™	**MEDIUM**
ValueTrend™	**NEGATIVE**
Cash Flow Generation	**STRONG**
Financial Leverage	**MEDIUM**
Growth	**MODEST**
Technical Evaluation	**BULLISH**
Relative Strength	**NEUTRAL**
Money Flow Index (MFI)	**NEUTRAL**
Upside/Downside Volume (U/D)	**BULLISH**
Near-term Technical Support, 10-week MA	**168.00**

DCF = Discounted Cash Flow; MFI, U/D = Please see glossary. MA = Moving Average

Company Vitals

Market Cap (USD)	$101,889
Avg Weekly Vol (30 wks)	13,077
30-week Range (USD)	131.12 - 175.43
Valuentum Sector	Industrials
5-week Return	7.4%
13-week Return	5.2%
30-week Return	17.8%
Dividend Yield %	3.4%
Dividends per Share	5.88
Forward Dividend Payout Ratio	67.8%
Est. Normal Diluted EPS	10.95
P/E on Est. Normal Diluted EPS	15.9
Est. Normal EBITDA	9,868
Forward EV/EBITDA	14.5
EV/Est. Normal EBITDA	12.1
Forward Revenue Growth (5-yr)	3.2%
Forward EPS Growth (5-yr)	11.6%

NMF = Not Meaningful; Est. = Estimated; FY = Fiscal Year

Returns Summary

3-year Historical Average

Return on Equity	47.0%
Return on Assets	13.1%
ROIC, with goodwill	20.3%
ROIC, without goodwill	33.2%

ROIC = Return on Invested Capital; NMF = Not Meaningful

Leverage, Coverage, and Liquidity

In Millions of USD

Total Debt	20,313
Net Debt	17,862
Total Debt/EBITDA	2.6
Net Debt/EBITDA	2.3
EBITDA/Interest	17.3
Current Ratio	1.4
Quick Ratio	0.8

NMF = Not Meaningful

Investment Highlights

• 3M is fundamentally a science-based company and holds over 100,000 patents. The company makes imaginative products, and it is a leader in many markets--from health care and highway safety to office products and abrasives and adhesives. 3M is perhaps among the most innovative firms in our coverage universe. Believe it or not, 3M started as a small mining venture in 1902.

• 3M has been scooping up assets to help it take advantage of the rapidly growing, regulatory driven market of workplace safety. Its top priorities for growth include connected safety, automotive electrification, advanced wound care, and data centers, among others.

• 3M has ambitious goals for the period 2019-2023. The conglomerate expects annual organic local-currency sales growth of 3-5%, annual earnings per share expansion of 8-11%, 20% return on invested capital, and 100% free cash flow conversion of net income. Its 'Healthcare' business is expected to lead top-line growth at 4%-6% per year, followed by 'Safety & Industrial' at 3%-5%.

• 3M has well laid-out capital allocation plan. In 2019-2023 it plans to allocate ~30% of capital to growth investments with R&D spending at ~6% of sales and capex at 5%-5.5% of sales. ~30% will be allocated to the dividend with the remaining ~40% going towards M&A and buybacks.

• 3M has accelerated its dividend growth in recent periods, and it has raised the annual payout in 62 consecutive years as of 2020. Management expects to grow the dividend in line with earnings over time. It also plans to maintain a minimum share repurchase threshold.

Business Quality

ValueCreation™

ValueRisk™	Very Poor	Poor	Good	Excellent
Low				
Medium				▨
High				
Very High				

Firms that generate economic profits with little operating variability score near the top right of the matrix.

Relative Valuation

	Forward P/E	PEG	Price / FV
Danaher	36.3	3.0	121.5%
Honeywell	28.8	1.7	101.3%
Lockheed Martin	15.0	2.3	96.3%
Union Pacific	25.9	1.4	119.1%
Peer Median	27.3	2.0	110.2%
3M	**20.1**	**1.9**	**99.5%**

Price / FV = Current Stock Price divided by Estimated Fair Value

Financial Summary

	----- Actual -----		Projected
Fiscal Year End:	Dec-18	Dec-19	Dec-20
Revenue	32,765	32,136	31,879
Revenue, YoY%	3.5%	-1.9%	-0.8%
Operating Income	6,660	6,174	6,665
Operating Margin %	20.3%	19.2%	20.9%
Net Income	5,349	4,570	5,026
Net Income Margin %	16.3%	14.2%	15.8%
Diluted EPS	8.89	7.81	8.68
Diluted EPS, YoY %	12.1%	-12.1%	11.1%
Free Cash Flow (CFO-capex)	4,862	5,371	5,775
Free Cash Flow Margin %	14.8%	16.7%	18.1%

In Millions of USD (except for per share items)

Structure of the Conglomerates Industry   GOOD

The industrial conglomerate industry is characterized by firms that operate various business lines on a global scale. Demand for industrial products tends to be cyclical in nature, and most firms couple their manufacturing operations with generally more stable services businesses to mitigate fundamental volatility. Firms tend to have bargaining power over suppliers due to industry dominance and boast substantial resources to adapt to changing conditions or competitive threats. Most sell products under powerful and recognizable brand names and look to emerging markets for future growth. We like the group.

VALUENTUM

Monster Beverage MNST   FAIRLY VALUED

Buying Index™   7   Value Rating ⬤

Economic Castle	Estimated Fair Value	Fair Value Range	Investment Style	Sector	Industry
Very Attractive	$80.00	$60.00 - $100.00	LARGE-CAP GROWTH	Next Generation	Disruptive Innovation

Monster Beverage has been one of the best-performing stocks during the past 20 years thanks to its tremendous innovation and brand development within the energy drink category.

Stock Chart (weekly)

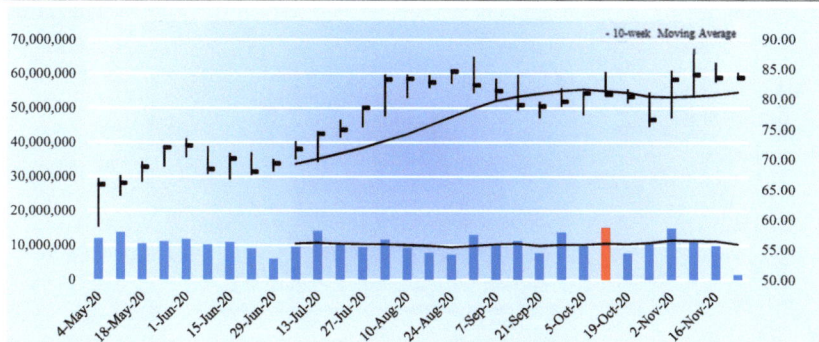

The week with the highest trading volume out of the last 30 weeks was a week of heavy selling, or distribution (red bar).

Company Vitals

Market Cap (USD)	$47,397
Avg Weekly Vol (30 wks)	10,377
30-week Range (USD)	58.73 - 88.41
Valuentum Sector	Next Generation
5-week Return	5.3%
13-week Return	-1.1%
30-week Return	41.0%
Dividend Yield %	0.0%
Dividends per Share	0.00
Forward Dividend Payout Ratio	0.0%
Est. Normal Diluted EPS	3.07
P/E on Est. Normal Diluted EPS	27.2
Est. Normal EBITDA	2,292
Forward EV/EBITDA	26.5
EV/Est. Normal EBITDA	20.1
Forward Revenue Growth (5-yr)	9.9%
Forward EPS Growth (5-yr)	14.2%

NMF = Not Meaningful; Est. = Estimated; FY = Fiscal Year

Returns Summary
3-year Historical Average

Return on Equity	25.9%
Return on Assets	20.9%
ROIC, with goodwill	34.5%
ROIC, without goodwill	61.7%

ROIC = Return on Invested Capital; NMF = Not Meaningful

Leverage, Coverage, and Liquidity
In Millions of USD

Total Debt	0
Net Debt	-1,331
Total Debt/EBITDA	0.0
Net Debt/EBITDA	NMF
EBITDA/Interest	Excellent
Current Ratio	3.5
Quick Ratio	2.8

NMF = Not Meaningful

Investment Highlights

• Monster Beverage is a leading marketer/distributor of energy drinks. The company makes Monster Energy brand energy drinks, Java Monster brand coffee+energy drinks, and other beverages. Its products are sold in 110+ countries on 6 continents. Coca-Cola holds a ~17% stake in the firm. The company was founded in 1985 and is headquartered in California.

• Monster Beverage faces heightened risk regarding product safety, given legal complaints alleging that the firm's beverages may not be safe. It continues to contest such claims. The firm also faces headwinds related to proposed taxes on sugary drinks, which may be gaining steam across the US.

• Monster Beverage continues to experience competition from new entrants in the energy drink and energy shot categories. The firm's products compete with Red Bull, Rockstar, No Fear, and Amp, while its Java Monster line competes with a number of Starbucks' products. Product innovation, as in its Ultra line extension, will remain key.

• We love the firm's balance sheet strength. Monster has a very nice cash position and no debt on its balance sheet. Such financial flexibility bodes well for a firm working to innovate and expand. Distribution and import costs (aluminum cans) have impacted margins recently.

• Monster will benefit from access to Coca-Cola's bottlers and international distribution network, which it is in the process of implementing into its operations in coming quarters. The company put up record sales and profits during the COVID-19 pandemic.

Investment Considerations

DCF Valuation	**FAIRLY VALUED**
Relative Valuation	**ATTRACTIVE**
ValueCreation™	**EXCELLENT**
ValueRisk™	**MEDIUM**
ValueTrend™	**POSITIVE**
Cash Flow Generation	**STRONG**
Financial Leverage	**LOW**
Growth	**HIGH**
Technical Evaluation	**BULLISH**
Relative Strength	**WEAK**
Money Flow Index (MFI)	**NEUTRAL**
Upside/Downside Volume (U/D)	**BEARISH**
Near-term Technical Support, 10-week MA	**81.00**

DCF = Discounted Cash Flow; MFI, U/D = Please see glossary. MA = Moving Average

Business Quality

ValueRisk™	ValueCreation™			
	Very Poor	Poor	Good	Excellent
Low				
Medium				▓
High				
Very High				

Firms that generate economic profits with little operating variability score near the top right of the matrix.

Relative Valuation

	Forward P/E	PEG	Price / FV
Wayfair	56.3	NMF	84.2%
Zoom Video	170.7	28.8	120.8%
Roku	-338.4	NMF	96.0%
Lululemon	81.5	1.9	99.9%
Peer Median	68.9	15.4	98.0%
Monster Beverage	**36.0**	**2.9**	**104.4%**

Price / FV = Current Stock Price divided by Estimated Fair Value

Financial Summary

	----- Actual -----		Projected
Fiscal Year End:	Dec-18	Dec-19	Dec-20
Revenue	3,807	4,201	4,524
Revenue, YoY%	13.0%	10.3%	7.7%
Operating Income	1,284	1,403	1,669
Operating Margin %	33.7%	33.4%	36.9%
Net Income	993	1,108	1,318
Net Income Margin %	26.1%	26.4%	29.1%
Diluted EPS	1.76	2.03	2.32
Diluted EPS, YoY %	23.8%	15.2%	14.6%
Free Cash Flow (CFO-capex)	1,087	1,012	1,290
Free Cash Flow Margin %	28.5%	24.1%	28.5%

In Millions of USD (except for per share items)

Structure of the Nonalcoholic Beverages Industry   **GOOD**

The nonalcoholic beverage segment of the commercial beverage industry is highly competitive, consisting of numerous companies that make various sparkling beverages, water products, juices, fruit drinks, energy and other performance-enhancing drinks. Pricing, advertising, product innovation, the availability of in-store private-label beverages, and health concerns about sugar-sweetened beverages are key drivers that impact demand. Leading brands with high levels of consumer acceptance and an expansive distribution network are sources of competitive strengths. We like the structure of the group.

Altria Group MO　FAIRLY VALUED

Buying Index™ **3**　**Value Rating** ◯

Economic Castle	Estimated Fair Value	Fair Value Range	Investment Style	Sector	Industry
Very Attractive	$42.00	$34.00 - $50.00	LARGE-CAP VALUE	Consumer Staples	Recession Resistant

Altria's attempt to pivot towards next generation smoking products has not panned out favorably. We recently lowered our fair value estimate.

Stock Chart (weekly)

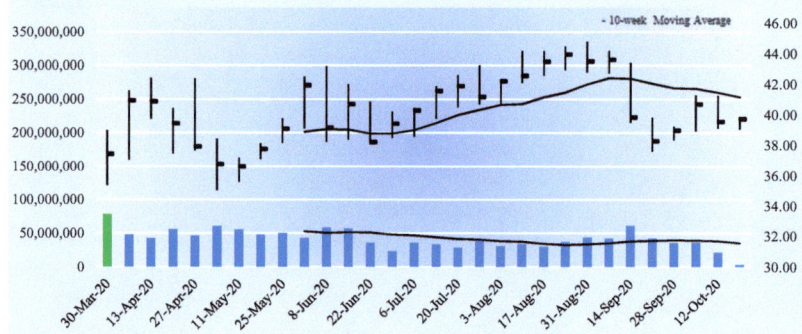

The week with the highest trading volume out of the last 30 weeks was a week of heavy selling, or distribution (red bar).

Company Vitals

Market Cap (USD)	$74,218
Avg Weekly Vol (30 wks)	41,660
30-week Range (USD)	35.02 - 44.77
Valuentum Sector	Consumer Staples
5-week Return	0.1%
13-week Return	-5.5%
30-week Return	7.7%
Dividend Yield %	8.7%
Dividends per Share	3.44
Forward Dividend Payout Ratio	91.1%
Est. Normal Diluted EPS	3.56
P/E on Est. Normal Diluted EPS	11.2
Est. Normal EBITDA	10,015
Forward EV/EBITDA	9.3
EV/Est. Normal EBITDA	10.0
Forward Revenue Growth (5-yr)	0.3%
Forward EPS Growth (5-yr)	-235.6%

NMF = Not Meaningful; Est. = Estimated; FY = Fiscal Year

Returns Summary
3-year Historical Average

Return on Equity	35.5%
Return on Assets	11.5%
ROIC, with goodwill	44.0%
ROIC, without goodwill	64.3%

ROIC = Return on Invested Capital; NMF = Not Meaningful

Leverage, Coverage, and Liquidity
In Millions of USD

Total Debt	28,042
Net Debt	25,925
Total Debt/EBITDA	2.6
Net Debt/EBITDA	2.4
EBITDA/Interest	8.4
Current Ratio	0.6
Quick Ratio	0.3

NMF = Not Meaningful

Investment Highlights

• Altria makes and sells cigarettes and smokeless products in the US. It owns the Marlboro brand, which holds ~43% retail cigarette share, and the Copenhagen and Skoal brands, which together own more than 50% retail smokeless share. The company was founded in 1919 and is headquartered in Richmond, Virginia.

• Altria has a ~10% equity interest in AB InBev, and it received ~$5.3 billion in pre-tax cash from the combination of AB InBev and SABMiller that created the global beer giant. Altria supported the deal, and we think it will be a long-term positive.

• Altria's recent investments did not pan out favorably. Altria posted large losses on its equity investment in Cronos Group, a leading cannabinoid company based in Toronto, and its equity stake in the embattled US e-cigarette market JUUL Labs. Those deals added a lot of debt to its balance sheet and significantly grew its annual interest expenses.

• Altria relies heavily on price increases to offset terminal declines in the consumption of cigarettes in the US. The firm is attempting to pivot towards next generation smoking products, with limited success so far. We like Altria's dominant market share position in the traditional US tobacco market.

• Recent initiatives from the FDA in cracking down on nicotine levels and menthol in tobacco products should be monitored, and the FDA is also working to regulate and reduce teen use of e-cigarettes. These actions have had a material impact on Altria's recent investments.

Investment Considerations

DCF Valuation	FAIRLY VALUED
Relative Valuation	NEUTRAL
ValueCreation™	EXCELLENT
ValueRisk™	LOW
ValueTrend™	POSITIVE
Cash Flow Generation	STRONG
Financial Leverage	MEDIUM
Growth	MODEST
Technical Evaluation	BEARISH
Relative Strength	WEAK
Money Flow Index (MFI)	NEUTRAL
Upside/Downside Volume (U/D)	DETERIORATING
Near-term Technical Resistance, 10-wk MA	41.00

DCF = Discounted Cash Flow; MFI, U/D = Please see glossary. MA = Moving Average

Business Quality
ValueCreation™

ValueRisk™	Very Poor	Poor	Good	Excellent
Low				■
Medium				
High				
Very High				

Firms that generate economic profits with little operating variability score near the top right of the matrix.

Relative Valuation

	Forward P/E	PEG	Price / FV
Coca-Cola	34.3	1.5	128.0%
Procter & Gamble	26.5	3.3	144.1%
Philip Morris	15.4	2.4	104.3%
Wal-Mart	26.8	2.3	130.2%
Peer Median	26.7	2.4	129.1%
Altria Group	**10.5**	**NMF**	**94.5%**

Price / FV = Current Stock Price divided by Estimated Fair Value

Financial Summary

	----- Actual -----		Projected
Fiscal Year End:	Dec-18	Dec-19	Dec-20
Revenue	19,627	19,796	20,489
Revenue, YoY%	0.7%	0.9%	3.5%
Operating Income	9,498	10,485	10,552
Operating Margin %	48.4%	53.0%	51.5%
Net Income	6,963	-1,293	6,959
Net Income Margin %	35.5%	-6.5%	34.0%
Diluted EPS	3.69	-0.69	3.78
Diluted EPS, YoY %	-30.7%	-118.8%	-646.0%
Free Cash Flow (CFO-capex)	8,153	7,591	7,375
Free Cash Flow Margin %	41.5%	38.3%	36.0%

In Millions of USD (except for per share items)

Structure of the Tobacco Industry　　　GOOD

The oligopolistic tobacco industry is attractive in a number of ways. Firms sell an "addictive" product (cigarettes and/or smokeless tobacco), have significant pricing power, generate high margins, and strong returns on invested capital. Still, declining trends in smoking in the US, threats of tobacco-related litigation, new tobacco regulation (labeling) that discourages tobacco use, and excise tax price shocks that may impact demand will always be concerns. In any case, we tend to like the structural characteristics of the tobacco industry and the shareholder-friendly policies of constituents.

Microsoft MSFT   FAIRLY VALUED

Buying Index™ 6   ***Value Rating*** ⬤

Economic Castle	Estimated Fair Value	Fair Value Range	Investment Style	Sector	Industry
Very Attractive	$236.00	$189.00 - $283.00	MEGA-CAP BLEND	Information Technology	Technology Giants

Microsoft continues to navigate the challenging environment caused by the COVID-19 pandemic quite well. We've raised our fair value estimate again, and we love its dividend growth profile.

Stock Chart (weekly)

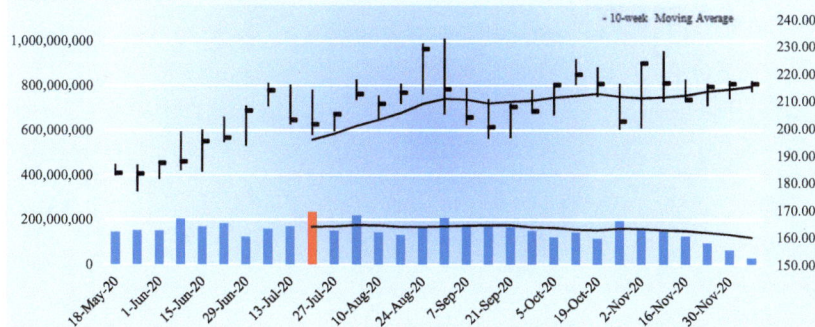

The week with the highest trading volume out of the last 30 weeks was a week of heavy selling, or distribution (red bar).

Investment Considerations

DCF Valuation	**FAIRLY VALUED**
Relative Valuation	**UNATTRACTIVE**
ValueCreation™	**EXCELLENT**
ValueRisk™	**LOW**
ValueTrend™	**POSITIVE**
Cash Flow Generation	**STRONG**
Financial Leverage	**LOW**
Growth	**HIGH**
Technical Evaluation	**BULLISH**
Relative Strength	**NEUTRAL**
Money Flow Index (MFI)	**NEUTRAL**
Upside/Downside Volume (U/D)	**BEARISH**
Near-term Technical Support, 10-week MA	**215.00**

DCF = Discounted Cash Flow; MFI, U/D = Please see glossary. MA = Moving Average

Company Vitals

Market Cap (USD)	$1,661,141
Avg Weekly Vol (30 wks)	151,832
30-week Range (USD)	176.60 - 232.86
Valuentum Sector	Information Technology
5-week Return	-3.7%
13-week Return	5.9%
30-week Return	16.4%
Dividend Yield %	1.0%
Dividends per Share	2.24
Forward Dividend Payout Ratio	32.8%
Est. Normal Diluted EPS	9.00
P/E on Est. Normal Diluted EPS	24.0
Est. Normal EBITDA	94,820
Forward EV/EBITDA	21.5
EV/Est. Normal EBITDA	16.7
Forward Revenue Growth (5-yr)	9.1%
Forward EPS Growth (5-yr)	14.9%

NMF = Not Meaningful; Est. = Estimated; FY = Fiscal Year

Returns Summary

3-year Historical Average

Return on Equity	34.6%
Return on Assets	12.0%
ROIC, with goodwill	41.3%
ROIC, without goodwill	66.9%

ROIC = Return on Invested Capital; NMF = Not Meaningful

Leverage, Coverage, and Liquidity

In Millions of USD

Total Debt	63,327
Net Debt	-76,165
Total Debt/EBITDA	1.0
Net Debt/EBITDA	NMF
EBITDA/Interest	25.4
Current Ratio	2.5
Quick Ratio	2.4

NMF = Not Meaningful

Investment Highlights

• Microsoft's products include operating systems, cloud services, server applications, desktop and server management tools, software development tools, video games, and online advertising. It also designs, manufactures and sells hardware, including PCs, tablets, gaming consoles, and other smart accessories that integrate with its cloud offerings.

• Microsoft can't scoop up its own shares fast enough through its massive buyback program. The firm floats debt with the best credit quality (Aaa), and we can't think of another firm with a better financial profile. Financial discipline and strong execution remain hallmarks of its business.

• Microsoft is not a tech dinosaur, and momentum behind new devices and platforms continues to build. Its cloud-based product suite, Office 365 and Azure, continues to catch favor among consumers and enterprises at impressive rates. This momentum has allowed it to achieve goals in commercial cloud annual recurring revenue well ahead of schedule.

• Microsoft acquired LinkedIn for over $26 billion in cash, and management believes the deal will expand its addressable market, while helping drive engagement across Office 365. The firm's impressive financial profile gives us confidence in it moving forward, and its tremendous free cash flow generating capacity has not wavered.

• Microsoft's Windows business has been the bread-and-butter of the company for such a long time, but investor focus has shifted to the company's other segments as its business model moves towards the cloud. Microsoft is helping drive the transition to cloud-based software products.

Business Quality

ValueRisk™	Very Poor	Poor	Good	Excellent
Low				▣
Medium				
High				
Very High				

ValueCreation™

Firms that generate economic profits with little operating variability score near the top right of the matrix.

Relative Valuation

	Forward P/E	PEG	Price / FV
Facebook	31.0	1.8	69.6%
Apple	29.8	2.4	85.0%
Alphabet	34.9	1.8	73.3%
Amazon.com	NMF	3.3	95.7%
Peer Median	31.0	2.1	79.2%
Microsoft	**31.6**	**2.5**	**91.6%**

Price / FV = Current Stock Price divided by Estimated Fair Value

Financial Summary

	----- Actual -----		Projected
Fiscal Year End:	Jun-19	Jun-20	Jun-21
Revenue	125,843	143,015	158,318
Revenue, YoY%	14.0%	13.6%	10.7%
Non-GAAP Operating Income	42,959	52,959	59,650
Non-GAAP EBIT %	34.1%	37.0%	37.7%
Non-GAAP Net Income	39,240	44,281	52,271
Non-GAAP NI Margin %	31.2%	31.0%	33.0%
Non-GAAP Diluted EPS	5.06	5.76	6.84
Non-GAAP Dil EPS, YoY %	138.1%	13.9%	18.6%
Non-GAAP FCF (CFO-capex)	38,260	45,234	59,746
Non-GAAP FCF Margin %	30.4%	31.6%	37.7%

In Millions of USD (except for per share items)

Structure of the Software Industry   **VERY GOOD**

Firms that serve the mature software markets—or those consisting of basic business applications—have powerful distribution channels, large installed bases, and fortress balance sheets. These entrenched competitors benefit from significant customer switching costs, which make it nearly impossible for new entrants to gain a foothold. Participants generally benefit from high-margin license revenue and generate significant returns on investment. Still, the shift to cloud computing has created both opportunities and challenges, and the enterprise software landscape continues to evolve. We like the group.

Mettler-Toledo MTD OVERVALUED 11.6%   *Buying Index*™ 4   *Value Rating* ✕

Economic Castle	Estimated Fair Value	Fair Value Range	Investment Style	Sector	Industry
Very Attractive	$870.00	$696.00 - $1044.00	LARGE-CAP CORE	Health Care	Health Care Bellwethers

We significantly increased our fair value estimate for Mettler-Toledo by building in optimistic assumptions, though shares are still generously valued.

Stock Chart (weekly)

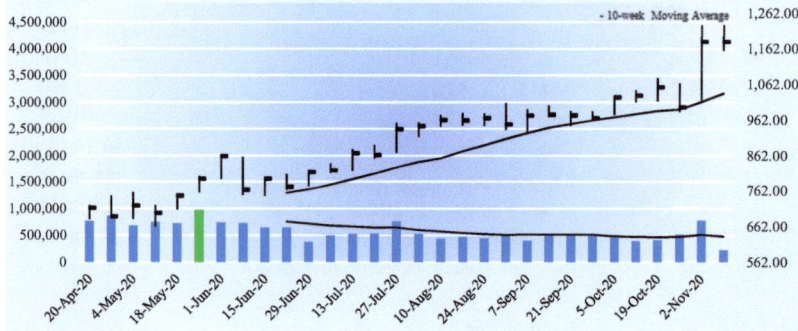

The week with the highest trading volume out of the last 30 weeks was a week of heavy selling, or distribution (red bar).

Company Vitals

Market Cap (USD)	$29,498
Avg Weekly Vol (30 wks)	578
30-week Range (USD)	661.32 - 1228.41
Valuentum Sector	Health Care
5-week Return	14.9%
13-week Return	22.4%
30-week Return	64.4%
Dividend Yield %	0.0%
Dividends per Share	0.00
Forward Dividend Payout Ratio	0.0%
Est. Normal Diluted EPS	35.72
P/E on Est. Normal Diluted EPS	33.1
Est. Normal EBITDA	1,112
Forward EV/EBITDA	39.0
EV/Est. Normal EBITDA	27.5
Forward Revenue Growth (5-yr)	6.4%
Forward EPS Growth (5-yr)	18.3%

NMF = Not Meaningful; Est. = Estimated; FY = Fiscal Year

Returns Summary
3-year Historical Average

Return on Equity	92.6%
Return on Assets	18.8%
ROIC, with goodwill	39.7%
ROIC, without goodwill	58.5%

ROIC = Return on Invested Capital; NMF = Not Meaningful

Leverage, Coverage, and Liquidity
In Millions of USD

Total Debt	1,291
Net Debt	1,083
Total Debt/EBITDA	1.6
Net Debt/EBITDA	1.3
EBITDA/Interest	22.1
Current Ratio	1.5
Quick Ratio	1.0

NMF = Not Meaningful

Investment Highlights

- Mettler-Toledo is a global manufacturer and marketer of precision instruments for use in laboratory (this segment generated ~52% of its net sales in 2019), industrial (~41%) and food retailing (~7%) applications. The firm is one of the largest providers of weighing instruments. The firm was founded in 1991 and is headquartered in Columbus, Ohio.

- Mettler-Toledo's services business is a competitive advantage. This segment typically generates over 20% of the company's net sales. The firm holds over 5,000 patents and trademarks, and its R&D spending is typically ~5% of its net sales.

- Please note that within our cash flow models, we have built in quite optimistic assumptions regarding Mettler-Toledo's medium- and long-term revenue growth rates and its future operating margins (we model in meaningful margin expansion). Even when assuming that the company achieves those financial targets, its shares still look expensive.

- Mettler-Toledo's business has been negatively impacted by the COVID-19 pandemic, though its long-term growth outlook is still promising. Demand from the end-markets Mettler-Toledo caters to has been negatively impacted by the pandemic, though not as bad as initially feared.

- Investors should be aware of Mettler-Toledo's exposure to China. As of 2019, ~30% of the firm's global production took place there, and ~18% of its sales and ~34% of its segment operating profit was generated in the country. Tariffs may pose headwinds.

Investment Considerations

DCF Valuation	**OVERVALUED**
Relative Valuation	**UNATTRACTIVE**
ValueCreation™	**EXCELLENT**
ValueRisk™	**LOW**
ValueTrend™	**POSITIVE**
Cash Flow Generation	**STRONG**
Financial Leverage	**MEDIUM**
Growth	**MODEST**
Technical Evaluation	**BULLISH**
Relative Strength	**STRONG**
Money Flow Index (MFI)	**NEUTRAL**
Upside/Downside Volume (U/D)	**DETERIORATING**
Near-term Technical Support, 10-week MA	**1036.00**

DCF = Discounted Cash Flow; MFI, U/D = Please see glossary. MA = Moving Average

Business Quality

ValueRisk™	Very Poor	Poor	Good	Excellent
Low				
Medium				
High				
Very High				

Firms that generate economic profits with little operating variability score near the top right of the matrix.

Relative Valuation

	Forward P/E	PEG	Price / FV
Johnson & Johnson	17.6	1.8	99.5%
Medtronic	25.6	2.2	109.0%
Merck	21.5	2.2	100.5%
Pfizer	20.1	0.8	93.3%
Peer Median	20.8	2.0	100.0%
Mettler-Toledo	**50.4**	**2.9**	**135.8%**

Price / FV = Current Stock Price divided by Estimated Fair Value

Financial Summary

	----- Actual -----		Projected
Fiscal Year End:	Dec-18	Dec-19	Dec-20
Revenue	2,936	3,009	2,958
Revenue, YoY%	7.7%	2.5%	-1.7%
Operating Income	705	728	695
Operating Margin %	24.0%	24.2%	23.5%
Net Income	513	561	579
Net Income Margin %	17.5%	18.6%	19.6%
Diluted EPS	19.88	22.47	23.41
Diluted EPS, YoY %	39.6%	13.0%	4.2%
Free Cash Flow (CFO-capex)	423	506	715
Free Cash Flow Margin %	14.4%	16.8%	24.2%

In Millions of USD (except for per share items)

Structure of the Medical Instruments Industry   GOOD

The medical instrument industry is heavily regulated and characterized by rapid technological change. Firms have been forced to compete on price due to economically-motivated buyers, consolidation among healthcare providers, and declining reimbursement rates. Healthcare reform measures have put additional pressure on procedure rates and market sizes. Still, firms can gain advantages by developing products with differentiated clinical outcomes or by creating patent-protected technology. Since most constituents hold important patents or trade secrets, we tend to like the group.

VALUENTUM

Micron Technology MU   FAIRLY VALUED

Buying Index™   7   Value Rating ◯

Economic Castle	Estimated Fair Value	Fair Value Range	Investment Style	Sector	Industry
Neutral	$64.00	$45.00 - $83.00	LARGE-CAP GROWTH	Information Technology	Technology Giants

We don't like the pricing pressures innate to Micron's business model. We apply a rather large margin of safety to our fair value estimate.

Stock Chart (weekly)

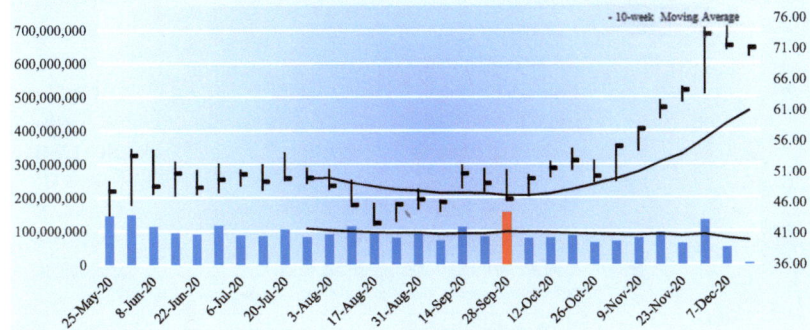

The week with the highest trading volume out of the last 30 weeks was a week of heavy selling, or distribution (red bar).

Investment Considerations

DCF Valuation	**FAIRLY VALUED**
Relative Valuation	**ATTRACTIVE**
ValueCreation™	**EXCELLENT**
ValueRisk™	**MEDIUM**
ValueTrend™	**NEGATIVE**
Cash Flow Generation	**STRONG**
Financial Leverage	**LOW**
Growth	**HIGH**
Technical Evaluation	**BULLISH**
Relative Strength	**STRONG**
Money Flow Index (MFI)	**NEUTRAL**
Upside/Downside Volume (U/D)	**BULLISH**
Near-term Technical Support, 10-week MA	**61.00**

DCF = Discounted Cash Flow; MFI, U/D = Please see glossary. MA = Moving Average

Business Quality

ValueRisk™	Very Poor	Poor	Good	Excellent
Low				
Medium				▮
High				
Very High				

Firms that generate economic profits with little operating variability score near the top right of the matrix.

Relative Valuation

	Forward P/E	PEG	Price / FV
Apple	29.8	2.4	85.0%
Alphabet	34.9	1.8	73.3%
Amazon.com	NMF	3.3	95.7%
Microsoft	31.6	2.5	91.6%
Peer Median	31.6	2.5	88.3%
Micron Technology	**18.9**	**1.1**	**111.1%**

Price / FV = Current Stock Price divided by Estimated Fair Value

Company Vitals

Market Cap (USD)	$79,996
Avg Weekly Vol (30 wks)	91,880
30-week Range (USD)	42.25 - 74.61
Valuentum Sector	Information Technology
5-week Return	19.0%
13-week Return	43.3%
30-week Return	53.8%
Dividend Yield %	0.0%
Dividends per Share	0.00
Forward Dividend Payout Ratio	0.0%
Est. Normal Diluted EPS	6.61
P/E on Est. Normal Diluted EPS	10.7
Est. Normal EBITDA	16,409
Forward EV/EBITDA	7.0
EV/Est. Normal EBITDA	4.7
Forward Revenue Growth (5-yr)	10.3%
Forward EPS Growth (5-yr)	26.4%

NMF = Not Meaningful; Est. = Estimated; FY = Fiscal Year

Returns Summary   3-year Historical Average

Return on Equity	27.1%
Return on Assets	18.3%
ROIC, with goodwill	25.2%
ROIC, without goodwill	26.3%

ROIC = Return on Invested Capital; NMF = Not Meaningful

Leverage, Coverage, and Liquidity
In Millions of USD

Total Debt	6,643
Net Debt	-2,547
Total Debt/EBITDA	0.8
Net Debt/EBITDA	NMF
EBITDA/Interest	44.6
Current Ratio	2.7
Quick Ratio	2.0

NMF = Not Meaningful

Investment Highlights

• Micron makes DRAM, NAND, 3D XPoint, and NOR memory solutions, as well as other innovative storage technologies for use in computing, consumer, networking, automotive, industrial, embedded and mobile products. A material portion of revenue comes from NAND and SSD products. The company was founded in 1978 and is headquartered in Boise, Idaho.

• Micron has historically traded at low earnings multiples. Though tempting, the low P/E isn't necessarily reflective of bargain-basement pricing, but more a reflection of concerns about the sustainability/cyclicality of its earnings stream given the competitive structure of its industry.

• Competition is fierce in the semiconductor memory market and includes Samsung, SK Hynix, and Kioxia (formerly Toshiba). Such intense rivalries have often resulted in industry overcapacity, pricing pressures, and painful cycles. Margins should be watched closely, especially in light of Intel entering the fray and the Western Digital-SanDisk combination.

• Those that are bullish on the Micron story point to a more rational memory market, supported by recent consolidation. Though the number of rivals has decreased, high-volume memory products are typically commoditized and made to industry specifications. There's little room for differentiation, but demand is diversifying and growing rapidly.

• Margins need to be watched closely. Average selling prices for DRAM and NAND have been extremely volatile during the past several years. Declines in average selling prices for DRAM and NAND of 30%-50% in a given year aren't unusual.

Financial Summary

	----- Actual -----		Projected
Fiscal Year End:	Aug-19	Sep-20	Sep-21
Revenue	23,406	21,435	24,114
Revenue, YoY%	-23.0%	-8.4%	12.5%
Operating Income	7,376	3,003	4,782
Operating Margin %	31.5%	14.0%	19.8%
Net Income	6,313	2,687	4,240
Net Income Margin %	27.0%	12.5%	17.6%
Diluted EPS	5.52	2.38	3.77
Diluted EPS, YoY %	NMF	NMF	58.6%
Free Cash Flow (CFO-capex)	3,409	83	192
Free Cash Flow Margin %	14.6%	0.4%	0.8%

In Millions of USD (except for per share items)

Structure of the Computers & Peripherals Industry   POOR

Firms in the computer and peripherals industry primarily make storage solutions, while others may offer custom-designed computer/mobile interface solutions or other ancillary computer/mobile products. The industry is characterized by rapid technological change, which has not only increased the adoption of technologies for use in a variety of devices but also has put significant pricing/gross-margin pressure on industry constituents. Competition is fierce, threats of over-supply are continuous, and the prospects for generating long-term competitive advantages are negligible. We don't like the structure of the group.

VALUENTUM

Netflix NFLX FAIRLY VALUED

VALUENTUM **Buying Index™** 6 VALUENTUM **Value Rating**

Economic Castle	Estimated Fair Value	Fair Value Range	Investment Style	Sector	Industry
Attractive	$488.00	$317.00 - $659.00	MEGA-CAP GROWTH	Consumer Discretionary	Discretionary Spending

We moderately increased our fair value estimate once again as Netflix has posted stellar net paid membership growth of late.

Stock Chart (weekly)

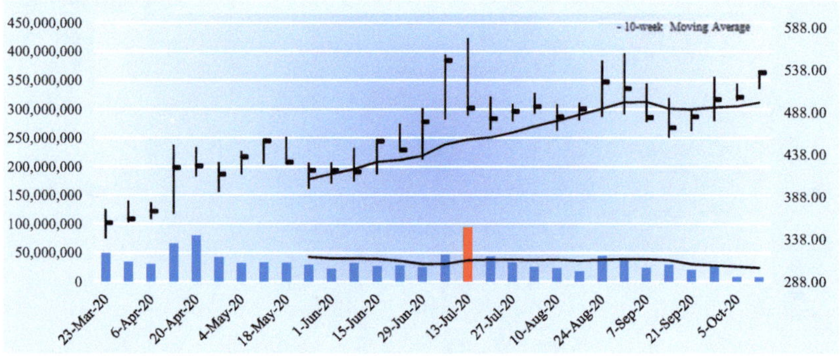

The week with the highest trading volume out of the last 30 weeks was a week of heavy selling, or distribution (red bar).

Investment Considerations

DCF Valuation	FAIRLY VALUED
Relative Valuation	UNATTRACTIVE
ValueCreation™	POOR
ValueRisk™	HIGH
ValueTrend™	POSITIVE
Cash Flow Generation	WEAK
Financial Leverage	MEDIUM
Growth	HIGH
Technical Evaluation	BULLISH
Relative Strength	WEAK
Money Flow Index (MFI)	NEUTRAL
Upside/Downside Volume (U/D)	BEARISH
Near-term Technical Support, 10-week MA	499.00

DCF = Discounted Cash Flow; MFI, U/D = Please see glossary. MA = Moving Average

Business Quality

ValueRisk™ / ValueCreation™	Very Poor	Poor	Good	Excellent
Low				
Medium				
High		■		
Very High				

Firms that generate economic profits with little operating variability score near the top right of the matrix.

Company Vitals

Market Cap (USD)	$241,541
Avg Weekly Vol (30 wks)	34,729
30-week Range (USD)	39.17 - 575.36
Valuentum Sector	Consumer Discretionary
5-week Return	11.2%
13-week Return	9.3%
30-week Return	53.7%
Dividend Yield %	0.0%
Dividends per Share	0.00
Forward Dividend Payout Ratio	0.0%
Est. Normal Diluted EPS	9.21
P/E on Est. Normal Diluted EPS	58.1
Est. Normal EBITDA	16,700
Forward EV/EBITDA	18.1
EV/Est. Normal EBITDA	15.0
Forward Revenue Growth (5-yr)	12.3%
Forward EPS Growth (5-yr)	23.7%

NMF = Not Meaningful; Est. = Estimated; FY = Fiscal Year

Returns Summary

	3-year Historical Average
Return on Equity	24.8%
Return on Assets	5.0%
ROIC, with goodwill	6.6%
ROIC, without goodwill	6.6%

ROIC = Return on Invested Capital; NMF = Not Meaningful

Leverage, Coverage, and Liquidity

In Millions of USD

Total Debt	14,759
Net Debt	9,741
Total Debt/EBITDA	1.2
Net Debt/EBITDA	0.8
EBITDA/Interest	19.0
Current Ratio	0.9
Quick Ratio	0.7

NMF = Not Meaningful

Investment Highlights

• Netflix is a video streaming service where subscribers can watch unlimited TV shows and movies streamed over the internet to their TVs, computers and mobile devices. It has over 190 million paid memberships with a large percentage located in the US. Its international growth runway is enormous, though its domestic operations are more profitable.

• Netflix's firmwide profitability is improving, but its free cash flow generation is not great. Should Netflix's paid membership growth stumble, its outlook would weaken materially. Its long-term debt load may balloon significantly in coming years.

• Though we've become more optimistic about Netflix's potential earnings leverage, it will continue to burn through cash for years to come. Free cash flow is expected to improve in coming years, however, aided by economies of scale. Netflix's total contractual obligations (debt, content, lease, and other purchase obligations) are simply enormous.

• We believe Netflix is a risky stock, and its junk-rated credit rating (Ba3/BB-) speaks to this. Competition is intensifying, and the company continues to spend robustly on creating and acquiring content. Subscriber performance will continue to make headlines, and price increases will help profitability.

• Netflix is investing heavily in original content to differentiate its service in the crowded industry it operates in. Netflix's paid membership growth in the recent past has simply been stellar, with COVID-19 driving up demand for at-home entertainment.

Relative Valuation

	Forward P/E	PEG	Price / FV
Disney	75.6	0.3	98.3%
Home Depot	22.9	1.9	106.7%
McDonald's	38.5	1.1	111.0%
Nike	52.8	2.5	104.9%
Peer Median	45.6	1.5	105.8%
Netflix	**85.5**	**5.5**	**109.6%**

Price / FV = Current Stock Price divided by Estimated Fair Value

Financial Summary

	----- Actual -----		Projected
Fiscal Year End:	Dec-18	Dec-19	Dec-20
Revenue	15,794	20,156	24,873
Revenue, YoY%	35.1%	27.6%	23.4%
Operating Income	1,605	2,604	4,104
Operating Margin %	10.2%	12.9%	16.5%
Net Income	1,211	1,867	2,852
Net Income Margin %	7.7%	9.3%	11.5%
Diluted EPS	2.68	4.13	6.25
Diluted EPS, YoY %	114.6%	54.0%	51.3%
Free Cash Flow (CFO-capex)	-2,893	-3,140	342
Free Cash Flow Margin %	-18.3%	-15.6%	1.4%

In Millions of USD (except for per share items)

Structure of the Internet Software & Services Industry — NEUTRAL

The Internet software/services industry is composed of a variety of companies with rapidly-changing business models. Most focus on improving the ways people connect with information, either via Internet search or by social media platforms, and generate revenue primarily by delivering cost-effective online advertising. Constituents earn significant returns on invested capital due to their capital-light operations, though competition remains fierce. We expect most companies in this group to look substantially different 10 years from now than they do today. Overall, we're neutral on the structure.

Nike NKE   FAIRLY VALUED

Buying Index™ 5   Value Rating

Economic Castle	Estimated Fair Value	Fair Value Range	Investment Style	Sector	Industry
Very Attractive	$124.00	$99.00 - $149.00	MEGA-CAP GROWTH	Consumer Discretionary	Discretionary Spending

We've significantly increased our fair value estimate for Nike as the firm has been firing on all cylinders of late.

Stock Chart (weekly)

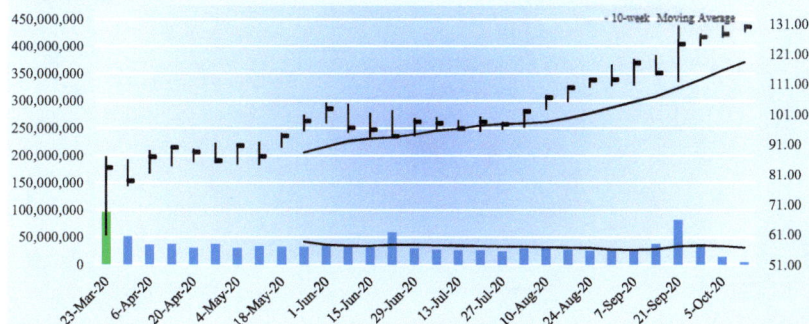

The week with the highest trading volume out of the last 30 weeks was a week of heavy selling, or distribution (red bar).

Investment Considerations

DCF Valuation	**FAIRLY VALUED**
Relative Valuation	**NEUTRAL**
ValueCreation™	**EXCELLENT**
ValueRisk™	**LOW**
ValueTrend™	**NEGATIVE**
Cash Flow Generation	**STRONG**
Financial Leverage	**MEDIUM**
Growth	**HIGH**
Technical Evaluation	**NEUTRAL**
Relative Strength	**STRONG**
Money Flow Index (MFI)	**OVERBOUGHT**
Upside/Downside Volume (U/D)	**BULLISH**
Near-term Technical Support, 10-week MA	**118.00**

DCF = Discounted Cash Flow; MFI, U/D = Please see glossary. MA = Moving Average

Company Vitals

Market Cap (USD)	$207,003
Avg Weekly Vol (30 wks)	35,171
30-week Range (USD)	60.58 - 130.44
Valuentum Sector	Consumer Discretionary
5-week Return	9.8%
13-week Return	36.2%
30-week Return	100.1%
Dividend Yield %	0.8%
Dividends per Share	0.98
Forward Dividend Payout Ratio	39.8%
Est. Normal Diluted EPS	4.40
P/E on Est. Normal Diluted EPS	29.5
Est. Normal EBITDA	8,932
Forward EV/EBITDA	39.0
EV/Est. Normal EBITDA	23.3
Forward Revenue Growth (5-yr)	10.0%
Forward EPS Growth (5-yr)	32.1%

NMF = Not Meaningful; Est. = Estimated; FY = Fiscal Year

Returns Summary
3-year Historical Average

Return on Equity	29.9%
Return on Assets	11.7%
ROIC, with goodwill	33.7%
ROIC, without goodwill	34.2%

ROIC = Return on Invested Capital; NMF = Not Meaningful

Leverage, Coverage, and Liquidity
In Millions of USD

Total Debt	9,657
Net Debt	870
Total Debt/EBITDA	2.5
Net Debt/EBITDA	0.2
EBITDA/Interest	Excellent
Current Ratio	2.5
Quick Ratio	1.4

NMF = Not Meaningful

Investment Highlights

• Nike focuses its 'Nike Brand' product offerings in the following categories: Running, Basketball, Football (Soccer), Men's Training, Women's Training, Nike Sportswear (sports-inspired lifestyle products), Action Sports, Gold, and the Jordan Brand. The breadth and depth of its product portfolio have translated into consistently strong results. Its long-term deal with Lebron James could spell upside.

• Nike is targeting material revenue growth. The company's internal long-term financial model indicates high single-digit to low double-digit revenue growth, mid-teens earnings per share growth and expanding returns on capital.

• Nike might not have the 'freshness' of a 'Lululemon' or 'Under Armour,' but we think Nike has the best business model and the most valuable brand among the three. Fiscal 2019 was its first full year of the Nike Consumer Direct Offense, and it has helped digital become its fastest growing channel in every geography of late. Digital has a favorable impact on gross margins.

• Nike's digital operations and direct-to-consumer sales helped enable the firm to continue meeting consumer demand during the early stages of the COVID-19 pandemic. Going forward, Nike's digital focus will support its long-term growth trajectory, as will its plan to grow its international sales.

• We don't expect any damages to the Nike or Jordan brands in the foreseeable future, but Adidas has done well in taking share in US athletic footwear. The gains have not come fully at the expense of Nike, but the strengthening rival is worth watching.

Business Quality

ValueRisk™	Very Poor	Poor	Good	Excellent
Low				■
Medium				
High				
Very High				

ValueCreation™

Firms that generate economic profits with little operating variability score near the top right of the matrix.

Relative Valuation

	Forward P/E	PEG	Price / FV
Disney	75.6	0.3	98.3%
Home Depot	22.9	1.9	106.7%
McDonald's	38.5	1.1	111.0%
Starbucks	92.2	0.6	110.6%
Peer Median	57.0	0.8	108.6%
Nike	**52.8**	**2.5**	**104.9%**

Price / FV = Current Stock Price divided by Estimated Fair Value

Financial Summary

	----- Actual -----		Projected
Fiscal Year End:	May-19	May-20	May-21
Revenue	39,117	37,403	39,722
Revenue, YoY%	7.5%	-4.4%	6.2%
Operating Income	4,772	3,115	4,568
Operating Margin %	12.2%	8.3%	11.5%
Net Income	4,029	2,539	3,883
Net Income Margin %	10.3%	6.8%	9.8%
Diluted EPS	2.49	1.60	2.46
Diluted EPS, YoY %	113.7%	-35.9%	54.5%
Free Cash Flow (CFO-capex)	4,784	1,399	4,088
Free Cash Flow Margin %	12.2%	3.7%	10.3%

In Millions of USD (except for per share items)

Structure of the Luxury Goods Industry   GOOD

Luxury goods firms differentiate themselves based on brand name, perception, and quality in order to generate excess returns on invested capital through the economic cycle. Building a large, successful luxury brand is difficult, leaving those that possess them with intangible competitive advantages that are not easily overcome by new entrants. Growth in emerging middle classes and China will be the key demand drivers going forward, though the strongest brands will also grow successfully via market share gains. Though changes in consumer preferences should be watched closely, we like the structure of the group.

Nvidia NVDA   FAIRLY VALUED

Buying Index™ 6   **Value Rating** ◯

Economic Castle	Estimated Fair Value	Fair Value Range	Investment Style	Sector	Industry
Very Attractive	$533.00	$394.00 - $672.00	MEGA-CAP GROWTH	Information Technology	Technology Giants

Nvidia is acquiring Arm Limited for ~$40 billion in a cash-and-stock deal. We raised our fair value estimate for Nvidia substantially due to its improving outlook. The company is 'firing on all cylinders.'

Stock Chart (weekly)

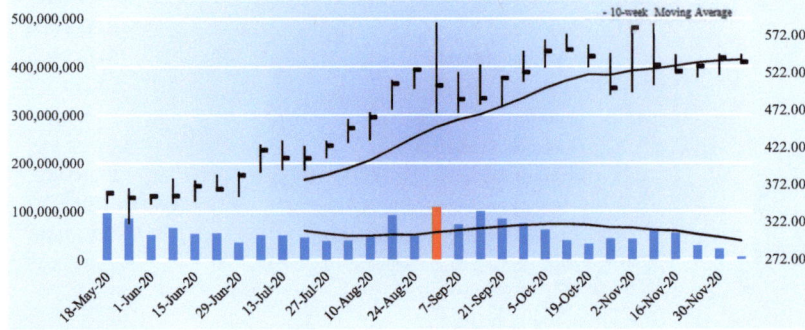

The week with the highest trading volume out of the last 30 weeks was a week of heavy selling, or distribution (red bar).

Company Vitals

Market Cap (USD)	$331,149
Avg Weekly Vol (30 wks)	55,865
30-week Range (USD)	319.87 - 589.07
Valuentum Sector	Information Technology
5-week Return	-7.9%
13-week Return	2.4%
30-week Return	52.9%
Dividend Yield %	0.1%
Dividends per Share	0.64
Forward Dividend Payout Ratio	6.5%
Est. Normal Diluted EPS	15.81
P/E on Est. Normal Diluted EPS	33.9
Est. Normal EBITDA	12,011
Forward EV/EBITDA	42.8
EV/Est. Normal EBITDA	26.8
Forward Revenue Growth (5-yr)	25.1%
Forward EPS Growth (5-yr)	38.7%

NMF = Not Meaningful; Est. = Estimated; FY = Fiscal Year

Returns Summary

3-year Historical Average

Return on Equity	40.4%
Return on Assets	27.0%
ROIC, with goodwill	107.5%
ROIC, without goodwill	133.5%

ROIC = Return on Invested Capital; NMF = Not Meaningful

Leverage, Coverage, and Liquidity

In Millions of USD

Total Debt	1,991
Net Debt	-8,906
Total Debt/EBITDA	0.6
Net Debt/EBITDA	NMF
EBITDA/Interest	62.1
Current Ratio	7.7
Quick Ratio	7.0

NMF = Not Meaningful

Investment Highlights

• Nvidia is a computer graphics company. Its business is based on two technologies: the GPU and the Tegra processor. GPUs are the engine of visual computing. Tegra processors incorporate multi-core GPUs and CPUs together with audio and video capabilities. The company was founded in 1993 and is headquartered in Santa Clara, California.

• Gaming has been a strong point for Nvidia as rapid demand growth in deep learning is pushing GPU (graphics processing unit) revenue higher. Its high-end graphics rendering platform, Nvidia RTX is setting new standards in gaming technology.

• In November 2020, Nvidia's management may have said it best about recent trends in its business in its third-quarter fiscal 2021 press release: 'Nvidia is firing on all cylinders, achieving record revenues in Gaming, Data Center and overall. The new Nvidia GeForce RTX GPU provides our largest-ever generational leap and demand is overwhelming.'

• Nvidia expects to be a significant player in autonomous driving. Hundreds of companies use its Drive AGX open computing platform, and the list includes many of the top names in next-gen car and truck manufacturing. Nvidia tabs autonomous vehicles as a $60 billion opportunity by 2035.

• We've traditionally been huge fans of Nvidia's net cash position, but that will likely change with its announcement to acquire Arm Limited from Softbank in a transaction priced at $40 billion. The deal has a $12 billion cash component.

Investment Considerations

DCF Valuation	FAIRLY VALUED
Relative Valuation	UNATTRACTIVE
ValueCreation™	EXCELLENT
ValueRisk™	MEDIUM
ValueTrend™	NEGATIVE
Cash Flow Generation	STRONG
Financial Leverage	LOW
Growth	AGGRESSIVE
Technical Evaluation	BULLISH
Relative Strength	NEUTRAL
Money Flow Index (MFI)	NEUTRAL
Upside/Downside Volume (U/D)	DETERIORATING
Near-term Technical Resistance, 10-wk MA	539.00

DCF = Discounted Cash Flow; MFI, U/D = Please see glossary. MA = Moving Average

Business Quality

ValueCreation™

ValueRisk™	Very Poor	Poor	Good	Excellent
Low				
Medium				▓
High				
Very High				

Firms that generate economic profits with little operating variability score near the top right of the matrix.

Relative Valuation

	Forward P/E	PEG	Price / FV
Apple	29.8	2.4	85.0%
Alphabet	34.9	1.8	73.3%
Amazon.com	NMF	3.3	95.7%
Microsoft	31.6	2.5	91.6%
Peer Median	31.6	2.5	88.3%
Nvidia	**54.6**	**3.1**	**100.5%**

Price / FV = Current Stock Price divided by Estimated Fair Value

Financial Summary

	----- Actual -----		Projected
Fiscal Year End:	Jan-19	Jan-20	Jan-21
Revenue	11,716	10,918	16,486
Revenue, YoY%	20.6%	-6.8%	51.0%
Operating Income	3,804	2,846	6,946
Operating Margin %	32.5%	26.1%	42.1%
Net Income	4,141	2,796	6,067
Net Income Margin %	35.3%	25.6%	36.8%
Diluted EPS	6.63	4.52	9.82
Diluted EPS, YoY %	37.4%	-31.7%	117.0%
Free Cash Flow (CFO-capex)	3,143	4,272	6,313
Free Cash Flow Margin %	26.8%	39.1%	38.3%

In Millions of USD (except for per share items)

Structure of the Integrated Circuits Industry

VERY POOR

Firms in the integrated circuits industry make components that form the electronic building blocks used in electronic systems and equipment. The industry is notoriously cyclical and subject to significant economic upturns and downturns, as well as rapid technological changes. Firms must innovate to survive, and products stocked in inventory can sometimes become obsolete before they are even shipped. Severe pricing competition and lengthy manufacturing cycles only add uncertainty to the mix. We're not fans of the structure of the integrated circuits space.

VALUENTUM

Oracle ORCL FAIRLY VALUED

Buying Index™ 6 **Value Rating** ○

Economic Castle	Estimated Fair Value	Fair Value Range	Investment Style	Sector	Industry
Very Attractive	$67.00	$54.00 - $80.00	LARGE-CAP VALUE	Information Technology	Technology Giants

Oracle's cloud applications businesses have started to perform better of late, which supports the firm's long-term outlook.

Stock Chart (weekly)

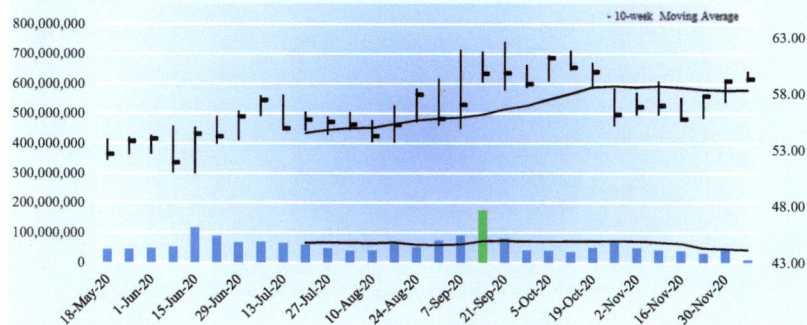

The week with the highest trading volume out of the last 30 weeks was a week of heavy selling, or distribution (red bar).

Company Vitals

Market Cap (USD)	$195,235
Avg Weekly Vol (30 wks)	59,028
30-week Range (USD)	50.91 - 62.60
Valuentum Sector	Information Technology
5-week Return	1.9%
13-week Return	-2.6%
30-week Return	9.9%
Dividend Yield %	1.6%
Dividends per Share	0.96
Forward Dividend Payout Ratio	22.6%
Est. Normal Diluted EPS	4.44
P/E on Est. Normal Diluted EPS	13.3
Est. Normal EBITDA	22,505
Forward EV/EBITDA	10.0
EV/Est. Normal EBITDA	9.9
Forward Revenue Growth (5-yr)	2.6%
Forward EPS Growth (5-yr)	7.2%

NMF = Not Meaningful; Est. = Estimated; FY = Fiscal Year

Returns Summary

3-year Historical Average

Return on Equity	33.5%
Return on Assets	7.0%
ROIC, with goodwill	21.3%
ROIC, without goodwill	66.8%

ROIC = Return on Invested Capital; NMF = Not Meaningful

Leverage, Coverage, and Liquidity

In Millions of USD

Total Debt	71,597
Net Debt	28,540
Total Debt/EBITDA	4.2
Net Debt/EBITDA	1.7
EBITDA/Interest	8.6
Current Ratio	3.0
Quick Ratio	2.8

NMF = Not Meaningful

Investment Highlights

• Oracle is shifting the complexity from IT, moving it out of the enterprise by engineering hardware and software to work together—in the cloud and in the data center. The company has three businesses, 'Cloud and License,' 'Hardware,' and 'Services,' which account for ~80%, ~10%, and ~10% of its total revenue. The firm was founded in 1977.

• Oracle has positioned its cloud applications businesses nicely. The company believes it is well on its way to becoming the leading provider in the enterprise SaaS market, and it continues to plow money into R&D, showcasing its dedication to innovation.

• Management expects overall top-line growth to accelerate moving forward as its cloud business becomes a larger portion of its total revenue. Competition remains fierce, but the firm is confident in its technology leadership, and the market is large enough for many winners. The number of its Fusion ERP and NetSuite ERP customers continue to surge.

• Oracle has reduced shares outstanding by an astounding 20%+ since fiscal 2011. Cash spent on share buybacks were $11.3 billion, $36.1 billion and $19.2 billion in fiscal 2020, fiscal 2019 and fiscal 2018, respectively (for comparison, cash dividend payments averaged ~$3 billion per year).

• Oracle's dividend payout speaks to its confidence in the free cash flow generating prowess of its business. However, its massive share buyback program has weakened its balance sheet, which now reveals a net debt position.

Investment Considerations

DCF Valuation	FAIRLY VALUED
Relative Valuation	NEUTRAL
ValueCreation™	EXCELLENT
ValueRisk™	LOW
ValueTrend™	NEGATIVE
Cash Flow Generation	STRONG
Financial Leverage	HIGH
Growth	MODEST
Technical Evaluation	VERY BULLISH
Relative Strength	WEAK
Money Flow Index (MFI)	NEUTRAL
Upside/Downside Volume (U/D)	BULLISH
Near-term Technical Support, 10-week MA	58.00

DCF = Discounted Cash Flow; MFI, U/D = Please see glossary. MA = Moving Average

Business Quality

ValueRisk™	ValueCreation™			
	Very Poor	Poor	Good	Excellent
Low				■
Medium				
High				
Very High				

Firms that generate economic profits with little operating variability score near the top right of the matrix.

Relative Valuation

	Forward P/E	PEG	Price / FV
Apple	29.8	2.4	85.0%
Alphabet	34.9	1.8	73.3%
Amazon.com	NMF	3.3	95.7%
Microsoft	31.6	2.5	91.6%
Peer Median	31.6	2.5	88.3%
Oracle	13.9	2.7	88.5%

Price / FV = Current Stock Price divided by Estimated Fair Value

Financial Summary

	----- Actual -----		Projected
Fiscal Year End:	May-19	May-20	May-21
Revenue	39,506	39,608	40,440
Revenue, YoY%	-0.8%	0.3%	2.1%
Operating Income	14,022	14,202	19,370
Operating Margin %	35.5%	35.9%	47.9%
Net Income	11,083	10,135	13,726
Net Income Margin %	28.1%	25.6%	33.9%
Diluted EPS	2.97	3.08	4.25
Diluted EPS, YoY %	229.0%	3.6%	38.2%
Free Cash Flow (CFO-capex)	12,891	11,575	16,092
Free Cash Flow Margin %	32.6%	29.2%	39.8%

In Millions of USD (except for per share items)

Structure of the Software Industry

VERY GOOD

Firms that serve the mature software markets—or those consisting of basic business applications—have powerful distribution channels, large installed bases, and fortress balance sheets. These entrenched competitors benefit from significant customer switching costs, which make it nearly impossible for new entrants to gain a foothold. Participants generally benefit from high-margin license revenue and generate significant returns on investment. Still, the shift to cloud computing has created both opportunities and challenges, and the enterprise software landscape continues to evolve. We like the group.

VALUENTUM

Palo Alto PANW   FAIRLY VALUED

Buying Index™ 5   **Value Rating** ◯

Economic Castle	Estimated Fair Value	Fair Value Range	Investment Style	Sector	Industry
Very Attractive	$357.00	$276.00 - $438.00	LARGE-CAP GROWTH	Next Generation	Disruptive Innovation

Palo Alto Networks' cybersecurity offerings secure networks, remote working environments, and public and private clouds. Subscription and support revenue accounts for more than half its business.

Stock Chart (weekly)

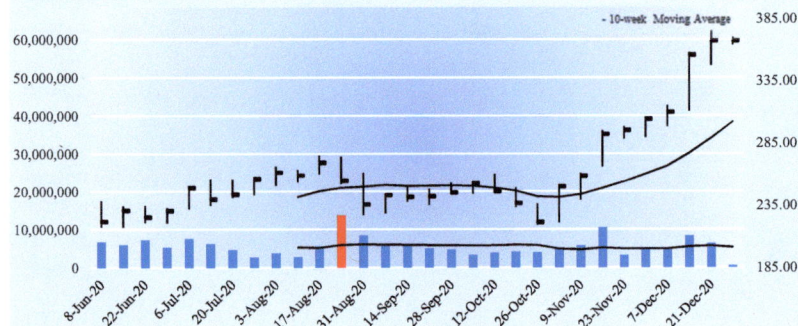

The week with the highest trading volume out of the last 30 weeks was a week of heavy selling, or distribution (red bar).

Company Vitals

Market Cap (USD)	$33,667
Avg Weekly Vol (30 wks)	5,532
30-week Range (USD)	217.48 - 375.00
Valuentum Sector	Next Generation
5-week Return	24.4%
13-week Return	49.4%
30-week Return	59.6%
Dividend Yield %	0.0%
Dividends per Share	0.00
Forward Dividend Payout Ratio	0.0%
Est. Normal Diluted EPS	3.41
P/E on Est. Normal Diluted EPS	107.7
Est. Normal EBITDA	612
Forward EV/EBITDA	367.0
EV/Est. Normal EBITDA	52.6
Forward Revenue Growth (5-yr)	19.6%
Forward EPS Growth (5-yr)	-237.9%

NMF = Not Meaningful; Est. = Estimated; FY = Fiscal Year

Returns Summary
3-year Historical Average

Return on Equity	-26.7%
Return on Assets	-6.6%
ROIC, with goodwill	46.6%
ROIC, without goodwill	67.2%

ROIC = Return on Invested Capital; NMF = Not Meaningful

Leverage, Coverage, and Liquidity
In Millions of USD

Total Debt	1,920
Net Debt	-1,483
Total Debt/EBITDA	NMF
Net Debt/EBITDA	NMF
EBITDA/Interest	-0.1
Current Ratio	1.9
Quick Ratio	1.8

NMF = Not Meaningful

Investment Highlights

• Palo Alto Networks is one of the fastest-growing cybersecurity companies with the largest firewall business. Its security platform protects enterprise, government, and service provider networks from intrusions. Its 'Cloud and AI' business is experiencing explosive growth, and the company brings together all security functions into its service from advanced threat protection to URL filtering. It was founded in 2005.

• Palo Alto Networks' reach, customer base, and potential upselling opportunities are tremendous. It has 42,500+ end-customers in over 150 countries, and its customer base includes some of the largest the Fortune 100 and Global 2000 companies across a broad range of industries.

• Some of the challenges facing Palo Alto currently include the need for continuous evolution to keep up with cybercriminals and the difficulty in balancing the limited insights of disjointed tools while keeping pace with business needs. The firm's platform is built for automation as it automates tasks using context and analytics, and subscription and support revenue account for more than half of total revenue.

• Some estimates peg the cybersecurity market to surpass $230 billion by 2022 from under $140 billion in 2017, but a changing and evolving landscape could make this figure much larger. Palo Alto Networks will have its hands in this large and growing pie, but competition will only intensify. Cisco, Check Point, Zscaler, Fortinet and Crowdstrike are rivals.

• Palo Alto Networks has a history of being significantly free cash flow positive, and we like this, but a good chunk of operating cash flow comes from compensation for equity-based awards. Profitability on a non-GAAP basis is robust, but GAAP profits have been elusive.

Investment Considerations

DCF Valuation	FAIRLY VALUED
Relative Valuation	NEUTRAL
ValueCreation™	EXCELLENT
ValueRisk™	MEDIUM
ValueTrend™	NEGATIVE
Cash Flow Generation	STRONG
Financial Leverage	LOW
Growth	AGGRESSIVE
Technical Evaluation	NEUTRAL
Relative Strength	STRONG
Money Flow Index (MFI)	OVERBOUGHT
Upside/Downside Volume (U/D)	BULLISH
Near-term Technical Support, 10-week MA	302.00

DCF = Discounted Cash Flow; MFI, U/D = Please see glossary. MA = Moving Average

Business Quality

ValueRisk™	ValueCreation™			
	Very Poor	Poor	Good	Excellent
Low				
Medium				▉
High				
Very High				

Firms that generate economic profits with little operating variability score near the top right of the matrix.

Relative Valuation

	Forward P/E	PEG	Price / FV
Wayfair	56.3	NMF	84.2%
Zoom Video	170.7	28.8	120.8%
Roku	-338.4	NMF	96.0%
Monster Beverage	36.0	2.9	104.4%
Peer Median	46.1	15.9	100.2%
Palo Alto	**-422.7**	**NMF**	**102.8%**

Price / FV = Current Stock Price divided by Estimated Fair Value

Financial Summary

	----- Actual -----		Projected
Fiscal Year End:	Jul-17	Jul-18	Jul-19
Revenue	1,762	2,273	2,900
Revenue, YoY%	27.8%	29.0%	27.6%
Non-GAAP Operating Income	-180	-129	-65
Non-GAAP EBIT %	-10.2%	-5.7%	-2.2%
Non-GAAP Net Income	-217	-148	-80
Non-GAAP NI Margin %	-12.3%	-6.5%	-2.8%
Non-GAAP Diluted EPS	-2.39	-1.61	-0.87
Non-GAAP Dil EPS, YoY %	-7.8%	-32.5%	NMF
Non-GAAP FCF (CFO-capex)	706	925	924
Free Cash Flow Margin %	40.1%	40.7%	31.9%

In Millions of USD (except for per share items)

Structure of the Software (security) Industry   NEUTRAL

Participants in the software security industry focus on protecting important information wherever it resides—whether in servers, computers, mobile devices, or in the cloud. The space is intensely competitive, and some companies may offer their technology for free, engage in aggressive marketing, or pursue competitive partnerships. Firms also face indirect competition from application/operating system providers that may embed security solutions/functions in their own products. Participants must continuously develop new and enhanced services to meet changing customer demands. We're neutral on the group.

Paychex PAYX FAIRLY VALUED

Buying Index™ 6   **Value Rating** 🟡

Economic Castle	Estimated Fair Value	Fair Value Range	Investment Style	Sector	Industry
Attractive	$76.00	$59.00 - $93.00	LARGE-CAP CORE	Information Technology	Technology Giants

Paychex has a highly diversified customer base. No one client has a material impact on its operations, and client retention has been solid. COVID-19 will cause a modest decline in adjusted EPS in fiscal 2021.

Stock Chart (weekly)

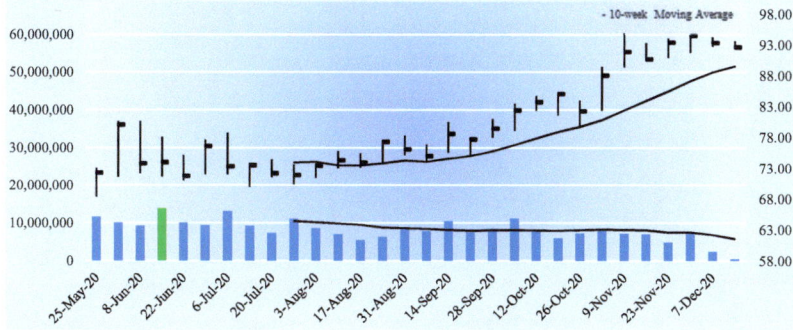

The week with the highest trading volume out of the last 30 weeks was a week of heavy selling, or distribution (red bar).

Investment Considerations

DCF Valuation	FAIRLY VALUED
Relative Valuation	UNATTRACTIVE
ValueCreation™	EXCELLENT
ValueRisk™	MEDIUM
ValueTrend™	NEGATIVE
Cash Flow Generation	STRONG
Financial Leverage	LOW
Growth	MODEST
Technical Evaluation	BULLISH
Relative Strength	STRONG
Money Flow Index (MFI)	NEUTRAL
Upside/Downside Volume (U/D)	BULLISH
Near-term Technical Support, 10-week MA	90.00

DCF = Discounted Cash Flow; MFI, U/D = Please see glossary. MA = Moving Average

Business Quality

ValueRisk™	Very Poor	Poor	Good	Excellent
Low				
Medium				▓
High				
Very High				

ValueCreation™

Firms that generate economic profits with little operating variability score near the top right of the matrix.

Company Vitals

Market Cap (USD)	$33,433
Avg Weekly Vol (30 wks)	8,153
30-week Range (USD)	68.39 - 94.95
Valuentum Sector	Information Technology
5-week Return	0.2%
13-week Return	19.4%
30-week Return	33.7%
Dividend Yield %	2.7%
Dividends per Share	2.48
Forward Dividend Payout Ratio	87.1%
Est. Normal Diluted EPS	3.31
P/E on Est. Normal Diluted EPS	28.0
Est. Normal EBITDA	2,062
Forward EV/EBITDA	18.3
EV/Est. Normal EBITDA	16.1
Forward Revenue Growth (5-yr)	3.8%
Forward EPS Growth (5-yr)	4.4%

NMF = Not Meaningful; Est. = Estimated; FY = Fiscal Year

Returns Summary

3-year Historical Average

Return on Equity	44.0%
Return on Assets	12.9%
ROIC, with goodwill	29.7%
ROIC, without goodwill	42.6%

ROIC = Return on Invested Capital; NMF = Not Meaningful

Leverage, Coverage, and Liquidity

In Millions of USD

Total Debt	802
Net Debt	-153
Total Debt/EBITDA	0.4
Net Debt/EBITDA	NMF
EBITDA/Interest	Excellent
Current Ratio	1.2
Quick Ratio	0.3

NMF = Not Meaningful

Investment Highlights

• Paychex is a leader in the payroll, human resource, and benefits outsourcing industry. With a wide range of services – including payroll processing, retirement services, insurance, and a fully outsourced human resource solution – Paychex customizes its offering to the clients' business. The company was founded in 1979 and is headquartered in New York.

• Paychex has a highly diversified customer base, and no one client has a material impact on its operations. Its agreements are generally terminable at any time, but client retention has been solid. The measure has hit record highs in recent years north of 80%. We like the 'stickiness' aspect of its operations.

• Paychex has two primary revenue sources: Payroll (~60% of sales) and Human Resource Services (~40%). Its payroll services target small businesses with 1-50 employees and mid-market businesses with 50-1,000 employees. Its HRS segment is a leader in complimentary services sold to payroll clients (retirement, insurance and HR).

• Investors should be aware that many of Paychex's services--specifically payroll tax administration services and employee benefit plan administration services--are designed in accordance with government regulations that are subject to continuous change. Adverse regulatory changes could impact performance and cannot be easily forecasted.

• Though its payout ratio (dividends paid per share divided by earnings per share) is high, Paychex boasts an excellent Dividend Cushion ratio. This is largely due to its fantastic, cash-rich balance sheet. The company offers a competitive dividend yield.

Relative Valuation

	Forward P/E	PEG	Price / FV
Apple	29.8	2.4	85.0%
Alphabet	34.9	1.8	73.3%
Amazon.com	NMF	3.3	95.7%
Microsoft	31.6	2.5	91.6%
Peer Median	31.6	2.5	88.3%
Paychex	32.5	4.2	121.9%

Price / FV = Current Stock Price divided by Estimated Fair Value

Financial Summary

	----- Actual -----		Projected
Fiscal Year End:	May-19	May-20	May-21
Revenue	3,773	4,041	3,944
Revenue, YoY%	11.6%	7.1%	-2.4%
Operating Income	1,371	1,461	1,385
Operating Margin %	36.3%	36.1%	35.1%
Net Income	1,034	1,098	1,028
Net Income Margin %	27.4%	27.2%	26.1%
Diluted EPS	2.86	3.04	2.85
Diluted EPS, YoY %	10.7%	6.4%	-6.4%
Free Cash Flow (CFO-capex)	1,148	1,314	1,342
Free Cash Flow Margin %	30.4%	32.5%	34.0%

In Millions of USD (except for per share items)

Structure of the Staffing Services Industry   NEUTRAL

The staffing services industry spans firms that provide business outsourcing services to those that offer talent management solutions. Providers of business outsourcing solutions compete with a variety of independent firms as well as captive in-house functions. Their businesses are characterized by long-term client relationships and recurring revenue. Talent management firms offer executive recruitment and consulting services and face emerging competition from professional networking website providers. Attracting consultants is particularly important for executive recruitment entities. We're neutral on the group.

Penn National PENN   FAIRLY VALUED

Buying Index™   **6**   **Value Rating**   ◐

Economic Castle	Estimated Fair Value	Fair Value Range	Investment Style	Sector	Industry
Attractive	$75.00	$56.00 - $94.00	MID-CAP VALUE	Next Generation	Disruptive Innovation

With its investment in Barstool Sports, Penn National is poised to take advantage of the nascent sports betting market.

Stock Chart (weekly)

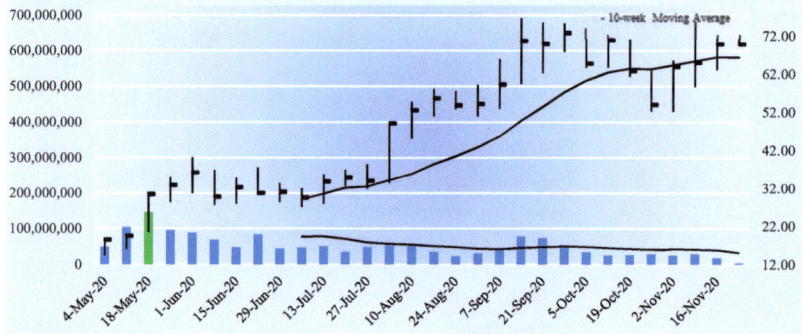

The week with the highest trading volume out of the last 30 weeks was a week of heavy selling, or distribution (red bar).

Company Vitals

Market Cap (USD)	$8,232
Avg Weekly Vol (30 wks)	51,641
30-week Range (USD)	14.31 - 76.62
Valuentum Sector	Next Generation
5-week Return	13.7%
13-week Return	29.6%
30-week Return	371.5%
Dividend Yield %	0.0%
Dividends per Share	0.00
Forward Dividend Payout Ratio	0.0%
Est. Normal Diluted EPS	2.59
P/E on Est. Normal Diluted EPS	27.0
Est. Normal EBITDA	1,374
Forward EV/EBITDA	357.2
EV/Est. Normal EBITDA	13.8
Forward Revenue Growth (5-yr)	5.8%
Forward EPS Growth (5-yr)	80.8%

NMF = Not Meaningful; Est. = Estimated; FY = Fiscal Year

Returns Summary
3-year Historical Average

Return on Equity	-40.3%
Return on Assets	3.6%
ROIC, with goodwill	6.5%
ROIC, without goodwill	7.8%

ROIC = Return on Invested Capital; NMF = Not Meaningful

Leverage, Coverage, and Liquidity
In Millions of USD

Total Debt	11,157
Net Debt	10,720
Total Debt/EBITDA	11.3
Net Debt/EBITDA	10.9
EBITDA/Interest	1.8
Current Ratio	0.7
Quick Ratio	0.6

NMF = Not Meaningful

Investment Highlights

• Penn National operates about 40 gaming and racing facilities in roughly 20 states. It completed a tax-free spin-off of Gaming and Leisure Properties (GLPI) in 2013, and most recently made big bets on Pinnacle (2018) and Barstool Sports (2020). The company was founded in 1972 and is headquartered in Pennsylvania.

• The big news with Penn National has been its investment in Barstool Sports, which launched its Sportsbook app in September 2020. App downloads have been encouraging, and handle has been impressive out of the gates.

• Penn National's strategy is multi-fold: 1) digitize brick-and-mortar through data analytics, launch in new states, support its Barstool integration, and roll out new product offerings. An omni-channel pursuit will be necessary in a post COVID-19 world where retail sportsbooks become mobile ones and regional casinos become iCasinos.

• Penn National's financial leverage is not comforting. Management estimates its lease-adjusted leverage is ~4.9x (down from 5.7x at the end of 2019). Total liquidity stood at ~$2.5 billion at the end of the third quarter of 2020, and traditional net debt measures have improved.

• Penn National may be a diversified operator of gaming and pari-mutuel businesses, but both segments remain economically-sensitive and exposed to intense competition. The legalization of sports gambling in the US is a clear positive, however.

Structure of the Gaming and Hotels Industry   NEUTRAL

The gaming industry is heavily regulated and particularly sensitive to discretionary spending. Significant future gaming revenue growth will come from the Asian markets, especially Macao. Possession of a gaming subconcession by the Chinese government is an advantage, though competition remains intense among existing Macao rivals. The hotels industry is highly competitive, with over 900 lodging management companies in the US alone. Demand for hotel rooms is very cyclical, and fluctuations in both occupancy rates and revenue per available room (RevPAR) should be expected. We're generally neutral on the structure of the group.

Investment Considerations

DCF Valuation	**FAIRLY VALUED**
Relative Valuation	**UNATTRACTIVE**
ValueCreation™	**POOR**
ValueRisk™	**MEDIUM**
ValueTrend™	**POSITIVE**
Cash Flow Generation	**STRONG**
Financial Leverage	**HIGH**
Growth	**MODEST**
Technical Evaluation	**VERY BULLISH**
Relative Strength	**STRONG**
Money Flow Index (MFI)	**NEUTRAL**
Upside/Downside Volume (U/D)	**DETERIORATING**
Near-term Technical Support, 10-week MA	**66.00**

DCF = Discounted Cash Flow; MFI, U/D = Please see glossary. MA = Moving Average

Business Quality

ValueRisk™	Very Poor	Poor	Good	Excellent
Low				
Medium		▉		
High				
Very High				

ValueCreation™

Firms that generate economic profits with little operating variability score near the top right of the matrix.

Relative Valuation

	Forward P/E	PEG	Price / FV
Wayfair	56.3	NMF	84.2%
Zoom Video	170.7	28.8	120.8%
Roku	-338.4	NMF	96.0%
Monster Beverage	36.0	2.9	104.4%
Peer Median	46.1	15.9	100.2%
Penn National	**NMF**	**NMF**	**93.2%**

Price / FV = Current Stock Price divided by Estimated Fair Value

Financial Summary

	----- Actual -----		Projected
Fiscal Year End:	Dec-18	Dec-19	Dec-20
Revenue	3,588	5,301	3,695
Revenue, YoY%	14.0%	47.8%	-30.3%
Operating Income	634	572	-236
Operating Margin %	17.7%	10.8%	-6.4%
Net Income	94	44	-585
Net Income Margin %	2.6%	0.8%	-15.8%
Diluted EPS	0.93	0.37	-4.87
Diluted EPS, YoY %	NMF	NMF	NMF
Free Cash Flow (CFO-capex)	260	514	-766
Free Cash Flow Margin %	7.2%	9.7%	-20.7%

In Millions of USD (except for per share items)

VALUENTUM

PepsiCo PEP FAIRLY VALUED

Buying Index™ 7 **Value Rating** ◯

Economic Castle	Estimated Fair Value	Fair Value Range	Investment Style	Sector	Industry
Attractive	$126.00	$101.00 - $151.00	LARGE-CAP CORE	Consumer Staples	Recession Resistant

We increased our fair value estimate for Pepsi and continue to like its business model, though we caution its net debt load is sizable.

Stock Chart (weekly)

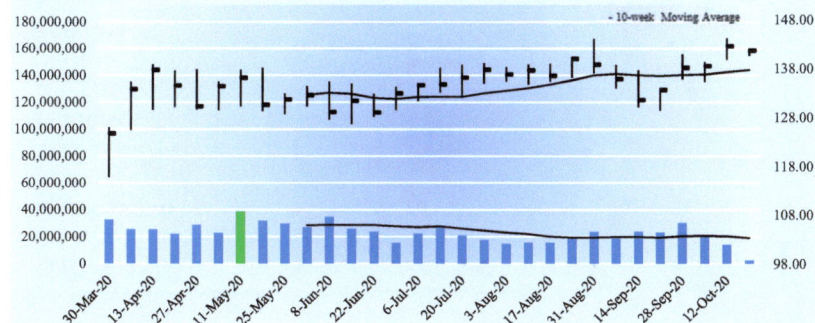

The week with the highest trading volume out of the last 30 weeks was a week of heavy selling, or distribution (red bar).

Investment Considerations

DCF Valuation	**FAIRLY VALUED**
Relative Valuation	**ATTRACTIVE**
ValueCreation™	**EXCELLENT**
ValueRisk™	**LOW**
ValueTrend™	**NEGATIVE**
Cash Flow Generation	**STRONG**
Financial Leverage	**MEDIUM**
Growth	**MODEST**
Technical Evaluation	**BULLISH**
Relative Strength	**WEAK**
Money Flow Index (MFI)	**NEUTRAL**
Upside/Downside Volume (U/D)	**BULLISH**
Near-term Technical Support, 10-week MA	**138.00**

DCF = Discounted Cash Flow; MFI, U/D = Please see glossary. MA = Moving Average

Company Vitals

Market Cap (USD)	$199,302
Avg Weekly Vol (30 wks)	23,121
30-week Range (USD)	15.66 - 144.11
Valuentum Sector	Consumer Staples
5-week Return	8.7%
13-week Return	4.5%
30-week Return	16.5%
Dividend Yield %	2.9%
Dividends per Share	4.09
Forward Dividend Payout Ratio	74.7%
Est. Normal Diluted EPS	7.26
P/E on Est. Normal Diluted EPS	19.5
Est. Normal EBITDA	16,381
Forward EV/EBITDA	16.9
EV/Est. Normal EBITDA	13.8
Forward Revenue Growth (5-yr)	4.6%
Forward EPS Growth (5-yr)	12.6%

NMF = Not Meaningful; Est. = Estimated; FY = Fiscal Year

Returns Summary

3-year Historical Average

Return on Equity	64.5%
Return on Assets	10.6%
ROIC, with goodwill	19.5%
ROIC, without goodwill	29.4%

ROIC = Return on Invested Capital; NMF = Not Meaningful

Leverage, Coverage, and Liquidity

In Millions of USD

Total Debt	32,068
Net Debt	26,330
Total Debt/EBITDA	2.5
Net Debt/EBITDA	2.1
EBITDA/Interest	11.2
Current Ratio	0.9
Quick Ratio	0.7

NMF = Not Meaningful

Investment Highlights

• Pepsi is a global food/beverage company with a plethora of respected brands. Its portfolio includes the namesake Pepsi, Mountain Dew, Gatorade, Lay's, Doritos, Cheetos, Tostitos, Ruffles, Quaker oatmeal, and Cap'n Crunch, among others. North America accounts for ~60% of its sales. The company was founded in 1898 and is headquartered in New York.

• Pepsi generates a little over half of its revenues from snacks and little under half of its revenues from beverages. Most of its revenues are generated in developed markets, though Pepsi has a long growth runway in emerging and developing markets.

• We're huge fans of Pepsi's brand portfolio, but competition remains fierce. Coca-Cola is its primary beverage competitor, while food and beverage rivals include Nestlé, Danone, Kellogg, General Mills, and Mondelēz. Pepsi has a scale advantage in North America, however, and has ~23 global brands that each bring in $1 billion in sales annually.

• Pepsi held up relatively well during the initial stages of the COVID-19 pandemic. The firm expects to generate ~4% in annual organic sales growth in fiscal 2020. Societal pressures as it concerns sugary drinks and snacks needs to be monitored, and Pepsi must continue to innovate to remain competitive.

• Pepsi seeks to optimize its logistics and manufacturing capabilities by increasing automated functions and reducing waste while improving its IT infrastructure to simply processes. At least some of the savings will be reinvested back into the business.

Business Quality

	ValueCreation™			
ValueRisk™	Very Poor	Poor	Good	Excellent
Low				■
Medium				
High				
Very High				

Firms that generate economic profits with little operating variability score near the top right of the matrix.

Relative Valuation

	Forward P/E	PEG	Price / FV
Coca-Cola	34.3	1.5	128.0%
Procter & Gamble	26.5	3.3	144.1%
Philip Morris	15.4	2.4	104.3%
Wal-Mart	26.8	2.3	130.2%
Peer Median	26.7	2.4	129.1%
PepsiCo	**25.9**	**2.2**	**112.4%**

Price / FV = Current Stock Price divided by Estimated Fair Value

Financial Summary

	----- Actual -----		Projected
Fiscal Year End:	Dec-18	Dec-19	Dec-20
Revenue	64,661	67,161	68,639
Revenue, YoY%	1.8%	3.9%	2.2%
Operating Income	10,110	10,291	10,841
Operating Margin %	15.6%	15.3%	15.8%
Net Income	12,515	7,314	7,629
Net Income Margin %	19.4%	10.9%	11.1%
Diluted EPS	8.78	5.20	5.47
Diluted EPS, YoY %	160.0%	-40.8%	5.3%
Free Cash Flow (CFO-capex)	6,133	5,417	5,719
Free Cash Flow Margin %	9.5%	8.1%	8.3%

In Millions of USD (except for per share items)

Structure of the Nonalcoholic Beverages Industry   GOOD

The nonalcoholic beverage segment of the commercial beverage industry is highly competitive, consisting of numerous companies that make various sparkling beverages, water products, juices, fruit drinks, energy and other performance-enhancing drinks. Pricing, advertising, product innovation, the availability of in-store private-label beverages, and health concerns about sugar-sweetened beverages are key drivers that impact demand. Leading brands with high levels of consumer acceptance and an expansive distribution network are sources of competitive strengths. We like the structure of the group.

Procter & Gamble PG OVERVALUED 16.8%

Buying Index™ 2   **Value Rating** ✗

Economic Castle	Estimated Fair Value	Fair Value Range	Investment Style	Sector	Industry
Attractive	$100.00	$80.00 - $120.00	MEGA-CAP CORE	Consumer Staples	Recession Resistant

We moderately increased our fair value estimate for Proctor & Gamble but shares still look expensive.

Stock Chart (weekly)

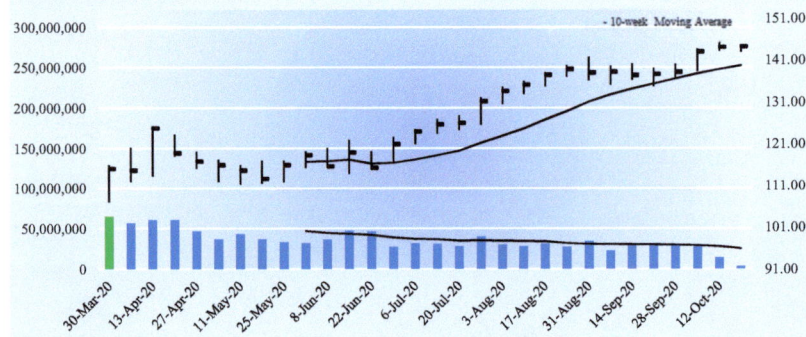

The week with the highest trading volume out of the last 30 weeks was a week of heavy selling, or distribution (red bar).

Investment Considerations

DCF Valuation	OVERVALUED
Relative Valuation	NEUTRAL
ValueCreation™	EXCELLENT
ValueRisk™	LOW
ValueTrend™	POSITIVE
Cash Flow Generation	STRONG
Financial Leverage	MEDIUM
Growth	MODEST
Technical Evaluation	NEUTRAL
Relative Strength	STRONG
Money Flow Index (MFI)	OVERBOUGHT
Upside/Downside Volume (U/D)	BULLISH
Near-term Technical Support, 10-week MA	140.00

DCF = Discounted Cash Flow; MFI, U/D = Please see glossary. MA = Moving Average

Company Vitals

Market Cap (USD)	$378,496
Avg Weekly Vol (30 wks)	35,518
30-week Range (USD)	107.00 - 145.33
Valuentum Sector	Consumer Staples
5-week Return	5.2%
13-week Return	14.7%
30-week Return	26.6%
Dividend Yield %	2.2%
Dividends per Share	3.16
Forward Dividend Payout Ratio	58.1%
Est. Normal Diluted EPS	6.44
P/E on Est. Normal Diluted EPS	22.4
Est. Normal EBITDA	24,006
Forward EV/EBITDA	18.6
EV/Est. Normal EBITDA	16.6
Forward Revenue Growth (5-yr)	4.0%
Forward EPS Growth (5-yr)	8.9%

NMF = Not Meaningful; Est. = Estimated; FY = Fiscal Year

Returns Summary
3-year Historical Average

Return on Equity	18.4%
Return on Assets	7.6%
ROIC, with goodwill	15.2%
ROIC, without goodwill	32.5%

ROIC = Return on Invested Capital; NMF = Not Meaningful

Leverage, Coverage, and Liquidity
In Millions of USD

Total Debt	34,720
Net Debt	18,539
Total Debt/EBITDA	1.9
Net Debt/EBITDA	1.0
EBITDA/Interest	40.3
Current Ratio	0.8
Quick Ratio	0.6

NMF = Not Meaningful

Investment Highlights

• Procter & Gamble boasts some of the most recognized branded consumer packaged goods. Though the markets in which its products are sold are highly competitive, the firm is well positioned in the industry and holds significant market share positions. The company was founded in 1837 and is headquartered in Cincinnati, Ohio.

• For a company with such established brands as Procter & Gamble, ongoing product innovation and compelling marketing strategies are vital to supporting its long-term sales growth trajectory. Improving its cost structure is another key focus.

• Procter & Gamble worked through a massive portfolio transformation during the past several years. P&G is now focused on ten categories where it holds leading market positions. In January 2020, P&G announced it was acquiring Billie, a women's shaving supplies and body care company, showing its willingness to grow inorganically.

• P&G's brands include Tide, Ariel, Gillette, Bounty, Charmin, Olay, Pampers, Crest, and Oral-B. The company's innovation pipeline is robust, and it markets the firm serves from 'Baby, Feminine, Family' to 'Health & Grooming' are massive and growing as the global middle class continues to grow.

• Procter & Gamble boasts 125+ consecutive years of dividend payments and 60+ consecutive years of dividend increases. Free cash flow productivity is generally targeted at 90%+, which is the core driver of its Dividend Cushion ratio given its net debt load.

Business Quality

ValueRisk™	Very Poor	Poor	Good	Excellent
Low				▓
Medium				
High				
Very High				

Firms that generate economic profits with little operating variability score near the top right of the matrix.

Relative Valuation

	Forward P/E	PEG	Price / FV
Anheuser-Busch InBev	27.2	0.5	101.7%
Coca-Cola	34.3	1.5	128.0%
Philip Morris	15.4	2.4	104.3%
Wal-Mart	26.8	2.3	130.2%
Peer Median	27.0	1.9	116.1%
Procter & Gamble	**26.5**	**3.3**	**144.1%**

Price / FV = Current Stock Price divided by Estimated Fair Value

Financial Summary

	----- Actual -----		Projected
Fiscal Year End:	Jun-19	Jun-20	Jun-21
Revenue	67,684	70,950	72,795
Revenue, YoY%	1.3%	4.8%	2.6%
Operating Income	13,832	15,706	18,294
Operating Margin %	20.4%	22.1%	25.1%
Net Income	3,637	13,027	14,009
Net Income Margin %	5.4%	18.4%	19.2%
Diluted EPS	1.43	4.96	5.44
Diluted EPS, YoY %	-61.0%	246.4%	9.7%
Free Cash Flow (CFO-capex)	12,155	14,330	14,649
Free Cash Flow Margin %	18.0%	20.2%	20.1%

In Millions of USD (except for per share items)

Structure of the Household Products Industry   GOOD

Firms in the household products industry sell some of the most recognized branded consumer packaged goods in the world and often hold a significant market share position in a variety of product categories. Though the industry is characterized by stiff competition from retailers' private-label brands, constituents tend to boast meaningful competitive advantages due to their brand strength/reputation and generate high returns on invested capital. Household products companies remain tied to the vicissitudes of consumer spending, but we tend to like the structure of the group.

VALUENTUM

Pinterest PINS   FAIRLY VALUED

Buying Index™   5   **Value Rating** 🟡

Economic Castle	Estimated Fair Value	Fair Value Range	Investment Style	Sector	Industry
Attractive	$71.00	$50.00 - $92.00	LARGE-CAP GROWTH	Next Generation	Disruptive Innovation

Pinterest is growing rapidly, but the company continues to generate net losses. We expect the firm to start generating meaningful free cash flow in the next few years, however.

Stock Chart (weekly)

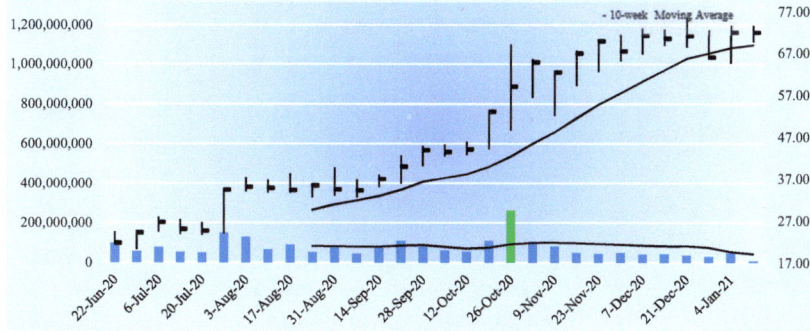

The week with the highest trading volume out of the last 30 weeks was a week of heavy selling, or distribution (red bar).

Investment Considerations

DCF Valuation	**FAIRLY VALUED**
Relative Valuation	**NEUTRAL**
ValueCreation™	**VERY POOR**
ValueRisk™	**MEDIUM**
ValueTrend™	**POSITIVE**
Cash Flow Generation	**WEAK**
Financial Leverage	**LOW**
Growth	**AGGRESSIVE**
Technical Evaluation	**NEUTRAL**
Relative Strength	**STRONG**
Money Flow Index (MFI)	**OVERBOUGHT**
Upside/Downside Volume (U/D)	**BULLISH**
Near-term Technical Support, 10-week MA	**69.00**

DCF = Discounted Cash Flow; MFI, U/D = Please see glossary. MA = Moving Average

Company Vitals

Market Cap (USD)	$30,219
Avg Weekly Vol (30 wks)	75,053
30-week Range (USD)	20.07 - 75.44
Valuentum Sector	Next Generation
5-week Return	-0.4%
13-week Return	62.6%
30-week Return	208.1%
Dividend Yield %	0.0%
Dividends per Share	0.00
Forward Dividend Payout Ratio	0.0%
Est. Normal Diluted EPS	0.21
P/E on Est. Normal Diluted EPS	349.9
Est. Normal EBITDA	252
Forward EV/EBITDA	-67.9
EV/Est. Normal EBITDA	113.1
Forward Revenue Growth (5-yr)	33.2%
Forward EPS Growth (5-yr)	-182.6%

NMF = Not Meaningful; Est. = Estimated; FY = Fiscal Year

Returns Summary
3-year Historical Average

Return on Equity	-52.7%
Return on Assets	-31.2%
ROIC, with goodwill	-23.3%
ROIC, without goodwill	-24.1%

ROIC = Return on Invested Capital; NMF = Not Meaningful

Leverage, Coverage, and Liquidity
In Millions of USD

Total Debt	0
Net Debt	-1,713
Total Debt/EBITDA	0.0
Net Debt/EBITDA	NMF
EBITDA/Interest	-636.9
Current Ratio	11.7
Quick Ratio	NA

NMF = Not Meaningful

Investment Highlights

- Pinterest is an online discovery engine that people use to find inspiration. It makes money from ads on its website and mobile applications. International revenue accounts for 15%-20% of business, with the balance coming from the US. Its website has 240+ billion pins (images/videos) organized across billions of 'boards.' It was incorporated in 2008 and is based in San Francisco, California.

- The number of monthly active users ('Pinners') continues to grow, totaling 442 million at the end of the third quarter of 2020, up from 335 million, 265 million and 216 million at the end of 2019, 2018, and 2017, respectively. Most revenue comes from the US, but 75%+ of its users are international.

- Through the first nine months of 2020, Pinterest generated positive adjusted EBITDA, but operating cash flow remained negative, indicating poor earnings quality. Adjusted EBITDA was $16.7 billion, -$39 billion, and -93 billion during 2019, 2018, and 2017, respectively. Pinterest has a bright future, but we prefer net cash rich and free cash flow powerhouse Facebook as our favorite consideration.

- The company's international monthly active users have been its growth engine. Pinterest's early efforts to focus on monetizing the US market have helped build a firm foundation, but its success in substantially monetizing non-US markets will be key for Pinterest to achieve the forecasts within our valuation model supporting our fair value estimate.

- Pinterest has a debt-free balance sheet and ample net cash, but it is generating material GAAP losses. Stagnant user growth in the US isn't great either. It had federal/state net operating loss carryforwards of $2.7 billion as of 2019, which should keep cash tax rates low for some time.

Business Quality

ValueRisk™	ValueCreation™			
	Very Poor	Poor	Good	Excellent
Low				
Medium	■			
High				
Very High				

Firms that generate economic profits with little operating variability score near the top right of the matrix.

Relative Valuation

	Forward P/E	PEG	Price / FV
Wayfair	56.3	NMF	84.2%
Zoom Video	170.7	28.8	120.8%
Roku	-338.4	NMF	96.0%
Monster Beverage	36.0	2.9	104.4%
Peer Median	46.1	15.9	100.2%
Pinterest	**-94.9**	**NMF**	**101.2%**

Price / FV = Current Stock Price divided by Estimated Fair Value

Financial Summary

	----- Actual -----		Projected
Fiscal Year End:	Dec-18	Dec-19	Dec-20
Revenue	756	1,143	1,631
Revenue, YoY%	59.9%	51.2%	42.7%
Operating Income	-75	-1,389	-460
Operating Margin %	-9.9%	-121.5%	-28.2%
Net Income	-63	-1,361	-446
Net Income Margin %	-8.3%	-119.1%	-27.3%
Diluted EPS	-0.50	-3.24	-0.76
Diluted EPS, YoY %	-51.8%	553.4%	-76.6%
Free Cash Flow (CFO-capex)	-83	-33	-137
Free Cash Flow Margin %	-10.9%	-2.9%	-8.4%

In Millions of USD (except for per share items)

Structure of the Internet & Catalog Retail Industry   **GOOD**

The Internet and catalog retail industry benefits as a whole from the secular trend toward consumer digital (online) consumption. The industry consists of a number of exclusive online retailers led by Amazon, which continues to disrupt the broader retail space, and businesses that offer Internet travel services such as Booking Holdings, while online auctions are dominated by eBay. The industry generates high returns on investment due to minimal capital costs, but the landscape will be vastly different in the decades ahead. Still, we like the group.

Philip Morris PM   FAIRLY VALUED

Buying Index™   **6**   **Value Rating**   ◯

Economic Castle	Estimated Fair Value	Fair Value Range	Investment Style	Sector	Industry
Very Attractive	$76.00	$61.00 - $91.00	LARGE-CAP CORE	Consumer Staples	Recession Resistant

Philip Morris' heated tobacco unit offerings have seen strong sales growth of late, helping offset declines of traditional cigarette sales by volume.

Stock Chart (weekly)

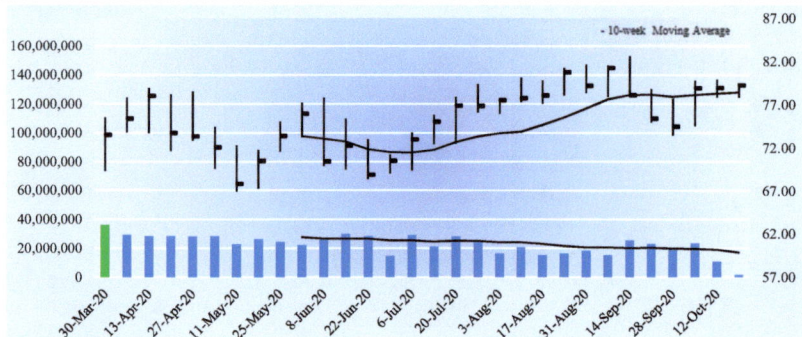

The week with the highest trading volume out of the last 30 weeks was a week of heavy selling, or distribution (red bar).

Company Vitals

Market Cap (USD)	$123,282
Avg Weekly Vol (30 wks)	22,682
30-week Range (USD)	66.84 - 82.58
Valuentum Sector	Consumer Staples
5-week Return	1.4%
13-week Return	3.2%
30-week Return	12.7%
Dividend Yield %	6.1%
Dividends per Share	4.80
Forward Dividend Payout Ratio	93.6%
Est. Normal Diluted EPS	6.02
P/E on Est. Normal Diluted EPS	13.2
Est. Normal EBITDA	14,325
Forward EV/EBITDA	11.9
EV/Est. Normal EBITDA	10.3
Forward Revenue Growth (5-yr)	3.4%
Forward EPS Growth (5-yr)	7.2%

NMF = Not Meaningful; Est. = Estimated; FY = Fiscal Year

Returns Summary
3-year Historical Average

Return on Equity	-60.3%
Return on Assets	18.0%
ROIC, with goodwill	47.2%
ROIC, without goodwill	79.7%

ROIC = Return on Invested Capital; NMF = Not Meaningful

Leverage, Coverage, and Liquidity
In Millions of USD

Total Debt	31,045
Net Debt	24,184
Total Debt/EBITDA	2.7
Net Debt/EBITDA	2.1
EBITDA/Interest	20.2
Current Ratio	1.1
Quick Ratio	0.6

NMF = Not Meaningful

Investment Highlights

• Philip Morris benefits from its exposure to faster-growing regions of the world, including Asia and EEMA. Still, it remains exposed to regulatory risk and excise price shocks that may impact demand for tobacco in certain countries. Currency fluctuations can pose stiff earnings headwinds at times and should not be ignored.

• Philip Morris aims to generate $1.0 billion in annualized savings with an eye towards reducing manufacturing costs and containing SG&A expenses. Digital investments may enable Philip Morris to unlock additional savings according to management.

• Pricing will be the main driver of Philip Morris' income growth. We like the company's ability to raise prices despite a challenging economic backdrop in several regions of the world. Longer term, Philip Morris expects its heated tobacco units, such as its IQOS offering, to support its cash flows as traditional tobacco sales by volume continue to shift lower.

• Philip Morris owns six of the 15 top selling cigarette brands worldwide including the Marlboro, L&M, Chesterfield, and Parliament brands. Ongoing strength at its Marlboro brand combined with surging heated tobacco unit sales enable the firm to control ~28% of the international (ex US and China) cigarette market.

• Philip Morris' capital expenditures have come down significantly in recent years, supporting its ability to generate meaningful free cash flows. Its financial and operational performance held up relatively well during the initial stages of COVID-19 pandemic.

Investment Considerations

DCF Valuation	**FAIRLY VALUED**
Relative Valuation	**NEUTRAL**
ValueCreation™	**EXCELLENT**
ValueRisk™	**LOW**
ValueTrend™	**NEGATIVE**
Cash Flow Generation	**STRONG**
Financial Leverage	**MEDIUM**
Growth	**MODEST**
Technical Evaluation	**VERY BULLISH**
Relative Strength	**WEAK**
Money Flow Index (MFI)	**NEUTRAL**
Upside/Downside Volume (U/D)	**DETERIORATING**
Near-term Technical Support, 10-week MA	**78.00**

DCF = Discounted Cash Flow; MFI; U/D = Please see glossary. MA = Moving Average

Business Quality
ValueCreation™

ValueRisk™	Very Poor	Poor	Good	Excellent
Low				▓
Medium				
High				
Very High				

Firms that generate economic profits with little operating variability score near the top right of the matrix.

Relative Valuation

	Forward P/E	PEG	Price / FV
Anheuser-Busch InBev	27.2	0.5	101.7%
Coca-Cola	34.3	1.5	128.0%
Procter & Gamble	26.5	3.3	144.1%
Wal-Mart	26.8	2.3	130.2%
Peer Median	27.0	1.9	129.1%
Philip Morris	**15.4**	**2.4**	**104.3%**

Price / FV = Current Stock Price divided by Estimated Fair Value

Financial Summary

	Actual		Projected
Fiscal Year End:	Dec-18	Dec-19	Dec-20
Revenue	29,625	29,805	28,643
Revenue, YoY%	3.1%	0.6%	-3.9%
Operating Income	11,377	10,531	11,461
Operating Margin %	38.4%	35.3%	40.0%
Net Income	7,910	7,185	7,992
Net Income Margin %	26.7%	24.1%	27.9%
Diluted EPS	5.09	4.62	5.13
Diluted EPS, YoY %	30.1%	-9.2%	11.1%
Free Cash Flow (CFO-capex)	8,041	9,238	8,884
Free Cash Flow Margin %	27.1%	31.0%	31.0%

In Millions of USD (except for per share items)

Structure of the Tobacco Industry   GOOD

The oligopolistic tobacco industry is attractive in a number of ways. Firms sell an "addictive" product (cigarettes and/or smokeless tobacco), have significant pricing power, generate high margins, and strong returns on invested capital. Still, declining trends in smoking in the US, threats of tobacco-related litigation, new tobacco regulation (labeling) that discourages tobacco use, and excise tax price shocks that may impact demand will always be concerns. In any case, we tend to like the structural characteristics of the tobacco industry and the shareholder-friendly policies of constituents.

Proto Labs PRLB FAIRLY VALUED

Buying Index™ 6 **Value Rating** ●

Economic Castle	Estimated Fair Value	Fair Value Range	Investment Style	Sector	Industry
Attractive	$146.00	$110.00 - $183.00	MID-CAP CORE	Next Generation	Disruptive Innovation

We significantly increased our fair value estimate for Proto Labs as its outlook has improved considerably, aided by its ongoing strategic initiatives.

Stock Chart (weekly)

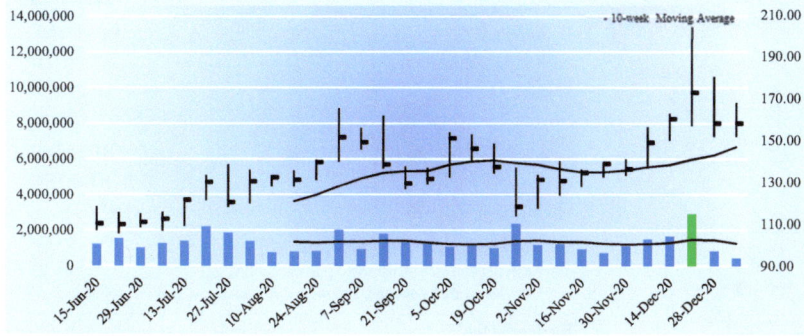

The week with the highest trading volume out of the last 30 weeks was a week of heavy selling, or distribution (red bar).

Investment Considerations

DCF Valuation	**FAIRLY VALUED**
Relative Valuation	**NEUTRAL**
ValueCreation™	**EXCELLENT**
ValueRisk™	**MEDIUM**
ValueTrend™	**NEGATIVE**
Cash Flow Generation	**STRONG**
Financial Leverage	**LOW**
Growth	**MODEST**
Technical Evaluation	**BULLISH**
Relative Strength	**NEUTRAL**
Money Flow Index (MFI)	**NEUTRAL**
Upside/Downside Volume (U/D)	**BULLISH**
Near-term Technical Support, 10-week MA	**147.00**

DCF = Discounted Cash Flow; MFI, U/D = Please see glossary. MA = Moving Average

Business Quality

ValueRisk™	Very Poor	Poor	Good	Excellent
			ValueCreation™	
Low				
Medium				■
High				
Very High				

Firms that generate economic profits with little operating variability score near the top right of the matrix.

Company Vitals

Market Cap (USD)	$4,274
Avg Weekly Vol (30 wks)	1,319
30-week Range (USD)	105.30 - 203.88
Valuentum Sector	Next Generation
5-week Return	15.4%
13-week Return	4.2%
30-week Return	47.0%
Dividend Yield %	0.0%
Dividends per Share	0.00
Forward Dividend Payout Ratio	0.0%
Est. Normal Diluted EPS	4.04
P/E on Est. Normal Diluted EPS	39.1
Est. Normal EBITDA	180
Forward EV/EBITDA	36.4
EV/Est. Normal EBITDA	22.9
Forward Revenue Growth (5-yr)	8.6%
Forward EPS Growth (5-yr)	22.9%

NMF = Not Meaningful; Est. = Estimated; FY = Fiscal Year

Returns Summary
3-year Historical Average

Return on Equity	13.0%
Return on Assets	11.5%
ROIC, with goodwill	21.8%
ROIC, without goodwill	31.6%

ROIC = Return on Invested Capital; NMF = Not Meaningful

Leverage, Coverage, and Liquidity
In Millions of USD

Total Debt	0
Net Debt	-161
Total Debt/EBITDA	0.0
Net Debt/EBITDA	NMF
EBITDA/Interest	Excellent
Current Ratio	4.9
Quick Ratio	4.5

NMF = Not Meaningful

Investment Highlights

• Proto Labs is a quick-turn manufacturer of custom parts for prototyping and short-run production. The firm utilizes computer numerical control, or CNC, machining and injection molding. Its technology eliminates the time-consuming and expensive labor required to make low-volume parts. The company was founded in 1999 and is headquartered in Minnesota.

• Proto Labs points to three mega-trends that are driving demand: shorter product lifecycles, the Internet of Things, and personalization and mass customization. It recently launched a new digital quoting platform in certain markets to improve its e-commerce operations.

• Proto Labs' market opportunity is tremendous, and the firm is growing at a rapid pace. The company is focused on its Protolabs 2.0 initiative, which among other things, aims to improve its e-commerce operations by investing in both consumer-facing and back-end operations. We think this initiative will improve the customer experience while making its business more scalable.

• Please be aware that our free cash flow model assumes that Proto Labs generates sizable revenue growth in the coming years on top of meaningful margin expansion, aided by its Protolabs 2.0 initiative. Should the firm stumble for any reason, its intrinsic value would face significant headwinds.

• Besides expanding its customer base, Proto Labs is broadening its part envelope and adding manufacturing processes to strengthen its value proposition. The company's net cash position on the balance sheet is a valuable asset as it continues to invest for growth.

Relative Valuation

	Forward P/E	PEG	Price / FV
Wayfair	56.3	NMF	84.2%
Zoom Video	170.7	28.8	120.8%
Roku	-338.4	NMF	96.0%
Monster Beverage	36.0	2.9	104.4%
Peer Median	46.1	15.9	100.2%
Proto Labs	**65.7**	**2.9**	**108.2%**

Price / FV = Current Stock Price divided by Estimated Fair Value

Financial Summary

	----- Actual -----		Projected
Fiscal Year End:	Dec-18	Dec-19	Dec-20
Revenue	446	459	431
Revenue, YoY%	29.3%	2.9%	-6.0%
Operating Income	89	80	84
Operating Margin %	20.0%	17.4%	19.5%
Net Income	77	64	65
Net Income Margin %	17.2%	13.8%	15.2%
Diluted EPS	2.81	2.35	2.40
Diluted EPS, YoY %	45.6%	-16.4%	2.4%
Free Cash Flow (CFO-capex)	36	54	52
Free Cash Flow Margin %	8.0%	11.8%	12.0%

In Millions of USD (except for per share items)

Structure of the Machinery & Tools Industry **GOOD**

The machinery and tools industry is fragmented and highly competitive. Most constituents offer a wide range of products in a myriad of markets. Firms are heavily exposed to fluctuating raw material prices (steel, resins, chemicals) and the vicissitudes of the global economic cycle, including customer capital/maintenance budgets. Several companies are recognized worldwide for their strong brand names and reputation for quality, innovation and value, and we view such attributes as material competitive advantages. Though pricing competition is not absent, we like the structural characteristics of the group.

VALUENTUM

Phillips 66 PSX　FAIRLY VALUED

			Buying Index™	**6**	Value Rating	○

Economic Castle	Estimated Fair Value	Fair Value Range	Investment Style	Sector	Industry
Attractive	$77.00	$58.00 - $96.00	LARGE-CAP VALUE	Energy	Oil & Gas Complex

We reduced our fair value estimate for Phillips 66 as the outlook for the refining industry has deteriorated due to the COVID-19 pandemic.

Stock Chart (weekly)

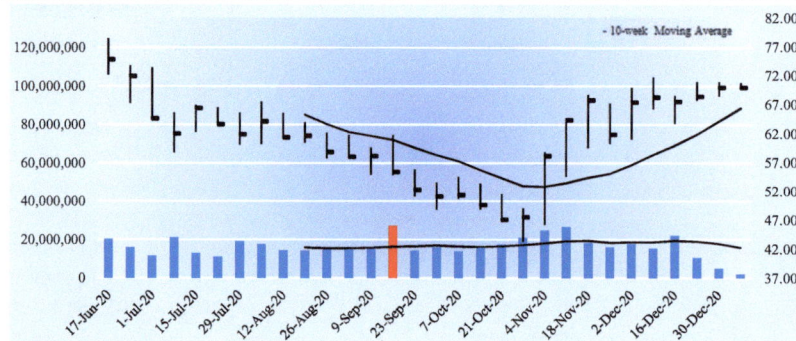

The week with the highest trading volume out of the last 30 weeks was a week of heavy selling, or distribution (red bar).

Investment Considerations

DCF Valuation	**FAIRLY VALUED**
Relative Valuation	**NEUTRAL**
ValueCreation™	**POOR**
ValueRisk™	**MEDIUM**
ValueTrend™	**POSITIVE**
Cash Flow Generation	**MEDIUM**
Financial Leverage	**MEDIUM**
Growth	**DECLINING**
Technical Evaluation	**BULLISH**
Relative Strength	**STRONG**
Money Flow Index (MFI)	**NEUTRAL**
Upside/Downside Volume (U/D)	**BULLISH**
Near-term Technical Support, 10-week MA	**66.00**

DCF = Discounted Cash Flow; MFI, U/D = Please see glossary. MA = Moving Average

Company Vitals

Market Cap (USD)	$31,745
Avg Weekly Vol (30 wks)	16,242
30-week Range (USD)	43.27 - 78.41
Valuentum Sector	Energy
5-week Return	2.2%
13-week Return	35.2%
30-week Return	NA
Dividend Yield %	5.1%
Dividends per Share	3.60
Forward Dividend Payout Ratio	NMF
Est. Normal Diluted EPS	5.03
P/E on Est. Normal Diluted EPS	13.9
Est. Normal EBITDA	4,600
Forward EV/EBITDA	26.7
EV/Est. Normal EBITDA	9.1
Forward Revenue Growth (5-yr)	-0.3%
Forward EPS Growth (5-yr)	5.7%

NMF = Not Meaningful; Est. = Estimated; FY = Fiscal Year

Returns Summary
3-year Historical Average

Return on Equity	19.8%
Return on Assets	8.9%
ROIC, with goodwill	8.0%
ROIC, without goodwill	9.0%

ROIC = Return on Invested Capital; NMF = Not Meaningful

Leverage, Coverage, and Liquidity
In Millions of USD

Total Debt	11,763
Net Debt	10,149
Total Debt/EBITDA	2.6
Net Debt/EBITDA	2.2
EBITDA/Interest	10.0
Current Ratio	1.2
Quick Ratio	0.9

NMF = Not Meaningful

Investment Highlights

• Phillips 66 was separated from ConocoPhillips back in 2012, and the new company is headquartered in Houston, Texas. Phillips 66 operates refineries, biofuel plants, petrochemical plants, and Phillips 66 has a significant midstream footprint (energy infrastructure) via its sizable economic stakes in DCP Midstream and Phillips 66 Partners LP.

• Phillips 66 sharply reduced its capital expenditure expectations in the wake of the COVID-19 pandemic. The outlook for refined petroleum product demand growth has been negatively impacted by the steep decline in commercial air travel seen of late.

• While material short-term headwinds remain, Phillips 66's long-term outlook is supported by the growing global middle class. Economic growth in China, India, and Southeast Asia over the coming decades supports the demand growth outlook for global refined petroleum and petrochemical products, with an eye towards growing demand for plastic products.

• Phillips 66 views its domestic operations as having access to cost advantaged feedstocks, a product of the North American energy production boom. That dynamic provies it with a key competitive advantage, though we caution that Phillips 66 is still highly levered to the state of the global economy.

• The trajectory of refining margins or "crack spreads" has an outsize impact on Phillips 66's financial performance. Rising raw energy resources pricing can create serious headwinds for its refining and petrochemical businesses (cost inflation).

Business Quality

	ValueCreation™			
ValueRisk™	Very Poor	Poor	Good	Excellent
Low				
Medium		▨		
High				
Very High				

Firms that generate economic profits with little operating variability score near the top right of the matrix.

Relative Valuation

	Forward P/E	PEG	Price / FV
Schlumberger	27.1	NMF	80.6%
Chevron	-198.5	NMF	111.0%
Exxon Mobil	-102.5	NMF	100.4%
Enterprise Product Partners	9.7	NMF	98.1%
Peer Median	-46.4	NMF	99.2%
Phillips 66	**-532.7**	**NMF**	**90.8%**

Price / FV = Current Stock Price divided by Estimated Fair Value

Financial Summary

	----- Actual -----		Projected
Fiscal Year End:	Dec-18	Dec-19	Dec-20
Revenue	111,461	107,293	62,981
Revenue, YoY%	6.5%	-3.7%	-41.3%
Operating Income	5,209	3,236	761
Operating Margin %	4.7%	3.0%	1.2%
Net Income	5,595	3,076	-58
Net Income Margin %	5.0%	2.9%	-0.1%
Diluted EPS	11.80	6.78	-0.13
Diluted EPS, YoY %	19.9%	-42.6%	-101.9%
Free Cash Flow (CFO-capex)	4,934	935	-555
Free Cash Flow Margin %	4.4%	0.9%	-0.9%

In Millions of USD (except for per share items)

Structure of the Refining Industry　　　　　　　　　　　　　　POOR

Results of firms in the refining industry are primarily affected by the relationship, or margin, between refined product prices and the prices for crude oil and other feedstocks. The cost to acquire feedstocks and the price at which refiners can sell refined products depends upon several factors beyond their control, including the supply/demand of crude oil and other refined products—which in turn depends on the availability of imports, production, inventories, political affairs and economic considerations. Refining margins are difficult to predict, and we expect them to continue to be volatile in the future.

PayPal PYPL   FAIRLY VALUED

Buying Index™   **6**   *Value Rating* ◯

Economic Castle	Estimated Fair Value	Fair Value Range	Investment Style	Sector	Industry
Very Attractive	$215.00	$172.00 - $258.00	MEGA-CAP BLEND	Information Technology	Technology Giants

We recently raised our fair value estimate of PayPal to over $200 per share, but there is more upside based on the high end of our fair value estimate range. The company remains one of our favorite ideas.

Stock Chart (weekly)

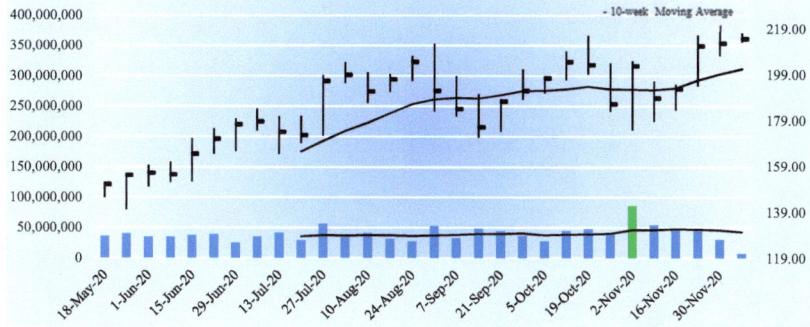

The week with the highest trading volume out of the last 30 weeks was a week of heavy selling, or distribution (red bar).

Investment Considerations

DCF Valuation	FAIRLY VALUED
Relative Valuation	UNATTRACTIVE
ValueCreation™	EXCELLENT
ValueRisk™	LOW
ValueTrend™	POSITIVE
Cash Flow Generation	STRONG
Financial Leverage	LOW
Growth	AGGRESSIVE
Technical Evaluation	BULLISH
Relative Strength	STRONG
Money Flow Index (MFI)	NEUTRAL
Upside/Downside Volume (U/D)	DETERIORATING
Near-term Technical Support, 10-week MA	201.00

DCF = Discounted Cash Flow; MFI, U/D = Please see glossary. MA = Moving Average

Business Quality

ValueRisk™	ValueCreation™			
	Very Poor	Poor	Good	Excellent
Low				■
Medium				
High				
Very High				

Firms that generate economic profits with little operating variability score near the top right of the matrix.

Company Vitals

Market Cap (USD)	$254,874
Avg Weekly Vol (30 wks)	39,489
30-week Range (USD)	140.02 - 220.57
Valuentum Sector	Information Technology
5-week Return	9.6%
13-week Return	15.3%
30-week Return	44.8%
Dividend Yield %	0.0%
Dividends per Share	0.00
Forward Dividend Payout Ratio	0.0%
Est. Normal Diluted EPS	6.17
P/E on Est. Normal Diluted EPS	34.8
Est. Normal EBITDA	9,482
Forward EV/EBITDA	40.9
EV/Est. Normal EBITDA	26.3
Forward Revenue Growth (5-yr)	16.4%
Forward EPS Growth (5-yr)	34.6%

NMF = Not Meaningful; Est. = Estimated; FY = Fiscal Year

Returns Summary   *3-year Historical Average*

Return on Equity	13.3%
Return on Assets	5.0%
ROIC, with goodwill	34.2%
ROIC, without goodwill	63.6%

ROIC = Return on Invested Capital; NMF = Not Meaningful

Leverage, Coverage, and Liquidity

In Millions of USD

Total Debt	4,965
Net Debt	-5,796
Total Debt/EBITDA	1.4
Net Debt/EBITDA	NMF
EBITDA/Interest	Excellent
Current Ratio	1.4
Quick Ratio	1.3

NMF = Not Meaningful

Investment Highlights

- PayPal operates as a technology platform company that enables digital and mobile payments on behalf of consumers and merchants worldwide. Its platform allows customers to pay and get paid, transfer and withdraw funds to their bank accounts, and hold balances in their PayPal accounts in various currencies. PayPal was spun off from eBay in July 2015.

- PayPal will continue to innovate and update its products and platform, which will be necessary to remain effectively competitive. Venmo, its peer-to-peer platform, offers additional growth potential, and management is optimistic regarding its ability to further monetize the platform.

- PayPal's business is subject to extensive government regulation and oversight, as well as complex, overlapping and frequently changing rules, regulations and legal interpretations. Additionally, any factors that increase the costs of cross-border trade or restrict, delay, or make cross-border trade more difficult would lower its revenues and profits and could harm our business, providing additional geopolitical risk.

- PayPal continues to set itself up for long-term success. The firm has announced partnerships with Visa, MasterCard, and Discover that enhance customer service features, particularly in the area of digital payments. COVID-19 will pose challenges to its operations, but the company remains well-positioned, in our view.

- Competition is growing for PayPal, including the likes of Square, Stripe, and digital initiatives from credit card companies. Amazon is reportedly offering discounts to retailers using Amazon Pay. Shares have been volatile on news around its agreement with eBay, which was ultimately extended through 2023.

Relative Valuation

	Forward P/E	PEG	Price / FV
Apple	29.8	2.4	85.0%
Alphabet	34.9	1.8	73.3%
Amazon.com	NMF	3.3	95.7%
Microsoft	31.6	2.5	91.6%
Peer Median	31.6	2.5	88.3%
PayPal	**56.0**	**3.0**	**99.8%**

Price / FV = Current Stock Price divided by Estimated Fair Value

Financial Summary

	----- Actual -----		Projected
Fiscal Year End:	Dec-18	Dec-19	Dec-20
Revenue	15,451	17,772	21,415
Revenue, YoY%	18.0%	15.0%	20.5%
Non-GAAP Operating Income	2,503	2,719	5,027
Non-GAAP EBIT %	16.2%	15.3%	23.5%
Non-GAAP Net Income	2,057	2,459	4,510
Non-GAAP NI Margin %	13.3%	13.8%	21.1%
Non-GAAP Diluted EPS	1.71	2.07	3.83
Non-GAAP Dil EPS, YoY %	16.3%	21.1%	84.9%
Non-GAAP FCF (CFO-capex)	4,660	3,857	7,030
Non-GAAP FCF Margin %	30.2%	21.7%	32.8%

In Millions of USD (except for per share items)

Structure of the Financial Tech Services Industry   EXCELLENT

The financial tech services industry is primarily composed of firms that generate revenue by charging fees to customers for providing transaction processing and other payment-related services. Constituents operate in a rapidly-evolving legal/regulatory environment, particularly with respect to interchange fees, data protection, and information security. Several participants benefit from a significant competitive advantage – the network effect. As more consumers use credit/debit cards, more merchants accept them, thereby creating a virtuous cycle. The industry is one of the most attractive in our coverage.

QUALCOMM QCOM   FAIRLY VALUED

Buying Index™ 7   Value Rating 🌕

Economic Castle	Estimated Fair Value	Fair Value Range	Investment Style	Sector	Industry
Very Attractive	$164.00	$131.00 - $197.00	LARGE-CAP BLEND	Information Technology	Technology Giants

QUALCOMM recently concluded a lucrative patent dispute with Huawei. The company is working through the COVID-19 pandemic, but its future remains bright, in our view.

Stock Chart (weekly)

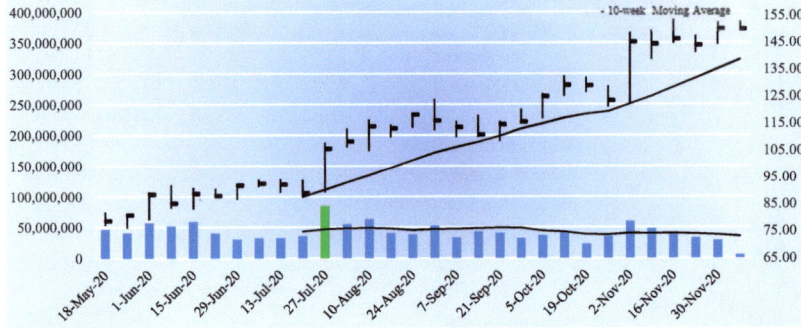

The week with the highest trading volume out of the last 30 weeks was a week of heavy selling, or distribution (red bar).

Company Vitals

Market Cap (USD)	$172,247
Avg Weekly Vol (30 wks)	41,921
30-week Range (USD)	76.16 - 153.33
Valuentum Sector	Information Technology
5-week Return	0.3%
13-week Return	30.1%
30-week Return	94.0%
Dividend Yield %	1.7%
Dividends per Share	2.60
Forward Dividend Payout Ratio	36.4%
Est. Normal Diluted EPS	9.30
P/E on Est. Normal Diluted EPS	16.1
Est. Normal EBITDA	13,560
Forward EV/EBITDA	15.9
EV/Est. Normal EBITDA	13.0
Forward Revenue Growth (5-yr)	12.3%
Forward EPS Growth (5-yr)	21.1%

NMF = Not Meaningful; Est. = Estimated; FY = Fiscal Year

Returns Summary   3-year Historical Average

Return on Equity	71.4%
Return on Assets	6.2%
ROIC, with goodwill	40.0%
ROIC, without goodwill	66.7%

ROIC = Return on Invested Capital; NMF = Not Meaningful

Leverage, Coverage, and Liquidity

In Millions of USD

Total Debt	15,726
Net Debt	4,512
Total Debt/EBITDA	2.1
Net Debt/EBITDA	0.6
EBITDA/Interest	12.7
Current Ratio	2.1
Quick Ratio	1.8

NMF = Not Meaningful

Investment Highlights

• QUALCOMM has revolutionized the mobile phone industry. Through its own R&D and through partnerships with other firms, the company develops breakthrough technology and then licenses it. The firm has one of the strongest Economic Castles in our coverage. It was founded in 1985 and is headquartered in San Diego, California.

• Broadcom withdrew its hostile bid for QUALCOMM after President Trump issued an order to block the deal on grounds that the merger could impair US national security. Since then reports have surfaced that its former chairman and CEO is seeking funding to take QUALCOMM private.

• Sentiment surrounding QUALCOMM has turned following Apple's agreement to drop all pending litigation and the formation of a multiyear licensing and chipset supply agreement. The company's strength in 5G has it well-positioned for growth moving forward and likely played a role in the settlement, which management expects to add $2 per share to earnings as shipments ramp.

• You know a firm's IP is one-of-a-kind when it continues to face antitrust lawsuits. However, serious concerns arose after the FTC filed charges against QUALCOMM for anticompetitive behavior. The FTC claims the firm disrupted the supply of baseband processors to obtain elevated royalties and other favorable terms.

• QUALCOMM recently concluded a lucrative patent dispute with Huawei. The COVID-19 pandemic has impacted handset sales, but the company's future remains bright, in our view. It is included in our Dividend Growth Newsletter portfolio.

Investment Considerations

DCF Valuation	FAIRLY VALUED
Relative Valuation	ATTRACTIVE
ValueCreation™	EXCELLENT
ValueRisk™	LOW
ValueTrend™	NEGATIVE
Cash Flow Generation	STRONG
Financial Leverage	MEDIUM
Growth	HIGH
Technical Evaluation	BULLISH
Relative Strength	STRONG
Money Flow Index (MFI)	NEUTRAL
Upside/Downside Volume (U/D)	DETERIORATING
Near-term Technical Support, 10-week MA	139.00

DCF = Discounted Cash Flow; MFI, U/D = Please see glossary. MA = Moving Average

Business Quality   ValueCreation™

ValueRisk™	Very Poor	Poor	Good	Excellent
Low				■
Medium				
High				
Very High				

Firms that generate economic profits with little operating variability score near the top right of the matrix.

Relative Valuation

	Forward P/E	PEG	Price / FV
Apple	29.8	2.4	85.0%
Alphabet	34.9	1.8	73.3%
Amazon.com	NMF	3.3	95.7%
Microsoft	31.6	2.5	91.6%
Peer Median	31.6	2.5	88.3%
QUALCOMM	**21.0**	**1.6**	**91.4%**

Price / FV = Current Stock Price divided by Estimated Fair Value

Financial Summary

	----- Actual -----		Projected
Fiscal Year End:	Sep-18	Sep-20	Sep-21
Revenue	24,273	23,531	32,708
Revenue, YoY%	6.8%	-3.1%	39.0%
Operating Income	7,667	6,255	9,393
Operating Margin %	31.6%	26.6%	28.7%
Net Income	4,386	5,198	8,041
Net Income Margin %	18.1%	22.1%	24.6%
Diluted EPS	3.60	4.52	7.14
Diluted EPS, YoY %	-208.1%	25.8%	57.8%
Free Cash Flow (CFO-capex)	6,399	4,407	8,612
Free Cash Flow Margin %	26.4%	18.7%	26.3%

In Millions of USD (except for per share items)

Structure of the Communications Equipment Industry   VERY POOR

The communications equipment industry continues to undergo rapid change, as network traffic expands, new service offerings are introduced, and end user demand shifts. Competition among communication network solution vendors remains intense, as securing new opportunities often requires agreeing to less favorable commercial terms and pricing. Rivalry among constituents will only increase in coming years, as Chinese equipment vendors gain entry into the US market and incumbent competitors strive to retain share. We don't think such conditions are favorable to generating long-term economic profit.

Roku ROKU   FAIRLY VALUED

Buying Index™   6   **Value Rating**   ◯

Economic Castle	Estimated Fair Value	Fair Value Range	Investment Style	Sector	Industry
Very Attractive	$274.00	$206.00 - $343.00	LARGE-CAP BLEND	Next Generation	Disruptive Innovation

Roku is disrupting linear television, and its users stream tens of billions of hours of content each year. Profits have been elusive, however.

Stock Chart (weekly)

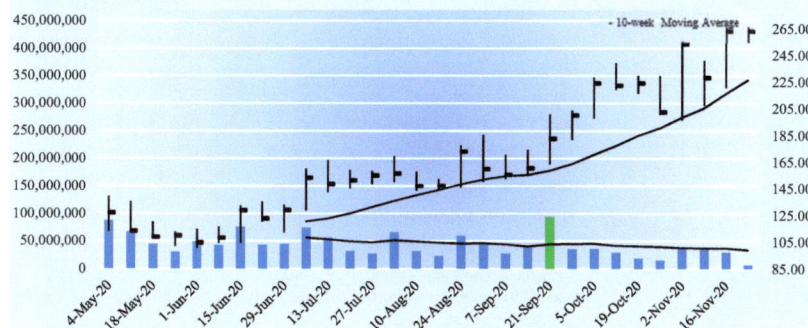

The week with the highest trading volume out of the last 30 weeks was a week of heavy selling, or distribution (red bar).

Company Vitals

Market Cap (USD)	$30,318
Avg Weekly Vol (30 wks)	43,437
30-week Range (USD)	100.19 - 265.97
Valuentum Sector	Next Generation
5-week Return	17.7%
13-week Return	52.5%
30-week Return	131.9%
Dividend Yield %	0.0%
Dividends per Share	0.00
Forward Dividend Payout Ratio	0.0%
Est. Normal Diluted EPS	1.39
P/E on Est. Normal Diluted EPS	189.7
Est. Normal EBITDA	320
Forward EV/EBITDA	-363.0
EV/Est. Normal EBITDA	93.4
Forward Revenue Growth (5-yr)	35.8%
Forward EPS Growth (5-yr)	-247.7%

NMF = Not Meaningful; Est. = Estimated; FY = Fiscal Year

Returns Summary

3-year Historical Average

Return on Equity	-19.6%
Return on Assets	-10.5%
ROIC, with goodwill	-207.3%
ROIC, without goodwill	-236.2%

ROIC = Return on Invested Capital; NMF = Not Meaningful

Leverage, Coverage, and Liquidity

In Millions of USD

Total Debt	100
Net Debt	-418
Total Debt/EBITDA	NMF
Net Debt/EBITDA	NMF
EBITDA/Interest	-21.0
Current Ratio	2.6
Quick Ratio	NA

NMF = Not Meaningful

Investment Highlights

• Roku traces its roots back to 2002, and its mission is 'to be the TV streaming platform that connects the entire TV ecosystem around the world.' The company sells streaming players through retailers and works with brand partners that license its operating system. Roughly one third of smart TVs that were sold in the US during 2019 was a Roku TV.

• Roku puts up impressive stats. Its users stream over 40 billion hours of content every year, and its active accounts keep growing rapidly. Roku added 2.6 million accounts in the third quarter of 2020 alone; it has ~50 million accounts in all.

• Roku gets paid through video advertising, sales through subscription services, via brand sponsorships, and from other billing services. Average revenue per user (ARPU) continues to increase. On a trailing 12-month basis through the third quarter of 2020, it totaled ~$27; this is up from $23.14 during the same period in 2019.

• Our fair value estimate is based on very optimistic assumptions, and most of the value we ascribe to the stock comes from long-run expectations. The current reality for Roku, however, is that it has lost money every year since its founding. Roku is an incredibly risky investment idea.

• Technology changes fast. Amazon, Apple and Google have TV streaming devices that compete with Roku TV. Roku is as much an acquisition candidate for these companies as it is at risk of the perils of intense competition from these tech giants.

Investment Considerations

DCF Valuation	FAIRLY VALUED
Relative Valuation	NEUTRAL
ValueCreation™	VERY POOR
ValueRisk™	MEDIUM
ValueTrend™	POSITIVE
Cash Flow Generation	WEAK
Financial Leverage	LOW
Growth	AGGRESSIVE
Technical Evaluation	BULLISH
Relative Strength	STRONG
Money Flow Index (MFI)	NEUTRAL
Upside/Downside Volume (U/D)	BULLISH
Near-term Technical Support, 10-week MA	226.00

DCF = Discounted Cash Flow; MFI, U/D = Please see glossary. MA = Moving Average

Business Quality

ValueCreation™

ValueRisk™	Very Poor	Poor	Good	Excellent
Low				
Medium	▓			
High				
Very High				

Firms that generate economic profits with little operating variability score near the top right of the matrix.

Relative Valuation

	Forward P/E	PEG	Price / FV
Wayfair	56.3	NMF	84.2%
Zoom Video	170.7	28.8	120.8%
Monster Beverage	36.0	2.9	104.4%
Lululemon	81.5	1.9	99.9%
Peer Median	68.9	2.9	102.2%
Roku	**-338.4**	**NMF**	**96.0%**

Price / FV = Current Stock Price divided by Estimated Fair Value

Financial Summary

	----- Actual -----		Projected
Fiscal Year End:	Dec-18	Dec-19	Dec-20
Revenue	743	1,129	1,731
Revenue, YoY%	44.8%	52.0%	53.3%
Operating Income	-13	-65	-106
Operating Margin %	-1.8%	-5.8%	-6.1%
Net Income	-9	-60	-103
Net Income Margin %	-1.2%	-5.3%	-6.0%
Diluted EPS	-0.08	-0.52	-0.78
Diluted EPS, YoY %	-96.2%	514.5%	49.5%
Free Cash Flow (CFO-capex)	-4	-63	55
Free Cash Flow Margin %	-0.6%	-5.6%	3.2%

In Millions of USD (except for per share items)

Structure of the Internet Software & Services Industry   NEUTRAL

The Internet software/services industry is composed of a variety of companies with rapidly-changing business models. Most focus on improving the ways people connect with information, either via Internet search or by social media platforms, and generate revenue primarily by delivering cost-effective online advertising. Constituents earn significant returns on invested capital due to their capital-light operations, though competition remains fierce. We expect most companies in this group to look substantially different 10 years from now than they do today. Overall, we're neutral on the structure.

Boston Beer SAM   FAIRLY VALUED

Buying Index™ 6 Value Rating ⦿

Economic Castle	Estimated Fair Value	Fair Value Range	Investment Style	Sector	Industry
Attractive	$949.00	$688.00 - $1210.00	LARGE-CAP BLEND	Next Generation	Disruptive Innovation

Boston Beer is experiencing unprecedented levels of demand as consumers stay at home during the COVID-19 pandemic. We've raised our fair value estimate materially.

Stock Chart (weekly)

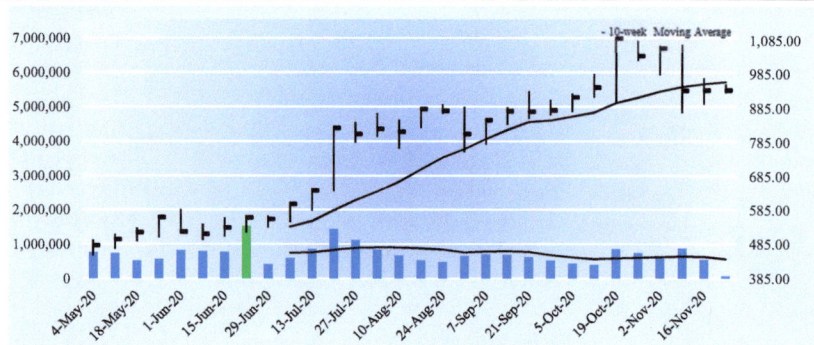

The week with the highest trading volume out of the last 30 weeks was a week of heavy selling, or distribution (red bar).

Investment Considerations

DCF Valuation	**FAIRLY VALUED**
Relative Valuation	**NEUTRAL**
ValueCreation™	**EXCELLENT**
ValueRisk™	**MEDIUM**
ValueTrend™	**NEGATIVE**
Cash Flow Generation	**STRONG**
Financial Leverage	**LOW**
Growth	**AGGRESSIVE**
Technical Evaluation	**BULLISH**
Relative Strength	**NEUTRAL**
Money Flow Index (MFI)	**NEUTRAL**
Upside/Downside Volume (U/D)	**DETERIORATING**
Near-term Technical Resistance, 10-wk MA	**963.00**

DCF = Discounted Cash Flow; MFI, U/D = Please see glossary. MA = Moving Average

Company Vitals

Market Cap (USD)	$11,173
Avg Weekly Vol (30 wks)	701
30-week Range (USD)	452.45 - 1,092.80
Valuentum Sector	Next Generation
5-week Return	-13.2%
13-week Return	6.5%
30-week Return	106.4%
Dividend Yield %	0.0%
Dividends per Share	0.00
Forward Dividend Payout Ratio	0.0%
Est. Normal Diluted EPS	33.68
P/E on Est. Normal Diluted EPS	27.9
Est. Normal EBITDA	614
Forward EV/EBITDA	36.2
EV/Est. Normal EBITDA	18.1
Forward Revenue Growth (5-yr)	25.8%
Forward EPS Growth (5-yr)	42.2%

NMF = Not Meaningful; Est. = Estimated; FY = Fiscal Year

Returns Summary

3-year Historical Average

Return on Equity	20.7%
Return on Assets	15.0%
ROIC, with goodwill	24.3%
ROIC, without goodwill	25.3%

ROIC = Return on Invested Capital; NMF = Not Meaningful

Leverage, Coverage, and Liquidity

In Millions of USD

Total Debt	0
Net Debt	-37
Total Debt/EBITDA	0.0
Net Debt/EBITDA	NMF
EBITDA/Interest	-310.9
Current Ratio	1.2
Quick Ratio	0.5

NMF = Not Meaningful

Investment Highlights

• Boston Beer brews handcrafted, full-flavored beers. Its Samuel Adams brand is among the US' largest brands in the Better Beer category, which accounts for 20%+ of US beer consumption by volume. The firm brews over 60 different styles of beer and sells million of barrels of its products each year. It was founded in 1984 and is headquartered in Boston.

• Concerns had been cropping up that the 'Better Beer' market may be reaching a saturation point. Smaller breweries had been gaining share, but the COVID-19 pandemic served as a catalyst for volumes to surge. Boston Beer has benefited greatly.

• Boston Beer is focused on innovating within the Samuel Adams family, integrating persuasive drinker programming across point of sale, promotions, and media for all brands while prioritizing the core styles of its new Truly brand, Angry Orchard, Twisted Tea, Traveler, and Coney Island Hard Root Beer. The performance of these styles will be key.

• For 2020, Boston Beer is expecting depletions and shipments growth rate to be 27%-35%. Gross margin guidance is targeted at 46%-48% for the year with growth driven in part by its new Truly brand. Higher supply and transportation costs have impacted margins of late.

• Due to its lower market share and the high amount of taxes it pays, Boston Beer may be a takeout candidate for a large foreign brewer. Founder Jim Koch said that he is likely the last American owner of Boston Beer.

Business Quality

ValueCreation™

ValueRisk™	Very Poor	Poor	Good	Excellent
Low				
Medium				▓
High				
Very High				

Firms that generate economic profits with little operating variability score near the top right of the matrix.

Relative Valuation

	Forward P/E	PEG	Price / FV
Wayfair	56.3	NMF	84.2%
Zoom Video	170.7	28.8	120.8%
Roku	-338.4	NMF	96.0%
Monster Beverage	36.0	2.9	104.4%
Peer Median	46.1	15.9	100.2%
Boston Beer	**60.1**	**2.4**	**98.9%**

Price / FV = Current Stock Price divided by Estimated Fair Value

Financial Summary

	----- Actual -----		Projected
Fiscal Year End:	Dec-18	Dec-19	Dec-20
Revenue	996	1,250	1,735
Revenue, YoY%	15.4%	25.5%	38.8%
Operating Income	117	145	229
Operating Margin %	11.7%	11.6%	13.2%
Net Income	93	110	184
Net Income Margin %	9.3%	8.8%	10.6%
Diluted EPS	7.64	9.24	15.61
Diluted EPS, YoY %	-6.1%	21.0%	69.0%
Free Cash Flow (CFO-capex)	108	85	153
Free Cash Flow Margin %	10.8%	6.8%	8.8%

In Millions of USD (except for per share items)

Structure of the Beverages (alcoholic) Industry

GOOD

The beer industry is structured as an oligopoly, with three players generating over half of industry profits. Though smaller industry constituents may price competitively at times, we view the overall industry structure as a rational oligopoly. Further consolidation in the space cannot be ruled out, and we would not be surprised to see larger players continuing to participate. Global operators will benefit from exposure to Asia, Africa, and Latin America, where beer consumption is growing at a pace several times that of mature markets such as North America and Western Europe. We like the structure of the group.

SBA Comm SBAC   FAIRLY VALUED

Buying Index™ 3   **Value Rating** ⬤

Economic Castle	Estimated Fair Value	Fair Value Range	Investment Style	Sector	Industry
Attractive	$229.00	$172.00 - $286.00	LARGE-CAP CORE	Telecom Services	elecom Services - diversific

We significantly increased our fair value estimate for SBA Communications as its global growth runway continues to impress.

Stock Chart (weekly)

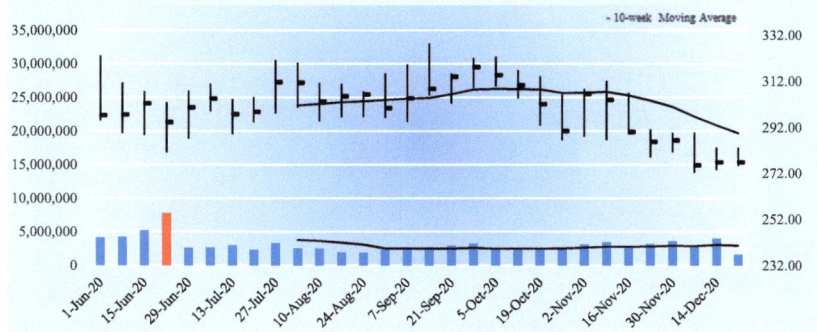

The week with the highest trading volume out of the last 30 weeks was a week of heavy selling, or distribution (red bar).

Company Vitals

Market Cap (USD)	$31,444
Avg Weekly Vol (30 wks)	3,084
30-week Range (USD)	272.36 - 328.37
Valuentum Sector	Telecom Services
5-week Return	-4.6%
13-week Return	-12.6%
30-week Return	-12.0%
Dividend Yield %	0.7%
Dividends per Share	1.86
Forward Dividend Payout Ratio	19.8%
Est. Normal Diluted EPS	4.70
P/E on Est. Normal Diluted EPS	58.9
Est. Normal EBITDA	1,936
Forward EV/EBITDA	26.7
EV/Est. Normal EBITDA	21.5
Forward Revenue Growth (5-yr)	8.6%
Forward EPS Growth (5-yr)	40.4%

NMF = Not Meaningful; Est. = Estimated; FY = Fiscal Year

Returns Summary   3-year Historical Average

Return on Equity	-3.4%
Return on Assets	1.3%
ROIC, with goodwill	12.1%
ROIC, without goodwill	12.1%

ROIC = Return on Invested Capital; NMF = Not Meaningful

Leverage, Coverage, and Liquidity
In Millions of USD

Total Debt	10,334
Net Debt	10,196
Total Debt/EBITDA	7.7
Net Debt/EBITDA	7.6
EBITDA/Interest	3.5
Current Ratio	0.3
Quick Ratio	0.3

NMF = Not Meaningful

Investment Highlights

• SBA Communications is a REIT that owns and operates wireless communications infrastructure across North, Central and South America. It generates revenue from site leasing and site development services. SBA Communications owns and operates over 32,000 towers. The company was founded in 1989 and is headquartered in Boca Raton, Florida.

• Though accounting earnings are negligible, SBA Communications generates a significant amount of free cash flow, the foundation of our estimate of its intrinsic value. SBA Communications converted its business to a REIT in January 2017.

• The attractive characteristics of scalable tower operations (operating leverage), long-term contracts, built-in escalators, high operating margins, and low customer churn make for a nice business model. SBA Communications' global growth runway is impressive, which supports our forecasts that the REIT will generate meaningful revenue growth going forward.

• SBA Communications initiated a quarterly common dividend program in 2019. Since then, the REIT's dividend has grown substantially, though these are still early days. We caution that its total debt load is quite large, and the REIT must retain constant access to capital markets to refinance its maturing debt.

• Readers should be cognizant that we are building significant operating leverage into the model with respect to profitability improvements. Should SBA Communications stumble for any reason, its intrinsic value would face significant pressures.

Investment Considerations

DCF Valuation	FAIRLY VALUED
Relative Valuation	NEUTRAL
ValueCreation™	GOOD
ValueRisk™	MEDIUM
ValueTrend™	NEGATIVE
Cash Flow Generation	STRONG
Financial Leverage	HIGH
Growth	MODEST
Technical Evaluation	BEARISH
Relative Strength	WEAK
Money Flow Index (MFI)	NEUTRAL
Upside/Downside Volume (U/D)	BEARISH
Near-term Technical Resistance, 10-wk MA	289.00

DCF = Discounted Cash Flow; MFI, U/D = Please see glossary. MA = Moving Average

Business Quality   ValueCreation™

ValueRisk™	Very Poor	Poor	Good	Excellent
Low				
Medium			▓	
High				
Very High				

Firms that generate economic profits with little operating variability score near the top right of the matrix.

Relative Valuation

	Forward P/E	PEG	Price / FV
AT&T	12.1	4.3	89.1%
Comcast	20.0	1.2	110.7%
Verizon	12.3	3.1	100.8%
American Tower	26.9	1.8	95.1%
Peer Median	16.2	2.5	97.9%
SBA Comm	**29.5**	**0.8**	**120.9%**

Price / FV = Current Stock Price divided by Estimated Fair Value

Financial Summary

	----- Actual -----		Projected
Fiscal Year End:	Dec-18	Dec-19	Dec-20
Revenue	1,866	2,015	2,096
Revenue, YoY%	7.9%	8.0%	4.0%
Adjusted Operating Income	582	632	817
Adj. Operating Margin %	31.2%	31.4%	39.0%
Funds from Operations	885	972	1,066
FFO Margin %	47.4%	48.2%	50.9%
Diluted FFO per share	7.60	8.47	9.39
Diluted FFO, YoY %	9.3%	11.6%	10.8%
Free Cash Flow (CFO-capex)	701	816	1,027
Free Cash Flow Margin %	37.6%	40.5%	49.0%

In Millions of USD (except for per share items)

Structure of the Wireless Telecom Services Industry   GOOD

Most firms in the wireless telecom services industry lease antenna space on communication sites/towers to wireless service providers, radio and television broadcast companies, and tenants in other industries. Tenant leases are typically long-term, non-cancellable, have high renewal rates (98%+) and include attractive built-in annual rent escalations. Tower operators enjoy consistent demand for their sites, have high operating leverage (incremental costs to add new tenants are minimal), and require little capital expenditures to maintain their communication sites. We like the structure of the group.

Starbucks SBUX FAIRLY VALUED

Buying Index™   **6**   **Value Rating** ⬤

Economic Castle	Estimated Fair Value	Fair Value Range	Investment Style	Sector	Industry
Very Attractive	$80.00	$60.00 - $100.00	LARGE-CAP GROWTH	Consumer Discretionary	Discretionary Spending

Starbucks' outlook is improving, and the firm is investing heavily in its digital operations, though significant headwinds remain.

Stock Chart (weekly)

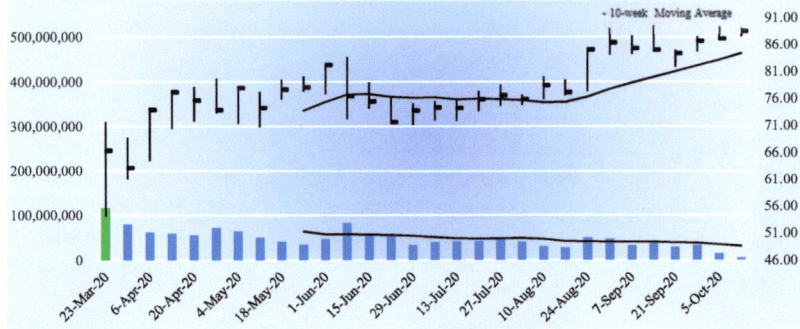

The week with the highest trading volume out of the last 30 weeks was a week of heavy selling, or distribution (red bar).

Company Vitals

Market Cap (USD)	$109,077
Avg Weekly Vol (30 wks)	47,632
30-week Range (USD)	54.00 - 89.43
Valuentum Sector	Consumer Discretionary
5-week Return	3.1%
13-week Return	19.3%
30-week Return	54.6%
Dividend Yield %	1.9%
Dividends per Share	1.64
Forward Dividend Payout Ratio	170.9%
Est. Normal Diluted EPS	3.30
P/E on Est. Normal Diluted EPS	26.8
Est. Normal EBITDA	6,987
Forward EV/EBITDA	38.9
EV/Est. Normal EBITDA	16.8
Forward Revenue Growth (5-yr)	9.1%
Forward EPS Growth (5-yr)	11.5%

NMF = Not Meaningful; Est. = Estimated; FY = Fiscal Year

Returns Summary   3-year Historical Average

Return on Equity	15.1%
Return on Assets	20.0%
ROIC, with goodwill	41.9%
ROIC, without goodwill	62.4%

ROIC = Return on Invested Capital; NMF = Not Meaningful

Leverage, Coverage, and Liquidity

In Millions of USD

Total Debt	11,167
Net Debt	8,409
Total Debt/EBITDA	2.1
Net Debt/EBITDA	1.6
EBITDA/Interest	15.9
Current Ratio	0.9
Quick Ratio	0.6

NMF = Not Meaningful

Investment Highlights

• Starbucks purchases and roasts high-quality coffees that it sells, along with handcrafted coffee, tea and other beverages and a variety of fresh food items, through its company-operated stores. Global comparable sales growth has averaged in the mid-to-high single digits per annum during the past few years. The company continues to innovate with ordering and other forms of customer-centric technology.

• Starbucks' China division is growing at a tremendous overall pace, as the firm is opening a store in China almost every day. Management expects its China business will eventually be larger than its US business. Performance in the region has been solid.

• Starbucks is investing in its digital capabilities, which we think may provide it with a unique advantage with younger consumers when coupled with its brand strength. The working-from-home trend during the COVID-19 pandemic has weighed negatively on Starbucks' financial performance, though its outlook is starting to improve.

• Starbucks has one of the strongest and most-recognized brands in the world, which we think is largely responsible for it being able to charge lofty prices, despite significant competition in its markets. Annual price increases across the menu appear to have become commonplace. We also like ongoing beverage innovation and recent step-change in food quality.

• Investors should be cognizant that input (coffee) costs can be volatile. A variety of factors can influence the price of coffee, such as the strength of South American currencies relative to the dollar and weather patterns. Wage/labor cost pressures should be monitored as well.

Investment Considerations

DCF Valuation	FAIRLY VALUED
Relative Valuation	NEUTRAL
ValueCreation™	EXCELLENT
ValueRisk™	MEDIUM
ValueTrend™	NEGATIVE
Cash Flow Generation	STRONG
Financial Leverage	MEDIUM
Growth	HIGH
Technical Evaluation	BULLISH
Relative Strength	STRONG
Money Flow Index (MFI)	NEUTRAL
Upside/Downside Volume (U/D)	BULLISH
Near-term Technical Support, 10-week MA	84.00

DCF = Discounted Cash Flow; MFI, U/D = Please see glossary. MA = Moving Average

Business Quality   ValueCreation™

ValueRisk™	Very Poor	Poor	Good	Excellent
Low				
Medium				▉
High				
Very High				

Firms that generate economic profits with little operating variability score near the top right of the matrix.

Relative Valuation

	Forward P/E	PEG	Price / FV
Disney	75.6	0.3	98.3%
Home Depot	22.9	1.9	106.7%
McDonald's	38.5	1.1	111.0%
Nike	52.8	2.5	104.9%
Peer Median	45.6	1.5	105.8%
Starbucks	**92.2**	**0.6**	**110.6%**

Price / FV = Current Stock Price divided by Estimated Fair Value

Financial Summary

	----- Actual -----		Projected
Fiscal Year End:	Sep-18	Sep-19	Sep-20
Revenue	24,720	26,509	23,328
Revenue, YoY%	10.4%	7.2%	-12.0%
Operating Income	3,807	3,886	1,808
Operating Margin %	15.4%	14.7%	7.8%
Net Income	4,518	3,599	1,171
Net Income Margin %	18.3%	13.6%	5.0%
Diluted EPS	3.24	2.92	0.96
Diluted EPS, YoY %	64.1%	-9.9%	-67.1%
Free Cash Flow (CFO-capex)	9,962	3,240	550
Free Cash Flow Margin %	40.3%	12.2%	2.4%

In Millions of USD (except for per share items)

Structure of the Restaurants Industry - Fast Food & Coffee   NEUTRAL

The restaurant industry has benefited from a long-term trend toward eating out, but the space has become increasingly more competitive as new concepts are introduced and successful chains expand. Not only are there pricing pressures and trade-down threats, but rising costs for commodities and labor have pressured profits. Barriers to entry are low, and many constituents have a difficult time differentiating themselves. We tend to like larger chains that benefit from scale advantages and international expansion opportunities, though niche franchises can be appealing. We're neutral on the structure of the group.

Stitch Fix SFIX FAIRLY VALUED

Valuentum **Buying Index™** 6 | Valuentum **Value Rating**

Economic Castle	Estimated Fair Value	Fair Value Range	Investment Style	Sector	Industry
Very Attractive	$52.00	$39.00 - $65.00	MID-CAP BLEND	Next Generation	Disruptive Innovation

Stitch Fix is reinventing the shopping experience through one-to-one personalization with its customers. The company's business is gaining momentum, and its asset-light model is attractive.

Stock Chart (weekly)

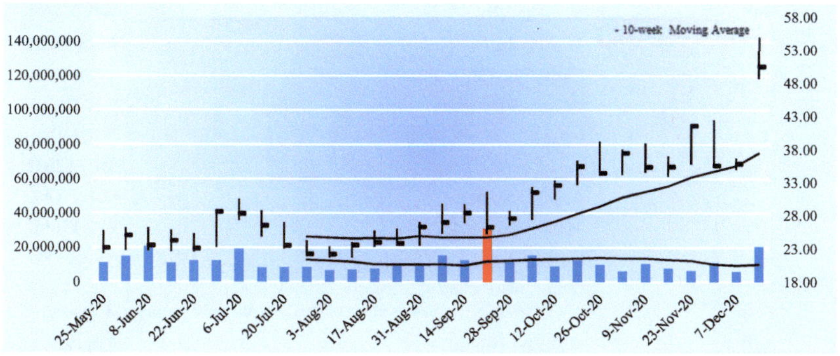

The week with the highest trading volume out of the last 30 weeks was a week of heavy selling, or distribution (red bar).

Investment Considerations

DCF Valuation	FAIRLY VALUED
Relative Valuation	UNATTRACTIVE
ValueCreation™	EXCELLENT
ValueRisk™	MEDIUM
ValueTrend™	POSITIVE
Cash Flow Generation	MEDIUM
Financial Leverage	LOW
Growth	AGGRESSIVE
Technical Evaluation	BULLISH
Relative Strength	STRONG
Money Flow Index (MFI)	NEUTRAL
Upside/Downside Volume (U/D)	BULLISH
Near-term Technical Support, 10-week MA	37.00

DCF = Discounted Cash Flow; MFI, U/D = Please see glossary. MA = Moving Average

Business Quality

ValueRisk™ \ ValueCreation™	Very Poor	Poor	Good	Excellent
Low				
Medium				■
High				
Very High				

Firms that generate economic profits with little operating variability score near the top right of the matrix.

Company Vitals

Market Cap (USD)	$5,168
Avg Weekly Vol (30 wks)	11,843
30-week Range (USD)	21.60 - 54.94
Valuentum Sector	Next Generation
5-week Return	44.0%
13-week Return	82.8%
30-week Return	107.2%
Dividend Yield %	0.0%
Dividends per Share	0.00
Forward Dividend Payout Ratio	0.0%
Est. Normal Diluted EPS	0.86
P/E on Est. Normal Diluted EPS	58.9
Est. Normal EBITDA	138
Forward EV/EBITDA	169.4
EV/Est. Normal EBITDA	35.5
Forward Revenue Growth (5-yr)	17.8%
Forward EPS Growth (5-yr)	-224.8%

NMF = Not Meaningful; Est. = Estimated; FY = Fiscal Year

Returns Summary

3-year Historical Average	
Return on Equity	1.3%
Return on Assets	1.2%
ROIC, with goodwill	42.8%
ROIC, without goodwill	42.8%

ROIC = Return on Invested Capital; NMF = Not Meaningful

Leverage, Coverage, and Liquidity

In Millions of USD

Total Debt	0
Net Debt	-286
Total Debt/EBITDA	0.0
Net Debt/EBITDA	NMF
EBITDA/Interest	NMF
Current Ratio	2.2
Quick Ratio	NA

NMF = Not Meaningful

Investment Highlights

• Stitch Fix was founded in 2011 and provides customers with personalized shipments ('Fixes') of apparel, shoes and other items that are hand-picked by the company's stylists. It doesn't have physical store locations and makes money by charging styling fees on purchased items and from selling annual Style Passes online. Stitch Fix operates in the US and UK and has roughly 3.8 million active clients.

• Though Stitch Fix has encountered GAAP losses more recently, it has been free-cash-flow positive, averaging $40 million during the past three fiscal years (2018-2020). Cash flow trends look encouraging in fiscal 2021, with the company off to a strong start.

• Stitch Fix's business is gaining momentum. During the first quarter of its fiscal 2021, for example, the company set a number of new records, including one for sequential-quarter client additions. Management believes its outlook is bright and is guiding fiscal 2021 revenue expansion to the range of 20%-25%. We think the company will hit the high end of its target.

• Initially, Stitch Fix focused on women's apparel, but it has since expanded into other segments, including men's and kid's apparel, shoes and accessories. These markets are absolutely huge, and Stitch Fix is tapping into connecting with customers on a personal level to drive demand. Data science remains integral to its business model.

• Providing people with apparel, shoes, and accessories they love in a personalized way is a great way to do business, but competition is fierce across both brick-and-mortar and e-commerce. Nevertheless, we think Stitch Fix has found a growing niche in a massive industry.

Relative Valuation

	Forward P/E	PEG	Price / FV
Wayfair	56.3	NMF	84.2%
Zoom Video	170.7	28.8	120.8%
Roku	-338.4	NMF	96.0%
Monster Beverage	36.0	2.9	104.4%
Peer Median	46.1	15.9	100.2%
Stitch Fix	**NMF**	**NMF**	**97.1%**

Price / FV = Current Stock Price divided by Estimated Fair Value

Financial Summary

Fiscal Year End:	Aug-19 (Actual)	Aug-20 (Actual)	Aug-21 (Projected)
Revenue	1,578	1,712	2,140
Revenue, YoY%	28.6%	8.5%	25.0%
Operating Income	23	-52	1
Operating Margin %	1.5%	-3.0%	0.0%
Net Income	37	-67	5
Net Income Margin %	2.3%	-3.9%	0.2%
Diluted EPS	0.36	-0.66	0.05
Diluted EPS, YoY %	-35.6%	-284.2%	-107.7%
Free Cash Flow (CFO-capex)	48	13	96
Free Cash Flow Margin %	3.0%	0.7%	4.5%

In Millions of USD (except for per share items)

Structure of the Internet & Catalog Retail Industry — GOOD

The Internet and catalog retail industry benefits as a whole from the secular trend toward consumer digital (online) consumption. The industry consists of a number of exclusive online retailers led by Amazon, which continues to disrupt the broader retail space, and businesses that offer Internet travel services such as Booking Holdings, while online auctions are dominated by eBay. The industry generates high returns on investment due to minimal capital costs, but the landscape will be vastly different in the decades ahead. Still, we like the group.

Sherwin-Williams SHW   OVERVALUED 4.8%

Buying Index™ 4   **Value Rating** ✕

Economic Castle	Estimated Fair Value	Fair Value Range	Investment Style	Sector	Industry
Attractive	$552.00	$414.00 - $690.00	LARGE-CAP CORE	Materials	Mining & Chemicals

The acquisition of Valspar has given Sherwin-Williams additional growth opportunities including in the areas of coil and packaging. The company's free cash flow generation is robust, and its dividend growth remains solid.

Stock Chart (weekly)

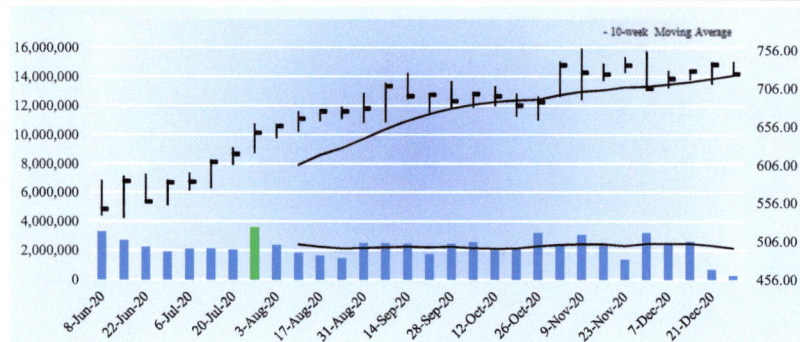

The week with the highest trading volume out of the last 30 weeks was a week of heavy selling, or distribution (red bar).

Company Vitals

Market Cap (USD)	$68,814
Avg Weekly Vol (30 wks)	2,233
30-week Range (USD)	535.97 - 758.00
Valuentum Sector	Materials
5-week Return	-1.3%
13-week Return	4.5%
30-week Return	24.2%
Dividend Yield %	0.7%
Dividends per Share	5.36
Forward Dividend Payout Ratio	32.5%
Est. Normal Diluted EPS	27.68
P/E on Est. Normal Diluted EPS	26.2
Est. Normal EBITDA	4,071
Forward EV/EBITDA	28.4
EV/Est. Normal EBITDA	19.2
Forward Revenue Growth (5-yr)	3.7%
Forward EPS Growth (5-yr)	25.7%

NMF = Not Meaningful; Est. = Estimated; FY = Fiscal Year

Returns Summary
3-year Historical Average

Return on Equity	59.2%
Return on Assets	12.4%
ROIC, with goodwill	30.4%
ROIC, without goodwill	51.2%

ROIC = Return on Invested Capital; NMF = Not Meaningful

Leverage, Coverage, and Liquidity
In Millions of USD

Total Debt	9,344
Net Debt	9,188
Total Debt/EBITDA	3.5
Net Debt/EBITDA	3.5
EBITDA/Interest	7.3
Current Ratio	1.0
Quick Ratio	0.5

NMF = Not Meaningful

Investment Highlights

• Sherwin-Williams makes and sells paint, coatings and related products to professional, industrial, commercial and retail customers primarily in North and South America with additional operations in the Caribbean region, Europe and Asia. It has over 4,750 stores in 120+ countries. The company was founded in 1866 and is headquartered in Cleveland, Ohio.

• Sherwin-Williams bought Valspar for ~$11.3 billion in an all-cash transaction in 2017. It has achieved hundreds of millions in annual run-rate cost synergies. Meaningful cash flow improvements have been evident, too. Free cash flow advanced to ~$1.57 billion in 2019 from ~$1.37 billion in 2018.

• Valspar's business brings with it new growth opportunities including in the areas of coil and packaging, as well as an enhanced geographic footprint in growth markets such as Asia-Pacific. Management has its work cut out for it in deleveraging the balance sheet, however. Net debt remains elevated and stood at $8.5+ billion at the end of 2019.

• Sherwin-Williams has brand power. It has the #1 architectural paint brand (SWP), the #1 stain (Minwax), the #1 aerosol paint (Krylon), the #1 auto specialty paint (Dupli-Color), the #1 painting tool brand (Purdy), and the #1 wood sealer (Thompson's). It's hard to find a better line-up of paint, coating and sealer brands than those of Sherwin-Williams.

• Sherwin-Williams' has raised its dividend in each of the past 40+ years. Management doesn't like to hold cash and has completed over a dozen acquisitions in the last decade. Capex requirements are modest, however, and buybacks are also common.

Investment Considerations

DCF Valuation	OVERVALUED
Relative Valuation	UNATTRACTIVE
ValueCreation™	EXCELLENT
ValueRisk™	MEDIUM
ValueTrend™	NEGATIVE
Cash Flow Generation	STRONG
Financial Leverage	HIGH
Growth	MODEST
Technical Evaluation	BULLISH
Relative Strength	NEUTRAL
Money Flow Index (MFI)	NEUTRAL
Upside/Downside Volume (U/D)	DETERIORATING
Near-term Technical Support, 10-week MA	722.00

DCF = Discounted Cash Flow; MFI, U/D = Please see glossary. MA = Moving Average

Business Quality
ValueCreation™

ValueRisk™	Very Poor	Poor	Good	Excellent
Low				
Medium				▉
High				
Very High				

Firms that generate economic profits with little operating variability score near the top right of the matrix.

Relative Valuation

	Forward P/E	PEG	Price / FV
Air Products & Chemicals	27.5	2.3	130.9%
DuPont	29.2	3.7	108.9%
BHP Billiton	20.3	1.9	107.6%
Compass Minerals	23.5	1.7	125.8%
Peer Median	25.5	2.1	117.3%
Sherwin-Williams	**43.9**	**2.4**	**131.2%**

Price / FV = Current Stock Price divided by Estimated Fair Value

Financial Summary

	----- Actual -----		Projected
Fiscal Year End:	Dec-17	Dec-18	Dec-19
Revenue	14,984	17,534	17,901
Revenue, YoY%	26.4%	17.0%	2.1%
Operating Income	1,768	2,067	2,283
Operating Margin %	11.8%	11.8%	12.8%
Net Income	1,814	1,109	1,567
Net Income Margin %	12.1%	6.3%	8.8%
Diluted EPS	19.11	11.67	16.49
Diluted EPS, YoY %	59.4%	-38.9%	41.3%
Free Cash Flow (CFO-capex)	1,662	1,693	1,994
Free Cash Flow Margin %	11.1%	9.7%	11.1%

In Millions of USD (except for per share items)

Structure of the Specialty Retailers Industry   NEUTRAL

The specialty retail segment is fragmented, highly competitive, and economically-sensitive. The group covers a broad array of businesses and is dominated by retailers with large brick-and-mortar store footprints. Though some constituents may be insulated from e-commerce competition, others risk obsolescence as product distribution moves to digital means, and online retailers offer lower prices for identical goods and services. We're fairly neutral on the structure of the industry, though some constituents will inevitably face secular and permanent declines.

Smucker SJM FAIRLY VALUED

Buying Index™ 6 **Value Rating** ○

Economic Castle	Estimated Fair Value	Fair Value Range	Investment Style	Sector	Industry
Attractive	$105.00	$84.00 - $126.00	LARGE-CAP CORE	Consumer Staples	Recession Resistant

J.M. Smucker's long-term strategy is built around growing its coffee and pet food businesses.

Stock Chart (weekly)

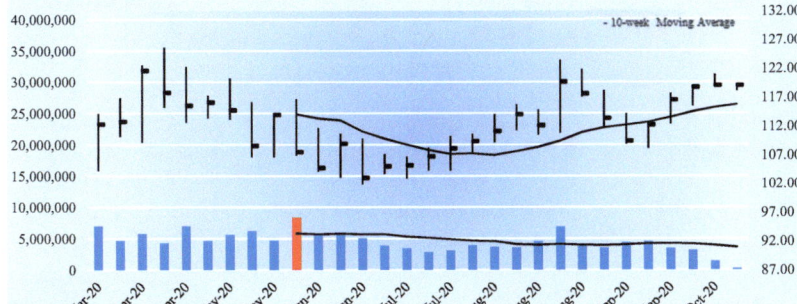

The week with the highest trading volume out of the last 30 weeks was a week of heavy selling, or distribution (red bar).

Investment Considerations

DCF Valuation	FAIRLY VALUED
Relative Valuation	NEUTRAL
ValueCreation™	GOOD
ValueRisk™	LOW
ValueTrend™	NEGATIVE
Cash Flow Generation	STRONG
Financial Leverage	HIGH
Growth	MODEST
Technical Evaluation	BULLISH
Relative Strength	NEUTRAL
Money Flow Index (MFI)	NEUTRAL
Upside/Downside Volume (U/D)	BULLISH
Near-term Technical Support, 10-week MA	116.00

DCF = Discounted Cash Flow; MFI, U/D = Please see glossary. MA = Moving Average

Company Vitals

Market Cap (USD)	$13,570
Avg Weekly Vol (30 wks)	4,482
30-week Range (USD	101.88 - 125.62
Valuentum Sector	Consumer Staples
5-week Return	9.3%
13-week Return	10.2%
30-week Return	14.1%
Dividend Yield %	3.0%
Dividends per Share	3.60
Forward Dividend Payout Ratio	40.0%
Est. Normal Diluted EPS	9.00
P/E on Est. Normal Diluted EPS	13.2
Est. Normal EBITDA	2,010
Forward EV/EBITDA	9.4
EV/Est. Normal EBITDA	9.4
Forward Revenue Growth (5-yr)	0.9%
Forward EPS Growth (5-yr)	6.8%

NMF = Not Meaningful; Est. = Estimated; FY = Fiscal Year

Returns Summary

	3-year Historical Average
Return on Equity	11.4%
Return on Assets	5.5%
ROIC, with goodwill	8.2%
ROIC, without goodwill	14.0%

ROIC = Return on Invested Capital; NMF = Not Meaningful

Leverage, Coverage, and Liquidity
In Millions of USD

Total Debt	5,621
Net Debt	5,230
Total Debt/EBITDA	3.2
Net Debt/EBITDA	3.0
EBITDA/Interest	9.2
Current Ratio	1.2
Quick Ratio	0.6

NMF = Not Meaningful

Investment Highlights

- J.M. Smucker manufactures and markets branded food products on a worldwide basis. Its key products include coffee, peanut butter, snacks, and pet food products. Smucker's 40+ brands are present in over 90% of US homes. It completed its merger with Folgers in 2008. The J.M. Smucker Company was founded in 1897 and is headquartered in Ohio.

- Smucker is looking to capitalize on the trend of the humanization of pets. The US pet population continues to expand, and e-commerce opportunities enhance the potential of the space. Its pet product brands include Meow Mix, Pup-Peroni, and Nature's Recipe.

- Smucker owns a large chunk of the US at-home retail coffee market via its Folgers, Cafe Bustelo, and Dunkin' Donuts brands. Coffee represents one of Smucker's major growth opportunities. Smucker has also been steadily growing its pet food and nutrition business, assisted by acquisitions. In May 2018, Smucker acquired Ainsworth Pet Nutrition.

- Smucker sold its US baking business in August 2018, including its Pillsbury and Hungry Jack brands, to focus more of its attention towards coffee and pet food products. The US retail market represents the source of over 85% of its revenues and its top ten customers account for ~60% of its net sales.

- Smucker's segment-level operating margin improved at its pet food and coffee operations (its two most promising segments) in fiscal 2020 versus fiscal 2019 levels, though net sales at both segments were broadly flat year-over-year.

Business Quality

ValueRisk™	Very Poor	Poor	Good	Excellent
Low			▓	
Medium				
High				
Very High				

ValueCreation™

Firms that generate economic profits with little operating variability score near the top right of the matrix.

Relative Valuation

	Forward P/E	PEG	Price / FV
Coca-Cola	34.3	1.5	128.0%
Procter & Gamble	26.5	3.3	144.1%
Philip Morris	15.4	2.4	104.3%
Wal-Mart	26.8	2.3	130.2%
Peer Median	26.7	2.4	129.1%
Smucker	13.2	2.5	113.3%

Price / FV = Current Stock Price divided by Estimated Fair Value

Financial Summary

	----- Actual -----		Projected
Fiscal Year End:	Apr-19	Apr-20	Apr-21
Revenue	7,838	7,801	7,863
Revenue, YoY%	6.5%	-0.5%	0.8%
Operating Income	1,167	1,291	1,557
Operating Margin %	14.9%	16.5%	19.8%
Net Income	514	780	1,026
Net Income Margin %	6.6%	10.0%	13.0%
Diluted EPS	4.55	6.84	9.00
Diluted EPS, YoY %	-61.4%	50.4%	31.5%
Free Cash Flow (CFO-capex)	781	986	973
Free Cash Flow Margin %	10.0%	12.6%	12.4%

In Millions of USD (except for per share items)

Structure of the Food Products Industry

NEUTRAL

The food products industry is composed of a number of firms with strong brand names. However, market supply/demand dynamics and intense competition still impact product prices, while fluctuations in commodity costs can make earnings quite volatile. Private-label competition, competitors' promotional spending, and changing consumer preferences often drive demand trends. The group's customers—such as supermarkets, warehouses, and food distributors—continue to consolidate, increasing buying power over constituents and hurting margins. Still, we're generally neutral on the group.

VALUENTUM

Virgin Galactic SPCE   FAIRLY VALUED

Buying Index™ 6

Value Rating ⬤

Economic Castle	Estimated Fair Value	Fair Value Range	Investment Style	Sector	Industry
Unattractive	$25.00	$13.00 - $38.00	MID-CAP BLEND	Next Generation	Disruptive Innovation

Virgin Galactic is working to capitalize on the new and untapped market for commercial human spaceflight for everyday people.

Stock Chart (weekly)

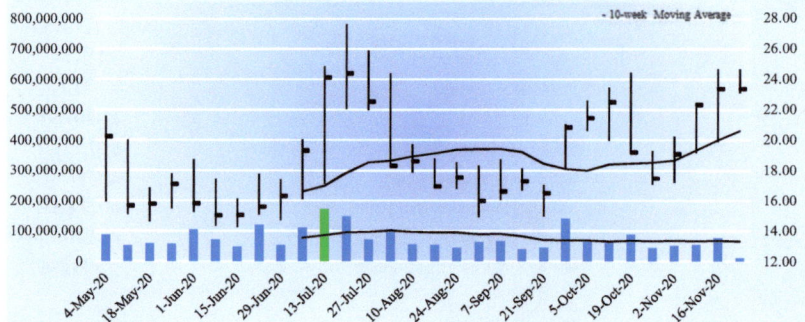

The week with the highest trading volume out of the last 30 weeks was a week of heavy selling, or distribution (red bar).

Investment Considerations

DCF Valuation	**FAIRLY VALUED**
Relative Valuation	**NEUTRAL**
ValueCreation™	**POOR**
ValueRisk™	**VERY HIGH**
ValueTrend™	**NEGATIVE**
Cash Flow Generation	**WEAK**
Financial Leverage	**LOW**
Growth	**AGGRESSIVE**
Technical Evaluation	**BULLISH**
Relative Strength	**STRONG**
Money Flow Index (MFI)	**NEUTRAL**
Upside/Downside Volume (U/D)	**DETERIORATING**
Near-term Technical Support, 10-week MA	**21.00**

DCF = Discounted Cash Flow; MFI, U/D = Please see glossary. MA = Moving Average

Company Vitals

Market Cap (USD)	$4,531
Avg Weekly Vol (30 wks)	73,919
30-week Range (USD)	14.21 - 27.55
Valuentum Sector	Next Generation
5-week Return	22.7%
13-week Return	28.6%
30-week Return	37.4%
Dividend Yield %	0.0%
Dividends per Share	0.00
Forward Dividend Payout Ratio	0.0%
Est. Normal Diluted EPS	1.27
P/E on Est. Normal Diluted EPS	18.4
Est. Normal EBITDA	373
Forward EV/EBITDA	-15.4
EV/Est. Normal EBITDA	10.8
Forward Revenue Growth (5-yr)	267.3%
Forward EPS Growth (5-yr)	-202.2%

NMF = Not Meaningful; Est. = Estimated; FY = Fiscal Year

Returns Summary

	3-year Historical Average
Return on Equity	-249.2%
Return on Assets	-77.7%
ROIC, with goodwill	Negative IC
ROIC, without goodwill	Negative IC

ROIC = Return on Invested Capital; NMF = Not Meaningful

Leverage, Coverage, and Liquidity

In Millions of USD

Total Debt	0
Net Debt	-493
Total Debt/EBITDA	0.0
Net Debt/EBITDA	NMF
EBITDA/Interest	Excellent
Current Ratio	4.6
Quick Ratio	NA

NMF = Not Meaningful

Investment Highlights

• Virgin Galactic is an aerospace entity that is pioneering space flight, not just for astronauts, but for everyday private individuals like you and me. Its space vehicles will allow customers a multi-day flight to experience weightlessness and view the Earth from space. The Virgin brand is a key asset when it may come to capital raising.

• Our fair value estimate range is huge because Virgin Galactic is a risky stock with hard-to-predict future forecasts. Operating costs to fly into space may be uneconomical, and one tragedy similar to the Challenger disaster could derail the entire business.

• According to the US Chamber of Commerce, as noted in Virgin Galactic's regulatory filings, 'the commercial space market is expected to grow 6% per year, from $385 billion in 2017 to at least $1.5 trillion by 2040, reaching 5% of US gross domestic product (SPCE 10-K). The company is investing heavily, but barriers to success are enormous.

• The market for commercial human spaceflight for private individuals is brand new, with fewer than 600 people ever having traveled into space. Virgin Galactic sees a huge opportunity for high net worth individuals to provide a spaceflight experience. Tickets may cost $250,000+ each.

• Other companies are trying to do what Virgin Galactic is attempting. Blue Origin (private). SpaceX and Boeing are others. The current reality for Virgin Galactic is that it continues to rack up losses and its future success is far from likely, in our view.

Business Quality

ValueRisk™	ValueCreation™			
	Very Poor	Poor	Good	Excellent
Low				
Medium				
High				
Very High		▓		

Firms that generate economic profits with little operating variability score near the top right of the matrix.

Relative Valuation

	Forward P/E	PEG	Price / FV
Wayfair	56.3	NMF	84.2%
Zoom Video	170.7	28.8	120.8%
Roku	-338.4	NMF	96.0%
Monster Beverage	36.0	2.9	104.4%
Peer Median	46.1	15.9	100.2%
Virgin Galactic	**-18.5**	**NMF**	**93.2%**

Price / FV = Current Stock Price divided by Estimated Fair Value

Financial Summary

	----- Actual -----		Projected
Fiscal Year End:	Dec-18	Dec-19	Dec-20
Revenue	3	4	2
Revenue, YoY%	62.4%	32.7%	-56.6%
Operating Income	-167	-213	-265
Operating Margin %	-5868.2%	-5640.4%	-16165.2%
Net Income	-138	-211	-258
Net Income Margin %	-4848.0%	-5576.9%	-15702.6%
Diluted EPS	-0.71	-1.08	-1.26
Diluted EPS, YoY %	0.0%	52.1%	16.4%
Free Cash Flow (CFO-capex)	-156	-223	-245
Free Cash Flow Margin %	-5485.9%	-5897.0%	-14910.6%

In Millions of USD (except for per share items)

Structure of the Aerospace and Defense Industry

GOOD

The global commercial aerospace duopoly is being challenged by encroaching international competitors who are intent on increasing market share, but Boeing and Airbus continue to dominate the large commercial aircraft segment. Long-term demand for commercial aircraft is cyclical and depends on the health of the credit markets, airline customers, and lessors, but massive backlogs and a strong multi-decade demand outlook are reasons for confidence. The defense industry has strong competition in all market segments and remains dependent on government funding decisions and competing budget priorities.

VALUENTUM

Splunk SPLK   FAIRLY VALUED

Buying Index™ 6   **Value Rating** ○

Economic Castle	Estimated Fair Value	Fair Value Range	Investment Style	Sector	Industry
Attractive	$228.00	$171.00 - $285.00	LARGE-CAP BLEND	Next Generation	Disruptive Innovation

We've raised our fair value estimate of Splunk considerably since our last update. We're now factoring in faster adoption of its cloud offering, greater margin leverage, and better long-term free cash flow generation.

Stock Chart (weekly)

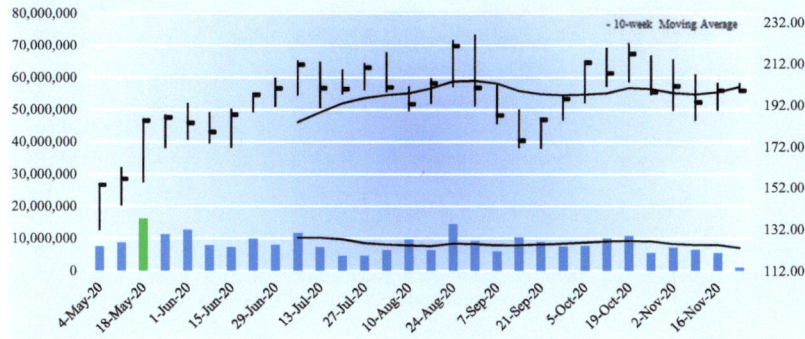

The week with the highest trading volume out of the last 30 weeks was a week of heavy selling, or distribution (red bar).

Investment Considerations

DCF Valuation	**FAIRLY VALUED**
Relative Valuation	**UNATTRACTIVE**
ValueCreation™	**EXCELLENT**
ValueRisk™	**MEDIUM**
ValueTrend™	**NEGATIVE**
Cash Flow Generation	**STRONG**
Financial Leverage	**LOW**
Growth	**AGGRESSIVE**
Technical Evaluation	**BULLISH**
Relative Strength	**WEAK**
Money Flow Index (MFI)	**NEUTRAL**
Upside/Downside Volume (U/D)	**BULLISH**
Near-term Technical Resistance, 10-wk MA	**201.00**

DCF = Discounted Cash Flow; MFI, U/D = Please see glossary. MA = Moving Average

Company Vitals

Market Cap (USD)	$30,229
Avg Weekly Vol (30 wks)	8,355
30-week Range (USD)	131.34 - 225.89
Valuentum Sector	Next Generation
5-week Return	-6.6%
13-week Return	-9.6%
30-week Return	50.2%
Dividend Yield %	0.0%
Dividends per Share	0.00
Forward Dividend Payout Ratio	0.0%
Est. Normal Diluted EPS	3.11
P/E on Est. Normal Diluted EPS	64.0
Est. Normal EBITDA	878
Forward EV/EBITDA	65.7
EV/Est. Normal EBITDA	32.4
Forward Revenue Growth (5-yr)	16.5%
Forward EPS Growth (5-yr)	-221.3%

NMF = Not Meaningful; Est. = Estimated; FY = Fiscal Year

Returns Summary
3-year Historical Average

Return on Equity	-22.2%
Return on Assets	-8.4%
ROIC, with goodwill	25.5%
ROIC, without goodwill	33.8%

ROIC = Return on Invested Capital; NMF = Not Meaningful

Leverage, Coverage, and Liquidity
In Millions of USD

Total Debt	0
Net Debt	-1,755
Total Debt/EBITDA	0.0
Net Debt/EBITDA	NMF
EBITDA/Interest	-1.3
Current Ratio	2.2
Quick Ratio	2.0

NMF = Not Meaningful

Investment Highlights

• Splunk provides the engine for machine data. Its software collects and indexes the machine-generated big data coming from websites, servers, networks and mobile devices that power businesses. The firm's software enables organizations to monitor, search, analyze, visualize and act on massive streams of real-time and historical machine data.

• Splunk is growing like a weed. The firm's software is designed to accelerate adoption and return on investment. It does not require customization or extensive professional services. Users can simply download and install the software in a matter of hours.

• Splunk expects its total addressable market (TAM) to grow to $144 billion in 2023 from $81 billion in 2020. Data production is soaring, and the number of devices connected to IP networks is proliferating. These trends present substantial opportunity for Splunk's hybrid cloud offerings. Its share of its addressable TAM is just ~2-3%.

• The company's total addressable market breaks down into four key areas: 1) observability/DevOps, 2) security, compliance, and fraud, 3) IT operations, and 4) platform/other. Splunk has ~400 customers that generate annual recurring revenue north of $1 million.

• Its long-range plan is impressive and includes massive gross margin leverage and 40% compound growth in annual recurring revenue. Management expects operating cash flow to surge in the coming years.

Business Quality

ValueCreation™

ValueRisk™	Very Poor	Poor	Good	Excellent
Low				
Medium				■
High				
Very High				

Firms that generate economic profits with little operating variability score near the top right of the matrix.

Relative Valuation

	Forward P/E	PEG	Price / FV
Wayfair	56.3	NMF	84.2%
Zoom Video	170.7	28.8	120.8%
Roku	-338.4	NMF	96.0%
Monster Beverage	36.0	2.9	104.4%
Peer Median	46.1	15.9	100.2%
Splunk	**168.4**	**NMF**	**87.3%**

Price / FV = Current Stock Price divided by Estimated Fair Value

Financial Summary

	----- Actual -----		Projected
Fiscal Year End:	Jan-19	Jan-20	Jan-21
Revenue	1,809	2,359	2,319
Revenue, YoY%	38.2%	30.4%	-1.7%
Operating Income	-251	-287	271
Operating Margin %	-13.9%	-12.2%	11.7%
Net Income	-276	-337	183
Net Income Margin %	-15.2%	-14.3%	7.9%
Diluted EPS	-1.89	-2.22	1.18
Diluted EPS, YoY %	39.1%	17.1%	NMF
Free Cash Flow (CFO-capex)	273	-389	669
Free Cash Flow Margin %	15.1%	-16.5%	28.8%

In Millions of USD (except for per share items)

Structure of the Software Industry

VERY GOOD

Firms that serve the mature software markets—or those consisting of basic business applications—have powerful distribution channels, large installed bases, and fortress balance sheets. These entrenched competitors benefit from significant customer switching costs, which make it nearly impossible for new entrants to gain a foothold. Participants generally benefit from high-margin license revenue and generate significant returns on investment. Still, the shift to cloud computing has created both opportunities and challenges, and the enterprise software landscape continues to evolve. We like the group.

Stryker SYK   FAIRLY VALUED

Buying Index™ 6   **Value Rating** 🟡

Economic Castle	Estimated Fair Value	Fair Value Range	Investment Style	Sector	Industry
Attractive	$209.00	$157.00 - $261.00	LARGE-CAP CORE	Health Care	Health Care Bellwethers

Stryker is in the process of acquiring Wright Medical through a deal worth ~$5.4 billion by enterprise value. We increased our fair value estimate.

Stock Chart (weekly)

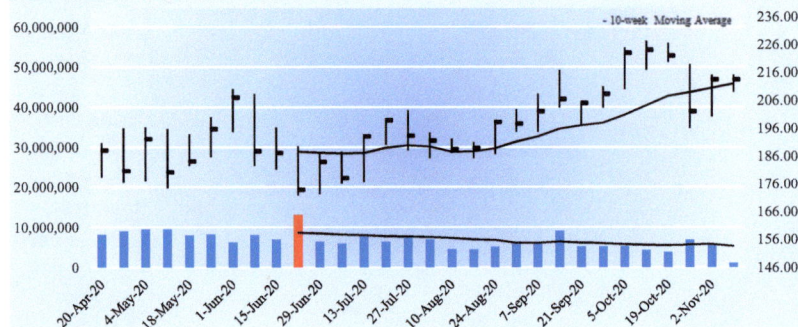

The week with the highest trading volume out of the last 30 weeks was a week of heavy selling, or distribution (red bar).

Investment Considerations

DCF Valuation	FAIRLY VALUED
Relative Valuation	UNATTRACTIVE
ValueCreation™	EXCELLENT
ValueRisk™	MEDIUM
ValueTrend™	POSITIVE
Cash Flow Generation	STRONG
Financial Leverage	HIGH
Growth	MODEST
Technical Evaluation	BULLISH
Relative Strength	NEUTRAL
Money Flow Index (MFI)	NEUTRAL
Upside/Downside Volume (U/D)	BULLISH
Near-term Technical Support, 10-week MA	212.00

DCF = Discounted Cash Flow; MFI, U/D = Please see glossary. MA = Moving Average

Business Quality

ValueRisk™	Very Poor	Poor	Good	Excellent
Low				
Medium				▓
High				
Very High				

ValueCreation™ (column header)

Firms that generate economic profits with little operating variability score near the top right of the matrix.

Company Vitals

Market Cap (USD)	$81,086
Avg Weekly Vol (30 wks)	6,649
30-week Range (USD)	171.75 - 227.38
Valuentum Sector	Health Care
5-week Return	-5.1%
13-week Return	13.1%
30-week Return	14.1%
Dividend Yield %	1.1%
Dividends per Share	2.30
Forward Dividend Payout Ratio	31.7%
Est. Normal Diluted EPS	9.86
P/E on Est. Normal Diluted EPS	21.7
Est. Normal EBITDA	5,081
Forward EV/EBITDA	22.5
EV/Est. Normal EBITDA	17.3
Forward Revenue Growth (5-yr)	5.5%
Forward EPS Growth (5-yr)	16.8%

NMF = Not Meaningful; Est. = Estimated; FY = Fiscal Year

Investment Highlights

• Stryker is one of the world's leading medical technology companies. The company offers reconstructive, medical, and surgical, and neurotechnology and spine products. Neurotechnology revenues represents ~65% of its annual net sales. Stryker owns over 8,880 patents globally. It was founded in 1941 and is headquartered in Michigan.

• The deferral of elective medical procedures as a result of the COVID-19 outbreak has impacted Stryker's results. Performance has held up, however, and the company is working with customers to meet the expected pent-up demand.

• Stryker is in the process of acquiring Wright Medical Group through an all-cash deal worth ~$5.4 billion by enterprise value when including convertible note considerations. Wright Medical has a complementary medical device portfolio that is focused on extremities and biologics. Stryker is an acquisitive company and will likely pursue additional M&A deals.

• Management continues to have a high level of conviction regarding the long-term growth potential for robotics in orthopedics, and MAKO continues to be a standout (Stryker acquired MAKO back in 2013). We're expecting big things, and innovation continues to be driven by R&D spending of ~6-7% of net sales.

• When elective surgeries resume in earnest worldwide, Styrker's near-term outlook should improve considerably. The potential for additional lockdowns to contain the COVID-19 pandemic remains a major concern, however.

Returns Summary
3-year Historical Average

Return on Equity	20.1%
Return on Assets	8.8%
ROIC, with goodwill	12.6%
ROIC, without goodwill	23.4%

ROIC = Return on Invested Capital; NMF = Not Meaningful

Leverage, Coverage, and Liquidity
In Millions of USD

Total Debt	11,090
Net Debt	6,665
Total Debt/EBITDA	3.2
Net Debt/EBITDA	1.9
EBITDA/Interest	Excellent
Current Ratio	2.6
Quick Ratio	1.7

NMF = Not Meaningful

Relative Valuation

	Forward P/E	PEG	Price / FV
Johnson & Johnson	17.6	1.8	99.5%
Medtronic	25.6	2.2	109.0%
Merck	21.5	2.2	100.5%
Pfizer	20.1	0.8	93.3%
Peer Median	20.8	2.0	100.0%
Stryker	**29.4**	**2.3**	**102.1%**

Price / FV = Current Stock Price divided by Estimated Fair Value

Financial Summary

	----- Actual -----		Projected
Fiscal Year End:	Dec-18	Dec-19	Dec-20
Revenue	13,601	14,884	14,393
Revenue, YoY%	9.3%	9.4%	-3.3%
Operating Income	2,537	2,713	3,135
Operating Margin %	18.7%	18.2%	21.8%
Net Income	3,553	2,083	2,759
Net Income Margin %	26.1%	14.0%	19.2%
Diluted EPS	9.34	5.48	7.26
Diluted EPS, YoY %	248.2%	-41.3%	32.4%
Free Cash Flow (CFO-capex)	2,038	1,542	4,021
Free Cash Flow Margin %	15.0%	10.4%	27.9%

In Millions of USD (except for per share items)

Structure of the Medical Instruments Industry   GOOD

The medical instrument industry is heavily regulated and characterized by rapid technological change. Firms have been forced to compete on price due to economically-motivated buyers, consolidation among healthcare providers, and declining reimbursement rates. Healthcare reform measures have put additional pressure on procedure rates and market sizes. Still, firms can gain advantages by developing products with differentiated clinical outcomes or by creating patent-protected technology. Since most constituents hold important patents or trade secrets, we tend to like the group.

Sysco SYY FAIRLY VALUED

Buying Index™ 6 **Value Rating** ◯

Economic Castle	Estimated Fair Value	Fair Value Range	Investment Style	Sector	Industry
Attractive	$74.00	$57.00 - $91.00	LARGE-CAP VALUE	Consumer Staples	Recession Resistant

Sysco has a broad customer base and a wide range of products. Its sales are still heavily weighted toward restaurants, however. The company has a very impressive track record of consecutive annual dividend increases.

Stock Chart (weekly)

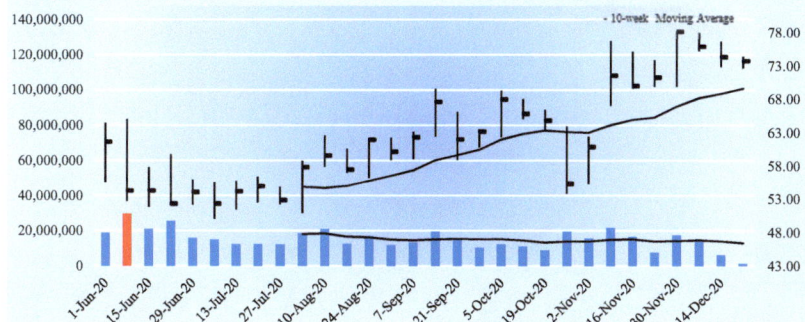

The week with the highest trading volume out of the last 30 weeks was a week of heavy selling, or distribution (red bar).

Company Vitals

Market Cap (USD)	$37,883
Avg Weekly Vol (30 wks)	15,168
30-week Range (USD)	50.03 - 78.14
Valuentum Sector	Consumer Staples
5-week Return	4.4%
13-week Return	16.8%
30-week Return	31.3%
Dividend Yield %	2.4%
Dividends per Share	1.80
Forward Dividend Payout Ratio	96.3%
Est. Normal Diluted EPS	3.92
P/E on Est. Normal Diluted EPS	18.8
Est. Normal EBITDA	3,758
Forward EV/EBITDA	19.3
EV/Est. Normal EBITDA	12.3
Forward Revenue Growth (5-yr)	5.3%
Forward EPS Growth (5-yr)	68.1%

NMF = Not Meaningful; Est. = Estimated; FY = Fiscal Year

Returns Summary
3-year Historical Average

Return on Equity	45.7%
Return on Assets	6.1%
ROIC, with goodwill	15.5%
ROIC, without goodwill	24.0%

ROIC = Return on Invested Capital; NMF = Not Meaningful

Leverage, Coverage, and Liquidity
In Millions of USD

Total Debt	14,447
Net Debt	8,387
Total Debt/EBITDA	9.2
Net Debt/EBITDA	5.3
EBITDA/Interest	3.9
Current Ratio	1.8
Quick Ratio	1.3

NMF = Not Meaningful

Investment Highlights

• Sysco is the largest North American distributor of food and related products primarily to the foodservice and restaurant industry. The US foodservice market is gigantic, and we think the firm has a long runway of growth ahead of it. The company estimates that it holds roughly 15%-20% share of the US foodservice market, but it is not without competition.

• Sysco has a broad customer base and a wide range of products. Restaurants account for more than half of sales, however. The balance of revenue is generated in healthcare; education and government; travel, leisure, and retail; and other. Fresh/frozen meats and canned/dry vegetables are its key product categories.

• Sysco wants to get bigger. In 2015, the company attempted to merge with peer US Foods, but regulators sued to block the transaction, and Sysco was forced to pull the plug on the tie-up. The deal's termination cost Sysco nearly $700 million, but it has not deterred management from acquisitive growth. It has spent nearly a half billion dollars on deals during the past three fiscal years (2018-2020).

• We're huge fans of Sysco's expansive distribution network, which would be incredibly difficult for new entrants to replicate. The company operates more than 325 distribution facilities serving ~625,000 customer locations. It delivers over 1 billion cases every year. Sysco has staying power and huge competitive advantages.

• The company is working through the COVID-19 crisis and has shored up liquidity, but earnings have been under material pressure. Fiscal 2021 won't be a great year for Sysco, but the company has shown it can generate strong free cash flow, despite sales pressure.

Investment Considerations

DCF Valuation	FAIRLY VALUED
Relative Valuation	UNATTRACTIVE
ValueCreation™	EXCELLENT
ValueRisk™	MEDIUM
ValueTrend™	NEGATIVE
Cash Flow Generation	MEDIUM
Financial Leverage	HIGH
Growth	MODEST
Technical Evaluation	BULLISH
Relative Strength	STRONG
Money Flow Index (MFI)	NEUTRAL
Upside/Downside Volume (U/D)	DETERIORATING
Near-term Technical Support, 10-week MA	70.00

DCF = Discounted Cash Flow; MFI, U/D = Please see glossary. MA = Moving Average

Business Quality

ValueRisk™	ValueCreation™			
	Very Poor	Poor	Good	Excellent
Low				
Medium				▓
High				
Very High				

Firms that generate economic profits with little operating variability score near the top right of the matrix.

Relative Valuation

	Forward P/E	PEG	Price / FV
Coca-Cola	34.3	1.5	128.0%
Procter & Gamble	26.5	3.3	144.1%
Philip Morris	15.4	2.4	104.3%
Wal-Mart	26.8	2.3	130.2%
Peer Median	26.7	2.4	129.1%
Sysco	39.4	2.6	99.6%

Price / FV = Current Stock Price divided by Estimated Fair Value

Financial Summary

	----- Actual -----		Projected
Fiscal Year End:	Jun-19	Jun-20	Jun-21
Revenue	60,114	52,893	51,095
Revenue, YoY%	2.4%	-12.0%	-3.4%
Operating Income	2,330	750	1,591
Operating Margin %	3.9%	1.4%	3.1%
Net Income	1,674	215	946
Net Income Margin %	2.8%	0.4%	1.9%
Diluted EPS	3.20	0.42	1.87
Diluted EPS, YoY %	18.3%	-86.9%	345.7%
Free Cash Flow (CFO-capex)	1,718	898	1,223
Free Cash Flow Margin %	2.9%	1.7%	2.4%

In Millions of USD (except for per share items)

Structure of the Food Retailers Industry
NEUTRAL

Firms in the mature food retailers industry generally have slim profit margins and face significant competition from brick-and-mortar locations (discount, department, drug, dollar, warehouse clubs and supermarkets) as well as Internet-based retailers (including Amazon). Though the industry is not terribly cyclical, economic conditions, disposable income, credit availability, fuel prices, and unemployment levels drive ticket size and traffic trends. Offering consumers a compelling value proposition is a must, even as higher-priced organic food offerings proliferate. We're generally neutral on the group.

Teradyne TER   FAIRLY VALUED

Buying Index™   5   Value Rating ⬤

Economic Castle	Estimated Fair Value	Fair Value Range	Investment Style	Sector	Industry
Very Attractive	$97.00	$73.00 - $121.00	LARGE-CAP GROWTH	Next Generation	Disruptive Innovation

Teradyne's industrial robotics technology is exciting. It's also benefiting from semiconductor test strength across the 'Memory,' 'Storage,' and 'SOC' markets. We also like its net-cash rich balance sheet.

Stock Chart (weekly)

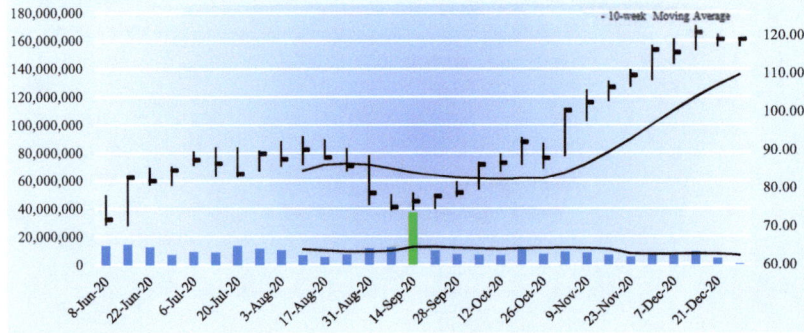

The week with the highest trading volume out of the last 30 weeks was a week of heavy selling, or distribution (red bar).

Investment Considerations

DCF Valuation	**FAIRLY VALUED**
Relative Valuation	**ATTRACTIVE**
ValueCreation™	**EXCELLENT**
ValueRisk™	**MEDIUM**
ValueTrend™	**NEGATIVE**
Cash Flow Generation	**STRONG**
Financial Leverage	**LOW**
Growth	**HIGH**
Technical Evaluation	**NEUTRAL**
Relative Strength	**STRONG**
Money Flow Index (MFI)	**OVERBOUGHT**
Upside/Downside Volume (U/D)	**BULLISH**
Near-term Technical Support, 10-week MA	**110.00**

DCF = Discounted Cash Flow; MFI, U/D = Please see glossary. MA = Moving Average

Company Vitals

Market Cap (USD)	$22,897
Avg Weekly Vol (30 wks)	9,496
30-week Range (USD)	70.06 - 122.37
Valuentum Sector	Next Generation
5-week Return	8.1%
13-week Return	49.5%
30-week Return	52.4%
Dividend Yield %	0.3%
Dividends per Share	0.40
Forward Dividend Payout Ratio	15.4%
Est. Normal Diluted EPS	4.73
P/E on Est. Normal Diluted EPS	25.1
Est. Normal EBITDA	1,142
Forward EV/EBITDA	33.6
EV/Est. Normal EBITDA	19.4
Forward Revenue Growth (5-yr)	11.5%
Forward EPS Growth (5-yr)	20.8%

NMF = Not Meaningful; Est. = Estimated; FY = Fiscal Year

Returns Summary
3-year Historical Average

Return on Equity	12.4%
Return on Assets	7.6%
ROIC, with goodwill	68.9%
ROIC, without goodwill	106.7%

ROIC = Return on Invested Capital; NMF = Not Meaningful

Leverage, Coverage, and Liquidity
In Millions of USD

Total Debt	380
Net Debt	-737
Total Debt/EBITDA	0.6
Net Debt/EBITDA	NMF
EBITDA/Interest	19.3
Current Ratio	3.6
Quick Ratio	3.0

NMF = Not Meaningful

Investment Highlights

• Teradyne sells automatic test equipment used to test semiconductors, wireless products, data storage and complex electronic systems that serve consumer, communications, industrial and government customers. Its industrial products include robotic arms, mobile robots and robotic control software. The company was founded in 1960 and is headquartered in Massachusetts.

• We're huge fans of Teradyne's balance sheet health, which provides its operations with a nice cushion. As of the end of 2019, the company had a cash and marketable securities position of ~$911 million compared to ~$395 million in long-term debt on the books. We like the financial flexibility.

• Teradyne has achieved prior non-GAAP EPS targets years ahead of schedule and now has even loftier goals for the future. Growing device complexity, integrated circuit unit growth, and rising quality requirements are expected to continue driving its 'Semiconductor Test' business, while its 'Universal Robots' business is expected to grow at a 50%+ clip for years to come.

• Teradyne's robotics technology is exciting. It makes collaborative robots (UR3, UR5, UR10) that mimic the motion of a human arm and can work side-by-side with workers. It makes autonomous mobile industrial robots (MiR), which increase warehouse efficiency and reduce customer costs. It also has opportunities in robotic software and in the forklift market.

• Recent trends have been very encouraging for Teradyne. For example, its its third quarter of 2020, test revenue advanced 46% thanks to strength in 'Memory,' 'Storage,' and 'System on Chip (SOC)' test demand. The company is benefiting from multiple drivers.

Business Quality
ValueCreation™

ValueRisk™	Very Poor	Poor	Good	Excellent
Low				
Medium				▨
High				
Very High				

Firms that generate economic profits with little operating variability score near the top right of the matrix.

Relative Valuation

	Forward P/E	PEG	Price / FV
Wayfair	56.3	NMF	84.2%
Zoom Video	170.7	28.8	120.8%
Roku	-338.4	NMF	96.0%
Monster Beverage	36.0	2.9	104.4%
Peer Median	46.1	15.9	100.2%
Teradyne	**45.8**	**2.4**	**122.6%**

Price / FV = Current Stock Price divided by Estimated Fair Value

Financial Summary

	----- Actual -----		Projected
Fiscal Year End:	Dec-17	Dec-18	Dec-19
Revenue	2,137	2,101	2,294
Revenue, YoY%	21.9%	-1.7%	9.2%
Operating Income	539	489	587
Operating Margin %	25.2%	23.3%	25.6%
Net Income	258	452	495
Net Income Margin %	12.1%	21.5%	21.6%
Diluted EPS	1.28	2.35	2.60
Diluted EPS, YoY %	NMF	83.5%	10.7%
Free Cash Flow (CFO-capex)	521	362	444
Free Cash Flow Margin %	24.4%	17.3%	19.3%

In Millions of USD (except for per share items)

Structure of the Semiconductor Equipment Industry   VERY POOR

The semiconductor equipment industry is highly competitive and characterized by rapid technological change. Success hinges on the ability to commercialize new technology in a timely manner, continuously enhance products to improve efficiency of customer fab operations, and manage costs and inventory effectively. Performance of constituents is heavily influenced by manufacturing capacity and fab utilization rates, which together create volatile demand cycles. The potential for unexpected shifts in demand for the group's products leaves us unexcited about the industry's structural characteristics.

Target TGT   FAIRLY VALUED

Buying Index™   **5**   **Value Rating** ○

Economic Castle	Estimated Fair Value	Fair Value Range	Investment Style	Sector	Industry
Attractive	$152.00	$122.00 - $182.00	LARGE-CAP CORE	Consumer Staples	Recession Resistant

Target's digital initiatives are paying off, enabling the retailer to grow its market share.

Stock Chart (weekly)

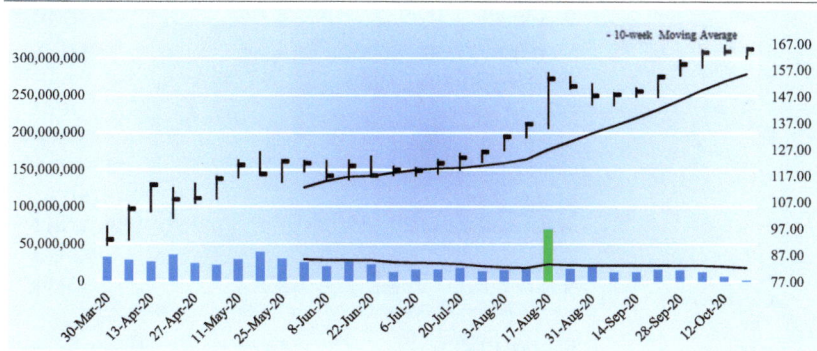

The week with the highest trading volume out of the last 30 weeks was a week of heavy selling, or distribution (red bar).

Investment Considerations

DCF Valuation	**FAIRLY VALUED**
Relative Valuation	**NEUTRAL**
ValueCreation™	**EXCELLENT**
ValueRisk™	**LOW**
ValueTrend™	**NEGATIVE**
Cash Flow Generation	**MEDIUM**
Financial Leverage	**MEDIUM**
Growth	**MODEST**
Technical Evaluation	**NEUTRAL**
Relative Strength	**STRONG**
Money Flow Index (MFI)	**OVERBOUGHT**
Upside/Downside Volume (U/D)	**BULLISH**
Near-term Technical Support, 10-week MA	**155.00**

DCF = Discounted Cash Flow; MFI, U/D = Please see glossary. MA = Moving Average

Business Quality

ValueRisk™	Very Poor	Poor	Good	Excellent
Low				■
Medium				
High				
Very High				

ValueCreation™ (column header)

Firms that generate economic profits with little operating variability score near the top right of the matrix.

Company Vitals

Market Cap (USD)	$85,087
Avg Weekly Vol (30 wks)	21,845
30-week Range (USD)	90.16 - 166.67
Valuentum Sector	Consumer Staples
5-week Return	11.0%
13-week Return	32.8%
30-week Return	71.6%
Dividend Yield %	1.6%
Dividends per Share	2.72
Forward Dividend Payout Ratio	37.5%
Est. Normal Diluted EPS	8.72
P/E on Est. Normal Diluted EPS	18.9
Est. Normal EBITDA	8,476
Forward EV/EBITDA	12.2
EV/Est. Normal EBITDA	11.1
Forward Revenue Growth (5-yr)	4.1%
Forward EPS Growth (5-yr)	10.8%

NMF = Not Meaningful; Est. = Estimated; FY = Fiscal Year

Returns Summary   3-year Historical Average

Return on Equity	26.5%
Return on Assets	7.6%
ROIC, with goodwill	16.5%
ROIC, without goodwill	17.0%

ROIC = Return on Invested Capital; NMF = Not Meaningful

Leverage, Coverage, and Liquidity

In Millions of USD

Total Debt	11,499
Net Debt	8,922
Total Debt/EBITDA	1.6
Net Debt/EBITDA	1.3
EBITDA/Interest	14.7
Current Ratio	0.9
Quick Ratio	0.2

NMF = Not Meaningful

Investment Highlights

• Target sells everyday essentials and differentiated items at discounted prices. Approximately one third of total sales are related to its owned (Archer Farms, Circo, etc.) and exclusive brands (Fieldcrest, Nick & Nora, etc.). The company experienced one of its best years in 2019, and it has done even better during the COVID-19 pandemic.

• Target's omni-channel sales strategy has performed very well recently, allowing it to take market share. Consumers are increasingly utilizing its digitally-oriented home delivery, curbside pickup, and order online and pickup in-store fulfillment options.

• The company faces tough competition from Walmart and other rapidly-expanding online retailers, namely Amazon, which is now looking to disrupt food retail via its acquisition of Whole Foods. Pricing competition is intense, and Target's margins are paying the price. Target remains one of the premier retailers within the industry, however.

• In the second quarter of fiscal 2020, Target's digital comparable sales grew by 195% year-over-year, enabling company-wide comparable store sales growth of 24.3% year-over-year. Target's financial and operational performance has proved resilient during the initial phases of the COVID-19 pandemic.

• Please be aware that our cash flow models for Target assume the retailer puts up decent revenue growth and steady margin expansion over time, underpinned by Target's digital initiatives and recent market share gains. Target will need to deliver on those fronts.

Relative Valuation

	Forward P/E	PEG	Price / FV
Coca-Cola	34.3	1.5	128.0%
Procter & Gamble	26.5	3.3	144.1%
Philip Morris	15.4	2.4	104.3%
Wal-Mart	26.8	2.3	130.2%
Peer Median	26.7	2.4	129.1%
Target	**22.8**	**2.4**	**108.6%**

Price / FV = Current Stock Price divided by Estimated Fair Value

Financial Summary

	----- Actual -----		Projected
Fiscal Year End:	Jan-19	Jan-20	Jan-21
Revenue	75,356	78,112	88,188
Revenue, YoY%	4.8%	3.7%	12.9%
Operating Income	4,110	4,658	5,057
Operating Margin %	5.5%	6.0%	5.7%
Net Income	2,930	3,269	3,664
Net Income Margin %	3.9%	4.2%	4.2%
Diluted EPS	5.50	6.34	7.25
Diluted EPS, YoY %	3.3%	15.4%	14.4%
Free Cash Flow (CFO-capex)	2,457	4,090	4,281
Free Cash Flow Margin %	3.3%	5.2%	4.9%

In Millions of USD (except for per share items)

Structure of the Food Retailers Industry   NEUTRAL

Firms in the mature food retailers industry generally have slim profit margins and face significant competition from brick-and-mortar locations (discount, department, drug, dollar, warehouse clubs and supermarkets) as well as Internet-based retailers (including Amazon). Though the industry is not terribly cyclical, economic conditions, disposable income, credit availability, fuel prices, and unemployment levels drive ticket size and traffic trends. Offering consumers a compelling value proposition is a must, even as higher-priced organic food offerings proliferate. We're generally neutral on the group.

Tesla TSLA OVERVALUED 20.9%

Buying Index™ 2 Value Rating ✗

Economic Castle	Estimated Fair Value	Fair Value Range	Investment Style	Sector	Industry
Neutral	$515.00	$335.00 - $695.00	MEGA-CAP GROWTH	Consumer Discretionary	Discretionary Spending

Tesla's growth runway is enormous, and economies of scale will eventually enable the firm to generate substantial free cash flow. We've raised our fair value estimate since the last update.

Stock Chart (weekly)

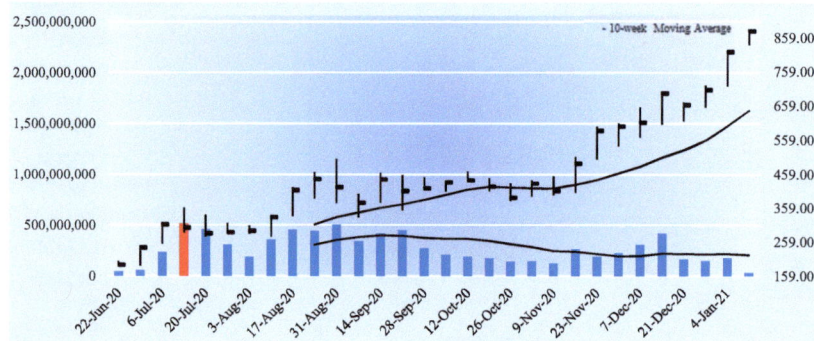

The week with the highest trading volume out of the last 30 weeks was a week of heavy selling, or distribution (red bar).

Investment Considerations

DCF Valuation	OVERVALUED
Relative Valuation	UNATTRACTIVE
ValueCreation™	POOR
ValueRisk™	HIGH
ValueTrend™	POSITIVE
Cash Flow Generation	WEAK
Financial Leverage	HIGH
Growth	AGGRESSIVE
Technical Evaluation	NEUTRAL
Relative Strength	STRONG
Money Flow Index (MFI)	OVERBOUGHT
Upside/Downside Volume (U/D)	BULLISH
Near-term Technical Support, 10-week MA	645.00

DCF = Discounted Cash Flow; MFI, U/D = Please see glossary. MA = Moving Average

Company Vitals

Market Cap (USD)	$777,437
Avg Weekly Vol (30 wks)	264,043
30-week Range (USD)	187.43 - 879.00
Valuentum Sector	Consumer Discretionary
5-week Return	41.9%
13-week Return	96.9%
30-week Return	339.3%
Dividend Yield %	0.0%
Dividends per Share	0.00
Forward Dividend Payout Ratio	0.0%
Est. Normal Diluted EPS	6.40
P/E on Est. Normal Diluted EPS	137.3
Est. Normal EBITDA	12,674
Forward EV/EBITDA	153.5
EV/Est. Normal EBITDA	61.9
Forward Revenue Growth (5-yr)	32.4%
Forward EPS Growth (5-yr)	-265.3%

NMF = Not Meaningful; Est. = Estimated; FY = Fiscal Year

Returns Summary
3-year Historical Average

Return on Equity	-28.8%
Return on Assets	-4.9%
ROIC, with goodwill	7.6%
ROIC, without goodwill	7.7%

ROIC = Return on Invested Capital; NMF = Not Meaningful

Leverage, Coverage, and Liquidity
In Millions of USD

Total Debt	13,419
Net Debt	6,905
Total Debt/EBITDA	5.2
Net Debt/EBITDA	2.7
EBITDA/Interest	3.7
Current Ratio	1.1
Quick Ratio	0.7

NMF = Not Meaningful

Investment Highlights

• Tesla's strategy is to accelerate the transition to electric vehicles with a range of affordable electric cars. The Model S, the world's first premium sedan to be engineered from the ground up as an electric vehicle, began deliveries in June 2012. CEO Elon Musk is dreaming big, but public relations missteps have impacted shareholder confidence at times. Stock market bulls are currently in charge at the moment.

• Tesla's stock volatility is not for the faint of heart. Shares have been on a roller coaster ride, and investor expectations have been ratcheted higher. Its competition continues to grow and will only intensify from here. Still, we're expecting substantial free cash flow generation in the coming years.

• Tesla is transitioning into a mass production car company. At the beginning of the third quarter 2012, it was producing just 5 cars per week. By the end of that quarter, it was making 100 cars per week. Fast-forward to 2020, and Tesla delivered ~500,000 vehicles in the year. Production continues to increase to this day, and management is targeting production of 20 million vehicles annually by 2030.

• Tesla was GAAP profitable in the first quarter of 2013 for the first time in its history thanks to the company exceeding its own targets for deliveries and gross margin. Tesla posted four consecutive quarters of GAAP profitability for the first time in the second quarter of 2020, and we expect profits and free cash flow to continue to expand in coming years.

• Tesla's thirst for innovation is among the best in our coverage universe. In 2019, Tesla acquired Maxwell (a leader in the development of cost-effective energy and power delivery systems) in a cash and stock deal. We wouldn't be surprised if CEO Elon Musk scoops up other strategic assets.

Business Quality

ValueRisk™	Very Poor	Poor	Good	Excellent
Low				
Medium				
High		▨		
Very High				

ValueCreation™

Firms that generate economic profits with little operating variability score near the top right of the matrix.

Relative Valuation

	Forward P/E	PEG	Price / FV
Disney	104.2	NMF	117.1%
Home Depot	22.9	1.9	106.7%
McDonald's	38.5	1.1	111.0%
Nike	52.8	2.5	104.9%
Peer Median	45.6	1.9	108.9%
Tesla	**NMF**	**NMF**	**170.6%**

Price / FV = Current Stock Price divided by Estimated Fair Value

Financial Summary

	----- Actual -----		Projected
Fiscal Year End:	Dec-18	Dec-19	Dec-20
Revenue	21,461	24,578	31,042
Revenue, YoY%	82.5%	14.5%	26.3%
Operating Income	-253	80	2,483
Operating Margin %	-1.2%	0.3%	8.0%
Net Income	-976	-862	1,350
Net Income Margin %	-4.5%	-3.5%	4.3%
Diluted EPS	-1.14	-0.97	1.50
Diluted EPS, YoY %	-51.6%	-14.9%	-253.6%
Free Cash Flow (CFO-capex)	-222	973	2,627
Free Cash Flow Margin %	-1.0%	4.0%	8.5%

In Millions of USD (except for per share items)

Structure of the Auto Manufacturers Industry VERY POOR

The auto manufacturers industry is characterized by high fixed costs, substantial operating leverage, and intense competition. Vehicle sales are impacted by general economic conditions, which are largely out of the control of participants, and by the cost of credit and fuel. Excess capacity, price discounting and other marketing initiatives can pressure the top line, while rising raw material and labor costs can squeeze the bottom line. Changing consumer preferences in type, model and fuel-efficiency can cause abrupt shifts in market share. The structural characteristics of the group are very poor.

Taiwan Semiconductor TSM FAIRLY VALUED

				Buying Index™	5	Value Rating	

Economic Castle	Estimated Fair Value	Fair Value Range	Investment Style	Sector	Industry
Attractive	$94.00	$71.00 - $118.00	MEGA-CAP GROWTH	Information Technology	Technology Giants

We raised our fair value estimate (again) for Taiwan Semiconductor as it remains an industry leader. The firm's long-term growth outlook is bright.

Stock Chart (weekly)

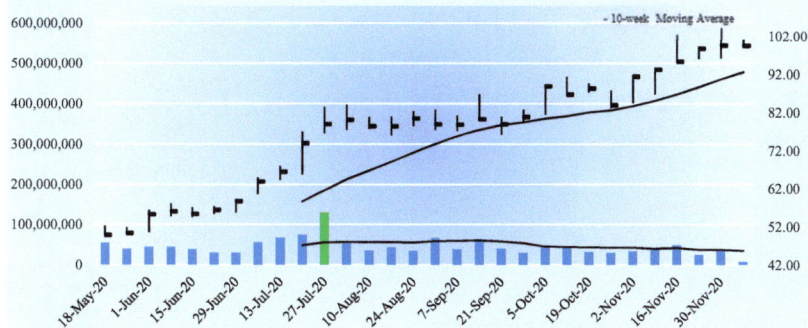

The week with the highest trading volume out of the last 30 weeks was a week of heavy selling, or distribution (red bar).

Investment Considerations

DCF Valuation	FAIRLY VALUED
Relative Valuation	ATTRACTIVE
ValueCreation™	EXCELLENT
ValueRisk™	MEDIUM
ValueTrend™	NEGATIVE
Cash Flow Generation	STRONG
Financial Leverage	LOW
Growth	HIGH
Technical Evaluation	NEUTRAL
Relative Strength	STRONG
Money Flow Index (MFI)	OVERBOUGHT
Upside/Downside Volume (U/D)	DETERIORATING
Near-term Technical Support, 10-week MA	93.00

DCF = Discounted Cash Flow; MFI, U/D = Please see glossary. MA = Moving Average

Company Vitals

Market Cap (USD)	$516,007
Avg Weekly Vol (30 wks)	45,377
30-week Range (USD)	49.61 - 104.30
Valuentum Sector	Information Technology
5-week Return	7.9%
13-week Return	23.6%
30-week Return	95.3%
Dividend Yield %	1.7%
Dividends per Share	1.69
Forward Dividend Payout Ratio	49.0%
Est. Normal Diluted EPS	4.63
P/E on Est. Normal Diluted EPS	21.5
Est. Normal EBITDA	42,448
Forward EV/EBITDA	15.3
EV/Est. Normal EBITDA	11.8
Forward Revenue Growth (5-yr)	14.8%
Forward EPS Growth (5-yr)	22.6%

NMF = Not Meaningful; Est. = Estimated; FY = Fiscal Year

Returns Summary

3-year Historical Average

Return on Equity	23.2%
Return on Assets	17.5%
ROIC, with goodwill	29.6%
ROIC, without goodwill	29.6%

ROIC = Return on Invested Capital; NMF = Not Meaningful

Leverage, Coverage, and Liquidity

In Millions of USD

Total Debt	4,832
Net Debt	-14,675
Total Debt/EBITDA	0.2
Net Debt/EBITDA	NMF
EBITDA/Interest	202.5
Current Ratio	1.4
Quick Ratio	1.2

NMF = Not Meaningful

Investment Highlights

- Taiwan Semiconductor is a foundry that makes semiconductors using manufacturing processes for its customers based on their own or third parties' proprietary integrated circuit designs. The company is heavily dependent on the highly cyclical semiconductor and microelectronics industries. It was founded in 1987 and is headquartered in Taiwan.

- Taiwan Semi is expanding 7-nanometer capacity to meet demand. It then expects to use that same technology to help finalize the development of its 5-nanometer technology. Such rapid development is necessary to compete successfully in the high-end mobile and smartphone markets.

- The smartphone market had been a source of strength for Taiwan Semi, but volume concerns at key customers have impacted expectations. Weakness in high-end smartphone demand has resulted in an inventory build, and this is expected to persist until the next round of new device launches. The firm has customer concentration risk as its top ten customers accounted for ~67% of revenue.

- The credit rating agencies rate Taiwan Semi's debt as investment grade (A+/Aa3), and we like its net cash position. Still, the participants in the industry that it operates in aren't necessarily benign. From time to time, rivals can undertake aggressive pricing initiatives for share gains, decreasing Taiwan Semi's customer base, or its average selling price, or both.

- Taiwan Semiconductor's relatively steady dividend recently experienced some significant jumps. After payouts hovering around 3NT$ for years, it jumped to ~4.5NT$ in 2015, then to ~6NT$ in 2016, ~7NT$ in 2017, and ~8NT$ in 2018. We think the company has the capacity to further increase the payout.

Business Quality

ValueRisk™	ValueCreation™ Very Poor	Poor	Good	Excellent
Low				
Medium				▓
High				
Very High				

Firms that generate economic profits with little operating variability score near the top right of the matrix.

Relative Valuation

	Forward P/E	PEG	Price / FV
Apple	29.8	2.4	85.0%
Alphabet	34.9	1.8	73.3%
Amazon.com	NMF	3.3	95.7%
Microsoft	31.6	2.5	91.6%
Peer Median	31.6	2.5	88.3%
Taiwan Semiconductor	28.8	1.9	105.9%

Price / FV = Current Stock Price divided by Estimated Fair Value

Financial Summary

	----- Actual -----		Projected
Fiscal Year End:	Dec-18	Dec-19	Dec-20
Revenue	33,697	35,774	48,080
Revenue, YoY%	2.2%	6.2%	34.4%
Operating Income	12,533	12,477	19,835
Operating Margin %	37.2%	34.9%	41.3%
Net Income	11,862	11,837	17,913
Net Income Margin %	35.2%	33.1%	37.3%
Diluted EPS	2.29	2.28	3.45
Diluted EPS, YoY %	1.9%	-0.2%	51.3%
Free Cash Flow (CFO-capex)	8,441	5,172	14,734
Free Cash Flow Margin %	25.0%	14.5%	30.6%

In Millions of USD (except for per share items)

Structure of the Integrated Circuits Industry   VERY POOR

Firms in the integrated circuits industry make components that form the electronic building blocks used in electronic systems and equipment. The industry is notoriously cyclical and subject to significant economic upturns and downturns, as well as rapid technological changes. Firms must innovate to survive, and products stocked in inventory can sometimes become obsolete before they are even shipped. Severe pricing competition and lengthy manufacturing cycles only add uncertainty to the mix. We're not fans of the structure of the integrated circuits space.

Twitter TWTR FAIRLY VALUED

Buying Index™ 6   **Value Rating** ◯

Economic Castle	Estimated Fair Value	Fair Value Range	Investment Style	Sector	Industry
Attractive	$47.00	$35.00 - $59.00	LARGE-CAP GROWTH	Information Technology	Technology Giants

Advertisers continue to spend heavily on the Twitter platform, and the company is working hard to improve its brand image and usability. New website features could further drive the company's user growth.

Stock Chart (weekly)

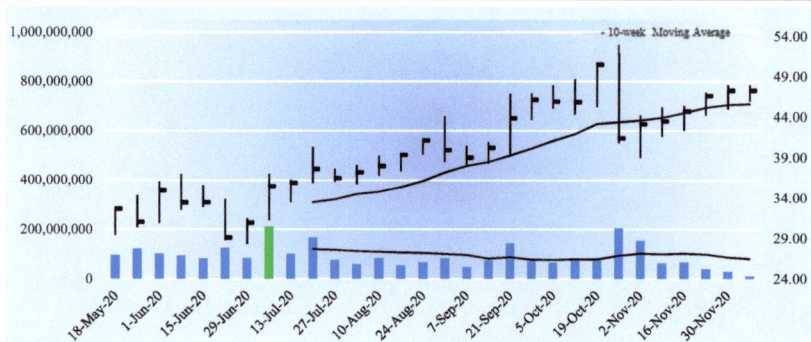

The week with the highest trading volume out of the last 30 weeks was a week of heavy selling, or distribution (red bar).

Investment Considerations

DCF Valuation	**FAIRLY VALUED**
Relative Valuation	**NEUTRAL**
ValueCreation™	**EXCELLENT**
ValueRisk™	**MEDIUM**
ValueTrend™	**NEGATIVE**
Cash Flow Generation	**STRONG**
Financial Leverage	**LOW**
Growth	**HIGH**
Technical Evaluation	**BULLISH**
Relative Strength	**STRONG**
Money Flow Index (MFI)	**NEUTRAL**
Upside/Downside Volume (U/D)	**DETERIORATING**
Near-term Technical Support, 10-week MA	**46.00**

DCF = Discounted Cash Flow; MFI, U/D = Please see glossary. MA = Moving Average

Company Vitals

Market Cap (USD)	$37,101
Avg Weekly Vol (30 wks)	91,145
30-week Range (USD)	28.23 - 52.93
Valuentum Sector	Information Technology
5-week Return	7.4%
13-week Return	19.8%
30-week Return	59.0%
Dividend Yield %	0.0%
Dividends per Share	0.00
Forward Dividend Payout Ratio	0.0%
Est. Normal Diluted EPS	1.05
P/E on Est. Normal Diluted EPS	45.0
Est. Normal EBITDA	1,779
Forward EV/EBITDA	-445.6
EV/Est. Normal EBITDA	17.5
Forward Revenue Growth (5-yr)	13.4%
Forward EPS Growth (5-yr)	2.5%

NMF = Not Meaningful; Est. = Estimated; FY = Fiscal Year

Returns Summary

	3-year Historical Average
Return on Equity	12.3%
Return on Assets	8.3%
ROIC, with goodwill	16.2%
ROIC, without goodwill	30.6%

ROIC = Return on Invested Capital; NMF = Not Meaningful

Leverage, Coverage, and Liquidity

In Millions of USD

Total Debt	692
Net Debt	-5,947
Total Debt/EBITDA	0.7
Net Debt/EBITDA	NMF
EBITDA/Interest	6.8
Current Ratio	9.2
Quick Ratio	9.0

NMF = Not Meaningful

Investment Highlights

• Twitter is an online platform for public self-expression and conversation in real time. The firm's website is unique in its simplicity: Tweets are limited to 280 characters of text. Users can quickly create and distribute content that is consistent across its platform and optimized for mobile devices. The company was founded in 2006 and is based in San Francisco, California.

• Twitter generates revenue from promoted products (e.g. an advertiser pays to promote a Tweet that appears in a desired target market's timeline). It has been using machine learning and enhancing its algorithms to improve both users' and advertisers' experiences.

• Modest expansion in the US has been an issue for Twitter, and social concerns have cropped up as it increases spending to police/protect its users. This will undoubtedly impact its long-term cost profile, and Congressional hearings have become common regarding customer privacy, security, and content moderation (propagation of misinformation).

• Mobile has become the primary driver of Twitter's business. Mobile products are critical to the value it creates for users, and they enable its users to create, distribute and discover content in the moment and on-the-go. Advertisers continue to substantially increase their marketing dollars on Twitter to reach users.

• Twitter has incurred material operating losses in the past, though we note it was profitabile on a GAAP basis in 2018 and 2019. The company has a nice net cash position and strong expected free cash flow, both of which support our valuation of the equity.

Business Quality

ValueRisk™	Very Poor	Poor	Good	Excellent
Low				
Medium				■
High				
Very High				

ValueCreation™

Firms that generate economic profits with little operating variability score near the top right of the matrix.

Relative Valuation

	Forward P/E	PEG	Price / FV
Apple	29.8	2.4	85.0%
Alphabet	34.9	1.8	73.3%
Amazon.com	NMF	3.3	95.7%
Microsoft	31.6	2.5	91.6%
Peer Median	31.6	2.5	88.3%
Twitter	**-65.9**	**NMF**	**100.5%**

Price / FV = Current Stock Price divided by Estimated Fair Value

Financial Summary

	----- Actual -----		Projected
Fiscal Year End:	Dec-18	Dec-19	Dec-20
Revenue	3,042	3,459	3,612
Revenue, YoY%	24.5%	13.7%	4.4%
Non-GAAP Operating Income	453	366	-669
Non-GAAP EBIT %	14.9%	10.6%	-18.5%
Non-GAAP Net Income	1,206	1,466	-572
Non-GAAP NI Margin %	39.6%	42.4%	-15.8%
Non-GAAP Diluted EPS	1.56	1.87	-0.72
Non-GAAP Dil EPS, YoY %	-1157.9%	NMF	NMF
Non-GAAP Free Cash Flow	856	762	186
Non-GAAP FCF Margin %	28.1%	22.0%	5.1%

In Millions of USD (except for per share items)

Structure of the Internet Software & Services Industry   NEUTRAL

The Internet software/services industry is composed of a variety of companies with rapidly-changing business models. Most focus on improving the ways people connect with information, either via Internet search or by social media platforms, and generate revenue primarily by delivering cost-effective online advertising. Constituents earn significant returns on invested capital due to their capital-light operations, though competition remains fierce. We expect most companies in this group to look substantially different 10 years from now than they do today. Overall, we're neutral on the structure.

VALUENTUM

Texas Instruments TXN   FAIRLY VALUED

Buying Index™   6   Value Rating   ○

Economic Castle	Estimated Fair Value	Fair Value Range	Investment Style	Sector	Industry
Very Attractive	$147.00	$107.00 - $187.00	LARGE-CAP CORE	Information Technology	Technology Giants

We increased Texas Instruments' fair value estimate on the back of its improving outlook. Its 300mm chip offerings are very cost-competitive.

Stock Chart (weekly)

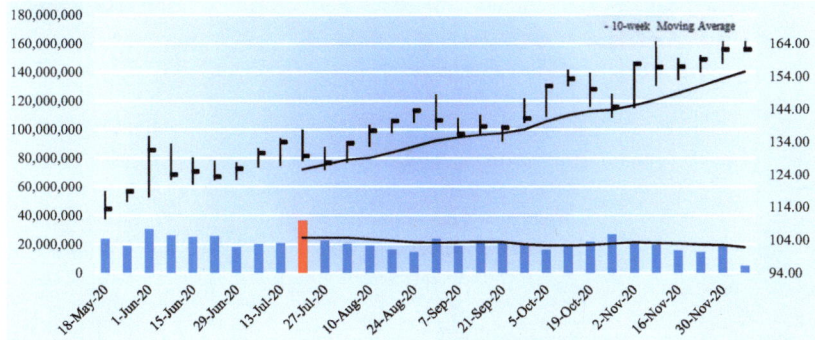

The week with the highest trading volume out of the last 30 weeks was a week of heavy selling, or distribution (red bar).

Investment Considerations

DCF Valuation	FAIRLY VALUED
Relative Valuation	NEUTRAL
ValueCreation™	EXCELLENT
ValueRisk™	MEDIUM
ValueTrend™	POSITIVE
Cash Flow Generation	STRONG
Financial Leverage	LOW
Growth	MODEST
Technical Evaluation	BULLISH
Relative Strength	STRONG
Money Flow Index (MFI)	NEUTRAL
Upside/Downside Volume (U/D)	DETERIORATING
Near-term Technical Support, 10-week MA	155.00

DCF = Discounted Cash Flow; MFI, U/D = Please see glossary. MA = Moving Average

Business Quality

	ValueCreation™			
ValueRisk™	Very Poor	Poor	Good	Excellent
Low				
Medium				▓
High				
Very High				

Firms that generate economic profits with little operating variability score near the top right of the matrix.

Company Vitals

Market Cap (USD)	$154,205
Avg Weekly Vol (30 wks)	20,646
30-week Range (USD)	110.26 - 164.63
Valuentum Sector	Information Technology
5-week Return	0.0%
13-week Return	17.1%
30-week Return	45.7%
Dividend Yield %	2.5%
Dividends per Share	4.08
Forward Dividend Payout Ratio	73.6%
Est. Normal Diluted EPS	7.18
P/E on Est. Normal Diluted EPS	22.6
Est. Normal EBITDA	9,127
Forward EV/EBITDA	21.0
EV/Est. Normal EBITDA	16.9
Forward Revenue Growth (5-yr)	6.5%
Forward EPS Growth (5-yr)	11.5%

NMF = Not Meaningful; Est. = Estimated; FY = Fiscal Year

Returns Summary

3-year Historical Average

Return on Equity	49.7%
Return on Assets	27.4%
ROIC, with goodwill	58.9%
ROIC, without goodwill	100.0%

ROIC = Return on Invested Capital; NMF = Not Meaningful

Leverage, Coverage, and Liquidity

In Millions of USD

Total Debt	5,803
Net Debt	416
Total Debt/EBITDA	0.8
Net Debt/EBITDA	0.1
EBITDA/Interest	41.3
Current Ratio	4.1
Quick Ratio	3.0

NMF = Not Meaningful

Investment Highlights

• Texas Instruments designs and makes semiconductors and sells them to electronics designers and manufacturers all over the world. It has four segments: Analog, Embedded Processing, Wireless and Other. The firm is #1 in analog and embedded combined, but it still has room to grow. It was founded in 1930 and is headquartered in Dallas, Texas.

• Over the long haul, Texas Instruments aims to convert 25%-35% of its annual revenues into free cash flow. To do so, the company's long-term goal is to spend ~6% of its annual revenues on capital expenditures. Inventory management is also key here.

• TI boasts a diverse product portfolio, but it faces intense competition from a long list of rivals: Analog Devices, Freescale Semi, Intersil Corp, and NXP Semi, among others. Pricing pressure will continue across much of its product line-up, but we're confident the company can navigate the landscape effectively, as it has done so effectively for the past 80+ years.

• Organic growth remains Texas Instruments' top priority for use of capital, and automotive and industrial R&D spending has led the way in recent years. The company's financials have held up relatively well so far during the COVID-19 pandemic, though serious headwinds remain.

• Rebounding automotive production and an uneven recovering in global industrial activity has improved Texas Instruments' medium-term outlook. The firm's outlook is supported by the cost-competitive nature of its 300mm chip offerings.

Relative Valuation

	Forward P/E	PEG	Price / FV
Apple	29.8	2.4	85.0%
Alphabet	34.9	1.8	73.3%
Amazon.com	NMF	3.3	95.7%
Microsoft	31.6	2.5	91.6%
Peer Median	31.6	2.5	88.3%
Texas Instruments	**29.2**	**2.7**	**110.2%**

Price / FV = Current Stock Price divided by Estimated Fair Value

Financial Summary

	----- Actual -----		Projected
Fiscal Year End:	Dec-18	Dec-19	Dec-20
Revenue	15,784	14,383	13,966
Revenue, YoY%	5.5%	-8.9%	-2.9%
Operating Income	6,713	5,975	6,318
Operating Margin %	42.5%	41.5%	45.2%
Net Income	5,580	5,017	5,226
Net Income Margin %	35.4%	34.9%	37.4%
Diluted EPS	5.64	5.27	5.54
Diluted EPS, YoY %	54.9%	-6.5%	5.2%
Free Cash Flow (CFO-capex)	6,058	5,802	6,280
Free Cash Flow Margin %	38.4%	40.3%	45.0%

In Millions of USD (except for per share items)

Structure of the Broad Line Semiconductor Industry   POOR

The broad line semiconductor industry is characterized by intense competition, rapid technological change, and frequent product introductions. The number and variety of computing devices have expanded rapidly, creating a connected landscape between suppliers and competitors. New market segments have emerged rapidly (smartphones, tablets), and constituents must continuously innovate to maintain share as traditional PC demand faces pressure. Though some firms may gain advantages via the combination of their manufacturing/test facilities with their design teams, we think the structure of the group is poor.

Uber UBER   FAIRLY VALUED

Buying Index™ 5   **Value Rating** ●

Economic Castle	Estimated Fair Value	Fair Value Range	Investment Style	Sector	Industry
Unattractive	$58.00	$29.00 - $87.00	LARGE-CAP BLEND	Next Generation	Disruptive Innovation

Losses continue to pile up at Uber. Our fair value estimate assumes the company is successful in the long run, something that is not guaranteed. Our large fair value estimate range reflects such uncertainty.

Stock Chart (weekly)

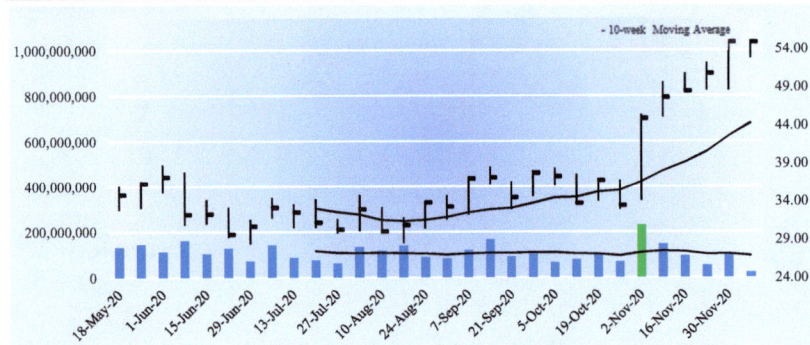

The week with the highest trading volume out of the last 30 weeks was a week of heavy selling, or distribution (red bar).

Company Vitals

Market Cap (USD)	$68,485
Avg Weekly Vol (30 wks)	106,824
30-week Range (USD)	28.39 - 54.86
Valuentum Sector	Next Generation
5-week Return	14.3%
13-week Return	47.9%
30-week Return	62.8%
Dividend Yield %	0.0%
Dividends per Share	0.00
Forward Dividend Payout Ratio	0.0%
Est. Normal Diluted EPS	-1.20
P/E on Est. Normal Diluted EPS	NMF
Est. Normal EBITDA	-1,964
Forward EV/EBITDA	-6.4
EV/Est. Normal EBITDA	-31.6
Forward Revenue Growth (5-yr)	19.4%
Forward EPS Growth (5-yr)	-167.2%

NMF = Not Meaningful; Est. = Estimated; FY = Fiscal Year

Returns Summary
3-year Historical Average

Return on Equity	-69.5%
Return on Assets	-14.3%
ROIC, with goodwill	-37.9%
ROIC, without goodwill	-38.4%

ROIC = Return on Invested Capital; NMF = Not Meaningful

Leverage, Coverage, and Liquidity
In Millions of USD

Total Debt	5,707
Net Debt	-6,360
Total Debt/EBITDA	NMF
Net Debt/EBITDA	NMF
EBITDA/Interest	-14.5
Current Ratio	2.5
Quick Ratio	NA

NMF = Not Meaningful

Investment Highlights

• Uber Tech first started in 2010 to make it easy for people to get a ride from point A to point B with the simple touch of a button. The company operates applications that connect consumers with independent drivers for ride sharing services. Its platform also connects consumers with restaurants for food delivery services. Uber has incurred billions in losses since its founding.

• The company has five operating segments: Rides, Eats, Freight, Other Bets, Advanced Technologies Group, and Other Technology Programs, the latter two focused on commercializing autonomous vehicle ridesharing solutions. Its Rides segment accounts for the vast majority of current revenue (~75%).

• The ridesharing and meal delivery businesses have low barriers to entry, and competition is intense. In its Rides segment, it competes with Lyft, OLA, Didi, and Taxify, while in its Eats segment, key rivals include GrubHub, DoorDash, and even Amazon, to an extent. Its business model and cost profile are also vulnerable to changing labor laws as it classifies its drivers as independent contractors (not employees).

• Operating losses continue to pile up at Uber, and at the end of 2019, the company had an accumulated deficit of $16.4 billion. Uber expects to continue to rack up losses in the near term as it continues to promote its platform. Our fair value estimate assumes Uber is successful in the long run, something that is not guaranteed.

• In December 2020, Uber acquired Postmates, an on-demand food delivery provider in all 50 states with a top share position in Los Angeles. The $2.65 billion all-stock tie-up unites Uber's global Rides and Eats businesses with Postmates' 'delivery-as-a-service' operations.

Investment Considerations

DCF Valuation	FAIRLY VALUED
Relative Valuation	NEUTRAL
ValueCreation™	VERY POOR
ValueRisk™	VERY HIGH
ValueTrend™	NEGATIVE
Cash Flow Generation	WEAK
Financial Leverage	LOW
Growth	AGGRESSIVE
Technical Evaluation	NEUTRAL
Relative Strength	STRONG
Money Flow Index (MFI)	OVERBOUGHT
Upside/Downside Volume (U/D)	BULLISH
Near-term Technical Support, 10-week MA	44.00

DCF = Discounted Cash Flow; MFI, U/D = Please see glossary. MA = Moving Average

Business Quality

ValueRisk™	Very Poor	Poor	Good	Excellent
Low				
Medium				
High				
Very High	■			

Firms that generate economic profits with little operating variability score near the top right of the matrix.

Relative Valuation

	Forward P/E	PEG	Price / FV
Wayfair	56.3	NMF	84.2%
Zoom Video	170.7	28.8	120.8%
Roku	-338.4	NMF	96.0%
Monster Beverage	36.0	2.9	104.4%
Peer Median	46.1	15.9	100.2%
Uber	**-14.1**	**NMF**	**94.6%**

Price / FV = Current Stock Price divided by Estimated Fair Value

Financial Summary

	----- Actual -----		Projected
Fiscal Year End:	Dec-18	Dec-19	Dec-20
Revenue	11,270	14,147	12,506
Revenue, YoY%	42.1%	25.5%	-11.6%
Operating Income	-3,033	-8,596	-10,158
Operating Margin %	-26.9%	-60.8%	-81.2%
Net Income	1,039	-8,472	-6,692
Net Income Margin %	9.2%	-59.9%	-53.5%
Diluted EPS	2.17	-6.79	-3.90
Diluted EPS, YoY %	-122.9%	-412.9%	-42.6%
Free Cash Flow (CFO-capex)	-2,099	-4,909	-5,101
Free Cash Flow Margin %	-18.6%	-34.7%	-40.8%

In Millions of USD (except for per share items)

Structure of the Internet Software & Services Industry
NEUTRAL

The Internet software/services industry is composed of a variety of companies with rapidly-changing business models. Most focus on improving the ways people connect with information, either via Internet search or by social media platforms, and generate revenue primarily by delivering cost-effective online advertising. Constituents earn significant returns on invested capital due to their capital-light operations, though competition remains fierce. We expect most companies in this group to look substantially different 10 years from now than they do today. Overall, we're neutral on the structure.

UnitedHealth Group UNH   FAIRLY VALUED

Buying Index™   7   **Value Rating**   ◯

Economic Castle	Estimated Fair Value	Fair Value Range	Investment Style	Sector	Industry
Very Attractive	$321.00	$241.00 - $401.00	MEGA-CAP CORE	Health Care	Health Care Bellwethers

We increased our fair value estimate for UnitedHealth Group on the back on strong forecasted revenue growth and margin expansion potential.

Stock Chart (weekly)

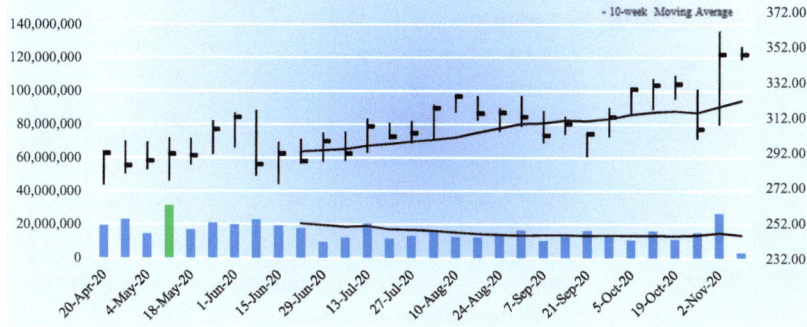

The week with the highest trading volume out of the last 30 weeks was a week of heavy selling, or distribution (red bar).

Investment Considerations

DCF Valuation	FAIRLY VALUED
Relative Valuation	ATTRACTIVE
ValueCreation™	EXCELLENT
ValueRisk™	MEDIUM
ValueTrend™	NEGATIVE
Cash Flow Generation	STRONG
Financial Leverage	MEDIUM
Growth	MODEST
Technical Evaluation	BULLISH
Relative Strength	WEAK
Money Flow Index (MFI)	NEUTRAL
Upside/Downside Volume (U/D)	BULLISH
Near-term Technical Support, 10-week MA	321.00

DCF = Discounted Cash Flow; MFI, U/D = Please see glossary. MA = Moving Average

Company Vitals

Market Cap (USD)	$335,646
Avg Weekly Vol (30 wks)	15,878
30-week Range (USD)	273.25 - 360.98
Valuentum Sector	Health Care
5-week Return	5.6%
13-week Return	8.1%
30-week Return	21.8%
Dividend Yield %	1.4%
Dividends per Share	5.00
Forward Dividend Payout Ratio	29.6%
Est. Normal Diluted EPS	21.73
P/E on Est. Normal Diluted EPS	16.0
Est. Normal EBITDA	32,074
Forward EV/EBITDA	14.1
EV/Est. Normal EBITDA	11.3
Forward Revenue Growth (5-yr)	6.8%
Forward EPS Growth (5-yr)	13.6%

NMF = Not Meaningful; Est. = Estimated; FY = Fiscal Year

Returns Summary   3-year Historical Average

Return on Equity	25.4%
Return on Assets	8.5%
ROIC, with goodwill	17.8%
ROIC, without goodwill	65.6%

ROIC = Return on Invested Capital; NMF = Not Meaningful

Leverage, Coverage, and Liquidity
In Millions of USD

Total Debt	40,678
Net Debt	26,433
Total Debt/EBITDA	1.8
Net Debt/EBITDA	1.2
EBITDA/Interest	13.1
Current Ratio	0.7
Quick Ratio	0.6

NMF = Not Meaningful

Investment Highlights

• UnitedHealth Group is a diversified healthcare and well-being company, and the firm provides health care benefits to a wide range of customers in an array of markets. Its two business platforms operate through four segments: UnitedHealthcare, OptumHealth, OptumInsight, and OptumRx. The company was founded in 1974 and is headquartered in Minnesota.

• The firm's UnitedHealthcare segment can be broken down into four operating divisions: Employer & Individual, Medicare & Retirement, Community & State, and Global. UnitedHealth is the largest health insurance provider in the US.

• Though UnitedHealth Group is a behemoth, it is not without its fair share of competition, which in its case comes from a variety of sources. Managed health care companies, insurance companies, HMOs, TPAs, PBMs, and business services outsourcing companies all provide similar services to any one of its businesses. The firm's significant scale is an advantage.

• UnitedHealth Group continued to be a free cash flow cow in 2020 and adeptly navigated headwinds created by the COVID-19 pandemic. The company's UnitedHealthcare and Optum businesses both posted solid revenue and operating income growth during the first three quarters of 2020.

• The company's Optum businesses, which focus on improving the healthcare system itself, have been performing extremely well of late. The firm was sued by the US DoJ over alleged Medicare overcharges, but most of those charges were dropped in 2018.

Business Quality   ValueCreation™

ValueRisk™	Very Poor	Poor	Good	Excellent
Low				
Medium				■
High				
Very High				

Firms that generate economic profits with little operating variability score near the top right of the matrix.

Relative Valuation

	Forward P/E	PEG	Price / FV
Johnson & Johnson	17.6	1.8	99.5%
Medtronic	25.6	2.2	109.0%
Merck	21.5	2.2	100.5%
Pfizer	20.1	0.8	93.3%
Peer Median	20.8	2.0	100.0%
UnitedHealth Group	**20.6**	**1.8**	**108.2%**

Price / FV = Current Stock Price divided by Estimated Fair Value

Financial Summary

	----- Actual -----		Projected
Fiscal Year End:	Dec-18	Dec-19	Dec-20
Revenue	226,247	242,155	256,684
Revenue, YoY%	12.5%	7.0%	6.0%
Operating Income	17,344	19,685	22,809
Operating Margin %	7.7%	8.1%	8.9%
Net Income	11,986	13,839	16,313
Net Income Margin %	5.3%	5.7%	6.4%
Diluted EPS	12.19	14.33	16.89
Diluted EPS, YoY %	13.8%	17.5%	17.9%
Free Cash Flow (CFO-capex)	13,650	16,392	18,037
Free Cash Flow Margin %	6.0%	6.8%	7.0%

In Millions of USD (except for per share items)

Structure of the Healthcare Services Industry   NEUTRAL

The healthcare services industry consists of firms that operate traditional hospitals, inpatient rehabilitation hospitals, and other specialized healthcare facilities. Demand for the group's services continues to increase as the US population ages and life expectancies rise. Inpatient rehabilitation care is growing at a 2-3% annual rate, while the expansion of patients with end stage renal disease continues at a slightly faster pace. Improvement in clinical practices and pharmacology and reimbursement policies of third-party payors have also impacted hospital utilization/occupancy. We're neutral on the group.

Visa V FAIRLY VALUED

Buying Index™ 6 **Value Rating** ◐

Economic Castle	Estimated Fair Value	Fair Value Range	Investment Style	Sector	Industry
Very Attractive	$219.00	$175.00 - $263.00	MEGA-CAP BLEND	Information Technology	Technology Giants

We moderately increased our fair value estimate for Visa as the company is well-positioned to capitalize on surging e-commerce demand.

Stock Chart (weekly)

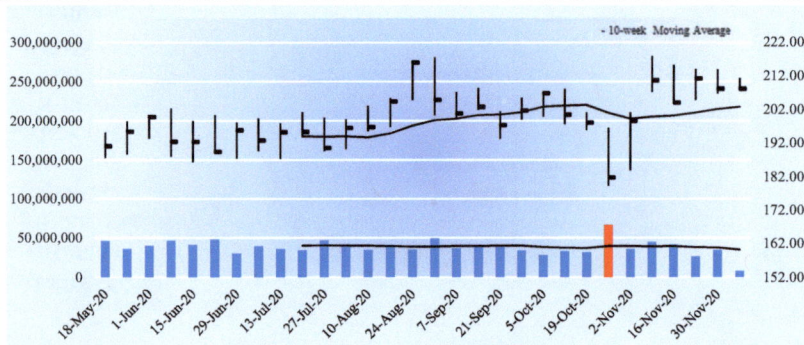

The week with the highest trading volume out of the last 30 weeks was a week of heavy selling, or distribution (red bar).

Investment Considerations

DCF Valuation	**FAIRLY VALUED**
Relative Valuation	**NEUTRAL**
ValueCreation™	**EXCELLENT**
ValueRisk™	**LOW**
ValueTrend™	**NEGATIVE**
Cash Flow Generation	**STRONG**
Financial Leverage	**MEDIUM**
Growth	**HIGH**
Technical Evaluation	**BULLISH**
Relative Strength	**NEUTRAL**
Money Flow Index (MFI)	**NEUTRAL**
Upside/Downside Volume (U/D)	**BEARISH**
Near-term Technical Support, 10-week MA	**203.00**

DCF = Discounted Cash Flow; MFI, U/D = Please see glossary. MA = Moving Average

Company Vitals

Market Cap (USD)	$462,495
Avg Weekly Vol (30 wks)	38,144
30-week Range (USD)	179.23 - 217.65
Valuentum Sector	Information Technology
5-week Return	-3.1%
13-week Return	2.3%
30-week Return	10.7%
Dividend Yield %	0.6%
Dividends per Share	1.28
Forward Dividend Payout Ratio	23.2%
Est. Normal Diluted EPS	8.44
P/E on Est. Normal Diluted EPS	24.6
Est. Normal EBITDA	21,934
Forward EV/EBITDA	30.6
EV/Est. Normal EBITDA	21.5
Forward Revenue Growth (5-yr)	12.7%
Forward EPS Growth (5-yr)	18.9%

NMF = Not Meaningful; Est. = Estimated; FY = Fiscal Year

Returns Summary *3-year Historical Average*

Return on Equity	38.3%
Return on Assets	15.4%
ROIC, with goodwill	34.4%
ROIC, without goodwill	55.9%

ROIC = Return on Invested Capital; NMF = Not Meaningful

Leverage, Coverage, and Liquidity
In Millions of USD

Total Debt	24,070
Net Debt	3,128
Total Debt/EBITDA	1.6
Net Debt/EBITDA	0.2
EBITDA/Interest	28.8
Current Ratio	1.9
Quick Ratio	1.6

NMF = Not Meaningful

Investment Highlights

• Visa is the largest retail electronic payments network based on payments volume, total volume and number of transactions. The company benefits from one of the strongest competitive advantages out there – the network effect. As more consumers use credit/debit cards, more merchants accept them, thereby creating a virtuous cycle.

• Visa is not a bank and does not issue credit cards. Visa takes on no credit risk--unlike American Express and Discover Financial--yet it is an integral part of the growing cashless society. Sales are primarily generated from payments volume on Visa-branded cards.

• Visa acquired Visa Europe through a transaction valued at $23+ billion back in June 2016 which unified the brand globally. Visa is in the process of acquiring Plaid for a total consideration of ~$5.3 billion, though the US DoJ has filed a civil antitrust lawsuit to prevent the deal from happening. Visa's growth outlook is promising with or without the Plaid deal closing.

• Visa is well-positioned to capitalize on the ongoing shift towards a cashless society. Surging e-commerce demand represents a major growth opportunity for Visa. Please note our cash flow models assume Visa significantly grows its revenues over the coming fiscal years, aided by secular growth tailwinds.

• Visa is a stellar company with a rock-solid cash flow profile, ample liquidity on hand, impressive operating margins, promising growth outlook and numerous competitive advantages. This company is one of the best operators in one of the strongest industries.

Business Quality *ValueCreation™*

ValueRisk™	Very Poor	Poor	Good	Excellent
Low				■
Medium				
High				
Very High				

Firms that generate economic profits with little operating variability score near the top right of the matrix.

Relative Valuation

	Forward P/E	PEG	Price / FV
Apple	29.8	2.4	85.0%
Alphabet	34.9	1.8	73.3%
Amazon.com	NMF	3.3	95.7%
Microsoft	31.6	2.5	91.6%
Peer Median	31.6	2.5	88.3%
Visa	**37.7**	**2.3**	**95.0%**

Price / FV = Current Stock Price divided by Estimated Fair Value

Financial Summary

	----- Actual -----		Projected
Fiscal Year End:	Sep-19	Sep-20	Sep-21
Revenue	22,977	21,846	23,222
Revenue, YoY%	11.5%	-4.9%	6.3%
Non-GAAP Operating Income	15,401	14,092	14,584
Non-GAAP EBIT %	67.0%	64.5%	62.8%
Net Income	12,080	10,866	11,958
Net Income Margin %	52.6%	49.7%	51.5%
Diluted EPS	5.32	4.89	5.51
Diluted EPS, YoY %	20.2%	-8.1%	12.8%
Free Cash Flow (CFO-capex)	12,028	9,704	14,709
Free Cash Flow Margin %	52.3%	44.4%	63.3%

In Millions of USD (except for per share items)

Structure of the Financial Tech Services Industry **EXCELLENT**

The financial tech services industry is primarily composed of firms that generate revenue by charging fees to customers for providing transaction processing and other payment-related services. Constituents operate in a rapidly-evolving legal/regulatory environment, particularly with respect to interchange fees, data protection, and information security. Several participants benefit from a significant competitive advantage – the network effect. As more consumers use credit/debit cards, more merchants accept them, thereby creating a virtuous cycle. The industry is one of the most attractive in our coverage.

VF Corp VFC   FAIRLY VALUED

Buying Index™   **6**   **Value Rating**   🌕

Economic Castle	Estimated Fair Value	Fair Value Range	Investment Style	Sector	Industry
Attractive	$87.00	$70.00 - $104.00	LARGE-CAP VALUE	Consumer Discretionary	Discretionary Spending

Its hard not to like VF Corp's top brands including The North Face, Vans, Timberland, and Wrangler. The company's dividend growth track record is excellent, and we expect it to continue.

Stock Chart (weekly)

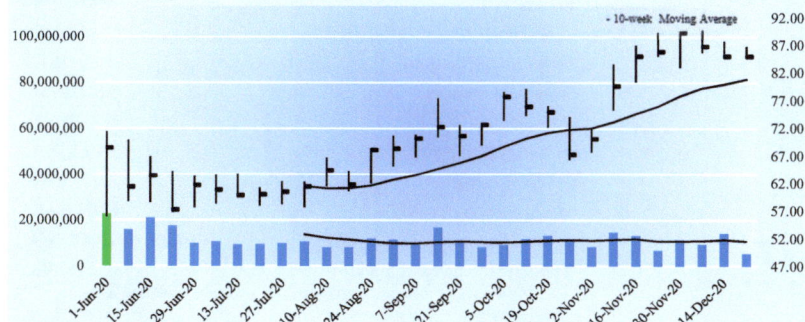

The week with the highest trading volume out of the last 30 weeks was a week of heavy selling, or distribution (red bar).

Investment Considerations

DCF Valuation	**FAIRLY VALUED**
Relative Valuation	**NEUTRAL**
ValueCreation™	**EXCELLENT**
ValueRisk™	**LOW**
ValueTrend™	**NEGATIVE**
Cash Flow Generation	**STRONG**
Financial Leverage	**MEDIUM**
Growth	**MODEST**
Technical Evaluation	**BULLISH**
Relative Strength	**STRONG**
Money Flow Index (MFI)	**NEUTRAL**
Upside/Downside Volume (U/D)	**DETERIORATING**
Near-term Technical Support, 10-week MA	**81.00**

DCF = Discounted Cash Flow; MFI, U/D = Please see glossary. MA = Moving Average

Business Quality

ValueRisk™	ValueCreation™			
	Very Poor	Poor	Good	Excellent
Low				▓
Medium				
High				
Very High				

Firms that generate economic profits with little operating variability score near the top right of the matrix.

Relative Valuation

	Forward P/E	PEG	Price / FV
Disney	104.2	NMF	117.1%
Home Depot	22.9	1.9	106.7%
McDonald's	38.5	1.1	111.0%
Nike	52.8	2.5	104.9%
Peer Median	45.6	1.9	108.9%
VF Corp	**31.7**	**3.4**	**97.6%**

Price / FV = Current Stock Price divided by Estimated Fair Value

Company Vitals

Market Cap (USD)	$33,927
Avg Weekly Vol (30 wks)	11,695
30-week Range (USD)	55.85 - 89.64
Valuentum Sector	Consumer Discretionary
5-week Return	-0.9%
13-week Return	18.2%
30-week Return	51.1%
Dividend Yield %	2.3%
Dividends per Share	1.96
Forward Dividend Payout Ratio	73.2%
Est. Normal Diluted EPS	2.73
P/E on Est. Normal Diluted EPS	31.1
Est. Normal EBITDA	1,609
Forward EV/EBITDA	22.8
EV/Est. Normal EBITDA	22.6
Forward Revenue Growth (5-yr)	2.5%
Forward EPS Growth (5-yr)	9.5%

NMF = Not Meaningful; Est. = Estimated; FY = Fiscal Year

Returns Summary
3-year Historical Average

Return on Equity	22.5%
Return on Assets	10.0%
ROIC, with goodwill	26.1%
ROIC, without goodwill	35.4%

ROIC = Return on Invested Capital; NMF = Not Meaningful

Leverage, Coverage, and Liquidity
In Millions of USD

Total Debt	2,923
Net Debt	2,357
Total Debt/EBITDA	1.8
Net Debt/EBITDA	1.5
EBITDA/Interest	16.4
Current Ratio	1.6
Quick Ratio	0.7

NMF = Not Meaningful

Investment Highlights

• VF Corp is an apparel and footwear powerhouse. The firm serves consumers with over 30 brands, multiple channels of distribution and geographies organized by five distinct coalitions: Outdoor & Actions Sports, Jeanswear, Imagewear, Sportswear and Contemporary Brands. The company traces its roots back to the 19th century.

• Its hard not to like the company's top brands including The North Face, Vans, Timberland, and Wrangler. However, US-China trade relations should be watched as ~11% of its cost of goods sold come directly to the US from China, and its jeans business has faced top-line pressure of late.

• VF Corp is targeting a 4%-6% revenue CAGR and an EPS CAGR of 10%-12% through 2021. It expects its sales channel breakdown to be 64% wholesale, 23% direct-to-consumer (DTC) stores, and 13% DTC digital in 2021, compared to 71% wholesale, 24% DTC stores, and 5% DTC digital in 2016. 85%+ of growth through 2021 is expected to be driven by growth in digital and owned DTC.

• VF Corp also expects margin expansion through 2021. It is targeting gross margin of 51.5% (220 basis points above 2016), 16% operating margin (210 bps above 2016), and ROIC of 20%+. Cumulative free cash flow for 2017-2021 is expected to be ~$8 billion, which it plans to return to shareholders via a 50/50 mix of dividends and buybacks.

• VF Corp recently acquired Williamson-Dickie Manufacturing, maker of Dickies work apparel, for $820 million. Though it is not a flashy business, the Dickies brand presents a relatively stable business with access to high growth sectors such as services and medical.

Financial Summary

	Actual		Projected
Fiscal Year End:	Mar-17	Mar-19	Mar-20
Revenue	11,811	12,181	10,448
Revenue, YoY%	-1.7%	3.1%	-14.2%
Operating Income	1,503	1,311	1,344
Operating Margin %	12.7%	10.8%	12.9%
Net Income	721	1,045	1,059
Net Income Margin %	6.1%	8.6%	10.1%
Diluted EPS	1.79	2.61	2.68
Diluted EPS, YoY %	-35.7%	46.2%	2.4%
Free Cash Flow (CFO-capex)	1,241	1,632	1,959
Free Cash Flow Margin %	10.5%	13.4%	18.7%

In Millions of USD (except for per share items)

Structure of the Luxury Goods Industry   **GOOD**

Luxury goods firms differentiate themselves based on brand name, perception, and quality in order to generate excess returns on invested capital through the economic cycle. Building a large, successful luxury brand is difficult, leaving those that possess them with intangible competitive advantages that are not easily overcome by new entrants. Growth in emerging middle classes and China will be the key demand drivers going forward, though the strongest brands will also grow successfully via market share gains. Though changes in consumer preferences should be watched closely, we like the structure of the group.

Verisk VRSK   FAIRLY VALUED

Buying Index™   **7**   **Value Rating** ○

Economic Castle	Estimated Fair Value	Fair Value Range	Investment Style	Sector	Industry
Very Attractive	$198.00	$149.00 - $248.00	LARGE-CAP CORE	Next Generation	Disruptive Innovation

Verisk's data analytics solutions continue to be in high demand, and the firm recently initiated a dividend.

Stock Chart (weekly)

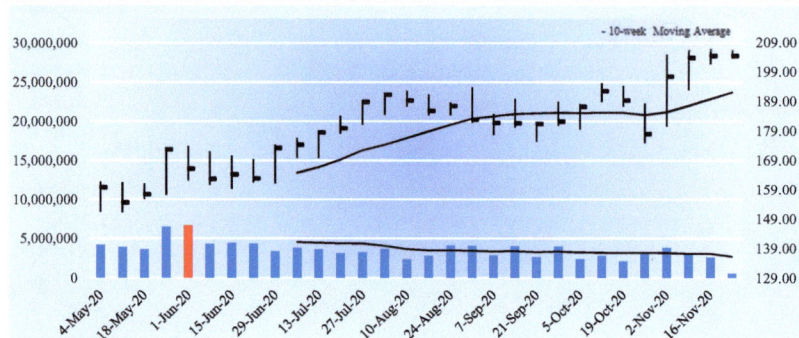

The week with the highest trading volume out of the last 30 weeks was a week of heavy selling, or distribution (red bar).

Investment Considerations

DCF Valuation	**FAIRLY VALUED**
Relative Valuation	**ATTRACTIVE**
ValueCreation™	**EXCELLENT**
ValueRisk™	**MEDIUM**
ValueTrend™	**POSITIVE**
Cash Flow Generation	**STRONG**
Financial Leverage	**MEDIUM**
Growth	**MODEST**
Technical Evaluation	**BULLISH**
Relative Strength	**STRONG**
Money Flow Index (MFI)	**NEUTRAL**
Upside/Downside Volume (U/D)	**DETERIORATING**
Near-term Technical Support, 10-week MA	**192.00**

DCF = Discounted Cash Flow; MFI, U/D = Please see glossary. MA = Moving Average

Company Vitals

Market Cap (USD)	$34,040
Avg Weekly Vol (30 wks)	3,535
30-week Range (USD)	151.18 - 206.83
Valuentum Sector	Next Generation
5-week Return	9.0%
13-week Return	9.3%
30-week Return	34.2%
Dividend Yield %	0.5%
Dividends per Share	1.08
Forward Dividend Payout Ratio	21.0%
Est. Normal Diluted EPS	6.71
P/E on Est. Normal Diluted EPS	30.5
Est. Normal EBITDA	1,821
Forward EV/EBITDA	24.7
EV/Est. Normal EBITDA	20.3
Forward Revenue Growth (5-yr)	8.1%
Forward EPS Growth (5-yr)	27.1%

NMF = Not Meaningful; Est. = Estimated; FY = Fiscal Year

Returns Summary
3-year Historical Average

Return on Equity	28.3%
Return on Assets	9.1%
ROIC, with goodwill	17.5%
ROIC, without goodwill	54.5%

ROIC = Return on Invested Capital; NMF = Not Meaningful

Leverage, Coverage, and Liquidity
In Millions of USD

Total Debt	3,151
Net Debt	2,966
Total Debt/EBITDA	3.1
Net Debt/EBITDA	2.9
EBITDA/Interest	8.0
Current Ratio	0.5
Quick Ratio	0.4

NMF = Not Meaningful

Investment Highlights

• Verisk is a leading source of information about risk. The firm offers risk-assessment services and decision analytics to professionals in many fields. Subscription revenue accounts for ~80% of its business and is typically secured under long-term contracts. Verisk has a strong business model.

• Verisk benefits from high customer retention, long-standing customer relationships, and high incremental margins. The firm's business model is 'build once, sell many times' with very little incremental cost to add a new customer.

• Verisk is targeting organic revenue growth of 7%-8% on average, over time, as well as organic EBITDA growth 1-2 percentage points faster than revenue growth, and double digit growth in adjusted EPS. Management expects its global presence, vertical expertise, contributory data, deeply integrated business model, and deal synergies to drive results.

• Verisk has a degree of revenue diversity, and it recently realigned its operating segments. Its 'Insurance' segment accounts for the largest portion of revenue, and its 'Energy & Specialized Markets' segment accounts for ~20% of revenue. 'Financial Services' makes up the balance.

• As of the third quarter of 2020, the company's debt/EBITDA stood at 2.26x. S&P, Moody's, and Fitch rate the firm investment grade (BBB/Baa2/BBB+). The company's target leverage is 2-3x.

Business Quality

ValueRisk™	Very Poor	Poor	Good	Excellent
Low				
Medium				■
High				
Very High				

ValueCreation™

Firms that generate economic profits with little operating variability score near the top right of the matrix.

Relative Valuation

	Forward P/E	PEG	Price / FV
Wayfair	56.3	NMF	84.2%
Zoom Video	170.7	28.8	120.8%
Roku	-338.4	NMF	96.0%
Monster Beverage	36.0	2.9	104.4%
Peer Median	46.1	15.9	100.2%
Verisk	**39.8**	**2.8**	**103.2%**

Price / FV = Current Stock Price divided by Estimated Fair Value

Financial Summary

	----- Actual -----		Projected
Fiscal Year End:	Dec-18	Dec-19	Dec-20
Revenue	2,395	2,607	2,787
Revenue, YoY%	11.6%	8.9%	6.9%
Operating Income	834	697	1,161
Operating Margin %	34.8%	26.7%	41.7%
Net Income	599	450	847
Net Income Margin %	25.0%	17.3%	30.4%
Diluted EPS	3.56	2.70	5.13
Diluted EPS, YoY %	8.1%	-24.1%	90.0%
Free Cash Flow (CFO-capex)	703	739	1,214
Free Cash Flow Margin %	29.4%	28.3%	43.6%

In Millions of USD (except for per share items)

Structure of the Financial Tech Services Industry   **EXCELLENT**

The financial tech services industry is primarily composed of firms that generate revenue by charging fees to customers for providing transaction processing and other payment-related services. Constituents operate in a rapidly-evolving legal/regulatory environment, particularly with respect to interchange fees, data protection, and information security. Several participants benefit from a significant competitive advantage – the network effect. As more consumers use credit/debit cards, more merchants accept them, thereby creating a virtuous cycle. The industry is one of the most attractive in our coverage.

VALUENTUM

VeriSign VRSN FAIRLY VALUED

Buying Index™ 7 **Value Rating** ○

Economic Castle	Estimated Fair Value	Fair Value Range	Investment Style	Sector	Industry
Highest Rated	$172.00	$129.00 - $215.00	LARGE-CAP CORE	Next Generation	Disruptive Innovation

Domain name registrations continue to advance at a steady clip, offering continued opportunities for VeriSign. The company generates strong free cash flow.

Stock Chart (weekly)

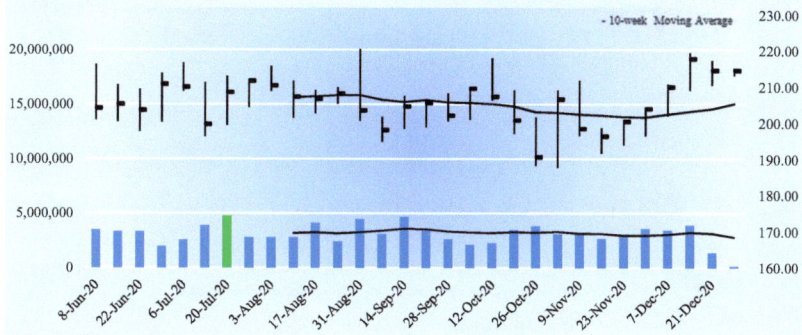

The week with the highest trading volume out of the last 30 weeks was a week of heavy selling, or distribution (red bar).

Investment Considerations

DCF Valuation	**FAIRLY VALUED**
Relative Valuation	**ATTRACTIVE**
ValueCreation™	**EXCELLENT**
ValueRisk™	**MEDIUM**
ValueTrend™	**NEGATIVE**
Cash Flow Generation	**STRONG**
Financial Leverage	**MEDIUM**
Growth	**MODEST**
Technical Evaluation	**BULLISH**
Relative Strength	**NEUTRAL**
Money Flow Index (MFI)	**NEUTRAL**
Upside/Downside Volume (U/D)	**BULLISH**
Near-term Technical Support, 10-week MA	**205.00**

DCF = Discounted Cash Flow; MFI, U/D = Please see glossary. MA = Moving Average

Company Vitals

Market Cap (USD)	$26,322
Avg Weekly Vol (30 wks)	3,081
30-week Range (USD)	187.83 - 220.51
Valuentum Sector	Next Generation
5-week Return	7.4%
13-week Return	6.0%
30-week Return	3.1%
Dividend Yield %	0.0%
Dividends per Share	0.00
Forward Dividend Payout Ratio	0.0%
Est. Normal Diluted EPS	6.38
P/E on Est. Normal Diluted EPS	33.7
Est. Normal EBITDA	1,075
Forward EV/EBITDA	29.7
EV/Est. Normal EBITDA	25.0
Forward Revenue Growth (5-yr)	5.5%
Forward EPS Growth (5-yr)	9.3%

NMF = Not Meaningful; Est. = Estimated; FY = Fiscal Year

Returns Summary
3-year Historical Average

Return on Equity	-40.0%
Return on Assets	20.0%
ROIC, with goodwill	171.6%
ROIC, without goodwill	200.0%

ROIC = Return on Invested Capital; NMF = Not Meaningful

Leverage, Coverage, and Liquidity
In Millions of USD

Total Debt	1,785
Net Debt	515
Total Debt/EBITDA	2.2
Net Debt/EBITDA	0.6
EBITDA/Interest	7.1
Current Ratio	1.4
Quick Ratio	1.3

NMF = Not Meaningful

Investment Highlights

• VeriSign powers the invisible navigation that takes people to where they want to go on the Internet. The firm operates the infrastructure for a portfolio of top-level domains that today include .com, .net, .tv, .edu, .gov, .jobs, .name and .cc. The company was founded in 1995 and is headquartered in Virginia. Most of its revenue is derived from registry services and from US customers.

• VeriSign's revenue and non-GAAP operating margin have showed steady improvement since early 2019. For one, quarterly revenue has jumped from under $150 million to over $300 million, while its non-GAAP operating margin has roughly doubled to 65%+.

• The firm is the exclusive registry of domain names within the .com, .net and .name generic top-level domains. Domain name registrations continue to advance at a nice and steady clip, with the base (.com/.net) standing at 163+ million, and VeriSign expects domain name base growth to remain resilient. Renewal rates have consistently been above 70% in recent years.

• The US National Telecommunications & Information Administration recently agreed to allow it to raise domain name prices by up to 7% in each of the last four years of a six year registry agreement. It recently extended its .net registry agreement with the DoC through mid-2023. Vertical integration is still forbidden.

• The outbreak of COVID-19 has accelerated the secular transition to e-commerce services, playing into VeriSign's wheelhouse. The company is significantly free cash flow positive, hauling in ~$714 million in 2019 and ~$661 million in 2018. Free cash flow will remain robust.

Business Quality
ValueCreation™

ValueRisk™	Very Poor	Poor	Good	Excellent
Low				
Medium				■
High				
Very High				

Firms that generate economic profits with little operating variability score near the top right of the matrix.

Relative Valuation

	Forward P/E	PEG	Price / FV
Wayfair	56.3	NMF	84.2%
Zoom Video	170.7	28.8	120.8%
Roku	-338.4	NMF	96.0%
Monster Beverage	36.0	2.9	104.4%
Peer Median	46.1	15.9	100.2%
VeriSign	**41.7**	**4.8**	**124.8%**

Price / FV = Current Stock Price divided by Estimated Fair Value

Financial Summary

	----- Actual -----		Projected
Fiscal Year End:	Dec-17	Dec-18	Dec-19
Revenue	1,165	1,215	1,219
Revenue, YoY%	2.0%	4.3%	0.4%
Operating Income	708	767	854
Operating Margin %	60.7%	63.2%	70.1%
Net Income	457	582	629
Net Income Margin %	39.2%	47.9%	51.6%
Diluted EPS	3.68	4.75	5.15
Diluted EPS, YoY %	7.7%	29.0%	8.5%
Free Cash Flow (CFO-capex)	653	661	714
Free Cash Flow Margin %	56.1%	54.4%	58.5%

In Millions of USD (except for per share items)

Structure of the Software (security) Industry
NEUTRAL

Participants in the software security industry focus on protecting important information wherever it resides—whether in servers, computers, mobile devices, or in the cloud. The space is intensely competitive, and some companies may offer their technology for free, engage in aggressive marketing, or pursue competitive partnerships. Firms also face indirect competition from application/operating system providers that may embed security solutions/functions in their own products. Participants must continuously develop new and enhanced services to meet changing customer demands. We're neutral on the group.

Vertex Pharma VRTX   FAIRLY VALUED

Buying Index™ 3   **Value Rating** ◐

Economic Castle	Estimated Fair Value	Fair Value Range	Investment Style	Sector	Industry
Very Attractive	$229.00	$137.00 - $321.00	LARGE-CAP BLEND	Health Care	Health Care Bellwethers

We moderately reduced our fair value estimate, though Vertex's growth outlook still looks bright.

Stock Chart (weekly)

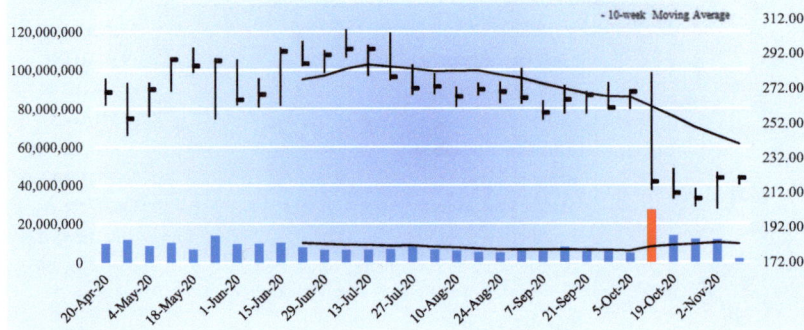

The week with the highest trading volume out of the last 30 weeks was a week of heavy selling, or distribution (red bar).

Company Vitals

Market Cap (USD)	$57,421
Avg Weekly Vol (30 wks)	8,564
30-week Range (USD)	202.57 - 306.07
Valuentum Sector	Health Care
5-week Return	-19.4%
13-week Return	-17.8%
30-week Return	-19.0%
Dividend Yield %	0.0%
Dividends per Share	0.00
Forward Dividend Payout Ratio	0.0%
Est. Normal Diluted EPS	9.60
P/E on Est. Normal Diluted EPS	22.9
Est. Normal EBITDA	3,410
Forward EV/EBITDA	25.2
EV/Est. Normal EBITDA	15.9
Forward Revenue Growth (5-yr)	18.8%
Forward EPS Growth (5-yr)	20.8%

NMF = Not Meaningful; Est. = Estimated; FY = Fiscal Year

Returns Summary

	3-year Historical Average
Return on Equity	30.9%
Return on Assets	20.5%
ROIC, with goodwill	35.0%
ROIC, without goodwill	37.8%

ROIC = Return on Invested Capital; NMF = Not Meaningful

Leverage, Coverage, and Liquidity

In Millions of USD

Total Debt	539
Net Debt	-3,269
Total Debt/EBITDA	0.4
Net Debt/EBITDA	NMF
EBITDA/Interest	22.2
Current Ratio	3.6
Quick Ratio	3.3

NMF = Not Meaningful

Investment Highlights

• Vertex discovers, develops, manufactures and commercializes small molecule drugs for patients with serious diseases. The company has obtained approval for four products that all treat certain forms of cystic fibrosis: TRIKAFTA, ORKAMBI, KALYDECO, and SYMDEKO. Vertex's long-term goal includes being able to treat up to 90% of cystic fibrosis patients.

• Vertex's efforts are primarily focused on cystic fibrosis and autoimmune diseases. The firm's drug pipeline includes treatments for sickle cell disease, beta-thalassemia, Type 1 diabetes, APOL1-mediated kidney diseases, pain management, and more.

• Vertex forecasts it will generate $6.0 billion - $6.2 billion in revenues from its cystic fibrosis products in 2020, aided by the launch of TRIKAFTA in the US. Vertex aims to broadly transform the treatment for cystic fibrosis. Clinical trials are underway to test out Vertex's cystic fibrosis treatments in children aged 2-5 and 6-11, which could significantly impact its outlook.

• Our cash flow models assume that Vertex's powerful revenue growth trajectory continues over the coming years, and that greater economies of scale leads to meaningful operating margin expansion. Should Vertex stumble for any reason, that would likely hurt its intrinsic value by a significant margin.

• Vertex's financial and operational performance has held up relatively well in the face of the COVID-19 pandemic. The firm benefits from its high quality cash flow profile. Its sizable free cash flows should allow Vertex to grow its cash balance over time.

Investment Considerations

DCF Valuation	FAIRLY VALUED
Relative Valuation	UNATTRACTIVE
ValueCreation™	EXCELLENT
ValueRisk™	HIGH
ValueTrend™	NEGATIVE
Cash Flow Generation	STRONG
Financial Leverage	LOW
Growth	AGGRESSIVE
Technical Evaluation	BEARISH
Relative Strength	WEAK
Money Flow Index (MFI)	NEUTRAL
Upside/Downside Volume (U/D)	BEARISH
Near-term Technical Resistance, 10-wk MA	240.00

DCF = Discounted Cash Flow; MFI, U/D = Please see glossary. MA = Moving Average

Business Quality

ValueRisk™	ValueCreation™			
	Very Poor	Poor	Good	Excellent
Low				
Medium				
High				▓
Very High				

Firms that generate economic profits with little operating variability score near the top right of the matrix.

Relative Valuation

	Forward P/E	PEG	Price / FV
Johnson & Johnson	17.6	1.8	99.5%
Medtronic	25.6	2.2	109.0%
Merck	21.5	2.2	100.5%
Pfizer	20.1	0.8	93.3%
Peer Median	20.8	2.0	100.0%
Vertex Pharma	**35.9**	**2.3**	**96.2%**

Price / FV = Current Stock Price divided by Estimated Fair Value

Financial Summary

	----- Actual -----		Projected
Fiscal Year End:	Dec-18	Dec-19	Dec-20
Revenue	3,048	4,163	6,374
Revenue, YoY%	22.5%	36.6%	53.1%
Operating Income	664	1,202	1,981
Operating Margin %	21.8%	28.9%	31.1%
Net Income	2,097	1,177	1,634
Net Income Margin %	68.8%	28.3%	25.6%
Diluted EPS	8.09	4.51	6.14
Diluted EPS, YoY %	NMF	NMF	NMF
Free Cash Flow (CFO-capex)	1,174	1,494	2,199
Free Cash Flow Margin %	38.5%	35.9%	34.5%

In Millions of USD (except for per share items)

Structure of the Pharma - Generic/Other - Industry   GOOD

The pharma (generic/other) industry is composed of makers of both brand and generic drugs. Intellectual property protection remains vital to the successful commercialization of safe/effective medicines, avoidance of pricing pressures, and offers brand firms competitive advantages over the life of such patents. Firms in the biotechnology industry face no certain future. Drug development is complex, difficult, and risky, and failure rates are high. Competition can be fierce when biosimilar products exist, though patents are material competitive advantages. We like the group, but the timing of expiration of patents should be watched closely.

Wayfair W   FAIRLY VALUED

Buying Index™   **3**   **Value Rating** ⬤

Economic Castle	Estimated Fair Value	Fair Value Range	Investment Style	Sector	Industry
Very Attractive	$300.00	$225.00 - $375.00	LARGE-CAP BLEND	Next Generation	Disruptive Innovation

Wayfair has carved out a niche and is disrupting the furniture and home goods market by capturing the secular shift from brick-and-mortar to online retail.

Stock Chart (weekly)

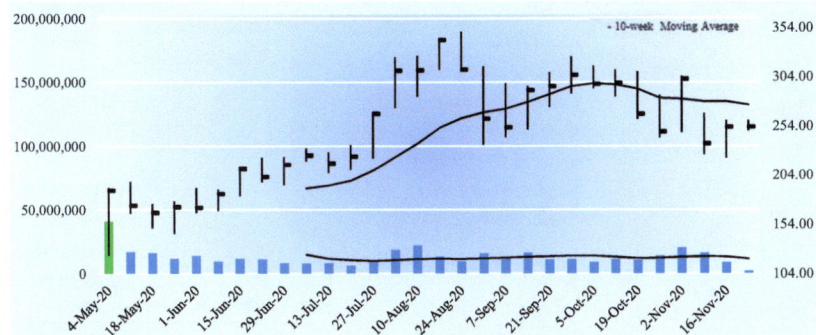

The week with the highest trading volume out of the last 30 weeks was a week of heavy selling, or distribution (red bar).

Investment Considerations

DCF Valuation	FAIRLY VALUED
Relative Valuation	NEUTRAL
ValueCreation™	EXCELLENT
ValueRisk™	MEDIUM
ValueTrend™	NEGATIVE
Cash Flow Generation	WEAK
Financial Leverage	LOW
Growth	AGGRESSIVE
Technical Evaluation	BEARISH
Relative Strength	WEAK
Money Flow Index (MFI)	NEUTRAL
Upside/Downside Volume (U/D)	DETERIORATING
Near-term Technical Resistance, 10-wk MA	275.00

DCF = Discounted Cash Flow; MFI, U/D = Please see glossary. MA = Moving Average

Business Quality

ValueRisk™	ValueCreation™			
	Very Poor	Poor	Good	Excellent
Low				
Medium				▨
High				
Very High				

Firms that generate economic profits with little operating variability score near the top right of the matrix.

Relative Valuation

	Forward P/E	PEG	Price / FV
Zoom Video	170.7	28.8	120.8%
Roku	-338.4	NMF	96.0%
Monster Beverage	36.0	2.9	104.4%
Lululemon	81.5	1.9	99.9%
Peer Median	58.7	2.9	102.2%
Wayfair	**56.3**	**NMF**	**84.2%**

Price / FV = Current Stock Price divided by Estimated Fair Value

Company Vitals

Market Cap (USD)	$23,284
Avg Weekly Vol (30 wks)	13,063
30-week Range (USD)	122.51 - 349.08
Valuentum Sector	Next Generation
5-week Return	-4.6%
13-week Return	-18.8%
30-week Return	102.5%
Dividend Yield %	0.0%
Dividends per Share	0.00
Forward Dividend Payout Ratio	0.0%
Est. Normal Diluted EPS	5.41
P/E on Est. Normal Diluted EPS	46.7
Est. Normal EBITDA	1,098
Forward EV/EBITDA	26.2
EV/Est. Normal EBITDA	21.6
Forward Revenue Growth (5-yr)	17.0%
Forward EPS Growth (5-yr)	-196.5%

NMF = Not Meaningful; Est. = Estimated; FY = Fiscal Year

Returns Summary   3-year Historical Average

Return on Equity	308.9%
Return on Assets	-32.8%
ROIC, with goodwill	26.2%
ROIC, without goodwill	26.3%

ROIC = Return on Invested Capital; NMF = Not Meaningful

Leverage, Coverage, and Liquidity
In Millions of USD

Total Debt	1,456
Net Debt	469
Total Debt/EBITDA	NMF
Net Debt/EBITDA	-0.7
EBITDA/Interest	-12.4
Current Ratio	0.9
Quick Ratio	NA

NMF = Not Meaningful

Investment Highlights

• Wayfair makes shopping for the home easy. The company has one of the largest online selections of home décor, including furniture, housewares, and other home accents. Wayfair's target customer is a 35- to 65- year old woman with above-average household income. Its offices are located in Boston, and the US is its largest market.

• Extensive experience in the home goods category, substantial investment in logistics and customer service, and the need to hold minimal inventory are key attributes of Wayfair's business model. The company thrives on convenience and value.

• The US home goods market is huge, estimated at nearly $300 billion, and offers Wayfair a long runway for continued growth. That said, traditional brick-and-mortar retail remains highly competitive. From Ashley Furniture, IKEA, Bed Bath and Beyond, and big box giants including Home Depot, Lowe's, Target and Walmart, the list of rivals is long.

• Increased engagement from existing customers will be key. It is estimated that more than half of Wayfair's orders in 2019 came from customers that have made three or more purchases before. It may be a matter of time before many more customers become comfortable with buying home goods online.

• In the long run, the company is guiding for 25%-27% gross margins and adjusted EBITDA margins in the range of 8-10%. We think its capital-efficient business model will lead to explosive growth in free cash flow.

Financial Summary

	----- Actual -----		Projected
Fiscal Year End:	Dec-18	Dec-19	Dec-20
Revenue	6,779	9,127	14,220
Revenue, YoY%	43.6%	34.6%	55.8%
Operating Income	-473	-930	545
Operating Margin %	-7.0%	-10.2%	3.8%
Net Income	-504	-985	420
Net Income Margin %	-7.4%	-10.8%	3.0%
Diluted EPS	-5.63	-10.68	4.48
Diluted EPS, YoY %	100.3%	89.5%	-142.0%
Free Cash Flow (CFO-capex)	-74	-469	1,172
Free Cash Flow Margin %	-1.1%	-5.1%	8.2%

In Millions of USD (except for per share items)

Structure of the Internet & Catalog Retail Industry   GOOD

The Internet and catalog retail industry benefits as a whole from the secular trend toward consumer digital (online) consumption. The industry consists of a number of exclusive online retailers led by Amazon, which continues to disrupt the broader retail space, and businesses that offer Internet travel services such as Booking Holdings, while online auctions are dominated by eBay. The industry generates high returns on investment due to minimal capital costs, but the landscape will be vastly different in the decades ahead. Still, we like the group.

Wal-Mart WMT   OVERVALUED 8%

Buying Index™ 4   **Value Rating** ✕

Economic Castle	Estimated Fair Value	Fair Value Range	Investment Style	Sector	Industry
Attractive	$111.00	$89.00 - $133.00	MEGA-CAP CORE	Consumer Staples	Recession Resistant

Wal-Mart recently launched its Walmart+ membership program which includes free home delivery services and discounts at its fuel stations.

Stock Chart (weekly)

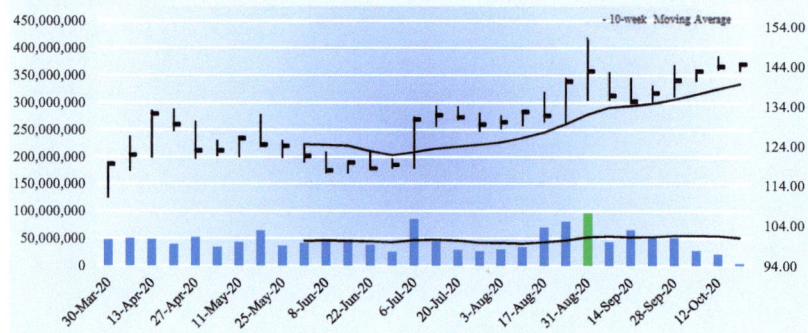

The week with the highest trading volume out of the last 30 weeks was a week of heavy selling, or distribution (red bar).

Investment Considerations

DCF Valuation	**OVERVALUED**
Relative Valuation	**UNATTRACTIVE**
ValueCreation™	**EXCELLENT**
ValueRisk™	**LOW**
ValueTrend™	**NEGATIVE**
Cash Flow Generation	**MEDIUM**
Financial Leverage	**MEDIUM**
Growth	**MODEST**
Technical Evaluation	**BULLISH**
Relative Strength	**NEUTRAL**
Money Flow Index (MFI)	**NEUTRAL**
Upside/Downside Volume (U/D)	**BULLISH**
Near-term Technical Support, 10-week MA	**140.00**

DCF = Discounted Cash Flow; MFI, U/D = Please see glossary. MA = Moving Average

Company Vitals

Market Cap (USD)	$414,483
Avg Weekly Vol (30 wks)	45,640
30-week Range (USD)	110.94 - 151.33
Valuentum Sector	Consumer Staples
5-week Return	5.9%
13-week Return	10.4%
30-week Return	29.2%
Dividend Yield %	1.5%
Dividends per Share	2.16
Forward Dividend Payout Ratio	40.1%
Est. Normal Diluted EPS	6.71
P/E on Est. Normal Diluted EPS	21.5
Est. Normal EBITDA	38,915
Forward EV/EBITDA	13.5
EV/Est. Normal EBITDA	11.8
Forward Revenue Growth (5-yr)	2.9%
Forward EPS Growth (5-yr)	13.7%

NMF = Not Meaningful; Est. = Estimated; FY = Fiscal Year

Returns Summary
3-year Historical Average

Return on Equity	13.7%
Return on Assets	4.8%
ROIC, with goodwill	17.1%
ROIC, without goodwill	21.4%

ROIC = Return on Invested Capital; NMF = Not Meaningful

Leverage, Coverage, and Liquidity
In Millions of USD

Total Debt	54,469
Net Debt	45,004
Total Debt/EBITDA	1.7
Net Debt/EBITDA	1.4
EBITDA/Interest	12.1
Current Ratio	0.8
Quick Ratio	0.2

NMF = Not Meaningful

Investment Highlights

• Wal-Mart operates retail stores. Its Wal-Mart US segment includes the company's mass merchant concept in the US. The firm recently launched its Wal-Mart+ membership program. Its Wal-Mart International segment consists of the company's operations outside of the US. The Sam's Club segment includes warehouse membership clubs and samsclub.com.

• Wal-Mart's business proved resilient during the initial phases of the COVID-19 pandemic as its domestic comparable store sales surged higher, supported by elevated demand for consumer staples products. The firm is well-positioned to ride out the storm.

• Gross margin pressures such as higher transportation costs, price investments, and mix effects from its growing e-commerce business are likely to persist in the near-term. The company is shifting its focus from store count growth to remodeling and supporting its digital initiatives as it works to keep its massive store base relevant and competitive.

• In 2018, Wal-Mart paid ~$16 billion for a 77% stake in Flipkart, an innovative e-commerce firm in India. Two years later, Wal-Mart sold Wal-Mart India to Flipkart, which enabled Flipkart to launch the Flipkart Wholesale digital marketplace. Wal-Mart's operations in India have a long growth runway.

• Over the past few years, Wal-Mart invested heavily in its domestic omni-channel sales capabilities. Wal-Mart US saw its e-commerce sales grow by 97% year-over-year in the second quarter of fiscal 2021, with strong demand seen across all sales channels.

Business Quality
ValueCreation™

ValueRisk™	Very Poor	Poor	Good	Excellent
Low				■
Medium				
High				
Very High				

Firms that generate economic profits with little operating variability score near the top right of the matrix.

Relative Valuation

	Forward P/E	PEG	Price / FV
Anheuser-Busch InBev	27.2	0.5	101.7%
Coca-Cola	34.3	1.5	128.0%
Procter & Gamble	26.5	3.3	144.1%
Philip Morris	15.4	2.4	104.3%
Peer Median	26.8	2.0	116.1%
Wal-Mart	**26.8**	**2.3**	**130.2%**

Price / FV = Current Stock Price divided by Estimated Fair Value

Financial Summary

	----- Actual -----		Projected
Fiscal Year End:	Jan-19	Jan-20	Jan-21
Revenue	514,405	523,964	549,638
Revenue, YoY%	2.8%	1.9%	4.9%
Operating Income	21,957	20,568	22,605
Operating Margin %	4.3%	3.9%	4.1%
Net Income	6,670	12,923	15,285
Net Income Margin %	1.3%	2.5%	2.8%
Diluted EPS	2.26	4.51	5.38
Diluted EPS, YoY %	-30.9%	98.9%	19.5%
Free Cash Flow (CFO-capex)	17,409	14,550	19,500
Free Cash Flow Margin %	3.4%	2.8%	3.5%

In Millions of USD (except for per share items)

Structure of the Food Retailers Industry   NEUTRAL

Firms in the mature food retailers industry generally have slim profit margins and face significant competition from brick-and-mortar locations (discount, department, drug, dollar, warehouse clubs and supermarkets) as well as Internet-based retailers (including Amazon). Though the industry is not terribly cyclical, economic conditions, disposable income, credit availability, fuel prices, and unemployment levels drive ticket size and traffic trends. Offering consumers a compelling value proposition is a must, even as higher-priced organic food offerings proliferate. We're generally neutral on the group.

Slack Tech WORK   FAIRLY VALUED

Buying Index™   **6**   **Value Rating** ●

Economic Castle	Estimated Fair Value	Fair Value Range	Investment Style	Sector	Industry
Attractive	$45.00	$34.00 - $56.00	LARGE-CAP BLEND	Next Generation	Disruptive Innovation

We've raised our fair value estimate of Slack to account for it being bought out by Salesforce. Slack shareholders will receive ~$27 in cash and 0.0776 Salesforce shares per share of Slack owned.

Stock Chart (weekly)

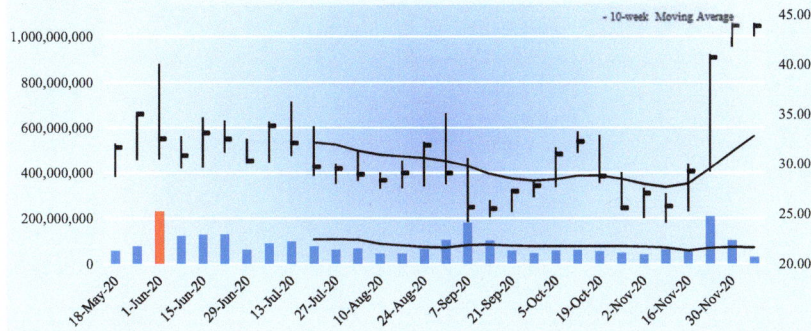

The week with the highest trading volume out of the last 30 weeks was a week of heavy selling, or distribution (red bar).

Investment Considerations

DCF Valuation	**FAIRLY VALUED**
Relative Valuation	**NEUTRAL**
ValueCreation™	**VERY POOR**
ValueRisk™	**MEDIUM**
ValueTrend™	**POSITIVE**
Cash Flow Generation	**WEAK**
Financial Leverage	**LOW**
Growth	**AGGRESSIVE**
Technical Evaluation	**BULLISH**
Relative Strength	**STRONG**
Money Flow Index (MFI)	**NEUTRAL**
Upside/Downside Volume (U/D)	**BULLISH**
Near-term Technical Support, 10-week MA	**33.00**

DCF = Discounted Cash Flow; MFI, U/D = Please see glossary. MA = Moving Average

Company Vitals

Market Cap (USD)	$17,512
Avg Weekly Vol (30 wks)	84,982
30-week Range (USD)	24.09 - 44.15
Valuentum Sector	Next Generation
5-week Return	71.3%
13-week Return	68.6%
30-week Return	40.2%
Dividend Yield %	0.0%
Dividends per Share	0.00
Forward Dividend Payout Ratio	0.0%
Est. Normal Diluted EPS	0.20
P/E on Est. Normal Diluted EPS	214.9
Est. Normal EBITDA	141
Forward EV/EBITDA	-676.8
EV/Est. Normal EBITDA	118.6
Forward Revenue Growth (5-yr)	27.9%
Forward EPS Growth (5-yr)	-188.2%

NMF = Not Meaningful; Est. = Estimated; FY = Fiscal Year

Returns Summary   3-year Historical Average

Return on Equity	-35.3%
Return on Assets	-22.3%
ROIC, with goodwill	-26.7%
ROIC, without goodwill	-30.4%

ROIC = Return on Invested Capital; NMF = Not Meaningful

Leverage, Coverage, and Liquidity

In Millions of USD

Total Debt	0
Net Debt	-769
Total Debt/EBITDA	0.0
Net Debt/EBITDA	NMF
EBITDA/Interest	NMF
Current Ratio	1.9
Quick Ratio	NA

NMF = Not Meaningful

Investment Highlights

- Slack is a channels-based messaging platform that is used to replace email within an enterprise or organization. The company's platform can be used in a countless number of tasks in the work environment, from reviewing job candidates to organizing disaster response plans and beyond. Its principal executive offices are in San Francisco.

- The company generates revenue primarily through subscriptions for Slack based on number of users. It has over 100,000 paying customers with three or more users, and hundreds of thousands more on its free subsription plan.

- Slack's platform solves a big problem. With traditional email, information is housed within individual inboxes, which limits team collaboration. With Slack's platform, the application allows records of conversations and workflows, and this helps retain valuable historical information as people join or leave a project.

- Slack's category is a relatively new one within the tech landscape. To achieve vast success, the company's platform has to disrupt entrenched players such as Microsoft, Google, Facebook, as well as communications providers such as Cisco. This won't be easy.

- The future may be incredibly bright for Slack, but current realities show a company that has incurred net losses since inception, including a massive $568.4 million loss in fiscal 2020. Its targeting free cash flow to be breakeven in fiscal 2021, however.

Business Quality   ValueCreation™

ValueRisk™	Very Poor	Poor	Good	Excellent
Low				
Medium	■			
High				
Very High				

Firms that generate economic profits with little operating variability score near the top right of the matrix.

Relative Valuation

	Forward P/E	PEG	Price / FV
Wayfair	56.3	NMF	84.2%
Zoom Video	170.7	28.8	120.8%
Roku	-338.4	NMF	96.0%
Monster Beverage	36.0	2.9	104.4%
Peer Median	46.1	15.9	100.2%
Slack Tech	**-361.7**	**NMF**	**97.4%**

Price / FV = Current Stock Price divided by Estimated Fair Value

Financial Summary

	----- Actual -----		Projected
Fiscal Year End:	Jan-19	Jan-20	Jan-21
Revenue	401	630	878
Revenue, YoY%	81.6%	57.4%	39.2%
Operating Income	-154	-588	-71
Operating Margin %	-38.5%	-93.3%	-8.1%
Net Income	-139	-568	-49
Net Income Margin %	-34.7%	-90.2%	-5.6%
Diluted EPS	-1.14	-1.42	-0.12
Diluted EPS, YoY %	0.1%	24.7%	-91.5%
Free Cash Flow (CFO-capex)	-97	-62	-63
Free Cash Flow Margin %	-24.3%	-9.8%	-7.2%

In Millions of USD (except for per share items)

Structure of the Internet & Catalog Retail Industry   GOOD

The Internet and catalog retail industry benefits as a whole from the secular trend toward consumer digital (online) consumption. The industry consists of a number of exclusive online retailers led by Amazon, which continues to disrupt the broader retail space, and businesses that offer Internet travel services such as Booking Holdings, while online auctions are dominated by eBay. The industry generates high returns on investment due to minimal capital costs, but the landscape will be vastly different in the decades ahead. Still, we like the group.

Williams-Sonoma WSM   FAIRLY VALUED

Buying Index™   7   Value Rating ◐

Economic Castle	Estimated Fair Value	Fair Value Range	Investment Style	Sector	Industry
Attractive	$117.00	$94.00 - $140.00	MID-CAP VALUE	Consumer Discretionary	Discretionary Spending

A key factor in Williams-Sonoma's omni-channel success is its exclusive product and lifestyle merchandising. Upcoming niche online marketplace ETSY is a key rival to watch, however.

Stock Chart (weekly)

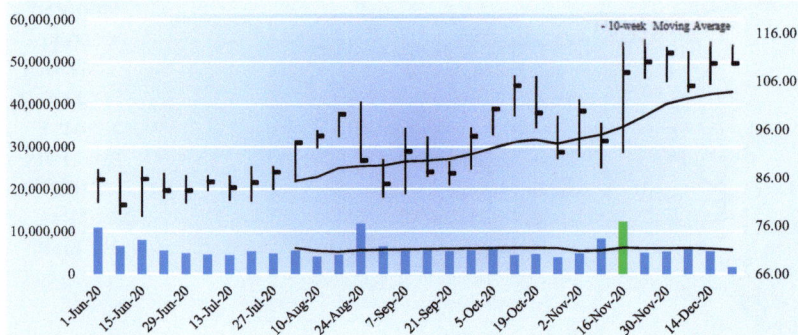

The week with the highest trading volume out of the last 30 weeks was a week of heavy selling, or distribution (red bar).

Investment Considerations

DCF Valuation	FAIRLY VALUED
Relative Valuation	ATTRACTIVE
ValueCreation™	EXCELLENT
ValueRisk™	LOW
ValueTrend™	NEGATIVE
Cash Flow Generation	STRONG
Financial Leverage	LOW
Growth	MODEST
Technical Evaluation	BULLISH
Relative Strength	STRONG
Money Flow Index (MFI)	NEUTRAL
Upside/Downside Volume (U/D)	BULLISH
Near-term Technical Support, 10-week MA	104.00

DCF = Discounted Cash Flow; MFI, U/D = Please see glossary. MA = Moving Average

Business Quality

ValueRisk™	Very Poor	Poor	Good	Excellent
Low				▨
Medium				
High				
Very High				

ValueCreation™

Firms that generate economic profits with little operating variability score near the top right of the matrix.

Company Vitals

Market Cap (USD)	$9,028
Avg Weekly Vol (30 wks)	5,876
30-week Range (USD)	77.79 - 114.65
Valuentum Sector	Consumer Discretionary
5-week Return	2.2%
13-week Return	24.8%
30-week Return	32.1%
Dividend Yield %	1.9%
Dividends per Share	2.12
Forward Dividend Payout Ratio	43.8%
Est. Normal Diluted EPS	7.61
P/E on Est. Normal Diluted EPS	14.4
Est. Normal EBITDA	994
Forward EV/EBITDA	12.7
EV/Est. Normal EBITDA	9.0
Forward Revenue Growth (5-yr)	5.0%
Forward EPS Growth (5-yr)	15.8%

NMF = Not Meaningful; Est. = Estimated; FY = Fiscal Year

Returns Summary   3-year Historical Average

Return on Equity	24.8%
Return on Assets	11.4%
ROIC, with goodwill	32.2%
ROIC, without goodwill	32.5%

ROIC = Return on Invested Capital; NMF = Not Meaningful

Leverage, Coverage, and Liquidity
In Millions of USD

Total Debt	300
Net Debt	-39
Total Debt/EBITDA	0.5
Net Debt/EBITDA	NMF
EBITDA/Interest	93.2
Current Ratio	1.6
Quick Ratio	0.4

NMF = Not Meaningful

Investment Highlights

- Williams-Sonoma is a multi-channel specialty retailer of high quality products for the home. Its brands include Williams-Sonoma, Pottery Barn, Pottery Barn Kids, West Elm, PBteen, Rejuvenation, and Mark and Graham. The company was founded in 1956 and is headquartered in San Francisco, California.

- A key factor in Williams-Sonoma's omni-channel success is its exclusive product and lifestyle merchandising. Almost all of the products the firm sells are directly sourced, offering a unique point of view on taste and style in addition to industry leading margins.

- One of the areas at Williams-Sonoma that we're huge fans of is its e-commerce operations. The company now generates more than half of its sales from that channel, a key competitive advantage. Omni-channel customers spend 5 times more than single-channel customers. Its e-commerce revenue has grown at a ~25% CAGR since 2000, and it carries a ~20% operating margin.

- Williams-Sonoma is a solid free cash flow generator, and its balance sheet is very healthy. Roughly 85% of sales in the home furnishing industry are still done in physical stores, but it is working to increase brand awareness and expand reach via digital ads. Rival ETSY is worth watching closely, however.

- The company retains a strong portfolio of brands, and we view its global supply chain as a competitive advantage. The firm has multiple opportunities to grow through brand extensions. Its vertical integration allows it to generate industry-leading gross margins.

Relative Valuation

	Forward P/E	PEG	Price / FV
Disney	104.2	NMF	117.1%
Home Depot	22.9	1.9	106.7%
McDonald's	38.5	1.1	111.0%
Nike	52.8	2.5	104.9%
Peer Median	45.6	1.9	108.9%
Williams-Sonoma	**22.7**	**1.7**	**93.7%**

Price / FV = Current Stock Price divided by Estimated Fair Value

Financial Summary

	----- Actual -----		Projected
Fiscal Year End:	Jan-18	Jan-19	Jan-20
Revenue	5,292	5,672	5,898
Revenue, YoY%	4.1%	7.2%	4.0%
Operating Income	454	436	510
Operating Margin %	8.6%	7.7%	8.6%
Net Income	260	334	392
Net Income Margin %	4.9%	5.9%	6.7%
Diluted EPS	3.02	4.05	4.84
Diluted EPS, YoY %	-11.7%	34.4%	19.4%
Free Cash Flow (CFO-capex)	310	396	431
Free Cash Flow Margin %	5.9%	7.0%	7.3%

In Millions of USD (except for per share items)

Structure of the Specialty Retailers Industry   NEUTRAL

The specialty retail segment is fragmented, highly competitive, and economically-sensitive. The group covers a broad array of businesses and is dominated by retailers with large brick-and-mortar store footprints. Though some constituents may be insulated from e-commerce competition, others risk obsolescence as product distribution moves to digital means, and online retailers offer lower prices for identical goods and services. We're fairly neutral on the structure of the industry, though some constituents will inevitably face secular and permanent declines.

Zimmer Biomet ZBH FAIRLY VALUED

Buying Index™ 3   **Value Rating** 🟡

Economic Castle	Estimated Fair Value	Fair Value Range	Investment Style	Sector	Industry
Attractive	$135.00	$108.00 - $162.00	LARGE-CAP CORE	Health Care	Health Care Bellwethers

We reduced our fair value estimate for Zimmer Biomet due to the significant headwinds created by the COVID-19 pandemic.

Stock Chart (weekly)

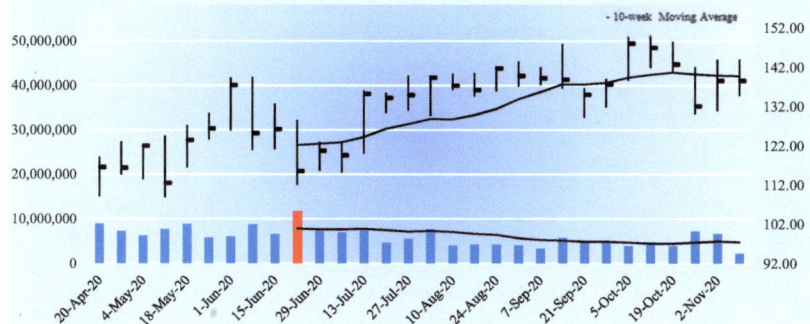

The week with the highest trading volume out of the last 30 weeks was a week of heavy selling, or distribution (red bar).

Company Vitals

Market Cap (USD)	$28,632
Avg Weekly Vol (30 wks)	6,056
30-week Range (USD)	108.77 - 150.08
Valuentum Sector	Health Care
5-week Return	-7.7%
13-week Return	0.6%
30-week Return	18.9%
Dividend Yield %	0.7%
Dividends per Share	0.96
Forward Dividend Payout Ratio	45.3%
Est. Normal Diluted EPS	7.98
P/E on Est. Normal Diluted EPS	17.4
Est. Normal EBITDA	2,966
Forward EV/EBITDA	24.6
EV/Est. Normal EBITDA	11.7
Forward Revenue Growth (5-yr)	4.2%
Forward EPS Growth (5-yr)	14.8%

NMF = Not Meaningful; Est. = Estimated; FY = Fiscal Year

Returns Summary
3-year Historical Average

Return on Equity	7.7%
Return on Assets	3.3%
ROIC, with goodwill	10.8%
ROIC, without goodwill	19.7%

ROIC = Return on Invested Capital; NMF = Not Meaningful

Leverage, Coverage, and Liquidity
In Millions of USD

Total Debt	6,721
Net Debt	6,103
Total Debt/EBITDA	3.0
Net Debt/EBITDA	2.7
EBITDA/Interest	10.0
Current Ratio	1.4
Quick Ratio	0.6

NMF = Not Meaningful

Investment Highlights

• Zimmer Biomet produces orthopedic reconstructive devices, spinal and trauma devices, biologics, dental implants, and related surgical products in the Americas, Europe, and Asia Pacific. The firm has been around for more than 85 years and is headquartered in northern Indiana. It was formed as a result of the merger of Zimmer and Biomet in 2015.

• There are multiple drivers of long-term sustainable growth present for Zimmer Biomet such as favorable global demographics (65+ age group growing), penetration opportunity in developed markets, and expanding access to healthcare in emerging markets.

• Knees, hips, S.E.T (sports medicine, extremities and trauma), and Dental, Spine & CMFT (craniomaxillofacial and thoracic) are Zimmer Biomet's four largest markets in terms of revenue generation. Recently, net sales at these business segments have faced significant headwinds due to the COVID-19 pandemic delaying elective surgeries.

• Zimmer Biomet has remained acquisitive since the big merger, though the acquisitions have been of the smaller, tuck-in variety. Some examples include the purchase of a Dutch developer of 3D range of motion technology and a musculoskeletal diagnostics testing firm. Its M&A is likely to continue going forward.

• The COVID-19 outbreak has resulted in the deferral of demand for elective surgeries. Zimmer Biomet is feeling the pain, but pent-up demand is looming on the other side of the pandemic. Significant near-term headwinds remain.

Investment Considerations

DCF Valuation	FAIRLY VALUED
Relative Valuation	UNATTRACTIVE
ValueCreation™	EXCELLENT
ValueRisk™	LOW
ValueTrend™	NEGATIVE
Cash Flow Generation	STRONG
Financial Leverage	MEDIUM
Growth	MODEST
Technical Evaluation	VERY BEARISH
Relative Strength	WEAK
Money Flow Index (MFI)	NEUTRAL
Upside/Downside Volume (U/D)	BEARISH
Near-term Technical Resistance, 10-wk MA	140.00

DCF = Discounted Cash Flow; MFI, U/D = Please see glossary. MA = Moving Average

Business Quality

	ValueCreation™			
ValueRisk™	Very Poor	Poor	Good	Excellent
Low				■
Medium				
High				
Very High				

Firms that generate economic profits with little operating variability score near the top right of the matrix.

Relative Valuation

	Forward P/E	PEG	Price / FV
Johnson & Johnson	17.6	1.8	99.5%
Medtronic	25.6	2.2	109.0%
Merck	21.5	2.2	100.5%
Pfizer	20.1	0.8	93.3%
Peer Median	20.8	2.0	100.0%
Zimmer Biomet	NMF	NMF	102.6%

Price / FV = Current Stock Price divided by Estimated Fair Value

Financial Summary

	----- Actual -----		Projected
Fiscal Year End:	Dec-18	Dec-19	Dec-20
Revenue	7,933	7,982	6,825
Revenue, YoY%	1.4%	0.6%	-14.5%
Non-GAAP Operating Income	1,743	1,270	754
Non-GAAP EBIT %	22.0%	15.9%	11.1%
Non-GAAP Net Income	-379	1,132	438
Non-GAAP NI Margin %	-4.8%	14.2%	6.4%
Non-GAAP Diluted EPS	-1.86	5.47	2.12
Non-GAAP Dil EPS, YoY %	-120.9%	-393.8%	-61.3%
Non-GAAP FCF (CFO-capex)	1,309	1,063	634
Non-GAAP FCF Margin %	16.5%	13.3%	9.3%

In Millions of USD (except for per share items)

Structure of the Medical Devices Industry   GOOD

The medical devices industry is heavily regulated and characterized by rapid technological change. Firms have been forced to compete on price due to economically-motivated buyers, consolidation among healthcare providers, and declining reimbursement rates. Healthcare reform measures have put additional pressure on procedure rates and market sizes. Still, firms can gain advantages by developing products with differentiated clinical outcomes or by creating patent-protected technology. Since most constituents hold important patents or trade secrets, we tend to like the group.

Zoom Video ZM   FAIRLY VALUED

Buying Index™ 3   **Value Rating** 🟡

Economic Castle	Estimated Fair Value	Fair Value Range	Investment Style	Sector	Industry
Highest Rated	$364.00	$273.00 - $455.00	LARGE-CAP GROWTH	Next Generation	Disruptive Innovation

Zoom Video is disrupting the video communications market.

Stock Chart (weekly)

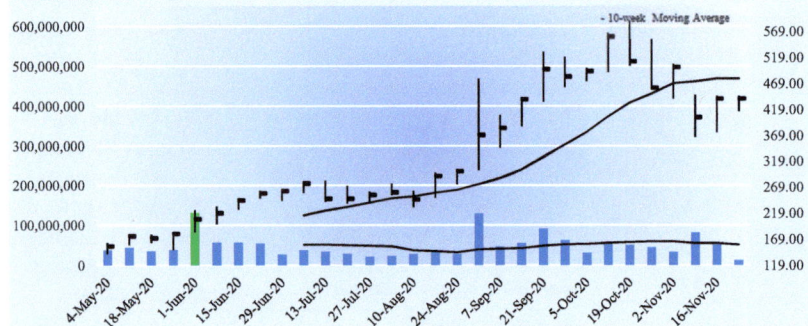

The week with the highest trading volume out of the last 30 weeks was a week of heavy selling, or distribution (red bar).

Company Vitals

Market Cap (USD)	$111,789
Avg Weekly Vol (30 wks)	48,543
30-week Range (USD)	140.45 - 588.84
Valuentum Sector	Next Generation
5-week Return	-15.5%
13-week Return	44.6%
30-week Return	212.3%
Dividend Yield %	0.0%
Dividends per Share	0.00
Forward Dividend Payout Ratio	0.0%
Est. Normal Diluted EPS	6.65
P/E on Est. Normal Diluted EPS	66.1
Est. Normal EBITDA	2,014
Forward EV/EBITDA	141.0
EV/Est. Normal EBITDA	55.1
Forward Revenue Growth (5-yr)	59.1%
Forward EPS Growth (5-yr)	153.4%

NMF = Not Meaningful; Est. = Estimated; FY = Fiscal Year

Returns Summary
3-year Historical Average

Return on Equity	-14.8%
Return on Assets	1.4%
ROIC, with goodwill	178.5%
ROIC, without goodwill	178.5%

ROIC = Return on Invested Capital; NMF = Not Meaningful

Leverage, Coverage, and Liquidity
In Millions of USD

Total Debt	0
Net Debt	-855
Total Debt/EBITDA	0.0
Net Debt/EBITDA	NMF
EBITDA/Interest	Excellent
Current Ratio	3.3
Quick Ratio	NA

NMF = Not Meaningful

Investment Highlights

• Zoom Video's goal is to make video communications frictionless. Its solutions enable thousands of people to be connected through voice and video in a single meeting across various devices and locations. Products include Zoom Meetings, Zoom Phone, Zoom Chat, and a variety of other services. It is based in San Jose, California.

• Zoom's strategy is multi-fold: 1) keep existing customers happy, 2) drive new customer acquisition, 3) expand within existing customers, 4) innovate its plaform continuously, 5) accelerate internationally, and 6) grow its partnership ecosystem (ZM 10-k).

• Zoom Video's stock price has surged, and that performance has perplexed some, but we want to stress that investors have bid up shares of ZM due to the sharp improvements in the firm's long-term free cash flow growth trajectory. Additionally, having a net cash position further supports its valuation, though in this case only to a modest degree.

• We're not interested in adding Zoom Video to our newsletter portfolios, though we applaud the firm for its strong operational and financial performance. Shares of ZM have already priced in the significant improvements in its long-term free cash flow growth trajectory, and shares have gone hyperbolic.

• Zoom's market is highly competitive. Cisco, Webex, and LogMeIn GoToMeeting are just a few competitors. Microsoft Teams and Google G Suite have their hands in this market, too. Technology changes fast, and the long run is difficult to predict.

Investment Considerations

DCF Valuation	**FAIRLY VALUED**
Relative Valuation	**UNATTRACTIVE**
ValueCreation™	**EXCELLENT**
ValueRisk™	**MEDIUM**
ValueTrend™	**POSITIVE**
Cash Flow Generation	**STRONG**
Financial Leverage	**LOW**
Growth	**AGGRESSIVE**
Technical Evaluation	**BEARISH**
Relative Strength	**STRONG**
Money Flow Index (MFI)	**NEUTRAL**
Upside/Downside Volume (U/D)	**DETERIORATING**
Near-term Technical Resistance, 10-wk MA	**479.00**

DCF = Discounted Cash Flow; MFI, U/D = Please see glossary. MA = Moving Average

Business Quality

ValueRisk™	ValueCreation™			
	Very Poor	Poor	Good	Excellent
Low				
Medium				▓
High				
Very High				

Firms that generate economic profits with little operating variability score near the top right of the matrix.

Relative Valuation

	Forward P/E	PEG	Price / FV
Wayfair	56.3	NMF	84.2%
Roku	-338.4	NMF	96.0%
Monster Beverage	36.0	2.9	104.4%
Lululemon	81.5	1.9	99.9%
Peer Median	46.1	2.4	98.0%
Zoom Video	**170.7**	**28.8**	**120.8%**

Price / FV = Current Stock Price divided by Estimated Fair Value

Financial Summary

	----- Actual -----			Projected
Fiscal Year End:		Jan-19	Jan-20	Jan-21
Revenue		331	623	2,413
Revenue, YoY%		118.2%	88.4%	287.5%
Operating Income		6	13	686
Operating Margin %		1.9%	2.0%	28.4%
Net Income		8	25	665
Net Income Margin %		2.3%	4.1%	27.6%
Diluted EPS		0.07	0.10	2.58
Diluted EPS, YoY %		-233.6%	52.2%	2488.2%
Free Cash Flow (CFO-capex)		23	114	1,179
Free Cash Flow Margin %		6.9%	18.3%	48.8%

In Millions of USD (except for per share items)

Structure of the Networking Equipment Industry
POOR

Firms in the networking equipment industry provide products for transporting data, voice, and video within businesses and around the world. Participants must adapt to address virtualization/cloud-driven needs in the enterprise data center market; the convergence of video, collaboration, and networked mobility technologies; and the move toward programmable, virtual networks. The industry is characterized by low barriers to entry, rapid technological change and significant pricing competition. Gross margins can be volatile and should be watched closely. We don't like the structure of the group.

Zoetis ZTS   FAIRLY VALUED

Buying Index™   6   Value Rating 🌕

Economic Castle	Estimated Fair Value	Fair Value Range	Investment Style	Sector	Industry
Attractive	$156.00	$109.00 - $203.00	LARGE-CAP CORE	Health Care	Health Care Bellwethers

We recently increased our fair value estimate for Zoetis. However, shares are not cheap, in our view.

Stock Chart (weekly)

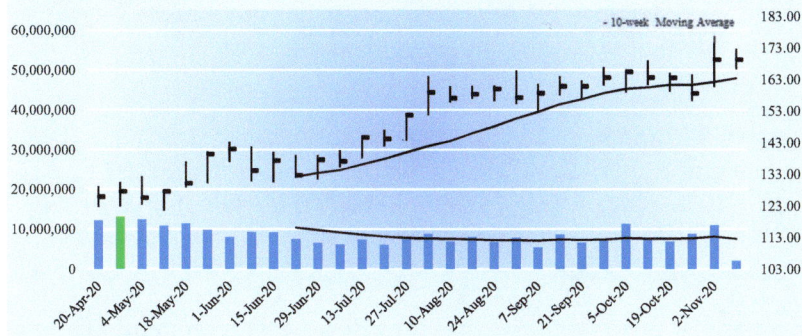

The week with the highest trading volume out of the last 30 weeks was a week of heavy selling, or distribution (red bar).

Company Vitals

Market Cap (USD)	$81,542
Avg Weekly Vol (30 wks)	8,382
30-week Range (USD)	121.50 - 176.63
Valuentum Sector	Health Care
5-week Return	1.3%
13-week Return	7.2%
30-week Return	31.5%
Dividend Yield %	0.5%
Dividends per Share	0.80
Forward Dividend Payout Ratio	21.5%
Est. Normal Diluted EPS	5.53
P/E on Est. Normal Diluted EPS	30.6
Est. Normal EBITDA	3,717
Forward EV/EBITDA	31.6
EV/Est. Normal EBITDA	23.2
Forward Revenue Growth (5-yr)	8.3%
Forward EPS Growth (5-yr)	20.5%

NMF = Not Meaningful; Est. = Estimated; FY = Fiscal Year

Returns Summary
3-year Historical Average

Return on Equity	62.1%
Return on Assets	12.9%
ROIC, with goodwill	24.1%
ROIC, without goodwill	32.5%

ROIC = Return on Invested Capital; NMF = Not Meaningful

Leverage, Coverage, and Liquidity
In Millions of USD

Total Debt	6,447
Net Debt	4,513
Total Debt/EBITDA	2.7
Net Debt/EBITDA	1.9
EBITDA/Interest	10.9
Current Ratio	2.6
Quick Ratio	1.7

NMF = Not Meaningful

Investment Highlights

• Zoetis is a leader in making animal health medicines and vaccines, with a focus on both livestock and companion animals. The company has five major product categories: anti-infectives, vaccines, parasiticides, medicated feed additives and other pharmaceutical products. Zoetis was spun off from Pfizer in early 2013.

• Zoetis is diversified from a geographical standpoint. The company has manufacturing facilities worldwide, including locations in Belgium, Brazil, Canada, China, Denmark, Italy, Norway, and the US. A little over half of Zoetis' revenues come from the US.

• The veterinary medicine industry is dominated by four players, making consolidation near the top of the industry unlikely. Zoetis is the worldwide animal health market leader in total revenue thanks in part to its durable and diverse portfolio. The average lifespan of its top 24 products is approximately 30 years, but they are not without risk of generic competition.

• Shares of Zoetis are not cheap. Please be aware our cash flow models assume the company generates significant revenue growth and operating margin expansion over the coming years. Should Zoetis stumble for any reason, its intrinsic value would face significant pressure.

• Things are looking solid at Zoetis and the firm's financial performance has been impressive of late. Demand for meat protein, new products, and the impact of its field force should drive growth at its livestock business over the long haul.

Investment Considerations

DCF Valuation	**FAIRLY VALUED**
Relative Valuation	**UNATTRACTIVE**
ValueCreation™	**EXCELLENT**
ValueRisk™	**MEDIUM**
ValueTrend™	**NEGATIVE**
Cash Flow Generation	**STRONG**
Financial Leverage	**MEDIUM**
Growth	**MODEST**
Technical Evaluation	**BULLISH**
Relative Strength	**WEAK**
Money Flow Index (MFI)	**NEUTRAL**
Upside/Downside Volume (U/D)	**DETERIORATING**
Near-term Technical Support, 10-week MA	**163.00**

DCF = Discounted Cash Flow; MFI, U/D = Please see glossary. MA = Moving Average

Business Quality

ValueRisk™	Very Poor	Poor	Good	Excellent
Low				
Medium				■
High				
Very High				

ValueCreation™

Firms that generate economic profits with little operating variability score near the top right of the matrix.

Relative Valuation

	Forward P/E	PEG	Price / FV
Johnson & Johnson	17.6	1.8	99.5%
Medtronic	25.6	2.2	109.0%
Merck	21.5	2.2	100.5%
Pfizer	20.1	0.8	93.3%
Peer Median	20.8	2.0	100.0%
Zoetis	**45.5**	**2.6**	**108.5%**

Price / FV = Current Stock Price divided by Estimated Fair Value

Financial Summary

	----- Actual -----		Projected
Fiscal Year End:	Dec-18	Dec-19	Dec-20
Revenue	5,825	6,260	6,479
Revenue, YoY%	9.8%	7.5%	3.5%
Non-GAAP Operating Income	1,881	2,018	2,306
Non-GAAP EBIT %	32.3%	32.2%	35.6%
Non-GAAP Net Income	1,428	1,500	1,771
Non-GAAP NI Margin %	24.5%	24.0%	27.3%
Non-GAAP Diluted EPS	2.93	3.11	3.72
Non-GAAP Dil EPS, YoY %	67.4%	6.2%	19.4%
Non-GAAP Free Cash Flow	1,452	1,335	1,915
Non-GAAP FCF Margin %	24.9%	21.3%	29.6%

In Millions of USD (except for per share items)

Structure of the Pharmaceuticals Industry   GOOD

The pharma (generic/other) industry is composed of makers of both brand and generic drugs. Intellectual property protection remains vital to the successful commercialization of safe/effective medicines, avoidance of pricing pressures, and offers brand firms competitive advantages over the life of such patents. Firms in the biotechnology industry face no certain future. Drug development is complex, difficult, and risky, and failure rates are high. Competition can be fierce when biosimilar products exist, though patents are material competitive advantages. We like the group, but the timing of expiration of patents should be watched closely.

Glossary of Valuentum Terms

Business Quality Matrix. We compare a stock's ValueCreation and ValueRisk ratings. The box is an easy way for investors to quickly assess the business quality of a company. Firms that generate economic profits with little operating variability score near the top right of the matrix.

Cash Flow Generation. A company's cash flow generation capacity is measured along the scale of STRONG, MEDIUM, and WEAK. A firm with a 3-year historical free cash flow margin (free cash flow divided by sales) greater than 5% receives a STRONG rating, while firms earning less than 1% of sales as free cash flow receive a WEAK rating.

Company Description. The description section provides a brief company profile and in the top right corner indicates the investment style that Valuentum assigns to the stock. Nano-cap: Less than $50 million; Micro-cap: Between $50 million and $200 million; Small-cap: Between $200 million and $2 billion; Mid-cap: Between $2 billion and $10 billion; Large-cap: Between $10 billion and $200 billion; Mega-cap: Over $200 billion. Blend: Stocks that we think are undervalued and exhibit high growth prospects (growth in excess of three times the rate of assumed inflation). Value: Stocks that we believe are undervalued, but do not exhibit high growth prospects. Growth: Stocks that are not undervalued, in our opinion, but exhibit high growth prospects. Core: Firms that are neither undervalued nor exhibit high growth prospects.

Company Vitals. In this section, we list key financial information and the sector and industry that Valuentum assigns to the stock. The P/E-Growth (5-yr), or PEG ratio, divides the current share price by last year's earnings (EPS) and then divides that quotient by our estimate of the firm's 5-year EPS growth rate. The estimated normalized diluted EPS and estimated normalized EBITDA represent the five-year forward average of these measures used in our discounted cash flow model. The P/E on estimated normalized EPS divides the current share price by estimated normalized diluted EPS. The EV/estimated normalized EBITDA considers the current enterprise value of the company and divides it by estimated normalized EBITDA. EV is defined as the firm's market capitalization plus total debt, minority interest, preferred stock less cash and cash equivalents.

Discounted Cash Flow (DCF) Valuation. We give our opinion on the company's valuation based on our discounted cash flow (DCF) process. Stocks that are trading with an appropriate discount to our fair value estimate receive an UNDERVALUED rating. Stocks that are trading within our fair value range receive a FAIRLY VALUED rating, while stocks that are trading above the upper bound of our fair value range receive an OVERVALUED rating.

Dividend Growth Potential. We blend our analysis of a stock's Dividend Safety with its historical Track Record, while also considering historical dividend growth trends. We believe such a combination captures a firm's capacity (cash flow) and willingness (track record) to raise its dividend in the future. Scale: EXCELLENT, GOOD, POOR, VERY POOR.

Dividend Safety. We measure the safety of a company's dividend by adding its net cash to our forecast of its future cash flows and divide that sum by our forecast of its future dividend payments. This process results in a ratio called the Valuentum Dividend Cushion™. Scale: Above 2.75 = EXCELLENT; Between 1.25 and 2.75 = GOOD; Between 0.5 and 1.25 = POOR; Below 0.5 = VERY POOR.

Dividend Strength. Our assessment of the stock's dividend strength is expressed in a matrix. If the safety of a firm's dividend is EXCELLENT and its growth prospects are also EXCELLENT, it scores high on our matrix (top right). If the firm's dividend safety and the potential future growth are VERY POOR, it scores lower on our scale (bottom left).

Dividend Track Record. We assess each company's dividend track record based on whether the fundamentals of the firm have ever forced it to cut its dividend. If the firm has ever cut its dividend (within the last 10 years), we view its track record as RISKY. If the company has maintained and/or raised its dividend each year (over the past 10 years), we view its track record as HEALTHY.

Economic Castle. A proprietary rating to Valuentum that assumes 'economic profit' (as measured by ROIC less WACC) is the primary factor in assessing the value that a company generates for shareholders. Whereas an economic moat assessment evaluates a company on the basis of the sustainability and durability of its economic value creation stream, the Economic Castle rating evaluates a firm on the basis of the magnitude of the economic profit that it will deliver to shareholders (as measured by its ROIC-less-WACC spread). Stocks with the best Valuentum Economic Castle ratings are poised to generate the most economic value for shareholders, regardless of their competitive positions.

Estimated Fair Value. This measure is an output of our discounted cash flow (DCF) valuation model and represents our opinion of the fair equity value per share of the company. We would expect a company's stock price to converge to this value within the next 3 years or so.

Fair Value Estimate Range. The fair value estimate range represents an upper bound and lower bound, between which we would consider the company to be fairly valued. The range considers our estimate of the firm's fair value and the margin of safety suggested by the volatility of key valuation drivers, including revenue, gross margin, earnings before interest, and enterprise free cash flow (the determinants behind our ValueRisk rating).

Financial Leverage. Based on the firm's normalized debt-to-EBITDA metric, we rank firms on the following scale: LOW, MEDIUM, and HIGH. Companies with a normalized debt-to-EBITDA ratio below 1.5 receive a LOW score, while those with a measure above 3 receive a HIGH score.

Money Flow Index (MFI). The MFI is a technical indicator that measures buying and selling pressure based on both price and volume. Traders typically use this measure to identify potential reversals with overbought and oversold levels. We use a 14-week measure to rank firms along the following scale: EXTREMELY OVERBOUGHT (>90), OVERBOUGHT (80-90), NEUTRAL (20-80), OVERSOLD (10-20), EXTREMELY OVERSOLD (0-10).

Range of Potential Outcomes. The company's margin of safety is shown in the graphic of a normal distribution. We consider a firm to be undervalued if its stock price falls along the green line and overvalued if the stock price falls along the red line. We consider the firm to be fairly valued if its stock price falls along the yellow line.

Relative Value. We compare the firm's forward price-to earnings (PE) ratio and its price/earnings-to-growth (PEG) ratio to that of its peers. If both measures fall below the peer median, the firm receives an ATTRACTIVE rating. If both are above the peer median, the firm receives an UNATTRACTIVE rating. Any other combination results in a NEUTRAL rating.

Return on Invested Capital. At Valuentum, we place considerable emphasis on return on invested capital (both with and without goodwill). The measure focuses on the return (earnings) the company is generating on its operating assets and is superior to return on equity and return on assets, which can be skewed by a company's leverage or excess cash balance, respectively.

Risk of Capital Loss. We think capital preservation is key for the dividend investor. As such, we evaluate the risk of capital loss by assessing the intrinsic value of each firm based on our discounted cash-flow process. If a firm is significantly OVERVALUED, we think the risk of capital loss is HIGH. If a company is FAIRLY VALUED, we think the risk of capital loss is MEDIUM, and if a firm is UNDERVALUED, we think the risk of capital loss is LOW.

Stock Price Relative Strength. We assess the performance of the company's stock during the past quarter, 13 weeks, relative to an ETF that mirrors the aggregate performance of constituents of the stock market. Firms are measured along the scale of STRONG, NEUTRAL, and WEAK. Companies that have outperformed the market index by more than 2.5% during this 13-week period receive a STRONG rating, while firms that trailed the market index by more than 2.5% during this 13-week period receive a WEAK rating.

Technical Evaluation. We evaluate a stock's near-term and medium-term moving averages and money flow index (MFI) to assign each firm a rating along the following scale: VERY BULLISH, BULLISH, NEUTRAL, BEARISH, and VERY BEARISH.

Timeliness Matrix. We compare the company's recent stock performance relative to the market benchmark with our assessment of its valuation. Firms that are experiencing near-term stock price outperformance and are undervalued by our estimate may represent timely buys.

Upside/Downside Volume. Heavy volume on up days and lower volume on down days suggests that institutions are heavily participating in a stock's upward advance. We use the trailing 14-week average of upside and downside volume to calculate an informative ratio. We rank each firm's U/D volume ratio along the following scale: BULLISH, IMPROVING, DETERIORATING, and BEARISH.

ValueCreation. This is a proprietary Valuentum measure. ValueCreation indicates the firm's historical track record in creating economic value for shareholders, taking the average difference between ROIC (without goodwill) and the firm's estimated WACC during the past three years. The company's performance is measured along the scale of EXCELLENT, GOOD, POOR, and VERY POOR. Those firms with EXCELLENT ratings have a demonstrated track record of creating economic value, while those that register a VERY POOR mark have been destroying economic value.

Valuentum Dividend Cushion. This is a proprietary Valuentum measure that drives our assessment of the firm's Dividend Safety rating. The forward-looking measure assesses dividend coverage via the cash characteristics of the business.

ValueRisk. This is a proprietary Valuentum measure. ValueRisk indicates the historical volatility of key valuation drivers, including revenue, gross margin, earnings before interest, and enterprise free cash flow. The standard deviation of each measure is calculated and scaled against last year's measure to arrive at a percentage deviation for each item. These percentage deviations are weighted equally to arrive at the corresponding fair value range for each stock, measured in percentage terms. The firm's performance is measured along the scale of LOW, MEDIUM, HIGH, and VERY HIGH. The ValueRisk™ rating for each firm also determines the fundamental beta of each firm along the following scale: LOW (0.85), MEDIUM (1), HIGH (1.15), VERY HIGH (1.3).

ValueTrend. This is a proprietary Valuentum measure. ValueTrend indicates the trajectory of the company's return on invested capital (ROIC). Firms that earned an ROIC last year that was greater than the 3-year average of the measure earn a POSITIVE rating. Stocks that earned an ROIC last year that was less than the 3-year average of the measure earn a NEGATIVE rating.

Disclosures, Disclaimers & Sources

To send us feedback or if you have any questions, please contact us at info@valuentum.com. We're always looking for ways to better serve your investment needs and improve our research.

www.ingramcontent.com/pod-product-compliance
Lightning Source LLC
Chambersburg PA
CBHW041706210326
41598CB00007B/554